THE CHIEF

THE CHIEF

The Life of Lord Northcliffe

ANDREW ROBERTS

**SIMON &
SCHUSTER**

London · New York · Sydney · Toronto · New Delhi

First published in Great Britain by Simon & Schuster UK Ltd, 2022
Copyright © Andrew Roberts, 2022

The right of Andrew Roberts to be identified as the author
of this work has been asserted in accordance with the
Copyright, Designs and Patents Act, 1988.

3 5 7 9 10 8 6 4 2

Simon & Schuster UK Ltd
1st Floor
222 Gray's Inn Road
London WC1X 8HB

www.simonandschuster.co.uk
www.simonandschuster.com.au
www.simonandschuster.co.in

Simon & Schuster Australia, Sydney
Simon & Schuster India, New Delhi

A CIP catalogue record for this book
is available from the British Library

Hardback ISBN: 978-1-3985-0869-9
eBook ISBN: 978-1-3985-0870-5

Typeset in Sabon by M Rules
Printed and Bound in the UK using 100% Renewable
Electricity at CPI Group (UK) Ltd

To Ian and Natalie Livingstone
Patrons of Literature

Contents

The Harmsworth Family

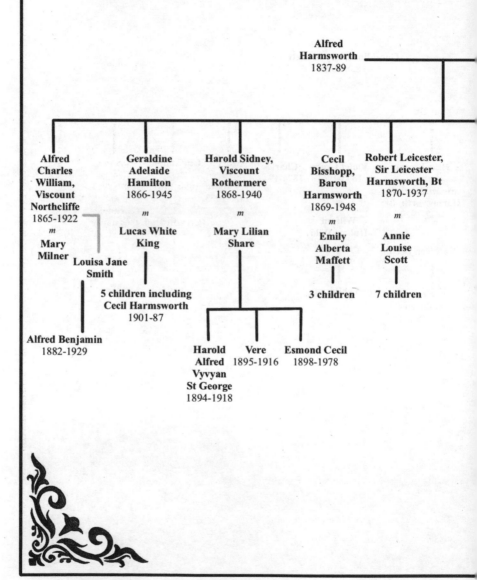

Alfred
Harmsworth
1837-89

Alfred
Charles
William,
Viscount
Northcliffe
1865-1922
m
Mary
Milner

Louisa Jane
Smith

Alfred Benjamin
1882-1929

Geraldine
Adelaide
Hamilton
1866-1945
m
Lucas White
King

5 children including
Cecil Harmsworth
1901-87

Harold Sidney,
Viscount
Rothermere
1868-1940
m
Mary Lilian
Share

Harold
Alfred
Vyvyan
St George
1894-1918

Vere
1895-1916

Esmond Cecil
1898-1978

Cecil
Bisshopp,
Baron
Harmsworth
1869-1948
m
Emily
Alberta
Maffett

3 children

Robert Leicester,
Sir Leicester
Harmsworth, Bt
1870-1937
m
Annie
Louise
Scott

7 children

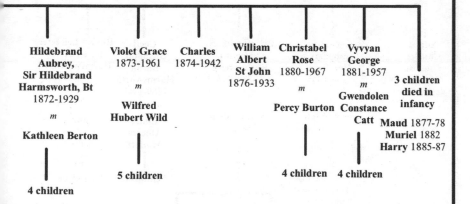

Geraldine Mary Maffett
1838-1925

Hildebrand Aubrey,
Sir Hildebrand Harmsworth, Bt
1872-1929

m

Kathleen Berton

4 children

Violet Grace
1873-1961

m

Wilfred Hubert Wild

5 children

Charles
1874-1942

William Albert St John
1876-1933

Christabel Rose
1880-1967

m

Percy Burton

4 children

Vyvyan George
1881-1957

m

Gwendolen Constance Catt

4 children

3 children died in infancy

Maud 1877-78
Muriel 1882
Harry 1885-87

INTRODUCTION

On the evening of Wednesday 4 November 1903, twelve men sat silently at a long table in a large, brightly lit room at Carmelite House in Blackfriars, London, the headquarters of the Harmsworth newspaper empire. On the table stood a Y-shaped 'Electrophone' – an ebonite and metal receiver-box with green cords attached to it. If their experiment came off, they would be making history, and they knew it.

At 8.10pm, a voice suddenly emanated from the box – a newly invented machine that, as was reported in the *Daily Mail* the next morning, 'marks the beginning of a change in the whole system of the world's reporting'.[1] The speaker's diction could be heard as 'clear as a bell, and eloquent, rising and falling, warning and persuading, pleading, insisting, proclaiming'.

More than a hundred miles away at Bingley Hall in Birmingham, the Liberal Unionist leader Joseph Chamberlain was unveiling his proposals for Imperial Preference, a radical plan to reform Britain's tariff system and end over half a century of free trade. Every word mattered, and for the shorthand-writers 'not only could they clearly hear the words of the speaker, they could also feel the emotion of the great meeting, they could hear the mighty waves of applause ... they could detect the slightest tremor in the voice of the statesman.'

The wires of the receiving-boxes on the speaker's platform at Bingley Hall had been connected by the National Telephone Company to the Birmingham Post Office, which in turn led onto to two trunk lines running to the Post Office headquarters in London, that then fed into the Electrophone room at Carmelite House. 'What was it like?' wrote the *Mail* journalist Filson Young about the experience of hearing human speech via this revolutionary process. 'Like nothing else in the world.'

The operation at Carmelite House was organised with perfectionist efficiency and split-second accuracy to take full advantage of this brand-new technological phenomenon. With the head of the reporting corps standing behind him with a stopwatch, the first shorthand writer took down Chamberlain's words for exactly two minutes and then started transcribing his notes into longhand for the printer at 8.12pm, whereupon the second shorthand writer took over for the next two minutes. So it continued around the table until the eleventh man, after whom the first was ready to start again. They kept this up throughout the one hundred and fifteen minutes of the speech.

The compositor was thus able to start setting up the first slip of newspaper copy at 8.22pm and, only five minutes after Chamberlain sat down at 10.05pm, the last reporter finished transcribing his notes. The *Evening News* was therefore able to hit the streets of London with a complete verbatim report of the speech at 10.32pm, a full hour and twenty-seven minutes before any other newspaper received the report of the speech down the telegraph wires.

'For the first time in the history of journalism,' the *Daily Mail* boasted, 'a speech was being reported simultaneously and verbatim by a staff of practised shorthand writers seated in a quiet room far away.'[2] The telephone had beaten the telegraph by eighty-seven minutes, and Chamberlain's words could be read on the streets of London on the very same night that they were delivered in the Midlands, rendering every other evening paper in the capital effectively obsolete.

The twelfth man sitting around the table was the thirty-eight-year-old Alfred Harmsworth, proprietor of the *Daily Mail*, *Evening News*, *Daily Mirror*, *Weekly Dispatch* and a large stable of other publications, and who, within five years, was to own *The Times* as well. 'Came to *Mail* office in the evening and listened to Chamberlain speech at Birmingham through the Electrophone,' he noted in his diary. 'Wonderful success. Heard the great man distinctly – distance

113 miles. *Evening News* brought out verbatim speech within half an hour of the finish.'[3] His attractive Irish secretary (and later one of his mistresses) Louise Owen recalled years afterwards how 'it seemed a miracle, so distinctly could I hear every word'.[4]

Harmsworth had been a journalist since he was fifteen. Ink ran in his veins. A man of ineffable charm, genuine journalistic genius and immense drive, he was also capable of utter ruthlessness and even, on occasion, cruelty. He and his brother Harold had founded the *Daily Mail* as Britain's first popular newspaper in 1896. By the time of Chamberlain's great speech, he was one of the richest men in Britain, and fewer than two years from becoming Britain's youngest peer: Lord Northcliffe.

Harmsworth had always embraced the latest technologies to improve the appearance, production and delivery of his newspapers – linotype, rotary presses, ticker-tape services, typewriters, motorised transport, and so on – and he was to continue to do so. Yet on that Wednesday evening in November 1903, it was not to be the new method of reporting Chamberlain's speech that was most profoundly to affect the career of Alfred Harmsworth, as much as what that statesman said in it.

The speech and the controversy that it launched over Britain's trading relations was to convulse the nation's politics for a decade, split one government and lead to a landslide election victory for another. It was also to catapult Northcliffe from the position of a highly successful businessman into the front-rank of international politics, where he became one of the most controversial figures of the era, loved and loathed alike. For after 4 November 1903 – and the decisions that he took in its immediate aftermath – nothing would be the same again for Northcliffe and his burgeoning, seemingly all-powerful press empire.

CHAPTER 1

YOUTH

July 1865–March 1886

'Northcliffe ... had known the pinch of poverty in his childhood, and with his usual directness appears to have made up his mind quite early in life that this obstruction to happiness must be put out of the way for himself and all his family before anything else was done.'[1]

J. A. SPENDER,
Life, Journalism and Politics 1927

Alfred Charles William Harmsworth was born on Saturday 15 July 1865 at Sunnybank Cottage in Chapelizod, a prosperous suburb of Dublin. It was a pretty, two thousand-square foot house with fine views of the city and a lawn that ran down to the River Liffey. He was the eldest child of his father, also called Alfred, an English-born schoolteacher, and his mother Geraldine, who was the daughter of a hard-bargaining Irish Protestant land agent.

Alfred Senior had put down 'Gentleman' as his occupation on his wedding certificate, and to all outward appearances the Harmsworths seemed like a comfortably off middle-class family. Yet in fact much of Alfred's childhood was spent in an atmosphere of quiet, submerged desperation. His family were indeed middle-class, but they were stricken with that species of Victorian genteel poverty by which genuine deprivation was hidden during a constant struggle to get by. The effect on Alfred was profound. 'As long ago as I can remember,' he said years later, 'I was determined to be rid of the perpetual and annoying question of money.'[2]

There ought to have been enough for Alfred to have enjoyed a relatively comfortable bourgeois upbringing, but three major factors militated against it. The first was that for all that Alfred Snr was a charming, engaging, literary and occasionally hard-working man, he was also an alcoholic who never fulfilled the potential that Geraldine had once seen in him. The second was that Geraldine's expected inheritance never materialised due to disputes over her father William Maffett's will, which ensured that the lawyers received more than the family.[3] The third great drain on the family resources was that Geraldine bore no fewer than fourteen children, eleven of whom lived past infancy.

Alfred Snr's father, Charles Harmsworth, had been a Regent's Park greengrocer and coal merchant who died, probably of cirrhosis, aged fifty-two.[4] By 1861, the twenty-four-year-old Arthur Snr was a teacher at the Royal Hibernian Military School in Phoenix Park, across the road from Sunnybank Cottage. The school, founded in 1769, overlooked Chapelizod and was a feeder for the British Army. This made Alfred Snr a possible target for the Fenians, the Irish republican terrorist movement, and while Alfred was an infant, his father would work at his desk with a sword resting on his knees.[5] Some have seen Alfred's intense British patriotism later in life as the subconscious result of this constant, if low-level, terrorist threat, but there is no direct evidence for that.[6]

It is easier to see from where Alfred Jnr's lifelong abhorrence of alcoholism originated. Alfred Snr was a dedicated but apologetic drunk: 'Made a fool of myself last evening. No more drink,' he would write in his diary, and, not long afterwards, 'Very seedy, my own fault, too much drink.'[7] It continued like that for years. The effect on his son of the disease that so nearly wrecked his family was predictable. 'Drunkenness disgusted him,' noted an employee years later, and no-one ever saw him drink to excess.[8]

The mainstay of the family was Geraldine, a formidable woman whose determination not to allow it to fall into financial disaster was tested almost to its limits by her unambitious, hopeless, but outgoing and popular husband. Her obituary mentioned 'her simple and direct nature', her Ulster Scots background, strict Protestant* faith, and powerful strength of character made her a force that kept the eight sons and three daughters of the family together, and ultimately led to two of her sons becoming viscounts, one a baron and two others baronets.[9] Her staunchly patriotic views were summed up when she refused to visit George Washington's grave at Mount Vernon in 1908, because she 'would not pay tribute to a rebel'.[10] A decade later, her family joked of her iron will that she would have made an excellent member of the War Cabinet.[11]

It was Geraldine, who was twenty-five at her wedding and a year older than Alfred Snr, who insisted that her husband escape what she saw as the provincialism and danger of Dublin to become a barrister in England, which led to the family leaving Ireland and moving to London in March 1867. He passed his Bar exams and took up a place at the Middle Temple in June 1869, before practising on the south-eastern circuit which took him to the Middlesex, Essex, Hertford, St Albans and Colchester Sessions, as well as at the Lord Mayors' Court at the City of London. He took a large number of briefs for small amounts – one pound, three shillings and sixpence was the standard fee.

Despite their modest accommodation at No 6 Alexandra Terrace in St John's Wood, money was always tight and Alfred Snr constantly teetered on the edge of bankruptcy. They borrowed from relatives, sold heirlooms and, one winter when blankets could not be afforded, Geraldine wrapped the children up (ironically enough) in newspapers. One baby was said to have slept in a cupboard drawer.[12] Their third child Harold recalled that they once lived on the same kind of fish for days because 'my mother couldn't afford to get us anything else'.[13] For more than twenty years, children were born every eighteen months or fewer, and all the children bar Alfred Jnr wore hand-me-down clothes. 'Having known in his early days what it was to be hard-up,' one of Alfred Jr's secretaries noted years later, 'he hated waste of any kind. I have been hauled

---

* Her forebears were Presbyterian though she was Anglican.

over the coals for carelessness, specially for omitting to switch off electric lights.'[14]

Alfred's mother Geraldine 'was not an adoring mother,' the journalist Hamilton Fyfe, who knew the family well, wrote. 'She was a critic, shrewd, kindly, frank.'[15] Once it became clear that her garrulous, genial, good-natured husband was not going to achieve her high ambitions for the growing Harmsworth family, she transferred them onto her eldest son. Meanwhile, her long, courageous struggles for her family kindled in Alfred Jnr a remarkable psychological and emotional bond between mother and son that lasted his whole life. 'Between them,' noted Fyfe, 'there appeared to be that complete confidence that sometimes exists between husband and wife.' Alfred often signed himself 'Your Firstborn' in his letters to his mother, to whom he wrote or telephoned every single day that they were apart.[16] 'She is a wonderful woman,' he said of her in 1916. 'Irish – and the only one who can keep me in my place. She *can* tell me off when she wishes.'[17]

Alfred Jr was to call his mother 'most darling one', 'Mum dear,' 'darling Mums', 'my sweet' and 'my pet' – while he called his wife 'dear' – and he has unsurprisingly been widely assumed to have had an Oedipus complex, yet their relationship was probably based on his admiration for her work in keeping the family solvent in hard times, rather than anything Freudian.[18] A private secretary noted that, even in Alfred's fifties, 'in the presence of his mother his attitude was not so much that of a grown-up son, but that of a child seeking guidance from her ... When he had to decide upon newspaper policy, he would consult his mother as well as newspaper colleagues.'[19] Another secretary noted that, 'If he had promised to dine or lunch with her, neither kings nor queens could keep him from that promise.'[20] Any hint of illness in his mother sent him 'quite hysterical' with fear. When she was eighty and he convinced himself, on no evidence other than her tiredness, that she had contracted cancer, he was 'quite beside himself' with anxiety and when several London specialists cleared her, he 'threw up his hands with relief'.[21]

Alfred Jr was nicknamed 'Sonny' and was described as a 'strangely quiet child' with 'solemn blue eyes'.[22] He had a large head, which

later in life he congratulated himself about, rather despising people
with heads that he considered too small to accommodate the necessary amount of brains. Yet, by the age of two, his head was causing
him trouble, and in August 1867 he was diagnosed by a doctor with
'congestion of the brain'.[23] He suffered what his father called 'little
Alfred's fits'. Prone to headaches later in life, he demanded silence
around him whenever possible, and sometimes worked from bed on
the basis that 'the blood doesn't have to make the effort of running
uphill to the brain'.[24] His childhood illnesses led to a profound hypochondria as an adult.

For all his father's general dreamy indolence and uselessness as a
paterfamilias, Alfred loved him as much as he despised the family's
genteel poverty. Alfred Snr wrote comic plays, satirical poems ('The
Wagga-Wagga Bone', 'A Hampshire Ballad'), pastiche-Tennyson
poems ('To a Young Widow', probably written for his sister Sarah),
short stories ('How We Escaped Collision' about a train nearly
crashing), and some poetry which was published in small-circulation
magazines and the *Dublin Review*. Alfred Snr's love letters to
Geraldine were full of passion and even literary merit, but they
buttered no parsnips.

In 1868, Alfred Snr and his friend Freddie Wood set up the Sylvan*
Debating Club, along with half a dozen others. It met at the Princess
of Wales tavern adjacent to Lord's cricket ground. By its second year,
the membership numbered fifty and later it averaged well over a hundred. Alfred Snr attended many of its thirty Monday-night meetings
a year, debating such issues as 'That the wrongs of Ireland justify a
spirit of dissatisfaction in its people'.[25] Alfred Jnr first attended aged
thirteen and enjoyed it; in 1896, he became its honorary treasurer
and he left it £100 in his will.

The family grew quickly in number after Alfred Jnr: Geraldine
(nicknamed 'Dot') was born in December 1866; Harold (nicknamed
'Bunny', somewhat incongruously for one who was to become a
great national power-monger in his own right) in April 1868; Cecil

---

* The name was chosen because of the idyllic nature of St John's Wood at the
time. The Club still exists today.

('Buffles' for his thick, buffalo-like hair) in September 1869; Leicester in September 1870. The growing family and Arthur Snr's lack of success at the Bar meant that, by 1870, he was late paying the butcher's bills and writing to the building society hoping to defer payments. 'Geraldine and I do not bear our troubles well,' he wrote in his diary in April 1870. 'My mind fearfully disturbed at our state.'[26] The next day: 'Very low spirited, never worse in my life.'[27] The next month they downsized, leaving leafy St John's Wood to relocate to Rose Cottage in the cheaper Vale of Health* at Hampstead Heath. A logical response to their downward mobility and more straitened circumstances might have been to slow the growth of the family, but Alfred and Geraldine did the opposite. Hildebrand Aubrey was born in March 1872 and Violet Grace in April 1873.

～

Alfred Jnr went to school for the first time aged eight; he was popular but did not shine intellectually. For his eighth birthday, a friend and debating companion of his father – George Jealous, the proprietor of the prestigious *Hampstead and Highgate Express*, then as now known as the *Ham & High* – gave him a bag of old, worn-out metal letters of newspaper type, from which he enjoyed making sentences.[28] Alfred later claimed that he had not been taught the alphabet before he was seven, but even if that were true he put it into printers' type soon afterwards. Mrs Jealous noticed that as soon as he could read, Alfred would curl up in armchairs with newspapers and journals.

By his early teens, Alfred Jnr was a handsome, blond-haired and blue-eyed boy: 'the Adonis of Hampstead', one admirer was later to call him.[29] Henry Arnholz, who Alfred Jnr saved from being bullied at school and who later became his lawyer and one of his closest confidants, said that he was so 'extraordinarily attractive' as a youth that people would stare at him in the street.[30]

'We [are] in great distress,' Alfred Snr wrote in his diary in August 1874, 'at lowest ebb, account overdrawn and without a shilling, and almost in despair. The money we depended upon from Ireland [that

---

* The name was an advertising promotion by a local builder in 1801.

is, from Geraldine's family] having sunk to £15. ... Nevertheless, full, though not so full as I could wish, of trust in God.'[31] Yet still the children kept coming: Charles in December 1874 and William Albert St John in May 1876. Maud Sarah died after eight months in 1878, but Christabel Rose was born in April 1880, to be followed by Vyvyan George in April 1881.

Having been appointed junior counsel for the Great Northern Railway in 1876, Alfred Snr could afford to move the family to No. 94 Boundary Road, St John's Wood, and to send his eleven-year-old eldest son to Browne's Grammar School in Stamford in Lincolnshire (today's Stamford School). Alfred Jnr hated the harsh disciplinary regime there; he was thrashed by the headmaster for playing marbles. Years later, he told a fundraising alumnus:

> I am sorry to say that, though I was educated at Stamford School,
> I have such unpleasant recollections of the place, and of the ill-
> treatment received by the boys from the then headmaster Mr
> Musson, that I never care to hear of it.[32]

Late in 1878, Alfred Jnr was allowed to leave Stamford and attend the much more easygoing Henley House School in St John's Wood as a day-boy. His headmaster, John Vine Milne (the father of A. A. Milne) thought him a good pupil, a useful cricketer and footballer, but also 'something of a puzzle'.[33] One of his teachers recalled that 'he was the handsomest boy I ever had and the most original. In one respect he was remarkably deficient. Arithmetic was a mystery to him, and as that was always compulsory for examinations, I never entered him for any and I am glad to think I never troubled him by them.'[34]

It was in March 1881 that the fifteen-year-old Alfred discovered the passion of his life, when he set up the *Henley House Magazine*, which he edited, largely wrote and set in type by arrangement with a printer in Kilburn called Ford. It was in Ford's shop that he learned how to make up a page of type so that 'it will leap to the eye'.[35] He discovered how there are 'dull flat pages' which 'seem to shrink from the reader', but also ways to 'raise' up type and make headlines.[36]

'The hours he spent in the composing-room,' wrote Hamilton Fyfe, 'in shirt-sleeves and white apron, picking the type rapidly from its slanting box with finger and thumb, putting it into his compositors' stick, were some of the happiest of his life.'[37]

The magazine was full of in-jokes and three-sentence paragraphs, painfully bad puns of the kind the Victorians enjoyed, requests for contributions, and Alfred's own poetry in blank verse, which has been described as 'of a most conventional sort'.[38] Importantly, on the back pages were questions sent in by pupils which were answered by Alfred, probably augmented by himself using pseudonyms. Self-promotion certainly came as second nature to him: in the 'Entre Nous' section, he wrote, 'I have it on the best authority that the H.H.S. Magazine is to be a marked success.'[39]

One of the reasons that the school magazine was indeed a success was that Alfred managed the business side as well as the editorial. He succeeded in selling a whole page of adverts to a sports shop in Holborn, and made the printers pay for advertising other products of theirs in spaces that would otherwise have been empty. A detractor has claimed that this showed the sixteen-year-old, whose nickname was 'Dodger', to be 'an unscrupulous mountebank', but in fact it merely showed shrewd business sense, and the nickname came from his nimbleness at football.[40] In the school holidays, Alfred took up part-time jobs working for George Jealous on the Ham & High. He also showed an entrepreneurial nature as a schoolboy – and here the charge of mountebank might indeed be levelled – when he claimed to have invented a mixture to 'revive' top hats and sold a patent remedy: 'Tonk's Pills – Cures all ills'.[41]

As well as journalism, Alfred had also discovered another passion: bicycling. Riding the high-wheeled penny-farthings required agility and even courage, and was largely restricted to athletic young men. 'For them,' writes an historian, 'showing off their bravery and virility added to the attraction of this macho "danger-machine".'[42] It was through bicycling that Alfred met Max Pemberton, another cyclist who was to become a close friend and eventually one of his many biographers. Pemberton later recalled 'a handsome and well-built boy' who rode a Timberlake bicycle with fifty-two-inch front and nineteen-inch back wheels, a feat requiring exceptional balance. Alfred was 'dressed in a grey knickerbocker suit* and wore a polo hat so placed that an obstinate forelock, almost golden in colour, could not fail to intrude itself on the notice of an observer'.[43]

Cycling required stamina, and although he would regularly ride with his club the sixty miles to Eastbourne or even a hundred miles to Bournemouth, this often required more strength than he possessed, and he would have to retire to bed for long periods afterwards, physically shattered. It was a sequence of over-exertion followed by collapse followed by periods of exhausted restitution that would re-emerge at intervals throughout his life. He was certainly a fanatical cyclist as a teenager; Pemberton recalled him cycling from St John's Wood to St Albans with Pemberton's brother one Saturday, returning at midnight, whereupon it was suggested that they cycle to Eastbourne for breakfast. 'The undaunted Harmsworth immediately accepted the invitation, and the pair set off amid cheers.'[44] Encountering a heavy mist, they slept in a hedge near Uckfield, reached Eastbourne at 10am, slept there until 5pm and then rode back to London, a round journey of 130 miles. When the club cycled around Surrey, a favoured route was down the Portsmouth Road past the Tudor stately home, Sutton Place.

In December 1881, aged sixteen, Alfred decided to leave school and try to make his living as a journalist. His father wanted him to go to university and then follow him into the law, telling him that if he went to Fleet Street instead, 'none of my friends will have anything to do with you'; journalism was not then practised by gentlemen.[45] It was true that the life of a freelance journalist in Victorian England was notoriously uncertain and hard-scrabble, and for the next six years Alfred had to work hard. He combined his two passions by writing about bicycling in the magazines *Bicycling News* (1882–88), *Wheel Life* (1884–85) and *Wheeling* (1885–88).

In order to break into Fleet Street, Alfred also took work wherever he could find it. 'I could turn my hand to anything,' he said later in

_____

* The uniform of the Stanhope bicycling club in St John's Wood, which had its own bugler.

life, 'as every capable journalist should be able to do. I could produce passable verse even. But I do not think I ever, after I left school, took any pleasure in writing for its own sake. I liked to turn out whatever I did in a workmanlike manner, but I very soon knew that writing was not to be the occupation of my life.'[46]

It was journalism rather than writing that interested Alfred, and he was constantly on the lookout for ways of turning ink into gold. When the great Victorian journalist George Augustus Sala advised him to give up writing and pursue something more lucrative, he did not realise that Alfred was constantly thinking of how journalism itself could be made lucrative and was saving as much money as possible for the time that he could invest in his own publication. He was an ardent advocate of the typewriter, the early models of which were worked with a pedal.

Alfred was willing to write about absolutely anything, regardless of whether he had any expertise in his subject. He had no discernible political bent at that period, and was just as ready to write for the Tory *Morning Post* as the Liberal *Pall Mall Gazette*. Ideology could come later, when he could afford it. Nor was he disheartened when editors rejected his work.[47] Often unable to afford public transport, Harmsworth tended to walk everywhere and deliver his copy to editors by hand if he could, allowing him to establish personal contact with them.

He quickly learned the importance of looking confident and dressing smartly, usually wearing a frock coat and shiny top hat. He took it in turns to wear the coat with his friend Herbert Ward when they roomed together, as they could not both afford one. It also helped that he was extremely good looking; the popular novelist Helen Mathers spoke of how 'he resembled a young Apollo'.[48] He smiled a lot, was not affected, and the adjective 'boyish' was often used about him, even into late middle age.[49] He had a pleasant though quiet voice, which one contemporary later thought 'served him greatly, radiating a personal charm far more powerful than any air of greatness'.[50]

The reason that he had to lodge with Ward rather than living at home was that, in early 1882, the sixteen-year-old Harmsworth had got the family's maidservant, Louisa Jane Smith, pregnant, and Mother had expelled him from the family home. As his nephew Cecil King was to put it eighty years later, Harmsworth had 'got the family servant in the family way'.[51] (The fact that they even had a servant underlines that the family were doing better than in the 1870s.)

Louisa was returned to her family in Essex to have the baby and hopefully minimise the scandal. Meanwhile, in April 1882, Harmsworth set off on an extended two-month cycling tour of France and Switzerland with the forty-three-year-old Cambridge-educated Reverend Edward Powys, the son of the Liberal politician Lord Lilford. They cycled to Aix-les-Bains via Dijon, and forty years later Powys recalled how Harmsworth's 'ready wit, his boyish joyousness, his remarkable personality were irresistible'.[52] He was obviously not too downcast at Louisa's predicament and the prospect of becoming a father.

On 5 November 1882, Louisa gave birth to Arthur Benjamin Smith. The birth certificate shows a gap where the name of the father should have been, and the signature of Louisa's mother Caroline Smith, who was present at the birth, was simply a cross, implying illiteracy.[53] The devout, church-going Geraldine was furious with her son over the sin (and probably also the potential scandal), but a financial arrangement was reached with the Smiths, and Arthur was brought up to be a carpenter's apprentice, with his father's identity kept secret.

That same year, 1882, Geraldine had gone through the trauma of losing another child, a boy oddly called Muriel, who only lived for a few days. In 1885, she was to lose her last, Harry, who lived for a year and a half. It is unclear how Alfred Harmsworth responded to either becoming a father or being forced to leave the family home aged seventeen, but it certainly did not affect his long-term worship of his mother, and vice-versa.

～

Although Harmsworth freelanced for prestigious established newspapers such as *The Globe*, *Morning Post* and *St James's Gazette*, and for magazines such as *Weekly Budget* and *Young Folks' Tales*,

it was George Newnes' new magazine *Tit-Bits*, founded in 1881
and funded by a vegetarian restaurant in Manchester, that made
the greatest impression on him. *Tit-Bits* contained strange facts,
light articles on a wide variety of subjects, very short stories, jokes
and puns, and paragraph-long pieces of information – what *Punch*
magazine described as 'giblets journalism'.

When Harmsworth and Max Pemberton visited Newnes in his
office in Farringdon Street, Pemberton recalled that Harmsworth
wore a tall hat. 'Not to wear a tall hat ... proclaims a man to be of
no account. This young man knows, none better than he, the value
of appearances.'[54] When Newnes asked what articles they would
write for *Tit-Bits*, Pemberton looked around the office and suggested
an article on jerry-building. Harmsworth wrote on 'Some Curious
Butterflies', 'How Some Fortunes are Made', 'Organ-Grinders
and Their Earnings' and 'QCs and How They Are Made'.[55] They
were paid a guinea* per column of seven hundred words. This was
already more than Alfred Snr was receiving for a brief that would
require him to read the papers and take him to St Albans magistrates
court and back.

Newnes was a master of promotion: *Tit-Bits* gave a house as a
prize for one of its competitions on the condition that it be called
Tit-Bits Villa. Although Harmsworth was impressed by Newnes'
business sense, overall the quality of Fleet Street proprietors and
editors left him profoundly underwhelmed. Three decades later, he
described how he had heard of a restaurant near Ludgate Circus
where the senior journalists ate:

> So I decided to go there and inspect them. Neither their eating
> nor their conversation impressed me. I was astonished to see such
> a collection of mediocrity. I said to myself, 'These are the giants
> of Fleet Street ... directors and editors and special writers.' I can
> remember now leaving that restaurant with the firm conviction
> that there was nothing to beat in that overfed gang, slipshod in
> food as well as work.[56]

---

* A guinea was worth twenty-one shillings, or one pound and one shilling.

Among the proprietors for whom he wrote were, he recalled, 'an unsuccessful draper who could not even spell, a Board School teacher, [and] an able bohemian who has since disappeared owing to his addiction to delirium tremens. It is quite rare to find a newspaper owned by the brain that made it.'[57]

In the half decade that he was a jobbing journalist, Harmsworth's own brain worked hard on how he was going to make his fortune, convinced that he could beat 'that overfed gang' at their own game. Meeting Pemberton on the steps of the British Museum one day in the late 1880s, he told his friend that:

> The Board Schools are turning out hundreds of thousands of boys and girls annually who are anxious to read. They have no interest in society, but they will read anything that is simple and sufficiently interesting. The man who has produced this *Tit-Bits* has got hold of a bigger thing than he imagines ... He is only at the very beginning of a development which is going to change the whole face of journalism. I shall try to get in with him. We could start one of those papers for a couple of thousand pounds, and we ought to be able to find the money. At any rate, I am going to make the attempt.[58]

In fact, scraping together a couple of thousand pounds was hard for a nineteen-year-old earning a guinea per column, whose family was broke and when £2-a-week wages had to cover board and lodging.

Harmsworth was right about the Board Schools, however, for in the 1870s a political development took place that was to change his fortunes forever. After the passing of the Second Reform Act in 1867, which gave the bulk of the lower-middle and upper-working class men the vote, it dawned on some of the governing class that, as Robert Lowe MP put it, 'We must educate our masters.' The result was W. E. Forster's Education Act of 1870, which provided for the teaching of reading and writing to all schoolchildren. When further legislation that decade made school attendance both free and compulsory, a vast new reading public was created.

In late 1882, Harmsworth wrote about another of his hobbies for

the magazine *Youth*, which was owned by Sir William Ingrams, proprietor of the prestigious *Illustrated London News*. In a long article
entitled 'Photography for Amateurs', he wrote that 'even a schoolboy
of average intelligence and with a trifling supply of pocket money
may become a moderately expert photographer in a few weeks,'
before giving his readers detailed practical explanations with sub-
headings such as 'Wet Plate Negatives and Printing' and 'Wet Plate
Solutions and the Dry Plate Process'.[59] Harmsworth was eclectic, but
he was never slapdash, and in the summer of 1883 he was appointed
assistant editor of *Youth* at a guinea and a half a week.

It was in that role in November 1883, and in particular in editing
the 'News From The Schools' section of *Youth*, that Harmsworth
became the target of a long-running hoax by a group of Etonian
sixth-formers. They invited him to Eton College and solemnly
informed him of various ancient school traditions and activities that
they had entirely invented, which he reported almost verbatim in the
magazine. It seems extraordinary that someone who later prided
himself on his highly developed sense for when his leg was being
pulled was not suspicious at some of the activities the pranksters
came up with or the aliases they used, such as R. A. S. Berry, T. T.
Vator, and A. S. Tute Goodheart. Nonetheless, he duly reported that
in the college dining hall, the 'curious custom' existed of 'Passing
The Green Stuff', in which boys chased anyone in the college dining
hall who asked for mint sauce around the school shouting military
commands.[60]

Harmsworth also completely swallowed the Etonians' claim that
there was a tradition called 'Slunching the Paddocks', when all the
pupils went to the school paddocks after dinner on a certain day to
throw puddings, called 'slunches', at each other. 'It is supposed to
be derived from the fact that when Queen Elizabeth visited Eton
College she lunched (s'lunched) in College Hall,' he was told, 'and
the students sprinkled the paddocks with dry rice in her honour.'*

---

* 'The Hon. C. Randegger-Devereux read a paper on Scandinavian Paleological
Researches' in which 'he derived the disputed word "slunch" from Schlunja,
patroness of baking among the Scandanavians.'

It was hardly cruel satire, but the Etonians kept it up for a good six months. If Harmsworth became sceptical about much of the British Establishment in later life, it might possibly be traced back to this early hoax played on him by some of its future members.

~

In October 1884, Ingrams hired him to edit *Youth* on £2 a week. One of his jobs as editor was to keep the content of *Youth* clean and wholesome, even if that meant it was somewhat self-righteous. He wanted to set *Youth* well apart from the popular 'penny dreadful' magazines, with their obsession with crime, torture, vampires and gothic murders. A. A. Milne sneered that Harmsworth 'killed the penny dreadful – by the simple process of producing a ha'penny dreadfuller' – but the accusation was simply untrue.[61]

When Herbert Ward left for the Congo and a life of exploration (where he met H. M. Stanley), his lodgings at 11 Boscable Gardens, between Baker Street and Lord's cricket ground, were taken by Max Pemberton, who had not yet become a novelist. It was there that Harmsworth taught himself the piano and, in May 1885, wrote 'The Ellen Terry Waltz', which was published to good reviews, such as 'deserves to become popular' (*The Architect*), 'graceful, poetic, charming' (*Oldham Chronicle*), 'lively and danceable' (*Daily Graphic*) and 'a very pleasing composition' (*The Metropolitan*).[62] It was not commercially successful, however, and Alfred Snr disapproved of his son writing popular music.

When Pemberton married, Harmsworth lodged with him and his wife at 34 Clifton Hill in St John's Wood. Years later, Pemberton recalled how they 'used to sally forth to Fleet Street to try and sell the product of their pens ... each sharing a top hat, one buttonhole, and paper cuffs which my mother cut for them.'[63] In January 1886, Harmsworth started a daily diary that lasted for two decades. It tells of his daily expenditure, and of his wooing of Mary 'Molly' Milner, whose brother Harry had been a friend since boyhood. She had large brown eyes and a beautiful head of hair, was vivacious, graceful and socially superior to him as her father, Robert Milner of Kidlington, Oxfordshire, was a prosperous sugar-broker.[64]

Alfred took Mary to church in January, to the London Scottish vs Richmond rugby match in February, and was 'awfully happy with my darling' in March. He worked furiously for *Lady's Pictorial*, *Bicycling News* and the *Young Folks Paper*, and was regularly hard on himself, recording in his diary over three days in late January 'a very bad day's work', 'a poor day's work', and 'did poor day's work'.[65] It could not have been too bad as his output was huge and varied, and it was not hack journalism either. Articles published in the first three months of 1886 included 'Famous Ventriloquists', 'Some Popular Delusions', 'How To Take a Photograph', 'Stage Villains', 'Sarini's Sapphire', 'The Origins of the Bicycle', 'Chinese Customs', 'The Tragedy of Doon Bay', 'What Shall I Be?' and 'The Secrets of Success'.[66] Harmsworth's strong sense that his family were inexorably sliding down the many declensions of middle-class life in Victorian Britain kept him working hard.

On 17 March 1886, the successful publisher William Iliffe, owner of the *Midland Daily Telegraph*, offered the twenty-year-old Harmsworth the editorship of *Bicycling News*, at fifty shillings a week. It meant that he would have to live in Coventry, far away from his sweetheart Mary, but it was the break he had been seeking.

CHAPTER 2

'SCHEMO MAGNIFICO'

March 1886–December 1891

GERALDINE: 'Those who ask shan't have, and those who
don't ask won't get.'

ALFRED: 'Yes, Mother, but I take.'[1]

Undated conversation from
Alfred Harmsworth's childhood

Coventry was the hub of Britain's bicycle industry, but before Alfred
Harmsworth became editor in March 1886, the sales of *Bicycling
News* had fallen to a few hundred per issue, far behind the market
leader *The Cyclist*. He therefore completely revamped the paper,
changing the typography, cutting paragraph lengths, introducing
short stories and hiring a female columnist, the Brooklyn-born
Lillias Campbell Davidson, who had an almost messianic belief in
the role of cycling in female liberation. Her popularity alerted him to
the potential for addressing female audiences later in his career.[2] He
also introduced a 'talking points' column, which encouraged readers
to discuss issues regarding bicycling amongst themselves, which was
also to become a key feature of his journalism.[3]

'When the bicycle was regarded as a toy,' Harmsworth later
said of William Iliffe, his proprietor, 'he saw that it would be the
beginning of a revolution.'[4] Harmsworth's revolution at *Bicycling
News*, and the fact that the blond-haired editor was so young, did
not make him popular with the staff, where he was nicknamed 'the

yellow-headed worm'.[5] Yet, before long, circulation rose and was soon to overtake that of *The Cyclist* itself. Nor was his contract with Iliffe exclusive; he also wrote two mass-market books for Newnes: *One Thousand Ways to Earn a Living** and *All About Railways*. He also tried to set up a journal called *The Private School Master*, which soon folded.

The 1880s and 1890s saw a technological revolution in printing.[6] It involved more efficient paper manufacture based on wood pulp, electricity-driven rotary presses that increased the speed of letterpress orienting, the hot-metal process that mechanised and automated type-pressing, and the invention of halftones which introduced photography into letterpresses.[7] Harmsworth embraced as many of these new processes as could be afforded by Iliffe, who in early 1887 offered him a small partnership in the firm. By then, however, a new opportunity had arisen, one that Harmsworth was determined to grasp.

W. Dargaville Carr was an Irish businessman whose mother was a friend of Geraldine and who had come into a small amount of money that he wanted to invest in a new publishing venture. Harmsworth had the idea of setting up a magazine based on the 'Answers to Correspondents' section of *Tit-Bits*, but had been unable to persuade Iliffe to invest in it. He had already had a Questions and Answers section in the *Henley House School Magazine* and *Bicycling News*, and saw it as a way of building a loyal readership.[8] Iliffe was willing to print the new venture on his Coventry presses on credit terms, however, which was an attractive incentive. The fortuitous convergence of Harmsworth's idea, Carr's seed-capital, and Iliffe's willingness to defer payment for printing costs until the new venture was successful, was about to bear remarkable fruit.

In June 1887, Carr and Co. started in first-floor offices at 26 Paternoster Square, under the shadow of St Paul's Cathedral. The partners were Carr; Harmsworth (who put in £1,000 of his own money); Edward Markwick, a barrister friend of Alfred Snr; and

---

* These went alphabetically, and the Cs included 'Care of the insane', 'Christmas card making' and 'Circus-riding'.

Markwick's half-sister Annie Rose Rowley, who worked as a secretary in the new venture. The following January, Markwick and Harmsworth persuaded Alexander Spink Beaumont to invest £1,000 of his wife's money in the venture. Beaumont, formerly a captain in the Royal Welch Fusiliers, was living in exile in Viareggio, Italy, after his trial for attempted sodomy (which had ended in acquittal).

Harmsworth's projected title for the new magazine was *Answers to Correspondents on Every Subject Under the Sun*, but the company was still £3,000 short of the capital needed to publish it. It was thus under severely straitened circumstances that he married the petite nineteen-year-old Mary Milner on Wednesday 11 April 1888. The ceremony was conducted by Harmsworth's bicycling friend Reverend Edward Powys in Hampstead, who recalled that 'It was the prettiest wedding imaginable, the extreme youth and good looks of the bride and bridegroom most attractive.'[9]

Harmsworth borrowed the money for the engagement ring from Markwick, his best man, and the honeymoon was spent in Folkestone. His sister Geraldine could only afford to spend twelve shillings and sixpence on a wedding present. 'My darling Mother,' he wrote the day after the wedding, 'Just a line to tell you how happy we are and how comfortable. What will please you I know is that we are having a very economical honeymoon ... we are living very simply. ... I cannot tell you how it pleased me to see you kiss my darling so affectionately. It is what I have wished for for years.'[10] In fact his mother was doubtful about the match, predicting 'They will have so many children and no money.'[11] It was the life she had had so far, but she could not have been more wrong on both counts.

The wedding report in the *Ham & High* stated that the couple were in Folkestone 'en route to the Continent', but in fact they were not en route to anywhere, except No. 31 Pandora Road, Dennington Park, in West Hampstead, a newly built terrace house then on the edge of the suburbs.[12] Mary had had a comfortable middle-class upbringing, with French and German governesses, foreign travel, music lessons and ponies, and when she told her father that she wanted to help her husband by working on *Answers*, he replied, 'Is it for this that I spent so much on your upbringing?'[13] On 19 April,

while the Harmsworths were on honeymoon, Markwick secured
the necessary extra funding for *Answers* from the Beaumonts. He
sent Harmsworth a one-word telegram from Italy to announce the
news: 'Joy'.[14]

On his return from honeymoon, Harmsworth flung himself
into editing *Answers to Correspondents*, a weekly magazine comprising sixteen pages and approximately 35,000 words, which
would be priced competitively at one penny. Subtitled 'A Journal of
Instruction, Literature and Amusement for Home and Train', the
first issue was published on 16 June 1888 after two practices with
dummy issues over the previous fortnight. Because it was new and
there were no correspondents yet, he and his small team, including
Mary, came up with the first questions themselves, which they attributed to non-existent readers. When one of his brothers went to work
on the magazine, he noticed that his material was published as from
'J. F. Smith from Birmingham'. Issues were published on a Saturday,
to coincide with rest days for the clerks and shop workers who were
the initial target audience.

Answers posed intriguing questions and then answered them,
whilst also running short articles on subjects as eclectic as 'How
Madmen Write', 'How to Cure Freckles', 'What The Queen Eats'
and 'Can Insects Feel Pain?'[15] There were endless facts, such as
that in 1795 all the flour that was used by hairdressers for wigs
could have made 5,314,280 loaves of bread.[16] *Answers* also offered
readers the chance to gain certificates in French and mathematics
as courses through the magazine, feeding the great demand for self-
improvement among its readers.[17]

Analysis of one edition of *Answers* taken at random – No 5, dated
30 June 1888 – illustrates its appeal. 'Interesting – Extraordinary –
Amusing' proclaimed its masthead, and it deserved all three
soubriquets. The first article on the front page was entitled 'Lord
Randolph Churchill's Height', which established that he was '5 feet
8 inches in his boots'. Below that was 'Are Whales Good to Eat?',
which was curiously inconclusive, but informed readers that roast
porpoise had been on the menu at King Henry V's wedding banquet.
Also on the front page was 'Inside Newgate', which mentioned the

prison's 'interesting collection of casts of murderers' heads taken after their execution'.[18]

On page 2, 'Rum Customer' asked why there were two buttons on the back of morning suits. (Answer: it was to button the coattails back for riding.) On the second and third pages were nineteen jokes, epithets and aperçus, such as 'There is a man in Birmingham who has been asleep seven years. This, we believe, beats the best yet done by any member of the Metropolitan Police Force.' The third page also listed the richest men of the century, led by Cornelius Vanderbilt ('His father began life as a bargee; he left £60,000,000'). On page 4 was a competition for 'A Free Continental Tour' which was 'open to all irrespective of age or position in life'. There was a 'prize for the reader following the most curious trade', a 'prize for the most curious love-letter' and a 'prize for a new way to make money'.[19] Elsewhere on page 4 were articles entitled 'About Girls Names' and 'Should Men Shave?'

Page 5 was almost completely covered with a biographical sketch of Charles Dickens, who had died eighteen years earlier, but it also fitted in a paragraph entitled 'The Effects of Smoking', which opined that 'smoking affects everyone in a different manner ... *excessive* is always bad'. Page 6 opened with 'Do Dogs Commit Suicide?' which might seem to conform to that long-established journalistic tradition of asking questions in headlines to which the answer is patently no, but in this case it argued that, if ill-treated, they would deliberately run in front of trains. On page 7 were the supposed maxims of the Rothschild family.[20]

To 'Jumpy', who wanted to be tattooed with a snake, the reply was, 'If he really wants to get disfigured in this way he had better go to Japan.' Page 8 had articles on 'The First Umbrella' (invented in Italy in 1611), 'How to Introduce People' ('the inferior is always introduced to the superior – the gentleman to the lady'), 'Human Leather' ('darker and more mottled than vellum, of a rather coarse textured surface, with holes in it like those of pigskin'), and 'The Pleasures of Carving'.

Page 9 discussed the penny journal market, explaining how only 7 per cent of the titles were profitable while 'The others exist feebly and then retire.' They made their profits, Harmsworth explained, 'by printing a huge number ... the cost of paper, print, editorial salaries and literary matter of each is reduced to six-tenths of a penny ... The newspaper proprietor, we will say, sells his paper to the news-agents for seven-tenths of a penny, thus making one-tenth profit ... If you will calculate what three or four hundred thousand tenths of a penny means you will find that the amount is a sum of very great proportions' which would 'make a remarkably handsome income'.[21] At that stage, *Answers*' circulation was twelve thousand, below the point at which it broke even. Harmsworth was unconcerned because of Iliffe's guarantee and, as Mary later recalled, 'He felt instinctively that success would come.'[22]

Pages 10, 11 and half of 12 of the fifth edition of *Answers* comprised a true crime story, and the rest of page 12 was covered with twenty-two more or less unfunny jokes. Letters to the editor covered page 13, including ones on tipping waiters and a 'Remarkable Case of Mesmerism'. The next two pages featured columns about famous fat people, what millionaires eat, 'The Destiny of Lost Luggage', 'Corns and their Cure', and whether the veteran French executioner Heindrich, who had guillotined one hundred and thirty-nine criminals, had seen anyone speak after decapitation? ('On one occasion, a woman's head made a faint effort to speak to him.')

The back page listed thirty-two 'Curious Facts', such as that Sir Arthur Sullivan wrote his comic operas between midnight and 4am, Fiji Islanders pray before and after playing cricket, and that Napoleon disliked cats. According to this section, 'kissing originated in England', 'betting men send more telegrams than any other class', and 'Mr Gladstone wears size nine boots'.[23] Anything hinting at sacrilege was blue-pencilled: a joke that went 'I knead thee every hour, as the baker said to the dough' was cut not because it was unfunny, but because it punned on the hymn *I need thee every hour, Most gracious Lord*.[24]

In the practice edition of 9 June, the week before going public, a question asked why the Prince of Wales was nicknamed Tum-Tum? 'The cause is understood to be the Prince's graceful rotundity of person,' was the answer, 'which is the more noticeable for the reason that he is well known to have a particular aversion to obesity.'[25] Of course, such lèse-majesté was never published; it was not going to be the route to the kind of rewards Harmsworth wanted in life, and when the comprehensive index to *Answers* was published, that question did not appear.

The *Answers to Correspondents* staff worked in one twelve-foot square room at Paternoster Square, rented at twelve shillings and sixpence a week. The first issues were printed in Coventry, but the operation moved to London once it became profitable, and on 3 November the title was shortened to *Answers*. As well as newsagents, it was sold by street vendors – 'hawkers' – who Harmsworth personally supervised. He also pioneered the practice whereby unsold copies were given away, to encourage word-of-mouth interest. On 1 December, *Answers* held its first major competition with a £100 note as the prize.

The early numbers of *Answers* provide an invaluable insight into Harmsworth's thinking and world-view at the time. The answer to the question 'Which is the Coming Race?' was America, although 'All serious foreign authorities admit that, politically and commercially, England is still the leading state.' In answer to 'Are the English Hated?', he wrote that 'the Germans regard us with envy, and perhaps some jealousy; the Russians do not dislike us half as much as we hate them'.[26] 'Do Jews Ride Bicycles?' asked a paragraph in the third issue, supposedly posed by a reader but almost certainly posed by Harmsworth himself as there were no readers yet. 'As a bicyclist of many years' riding,' the questioner states, 'I have never yet met a fellow-cyclist of the Hebrew persuasion.'[27]

'Horse-riding and athletic Hebrews are in plenty,' was *Answers*' reply to its own question:

but this race apparently does not like cycling. It is not only to bicycling that Jews evince an antipathy. We scour our memory to find examples of Jew butchers, bakers, hairdressers, chemists, bootmakers – in fact, there are a dozen occupations in which we cannot call to mind any Hebrew names. On the other hand it is remarkable how many Jew clothiers, fruiters, wholesale fishmongers, pickle manufacturers, second-hand booksellers, pawnbrokers, jewellers, tobacconists, artists, actors, authors and others there are.[28]

In the fifth issue, these ludicrous generalisations were fortunately contradicted by genuine readers, including by 'A Hebrew Cyclist' and a letter from Albert Myers of the Strand, who pointed out that there were in fact hundreds of Jewish bakers, bootmakers and hairdressers. Alfred Cohen, a cycling club treasurer, concluded that 'your rash correspondent' must have 'used his eyes and intelligence to very poor purpose'.[29] In the ninth issue, 'An Admirer of the Jews' reeled off a list of famous cyclists and medal-winners, such as A. H. Solomon, Victor Abraham and Philip Bernstein, whereupon Harmsworth closed the correspondence.

Answers tended to steer clear of political or contemporary controversies, as these could be bad for circulation. Between issues 13 and 24, Jack the Ripper was terrorising Whitechapel less than two miles away, but only one euphemistic mention was made of it. In an article entitled 'How to Buy a Slave', about Christians buying humans in Arab slave-markets in order to release them, *Answers* claimed that, 'under civilised training', former slaves often made excellent domestic servants, and the purchaser had 'the satisfaction of knowing that he had saved one human life from the possibility of a fate which even our own Whitechapel experiences can hardly hold a parallel'. Harmsworth concluded with the sentence: 'At the same time we must not be understood as advocating a domestic slave trade.'[30]

The articles in *Answers* were mostly fun, genuinely informative and very wide-ranging, with a strong interest in death. Others from the first six months of publication included 'Men with Horns', 'Who Invented Laughing Gas?', 'A Terrible Time with a Cobra', 'What a Dead Horse is Worth', 'Skeletons', 'Killed in the House of Commons', 'Terrors of Top Hats', 'Number of Bones in the Body' (around two hundred), 'Do Monkeys Smoke?' (not unless taught to, which is cruel), 'How to Find the Will', 'Sneezing Customs', 'Lion-Tamers at Work', 'Does The Queen Sing?' (not by then, but 'she still plays the piano capitally'), 'Some Celebrated Duels', 'Strange

Things Found in Tunnels', 'About Glass Eyes', 'Can Snakes Kill Pigs?' (no), 'Narrow Escape from Burial Alive', 'Why Don't Foreigners Use Soap?' (answer: 'they *do*'), 'About Misers', 'Can a Clergyman Marry Himself?' (no), 'Buried Money', 'Female Executioners', 'What Hanging is Like', and 'Performing Monstrosities'. Several of these are patently risible, but it was upon the financial success of *Answers*, and the Victorians' love of the 'interesting, extraordinary, amusing', that one of the greatest publishing enterprises in history was based.

Harmsworth paid his contributors two guineas a column, more than the normal Fleet Street rate, which ensured high-quality material. The headlines were chosen to attract attention, rather than merely reflecting what was in the article, and to become 'talking points' in themselves. Who would not want to read articles entitled 'A Terrible Time with a Tiger', 'Mysteries of a Hashish House', 'Horseflesh as Food'*, 'Narrow Escapes from Burial Alive' and 'An Electrical Flying Machine'?[31] There was a good deal of sensationalism and violent death. Statements made about what it was like to be hanged were very unlikely to be gainsaid. Criminals' confessions and stories of people falling under trains were regular staples.

For issue No. 14 on 1 September 1888, more than thirteen hundred readers wrote in to try to win the one-guinea prize with predictions of what Britain would be like in the year 1988. The winner was Marcus Morrison of Elmore Street in Canonbury, who predicted that the population would be 60 million (he deserved his prize; it was in fact 56.86 million); electric lighting would be in every house; there would be a Welsh parliament at Cardiff; capital punishment would have been abolished; there would be female MPs, astronomers and scientists, and trains, cars and buses would be propelled by electricity. Mr Morrison did make a few errors: he predicted that England would be a republic, weather forecasting would be an exact science, Ireland and France would be connected to England by tunnels and bridges, and cremation would be universal, as would the twenty-four hour clock.[32] Harmsworth himself joked that the most

---

* Staff members ate some but were unimpressed, and it was denounced as a Gallic practice.

interesting part of the centenary celebration of *Answers* would be 'the procession of literary men and women to the tomb of the first editor in Westminster Abbey'.[33]

Harmsworth had factored early losses into his business model and, by February 1889, *Answers* had not broken even, despite weekly sales hovering around 30,000.[34] He recognised the magazine needed advertisements as a necessary evil to keep the magazine profitable, but he always saw circulation as the key to financial success. *Answers* was operating in a highly competitive market: there were no fewer than two hundred periodicals being published in Britain in 1888.[35] Yet around this time, he spoke to his family about his 'Schemo Magnifico', which sadly neither he nor they wrote down.[36] It was his plan to succeed in publishing, although there is no evidence that it was what one detractor has called his plot to 'kill his opponents by pushing them out of the market-place by the weight of his enterprises'.[37] It was much more likely to be his project of using any profits from *Answers*, once they came, to invest in new enterprises, and gradually to increase the Harmsworth stakes vis à vis his sleeping partners the Carrs and the Beaumonts.

Max Pemberton became a roving correspondent for the paper, called 'Mr Answers': he went deep-sea diving in a diver's bell, up a steeple, and took a ride in a locomotive engine. When *Answers* expressed doubts that grass could grow properly in the inner city, readers sent lots of it into the magazine and Harmsworth had to pay ninepence on the postage of one forty-eight-pound bale of it, before discovering what it was. Blaming the initial low readership on the fact that fewer people were going outdoors because of Jack the Ripper, Harmsworth added interviews with famous people, more adventure stories and contests with prizes that included a junior editorship (which, out of ten thousand entrants, was won by a woman). Mary worked beside him and they walked the four miles to the office every weekday to save the bus fare. Although it was hard work, it was to be a happy period of their lives together to which they looked back with nostalgia.

Although *Answers* continued to struggle, Harmsworth believed implicitly in his Schemo Magnifico and understood how eye-catching competitions could increase circulation – *Tit-Bits* had even buried gold in the past. When Newnes made the somewhat macabre offer of £100 to the family of anyone killed in a railway crash who had *Tit-Bits* on their corpse, Harmsworth simply raised the stakes, offering £200 to the bereaved families of *Answers* readers. Puzzles were another circulation builder, such as 'Pigs in Clover', a free game comprising a small glass box with seven balls which, if carefully balanced inside, spelt 'answers'. The story goes that the original metal balls were too heavy to make marketing the puzzles practical on a large scale, and that Alfred, 'sadly reflecting on this hitch' as he walked down Fleet Street, noticed some much lighter sugar balls in a sweet-shop window and bought the entire stock.[38]

The puzzle phenomenon became a craze, with puzzle clubs mushrooming around the country and two hundred contestants competing at the *Answers* offices for a £50 national prize.[39] Sales rose to 45,000. Meanwhile, *Answers* sold toothache cures, a treatment to prevent blushing, growth pills and 'cures' for baldness. Free trips to the Paris Exhibition, for which Gustave Eiffel had built a special tower, proved popular prizes too.

~

On 10 May 1889, the twenty-one-year-old Harold Harmsworth threw up his secure job at the Mercantile Marine Office of the Board of Trade to join *Answers*. He had the financial acumen to make the Schemo Magnifico a success, by ruthlessly keeping costs down, dissuading Alfred from his more extravagant ideas, preventing Carr and Beaumont from demerging the Answers Co Ltd (of which he became company secretary) from Carr & Co, and constantly staying on the lookout for new publishing ventures, while learning every aspect of the business. The limelight stayed unwaveringly on Alfred with his acknowledged good looks, charisma, showmanship and journalistic genius, but the coming commercial success of the Harmsworth publications was just as much the brainchild of his younger brother Harold.

On Tuesday 16 July, Alfred Harmsworth Snr died of cirrhosis of the liver, a fortnight short of his fifty-second birthday, at his

home in Brondesbury. 'The dear father looked and was, his old
self,' Alfred Jnr explained to his brother Cecil about a garden party
held four days earlier. 'Nicely dressed, jolly and genial he made the
mother proud to be with him,' but back home, shortly after 7pm,
'she found him vomiting blood' and the doctor said there was no
hope for him. 'He lingered on peacefully and painlessly till 4.15am
on Tuesday when he died, looking, as Leicester told me, perfectly
happy.'[40] Mother was 'much shattered by the shock' and Alfred wrote
of himself that 'the shock was terrible'.

The loss strengthened the resolve of Alfred, the new head of the
family, to be successful, even though at the time he found it hard
even to cover the funeral costs. 'It will be a bit of a struggle to keep
our family in its place,' he wrote to Cecil, *but we will do it*, aye,
and we must make our folk powerful and prosperous, where the
father would have loved to have seen us. Our business grows apace.
Answers did 57,000 last week.'[41] He ended with these words: 'Do
not grow depressed at the terrible occurrence. There are many things
about it that make the father's death less of a trial than it should
otherwise have been. ... The turn of our financial tide has come.'

By then, Alfred was writing much of the magazine himself, and
often rewriting the serials, ensuring that the stories ended with exciting cliff-hangers and the tantalising words 'To be continued'. The
journalist J. A. Spender wrote of him that in this period of his life
he had 'a real respect for writers and artists. He read history with
a hungry eye for powerful characters and showed a queer kind of
unexpected knowledge in his talk.'[42]

What turned the tide for *Answers* was the success in October
1889 of its 'A Pound a Week for Life!' competition, which the mag-
azine touted as 'The Most Gigantic Competition the World Has
Ever Seen!' The idea came from a conversation that Alfred and
Harold had with a tramp they met while walking along the Thames
Embankment, who told them that would be his ultimate dream.
Contestants had to guess the value of the gold coinage held in the
Bank of England at the close of business on Wednesday 4 December
1889. Although the competition was free to enter, crucially all entries
had to come on postcards (which were inserted in the magazine) that

had to be witnessed by five people who were not relatives or living at the same address, which ensured that *Answers* became known to five times the number of people. It was a more popular idea than dying in a train accident, and no fewer than 718,218 cards were received at Paternoster Square. Geraldine (23), Cecil (20), Leicester (18) and Hildebrand (17) were all brought in to help in the circulation department.

On 4 December, the crowds thronging Threadneedle Street to read the Bank's official report of that day's gold coinage reserves were so huge that extra policemen had to be drafted to manage them. Sapper C. D. Austin of the Ordnance Survey Department of the Royal Engineers in Southampton guessed the amount to within two pounds, which was enough for him to marry his girlfriend early on his newfound wealth, giving *Answers* a warm human interest story into the bargain. The Christmas issue announcing the winner sold 205,000 copies. 'Great excitement in office', noted Alfred in his diary.[43] Had Austin enjoyed average longevity it would have cost *Answers* thousands, but in fact he died of tuberculosis eight years later. Alfred sent his widow a cheque for £50.

The Harmsworth brothers could not know it, but Britain was experiencing the beginning of a long boom in newspaper and journal circulations, which rose sharply from 1890 to 1910 before levelling off in the 1920s.[44] What has been called the 'New Journalism' of the 1890s used ground-breaking machinery, illustrations, investigative reporting, and news agencies. Although these had all existed earlier, they were taken to an advanced level in that decade, and other innovations that came into their own included catchy headlines, human interest stories and short, stand-alone paragraphs, which Alfred pioneered. Britain's extensive railways and increasingly motorised distribution systems greatly widened the speed and geographical reach of distribution around the country. Despite the fact that it was growing, however, the market was ruthlessly cut-throat and lived or died by early gains in circulation. If a title was quickly taken up by the public, it survived. If not, it swiftly folded.

In 1890, with weekly sales continuing at two hundred thousand despite the end of the competition, *Answers* branched out in its

marketing and produced a pipe, a waltz, a brand of cigarettes, foun-
tain pens, coffee, toffee and toothache cures, requiring considerable
entrepreneurship and Alfred and Harold's negotiating skills.[45] The
magazine was now producing a healthy profit, although nothing
like enough for the intensely competitive Harmsworths as *Tit-Bits*
sold half a million. In order to boost it, *Answers* offered a '£2 a
week for life' prize, which the Treasury declared illegal under the
Lotteries Act.* This led Markwick to question the validity of the
whole business model and to sell his shares in Answers Co Ltd to
the Harmsworths and Beaumont, easily the worst decision of his life.

In January, Carr moved to Dublin to manage the Irish subsidiary
of the business, and Alfred took on as his secretary the twenty-year-
old George Sutton, who became his most trusted confidant for the
rest of his life. In February and March 1890, after an attack of flu
that he ascribed to exhaustion, Alfred took a three-week holiday
to Paris, Basle, Milan, Turin, Genoa and to see the Beaumonts in
Viareggio. This established a pattern that was to recur throughout
his life, of overwork leading to long continental and international
holidays, only to return to London and plunge straight back into a
punishing work schedule.

The Schemo Magnifico took a major step forward on 17 May
1890 with Answers Co Ltd's publication of an eight-page half-penny
magazine entitled *Comic Cuts*, a mixture of picture strips, cartoons
and text whose first edition sold 118,864 copies and for which sales
swiftly rose to 300,000.[46] 'It is as large as any penny paper of the
kind published,' Alfred told readers, 'this you can prove by meas-
urement. It employs the best artists, is printed on good paper, is
published every Thursday, will give big prizes, is the first half-penny
illustrated ever issued, and has plenty of money behind it.'[47] It was
also heavily cross-promoted in *Answers*, as the Harmsworths always
well appreciated the advantage of free advertising.

With the subtitle 'Amusing without being vulgar,' *Comic Cuts* and

---

* On behalf of those readers who had already entered the competition, Answers
gave £250 to the Balaclava Heroes Fund for the survivors of the Charge of the
Light Brigade.

its immediate offshoot *Illustrated Chips* 'established the style and format of the medium for a generation'.[48] They had extraordinary longevity: *Comic Cuts* was published until 1943 and *Illustrated Chips* (later shortened to *Chips*) until 1952, bringing in huge annual revenues. *Chips'* most popular characters were the endearing tramps Weary Willie and Tired Tim, who got up to scrapes and who were reputed to have inspired Charlie Chaplin.

Throughout his life, Alfred Harmsworth had to contend with the sneers of the intelligentsia. H. G. Wells, who had been a schoolmaster at Henley House School when Alfred was a pupil there, was to call *Comic Cuts* an 'enormously profitable, nasty, taste-destroying appeal for the ha'pence of small boys'.[49] In fact it was not at all nasty, but good-natured and humorous. 'It was considered rather indecent to advertise anything except in a quiet, unobtrusive way,' Alfred recalled years later. 'The persistent prejudice against me all through the earlier part of my career was due to the shock I gave refined individuals by the methods I adopted to make unintellectual common or garden people buy *Answers*. I am sure of that.'[50]

Fortunately Harmsworth had the self-confidence not to let the prejudice of highbrow literati affect him one way or the other, especially later on when the criticism became extraordinarily vocal and political. For all that the intelligentsia, particularly of the political Left, came to despise Alfred, politicians – at least publicly – sought to cultivate him. 'I do not believe that literature would do anything but gain by the existence of *Answers*,' wrote Lord Randolph Churchill in a letter intended for publication. 'I am inclined to think that it will continue to flourish, and that, far from being evanescent, it will become – as it practically has – a permanent feature of the journalism of the day.'[51]

As early as 1891, Harmsworth became the target of satire by no less a figure than George Gissing in his novel *New Grub Street*, in which he appeared as Whelpdale, proprietor of *Chit-Chat* magazine, who orders that no article is to be more than two inches long and says, 'I would have the paper address itself to the quarter-educated; that is to say, the great new generation that is being turned out by the Board Schools, the young men and women who can just read,

but are incapable of sustained attention.' The fact that hard-working
people on their tram or train commute were reading magazines that
amused them rather than high literature continued to infuriate the
intelligentsia for decades, and Harmsworth became a focus for their
resentment.

The immediate and great success of the two comics that followed
the publication of *Answers* led to a huge increase in the number and
range of Harmsworth publications throughout the 1890s, during
which they created *Forget-Me-Not: A Pictorial Journal for Ladies*
(in 1891), *Boys' Own Journal*, *Halfpenny Marvel* (later *Marvel*
1893–1922, not to be confused with the American comic book of
the same name), *Home Sweet Home* (1893–1901), *Union Jack* (1894–
1933), *Pluck* (1894–1916), *Sunday Companion* (in 1894), *Boys'
Friend* (1895–1927), *Home Chat* ('The Daintiest Little Magazine in
the World' 1895–1958), *Funny Wonder* and *Comic Home Journal*.
All titles made money and soon the company moved from Paternoster
Square to much larger premises at No 108 Fleet Street, where Alfred
had a view of St Bride's church spire and Ludgate Circus.

Yet Alfred and Harold were quite prepared to walk away from purchases, turning down opportunities to buy *Admiralty*, *Horseguards
Gazette* and *Pictorial World* when they thought the price too high
or the opportunity for expanding readerships too limited. Harold
also had a good editorial eye. 'On Page 269 is repeated a joke that
appears on p.266,' he told his brother in September 1890 about issue
number 171 of *Answers*. 'Perhaps if you offer a guinea to the person
who points out what was extraordinary about no. 171, the readers
who notice the mistake may think it was an intentional one and thus
save us the stigma of carelessness.'[52]

In September 1890, Alfred bought Elmwood, a property near
Broadstairs in Kent. It cost £7,500, more than half of which was lent
by Captain and Mrs Beaumont. Although he was to live in grander
houses in later years, the relatively unprepossessing Elmwood,
which nonetheless had large gardens, was always where he felt most
comfortable. He had a bungalow built in the garden where he could
work in solitude and where he hung a blackboard on a wall, ruled
off with the names of his publications; when an idea occurred to

him, he would write it in the appropriate column.[53] The bungalow did not have a telephone, but in the main house there was a portable telephone the size of a sewing machine that had to be carried from room to room.[54]

Elmwood was damp in winter – the piano needed retuning every spring – but he loved the house. So too did his eight-year-old niece Enid, who recalled a summer holiday there in 1905 that 'was a paradise' and how they used to walk

> near the sea down a sandy track edged with poppy and wild barley to the beach, which was all our own, and where we played freely all day. The garden was more wonderful than any I had known. Auntie Mary was a most intelligent gardener . . . her exquisite taste was long before her time in this . . . Submerged in dark steaming water in a hot greenhouse hung with tropical plants lay a real live alligator, which hissed when we poked him with a stick. But, best of all, there was a swing in a shady sort of drive . . . The house was full of surprising treasures, and I thought the rooms the prettiest I have ever seen.[55]

Mary was the perfect hostess to the writers, journalists and employees whom Alfred often invited down, sometimes with almost no notice. The alligator was something of an affectation, perhaps, and allowing children to poke it with a stick sounds dangerous.

There is a possibly apocryphal story that, in his bathroom at Elmwood, Harmsworth had an aquarium which 'divided into two compartments; one contained goldfish, the other pike; when the spirit moved him he would lift the glass compartment between them', whereupon of course the pike would devour the goldfish.[56] The type of fish change with the storyteller – trout have also been mentioned as victims – but, if true, it supports Northcliffe's biographer Reginald Pound's private comment to Geoffrey Harmsworth that 'Most people who knew [Harmsworth] long enough recognised there was a vein of cruelty in him.'[57]

~

In January 1891, Alfred commissioned a story from Arthur Conan Doyle ('The Doings of Raffles Haw') and the next day wrote to his ultimate literary hero Thomas Hardy. He was arriving in the world, and in April one of Harold's weekly sales reports to him stated that total sales of all the publications had topped a quarter of a million copies. With his new-found wealth, Alfred bought No.112 Maida Vale for his mother, made a better provision for his illegitimate son Alfred Benjamin Smith, and paid for the educations of his brothers Leicester, Hildebrand and St. John at Oxford and for Vyvyan at Cambridge. His sister Geraldine, who had already married, was given a post-marriage dowry.[58] In due course, Alfred and Harold bought Poynters Hall, a Queen Anne mansion in Totteridge, north London with thirty-five acres designed by Capability Brown, for their mother. It cost £9,000 and they gave her a further £6,000 per annum for life, which helped pay for her liveried servants. She needed a large house as she was to have no fewer than thirty-seven grandchildren. (There were several more illegitimate ones, but they did not exist as far as she was concerned.)

Discussions over the founding of *Forget-Me-Not* in the autumn of 1891 gave the Harmsworth brothers the opportunity to cut the Beaumonts, who were only willing to pay £1,000 into the new company that was publishing it rather than the £2,500 it needed, out of the business. Negotiations became bitter, and the Harmsworths eventually bought out Beaumont and Miss Rowley in August 1892. There is no doubt that their behaviour was ruthless, and Captain Beaumont found it disloyal and unpleasant, but it was perfectly legal and there seems to be no evidence to support the serious allegation that Alfred hinted that he would expose Beaumont as a homosexual if he did not cooperate. (Since Beaumont had already been tried for sodomy, it would hardly have been a powerful blackmail tool.) Carr was not bought out until later but, from 1892, the Harmsworths were essentially working for themselves, having made good profits for their sleeping partners over the previous four years.

The first issue of *Forget-Me-Not* on 12 November 1891 'cleared out 50,000 copies in no time,' as Alfred recorded and, by the close of the following day, it had sold nearly 60,000.[59] It announced itself as cheaper, at a penny, yet superior to the established *Lady's Pictorial* and *Queen* magazines. It was aimed, like so many Harmsworth publications, at the striving lower-middle and middle classes, helping them to learn how to behave in society.

By June 1892, Alfred thought *Forget-Me-Not* to be 'far and away the most successful' of their publications.[60] It was tagged 'the most useful home paper' and carried fashion hints and articles on household management, as well as fiction. Although it carried advertising on the front, back and inside covers, it was mainly a mass of stories and information. In an edition chosen at random – 12 November 1892 – the contents included 'Flirtation, Courtship, Marriage', 'A Chat with a Famous Dressmaker', 'The Fashion in Perfumes' and 'Some Matrimonial Eccentricities', involving 'an extraordinary wedding occurred some years ago, being that of a blind girl to a man who was deaf and dumb'. There was an entire page full of tit-bits that informed readers that 'the ostrich quill pen is the latest American fad', that 'of sixty-seven Queens of France only thirteen have died without leaving a record of misery', and that 'the German Emperor has a pianoforte constructed for him entirely of bits of stags' horns'. Elsewhere, readers learned there were 140 female doctors in Britain and 275 lady clergymen in the United States, and that 'women who suffer from low spirits and despondency ought to have bright colours about them in their rooms. Scarlet draperies have been found to be a cure for these in many cases.'[61]

The articles in the Harmsworth women's magazines – such as 'How to Kiss and When to Kiss', 'Are Flirts Always Heartless?' and 'Diary of a Professional Beauty' – have been accused of 'grovelling to the proprieties' of Victorian prudery, because they recommended that women should not flirt and kiss however beautiful they were.[62] Yet it was not the magazine's duty to promote a more louche society, so much as to reflect the one in which people were actually living. So instead there were half-guinea prizes for recipes; poems that rhymed, scanned and made sense; a missing word competition; an advert for The Starving Little Ones' Fund; 'Secrets of a Beauty Doctor'; and advice about how to fight chicken pox, bronchitis and curvature of the spine.[63]

The magazine advertised itself as 'beautifully illustrated', and a guinea was given for the best love story. In the agony aunt column entitled 'Confidential Chat', readers' queries about courtship were answered. 'That your fiancé will not take your arm in public', it opined to someone with the pseudonym Puzzled, 'only shows that she does not care to flaunt her love-making in the eyes of other people – not that she does not care for you. I think her feeling in this subject does her credit.'[64] The article 'Do Women Always Mean "No"?' referred to marriage proposals, and concluded that the would-be groom 'should bide his time and try again, and in all probability the answer will be "Yes"'. It is of course easy to satirise such a combination of frippery and condescension, but it was an honest attempt to entertain and engage, and its eighteen pages for a penny (around £1.30 in today's money), constituted excellent value.

Magazines such as *Forget-Me-Not* were despised by the bohemian critics of bourgeois culture, partly because they were unashamedly aimed at those who aspired to better themselves in society. They spoke to the classes who were just about managing and insisted on keeping up appearances, which after all was the story of the first twenty-five years of Alfred's own life. Yet because the middle classes were also the backbone of Victorian England, magazines such as *Forget-Me-Not* had immense influence over the morals and manners of the country, being forces for propriety, hard work, restraint, politeness and the other positive aspects of what are today thought of as Victorian values. The Harmsworth publications showed 'empathy with the needs of the newly emergent reader group' and one that readers could tell was genuine.[65]

CHAPTER 3

'The Gospel of Loyalty
to the Empire'

February 1892–April 1896

'The only way to run a newspaper is to do it in the impersonal way. Friendships become costly luxuries to a publisher.'[1]

LORD NORTHCLIFFE to Isaac Marcosson

In February 1892, *Comic Cuts* overtook *Answers* as what Harold Harmsworth called 'the milch cow of the business', but his elder brother, who edited both, was feeling exhausted and was ready for another prolonged holiday.[2] After attending the opening night of Oscar Wilde's *Lady Windermere's Fan* at the St James's Theatre, and ordering Cecil and Leicester not to leave the office before 6pm except on business, on 22 February Alfred left with Mary for a seven-week tour of Cadiz, Seville, Tangier, Malaga, Nice, Monte Carlo, Syracuse, Cyprus, Beirut, Damascus, Jaffa, Suez, Cairo, Alexandria, Malta and Gibraltar.[3] They 'decided to miss out Jerusalem, having had quite enough of Palestine', but left Cairo with severe regrets 'having enjoyed the stay here as much as any period in our lives'.[4] He was gratified to see *Answers* being read in Sicily, Port Said and Gibraltar.

On 6 May 1892, the Amalgamated Press Co.'s combined weekly sales hit 1,002,500, beating even the great American combines owned by Joseph Pulitzer and William Randolph Hearst. It was a remarkable achievement considering that *Answers* had begun publication less than four years earlier. 'America is supposed to be monopolising the publication of English literature,' commented the *Manchester Guardian*, 'yet the attainment of the largest circulation of periodical journalism in the world can be ascribed to a British editor, Alfred C. Harmsworth'.[5]

Having observed that people enjoyed reading the same paper as each other, possibly because of the opening that gave to their talking points, Harmsworth hired chartered accountants to audit sales figures, recognising that knowledge of the very popularity of the Harmsworth titles added to their attraction. This in turn served to solidify their position. He was a great journalist, but a great psychologist too. He also appreciated how serialisations sold magazines and would on occasion start a story in one of his publications only to continue it in a different one, thus forcing readers to buy – and hopefully continue buying – both.

Harmsworth briefly considered standing in the 1892 general election, but this was more for the influence and status that being an MP would bring than for any political commitment, although he did vote for the Unionist candidate in his local constituency of Thanet. During the campaign, the Liberal prime minister William Gladstone said in an exclusive interview that he considered 'the gigantic circulation of *Answers* an undeniable proof of the growth of sound public taste for healthy and instructive reading. The journal must have vast influence.'[6] Just in case any Unionists thought the interview meant that *Answers* might have a Liberal bent, Harmsworth re-ran a positive comment that Lord Randolph Churchill had made about the magazine in March 1891.

Cecil Harmsworth, who became a Liberal MP, wrote that he 'often wondered what Alfred's politics really were'.[7] Although it was hard to discern much consistency in his domestic politics, Alfred's unwavering passion was to protect and expand the British Empire, which at that time spanned more than one-fifth of the world's land surface, dominated the oceans, and was by far the largest the world had ever known. He would have agreed wholeheartedly with Winston Churchill's first public speech in July 1897, in which he said that, despite the sceptical 'croakers', the Empire would 'continue to pursue that course marked out for us by an all-wise hand and carry out our mission of bearing peace, civilisation and good government to the uttermost ends of the earth'.[8]

By the mid-1890s, the threats to the primacy of the British Empire seemed to come from the United States in trade, Russia in Asia, but especially from Germany in the European military and increasingly naval spheres. It was therefore natural that Harmsworth should be drawn to Joseph Chamberlain, who was trying to draw the Empire together to meet these challenges while also extending it (especially in southern Africa), and supporting Lord Salisbury, the Unionist leader with whose Conservative party Chamberlain had coalesced the Liberal Unionists in opposing Irish Home Rule in 1886. 'Joe' was vigorous, a successful businessman, and not part of the Tory establishment, and had been Harmsworth's political hero long before he met him. An even greater hero was Cecil Rhodes, the prime minister of Cape Colony and chairman of the British South Africa Company, who was busily adding 150,000 square miles to the British Empire in southern Africa.

~

Overall circulation kept on growing with the immediate success of a new halfpenny publication called *Wonder*, which sold 140,000 copies after its launch on 23 July 1892, bringing the weekly total to 1.23 million. On its third issue, Harold predicted that 'The *Wonder* will be a very happy stroke of business for us.'[9] He was right; it too lasted until the Second World War. Alfred's success now brought him to the notice of the radical *Daily News*, which was to attack him throughout his life under six successive editors, the most aggressive of whom was A. G. Gardiner, who wrote of his 'sure instinct for the hunger of the rudimentary mind for information about the unimportant, for entertainment, and for cheap sentiment'.[10] Yet for all that the haut monde sneered at rudimentary minds, by early 1893 weekly circulation figures were regularly topping one and a half million and the often pessimistic Harold reported to his brother on 12 January that 'Business seems to be booming somewhat.'[11]

The trust and mutual respect between the two brothers is very evident from their correspondence, with Harold controlling the business and financial side – such as the timing of new publications and purchase of machinery – and Alfred organising everything to do with content.

~

By August 1893, the company was making profits of £50,000 a year, and was able to move into yet larger offices at No. 24 Tudor Street.[12] In mid-October, Alfred's doctor prescribed another holiday for his exhaustion, one that should last at least three months. Instead, on 8 November, the brothers launched the boys' magazine *Halfpenny Marvel*, which soon became *The Marvel,* featuring interesting facts, uplifting Wild West and British Empire tales of adventure and exploration, and detective stories. The detective Sexton Blake appeared for the first time in a story entitled 'The Missing Millionaire'. *Halfpenny Marvel* was another instant success, selling 138,000 copies of the second issue.

'This has been a good year for us in many ways,' Alfred noted in his diary on 30 November. 'We have practically completed our [new Linotype] printing works, my investments have considerably increased. I have settled Elmwood and £21,000 on my wife, £51,000 on my Mother, and have ... invested in the printing works and other securities something like £18,000.'[13] Yet his ambitions were not confined to magazines that brought in only halfpennies and pennies weekly. The next stage of the Schemo Magnifico would involve owning evening and national newspapers, which would daily bring in pennies and even threepennies, and bestow political power on their proprietor.

~

On 19 April 1893, Mary underwent surgery for her childlessness, five years after their marriage. 'This morning at 9 o'clock, Dr Dakin, Dr Raven and an anesthetist came to perform an operation on the wife,' Alfred noted in his diary. 'It was all over in half an hour and expect great things from the performance thereof.'[14] Tragically the operation was unsuccessful and the couple started to drift apart both sexually and emotionally. Victorian society being what it was, there could be no question of divorce, and they made an effort to stay on relatively good personal terms, despite both taking lovers. They still lived and holidayed together, and seemed never to notice the other's affairs, several of which lasted for many years.

It is impossible to be certain when it started, but at some period six years or so after their marriage, Mary began a long-running but possibly not exclusive affair with Reggie Nicholson, which Harmsworth not only did not mind but almost seems to have encouraged. Alfred and Nicholson managed to remain close friends; they regularly went on holiday together – sometimes with Mary present, sometimes not – and he later appointed Nicholson to important posts within his newspaper empire.

On 3 January 1894, Alfred, Mary and his secretary George Sutton departed from Liverpool on board the 10,000-ton *Teutonic* for a two-month tour of the United States and Canada. It was to be the first of twenty trips to the United States that Harmsworth made before the outbreak of the Great War, and they were to have a profound effect on him. They both convinced him of the vital importance of amity between the British Empire and the American republic – he adopted 'Atlantic' as one of his codenames during confidential business negotiations – and gave him endless ideas about how British journalism could develop.[15]

Often accused of merely plagiarising American journals and magazines, in fact there was a constant cross-pollination between the journalism of the two countries, and Harmsworth already had a reputation in the United States because of his huge audited circulation figures. Moreover, he was always popular with the American press because he was young, successful, unsnobbish, keen to learn, clearly pro-American, not a direct competitor and always ready with a quote for a reporter.

'Mr [J. Bruce] Ismay [chairman of the White Star Line] saw us off and gave us [the] use of private sitting room,' Harmsworth noted in his diary of this clear acknowledgement of his new-found social status.[16] In New York, he and Mary stayed at the Waldorf Hotel and visited the Stock Exchange, *Tribune* and *World* newspapers, *Cosmopolitan* magazine and various printing works, as well as Chinatown, the Bowery, Harlem and the Bronx, before those places were even fully paved.[17] At one lunch at a circulation agency, he was handed a cable from Harold simply stating: '*Answers*: 350,000'.[18] (Of course it is not impossible that that *coup de théatre* had been engineered between them.)

Harmsworth was impressed by Joseph Pulitzer and James Gordon Bennett Sr* and their huge newspaper sales. The American press tended to employ more imaginative headlines than Britain's – the *Chicago Times* had once headlined a story about the hanging of four praying murderers 'Jerked to Jesus' – but Harmsworth carefully studied the entire industry before heading off to the Niagara Falls, Montreal, Quebec and Boston, followed by a fishing holiday in Florida where he stayed at the Tampa Bay Hotel and caught a shark. He returned to Euston Station on 14 March, where he was met by his mother Geraldine.

Harmsworth was so struck by his trips to the United States that later on he spent large sums of money sending members of his various staffs there, 'not only to study methods of business,' wrote one employee, 'but also to grasp and understand the American outlook'.[19] Yet for all that he believed in the friendship of the English-speaking peoples, Harmsworth was intensely competitive and, when in New York, he heard of an American expedition being planned to the North Pole and decided to try to beat them to it. He contacted Frederick George Jackson, who the previous year had crossed three hundred miles of frozen Siberian tundra, and when they met on Harmsworth's return to London, he proposed a Jackson-Harmsworth Expedition to the Franz Josef Land archipelago in the Arctic, under the overall auspices of the Royal Geographical Society.

Harmsworth launched the expedition out of patriotism, but it was also an opportunity to break into high society. He was not overly impressed with the aristocracy per se, but he appreciated that they still wielded a good deal of real power in late-Victorian Britain.

---

* The person who inspired the exclamation of surprise: 'Gordon Bennett!'

Much of high society, including no fewer than seventeen knights, were present at Alfred and Mary's reception at the Grafton Galleries on 6 July to fete the explorers and view their equipment, people who would not normally have attended a party thrown by the owner of *Comic Cuts* and *Illustrated Chips*.

Mary in particular was excellent at socialising and engaging with high society – the dowager Queen Mary was to become a friend – and Alfred and she were both keen to translate their wealth into social status. On his 29th birthday at Cowes, while staying on Sir Allen Young's steam yacht the *Stella*, Alfred was contacted by Queen Victoria's son-in-law Prince Henry of Battenberg, who asked to meet him 'and congratulated me on the organisation of the Polar Expedition'.[20]

On 12 July 1894 they went to Greenhithe to see the nine-man Expedition set sail on the specially converted steamship *Windward* which he bought himself. There were two *Answers* reporters on board, which inevitably led detractors to claim that the expedition was all merely another Harmsworth advertising stunt, but in fact it was more like an adventure straight out of his *Boys' Own Journal* or *Union Jack* magazines. Although the explorers did not reach the North Pole, they probably saved the lives of the Norwegian explorers Fridtjof Nansen and Hjalmar Johansen whose kayaks had been attacked by walruses and had become lost. They hadn't been heard of for a year.[21]

Jackson paid tribute to the principal backer of the expedition by covering Franz Josef Land in place names honouring him and his family. Alfred Island* was 43 square miles in size, and there were also Cape Mary Harmsworth, Cape Cecil Harmsworth and the Harold Harmsworth Straits. Alfred's imperialism could also be discerned from the names Salisbury Island, Chamberlain Island and the Cecil Rhodes Fjord. When *Windward* finally returned in September 1896, Alfred had one of the lifeboats put in the garden at Elmwood, and for years afterwards when showing a stuffed polar

---

* Today called Ostrov Artura and in the Archangel administrative region of the Russian Federation.

bear to guests in the hall, he would wryly remark that the animal had cost him £30,000.[22]

~

The Harmsworths' chief commercial rival was Arthur Pearson, an alumnus of Winchester College who had won a sub-editorship on *Tit-Bits* as a competition prize and had set up *Pearson's Weekly* as soon as he saw that *Answers* was a success. When the Harmsworths published *Comic Cuts*, Pearson brought out *Funny Cuts*, and when the Harmsworths brought out *Home Chat*, Pearson published *Home Notes*. As far as plagiarism was concerned, the Harmsworths were far more sinned against than sinning. Yet they stayed on good personal terms with Pearson, occasionally entering into discussions of mutual interest, such as Alfred's proposal for an association of newspaper proprietors.[23] In June 1894, the Newspaper Defence Association held a meeting, with Sir William Ingram MP, proprietor of the *Illustrated London News*, in the chair.

Adam Smith declared that 'people of the same trade seldom meet together, even for merriment and diversion, but the conversation ends in a conspiracy against the public,' and that has been the accusation levelled against Harmsworth over what became the Association of Newspaper Proprietors. Yet in fact it and its predecessor were more of a conspiracy against the news agencies such as that of Baron Reuter, and the undersea cable and overhead telegraph companies that made publishing foreign news almost prohibitively expensive. Instead of creating a price-fixing cartel for journals, this association, Alfred's brainchild, was intended to smash an already-existing cartel. Moreover, he continued his price wars against his rivals, undercutting them whenever he safely could. By July, the Harmsworth publications had a combined weekly sale of 1.75 million, when the population of Britain was thirty million. When it came to naming the new printing works they had invested in heavily, only one proposal was considered: the Geraldine Press.

In 1894, London had nine evening papers; four sold for a halfpenny, five for a penny. Such competition meant that most were in financial difficulties, especially the Conservative-supporting

Evening News which, despite its 100,000 circulation, was facing bankruptcy.[24] In August, Louis Tracy, assistant editor at *The Sun*, and its chief sub-editor William Kennedy Jones approached the Harmsworths with a proposal that they buy the *Evening News*, only days before Tracy and Jones' option expired.

Alfred and Harold visited the offices to inspect the books on 23 August, but Alfred noted four days later that they were 'in great doubt all day as to whether we should get the *Evening News* or not, there being other competition and matters difficult to arrange'.[25] They had no experience of running a daily paper and Harold's view was that 'If we could pick the paper up for a song it would be worth our while to have it, but not otherwise.'[26] He felt that owning a Tory paper would also draw them into politics, which might be bad for the magazine business, telling Alfred that as a Liberal 'I have no wish to identify myself with the Conservative Party, and it would certainly not suit your purpose to do so either.'[27]

One of the employees of the *Evening News* later described the building in Whitefriars Street before the Harmsworths bought the paper as:

> old and dirty, and, as we worked, cockroaches fell off the ceiling into our books. We used to spear them with our pens, and, from time to time, staged some quite exciting races with the vermin as competitors. The publishing-room, where the papers were handed out – or rather thrown out to the street sellers ('runners') – stank dreadfully, in spite of liberal soakings with disinfectant, and at edition times, sheer pandemonium reigned.[28]

However, on 28 August 1894, the Harmsworths bought the *Evening News* for only £25,000.[29]

When Alfred went to Coutts Bank to liquidate some securities to raise the money, the manager solemnly informed him that in his experience 'there were several ways by which a man might be certain of losing his money and none of them was more certain than running a newspaper'.[30] Harold disagreed, telling his brother that there was money to be made after he had identified cuts that would reduce the costs from £33 to £25 per number. 'We think it a bargain,' Alfred told Cecil and Leicester later that year, 'inasmuch as we got all the machinery thrown in. Its circulation is 40,000 a day more than the *Star* and 60,000 more than the *Sun*.'[31]

Jones was installed as editor and Tracy as business manager; they each received 7.5 per cent of the profits, while Alfred acted as a very hands-on editor-in-chief. The abrasive Kennedy Jones, nicknamed 'KJ', was two months older than Alfred but had been born in the slums of Glasgow and had got a job on the *Birmingham Daily Mail* as a junior reporter, before working his way up. 'He had the reputation of being the best-hated man in Fleet Street,' recalled a colleague after Jones had become Alfred's principal lieutenant. 'He was a strong man, and his earlier experiences hardened his character. He often undertook unpleasant jobs which Northcliffe himself did not care to tackle, or which he knew KJ could do better.'[32]

Several of the changes made at the *Evening News* were ones Harmsworth and Jones instituted with future newspapers, such as putting articles in the same place in the paper every day so readers knew where to go. It seems obvious, but few other papers did it at the time. They also instituted bolder headlines, shorter leaders, a women's page, a fresher typeface, maps for foreign news items, short stories and feature articles on 'talking points' such as 'How Timetables are Made', 'Smoking in Cemeteries', and 'Is Crime a Mental Disease?'[33] It ran domestic murder trials in detail and broke the scoop of the death of Tsar Alexander III. The football and cricket coverage was greatly increased and a special Saturday edition delivered up-to-the-minute football scores.[34] The telegraph was used to keep readers up to score with the results of Test matches in Australia.

The *Evening News* had editorials on non-political subjects and vivid explanatory sub-headlines, something that had impressed Harmsworth in the United States. 'Killed by Rum' would be followed, for example, by 'A Fatal Xmas Drinking Bout by an Intemperate Woman', for example, or 'A Brave Teacher' would precede 'Successfully Defends Her School Children Against a Mountain Lion'. Under 'Head Torn Off', there was 'A Man Decapitated by Machinery in a Laundry'.[35] Copying *Answers*, the

Evening News featured snippets of information about things unconnected to current events, such as how navvies got their name,* how many people sat on Hindu juries (five), and the fact that Robert Browning started work at 7am.

'Freed from fad and prejudice,' ran a statement on 31 August,

> the *Evening News* will preach the gospel of loyalty to the Empire and faith in the combined efforts of the peoples united under the British flag. While strongly and unfalteringly Unionist in Imperial politics, the *Evening News* will occupy an advanced democratic platform on all social matters. It will be progressive in municipal reform; non-sectarian in all questions affecting the religious beliefs of the community, sympathetic towards labour and friendly towards every phase of communal advancement.[36]

These were Alfred's political principles, which have been described as a combination of 'Tory populism, Disraelian imperialism and a firm belief in "the Anglo-Saxon future"'[37] – to which should be added a strong opposition to Irish nationalism if it resulted in the island's separate existence outside the Empire.

Harold meanwhile analysed crowd movements around London, and sent his runners to where people were during rush-hour, rather than keeping them at stationary points throughout the day. Again it sounds obvious, but at the time was a brilliant innovation. Harold's forensic accounting discovered that the paper had been overpaying for newsprint for years, and a combination of increasing the circulation to 122,000 in six months and cutting costs meant the paper was soon back in profit. By the end of the first year ,its £9,000 loss had been turned into a £14,000 profit.[38] Within three years, the £25,000 cost of its purchase had been recovered, and by 1898 the paper was selling a staggering 800,000 copies daily and contributing £50,000 a year to the company. Small wonder that Harold came to call the *Evening News* 'our gold brick'.[39]

Although weekly magazines were always important to Alfred, and

---

* From having worked on Lincolnshire's inland navigational waterways.

throughout his life continued to make a huge financial contribution to the Harmsworth empire, after 1894 it was the immediacy and excitement of daily newspapers that came to dominate his life. For all the poverty of his early years, one advantage in having quite so many brothers was that there were always enough of them to superintend the magazine side of the business, allowing him to concentrate on newspapers.

~

'You should drop as much work as possible,' Harold told Alfred in early September 1894. 'At the present pace we shall be nervous tired-out men by the time we reach forty.'[40] It was not unusual for Alfred to stay up all night at the presses and sleep in his office. Sometimes he forewent the duties of an editor-in-chief and undertook some reporting himself, as on 26 September when he went 'down to Chelmsford Prison and saw Read the alleged Southend murderer'.[41] In June, the married thirty-nine-year-old James Canham Read had shot Florence Dennis, his pregnant eighteen-year-old mistress, in the head in woodland at Prittlewell, near Southend. 'During the past three days,' Harmsworth noted in his diary on 14 November, 'the *Evening News* has sold Monday 187,000, Tuesday 225,000, today 236,000, on account of the Read trial.'[42] On the last day of the trial, it sold 390,000, a testament to the Victorians' love of murder trials. Read was hanged on 4 December; his last words were 'Will it hurt?' Back in Paris on 18 October, Alfred went around 'the thieves' quarter' with a detective.[43] In a previous visit with Harold, he had visited the Paris morgue, recognising how real-life crime stories boosted newspaper sales.

Having informed Lord Salisbury of the turnaround in the profitability of the *Evening News*, the Unionist leader replied on 21 November that he was 'very glad to hear of the good prospects which have opened before the *Evening News* ... I believe that such organs of opinion may be of great value if they can be made financially to succeed.'[44] Harmsworth told Salisbury that his next project was to start a daily newspaper and, early in December 1894, Harold and Alfred dined together to map out the outlines of such a venture.

In the meantime, the magazine empire continued to expand. The *Union Jack Library* was published on 23 November; it immediately sold 196,000 and was later shortened to *Union Jack*. Its first editorial stated that 'there will be nothing of the "dreadful" type in our stories. No tales of boys rifling their employers' cash-boxes and making off to foreign lands, or other such highly immoral fiction products.' Several of the short story authors used pseudonyms, so as not to reveal how few people actually wrote the magazine. The magazine was filled by tales of imperial derring-do which today would be considered profoundly politically incorrect. Similarly, *Boys' Friend* was published two months later, which sold 205,000, 'the largest number we have ever done of a new publication', noted Alfred.[45] The magazine ('To amuse, to instruct and to advise boys') was a sixteen-page halfpenny weekly containing a serialised story, tips on cricket and football, Sexton Blake detective stories, seafaring and Wild West yarns, and tales by Charles Hamilton, who later created Billy Bunter for another Harmsworth magazine, *The Magnet*, which ran from 1908 until 1940. *Boys' Friend* ran for 1,717 issues until 1927. By late 1894, the weekly sales of the Harmsworth magazines had topped two million.

~

On 30 November 1894, Alfred had the opportunity to meet his hero, Cecil Rhodes, for breakfast at the Burlington Hotel in Mayfair. Also present was Rhodes' faithful lieutenant Dr Leander Starr Jameson, 'the Conqueror of Matabeleland'. They breakfasted again together a fortnight later. 'Their meeting left Alfred greatly impressed with the charismatic Rhodes,' writes the historian J. Lee Thompson, 'a self-made man like himself, who had followed his own path and helped to paint Africa red in the maps of empire the newspapers were fond of printing.'[46] These men devoutly believed that they were building the greatest empire in history since that of Rome, and Harmsworth viewed his mission in life to be to defend that empire against all-comers.

Many years later, after Rhodes' death, Harmsworth was asked who were the three greatest men he had ever met. He said

'unquestioningly' Rhodes was the greatest and then the Pasteur
Institute's Ilya Ilyich Mechnikov, a Jewish zoologist of Romanian
ancestry famed for his pioneering research in immunology, and after
them Alfred Deakin, the prime minister of Australia.[47] Harmsworth
also once told an extraordinary – and possibly untrue – story about
the first time he met Rhodes. He said he went to Rhodes' hotel and

> quite by accident got into the financier's bathroom. A strange
> sight met his gaze. Rhodes sat in his morning tub vainly trying to
> wash his back. Quick as a flash Northcliffe said: "You're wasting
> a lot of energy. I know of a brush with a long handle that is the
> best back-washer in the world." Rhodes was much interested in
> this suggestion ... The net result was that these two dominating
> personalities became intimate friends.[48]

A more believable story was of the first time that Mary sat next to the
multi-millionaire adventurer at a dinner party and said to him, 'Mr
Rhodes, I feel very nervous as I am told you are a woman-hater.'[49]
Rhodes replied that she need have no fears on that account. Even
if he were a misogynist, Rhodes was unlikely to have offended the
wife of someone who was poised to become his greatest supporter
in the British press. At the Sylvan Debating Society on 17 December,
Harmsworth spoke in favour of 'Mr Rhodes' policy', which at the
time envisaged British control of all the territory between Cairo and
the Cape of Good Hope.[50] He saw Rhodes again for ninety minutes
on 22 January for an 'interesting talk' during which Rhodes invited
him to southern Africa.[51]

On 25 March 1895, Captain Middleton, the chief agent of
the Conservative Party, asked Alfred to fight the constituency of
Portsmouth alongside the Hon. Evelyn Ashley, the Liberal Unionist
candidate. (The two parties had formed an alliance against the
Liberals in 1886 over Irish Home Rule.) Four days later, after visiting Portsmouth once, Harmsworth was unanimously adopted as
their candidate by the Portsmouth Conservative Association and,
over the next sixteen weeks, he visited the town regularly in the
afternoons and evenings. He toured the dockyards; spoke at each

of the wards (which he hated doing and at which he admitted that he was 'very bad'); was photographed at Debenhams; received deputations of postmen, naval coopers and chief petty officers; became an Apprentice Freemason of the United Brothers Lodge as well as a Forester, Buffalo, Oddfellow and even a Druid; went out on a destroyer; and watched the fire brigade turn out. On 30 May, 'In the afternoon, Wife opened Bazaar on the Clarence Pier when I was mesmerised.'[52] He made well-publicised donations to no fewer than forty-seven charities within the constituency, 'from the roof fund of an Anglican church to educational classes in Hebrew'.[53]

Harmsworth thoroughly disliked the whole process, particularly the endless speechifying, as he had a weak voice. 'It was like swimming in a sea of filth,' he told friends. Standing for Portsmouth, he naturally called for higher naval spending, although he had always genuinely believed in that and continued to advocate it strongly for the rest of his life, supporting the Navy League pressure group in his newspapers for years. George Goschen, the first lord of the admiralty, and St John Brodrick, a future secretary for war, came down to Portsmouth to speak for him.

A month before the election, the Harmsworths bought the Portsmouth *Evening Mail*, which then ran a serialised short story, 'The Siege of Portsmouth', about what would happen to the city if what the paper claimed was the Liberal government's underspending on the Royal Navy encouraged France and Russia to invade two years later. It ran weekly headlines such as 'The Battle of Eddystone' and 'The Battle of Spithead'. Field Marshal Lord Wolseley was captured in one episode, and real inhabitants of Portsmouth were mentioned as characters in the story.

It was not quite enough: on 16 July 1895, Harmsworth received 9,717 votes and Ashley 9,567, to the two Liberals' 10,451 and 10,255. In a turnout of more than 20,000 (every elector had two votes), he was only 538 votes behind his nearest opponent. What made the defeat sharper, as well as the money wasted on the *Evening Mail*, was that the Unionists won the general election in a landslide victory in which the Conservatives won 340 seats and the Liberal Unionists seventy. 'At my age defeat does one good,' he philosophically told the

Evening Mail. 'Too much success in life is bad for one.'[54] He consoled himself in his diary that he had outpolled the winner of 1892. 'My place is in the House of Lords where they don't fight elections,' he told journalists.[55] For all that it sounded hubristic, Lord Salisbury had already elevated two newspaper owners to the upper house. His failure at Portsmouth made him less respectful of politicians who were willing regularly to debase themselves for votes in the way that he had, although it is not true that it turned him against the entire democratic process, as has been alleged.

~

On 29 December 1895, Dr Jameson launched a raid from Bechuanaland into the Transvaal that was designed to arouse British miners, living under the Boers as second-class citizens, to rise up and overthrow the Afrikaans government of Paul Kruger. Known as Uitlanders (foreigners), the British and other non-Afrikaans workers in the Transvaal had few civil and no franchise rights, and the raid was intended to give them self-government in an area of the Transvaal where they were in the overwhelming majority. Harmsworth was so much in support of it that the *Evening News* even suggested that Chamberlain was 'blundering' when he denounced the Jameson Raid as soon as he was officially informed of it.[56] (Chamberlain in fact knew it was about to happen and he even told an official to tell Rhodes to 'hurry up'.) All that Harmsworth's diary records on 1 January was 'Transvaal Crisis', but he clearly saw the Jameson Raid as a brave, empire-building moment rather than an unwarranted invasion of the Boers' sovereign territory.[57] Of 'Brave Dr Jim', as the *Evening News* dubbed him, the paper wrote, 'May his march to the relief of our brothers and sisters in the Transvaal be crowned with success.'[58]

On the very same day that the *Evening News* was wishing his raid well – Thursday 2 January 1896 – Dr Jameson surrendered to the Transvaal army after a desultory shoot-out and went into ignominious captivity ten days later. Cecil Rhodes was forced to resign as prime minister of Cape Colony. On 3 January, Kaiser Wilhelm II of Germany sent a telegram to the Transvaal president Paul Kruger expressing his 'sincere congratulations that you and your people . . . have succeeded, by your own energetic action against the armed bands which invaded your country as disturbers of the peace, in restoring peace and in maintaining the independence of the country against attack from without'. The *Evening News* interpreted this as the German emperor congratulating the Boer president for having 'killed Englishmen'.[59]

The Kaiser had acceded to the throne of Germany on the death of his father Frederick III from throat cancer in June 1888. He has been accurately described as both 'a meddling amateur with a belief in the divine right of kings' and a 'peculiar mix of swaggering overconfidence and obvious insecurity'.[60] A powerful personal hatred of the Kaiser – whom he never met – was to become a lifelong passion of Harmsworth's. The telegram provoked huge indignation in London, where German shops had their windows smashed and German sailors on shore leave were assaulted. *The Times* also denounced the telegram, and the Royal Navy was briefly mobilised.

Harmsworth warned of the German threat to the British Empire long before most people spotted the danger inherent in the post-Bismarckian Reich. Detractors put this down to scaremongering in order to sell papers; in fact, it showed impressive prescience, as the naval budgets Germany passed in the late 1890s made it increasingly clear that their growing fleets were not intended solely to defend their own coastline and police their overseas empire.

In southern Africa, Harmsworth's support for the British adventurers was unconditional. On 4 February, the day that Rhodes and Frederick Rutherfoord Harris, the secretary of the British South Africa Company, arrived in London to defend the company against Liberal politicians who wanted to sanction it over the raid, Harmsworth spent two hours with the two men and their legal team, and another two hours six days later.[61] When Jameson was released by the Boers to stand trial in London, Harmsworth witnessed the arrival of the accused at Bow Street police court, where he was cheered by crowds in what Harmsworth recorded in his diary as 'a most extraordinary scene'.[62] On 28 February, he 'had a long chat with Dr Jameson' and dined with him on 20 April, prior to his receiving a fifteen-month sentence in June (of which he only had to serve six, through illness).[63] Alfred Harmsworth knew that patriotism sold newspapers, but it was nonetheless a patriotism that he felt profoundly.

CHAPTER 4

'WE'VE STRUCK A GOLDMINE': THE *DAILY MAIL*

April 1896–July 1899

'It is *hard news* that catches readers. Features hold them.'[1]

LORD NORTHCLIFFE to Tom Clarke

In 1896 Alfred Harmsworth set up what was to be his largest venture by far: the eight-page national daily broadsheet the *Daily Mail*. He later recalled of the period just before the *Daily Mail* was founded:

> *The Times* went on its own mysterious way in the warren of Printing House Square, the *Daily Telegraph* continued its gentle rivalry with the *Standard*, the *Morning Post* was alive, the *Daily News*, political and literary, was the leading Radical organ, and the *Daily Chronicle*, under [Henry] Massingham, was the most brilliant and enterprising. I hope I shall not offend my friends of these great dailies when I say that their lack of initiative, through which they had fallen from the highly competitive days of the Sixties, and their subservience to Party were a direct invitation to the assault administered by the *Daily Mail*.[2]

The American writer Sydney Brooks recalled how 'Into this easy-going and self-satisfied world there burst the *Daily Mail*.'[3]

Accounts differ on why the title was chosen: Harold Harmsworth
thought it derived from the *Glasgow Daily Mail & Record*, which
he had bought the previous year, William Kennedy Jones thought
it was in homage to his own alma mater, the *Birmingham Daily
Mail*, but Leicester Harmsworth might have been correct when he
recalled that it just sounded good when shouted by paper-sellers.[4]

On 28 April 1896, Alfred got into the office at 5am. The next day,
he did not leave it until 11pm. In order to save the commute from
Elmwood, in the weeks leading up to the launch of the *Daily Mail*,
he stayed in the houses of friends and of Harold. Nothing was to be
left to chance before the first copy went on sale on the morning of
Monday 4 May, and the paper went through no fewer than sixty-
five dummy editions before it hit the streets.[5] The upfront costs of
newsprint, staff salaries and wire services reached a phenomenal
£40,000. Not for nothing did he joke that the new venture would
lead to either 'bankruptcy or Berkeley Square'.[6]

The private dummy runs contained 'all manner of grotesque
features which were designed to delude rivals into whose hands
Harmsworth made certain they fell. His rivals were amused and not
at all apprehensive.'[7] Meanwhile, the sides of houses and railway
bridges were plastered with advertisements for the *Daily Mail*. 'After
a severe struggle got the papers to press with many misgivings at
1.20am,' Harmsworth noted in his diary.[8] The first copy that rolled
off the press, at a record-breaking 20mph, he autographed and had
couriered to his mother.

The Harmsworths had invested in the latest Linotype machines,
which revolutionised typesetting and allowed a small number of
skilled operators to set type far faster than before, using a ninety-
character keyboard. 'Sitting in front of a keyboard not unlike that
of a typewriter,' reported an impressed technician, 'the operator is
able, by merely striking a key for each letter he requires, to cast the
type in lines of solid metal from a heated reservoir at the top. The
Linotype not only does the work several times more rapidly than the
old hand compositor, but reduces the expense by about 25 per cent.'[9]

Yet it was the Harmsworths' revolutionary attitude to the paper's content that was to explain its phenomenal success. They knew their target audience – white-collar, hardworking, commuting middle classes, clerks and City workers – and concentrated on giving it a penny-quality newspaper for a halfpenny. 'Had Northcliffe designed the *Daily Mail* as a halfpenny paper, and sold it for that price,' writes an historian, 'its fate might not have been the same.'[10] The 'ears' (the top sections on either side of the title) proclaimed 'The Busy Man's Daily Journal' and 'A Penny Newspaper for One Halfpenny'. It was unashamedly aspirational; 'Harmsworth was fond of declaring that the average *Mail* reader only earned a hundred pounds a year but expected one day to earn a thousand.'[11] He was determined to cater for the then largely unsatisfied need for the ever-more-literate and growing population to read interesting material. A newsvendor at King's Cross Station noted how the *Mail* was being bought by 'thousands of working men who never bought a morning paper before'.[12]

Many of the newspapers of the day were simply boring. They spoke down to readers, felt obliged to print indigestible pages of speeches by backbench MPs, had very small fonts and long-winded sententious editorials. By total contrast, the *Daily* Mail's pre-publication advertisements promised 'four leading articles, a page of Parliament, and columns of speeches will NOT be found in the *Daily Mail* on 4 May, a halfpenny'.[13] During the first month, the *Daily Mail* ran Westminster reports that averaged only seven lines for the House of Lords and eight for the Commons. By the new century, it had given up reporting debates daily altogether.[14] The politicians complained of the lack of coverage, claiming it was bad for democracy, but Harmsworth suspected that people did not read political reports and editorials, so he only covered politics when it was intrinsically interesting. On 4 May 1896, therefore, while leading articles filled eighty-one inches in *The Times*, fifty-five inches in the *Daily Chronicle*, fifty-three inches in the *Morning Post*, and thirty-two inches in the *Daily Telegraph*, they only covered seventeen inches in the *Daily Mail*.[15]

Although the paper was politically Conservative, Harmsworth occasionally allowed socialists such as Robert Blatchford and Philip Snowden to contribute to it. For all that, pride in and support for the

British Empire was central to the *Daily Mail*'s success. As Kennedy
Jones wrote in his autobiography *Fleet Street and Downing Street*,
'If Kipling be called the Voice of Empire in English literature,
we may fairly claim to have been the Voice of Empire in London
journalism.'[16]

Harmsworth also concentrated on topics such as agriculture, new
technology (he had visited the 'moving pictures' the previous year
and spotted their potential), sports, food, fashion, entertainment
and high society. He ordered editors that his papers must 'touch
life at as many points as possible'.[17] He also invented the concept of
a dedicated Letters to the Editor section.* (He didn't like unsigned
letters because 'The public believe they are written up in the office,'
which indeed they quite often were.[18]) Reflecting his own interests,
the *Mail* was 'the first journal to perceive that the motor-car was not
merely a new toy or a new convenience but portended a complete
revolution in the methods of land transportation ... It was the first
journal, too, to foresee the possibilities of aviation.'[19]

Harmsworth's definition of news was 'anything out of the ordinary ... the only thing that will sell a newspaper'.[20] The main news
page he called 'the surprise page', insisting that readers should find
things there that were genuinely unexpected.[21] 'Each day we must
have a feature,' he ordered, 'something different ... a surprise.'[22]
Early examples included 'The Truth About Nightclubs', 'Do We Eat
Too Much?' and 'The Riddle of Spiritualism'[23] (Harmsworth did not
believe there was anything to the last), while star journalist Hannen
Swaffer wrote an article entitled 'Is Oatmeal a Poison?' The paper
was written consciously for a wide British audience: foreign cur-
rencies were turned into sterling; phrases like *fait accompli* became
'accomplished fact'.

Harmsworth believed contrast to be 'the salt of journalism', so
stories on the same subject were never allowed to be placed near one
another. Brevity was also prized, with no long columns and many
short paragraphs. 'He exploited the paragraph,' the historian A. J. P.
Taylor noted, 'the short, quickfire presentation which makes modern

---

* An early letter to the editor was entitled 'Should the Clergy Dance?'

newspapers readable, the greatest advance in communication since the abandonment of Latin for English.'[24] 'Explain, simplify, clarify!' Harmsworth would regularly tell his sub-editors.[25] Years later, he explained the secret of his success to an employee, Norman Angell: 'I determined to put as much care and genius in making things plain to the mill-girl (or her employer, often just as ignorant) as a *Times* leader writer takes in making things plain to the clubman.'[26] As with the *Evening News*, there were lots of maps and regular features that could be found in the same place every day.

With correspondents in New York and Paris, and the Post Office capable of transmitting cables at ten words a second, readers got foreign news quickly. Harmsworth's office was connected up to the eastern end of the transatlantic cable on Valentia Island off the Irish coast. Whereas the other papers covered pages with long legal reports, Harmsworth put American and Canadian news – and also that from France, India and Germany – into the *Daily Mail*. Such was the extent of the railway system by then that newsagents could pick up the papers in the early morning and distribute them by breakfast time all over the country. This wide distribution made the *Daily Mail* 'the first truly national newspaper'.[27] When a news editor spent a lot of money covering a story, Harmsworth told him: 'Better a wrong decision any time than no decision at all. And remember this in your newspaper career – you have got to spend money to make it.'[28]

'The three things which are always news are health things, sex things and money things,' Harmsworth told Norman Angell. 'Health and sex and money always; and quickly.'[29] He recognised the power of human interest stories, especially in the areas of love, murder, missing children, crime and divorce, which the upmarket broadsheets often took a superior view to publishing.[30] One of his reporters recalled how they 'were trained to see something of human interest behind the scenes or on the sidelines of a formal ceremony or pompous pageant. They were expected to get a good story by discovering some odd character or unknown phase of life, or the pathos and drama of the *comédie humaine*. This was the stuff which interested Harmsworth himself.'[31] Yet, as another of his employees recalled, 'he had no use for the gossip column. He would not have it in the *Daily Mail*. He liked Court and Society paragraphs which recorded facts; he liked news about people ... but his "fact mind" revolted against "we hear"s and intangible trivialities about precious nobodies and puff-seekers.'[32]

Harmsworth disliked euphemisms intended to spare the blushes of Victorian matrons. 'I could never understand the squeamishness which made us talk in our law reports of "misconduct" when we meant "adultery",' he once complained, 'which caused us for years to talk about "the hidden plague" instead of syphilis.'[33] He also believed that reports of illegal abortions should be printed 'to help stop race suicide'. Nor did he allow titillation. 'He hated vulgarity in its most crude sense and even at school he had disliked dirty stories.'[34] He rarely swore and could sometimes be prudish, not allowing words like 'rupture' or 'constipation' into adverts. 'He never published an indecent word in his life,' Hannen Swaffer once pointed out.[35] And of course there was always Mother, who read his publications avidly and often took him to task if she thought something was vulgar. She approved of the policy by which the Almighty was almost never referred to in print. 'There isn't room for two gods here,' one sub-editor joked.[36]

As well as eye-catching news items, the *Daily Mail* ran daily serials of novels over eight weeks that averaged 100,000 words in total. Harmsworth took enormous trouble over these, knowing how they built readership. He would demand rewrites if he thought anything needed explaining. A sentence that ran, 'One afternoon in November a tall, dark man walked along Bond Street' would have him commenting, 'Who knows Bond Street except Londoners? What of the great world beyond? London is *so* provincial. Say *where* Bond Street is and *what* it is.'[37] He would show an almost obsessive attention to detail and would lambast editors if they had not noticed discrepancies in stories, telling them, 'The Earl starts his career at twenty-eight and goes to the altar with the mill-girl at twenty-five.' He criticised editors of comics if they depicted policemen without paunches, because 'The public expect comic policemen to be fat,' just as hen-pecked husbands always had to be thin.[38]

'He had no time for the old-time editorial pomposity,' an employee recalled of Harmsworth, 'which looked down on such departments as circulation, advertising and production.'[39] The *Daily Mail* marked a turning point in British newspaper advertising which, unlike the classified adverts in other papers, started to ignore the limitations of columns, use different type, employ illustrations and look more like billboard displays than old-fashioned newspapers. These were American techniques and they met with success, although Harmsworth was in constant friction with his advertising managers when he thought they might be distracting readers' attention too much away from the news. He was also constantly complaining of the typefaces employed by the advertising department – 'overwhelming', 'bludgeoning' – especially when 'the block didn't print well, or a bit of it showed through to the next page and gave a society woman a moustache'.[40] The juxtaposition of advertisements mattered to Northcliffe, who once wrote to a manager: 'Why place a whisky advertisement right under a Church Charity appeal? Do you think either will help the other?'[41]

Thomas Wareham Smith joined the *Daily Mail* when it launched and soon became its advertising manager. He recalled how Harmsworth 'invented the use of the telegraph form to attract advertisements. The form was printed daily in the paper. The reader was invited to write on it his requirements and send it along to the office for publication at a halfpenny a word – the same price as the [Post Office] charged for telegraphing. The idea caught on. Forms poured in. We couldn't deal with the business fast enough.'[42] In 1899, when a million people were buying the paper daily, Harmsworth could choose which companies he wanted to advertise in his pages, telling Wareham Smith, 'Wait for them to come to you.'[43]

The use of audited circulation figures meant that once the paper was an immediate success – and its first edition sold 397,213, a world record for any newspaper – advertisers flocked to the *Daily Mail*, allowing profit margins to rise. This meant that Harmsworth could afford to pay for the best writers in Fleet Street, which created a virtuous circle for sales. He often boasted about how much better his employees and freelancers were paid than in the rest of Fleet Street, and how that attracted the best writers. Oxbridge graduates started to write for him, attracted by the salaries on offer, and the high pay meant that a virtual Who's Who of talented late Victorian and Edwardian journalists wrote for the *Mail* at various times, including Max Beerbohm, Philip Gibbs, Charles Hands, Lionel Springfield, Hannen Swaffer, Duncombe Jewell, George Warrington Steevens, Edgar Wallace, H. G. Wells and the explorer Harry Johnston.

Harmsworth also believed it helped journalists to have memorable names and would encourage his employees to write under different ones if theirs were not unusual enough. William Pollock had to write under 'Pollock Pollock', for example, although for obvious reasons Hannen Swaffer and Twells Brex were allowed to keep their names, whereas January Mortimer was completed invented.[44] Harmsworth changed Charles Robert Mackenzie's name to Crombert Mackenzie because he said there were too many Mackenzies in the office and 'It is unjust to my secretaries,' arguing that it was doing him a favour as 'It will look fine at the top of an article.'[45]

The downside of being paid high salaries was that he quickly fired under-performers, or those lacking in ambition. When, after one conference, Charles Hands hung back and asked for a £100 loan, Harmsworth replied, 'Certainly not. You know I never lend money, Charles, but I sometimes give it,' whereupon he wrote out a cheque for £100.[46] Nor did he mind journalists asking him for a pay rise, seeing it as a sign of ambition (although that did not guarantee he would grant one). The story was told of him asking a reporter what he earned, getting the reply eight pounds a week, and asking 'Are you satisfied?' 'Quite.' 'Then you'd better go. Nobody who thinks he is earning enough is any good here.'[47]

'If you see anyone walking down these passages and looking like a codfish, you'll know he was brought in by my brother Cecil,' he once told the writer Philip Gibbs. 'Then I have the unpleasant duty of hoiking him out again.'[48] Hannen Swaffer was hired and fired three times. Harmsworth had the reputation of hiring, as one employee put it, 'only good-looking men who dressed well, on the theory that such men would impress and please people and so get information most easily and possess a useful self-confidence'.[49] When reporters went to interview very important people such as royalty, he let them use his Rolls-Royce.

Yet Harmsworth's army of reporters would not get every assignment. 'He insisted on "experts",' recalled one sub-editor. 'An Etonian to describe the Fourth of June; a Roman Catholic to describe Lourdes; a Jew to report a Jewish wedding; an electrical engineer to criticise the telephones; an American to describe baseball; a Labour man to report on [the] Labour conference; a sailor to report yachting; a lawyer (if he could get him) to report a murder trial; and so on. One often wondered what was left for the ordinary routine journalist.'[50]

Philip Gibbs, the *Daily Mail*'s second literary editor, wrote a memoir more than sixty years later, in which he recalled Harmsworth:

> I knew him at his best, a man of great charm, good looks (always beautifully dressed in an easy, informal way) extraordinarily kind and generous to those he liked (though occasionally ruthless and even cruel), and with a sure touch of journalistic genius ... [He] was curiously democratic in his behavior to the youngest members of his staff. At the Conference [at 4.30pm] every afternoon the most junior reporter was encouraged to suggest any idea for the benefit of the next day's paper, and, if it happened to be a good one, was rewarded by a word of praise from the Chief. He had to risk a word of withering sarcasm if it were not so good.[51]

From the beginning, Harmsworth was known as 'the Chief' by everyone at the *Daily Mail* and it soon spread to his other publications. Even Mary, when writing to third parties, called him that, and it was how he usually signed himself in his communiqués to his workforce.

Like Napoleon, Harmsworth had a remarkable capacity for compartmentalisation. 'There was scarcely a minute's interval,' one of his secretaries recalled, 'and it surprised me how he could switch off so completely from one subject to another.'[52] A senior executive in the company noticed how 'one moment Alfred would focus the entire force of his concentration on the subject of the vital necessity of improving Anglo-American relations. The next he would switch, with equal vigour, to arranging the details of the *Daily Mail* Golden Slipper competition to be won by the actress with the smallest foot.'[53] Although the executive was critical of this ability, it was useful in a trade when the focus of news could change by the minute. It did not mean that Harmsworth's belief in Anglo-American cooperation was in any way lessened by his having to concentrate on finding the smallest-footed actress.

~

Harmsworth ensured that the *Daily Mail* was a campaigning newspaper, not always on political issues but in areas that touched people's lives. Over the years, he and his papers – particularly the *Daily Mail* – campaigned for pasteurised milk, slum clearance and better housing, a standard loaf of bread containing at least 80 per cent wheat, daylight saving,* compulsory rear-view mirrors in cars, motor-driven rather than horse-drawn fire-engines, new types of roses and larger sweet peas, and even a new style of man's hat. An early campaign was for police stations to be equipped with telephones, a concept that the Metropolitan Police commissioner initially rejected on the grounds that it would merely encourage the public to keep telephoning their local stations, and his men would spend all their time on the telephone rather than out on the street catching criminals.[54]

The *Mail* headed a campaign for people taking holidays earlier than August; bought a farm and selected a tenant to see if smallhold-ings could pay, and gave prizes for the best design for a cottage.[55] The last eventually became the Ideal Home Exhibition, which still exists. When some of these campaigns were denounced as 'stunts', he replied that: 'A stunt is merely what jealous newspapers call something their rival has done that they had not the brains to do themselves. It is mostly used by the pompous old ladies of the "supe-rior" press.'[56]

'The old-fashioned, stodgy papers were for men only,'

---

* Which was not introduced until 1972.

Harmsworth later recalled. 'They ignored the news of interest to women. Now we look out specially for it. Women are the greatest newspaper readers.'[57] The *Daily Mail* was the first newspaper in Britain to have an entire page dedicated to women, entitled 'Women's Realm'. Occasionally he would have his chef prepare dishes following precisely the recipes published in his papers – 'and woe betide the editor if they did not turn out well'.[58]

Harmsworth typically woke around 5.30am and read all the competition papers first. He had a series of coloured pencils by his bedside with which he would mark up his own papers, before telephoning his editors at breakfast-time to congratulate them on scoops or criticise them for missing stories. He would also let his views be known far wider; for many years, communiqués – essentially a stream of consciousness about what he thought of that day's papers – were telegraphed almost daily and circulated to the whole staff. The micro-management was extraordinary. 'They ranged over every detail in every department,' a senior editor later recalled.

> He would warn us with equal seriousness to "watch" Ireland, or the divorce courts, or the comic animals in our children's features.* He would report things he had heard and seen and suggest news stories about them ... sometimes he would criticise the paper page by page; he would ... demand explanations of faults and delays he had noticed; he would hit out at "some infernal idiot" in this or that department ... Very often these communiqués were embarrassingly personal, but if at times they blamed, they also praised. He never lost a chance of commending good work in any department, and his communiqués would now and then announce a surprise bonus to this or that individual.

He often varied the form of these messages; on one occasion, he wrote in the style of Samuel Pepys.

By the evening of 5 May 1896, the day after the publication of its first edition, 397,215 copies of the *Daily Mail* had been sold,

---

* There seem never to have been enough monkeys for his taste.

against an initial expectation of 100,000. 'Orders still pouring in,' Harmsworth told Kennedy Jones as he put on his coat and left for the Salisbury Hotel. 'We've struck a goldmine.'[59] 'A big success, I think, bigger than we anticipated,' he noted in his diary after the launch. 'Letters and telegrams of congratulation pouring in on the debut of the *Daily Mail*.'[60] He had believed that the *Daily Mail* would be the biggest thing to hit Fleet Street in four decades, since the *Daily Telegraph* had been launched as a penny daily in 1855, and he was proved right. 'The brothers found an old-fashioned, ramshackle business and transformed it into a modern, streamlined industry,' notes an historian. 'They converted Grub Street into Fleet Street.'[61] Although there was always a dip after the first day of publication, by 1 September the paper had retained daily sales of 222,405.[62] This rose to more than 400,000 in 1898, 500,000 in 1899, 989,255 in 1900 and, during the Boer War, it briefly touched a million, giving Harmsworth the largest daily sales of any newspaper in the world.[63]

From making a guinea an article eight years before, Harmsworth was already earning £80,000 a year in 1895 – nearly £11 million in today's money – and the *Daily Mail* was to make him one of the richest men in Britain.[64] Yet money was not the driving force in his life after he had rescued himself and his family from their shabby genteel poverty. His life blood flowed from being the most influential press proprietor in the British Empire. Someone who saw a good deal of him later in life noted how he 'liked being rich, partly because wealth gave him the power of doing what he wished to do, and partly because money represented the stakes for which his game of life was played, and to win money meant that he was winning the game'.[65] Yet it was always a means to an end, and the end was power.

The congratulatory letters and telegrams on the launch included one from Lord Salisbury, to which Harmsworth replied: 'Fortune has placed us in possession of a most sudden and unexpected success and we shall spare no pains to maintain and increase it.'[66] Salisbury's nephew and successor as Conservative party leader, Arthur Balfour, wrote 'to express my high appreciation of your new undertaking ... I cannot doubt that it will succeed, knowing the skill, the energy, the resource with which it is conducted.'[67] Even William Gladstone wrote to say that 'The *Daily Mail* appears to me a most interesting experiment to which I give my hearty good wishes.'[68]

In private, Lord Salisbury is widely believed to have dismissed the *Daily Mail* as 'a newspaper run by office boys for office boys'. If he ever genuinely said it, this was a classic example of the snobbery that the paper had to face throughout its existence.[69] Salisbury's possibly apocryphal gibe probably referred to Thackeray's character Arthur Pendennis's* remark that 'The *Pall Mall Gazette* is written by gentlemen for gentlemen.' Yet it missed the mark, since there was a huge social grouping looking for a newspaper that fitted their patriotic views and demand for readability but which did not cost a penny, let alone threepence like *The Times*.

Harmsworth intended his audience to be as wide as possible – far beyond office-boys – which is why he was attacked so much by those who came slowly to realise that the *Daily Mail* had filled a vast gap in the newspaper market, and was to do so for decades to come. In retrospect, it might seem obvious that introducing a new audience – especially women – to concise writing, interesting formats and attractive competitions and advertisements would pay dividends, especially at half the cover price of the competition. Yet genius partly lies in doing what others find obvious in retrospect, but no one else was doing at the time.

Because it was deliberately written for Middle England, for the upper-working, lower-middle and middle classes and the bourgeoisie, the *Daily Mail* was instantly loathed by the intelligentsia, which never let up on it. With characteristic intellectual snobbishness, the historian G. M. Trevelyan wrote that 'The printing press, following the law of supply and demand, now appeals to the uneducated mass of all classes.'[70] This was untrue; *Daily Mail* readers had attended the Board Schools created by the Education Act in 1870 and were thirsty for knowledge. Harmsworth was entirely comfortable with the sneers, later telling Hannen Swaffer that 'the *Daily Mail* is the

---

* When Harmsworth occasionally used pseudonyms in his journalism, he called himself Arthur Pendennis.

best-hated paper in the world. On the day it ceases to be, I'll change my staff.'[71]

When, on 24 May 1897, the P&O ship *Aden* sank off Socotra in the Yemen with much loss of life, the *Daily Mail* was informed about the tragedy by an Aden postmaster, who furnished the fullest details. When P&O, whose communications were inferior, indignantly denied that the ship had sunk, the rest of Fleet Street abused the paper for its invention and questions were asked in Parliament. 'It was at this time that there began,' Harmsworth later recalled, 'from the other newspapers, those showers of abuse which have helped to make the paper.'[72] It took some days before the *Mail*'s scoop was revealed to have been true in every particular. Meanwhile, the attacks had been free publicity for the paper. It certainly led to Harmsworth's firm and lifelong belief that the more the *Daily Mail* was attacked, the better it did commercially.

~

In the summer of 1897, an attempt seems to have been made by Joseph Warren, who married Louisa Smith in 1884, to blackmail Harmsworth because of his and Louisa's fourteen-year-old illegitimate son Alfred Benjamin Smith, who was then living with his maternal grandmother in Essex and apprenticed to a carpenter. We do not know the financial arrangement made between him and the Warrens, but Harmsworth seems to have removed the boy from Essex and put him into the care of F. Bluett Duff, a twenty-one-year-old graduate of King's College, Cambridge, and law student, who later became a barrister and who arranged for Smith's upbringing. He was given a tutor, sent to concerts, the theatre and on a tour of Europe. An undated monthly bill survives which was paid by Harmsworth for rent on a boarding house in Eastbourne, pocket money, rail fares and incidentals, and money for medicine and an optician, totalling £98 two shillings and twopence.[73]

According to the 1901 census, a nineteen-year-old Alfred Smith, born in Southminster, was staying in the Grand Hotel, Brighton, and was put down as a 'Student Cambridge', though he was eighteen at the time and there is no record of his having attended either school or university there. He seems to have got occasional work from the *Daily Mail* in 1903, 'gaining a certain amount of experience in different departments'.[74] Louise Owen, Harmsworth's secretary and later his mistress, recorded how 'it was most pathetic to see Northcliffe literally hungering for the affection of this boy'.[75] He seems to have gained it, as young Alfred told her often: 'You would be surprised if you knew what a wonderful father I have; he really is a great man.'

Much about Alfred Benjamin Smith's later life is frankly conjecture, including the manner and place of his death, which Bluett Duff stated to a Harmsworth family investigator in 1935 had taken place in a lunatic asylum in Australia by 1929, although no Australian death certificate of anyone of that name exists. If all this seems to raise more questions than it answers, we can at least be fairly certain that Alfred Benjamin Smith had a grander upbringing than that of a carpenter and that his father was willing to spend money on retaining the public respectability necessary for entering high society. There seems to be no evidence to confirm (or indeed refute) the long-standing family story that Smith worked for years as a doorman at Carmelite House, the *Daily Mail* headquarters.[76]

~

Three days after the founding of the *Daily Mail*, Harmsworth spoke about Cecil Rhodes at a meeting of the imperialist Anglo-Saxon Club, which met in the Trocadero Restaurant in Piccadilly. The next day, the Liberal Imperialist MP Sir Charles Dilke told the war correspondent George Warrington Steevens that he had 'met last night one of the most remarkable men I have ever seen', before expounding on the similarities between Harmsworth and Napoleon in his creative phase as First Consul.[77] This comparison was later to become so much of a commonplace that one of Harmsworth's biographies was subtitled 'Napoleon of Fleet Street'.[78] Harmsworth collected books on Napoleon, had already visited his tomb at Les Invalides, read Bourrienne's *Life of Napoleon* more than once by July 1903, and was said to have cultivated a curl on his forehead in the manner of the young Bonaparte.

'There is a popular myth that he was an ardent admirer of Napoleon and his genius,' Max Pemberton wrote of his friend, 'but this is in a sense untrue. What I may call the Napoleonic cult, as it was supposed to be followed by Lord Northcliffe, was wholly the creation of clever Mr E. V. Lucas.'[79] In his 1903 satirical squib *Wisdom While You Wait*, Lucas joked about the youthful ages of the Harmsworths, including 'Alfred Napoleon Harmsworth, 23'.[80] Yet that was hardly enough to create a popular myth, which was actually based on Alfred Harmsworth's genuine interest in Napoleon. In November 1903, the *Daily Mail* leader-writer H. W. Wilson sent Harmsworth a list of sixteen books on Napoleon.[81] Many are the writers who have ascribed his interest in Napoleon to an early symptom of megalomania, but it is just as likely that he admired the ultimate exemplar of the youthful ambitious self-made man.

In the months following the success of the *Daily Mail*'s launch, Harmsworth found himself both enjoying his entry into high society and being sought out by politicians. He joined the Carlton Club; attended Lady Salisbury's great annual reception for the Diplomat Corps at the Foreign Office; went to Royal Ascot; was invited on shooting weekends; and, in July, Lady Magdalene Bulkeley, the daughter of the 5th Earl of Hardwicke, wrote to one of Salisbury's secretaries to suggest that Harmsworth should receive a baronetcy for his services to the nation and the Unionist party. When a knighthood was offered instead, he took the risk of turning it down, preferring to wait for the far more prestigious baronetcy (although, as he had no legitimate children, the difference was one of prestige rather than practicality). The candidates' page of the prestigious Beefsteak Club for 1 January 1897 is further evidence of Harmsworth's new-found social acceptability, consisting of no fewer than twenty-one names of supporters, including the Marquess of Granby, Earl of Onslow and Disraeli's former private secretary Lord Rowton, as well as his proposer, the Prime Minister's private secretary Sir Schomberg McDonnell.[82]

On 8 October 1896, in his capacity as editor of the *Daily Mail*, Harmsworth travelled to Dalmeny House near Edinburgh to interview the former prime minister the Earl of Rosebery, a Liberal Imperialist who was still nominally the leader of the Liberal Party, although he had fallen out with its empire-sceptic Gladstonian majority and was only hours away from resignation. When Rosebery suggested that the *Daily Mail* was Conservative, Harmsworth corrected him, saying that it was 'independent and imperial'.[83] (He meant British imperial; his newspapers severely criticised the horrors being perpetrated by King Leopold II of the Belgians in the Congo.) While at Dalmeny, Harmsworth met Herbert Asquith, who had been Home Secretary in the Rosebery Government. 'Lunched and spent a pleasant time there,' he recorded of his visit. When Rosebery resigned the Liberal leadership soon afterwards, the *Daily Mail* headline read 'Well done Rosebery', and after Harmsworth attended Rosebery's speech in Edinburgh, he told his diary it had been 'about the best speech I have heard'.[84]

In early December, Harmsworth fulfilled his earlier prophecy when he bought No 36 Berkeley Square, next door to Lord Rosebery at No 38. Mary remembered years later how her husband and Rosebery would go for 'almost daily walks' in Hyde Park 'where they walked to a certain tree and tapped it with their sticks before returning'.[85] On one of these walks, Rosebery told him, 'apropos the mob who like to go round great houses on show days, "What they really want to do is to see into your bedroom."'[86]

By December, the sheer physical effort of editing had exhausted Harmsworth again, and his doctors advised him to take a long holiday, what he called 'filling up my mental accumulators with energy.'[87] When one doctor, who he called his 'quacktitioner', warned him about his blood pressure, he joked that 'my circulation is in my newspapers'.[88] He, Mary and Reggie Nicholson left London for Dover on 10 December and were in Bombay (modern-day Mumbai) by Christmas Eve, travelling via Calais, Brindisi, Port Said and Aden. Nicholson had once been the traffic manager of the Bengal-Nagpur railways, so he knew the sub-continent well, but the main purpose of his invitation seems to have been as Alfred's friend and Mary's lover.

Alfred enjoyed his first visit to India, where he caught a 42lb fish at

Dhin ('best fishing place I ever saw'), rode an elephant, failed to shoot
a tiger, visited temples and forts at Poona, attended race meetings,
heard jackals 'wailing at night', saw the Taj Mahal by moonlight,
visited the Indian Mutiny sites at Lucknow and Cawnpore (modern-
day Kanpur), watched people bathing in the Ganges, met the Holy
Man of Benares and visited the Monkey Temple,* before leaving
Bombay on 5 January 1897.[89]

   The city had been in the grip of a famine and a subsequent
outbreak of bubonic plague since July 1896, and between the
Harmsworths' arrival and departure after a month's sightseeing,
some 300,000 people had fled the city. Leaving Mary and Nicholson
to their own devices, Harmsworth visited famine camps with the city
magistrate and commissioner, and wrote powerful articles that were
published as a pamphlet in July 1897 entitled *Hard Truth from India*
in which he was highly critical of the British authorities. In Lucknow
he wrote of 'the spectres, the gaunt, shrivelled old men and women,
the babies who seem all head and staring eyes'.[90] He described the
articles as 'written hurriedly – for the most part in trains and in
camp – but they are the result of much labour interviewing in the
course of a 4,000-mile journey during the last cold season'.[91]

   Although Harmsworth had been told that the deaths in Bombay
were running at sixty a day, on his arrival he could immediately see
that the true numbers were far higher than that.[92] Thomas Bennett,
the proprietor of *The Times of India*, told him that in fact the plague
deaths were running at between 1,500 and 2,000 weekly, but were
put down as fever and pneumonia rather than plague because land-
lords bribed 'native doctors' so that they could re-let their properties.
Harmsworth was angry that the local newspapers conspired to help
minimise the tragedy 'to a ridiculous, nay, criminal, degree'.[93]

   The horror did not make him doubt the British Raj, though;
indeed, the opposite. 'I know of no more striking proof of the lack
of ability to govern displayed by the educated Hindu, Mohammedan,
and Parsee', he wrote,

---

* Durgaji Temple.

than their disgraceful flight from Bombay at this terrible time. As for the mob, I shall never forget a night I spent at the railway station witnessing the wild scramble to escape. Those who were able to get into line at the booking office were able to resell their tickets at a premium of 5, 10 and even 20 rupees ... They have bolted like roach before a pike.[94]

Meanwhile, Harmsworth was proud to note, 'There has been no panic among the English.'[95] He argued that more railways, canals and roads would result in fewer famines, 'for I need scarcely add that both famine and plague, previous to the British conquest, removed their millions with terrible frequency, and, it should be remarked, with an infinitely smaller population'.[96]

A modern historian, Chandrika Kaul, records that the Bombay plague and famine of 1896–97 affected more than thirty million people, and adds that the *Daily Mail*'s coverage

handled the tragedy with sensitivity and in depth. The newspaper accorded due weight to the economic and political implications of the famine ... devoted daily coverage to the calamity, covering a range of issues over a period of several months. In hard-hitting editorials it expressed the view that ... England was 'holding back from the task of giving help to the starving natives'.[97]

The paper accused the secretary of state and the government of being 'little concerned with the probable death of a few hundreds of thousands of insignificant black men in remote country districts' – a very serious charge to have made.[98] It also urged Britons to contribute to a relief fund 'helping India in her hour of bitter need', which raised £170,000 by the end of January 1897.[99]

Over the decades of Harmsworth's ownership, states Kaul, the paper's coverage of India 'reflects a more thoughtful and considered position' than its bellicose stances over, say, the Sudan and China.[100] Over the Amritsar massacre in 1919, for example, it supported the government against the supporters of General Dyer and called for 'the appeasement of moderate and loyal Indians as essential for the security of the Raj' through the Government of India Act of 1919.

By contrast, the *Daily Mail*'s coverage of the official inquiry into the Jameson Raid in February 1897 reflected Harmsworth's full support of 'the Great Man of Africa', as it called Cecil Rhodes, who resolutely refused to produce the cablegrams that would have proved that Joseph Chamberlain had been lying when he claimed to have had no prior knowledge of the Raid. 'Mr Rhodes Holds the Field' trumpeted the newspaper, which was delighted when no sanctions were imposed on the British South Africa Company. 'He has served his country nobly,' the paper said of Rhodes, 'and has taken his place for all time amongst the makers of the British Empire.'[101]

Harmsworth understood how imperialism sold newspapers. 'It had been overlooked in Fleet Street how largely the British Empire is a family affair,' Kennedy Jones wrote in his autobiography; 'that there is hardly a household or a family circle of any size that does not have one or more of its family members earning a livelihood somewhere in the outer wards ... The instant we lifted the Jameson Raid out of the miasmal fog of party politics and put it in the clear light of reason and honourable motive the heartiest support was accorded to our paper by all classes.'[102]

Harmsworth's vertiginous social advancement took a step forward on 17 May when he attended a levee at St James's Palace and was presented to Queen Victoria by Lord Arthur Hill. Her Diamond Jubilee on 22 June, which in many ways witnessed the moment of zenith for the British Empire, was celebrated by the Harmsworth press with massive coverage and a ten-part series entitled *Sixty Years a Queen*. The evening before the Jubilee procession, Alfred and Mary had given a glittering reception for the colonial premiers at Berkeley Square. It was almost a social apotheosis for them, with the noted Polish pianist Ignacy Jan Paderewski performing in the drawing room and the Australian operatic soprano Nellie Melba singing. A chef was brought over from Paris. 'The house was beautifully decorated and the party was, I think, a great success,' Harmsworth noted.[103] 'Saw the Jubilee Procession,' he wrote in his diary the next day, 'the most magnificent spectacle I ever beheld, or can ever behold.'[104] He rented No. 66 St James's Street so that he, Mary, Mother and eighteen guests could watch it all in comfort. The procession was notable for the way the Rhodesian Horse was cheered especially loudly by the patriotic crowds, whereas in some places Kaiser Wilhelm II was booed.

Speaking at the annual shareholders' meeting the following month, Harmsworth announced that 'we are Unionist and Imperialist' and that he 'felt no sympathy whatever with the politicians of the sixties, seventies or the eighties', meaning the Gladstonian Liberals who had been in power for the majority of that time. His papers stood for the 'unwritten alliance of the English-speaking peoples' and for the Royal Navy that protected it.[105] He supported Imperial Federation, reciprocal tariffs against foreign protectionism (known as fair trade) and worried about German commercial success vis à vis Britain. Whatever they might have thought of his politics, the shareholders were happy: in 1897, the net profits of Harmsworth Brothers Ltd stood at £178,000.[106]

~

In January 1898, Harmsworth and Mary went on another long holiday, encompassing Paris, Genoa, Florence, Rome, Brindisi, Port Said and Cairo. As with India, he mixed the pleasure of seeing the sights with the business of interviewing people about the issues facing the empire, in this case Lord Cromer, the British Agent in Egypt (effectively its governor-general), whom he described as 'a strong, practical man', combining two qualities he admired greatly.[107] Cromer was at the forefront of the Salisbury Government's plan to avenge the death of General Gordon in Khartoum at the hands of the Dervishes thirteen years earlier, a plan that received vocal support from the *Daily Mail*.

The Harmsworths spent a month seeing the Pyramids at Giza, cruising down the Nile, bird-shooting and photographing, visiting the temples at Karnak and Luxor, and going as far south as the First Cataract above Philae. Harmsworth sent back a piece of 4,000-year-old mummy cloth to a friend of his father, joking that 'As my dear father would have said, from journalism to robbing the dead is but

a natural and brief step.'[108] He also bought the *Daily Mail* journalist
G. W. Steevens some camels at Aswan. He adored sailing down the
river on a converted houseboat with what he called 'companions one
loves and a goodly store of books, I know nothing like it'.[109]

When the Spanish–American War broke out in April, the *Daily
Mail* supported the United States wholeheartedly, in part because
critics of American imperialism – at home and abroad – tended to
be the same people who criticised British imperialism, and partly
because Harmsworth believed the Americans would make far
better imperialists than the Spanish. Yet he found out that the
amount it cost to cover that war was not covered by increased
circulation; the British people were not particularly interested in
what was taking place in Cuba and Manila, however much his
papers emphasised co-sanguinity. With more than a dozen war
correspondents engaged in the Sudanese and Spanish–American
Wars by the end of 1898, Harmsworth calculated that he was
paying more in telegraph costs than any other British proprietor.
When General Kitchener won his decisive victory at the Battle of
Omdurman in September, he was congratulated by the *Daily Mail*,
while Steevens made reference to the 'magnificent heroism of the
doomed dervishes'.

On 1 November 1898, the Harmsworths brought all their publications together under one roof at Carmelite House on the corner
of Carmelite Street and Tallis Street, a five-storey red-brick building with mullioned windows. The spacious and ornate Room One
overlooking Tallis Street started off as Harmsworth's office before it
was later used as the main conference room. 'It is a vast hall rather
than a room,' recalled Tom Clarke, the *Daily Mail*'s news editor. 'I
remember the awful distance I had to walk from the door across a
silent desert of carpet to the Editor sitting afar off at a flat desk, his
eyes on me all those terrible moments it took to reach him.'[110] Clarke
later discovered that it had been deliberately planned that way, when
Harmsworth told him, 'You can learn a lot about a man by watching him walking at you across a room.' There were huge fireplaces
at each end, with massive mantelpieces and electric 'candles' with
crimson shades. At night, the room was illuminated by lights hidden

behind a cornice that ran around the mahogany-panelled walls and threw light upwards on to a green and gold strip.

As well as a portrait of Mary by Philip de Laszlo resting on an easel, Harmsworth had a bronze bust of Napoleon on a pedestal, looking towards his desk. Instead of weighty tomes, the bookshelves contained bound volumes of *Pluck*, the *Girls' Friend* and *Comic Cuts*, which Clarke thought 'appear to be rather incongruous ornaments to this editorial sanctum'.[111] For all that Harmsworth's office was intimidating, he expected people to come to see him if they had good ideas for the paper. 'I earn my living by being worried,' he told Clarke.

> I have no use for the man who is too busy to be seen. The really busy man always has time, because he has his work organised. The man at the top must always make time. If he has no time, it shows he is foolishly tied up with detail, which office-boys can look after, and is not doing what he is paid for – thinking, and receiving ideas from the outside. He is paid to be worried, not to barricade himself on an inaccessible throne.'[112]

Although at that period he sometimes bit his fingernails until they bled, he distinguished between being worried and getting rattled. 'I have no use for the man who gets rattled,' he told Clarke, mentioning one of his employees on another paper. 'I have been trying to rattle him for weeks. He is taking it splendidly. He will be a director one day.'[113] On New Year's Day 1900, in a characteristic act of willpower, he decided he would never bite his fingernails again, and never did.[114]

Near to Carmelite House, the Harmsworths owned three large buildings in Whitefriars Street whose presses could produce 600,000 papers a day. F. A. Mackenzie, a veteran *Daily Mail* employee, recalled that 'the main building is pervaded with the odour of printers' ink and engine grease; the air is full of vibration caused by the rapid movement of the printing-machines and the throbbing of the 120-horsepower engines; the noise is so great that one must shout to make even a person standing just by hear.'[115] The Harmsworths were already the largest owners and operators of rotary presses in the country. Key to their success was their determination to own every step of the production process, from the creation of the wood pulp through the printing and distribution of the papers, until the finished product got into the hands of the newsagents themselves.

Yet not everything the Harmsworths launched was automatically successful. When, in the spring of 1899, they tried to produce a Sunday edition of the *Daily Mail*, it foundered within two months under an avalanche of Sabbatarian abuse. Proving their capacity for cutting losses when necessary, they closed it after only six editions.

In 1899, G. W. Steevens wrote *The Tragedy of Alfred Dreyfus*, which highlighted how profoundly anti-Semitic Third Republic France was. When he was subjected to abuse for this, Harmsworth stood by him, despite his own anti-Semitism. 'I am not in the least afraid of public opinion,' he was later to state. 'I stood up against it here in the Dreyfus Case.'[116] Yet Kennedy Jones also told the story of Harmsworth telling him 'Jones, you're making too much of this Dreyfus Affair' when he was editing the *Evening News*. 'Alfred, did you ever hear of the crucifixion of Christ?' Jones replied. 'Well, this is the biggest news story since that.'[117]

In January 1899, the *Harmsworth Magazine* published a macabre short story entitled 'Man Overboard!' about a man who falls off a steamer in the Red Sea and which ends just before he is eaten by a shark. The author was Lord Randolph Churchill's son Winston who, despite being published by Harmsworth, snobbishly told his mother Jennie Jerome of 'Harmsworth's cheap Imperialist productions', adding that 'I don't say that they have not done good and paid but they are produced for thousands of vulgar people at a popular price.'[118] That July, Harmsworth drove to Oldham to support Churchill's first attempt to get into Parliament. He had just taken possession of a six-horsepower Panhard-Levassor motor car from Paris and there were several punctures and mechanical mishaps along the way, but he had shown willing for a young man who he saw as one of a promising new generation of Unionist Imperialists. After he came third out of the four candidates, Churchill wrote 'to thank you for your kindness in supporting me during the election in the *Daily Mail*, and for your adventurous expedition in the motor car. I'm sorry that neither of our enterprises were successful in connection to Oldham. But I don't expect my career or your car will be seriously damaged.'[119] Instead, a major watershed in the lives of both men was fast approaching.

CHAPTER 5

'WE BELIEVE IN ENGLAND': THE BOER WAR

April 1899–May 1902

'He had an uncanny flair as to what the public wanted.'[1]

SIR EVELYN WRENCH on Lord Northcliffe, 1934

The Jameson Raid failed to lead to any significant amelioration in the plight of the Uitlanders, so in mid-April 1899, Cecil Rhodes was back in London demanding vigorous action against the Boers. Harmsworth gave him a ready ear, dining with him then, and again on 5 May, after which the *Daily Mail* argued that it was 'England's Duty' to support the British population in the Transvaal. On 8 May, Rhodes was given a tour of Carmelite House, where he was shown his own draft obituary, and the next month the paper denounced Paul Kruger for refusing to make any meaningful concessions over the franchise or an independent judiciary.[2] The crisis kept Harmsworth working in the office until 1.30am on various occasions in June.

The political influence that the *Daily Mail* already exercised was reflected in the fact that, in September, Harmsworth was invited to the War Office to discuss the South African situation with George Wyndham, the under-secretary for war, and Lord Selborne, the under-secretary at the Colonial Office. Information began to be leaked to it from a government that knew it could be trusted in its solidly anti-Boer stance.

War was coming and Harmsworth was determined that the *Daily Mail* would cover it more fully than any other paper, whatever the cost. He sent no fewer than twenty-two war correspondents to South Africa, including G. W. Steevens, Charles Hands, the American Julian Ralph ('The War as an American Cousin Sees It') and Edgar Wallace. This marked the largest contingent from any British newspaper.[3] He offered Winston Churchill a job as a war correspondent, who used it as a lever to a bigger offer from Oliver Borthwick of the *Morning Post*.[4] Harmsworth instead hired Churchill's aunt Lady Sarah Wilson, daughter of the 7th Duke of Marlborough as the first female war correspondent. She did an outstanding job during the siege of Mafeking, where her husband was aide-de-camp to the commander Colonel Robert Baden-Powell.

By the end of 1899, the *Daily Mail* had a Cape Town office that, on a single night, sent cables costing £600. The paper chartered special trains at £200 per week to ensure that the news of the war hit the streets of Manchester four hours ahead of any rival.[5] From 1902, the *Daily Mail* and *Evening News* were also delivered by motorised transport, far faster than their horse-drawn competitors.[6]

For those looking for a conspiracy theory to explain Harmsworth's vocal support for the Boer War, his ownership of shares in Rhodes's British South Africa Company proved a godsend. A pamphlet was placed on every seat in the House of Commons, accusing Harmsworth of being in the pay of Cecil Rhodes.[7] 'Many years ago I was unwise enough to purchase a number of shares in the Chartered Company,' Harmsworth commented four years later.

> I was one of the fools, and still hold the shares, but, in addition to their depreciation in value, I have never received a dividend, and have been overwhelmed with abuse in Parliament and elsewhere. And quite rightly, I think. It never occurred to me when I purchased these shares that there would be a South African war, and, had it occurred to me, I should never have considered it possible that one's critics would suppose that such a property would bias one's judgement in national affairs.[8]

The pamphlet was published anonymously for libel reasons, but a strong suspicion must rest with Henry Labouchere, editor of the scurrilous and ill-named newspaper *Truth*. In fact, however, Harmsworth's belief in Britain's mission in South Africa, and his wish for vengeance after Britain's defeat in the First Anglo–Boer War of 1881, long predated and far outweighed any hope that his shares in Rhodes' company might ever return to the level of the £8 10 shillings that he paid for them. As we have seen, power and a belief in empire, rather than money, motivated Harmsworth once his family had been made financially secure a decade earlier.

On 9 October 1899, after a decade of worsening relations with Britain, President Kruger issued an ultimatum for British forces to be withdrawn from Cape Colony; two days later, the armies of the Transvaal and Orange Free State invaded Cape Colony and Natal, and the Second Anglo-Boer War began. For the past three and a half years, Harmsworth had been editing the *Daily Mail* with the help of S. J. Pryor, but on the outbreak of war, he brought in Thomas Marlowe, who was described by Philip Gibbs as 'looking like a good-natured bulldog'.[9] Gibbs recalled how 'Tom Marlowe, imperturbable, with just a faint twinkle now and then in his dark eyes, was a restraining influence on the impetuous genius of Alfred Harmsworth.'[10] (When Marlowe's son was born in 1904, he rather oleaginously was christened Anthony Alfred Harmsworth Marlowe.)

Yet Harmsworth did not quite strip Pryor of his de facto editing role, seeing the battle between Pryor and Marlowe as one of the survival of the fittest. 'It was now unclear which of them was in charge,' states an historian, 'so they would race each other every morning to get to the editor's chair first and stay there, with Harmsworth looking on and enjoying the joke. Marlowe emerged victorious: it is said he got up earlier and had the foresight to bring sandwiches for his lunch; maybe he also had the stronger bladder.'[11] This method of blurring roles and encouraging internal competition was something Harmsworth employed regularly, however much it understandably irritated his employees.

~

The Boer War started very badly for Britain. On 30 October, Piet Joubert defeated Sir George White at the battle of Nicholson's Nek and, three days later, Ladysmith in Natal fell under a punishing Boer siege. In 'Black Week' in December, the British were defeated at the battles of Stromberg on the 10th, Magersfontein on the 11th and Colenso on the 15th, collectively more than justifying the *Daily Mail*'s criticism of the British commander-in-chief General Sir Redvers Buller as insufficiently vigorous. For all that Harmsworth wanted a baronetcy from Lord Salisbury, he attacked the Unionist government with verve as the news arrived of debacle after debacle. Its readers recognised that the paper was on the side of the ordinary soldier rather than the generals or politicians, and by December it was attaining regular daily sales of a million. The paper reserved its most vitriolic criticism for those it called the 'Little Englanders' – anti-imperialists who opposed the war and wanted a peace that gave the Boers what their ultimatum had demanded. Harmsworth 'saw himself as an independent, incorruptible crusader for the common man and the interests of the British Empire', and his readers did too.[12]

Harmsworth's criticisms naturally infuriated government ministers, and the *Daily Mail* was threatened with being cut off from receiving official news. But other newspapers stood by Harmsworth, especially *The Times* and the members of the Newspaper Proprietors Association, seeing it as an attack on the press in general. When he was accused by St. John Brodrick, the secretary of state for war, of having gathered 'secret information', Harmsworth challenged him to 'express definitely on a public platform, where we can proceed against him for libel, that the *Daily Mail* has purloined public documents'.[13] Brodrick declined.

Edgar Wallace and Sarah Wilson also sometimes got into trouble with the generals and the government, but Harmsworth strongly supported them each time. 'He relished the battle, for, in waging it, he was conscious of having the old ghosts whom he reverenced at his back.'[14] These ghosts were men like John Delane, editor of *The Times* from 1841 to 1877, and William Howard Russell, its war correspondent in the Crimea, another conflict that had begun badly for Britain. Harmsworth was fascinated by the history of the British press and 'would pore for hours over old files of newspapers'.[15] He saw himself in the heroic tradition of Delane and Russell, and behaved accordingly, regardless of the embarrassment it caused the government and Unionist Party.

When the war broke out, Harmsworth offered Rudyard Kipling, the first poet of the British Empire, £10,000 to represent the paper as a war correspondent. Kipling declined, but he agreed instead to assist in the fundraising for the *Daily Mail*'s Soldiers' Families Fund, which raised money for tobacco, cocoa and soap for the troops, and clothing and food parcels for their dependents. Kipling wrote 'The Absent-Minded Beggar', a music-hall song that reminded audiences of the dependents of the 'gentlemen in khaki ordered south' and which urged audiences to 'pay – pay – pay!' It was published on 31 October 1899 and sold as a pamphlet, and once Sir Arthur Sullivan had set the words to rousing music, it became ubiquitous. As well as in music-halls, it was sung at concerts and recitals, and even to barrel-organs in the streets, while the words were printed on every kind of paper and on silk, satin, and linen.[16] Maud Tree, the wife of the impresario Herbert Beerbohm Tree, recited the poem every night for fourteen weeks, raising £70,000 for a fund that eventually came to more than £340,000,* further equating the *Daily Mail* with patriotism in the mind of the public. When Lily Langtry sang the lines 'pay – pay – pay!' at the Garrick Theatre, 'she was almost driven from the stage by the hail of silver thrown by the enthusiastic audience'.[17] When it was wound up in 1903, the Soldiers' Families Fund bought a 300-bed veterans hospital set in sixty-six acres in Alton, Hampshire, which it gave to the nation.

The fund also inaugurated a long friendship between Harmsworth and Kipling, in which the former introduced the latter to a love of motoring. Harmsworth visited Rudyard and Carrie Kipling at their country house at Rottingdean in East Sussex in a new Mercedes in October 1899. He said that being driven in a car was 'like being massaged at speed' and he took them on a twenty-minute trip, leaving them 'white with dust and dizzy with noise', but of which Kipling later

---

* Well over £10 million in today's money.

wrote in his autobiography *Something of Myself*, 'the poison worked from that hour'. The next year, after the *Daily Mail* had sponsored a Thousand Mile Trial for vehicles throughout the country, Kipling wrote *The Muse among the Motors*, fourteen poems which were published in series over seven days in the *Daily Mail* in February 1904.

A speech that the German Chancellor, Bernhard von Bülow, delivered in the Reichstag on 11 December 1899 – in which he said that during 'the coming century the German people will be a hammer or an anvil' – alarmed Harmsworth, echoing as it did Bülow's demand two years earlier for Germany to have 'a place for ourselves in the sun'. Before the end of the Boer War, in which the vast majority of Germans openly supported the Boers, Bülow said that 'We must continue to keep Germany so strong that, as is the case today, our friendship is worthwhile, and no-one can be indifferent to our enmity.'[18] Such Weltpolitik required a naval programme which made antagonism with Britain inevitable. Despite the fact that the British and German nations had long traditions of cooperation, reinforced by dynastic, cultural, religious and economic ties, a large German navy invited a clash.

Harmsworth did not mind that Germany wanted a colonial empire in places like Namibia, the Cameroons, East Africa and some Pacific islands, but he was suspicious of it building a far greater fleet than was necessary to service such places. Wilhelm II was, as one historian has put it:

> intent on transforming the international constellation of Great Powers with the clear aim of establishing German hegemony on the European continent. The traditional guarantor of the European balance of power, Britain, was to be neutralised through the naval programme orchestrated by [Germany's naval minister, Admiral Alfred von] Tirpitz. The Kaiser's support for the minister was a key factor in the unfolding naval race with Britain.[19]

It was a race that Harmsworth was determined that the Royal Navy should not lose.

Meanwhile, the *Daily Mail* kept up its fire on the War Office,

demanding 'Guns! More guns! Better guns!'[20] It denounced the
Ordnance Department for the fact that the Boers had superior
weaponry than the British Army, comparing their Krupp artillery
and Mauser rifles to their British equivalents. Widening its attack
on the Salisbury ministry, it also pointed out that so many ministers
were septuagenarians that it was, as one headline put it, 'The Oldest
Government on Record'. The troops themselves were depicted as
heroes gravely let down by the government, especially considering
what the *Daily Mail* called the 'Government's Inexplicable Delay'
in sending out enough reinforcements on the long journey south.

Sir Michael Hicks Beach, the veteran chancellor of the exchequer,
was blamed for not providing enough money for the campaign;
Lord Wolseley, the commander-in-chief of the British Army, was
implicitly blamed for the inferior armaments and equipment; and St
John Brodrick and his predecessor Lord Lansdowne were accused of
apathy and incompetence. (When Brodrick attempted to punish the
Daily Mail by refusing it permission to publish the casualty lists, it
ran them anyway.) Only the Colonial Office, led by Harmsworth's
hero Joseph Chamberlain, escaped unscathed. On 29 December, the
paper reported that the military authorities were 'even now, sending
obsolete guns to the Cape'. 'Can the Government be Saved?' the
paper asked on 12 January 1900, attacking Lord Salisbury's nephew
and political heir Arthur Balfour for his 'bland assurances'.

If it were going to be saved, it would be by General Frederick
Roberts and his chief of staff Herbert Kitchener, who had arrived in
the Cape on 10 January to supersede Buller and prepare for a long
war. These changes were hailed by the Harmsworth papers. Even
Harmsworth's great detractor A. G. Gardiner wrote of the *Daily
Mail* during the Boer War that 'people laughed and scoffed, but they
read it and insensibly were governed by it'.[21] The Boer War taught
Harmsworth that the Establishment, and the aristocracy that still
held tremendous sway in both the government and the British Army,
were not the supremely competent standard-bearers of Empire. It was
a lesson he was never to forget.

In 1900, a second printing and distribution plant was established in Manchester for the *Daily Mail*. The contents of the standard edition published in London was telegraphed via a private wire so the paper printed in Manchester was an exact replica of that produced in London, the first time such a thing had been done. Harmsworth explained to shareholders that the main reason for its success was 'its free use of cable and private wire'.[22] He constantly embraced new technology, saying, for example, 'Telephones multiply the man.'[23]

During this period, Harmsworth also assembled the managerial and editorial team that was to stay with him for the rest of his life. He already had George Sutton as his closest lieutenant, described by a contemporary as 'a Sphinx in the background, the Chief's right hand man ... Austere, uncommunicative, intense, a tall, thin-lipped man with black piercing eyes in a parchment face, a man of nerves and Oriental inscrutability, he was always an enigma.'[24] He had been with Harmsworth since joining as a twenty-year-old shorthand writer on *Answers*; by thirty-four, he was a director and, by forty-four, vice-chairman of Amalgamated Press. 'He knew all the Chief's secrets.'[25]

Harmsworth promoted Andrew (later Sir Andrew) Caird from the night editorship of the *Mail* to be put on the board in charge of day-to-day finances, 'a watcher of the halfpennies'.[26] A cautious Scot with a rough exterior and shrewd dark eyes, close-cropped hair and a bull neck, he kept an eye on Harmsworth's instinctive generosity. When Harmsworth characteristically told an employee to 'spend all the money you can', Caird was on hand shortly afterwards to ensure he did not take that literally.[27]

Much of the news organisation was in the hands of Walter Fish, 'the very embodiment of efficiency and drive'.[28] He must have got tired, however, of Harmsworth ringing him up to ask for the latest news with the words 'Anything fresh, Fish?'[29] Another key figure on the news side of the *Daily Mail* was Bernard Falk, who recalled in the 1950s how Harmsworth would feign anger to get results, describing him as 'a great actor in his way'.[30] Falk was Jewish and claimed that Harmsworth was not anti-Semitic. 'What would people say if they saw me walking in the park with you?'

Harmsworth once asked him. 'Tell 'em I'm young Rothschild,' Falk replied.[31] Falk was clearly pleased enough by his response to recall it half a century later, but it does not lessen the anti-Semitism inherent in the question.

Falk believed that all journalists should be thankful to Harmsworth for the way he raised salaries across Fleet Street and he spoke of his 'indescribable charm'.[32] The charm was undeniable, and perhaps some of the anger was faked, though that would not have made it any less disturbing for the person on the receiving end. The journalist Norman Angell never personally experienced the 'very rough side to his tongue' in ten years of working closely for Harmsworth, although he knew it existed and once heard 'a dose of Billingsgate* and tongue-lashing of which I have never heard the equal'.[33] Yet at least he felt guilt, telling Angell, that 'a man as powerful as I am ought not to let his temper get away with him'.[34]

Harmsworth was devastated when he heard that, on 15 January 1900, G.W. Steevens had died from enteric fever during the siege of Ladysmith. He had specially chosen him to cover the war, and he drove down to Merton Abbey near Wimbledon to give his con-dolences to Steevens' widow. Accompanied by the American war correspondent Richard Harding Davis, who would be sent to South Africa in Steevens' place, Harmsworth arrived in a 'very emotional condition', according to the art historian Charles Lewis Hind, who was also present, 'sobbing and saying that he could never forgive himself for sending George to Ladysmith and that the blow had destroyed his power to think and to work'.[35] Harmsworth gave Mrs Steevens a pension of £500 a year for life and established a scholar-ship in her husband's name.

True to his belief in American energy and enterprise, Harmsworth employed a large number of Americans over the years. As the veteran journalist John Hammerton recorded in his autobiography *With Northcliffe in Fleet Street*, 'his frequent transatlantic trips were regarded with some apprehension by his

---

* The London fish market famed for the profanity of its porters.

Carmelite colleagues' as very often 'the Chief returned from the United States with a bright new American journalist, who was to set Fleet Street in a flutter'.[36] He tended to drop them as easily as he had picked them up, but other examples of his American imports included Julian Ralph, Charles Balch, the illustrator Penrhyn Stanlaws, W. L. Warden (editor of the *Continental Daily Mail*), Marine Dubbs in the circulation department, Alexander Kenealy (who edited the *Daily Mirror* successfully) and, most importantly, Pomeroy Burton, the former editor of Joseph Pulitzer's *New York World* who became the general manager of Associated Newspapers. When it came to Anglo–American amity, Harmsworth practised what he preached.

~

The arrival of Field Marshal Lord Roberts and General Kitchener at Cape Town heralded a change of fortunes in the Boer War, with Kimberley relieved on 15 February, Piet Cronje surrendering to the British at Paardeberg on 18 February, the relief of Ladysmith ten days later, Roberts's capture of Bloemfontein on 10 March and the surrender of the Orange Free State a week after that. Freed from Kimberley, Cecil Rhodes lunched with Harmsworth on 19 April, approving of the *Daily Mail* headline of 'Peace with Dishonour' should Britain grant the Boers independence as the price of peace.

Celebrating its fourth anniversary on 4 May 1900, the *Daily Mail* defiantly stated that it was:

> the embodiment and mouthpiece of the imperial idea. Those who launched this journal had one definite aim and view. It was and is to be the articulate voice of British progress and dominion. We believe in England. We know that the advance of the Union Jack means protection for weaker races, justice for the oppressed and liberty for the downtrodden. Our Empire has not exhausted itself. Great tasks lie before it and great responsibilities have to be borne. It is for the power, the greatness, the supremacy of this Empire that we have stood. In the heart of every Englishman has dawned the consciousness that a still greater destiny awaits us. The glorious

pages of yesterday in our history are to be succeeded by brighter achievements tomorrow. Ours is no limited task. If the burdens of empire are great, the results are worthy.[37]

For all that these sentiments are profoundly politically incorrect today, they were held genuinely by patriots who believed that protecting and extending the British Empire was a noble calling, which did far more good to the world than harm, and that the only alternatives to it were not the peaceful self-determination of the native peoples of the empire, but either vicious communal and inter-tribal strife or German, Spanish, French, Dutch or Russian domination. The imperialists to whom Harmsworth wanted to appeal were those whose motives were essentially altruistic, and he would not have recognised the modern Marxist analysis that it was all a merely exploitative construct intended to mulct indigenous peoples.

The relief of Mafeking on 17 May 1900, after its 216-day siege, led to the greatest scenes of popular national jubilation since Trafalgar.[38] Crowds formed outside newspaper offices and the house of Robert Baden-Powell's mother. Harmsworth was staying at the Surrey house of St. Loe Strachey, the editor of the *Spectator* magazine and a fellow motoring enthusiast, when the news arrived, and noted that when he drove to a country house which he was renting – Calcot Park near Reading – 'the Mafeking celebrations [were] forming a remarkable sight on the road'.[39] The *Daily Mail*'s response was to summon up the Napoleonic Wars to celebrate the fact that 'John Bull is just as willing to fight in a just cause as he was in 1815.'[40] A few days later, however, Douglas Story of the *Daily Mail* broke the news in an interview with the Boer leader Marthinus Steyn that far from meaning victory, the war was set to continue, even though Britain annexed the Orange Free State on 24 May and took Pretoria, the capital of the Transvaal, on 5 June. Two days later, the *Daily Mail* called on Sir Alfred Milner, the Liberal Imperialist governor of Cape Colony whom Harmsworth greatly admired, to be given the task of reorganising southern Africa under the Crown after the eventual victory.

Just as an enormous audience had begun to trust the *Daily Mail* for the quality of its news, an event occurred that threatened to undermine it completely. The paper had covered the Boxer* Rebellion in China extensively and had got several important things right about the siege of the European Legations (embassies) in Pekin (modern-day Beijing). But on 13 July 1900, it ran a story entitled 'Pekin Massacre', which claimed that everyone in the Legations – including the British ambassador Sir Claude MacDonald – had been 'put to the sword'.[41] A shocked nation went into mourning, but just before a memorial service took place at St Paul's Cathedral on 23 July, the truth emerged that the Legations were still holding out. The next day, the *Daily Mail* proclaimed 'Legations Safe!' Harmsworth immediately sent off a reporter on the next boat to discover the truth. (Since he was not given enough time to go home to pack, he boarded ship wearing the tailcoat in which he had turned up to work.[42]) The *Daily Mail* was rightly lambasted by rival newspapers and in Parliament for its incorrect report that had caused so much anguish.

For a short period, circulation languished, but the paper's in-depth Boer War coverage helped revive it, especially once Roberts occupied Johannesburg on 31 August and Kruger fled the Transvaal for Europe on 11 September. Running a piece entitled 'The Boer Army's End' on 21 September proved to be over-optimistic; in fact, the Boers had decided to adopt guerilla tactics and continue the war as an insurgency.

Lord Salisbury called a snap general election in the first fort-night of October 1900. Known as the 'Khaki Election' for the way that the war dominated it, he was rewarded with the return of 334 Conservatives and sixty-eight Liberal Unionists, against an opposi-tion of only 186 Liberals and eighty-two Irish Nationalists. A new party, called Labour, won two seats. Three of the Harmsworth brothers – Hildebrand, Leicester and Cecil – stood in the election as Liberal Unionists, but only Leicester won, squeaking in at Caithness by twenty-eight votes. The *Daily Mail* supported them and also Winston Churchill, who this time was elected for Oldham.

On the last day of the election – 16 October – Harmsworth

---

* This fanatical Chinese secret society was also called the Society of the Righteous Harmonious Fists.

authorised R. D. Blumenfeld, a Wisconsin-born news editor at the
Mail, to offer Godfrey and Arthur Walter, the leading owners of
The Times, £1 million for the paper. 'Never mind,' Harmsworth
told Blumenfeld after the approach came to nothing. 'We'll get it
sooner or later.'[43]

~

In November 1900, Harmsworth, Mary and Reggie Nicholson left
for the United States on the RMS *Teutonic*, Alfred's first visit there
since 1894. 'Are you on business or pleasure?' Churchill asked.
'Perhaps one involves the other: it should in any well-conceived
existence.'[44] It was indeed both; as well as attending the Whitney
Ball along with the Astors, Vanderbilts, Jays and Harrimans,
Harmsworth made friends with the publisher Walter Hines Page,
visited Thomas Edison to inspect his inventions in New Jersey, found
Mark Twain on 'great form' at a book reading, and had a private
audience with President William McKinley.[45]

Harmsworth's greatest coup of that trip, however, came when
Joseph Pulitzer challenged him to guest-edit a special edition of his
New York World for the first day of the new century, to show what
'the newspaper of the future' would look like.[46] Harmsworth enthusi-
astically took up the opportunity. He cut the usual size by half, turning
the *World* into a four-column paper with twenty-four pages that were
eighteen inches high and nine wide. He called the size 'tabloid', which
he took from a chemists' term for an effervescent pill, and which stuck.
The longest story in the paper was only two hundred and fifty words,
and at midnight on New Year's Eve when it went to press, William H.
Merrill, the chief editorial writer, toasted Harmsworth in champagne
on the newsroom floor, proclaiming it 'an epoch-making international
episode in the history of journalism'. The *World* staff wore evening
dress to honour the Englishman, who told them: 'I don't suppose any
great newspaper proprietor in the world except Mr Pulitzer would
entrust his entire plant for one day to the discretion of a young man
who has no other recommendation than some little success three thousand miles away.'[47] He went on to compliment them on having been
able to produce a tabloid from a broadsheet with next to no warning.

One historian has commented that on New Year's Day 1901, Harmsworth 'in effect introduced tabloid journalism to the United States.'[48] 'New in size, new in form, new in style, new in appearance, picture and methods, but FULL OF NEWS', was the advertising plug, which turned out to be true in every particular.[49] Harmsworth also boasted that it had 'All The News In Sixty Seconds', which seems to have been appreciated by the public, as the World sold 100,000 extra copies.

Although Thomas Edison and some other publishers complimented Harmsworth on the edition, there was criticism which focused on the idea that a newspaper might condense the news rather than allow readers to decide for themselves what to read.[50] For all that, it made Harmsworth's name in the United States and, from then on, reporters were keen to interview him whenever he visited. He was exaggerating, however, when he told his 'darling Mum' that 'People say that no young man's coming has ever stirred up the United States so much before.'[51] He was to fall out with Pulitzer over the hiring of Pulitzer's secretary, Alfred Butes, six years later. 'I always knew you were a hard man,' Pulitzer told him, 'but I didn't think you would steal a dog from a blind man.'[52]

In an eighteen-page article entitled 'The Simultaneous Newspapers of the Future' for the January 1901 issue of the North American Review, Harmsworth set out his philosophy of journalism, thoughts about its future, and implicitly his own ambitions, which thus deserves examination at some length. The piece showed that he thought deeply about his profession and had revolutionary plans for it, with profound implications for the relationship between journalism, politics and business. Although he was ostensibly writing about the United States, his assumptions and predictions applied equally to Britain. In the article, he envisaged a continent-wide, non-partisan daily paper that played a powerful political role in the running of the country. Some of his predictions were borne out, others were not, but it is invaluable in analysing the thirty-five-year-old's vision for his industry at the dawn of the twentieth century.

Harmsworth traced the development of the newspaper since the seventeenth century, arguing that it was 'an essentially modern outgrowth of civilisation'. Telegraphy, telephony, electrotyping, process engraving and rapid transit by land and water were transforming the industry, and he further instanced the way the rotary press, mechanical typesetter, lightning stereotyping box, cablegram and use of wood pulp had fundamentally altered their appearance. Meanwhile, the development of the interview, the dedicated war correspondent, 'the more popular presentation of news and ideas' and 'the abundant use of illustrations' had totally changed their content.

Harmsworth was highly critical of the old-style papers, stating that 'the ordinary news-sheet is hopelessly clumsy in shape, verbose as to matter, and most imperfect as a record'.[53] He predicted that a global newspaper would soon be published simultaneously in different cities and even countries, especially considering that the newspapers in Paris, New York and London were surprisingly alike in view of 'the distinctions in temperament, modes of thought and methods of action which exist between the leading nations of the world'.[54] The major difference between British and American newspapers was the latter's 'unwieldy bulk, scare headlines and a greater directness of style', so that, 'When the American comes to England, the British journal sits as heavily on him as does the British climate.' He noted the fact that 'the best brains of the Anglo-Saxon countries' went into law or public service rather than journalism, citing John Morley (a newspaper editor who became a Cabinet minister) and Sir Alfred Milner (who had had a brief career on the *Pall Mall Gazette*).

'British and American newspapers are not always equal to the average intelligence of their readers,' Harmsworth opined. 'Newspaper opinion carries weight merely because of its known influence on the gentleman whom in England we call "the man in the street"', of whom it was assumed he had 'no interest in literature, and that a slangy colloquial style has most charms for him'. Harmsworth believed that the popularity of writers such as Rudyard Kipling and the late G. W. Steevens proved that to be wrong, and that in fact the public appreciated good writing.

'The instinct that tells what is news, and how the public will best take it, is not given to every writer,' Harmsworth wrote. 'There is a great art in feeling the pulse of the people.'[55] He believed that the future size of newspapers should be 'a small, portable and neatly indexed publication' rather than an inconveniently vast paper hard to read on a windy day, the 'relic of the days of the old and slow flat printing press'.[56]

'Given the man, the capital, the organisation, and the occasion, there seems to be no reason why one or two newspapers may not presently dominate great sections of the United States, or almost the whole of Britain,' Harmsworth thought (and probably hoped). 'Where there are now a multitude of papers – good, bad, and indifferent – there will then be one or two great journals.'[57] The simultaneous printing of papers would facilitate this universal paper, instancing the Hearst, Bennett and Pulitzer presses in the United States, and his own London and Manchester plants, which meant that the *Daily Mail* in 'two great centres of population 200 miles apart, by means of my own railroad trains, is read at breakfast tables 500 miles apart each morning'.[58]

Harmsworth's dream was for a paper edited by 'a man of the journalistic ability of John Delane', who was 'the greatest political editor in the history of journalism', and backed by 'an organisation as perfect as the Standard Oil Company' to be issued each morning in the thirteen major cities of Britain and the United States, for 'would not such a journal effectively revive the waning influence of the newspaper upon the life and thought of the nation?'[59] The market for news could be dominated by one great combine, for as he blatantly put it, 'What a Rockefeller can do in the matter of oil, with its hundred and one adjuncts, another Trust could effect in the way of news.'[60]

Harmsworth speculated about how such a monopolist transatlantic newspaper combine might go about dominating the market. The first step 'would be to buy the best brains, newspapers and machinery', whereupon 'the power to undersell would drive many newspapers into the combination, and little by little rival newspapers would be so weakened that, where they did not die a natural death, their purchase or absorption would be a comparatively easy and inexpensive step.'[61] Harmsworth's neo-Darwinian business principles were rarely more clearly displayed, although he never overtly stated that the combine should happen, merely that it could.

'Possessing its own cables, wires, dispatch boats and special trains, the simultaneous newspaper concern would soon have its own paper-mills, printing-ink factories, machinery shops and the like.'[62] That was already the case with *The Times*. Harmsworth foresaw the combine taking over railway news-stands to 'compel all newsagents to accept the position of agents of the combine'. The article posed as a warning, but it is hard to avoid the conclusion that it was also Harmsworth's dream, at least for Britain.

Any such monopoly, Harmsworth believed, 'would almost necessitate a series of weekly supplements' to deal with special subjects, instancing religion, science, education, finance, commerce, law, sport and medicine. The simultaneous newspaper would also be published in evening, weekly and monthly editions. 'It is no uncommon thing already for a great journal to equip a scientific expedition, to raise a war fund, or to carry through some great charitable exercise,' he wrote, although he forbore to mention that he had already done all three himself.[63]

'The existence of a gutter press cannot altogether be ignored,' Harmsworth admitted. Yet he believed that the sheer quality of the universal paper 'will promptly put an end to it, and will thus confer an additional benefit to the nation'. He believed that it was solely competition that forced editors to run 'some sensational but unelevating police case, because he knows full well that his rival will insert it, and will subsequently boast about his superior news-service!'[64] By contrast, 'a newspaper possessing a monopoly could absolutely boycott all items' that did not elevate the public discourse. 'Such a newspaper could maintain a high literary tone,' he continued, 'and thus become an educative institution of the greatest value.'

William Randolph Hearst's 'successful appeal to the people' over the Spanish–American War and the British press's support for the Boer War showed the power of the press. 'Imagine, then,' Harmsworth wrote, 'the influence which would be exerted if an overwhelming majority of the newspapers in the United States spoke with the same voice, supported the same principles, and enunciated the same policy!'[65] Whilst most believers in pluralism would recoil at such an idea, Harmsworth thought that 'Such a state of things would be a terror to evil-doers and to the supporters of anything inimical to the commonwealth.'

He then quoted Napoleon (apocryphally) as saying that 'Four hostile newspapers are more to be feared than a thousand bayonets,' and argued that 'a hostile press, issued simultaneously throughout the land, would be simply irresistible'.[66] He did not believe this would be dangerous because the 'thoroughly capable journalists' would always wish to represent the general will of the people, and because 'Mere capital, apart from journalistic ability, has never yet created a successful journal.' Indeed, he stressed, 'One of the prime essentials of a good newspaper leader is that he should be in intimate touch with his public. His finger must be on the pulse of the people, and his ear must be ever listening to their voice.'[67]

As for the idea of a monopoly being 'a fatal blow' to press freedom:

> I do not see the force of this. The Press would be raised to so commanding a position that its freedom would be greater than ever. One must remember that the freedom of the Press does not mean a license to say what we please ... but a freedom from outside interference or censorship. In my opinion, the party journals of the present day possess far less freedom than the simultaneous newspapers of the twentieth century will enjoy.[68]

After seventeen pages of almost uninterruptedly advocating a newspaper monopoly as being good for governance, journalism and even democracy and press freedom, Harmsworth then wrote: 'Let me repeat, however, that I am not advocating newspaper monopolies. I am only pointing out that they are practicable, and will probably soon become important factors in journalistic life.'[69] He ended on a positive note for the press in the coming century. 'Already, it is in touch with the people to an extent never attained before. Already, its influence has spread into the secret council chamber, as well as into the labourer's cottage. Already, it is leaving behind what is effete and antiquated, and is keeping step with the march of a progressive age.'[70]

The American trip ended badly when Harmsworth caught malaria when fishing in Florida in early March, after which he spent a week in St Augustine, depressed. The rest of the month was spent getting back to London via New York, and thereafter he suffered from prostate and back pain, not returning to work until 1 May. It was not until he was in Paris on 20 May that he was able to write in his diary: 'A lovely day and felt so well. Drove in Bois [de Boulogne]. Life worth living.'

~

By the turn of the century, Alfred Harmsworth's net worth stood at £886,000, approximately £111 million in today's money. At Christmas 1900, he took a long lease on Sutton Place near Guildford, one of the most splendid Tudor houses of England and where Henry VIII was thought to have first met Anne Boleyn. Because of the £70,000 he spent on refurbishment and laying out gardens, it took eight months to move in.[71] One of the few portraits that Harmsworth brought to Sutton Place – which was described by a contemporary as 'an ecstasy of oak panelings, quaint furniture, nooks and wonderful stairways, surrounded by park and gardens' – was a full-length portrait of Cecil Rhodes.[72]

Mary never had shares in the family businesses, but she did have what she later called an 'enormous' allowance. She was an accomplished hostess at Sutton Place, a house she loved. Although his detractors allege that Harmsworth was 'unhappy in the company of his social and intellectual superiors', that myth is exploded by the list of people he invited to Sutton Place over nearly two decades.[73] Guests included Joseph Chamberlain, the American orator William Jennings Bryan, Winston Churchill, the noted cricketer Maharajah Jam Sahib of Nawanagar, 'a large contingent of the Russian Duma', ex-president Theodore Roosevelt, Lord Roberts, the octogenarian and noted conversationalist Lady Dorothy Nevill,* the former French foreign minister Théophile Delcassé, and the cream of Britain's intellectual journalists, such as J. A. Spender, J. L. Garvin and Leo Maxse. They

---

* Nevill would reminisce about her friendships with people like Disraeli, but Queen Victoria never received her after the unchaperoned Nevill was involved in an amorous incident in a summer house with George Smythe MP.

discussed imperial and foreign affairs in the large halls and dining rooms, for as Harmsworth somewhat pompously told an employee on New Year's Day 1912, 'Little rooms are no good for big ideas.'[74]

'The hospitality there was simple and charming,' recalled J. A. Spender, 'and without the slightest suspicion of social climbing.'[75] Harmsworth wanted to conquer the social heights, but only on his terms. He was always to think of himself as an anti-Establishment outsider, and was unimpressed by the aristocracy whom he thought to be too effete to be entrusted with the destinies of the greatest empire since Rome. Aristocrats were invited to Sutton Place, but only those who had other things to contribute to the conversation besides their lineage.

'You look after me and I'll look after you,' Harmsworth told the nineteen-year-old Manxman Harry Pine, who had been wounded in the leg in the Boer War, as he hired him as his chauffeur at Sutton Place.[76] Within a few weeks, Pine was put in charge of seven men and ten cars there, including a forty-horsepower Mercedes, the super-car of its day. He recalled in an interview in 1946 that his employer sometimes had a bad temper and was a terrible back-seat driver, but would say charming things at the end of a journey such as 'a hungry man in a temper is a hellish thing, isn't it Pine?'[77]

On 31 May 1902, the Treaty of Vereeniging finally brought the Boer War to an end. To the authorities' fury, the *Daily Mail* broke the news before it was officially announced, when Edgar Wallace 'suborned one of his old soldier pals who was guarding the encampment to send him coded messages by waving different-coloured handkerchiefs'.[78] Sir Alfred Milner stayed in South Africa to rebuild the region, which he achieved remarkably quickly, aided by a coterie of bright, young and highly educated imperialists who soon gained the nickname – with a nod to the high commissioner's German ancestry and upbringing – 'Milner's Kindergarten'. Having loyally taken the paper during twenty-nine months of war, the *Daily Mail*'s readership held up well after the peace, remaining at more than one million, the largest circulation of any newspaper in the world.

CHAPTER 6

THE *MIRROR* AND A
MYSTERY WOMAN

August 1902–November 1904

'Northcliffe knew his own mind at any given moment,
though his mind may change with startling rapidity.'[1]

JOHN WALTER IV

With the coronation of King Edward VII postponed to 9 August
1902 due to appendicitis, Harmsworth visited Germany for the first
time in July, travelling from Strasbourg to Stuttgart to visit two of
his maternal aunts, Grace and Caroline Maffett, who were both
married to Germans. He returned even more convinced than before
that Germany – whose Second Naval Act of June 1900 countenanced
a fleet of thirty-eight battleships by 1920 – posed a serious threat
to the British Empire. To counter it, Harmsworth hoped to use the
gathering of colonial prime ministers for the coronation to encourage
imperial federation, at least in the realm of defence. The *Daily Mail*
warned in its coverage of the coronation's naval review at Spithead
that, since the one marking Queen Victoria's Diamond Jubilee in
1897, 'a powerful navy has grown up in the North Sea which has to
be considered in the balance of power'.[2] That autumn, while staying
at the Paris Ritz for three weeks, Harmsworth gave an interview to
Le Matin in which he said: 'Yes, we detest the Germans, we detest
them cordially and they make themselves detested by the whole of

Europe. I will not permit the least thing that might injure France to appear in my paper, but should not like for anything to appear in it that might be agreeable to Germany.'[3]

'In this life of competition between nations, time is everything,' warned the *Daily Mail* on 12 August 1902.[4] Yet although the premiers gladly accepted Harmsworth's invitations to Berkeley Square dinners and Sutton Place receptions, and warmly applauded Joseph Chamberlain's speech at the Imperial Conference held at the Colonial Office, almost nothing of substance was agreed beyond that they would meet again within four years. The premiers suspected (correctly) that Britain wanted them to contribute much-needed manpower to an imperial army and navy, and that Chamberlain wanted a customs union that would turn the British Empire into a unified world power and which might stymie the colonies' commerce with the outside world.[5] In particular, Wilfrid Laurier of Canada, the most powerful of the premiers, proved reluctant to promise anything that might compromise Canada's trading relationship with the United States.

The resignation of Lord Salisbury after the coronation, and the promotion of his nephew Arthur Balfour to the premiership, sped up the process by which the Unionist government was starting to split between those who supported Imperial Preference, led by Chamberlain, and those who continued to support free trade, led by C. T. Ritchie, the Chancellor of the Exchequer. Chamberlain wanted to levy a protective tariff on food entering Britain from outside the Empire. 'Britain's world power status would be sustained by harnessing the rich natural and human resources of this efficient and integrated imperial economic bloc,' as an historian puts it.[6] Harmsworth had not yet met Chamberlain, and would not do so until visiting his house in Prince's Gardens, Kensington, in December 1903. Despite his reverence for Chamberlain's overall message, he recognised that the struggle was going to be tough, because the free trade system adopted since the repeal of the Corn Laws half a century earlier was widely seen as the foundation of British economic success.

If there were a war against Germany, as Harmsworth was already starting to predict, it was essential that his publishing empire continued to have access to a limitless and dependable supply of cheap paper, which would not be able to come from Scandinavia as at present. In the manner of American titans like John D. Rockefeller, who used 'vertical integration' to control all facets of their operations, in 1903 the Harmsworths conceived a remarkably ambitious scheme to construct the largest pulp and paper mill in the world on the banks of the Exploits River in Newfoundland. Mayson Beeton, who they sent out to choose the siting of the mill, became the first president of the Anglo–Newfoundland Development Company.

The scale of the enterprise was truly extraordinary; the company bought 3,100 square miles of territory – an area exceeding the size of Sussex, Surrey and Kent put together – as well as building railways, dams and harbours. It worried Harold deeply, who was counting the costs involved in the project, but Alfred insisted on the money being found. He imported reindeer to populate the woodland, replaced herds of tuberculosis-infected cattle, ordered axemen to wash daily and stop spitting, and sent shiploads of Devonshire earth to lay out an English garden for his manager's house there, for which Mark Twain had sent the plans.

When it opened in 1905, the brand-new town of Grand Falls had well-designed houses, a school, church, baseball team, arts and culture centre, and hospital (named after Mary). Over the coming years, there were also electricity, street-lamps, telephones, a public library, bank, theatre, cinema and wireless. The official opening of Grand Falls in October was attended by Lord Grey and Sir Edward Morris, the premier of Newfoundland, but the words spelt out by the town's lights were 'Welcome to The Chief'.

What was described at the time in the American press as 'a bold gamble in the wilderness' paid off handsomely; the paper mill only closed in 2009, and today Grand Falls is still a thriving community.[7] There were 'dreadful' mosquitoes at Grand Falls, but in time the Anglo–Newfoundland Development Company dealt with them too. Although Northcliffe was slightingly described as 'the Robinson Crusoe of his new found land of paper' in the American press at the outset of the project, none could doubt its success by the time of the Great War, when the Harmsworth press was the only large newspaper group not to experience severe paper shortages.[8] On one visit in September 1913, to welcome him the Anglo-Newfoundland Development Company had built an 'N' – for Northcliffe – in lights with a coronet on the top of a tower thirty-five feet high. 'It looks brilliant and can be seen twenty miles away in the forest,' he told Mother.[9]

In 1903, Alfred Harmsworth contributed an essay, 'The Making of a Newspaper', to a book entitled *Journalism as a Profession*, edited by Arthur Lawrence. As with his *Atlantic Monthly* article, it allows insights into his thinking that justify an in-depth analysis. 'Few businesses have made more rapid strides during the past few years than that of the making of newspapers,' he began. 'Few vocations afford more opportunity for the investment of brain than newspaper-making.'[10] He argued that journalism had been transformed from the days when 'Grub Street was not a thoroughfare for respectable wayfarers' into a steady, well-paid and interesting calling for someone 'of imagination and judgement'.[11] Lord Salisbury had once been a journalist, he pointed out, adding that 'few politicians would care to attempt to govern without the assistance of newspapers'.[12] Several of the predictions in the article proved accurate, such as: 'It may be quite possible in the next few years to print photographs really well in a morning newspaper.'[13]

One sentence in his eulogy to his profession failed to ring true, however, when he wrote that 'it is not necessary today, as it was in the past, to use the newspaper as a stepping stone to influence.'[14] Instead, he argued, 'the controller of a newspaper who wishes to retain his independence must be a hermit.'[15] Harmsworth wrote that 'a wide circle of acquaintance among people like politicians is specially to be avoided by a newspaper proprietor for many reasons.' When cabinet ministers told him things in confidence that his reporters then discovered by legitimate means, he was criticised for breaking a confidence. 'Politicians and newspaper owners are best apart. The newspaper owner should always remember that, while the politicians have nothing to give him, they have much to gain from his newspaper.'[16]

~

Joseph Chamberlain unveiled his detailed tariff reform – that is, Imperial Preference – proposals at a major speech in Birmingham on 15 May 1903. He was convinced that his proposals would deliver both imperial unity and domestic prosperity, but instead they united the Liberal Party behind free trade and split the Unionist party in two. Harmsworth was initially unsure of how to respond, a very unusual state for someone who was usually so decisive. He had long favoured protectionism – J. A. Spender recalled how Harmsworth 'unhesitatingly ascribed what he called the "colossal success" of Germany and the United States to their tariffs' – but his political intuition told him that the British people would never accept the taxes on food from outside the empire, which were an essential feature of Chamberlain's programme.[17]

On 19 May, the *Evening News* announced its opposition to 'a food tax which would raise the cost of living – in other words … a stomach tax'.[18] With his instinctive ability to get to the nub of the matter, Harmsworth's coining of the phrase 'stomach tax' proved devastating.[19] Ten days later, the *Daily Mail* supported Chamberlain's proposed tariffs on manufactured goods, but not on foodstuffs. Harmsworth had spotted the Achilles heel in Chamberlain's tariff reform campaign, and he put his readers' views first.[20]

In August, the *Daily Mail* conducted 2,000 interviews with the public, with an army of reporters, which the paper called 'walking inquirers', spreading across the country to listen to the man in the street and the pub, and carefully record what they heard in small black notebooks. One of the inquirers in Colchester was Alfred Benjamin Smith, Harmsworth's illegitimate son. The notebooks were returned to Carmelite House and revealed that one fifth of people had not heard of Chamberlain's proposals but that, among those who had, almost everyone was hostile to them, with virtually no-one in favour.

'Until Chamberlain spoke out,' an historian of the tariff reform campaign states,

Alfred Harmsworth was content to conduct his newspapers as business enterprises. However, when Chamberlain challenged British opinion at Birmingham, Harmsworth became convinced that the campaign for tariff reform provided him with an opportunity to assert his own position as a person of importance in national affairs ... His large appetites ... could no longer be sated by mere commercial success. In 1903, for the first time, he began to desire a substantial measure of political power. And he believed that Chamberlain's new course furnished him with an opportunity to clutch at that power on a scale he had never contemplated before.[21]

When it became clear that Chamberlain would not drop food taxes and that the new premier Arthur Balfour did not have the power – nor, seemingly, the inclination – to present an alternative policy, Harmsworth suggested to the Liberal Imperialist Lord Rosebery in a letter of 1 September that they start a nationwide campaign together. With Rosebery giving the speeches and Harmsworth providing the coverage, the partnership would 'counteract the effect not only of the Tariff speeches of the Protectionists, but also of the endeavours of [the Liberal Party leader] Sir Henry Campbell-Bannerman and others'.[22] He wanted a national government under Rosebery, whom he hoped would make ten speeches before Christmas in a campaign coordinated by Harmsworth himself. All he asked was an indication of 'support from you equal to the very urgent need of the occasion'.[23]

'I am not ambitious, as you know,' Rosebery replied, 'and, even if I were, I could not sacrifice my liberty of action.' He added that if it became known that 'a great newspaper proprietor' was conducting his campaign, 'It would be said, not unnaturally, that I was being "run" by him.'[24] This led Harmsworth to conclude that Rosebery 'was as impossible as all the other Liberal leaders, and that no one in his senses would go tiger-hunting with any of them'.[25] J. A. Spender noted how Harmsworth 'never wavered in his belief that the Tory Party were going to smash over the business' of tariff reform, 'and he told me more than once that I greatly underestimated the coming Liberal majority'.[26]

'I almost despair of politics at the present time,' Harmsworth told Churchill, an ardent free trader, on 14 September. 'Unless I see some party to which to attach myself, I shall give up politics and go in for buying and organising more newspapers.'[27] The next day, the *Daily Mail* stated that it had 'no hesitation in saying that any policy based upon the taxation of the foodstuffs of the people is doomed to failure. The consensus of opinion from all sides is overwhelming.'[28] Two days later, Chamberlain resigned as colonial secretary to fight for tariff reform from outside the cabinet, and at the same time five other cabinet ministers led by Ritchie the chancellor also resigned in order to fight against it. The *Daily Mail* expressed 'sincere admiration and heartfelt regret' at Chamberlain's action, both of which were genuine.

On 26 September, Harmsworth organised a debate on tariff reform at Sutton Place – what he called a Fiscal Conference – in which Churchill took part. It was inconclusive, but Harmsworth's stance was clear from the *Daily Mail*'s first leader that morning: 'Any Unionist member of parliament who has been among his constituents recently must know that almost to a man they are in favour of putting a tax on foreign manufactured imports.'[29] But not on food. Harmsworth wrote to Chamberlain saying that he was 'hoping that your policy will provide for the extinction of the food taxes because then I shall be able to support you as warmly as I did during the Boer War'.[30]

Writing to Leo Maxse, the pro-tariff reform proprietor-editor of the *National Review* magazine in early October, Harmsworth said:

You may know that my family are making what, perhaps, is the largest fortune now being made in England, and almost every penny of it comes from the poor. Not unnaturally, therefore I have made some study of the lives of these people, and I feel it would be criminal of me, knowing their circumstances as I do, and deriving the money I do from them, were I to adopt any other course ... I cannot and will not support preferential tariffs, unless a very large proportion of the money received from the taxation of foreign manufactured articles is allocated to the practical extermination of food taxes.[31]

It was not true that the family's income derived from 'the poor', so much as the lower-middle and middle classes, but understandably he did not want the pennies and halfpennies presently spent on his publications to go towards buying dearer food instead.

On 7 October, Harmsworth wrote what looked like a pro-tariff reform article under his own name in the *Daily Mail*, but it demanded that 'the taxation of foreign manufactures should precede, it seems to me, the taxation of food ... The danger is that if the two different parts of the scheme are applied at the same moment the worker will reject both, because he sees and knows only his present loss and is doubtful of the future gain.'[32] He likened Joseph Chamberlain to Bismarck and Gladstone, and described tariff reform as 'a vast programme constructive and destructive, a social and commercial revolution. It involves the uprooting of our beliefs and old principles ... while the national life is being adapted to the changed condition of modern existence.'[33]

Harmsworth certainly did not believe in the status quo, describing Britain's position as 'impossible' in a world where foreign goods imported into the country attracted nil tariffs, while similar British goods going to Russia attracted 123 per cent duties, the USA 73 per cent, France 34 per cent and Germany 25 per cent, 'with all the damage that caused British manufacturers and exporters'.[34] He believed that 'By protection alone we can obtain some means of replying to foreign powers ... we can give security to capital and labour.' The article sought to remove the issue from partisan politics by establishing a committee of businessmen to inquire into it, one of those few instances where he was being naïve, because it could only ever be highly political, as the resignation of half the cabinet showed. Harmsworth considered himself 'a very keen tariff reformer', although he turned down the chairmanship of the Tariff Reform League. The *Daily Mail* meanwhile attacked free trader advocates as 'Little Englanders' who were 'alienating the sister states of the Empire, and destroying in one generation the glorious work of centuries of toil and self-sacrifice'.[35]

Until 1903, wrote Max Pemberton, Harmsworth 'still took the business side of a newspaper as a much more serious side than the politics. I can never remember that he ever seemed violently concerned about domestic politics, at all events before Chamberlain divided the country on the question of tariff reform.'[36] By the autumn of that year, Chamberlain had captured the extra-parliamentary organisation of the Unionist Party; by 1907, tariff reform was accepted as official party policy; and by January 1910 it was the main platform of the Unionist campaign.[37] Yet although his heart drew him towards Imperial Preference, Harmsworth's head told him that food taxes were a certain election loser for the Unionists.

~

On 1 November, the Harmsworths launched the *Daily Mirror*, which described itself in its huge advertising campaign as 'The First Daily Newspaper for Gentlewomen'. Not only was it for women, but it was almost entirely staffed by them; the editor was Mary Howarth, the director of the *Daily Mail*'s women's page, who was only the third female editor of a national daily in British history. Virtually the only man on the editorial team was Hamilton Fyfe, a charming and capable man who later became a playwright, war correspondent and Harmsworth's biographer.

'It is unlike any other newspaper because it attempts what no other newspaper has ever attempted,' stated the *Mirror*'s opening editorial. 'It is no mere bulletin of fashion, but a reflection of women's interests, women's thoughts, women's work.'[38] William Kennedy Jones recalled that as 'it was to be a reflection of feminine interests; what more suitable than a mirror?'[39] One of his jobs was to keep an eye out for sexual innuendo: 'Our French Letter' was changed to 'Yesterday in Paris', for example.[40] 'After the usual pangs of childbirth, produced the first copy at 9.50pm,' Harmsworth noted in his diary on 1 November. 'It looks a promising child, but time will show whether we are a winner or not.'[41]

It was not. Although its first number sold 265,217 copies, this had dropped to 131,000 on the second, and soon it was down to 24,800 and the penny paper was losing £3,000 a week.[42] It was the first time Alfred Harmsworth had failed at anything important, and was to be a serious test of character. Various explanations have been given for why the project failed, one being 'the drawing-room-and-university background' of the 'gentlewomen' chosen to edit it who supposedly did not understand the preoccupations of women in the populous industrial suburbs that the paper needed for a mass readership.[43] With his customary eye for the bottom line, Harold understandably suggested they close it immediately but instead, on 23 November, Fyfe was appointed editor, Howarth returned to the *Mail*, and the female staff were fired with three months' severance pay, a process Fyfe later likened to 'drowning kittens'.[44] Alfred's summation was that 'it was simply another failure made by mere man in diagnosing women's needs!'[45]

Instead of closing the paper, Alfred decided it would be re-launched on 28 January 1904 as the *Daily Illustrated Mirror*, a halfpenny 'Paper for Men and Women'. It was fortunate that the Russo–Japanese War broke out ten days after the relaunch, which greatly increased the demand for war illustrations. The paper was a success, and was selling five million copies by 1922. A year after the initial launch, Harmsworth wrote an article under his own name entitled 'How I Dropped £100,000 on the *Mirror*' in which he admitted that he had thought it would be 'the only journalistic failure with which I have been associated'.[46] He only wrote it because by then it was clear that it was not. Nor was the *Mirror* his only venture in 1903; that year he also bought the near-bankrupted *Weekly Dispatch* from the Newnes family, which he turned into a successful paper in the cheaper end of the market, even though he was soon complaining to the editor about the 'common-looking babies' in its Beautiful Babies competition.[47]

In November 1903, Harmsworth hired Evelyn Wrench, an Old Etonian who had left the Diplomatic Service in order to set up a post-card company that, at its height, had sold three million postcards a month, but which had gone into liquidation through over-expansion and lack of capital. Harmsworth did not share Edwardian socie-ty's horror and stigmatisation of bankruptcy, instead recognising it as a possible sign of entrepreneurship. 'Remember, my boy,' he told twenty-one-year-old Wrench, 'when you grow older, always surround yourself with young people. Businesses grow old rapidly.

Make a rule never to bring in anyone from outside over the age of twenty-five.'[48]

A year later, Wrench had published the *Overseas Daily Mail*, a fourteen-page weekly penny paper that gave news of the British Empire to readers in Canada, India, Australia and, as Harmsworth put it in its first edition, 'other foreign countries in which the lonely Englishman is found'.[49] Wrench was a proselytiser for the empire who later travelled 64,000 miles within it and set up the Royal Overseas League and the English-Speaking Union, both of which Harmsworth supported financially. Wrench also found him generous in paying off half of his liabilities from the postcard debacle, and later wrote that Harmsworth was 'like a light-hearted young uncle or elder brother ... and would talk about life, politics, ambition, history, America, "the fair sex" and the Empire'.[50]

Meanwhile the financial acumen that Wrench ascribed to Harold was on show in November 1903 when, at the Amalgamated Press' shareholders' meeting and with fifty shareholders present, the brothers announced annual profits of £266,223, and a 40 per cent dividend.[51] Between 1902 and 1921, net profits increased every year bar two (when they were still stable) and a 40 per cent dividend was paid every year bar one, when it was 35 per cent.[52] Investing in the success of the Harmsworth press empire was a very profitable thing to do.

'The name of Mr Alfred Harmsworth has been mentioned to me for an honour,' King Edward VII wrote to Arthur Balfour on Christmas Day 1903. 'It seems that Lord Salisbury offered him once a knighthood, which he declined; but I understand that he is most anxious for a baronetcy. He is a great power in the Press and strongly supports the government as well as Mr Chamberlain's policy. Should you wish to recommend his name to me, I will certainly give my consent. He is married, but has no children.'[53]

The baronetcy was announced on 22 June 1904, whereupon more than 200 congratulatory telegrams were received at Berkeley Square. 'Such a day of congratulations as amazed me,' the new Sir Alfred Harmsworth noted.[54] He clearly did not think it was his last honour, as was clear from his joke to St.Loe Strachey about how he was 'starting to learn Yiddish with a view to speechmaking in the Lords', a reference to the number of Jews who had been given peerages.[55] 'My Darling "Sir Alfred",' wrote Mary from Sutton Place where he had wired her the news of the baronetcy, 'I must be the first to tell you how glad and happy I am to know that you have gained recognition for the hard work of years. No-one, dear, deserves it more than you – but the happiest thought of all to me is that *we began* life together and have been together through all the years of work which have earned you distinction and fortune so young. My fond love and every congratulation from your loving *Wife*.'[56]

Mary was indeed a loving (if unfaithful) wife, and Alfred admired her social gifts and appreciated everything she did to help him, but their failure to have children undermined what had originally been a genuine love match. 'Nobody gets everything,' Alfred would remark.[57] 'She did everything in her power to give Uncle Alfred a child without success,' recalled his niece Enid Stokes, 'enduring very painful treatment.' In 1956, Mary told a nephew that she thought 'the story would have been different if they had children. She said that she had consulted all the leading doctors at home and abroad and they said there was no physical reason why she could not bear children.'[58]

By the spring of 1904, it is very likely that Harmsworth had started an affair with a woman who called herself Kathleen Wrohan, and on occasion Lady Cathleen Wrohan. The true identity of his mistress has been a mystery until now. Mistresses are notoriously difficult for historians to track down after over a century, but harder still when the most powerful press proprietor in British history wants to keep her hidden. Yet there are clues to Mrs Wrohan's life that can be pieced together from legal papers, Post Office directories, income tax returns, some provincial and foreign (that is, non-Northcliffe) press, passenger manifests, immigration records, electoral rolls and baptism registers that at least can place her in certain locations.

She was recorded as staying at the Grand Hotel du Louvre in Paris in April 1904, and gave her address as the Savoy Hotel in London when she was arraigned on a speeding charge in Surrey that June. ('I am very sorry,' she told the court, 'I know I was going too fast, but

I wanted to get home. Can I pay the fine now?') In November 1904, her chauffeur was fined for speeding in Yorkshire in a car registered to her as the owner. She was unlikely to have been able to afford a room at the Savoy, let alone a motor car and chauffeur, on her own slender resources, but by contrast once Associated Newspapers was incorporated in April 1904, Harmsworth enjoyed a net income of £115,000 and stock worth £300,000 outside the family businesses. Five years later, his annual income was £200,000, making him one of the highest income earners in Britain.[59]

Mrs Wrohan was reported by the *Brighton Gazette* to have been a guest at the Hotel Metropole there in July and October 1905, and in June 1906, and there was a Mrs Wrohan (which is a surprisingly rare name) listed in the 1905 Post Office directory as living on the west side of Gray's Inn Gateway, a fifteen-minute walk from Harmsworth's offices at Carmelite House. Like so much else about Kathleen Wrohan, it is not known where she met Harmsworth or under what circumstances. It has been suggested that they met through a typewriting agency that she is said to have managed, although Louise Owen – a later, possibly overlapping mistress who thoroughly disliked her – claimed that Wrohan had been employed to do contract typing, a low-level clerical job whose large (£25) expenses Owen questioned but Harmsworth confirmed.[60]

Other rumours about Wrohan include that she was the illegitimate daughter of King Edward VII or the Countess of Glasgow, or both. In July 1907, she appeared on the electoral roll as the only occupant at 102 Savoy Court on the Strand. Savoy Court was a very prestigious block of flats and offices at the back of the Savoy Hotel. In the *Evening Standard* in April 1908, she was named as having been one of the guests at Bertolini's Palace Hotel in Naples.[61] In February 1909, she was listed as staying at the Hermitage in Monte Carlo and 'entertaining in the Salle Blanche of the Hotel de Paris' where the Earl and Countess of Glasgow were also staying.[62] On 14 July 1909, by which time she was living at 33 Dover Street in Mayfair, the Court Circular noted that 'Her Majesty the Queen received Mrs. Wrohan (from Australia) and Madame Ferrari (the composer) this morning',[63] When she attended the King's Levee the following March – presented by Lady Glasgow – she was said by the Australian press to be from Victoria. Yet all accounts from contemporaries record her speaking with a strong Irish accent.

Fortunately, the Northcliffe Archive Papers held privately by the Harmsworth family provide a crucial clue to Mrs Wrohan's true identity, which can now be revealed. On 5 May 1907, she wrote a letter from 39 Lennox Gardens in London to Alfred Harmsworth's trusted friend and solicitor Henry Arnholz, asking him

> to procure for me a copy of the birth certificate of a child (one of twins) called Beatrice Maud Cromie born about the year 1872 at Tamniarin, Dungiven, C[ounty] Derry, Ireland. The parents' names were Henry James Cromie and Annie Cromie ... I have just come back from Paris where we had the most delicious sunshine and heat.'[64]

She then arranged for a quarterly stipend to be paid to Maud Cromie's aunt Isabella Osborne, albeit with the proviso 'Will you kindly let her know that this is going to be done without giving her any idea from whom it comes? My address from the end of August will be Elmwood, St Peter's, Thanet.'[65] (By then, Harmsworth had bought Mary a house in Crowborough, East Sussex, and she no longer visited Elmwood.) On 10 September 1908, Arnholz drew up an annuity of £6,000 per annum for Mrs Wrohan, equivalent to almost three quarters of a million pounds today.

Between December 1911 and February 1912, a notice was placed in the 'Missing Relatives' column of numerous newspapers by Revd J. A. Tyney, a relative of Isabel Tyney. Isabel had been growing increasingly suspicious about her new husband Francis Waters, head constable of the Royal Irish Constabulary stationed at Belfast, since their marriage on 23 August 1911. He had claimed that his first wife, Beatrice Maud Cromie, whom he had married in 1895, had died, although no death certificate existed for her (or indeed has ever come to light to this day). Isabel Tyney feared that Waters might be a bigamist. The rumours and theories about how Beatrice Cromie supposedly met her end were many and varied. She was allegedly 'lost at sea' in the Bay of Biscay in 1895, according to one family story. Her Aunt Florence claimed that 'Maud ran off to South Africa with an actor and was drowned.'[66] In Revd Tyney's appeal for information about Beatrice Cromie, her height is given as five feet and three inches, close to the five feet and four inches given for the person described as 'Cathleen Wrohan' when she crossed into New York State from Canada on 16 July 1906. (She had been 'Lady Cathleen Wrohan' when she arrived in Quebec nine days earlier.[67])

On 18 December 1911, four years after Mrs Wrohan's money had started to arrive, Isabella Osborne wrote to Henry Arnholz stating her belief that her secret benefactress was 'the niece referred to in my last [letter] & whose husband [ie Francis Waters] re-married this last August ... She disappeared from me also & does not evidently wish her whereabouts known.' Isabella confessed that she 'would be most thankful to know that she's alive', but asked the solicitor not to let his client know that she has enquired about her, as 'supposing she still wishes to keep out of sight which I believe she does she would be very angry with me naturally & might cause the withdrawal of my allowance'. Nevertheless, she asked Arnholz to apprise his client of her erstwhile husband's (bigamous) remarriage. Though no names were mentioned in Isabella's letter, there can be no doubt of whom she was writing, and if we can assume that Arnholz did indeed pass on the news to Mrs Wrohan, she would have known that her husband had committed bigamy.

In February 1912, Francis Waters was charged with making false declarations for the purposes of obtaining a marriage licence, and was tried in June 1912 at Denbighshire Assize Court. ('Policeman's Romance' was the title of the *Belfast Weekly Telegraph* report.) Although Waters was specifically not charged with bigamy, establishing whether Beatrice was still alive was material to the case, as it affected the validity of the second marriage and thus whether his new 'wife' could testify against him. He stated at his trial that Beatrice Maud had been working as a typist when she left him and went to London.[68] Isabella Osborne appeared as a witness to help clarify the situation regarding his first wife. She said that when Beatrice Maud left Ireland, she had written to her stating, 'I am simply disappearing from everybody, but if I ever become better off I may reappear.'

By then, Isabella had more than a strong hunch that her niece was alive and prospering, but she did not tell the court that. Germane to the case was the will that Mrs Wrohan drew up in 1907, in which Mrs Isabella Osborne (née Cromie) was a beneficiary and described as 'my distant relative'. In a subsequent version written in 1912, Kathleen made Isabella the recipient of a third of her estate, but she was not mentioned in Kathleen's final will in 1917. The evidence, though circumstantial, overwhelmingly supports the conclusion that Alfred Harmsworth's mistress Kathleen Wrohan was in fact Beatrice Maude Waters (née Cromie), an Irishwoman who had left her native country, aged about thirty-two, to escape her husband and find a better life.

CHAPTER 7

LIBERAL DAWN

May 1905–December 1907

'He was never at ease in the old system; his peerage had
not bought him ... There were times when he reminded
me of a big bumblebee puzzled by a pane of glass.'[1]

H. G. WELLS on Lord Northcliffe,
Experiment in Autobiography 1934

'Purchased *Observer*' was Sir Alfred Harmsworth's typically laconic
diary entry for 3 May 1905.[2] *The Observer* was Britain's oldest surviving Sunday paper (it was founded in 1791) and his purchase of
it for a mere £4,000 probably saved the high-quality but very low-
circulation publication from extinction, as it was losing £15,000 a
year.[3] Harmsworth later said it 'lay derelict in the Fleet Ditch'.* He
offered the editorship to the famous political journalist and tariff
reformer James Louis Garvin, who refused it, as did his fellow tariff
reformer Leo Amery, who hoped to follow the veteran G. E. Buckle
as editor of *The Times*. Harmsworth ended up settling on Arthur
Harrison, who steadily increased circulation before Garvin was
persuaded to take it on in 1908, whereupon sales leapt to 40,000
by 1909. Garvin saw journalism differently from Harmsworth,

---

* The Ditch was what remained after the River Fleet had dried up, before it was
enclosed in the nineteenth century. It still flows from under Hampstead Heath
into the Thames today.

believing it had a didactic duty and once telling him that *The Observer* should give the public what it did *not* want. 'Are you a fisherman?' Harmsworth replied. 'When you go fishing, you bait the hook with what the fish wants, not what you want him to want.'[4]

Only nineteen days after buying *The Observer*, Harmsworth launched the *Continental Daily Mail*, which was initially published in Paris but soon spread out across Europe. It was edited by Ralph Lane, who used his middle names to write books under the name Norman Angell, and who became the only person to win the Nobel Peace Prize for publishing a book. *The Great Illusion*, published in 1910, predicted that Britain and Germany could not go to war because the world was too interconnected commercially for it to be possible, yet he won the Prize in 1933, nearly two decades after it had been proven incontrovertibly wrong.

Angell had originally hoped Harmsworth would buy the French journal *The Messenger*, which he edited, so he visited 'the young Napoleon of Fleet Street' in his office and 'was shown into his big room with the thick carpet, the ornate desk at one end, the shaded lights and all the other stage effects'.[5] At one point during the discussions about the minor shareholders, Harmsworth asked: 'Have you offered these people five thousand pounds spot cash? It's wonderful what a cheque for five thousand pounds flourished under a man's nose will do.'[6] Angell was unable to do that, and eventually Harmsworth said, 'I would not buy your paper but I'm prepared to buy you ... You will be head of the whole Continental organisation. You can make three major mistakes and I will not hold it against you. After that we'll see.'[7]

Angell, who had written worthy Liberal books on the importance of rationalism in politics, claims to have stammered out that not only were their politics different but 'I regard you as the most mischievous person in Britain,' a strange stance to have taken if he wanted Harmsworth's financial support. 'What's that got to do with it?' Harmsworth replied. 'I'm not asking you to write the leaders of the *Mail* or become responsible for its politics ... As a matter of fact, most of the chief Conservative newspapers in England seem to be run on the business side by extreme Scotch Radicals.'[8] He went on:

'You understand people, which is the main thing in administration. If you want a thing done well you must get other people to do it. You can't possibly do it yourself in a big business. Choose the right people and treat them so as to get the most out of them.'[9]

Harmsworth was as good as his word. When Angell set up the *Continental Daily Mail* in Paris and sought permission to take a twenty-year lease on a printing and editorial building and then spend £5,000 altering it, Harmsworth replied: 'I thought that the arrangement between us was that you should decide these things and take the consequences. If you make a mistake in a decision of that character it will be a very black mark against you. Decide it.'[10] The *Continental Daily Mail* proved a major commercial success, although the French government did not allow it to report on domestic French politics, to which Harmsworth acceded, saying, 'It is not polite to discuss our hosts' internal affairs.'[11] He loved France just as powerfully as he feared Germany, and when the Kaiser's inflammatory visit to Tangier in the spring of 1905 sparked the First Moroccan Crisis, his papers took a resolutely pro-French stance. The Kaiser described Morocco as independent, inflaming Arab nationalism there, and the *Mail* criticised 'schemes of political adventure on the part of German statesmanship'.[12]

On 4 December 1905, unable to keep his party together any longer over tariff reform, Arthur Balfour resigned the premiership and Henry Campbell-Bannerman became prime minister of a Liberal government that included Herbert Asquith, Sir Edward Grey and Lord Haldane. When Balfour presented his resignation honours list to Edward VII, the king requested that Harmsworth be awarded a peerage. Balfour replied that although he had received a baronetcy only the previous year, he would 'be happy to add' his name to the list.[13] The chief whip, Alexander Acland-Hood, told J. S. Sandars, Balfour's private secretary, 'I very much dislike the business, but as we *can't* stop it in the future why make so handsome a present to the other side! Of course some of our men will be furious and I can't blame them ... I think in this case we must allow our virtue to be raped.'[14]

Harmsworth had joked, 'When I want a peerage I will buy one, like an honest man,' and it was not long before rumours swirled that money had indeed been involved.[15] Acland-Hood told the Tory MP Robert Sanders that Harmsworth had 'offered a very large cheque to the Conservative Party' which Acland-Hood had refused.[16] Conversely, Lord Beaverbrook was decades later to tell Stanley Morison, the editor of *The History of The Times*, that Harmsworth had been offered a peerage for £110,000 but had refused to pay.[17] The fact remains that neither of these stories, if true, would have resulted in the honour actually being conferred.

A further rumour was that both Harmsworth and the banker Sir Herbert Stern (who had become Lord Michelham) were being rewarded for the financial assistance they had given Alice Keppel, the king's mistress.[18] This theory was supported in the diary entry of the newspaper proprietor Cecil King, Harmsworth's nephew, of 16 February 1974, which records a lunch with Leicester Harmsworth's son Geoffrey, who 'confirmed the suspicion that Northcliffe bought his peerage from Edward VII for a hundred £1,000 notes. The money was needed for Mrs Keppel. Geoffrey says Stern's barony of Michelham was bought at the same time. What is known is that Northcliffe's peerage was pressed on Balfour by Edward.'[19]

That seven-decades-old and third-hand information cannot be taken as necessarily accurate, however. Cecil King was notoriously biased against his own family, as shown in his autobiography *Strictly Personal* which was highly critical of them, and he might well have presented Geoffrey's gossipy speculations as truth. A more likely explanation was that, having created the best-selling newspaper in the world, and a conglomerate that was growing strongly – the *World* newspaper had been bought for £14,000 the previous month – it was recognised that Harmsworth was enough of a power in the land to justify a peerage. Moreover, if the Tories did not bestow it, then the Liberals might, with potentially disastrous political consequences at a critical time.[20] Certainly, when Mary was questioned on it by Geoffrey Harmsworth in 1956, she 'unhesitatingly and with conviction' said that Alfred had not bought the peerage.

However it was obtained, on 9 December 1905 Harmsworth was created Baron Northcliffe of the Isle of Thanet. He and Mary

were staying with Reggie Nicholson at Hurley in Berkshire when
his mother's telegram arrived saying 'I am feeling very proud today
fond love to both – Mother'.[21] Later, the normally undemonstrative
Balfour put his hand around Northcliffe's shoulder and congratulated him on becoming the youngest peer ever created. If Northcliffe
knew that it had been the king who had suggested it, he was too
polite (or politic) to mention it.

Overall, Balfour's resignation honours list received a bad press,
with *Truth* running a mocking piece about 'the Title Boom' and the
Saturday Review discussing 'The Adulteration of the Peerage', saying
that Northcliffe had done

> more than any man of his generation to pervert and enfeeble the
> mind of the multitude. ... he has been true to no party, and has
> made himself at different times the mouthpiece of Lord Rosebery,
> Mr Chamberlain, and Mr Balfour. ... We fail to discover in his
> record any performance of those higher duties to the State or those
> wider services to humanity, which alone entitle a citizen to become
> a peer ... The "fountain of honour" has become ... a spring of
> dishonour.[22]

Such criticism was typical of the Radical reaction to Northcliffe's
peerage, and also unfair. It was not the duty of a newspaper proprietor to be true to either a party or a particular politician, and as
for higher duties to the state, there was the Jackson–Harmsworth
Expedition; the warnings about Wilhelmine Germany; the holding of the government to account in the Boer War; the creation of
several thousand jobs and the introduction of technological innovation in Fleet Street; the plethora of new newspapers such as the
Daily Mail, the *Daily Mirror*, *The Observer*, the *Evening News*,
the *Overseas Daily Mail* and the *Continental Daily Mail*; the support of the British Empire; the promotion of Anglo–French and
Anglo–American amity; the development of Newfoundland; the
encouragement of motoring and flying by sponsoring international
prizes and competitions; the philanthropy along the lines of the
Daily Mail's 'Christmas Stocking Fund' for poor children; and the

ongoing professionalisation and increased status of journalism as an industry.

Northcliffe did not take the title Elmwood because it was a wood traditionally used for making coffins. He might have been Lord Broadstairs or Lord Kingsgate, but instead he decided upon Northcliffe, which forms part of the Kent coast near Elmwood. It was widely alleged that he chose it because it gave him the same initial as Napoleon, and he could sign letters 'N' in the way the emperor sometimes did.[23] He also incorporated bees into his coat of arms, which are a Napoleonic symbol, but that also might have been a reference to his bee-keeping at Elmwood. (He collected twenty-six pounds of honey on one evening in June 1896.[24])

Arthur Pearson, the owner of the *Standard* and *Daily Express* and Northcliffe's greatest rival, wrote to him to say that 'we don't seem to have been on the best of terms lately, but all the same I should like to congratulate you very sincerely on the great distinction which has been conferred on you ... I should like to feel that if we cannot be close friends, at all events we need not be enemies.'[25] An altogether more baleful observer who also noticed Northcliffe's peerage was Kaiser Wilhelm II, who complained to Count von Bülow about the British 'jingo press' of Harmsworth, 'who His Majesty has now made a lord'.[26]

~

For a sense of how Northcliffe divided his time in this period, taking 1906 as a typical year, he spent 110 days in the office, a month in the United States, several days visiting the Manchester office of the *Daily Mail* and his Imperial Paper Mills company at Gravesend, eleven days in Monte Carlo, most weekends at Sutton Place but some at Elmwood and Totteridge, and a few staying with Lord Montagu at Beaulieu. Northcliffe spent thirty-nine days motoring around France in seven trips, some with Mary but most without (and possibly with Mrs Wrohan). He rarely went to the House of Lords, believing that he could propagate his views far better through his publications than there. 'To the House of Lords for the King's Speech at the Opening of Parliament,' he noted on 19 March 1906. 'Afterwards to the Office.'[27] He had been introduced as a peer by Montagu, who was the editor of *Car Illustrated* and whose mistress Eleanor Thornton was the model for the Spirit of Ecstasy figurine on the bonnet of Rolls-Royces.

The 1906 General Election was fought on tariff reform, which the *Daily Mail* argued, exaggeratedly, 'must prevail unless the Empire is to go down and the country become bankrupt'.[28] The paper supported Balfour's compromise plan for protectionism, rather than Chamberlain's full-blown model. Balfour was opposed to a general tariff and stated that the Unionists were not protectionist, but the Liberals managed to keep the focus on the 'stomach taxes' aspects of the proposals during the campaign, which also threw light on the Unionists' chronic split on the issue. Campbell-Bannerman won one of the greatest landslide victories of British political history. 'First day of the General Election,' Northcliffe noted in his diary on 13 January. 'Mr Balfour defeated at Manchester.'[29] As the results came through, the *Daily Mail* projected them by 'magic lantern' onto buildings on the Embankment and Trafalgar Square, and fired signal rockets of differing colours to represent the parties of MPs who were elected.

By the end, the Liberals had won 400 seats, the Unionists 137, the Liberal Unionists twenty-five, Irish Nationalists eighty-three, and the Labour Party, with whom the Liberals had done a pre-election deal, thirty. One of the issues in the campaign had been Votes for Women, and the *Daily Mail* had coined the neologism 'suffragette'. As so often in history, what had been intended as a jibe stuck, and became a label that women wore with pride.

Northcliffe had long been predicting a Tory defeat, although he had not foreseen the quintupling of the Labour vote from 63,304 in the last election to 329,748 in this one. In a letter to Northcliffe, Balfour described it as 'a reflection in this country – faint I hope – of what is going on in the Continent'.[30] This was a reference to the powerful socialist movements in France and Germany, and a general strike and revolution in Russia.

During the election, Winston Churchill attacked Northcliffe in a speech at Wolverhampton on 16 January. 'I condemn retaliatory duties on foods coming into this country,' he said.

Who will we retaliate against? We are told to retaliate against
Germany. Well, Mr Chamberlain does not like Germany, and the
proprietor of the *Daily Mail* does not like Germany. All the proprietors of the papers patronised by Mr Balfour have been made
noble lords. The proprietor of the *Daily Mail* dislikes Germany
because he has a quarrel with some German newspaper, and
they are trying to show how patriotic each of them can be for a
halfpenny.[31]

Northcliffe never minded attacks against him by Churchill – who
at this stage he regarded as a friend – so long as he was allowed to
retaliate, which he rarely failed to do.

~

In March 1906, the *Daily Mail* published the first instalment of
William Le Queux's novel *The Invasion of 1910,* the book version
of which was subtitled *With a Full Account of the Siege of London.*
Lord Roberts, Boer War hero and now the president of the National
Service League, contributed a preface to the book, and the *Daily
Mail* leader writer H. W. Wilson wrote the naval chapters. In the
550-page book, illustrated by twenty-one maps, the Germans land
at Weybourne in Norfolk, along the Essex coast and at Goole
in Yorkshire. Battles take place in Purleigh, Sheffield, Royston,
Chelmsford, Epping and Harlow, after which London is captured.
Chapter titles give the sense of the story, and the politics behind
it: 'The Surprise', 'Our Fleet Taken Unawares', 'How the Enemy
Dealt the Blow', 'Bombardment of London', 'Germans Sacking the
Banks', 'Revolts in Shoreditch and Islington', 'Massacre of Germans
in London', and so on.

The book was denounced as paranoiac by liberals and radicals, but
was also extremely readable, from the opening scene of two newspaper sub-editors noting that the telegraph and telephone connections
in London had gone down, to the truce at Hampstead after millions
of Britons had perished, and the subsequent peace treaty in January
1911 when 'practically the entire cost of the war had been borne by
England'. The moral of the book was clear throughout: 'The British

nation had been warned against the danger; it disregarded the warning ... In the teeth of all entreaties it reduced in 1906 the outlay upon
its army and its fleet, to expend the money thus saved upon its own
comfort. The battalions, batteries, and battleships sacrificed might
well have averted invasion, indeed, have prevented war.'[32]

Le Queux had spent four months touring southern England to
spot the likeliest places for the Germans' invasion, but their strategy
was altered by Northcliffe in view of the marketing for the serial
of the book, who ordered that the German army should 'not keep
to remote one-eyed villages where there was no possibility of large
Daily Mail sales'.[33] Meanwhile, the advertising department dressed
actors in spiked helmets and Prussian-looking uniforms and marched
them down Oxford Street with sandwich boards announcing the
forthcoming articles in the *Daily Mail*.[34] When the book came out, it
was one of the greatest bestsellers of the era, selling a million copies.

The invasion genre was well-established, usually written by army
and navy officers, and not invented by Northcliffe. This popular
genre fitted in well, however, with Harmsworth's call to be ready
once Germany unveiled its plan to hegemonise Europe; the *Daily
Mail* had first called for compulsory military service in 1904, and
by 1908 it began actively to campaign for it.

On 27 June 1906, Northcliffe left for New York on board the liner
Kaiser Wilhelm der Grosse – named after the Kaiser's grandfather –
for a tour of New York, Newport, Boston, Montreal and Quebec,
before heading to Grand Falls, Newfoundland. As usual, he travelled
in style, with a large entourage, although Mary did not come on this
trip, and his time in Quebec overlapped for three days with the visit
there of 'Lady Cathleen Wrohan'.

Northcliffe was forced to return home sooner than he expected,
however, after he received a telegram to say that his thirty-year-
old sixth brother St. John (aka 'Bonchie') – whom Evelyn Wrench
thought was Northcliffe's favourite sibling – had suffered a debilitating motoring accident near Hatfield when being driven home to
London from Harold's house, Horsey Hall in Norfolk.[35] The chauffeur had missed the road in the darkness and St. John fractured his
spine in the crash and was paralysed from the waist down for the

rest of his life.* Thereafter, Northcliffe 'constantly referred to his brother St. John's fortitude and courage in taking up the threads of his life and making good, in spite of the terrible motor accident, which crippled him'.[36]

The Indian clubs, a type of exercise equipment that St. John used for his physiotherapy, gave him the idea for the shape of the bottles for the Perrier mineral water company that he bought with Northcliffe's help, and which proved a commercial success.[37] (Northcliffe always insisted on Perrier being the water drunk at his formal dinners.) After the Great War, St. John's state-of-the-art bottling works† produced five million bottles of Perrier a year. 'His brother's accident affected Northcliffe more than anything that ever happened to him,' Wrench recalled. 'I do not think he was ever quite the same again.'[38]

Despite having almost certainly seen Kathleen Wrohan in Quebec in July 1906, Northcliffe had already embarked on an affair with the Pennsylvania-born beauty and novelist Baroness Bettina 'Betsy' von Hutten zum Stolzenberg, who was married to a German. 'Escorted Baroness von Hutten to Queenborough,' Evelyn Wrench noted in his diary on 19 June. 'Northcliffe told me he would only entrust this mission to either Reggie Nicholson, George Sutton or myself.'[39] Queenborough is a small town on the Isle of Sheppey. Two days later, Wrench noted, 'I think the Chief was very pleased with the way I carried out my instructions the other day.'

Northcliffe could trust Sutton as his confidential right-hand man, but the choice of Nicholson, his wife's lover, as a person to help facilitate his affairs implies a truly Edwardian attitude towards the hypocrisy then surrounding marital infidelity. To have three enablers in Wrench, Sutton and Nicholson helped enormously, although Wrench, who thought of himself as a budding hero of the British Empire rather than a sexual facilitator, came to dislike his role. Northcliffe's affair with Hutten did not last long, and later she

---

* The motorcyclist who found St. John by the side of the road was rewarded with a pound a week for the next twenty-seven years.
† One of the stonemasons who worked on it was Benito Mussolini.

would tell stories about his histrionics, although how truthful they were is impossible to say. Did he really slap an editor's face in a Paris restaurant and challenge him to a duel, for example? Did he really fall on the carpet of a hotel in a fit of uncontrollable rage, only to tidy his hair with the comb that she offered him?[40] Perhaps – but then again, she *was* a novelist.

When Hutten visited England on 11 October 1906, Wrench was sent to 'offer her a cordial welcome back to England'.[41] She was at Sutton Place nine days later, and then back again at Sutton Place on 4 November. In September 1953, Wrench told one of Northcliffe's biographers, Reginald Pound, that the affair with Hutten 'disgusted the Spenders and was unfortunate for Northcliffe in a far more serious way which had better not be written down for idle eyes to see'.[42] Pound speculated that he meant that Northcliffe had caught venereal disease from her, but there is no evidence for this. The affair certainly seems to have ended before her divorce from the baron in 1909, by which time she was said to have been in love with the Italian tenor Francesco Guardabassi.

'The first time I ever saw the ugly side of his nature was in 1908,' Wrench recalled of Northcliffe in his autobiography, *Uphill*, many years later.

I had unintentionally learnt about something he wished to keep private.* Naturally I would never have said a thing to a soul. He was very disturbed about the whole thing, not with me, for I had nothing to say on it, but he vented his spleen on me. He came into my room and said, 'If you ever tell a soul, I will sack you on the spot.' I could hardly believe my ears, that the Chief should speak to me like that. The next time I saw him, he went out of his way to be nice to me.[43]

Yet the spell Northcliffe had cast over Wrench was broken. 'I began to see my idol had feet of clay.'

---

* Wrench had caught Lady Northcliffe in flagrante with Reggie Nicholson. [Taylor, *Great Outsiders*, p.84]

'There was a cruel side to Northcliffe's character,' Wrench later wrote. 'If he had his knife in anyone he was ruthless and relentless.'[44] Yet, in 1908, Northcliffe gave Wrench a percentage of the net profits of the *Continental Daily Mail* and, in January 1909, he and Harold put Wrench (who Northcliffe called 'My dear Evelyn') in charge of the entire sales side of the Amalgamated Press on a salary of nearly £2,000 a year. Wrench organised a nationwide house-to-house distribution of millions of leaflets featuring instalments from the weeklies. Explaining the moral imperatives behind the serialisations, he wrote: 'If the villain seduced the virtuous maiden, he was always brought to book. The hardworking hero always ended up as head of the firm. True love was always requited.'[45] Northcliffe also entrusted Wrench to produce a braille edition of the *Daily Mail*, a loss-making enterprise that Northcliffe undertook philanthropically.[46]

In December 1906, Northcliffe sold No. 36 Berkeley Square and took a nine-year lease on No. 22 St James's Place, overlooking Green Park, which Tom Clarke described as a 'little cul-de-sac of aristocracy'.[47] The house was designed by James Wyatt, with cornices and chimney pieces by John Flaxman, and Northcliffe was proud that when the poet Samuel Rogers had lived there from 1803 to 1855 his guests had included Richard Brinsley Sheridan, William Wordsworth, Madame de Staël, Sydney Smith, Walter Scott and J. M. W. Turner.

~

In 1901, Northcliffe had written of his projected newspaper combine that 'after the fashion of the great commercial Trusts of the United States, they could simply stamp out opposition and rivalry'.[48] Five years later, he began to worry that combines were about to extinguish competition in Britain, and that he was going to be a victim of it. 'One day in October 1906 the Chief sent for me,' recalled Wareham Smith, and said to him, 'We have had the tobacco combine. We now have the soap combine. Other interests will follow. If competition is stopped, people won't advertise. And anyhow Trusts are bad for the public. It must be stopped.'[49]

The way that Northcliffe attempted to stop it was by waging an aggressive newspaper campaign against Lever Brothers, who manufactured Lux and Lifebuoy soap at their Wirral factory, Port Sunlight. Since some raw materials had increased in price owing to them also being used to make margarine, William Lever had decided to reduce the size of the threepenny bar of soap from 16oz to 15oz, while keeping the price the same. Northcliffe believed that Lever was also attempting to establish a cartel in soap, which would streamline the industry and ultimately lead to cuts in advertising expenditure.[50] It is hard to believe that Northcliffe would have launched so virulent a campaign against the Lever brothers had they not been Jewish.

Northcliffe wrote some of the anti-Lever leaders in the *Daily Mail* himself, and they were unsparing, with headlines such as 'Squeezing the Public' and 'Cruel Blow to the Poor'. There were also cartoons directed against the Levers that employed blatantly anti-Semitic tropes and attributed slogans such as 'We don't care about you, We want more of your money.'[51] Lever Brothers' share price dropped by 25 per cent and sales by 60 per cent before the company issued a libel writ against Associated Newspapers, and hired Edward Carson and the young F. E. Smith to represent them.[52] Meanwhile, Northcliffe engaged the equally brilliant (and Jewish) barrister Rufus Isaacs in his defence.

The case entered legal folklore. According to Smith's account, he was summoned back from a hunting weekend in Leicestershire to a room at the Savoy at 9.30pm to find a four-foot-high stack of legal papers relating to the case, whereupon he ordered a bottle of champagne and two dozen oysters. By 8.30am the next morning, he opined, 'There is no answer to this action for libel. The damages must be enormous. F.E. Smith.'[53] They certainly were. Carson destroyed Associated's case in a five-hour opening speech on 17 July 1907, after which he called William Lever, who defended himself superbly under cross-examination by Isaacs, who then 'in an audible whisper' offered £15,000 damages.[54] Carson scorned the offer – and also those of £20,000, then £30,000, then £40,000 – only finally accepting £50,000, at that time one of the largest sums ever awarded to a successful litigant in the English courts.[55]

'We had to climb down unconditionally,' Wrench noted in his diary. 'All the office rather depressed.'[56] The opposite was true at

Port Sunlight where the workers were given a day's paid holiday to celebrate, and Levers publicly donated the money to the Tropical Medicine, Russian Studies and Town Planning departments of Liverpool University. Nor did they let up, suing over material damages to their individual businesses until, by the end of all the litigation, Associated Newspapers had lost at least £141,000.[57]

Northcliffe paid many of the costs of the case out of his own pocket in order not to affect his employees' profit-sharing scheme. It was an indication that he recognised his personal involvement – he had dictated many of the worst libels personally – but it also reflected his protectiveness towards his employees, and of course also the sheer extent of his personal wealth by then. He has been accused of 'overweening arrogance that perhaps portended his later madness' over the case, but this goes too far.[58] He learnt his lesson and 'was sufficiently chastened by the Lever affair never again to indulge in vendettas against rich individuals in the business community'.[59] The only good to come of it was a lifelong friendship with Rufus Isaacs.

~

Northcliffe was particularly fearful of the use the Germans might make of air power, which hitherto had hardly been considered by the Admiralty or War Office, despite Orville and Wilbur Wright first flying in December 1903. On 12 November 1906, the Brazilian Alberto Santos-Dumont flew an aeroplane a distance of 700 feet in twenty-one seconds, just fifteen feet above the ground in Paris. Northcliffe described it as an 'aerial motor-car' and, in a leader in the Daily Mail, predicted that

New difficulties of every kind will arise, not the least being the military problem caused by the virtual annihilation of frontiers and the acquisition of the power to pass readily through the air above the sea. The isolation of the United Kingdom may disappear, and thus the success of M. Santos-Dumont has an international importance. They are not mere dreamers who hold that the time is at hand when air power will be an even more important thing than sea power.[60]

He added to one of his editors, 'England is no longer an island. There will be no more sleeping safely behind the wooden walls of old England with the Channel our safety moat.'[61]

Northcliffe was a visionary when it came to the role that air power was to play in the twentieth century. His predictions came months before H. G. Wells wrote his ground-breaking 1907 novel *The War in the Air*. Northcliffe was determined that Britain and her ally France should be in the forefront of aerial technical innovation. The best way he could advance this was by instigating flying competitions with large cash prizes from the *Daily Mail*. He offered £1,000 to the first person to fly across the English Channel; in February 1909, he offered £10,000 for flying from London to Manchester* within a period of twenty-four hours and with only two stops en route; in 1911, he offered £10,000 for a flight around Britain, and so on. When, on 1 April 1913, the *Daily Mail* offered a prize of £10,000 for the first direct flight across the Atlantic, many readers and rival newspapers assumed it was an April Fools' Day prank or a mere circulation-boosting gimmick. *Punch* magazine offered the same money for a flight to Mars.[62]

Harold Harmsworth fully supported the initiative and, over the years, the *Daily Mail* paid out over £60,000 in prizes for the aerial exploits of many of the greatest pioneers of early aviation, including Louis Paulhan, Louis Blériot, John Moore-Brabazon, Thomas Sopwith, John Alcock and Arthur Whitten Brown, and Amy Johnson. Other newspapers mocked these prizes, but Santos-Dumont wrote to Northcliffe praising him for the way it encouraged the aviation industry. Every time a great milestone was achieved and a prize won, the *Daily Mail* would remind its readers of the strategic considerations involved. For example, after Northcliffe presented Louis Blériot with the £1,000 prize for flying across the Channel at a celebratory lunch at the Savoy on 26 July 1909, the *Daily Mail* rammed home the point that 'the British people have hitherto dwelt secure in their islands ... locomotion is now being transferred to an element where Dreadnoughts are useless and sea power no shield against attack'.

---

* Not coincidentally, the two places where the *Daily Mail* was printed.

~

In December 1907, Alfred and Mary Northcliffe were invited by a friend to hear Ignacy Jan Paderewski play the piano and they motored up from Sutton Place for the occasion. By the time they reached Berkeley Square, it was so foggy that they felt it would be foolish to drive further, and they stopped and telephoned their regrets to their friend.' The friend nonetheless insisted, so much against their will, they groped their way to his house.[63] During an interval in the recital, Northcliffe congratulated the financier Sir Alexander Henderson – who as well as sitting on one of Arthur Pearson's boards was connected with the Great Central Railway – on having succeeded in amalgamating the Great Central with the prosperous Midland Railway. Henderson revealed that he was 'doing something better than that' and that there was a plan afoot for Pearson's *Standard* to take control of *The Times*.[64]

Without betraying more than normal interest in the news, Northcliffe returned to the second half of the recital, and soon afterwards left for France, thereby giving the impression that he was not concerned that his greatest rival Arthur Pearson was about to buy the most respected and politically influential newspaper in the British Empire. Privately, however, he instructed Sir George Lewis, his discreet and well-connected solicitor, to 'find out what you can'.[65] Had he been turned back by the pea-souper fog that December evening, Lord Northcliffe might never have made the decision that led to him taking control of *The Times*.

CHAPTER 8

TAKING *THE TIMES*

January–March 1908

'Northcliffe ... indisputably saved *The Times*.'[1]

DERWENT MAY, *Critical Times: The History of the
Times Literary Supplement* 2001

The Times, which had been founded in 1785 as the *Universal Daily Register*, was by far the most prestigious newspaper in Britain, and Northcliffe saw it as the pinnacle of his career to own it. Among his heroes were John Walter II, son of *The Times* founder; Thomas Barnes, the editor from 1817 until 1841, who had laid down the rule that leading articles should be 'designed to be acted upon'; and perhaps the greatest newspaperman of the nineteenth century, John Delane. It was the paper Alfred Harmsworth Snr had read.

The Times was read by virtually the entire British Establishment and was greatly respected abroad, where the chancelleries of Europe considered that it represented the national view. To own the paper automatically bestowed huge power, although the Walter family had chosen not to exercise it over the previous four generations. Buying *The Times* was 'a very poor use of capital judged by purely commercial criteria, but a rational step to take given Northcliffe's wish to influence policy-making at the highest level'.[2]

Fortunately for Northcliffe, although it was hugely esteemed, *The Times* made dull reading and had a circulation of only 38,000, which was 50 per cent down on the days of Delane. It was inefficiently run, could not afford modern printing machinery, had old-fashioned typefaces and byzantine financial practices. In addition, the present proprietors – Arthur Walter and his brother John Walter V (the family took Roman numerals in the manner of monarchs) – recognised that the paper's problems could be resolved only by what he called 'a revolution or earthquake at Printing House Square', where it was published.[3] The paper's decline in financial viability had been greatly accelerated in 1888 by the disastrous decision of the editor C. E. Buckle to publish letters that seemed to implicate the Irish nationalist leader Charles Parnell in terrorism. These turned out to have been forged and the debacle cost the paper a quarter of a million pounds in libel damages and legal fees.

Northcliffe had considered investing in *The Times* in June 1898. He spoke to Arthur Walter and the managing director Charles Moberly Bell about it, but nothing came of it as only 2.5 per cent of the shares seemed to be on offer. Then in July 1907 – coincidentally the same month as the Lever Brothers judgement was handed down – a decision in an entirely different courtroom suddenly opened up an opportunity for any determined and cash-rich would-be proprietor. Since the mid-1880s, the Walter family had demanded that owners of *Times* equity, which after a century numbered over eighty of their very extended family, including their cousins the Sibley family, could not sell their shares on the open market. Yet after many years of dwindling profits, the Sibleys and other minority shareholders wanted to sell their stock before the paper went bankrupt. By 1908, the newspaper was only kept afloat by the sale of its subsidiary's ownership of the *Encyclopedia Britannica* and *The Times Atlas*. In the case of *Sibley v Walter*, the Court of Chancery ordered *The Times* to be reorganised as a limited liability company. Suddenly, after 123 years, one of the greatest newspapers in the world, and the only one to cost threepence rather than a penny, was up for grabs.

For all his feigned nonchalance at the Paderewski recital, Northcliffe recognised that here was a defining, possibly once-in-a-lifetime moment for him. This was not only because he had always wanted to own Britain's premier highbrow paper himself, but also because if Pearson owned *The Times* as well as his current papers

the *Standard, Daily Express* and several regional papers and magazines, he would enjoy a journalistic pre-eminence and political power
that Northcliffe probably never would, however many successful
middlebrow papers he owned. Pearson's constant plagiarising of his
magazine titles in the 1890s possibly rankled, and Northcliffe also
might have feared that in the coming winnowing out of Fleet Street
into one great monopoly that he had predicted in 1901, he would be
victim rather than predator.

On 5 January 1908, while in Paris, Northcliffe inserted a sentence in
The Observer based on what Sir George Lewis and his informers in
the industry had managed to glean about Pearson and the Walters.
Under the headline 'The Future of *The Times*', it declared that 'it
is understood that important negotiations are taking place which
will place the direction of *The Times* in the hands of a very capable
proprietor of several popular magazines and newspapers'.[4] That
could only mean one of two people at that time: Arthur Pearson or
Northcliffe himself. Since the latter was *The Observer*'s proprietor
and hardly likely to leak the news against himself, and was anyway
known to be holidaying abroad, it must mean Pearson. The revelation that talks were underway severely upset the Walter brothers'
plans to sell to Pearson, because they had not previously informed
either Charles Moberley Bell or George Earle Buckle, *The Times*'
veteran editor of twenty-four years.

Buckle was the son of a scholarly clergyman; he had taken a
double-first from New College, Oxford, and was a Fellow of All
Souls. He was conscientious, popular, hard-working, devoted to
the paper, and firmly believed that *The Times*'s duty was to support whichever government was in power at the time, although his
personal politics were those of Disraelian Toryism. (Indeed, he was
later to become Disraeli's official biographer.) Rather old-fashioned
for his fifty-four years, he wrote all his letters himself by hand, kept
no records of his correspondence, and no notes of conversations.
'He had little interest in modern organisation and disdained changes
in routine. The telephone and typewriter and other such technical

innovations might as well have been intended as mechanical ornaments. ... He never acquired the knack of dictation and for many
years even avoided having a secretary.'[5]

The key figure in the looming takeover battle was not Buckle but
Charles Moberley Bell, who was sixty-one, and had managed *The
Times* since 1890, as well as being a *Times* correspondent during
General Gordon's expedition to Khartoum. When running to catch
a troop train, he had caught his foot in the rail line and his ankle-
ball – the astragalus – had to be removed, leaving him walking with a
limp for the rest of his life. (He had the bone mounted in his walking
stick, saying, 'I'll make my astragalus work for me somehow.'[6]) Like
Buckle, Bell kept long hours at *The Times*, but despite all their hard
work, the paper lost money.

In their negotiations with Pearson, the Walter brothers had kept
Buckle and Bell in the dark, treating it as a purely commercial decision that would be presented to the staff later as a fait accompli.
Indeed, Arthur Walter entered into an agreement with Pearson by
which he would become chairman of a new company, *The Times* Ltd,
with Pearson as the managing director and majority shareholder.

On reading the *Observer* story, Buckle and Bell naturally protested
to Arthur Walter, demanding that it be announced in *The Times* that
Pearson was indeed the prospective buyer. Both men knew that they
were unlikely to survive long in their jobs under a Pearson regime,
and when Harcourt Kitchin, Bell's deputy, asked him, 'What are you
going to do about this Pearson business?', Bell replied, 'Smash it.'[7]
Bell's first thought was to set up a new paper with all the old *Times*
staff; as the senior foreign correspondent Henry Wickham Steed
pointed out to him, 'If the announcement is made, no one is likely
to bid for the mere name of *The Times*.'[8]

On 7 January, it was stated in *The Times* that 'negotiations are in
progress whereby it is contemplated that *The Times* newspaper shall
be formed into a limited company [and] ... the business management
will be reorganised by Mr C. Arthur Pearson, the proposed managing director'.[9] Northcliffe wrote from Paris to congratulate Pearson
on the takeover, suggesting that the *Daily Mail* run an interview with

him, which Pearson refused as he did not want to 'rub things in' or
to 'push myself at all'.[10] It had the effect of making Pearson believe
that his purchase was all over bar the signing of the contract and
other legal formalities.

The next day, Northcliffe wrote an anonymous profile on page
four of the *Daily Mail* under the pseudonym 'X' entitled 'Mr Pearson
of *The Times* – An Appreciation by An Opponent'. This praised the
'vigour and determination' of a figure who was 'above all things, not
easily deterred by seeming difficulties', and was 'a typical man of
the new century'.[11] 'In this handsome young Englishman you have
one of the best specimens of a well-born man of his race who has
passed through a working public school – Winchester,' Harmsworth
enthused, before slipping in the information that Joseph Chamberlain
had referred to Pearson as a 'Champion Hustler'. The rest of the article was as positive as the start, about how Pearson would 'greatly
improve' *The Times*, but the stiletto had been deftly inserted.

Chamberlain had suffered a debilitating stroke in December 1906
which rendered him incapable of speech, and so it was impossible
to know whether he really had described Pearson as a hustler, but
Northcliffe knew that the extended Walter family and the political
world would probably not want to sell their venerable institution
to someone with that reputation. When Buckle took soundings,
he discovered that Arthur Balfour, Lord Lansdowne, Joseph
Chamberlain's son Austen, Lord Curzon, Sir Edward Grey and John
Morley all deplored the idea of *The Times* falling to Pearson (who
Northcliffe had also usefully pointed out had worked for *Tit-Bits*).[12]
Pearson realised only when it was too late that Northcliffe had
emphasised everything most likely to worry *The Times* proprietors
and the political heavyweights of both parties.

Northcliffe had written the piece from the Ritz Hotel in Paris and
telegraphed it to Kennedy Jones and George Sutton in the name of
'Brunnbauer'. (Joseph Brunnbauer was his Austrian valet, of whom
Evelyn Wrench recalled in 1955 that he 'used to glide about the
passages of Sutton Place wearing fur-lined slippers, and occupied a
privileged position in the establishment, for Northcliffe used him for
many errands'.[13]) During the coming negotiations, absolute secrecy

was maintained by the extensive use of codenames: Northcliffe was 'Atlantic' (either for his pro-Americanism or possibly in mockery of the Kaiser's self-styling as 'Emperor of the Atlantic'); Printing House Square, *The Times'* premises in Blackfriars, was 'The Cenotaph', which before the Great War merely meant empty tomb*; Bell was 'Canton'; Harold was 'Abigail'; General John Sterling was 'Caesar'; Sutton was 'Buffalo', and Kennedy Jones 'Alberta'. When Bell visited Northcliffe at the Hôtel Christol in Boulogne for face-to-face meetings in the era before passports were required, he travelled under the (hardly impenetrable) name of 'Mr Charles Ball'.[14]

On one occasion when trans-Channel telephone connections went down, Wrench had to take a note to Sutton about the takeover during 'one of the stormiest crossings I have ever made'.[15] It might seem paranoiac but Pearson did employ scores of reporters, and at that time it was impossible to prevent telephonists from listening in to conversations and telegraphists from reading telegrams. In order to throw people off the scent, Northcliffe had news items inserted in his papers saying he was on holiday in the south of France when he was in fact organising the bid at locations in Versailles, Paris, Boulogne and London. When in London, he did not go to St James's Place but stayed incognito (possibly with Mrs Wrohan) or with Sutton at his house in Belsize Park.[16]

On 12 January, another seemingly promotional article in *The Observer* said of Pearson that 'He has done strong as well as sensational things.'[17] The term sensational was a pejorative one in business, and the Walters began to worry about what might happen to their stately paper under this sensationalist hustler Arthur Pearson. Without the deal having been signed, Pearson then made the stunning error of throwing a celebratory dinner at the Savoy Hotel, complete with an ice sculpture of Printing House Square.[18] He was anticipating a positive result from a Court of Chancery hearing scheduled for late January, at which Pearson was to be approved

---

* And which Derwent May, the biographer of the *Times Literary Supplement*, surely correctly thought was 'perhaps a Northcliffe joke'. [May, *Critical Times*, p.61]

by Mr Justice Warrington as *The Times*' new owner. Yet before that took place, Bell approached Kennedy Jones to ask whether Northcliffe would be interested in investing in *The Times*, in such a way that would preserve the paper's character and save his and Buckle's jobs.

'No sale of *The Times* has yet been effected,' announced *The Times* on 18 January, 'nor has any decision been arrived at as to the mode or terms of any such sale.'[19] Bell now busied himself undermining the Pearson bid from within, persuading partners such as General John Sterling, the largest non-Walter shareholder, and Sir Edward Tennant to change their minds. Rumours about counterbids swirled around the City and Westminster. Would the Prime Minister, Sir Henry Campbell-Bannerman, be able to put together a pro-Free Trade bid under which the paper would be edited by J. A. Spender? Were the Americans about to step in to support what looked like a Bell–Sterling combination? Might the Kaiser be getting involved, through the involvement of the Austrian banking group the Wiener Bankverein? Bell cunningly let Northcliffe think the last was a possibility, and Northcliffe afterwards told Harcourt Kitchin that he had 'saved *The Times* from the German Emperor'.[20]

Just as he had signed his *Daily Mail* article 'X', so Northcliffe insisted to Bell as a precondition to making an offer that his name should not be revealed to anyone as the alternative to Pearson. This meant that Bell could not consult anyone on the editorial side of *The Times* (including Buckle) or outside the office, so, as Bell's daughter later recalled,

he hit upon one expedient to help him to a decision. He made a list in alphabetic order of all the prominent people known to possess sufficient wealth to be possible purchasers of *The Times*, and submitted it to Lord Cromer, to some of the Rothschilds, and to various others ... asking them to cross off the names of any to whose connection with *The Times* they would take serious exception. No-one crossed off Northcliffe's name. Fortified by that, and because he believed he could do something to save the independence of the paper, he promised his support to Northcliffe.[21]

By 29 January, Bell was able to tell Northcliffe that 'W[alter] is openly (to me) anxious to get out of the P[earson] agreement, and is indignant with his brother for getting him into it.' Bell told Walter that if Northcliffe bought *The Times*, 'The only serious change that will be made is in the machinery and printing.'[22] If Bell truly thought that Northcliffe was only interested in altering those two aspects of the paper, he was being unusually naïve. 'I must see you,' Bell continued.

> How can it be managed? If W[alter] were not so desperately weak I believe I could get him in, even giving your name, but that would be dangerous now ... Where can I see you? Couldn't I come out to some suburb and you pick me up in a motor – or I will come to you like Nicodemus by night! I ... could get to St James' Place by midnight. I see no signs of being shadowed yet.[23]

Wherever it was they met – not at St James's Place, which Northcliffe feared might be watched by Pearson reporters – the next day Bell warned Northcliffe of the financier William Sharp's plan for three rich Free Traders – Lord Brassey, Sir Hugh Bell and Yates Thompson – to buy *The Times*.[24] (Sharp was promptly codenamed 'Naples'.) Bell started writing Northcliffe long, coded letters almost daily keeping him informed of what the Walters were telling him. Claiming to be expressing his personal views 'and not as Manager of *The Times*' – which was all the more absurd when written on *Times* writing paper – Bell told Sharp that the Pearson bid 'spells disaster to the interests of *The Times*. I oppose it openly and avowedly ... The only remedy lies in reassuring the public that there will be no change in the whole tone of the paper. (I do not say no mechanical change).'[25]

On 4 February, Northcliffe met Bell at the Sackville Street offices of T. E. Mackenzie, Northcliffe's accountant. When Bell asked Northcliffe what he wanted to do with *The Times*, he received the reply – at least according to Bell's recollection two years later:

> I want to make it worth threepence. I think the printing is bad and the make-up abominable. Your law reports and Parliamentary

reports are good, but they ought to be fuller. Your City news can be greatly improved ... You do not give enough space to foreign news – in fact, I want to improve every department of the paper, but as to the policy of the paper, I do not want to interfere at all – that is a matter for the Editor.[26]

He guaranteed senior management in their jobs – 'I do not want to get rid of anyone who does his work well, I want as little change as possible' – especially Buckle, Bell and Valentine Chirol, the foreign editor who had an encyclopaedic knowledge of the international scene.

Negotiations continued, and when, on 9 February, Bell tried to impose further conditions, Northcliffe threatened to withdraw altogether. One morning around this time an emissary from Northcliffe – probably Kennedy Jones or Sutton – visited Bell at home before he was dressed. Bell went downstairs in his dressing gown to be presented with an ultimatum that unless Bell signed a letter to Northcliffe, the deal was off. 'It is understood,' the letter stated, 'that in the event of your acquiring *The Times* newspaper, I shall act as your managing director for five years and carry out your absolute instructions.'[27] Bell signed it, which effectively gave Northcliffe control of the management in return for a renewal of Bell's lucrative five-year contract, but he never told Buckle, Chirol or anyone else that he had.[28]

Before Northcliffe could seal any deal, however, a rival bid from the financiers William Koch de Gooreynd and Sir Edgar Speyer had to be dealt with. Speyer was a German-born banker who took British citizenship in 1892. A friend of Asquith and Churchill, he was a baronet and privy councillor, and in 1902 had saved the Proms from bankruptcy. Koch de Gooreynd was Belgian. A mixture of anti-foreigner and anti-Semitic prejudice was mobilised by Bell and Steed to stymie their takeover hopes. On 24 February, Bell wrote to Steed, *The Times* correspondent in Austria, with heavy sarcasm to say that a consortium supported 'by Britons of the name of Koch and Speyer' were working hard to take over *The Times* after the failure of the Pearson bid.[29] Steed replied from Vienna:

I fear Speyer and Koch. Even if they have no direct commission from the German Government, they are German Jews, and five years' experience here has taught me one thing – for some hitherto unexplained reason, interest, clannishness, unconscious linguistic or racial fanaticism, every Jew in this part of the world is a strong pro-German who looks towards Berlin as a Musselman [Muslim] towards Mecca. I have studied them, high and low, rich and poor, learned and unlearned – in their heart of hearts they are pro-German to a man.[30]

Steed, a virulent lifelong anti-Semite, suggested that Bell commission an article about Speyer and Koch, as 'the more light that is let in upon them the less lovely are they likely to appear to their confederates or dupes'.[31] He suggested a plebiscite or strike among the staff 'in case of purchase by the Speyers … If it were noised abroad that the staff would not stand being sold to the Hebrews like a flock of sheep or a drove of pigs, would not the prospective bidders tremble for the safety of their prospective investment?' It cannot be doubted that Northcliffe's being a Gentile was one of the reasons his takeover of *The Times* came off in the way that it did.

On 8 March, Northcliffe finally authorised Bell to inform Arthur Walter of his identity as the bidder. Walter did not seem shocked, and indeed told Bell that Northcliffe would be 'all right' as a proprietor.[32] Bell then persuaded Buckle and Chirol – who initially certainly did not think it would be all right to become employees of Northcliffe – that of all the deals on offer, this was the best. Buckle professed it a 'bitter pill to swallow'.[33] Discussing where the money needed to come from to escape Pearson or Speyer, however, Chirol told Bell, 'I should take it from the Devil himself!'. In a quite remarkable twist, it was agreed that even after the deal went through, it would not be publicly stated that Northcliffe owned the controlling stake, but that his identity would remain secret for years.

The only members of his family that Northcliffe told about the bid were Harold, Mary and Mother. 'Exactly when we shall return depends upon events,' he told his mother from the Hotel des Reservoirs in Versailles on 12 March, of which you know the purport. So far these affairs go well though there have been, already, rumours of indiscreet talk on the part of members of our family – who certainly *know* nothing. The very appearance of your firstborn on the scene of a struggle of this kind brings in others ... We are most anxious that if the thing is accomplished it shall not be known for several years, until we have time to demonstrate that we are not so erratic as our enemies suppose ... I shall be very glad when I am able to relinquish the life of an exile.[34]

Four days later, Bell wired Northcliffe at Versailles – 'Gone through as we wanted' – whereupon Northcliffe wrote to his mother. 'I could not wire you that I have been successful ... as the Post Office is a sure way of revealing secrets, but I have just received a telegram saying so. I shall try to make the work worthy of you my dear, but *it is a secret*.'[35] Her comment on her son acquiring *The Times* was somewhat philosophical, commiserating with him for attaining his ultimate dream so early in life. 'I'm sorry, Alfred,' she said. 'You have lost your horizon.'[36]

On 17 March 1908, Lord Northcliffe bought *The Times* for £320,000 in cash, in the names of Moberley Bell and General Sterling. (He had been ready to go up to £400,000.) Ahead of the sale, the money was placed in Bell's private bank account without any sort of condition or safeguard, which Bell's daughter stated was 'a confidence which [Bell] warmly appreciated'.[37] Northcliffe later told Kitchin that he did this because he 'wanted to please old Bell and to show that I, at any rate, believed in him. He made all sorts of conditions for *The Times* and for the staff, yet he made no condition for himself.'[38] This was untrue; Bell's five-year contract had been agreed beforehand.

As Pearson's bid was to have been financed by a stock offering, the Court of Chancery preferred the Bell–Sterling all-cash offer, which went through officially one week later after no appeals were received. As far as the world was concerned, therefore, it was the Bell–Sterling consortium who were buying *The Times*, whose major backer remained anonymous, since Northcliffe did not want a backlash of hostile and mocking publicity along the lines that Printing House Square, the bastion of British high-class journalism, had fallen to the publisher of *Comic Cuts*. This was not out of any personal sensitivity, but because he did not want *The Times* to lose circulation. Despite his 51 per cent stake, Northcliffe did not join the board for four years, and never even set foot in Printing House Square for the first year of his ownership.[39]

Louise Owen recalled how 'March 17 was a momentous day for us, for *The Times* is the most powerful thing in the world.' That day, *The Times* announced: 'There will be no change whatever in the political or editorial direction of the paper, which will be conducted by the same Staff on the independent lines pursued uninterruptedly for so many years.'[40] Readers were told that the new board of directors would be John Walter V as chairman, Buckle as editor, Bell as managing director, Valentine Chirol as foreign editor, and Buckle's former assistant, William Monypenny. When the *Daily Chronicle* announced that Northcliffe was the buyer, it was not believed. Sometime later, Bell told Northcliffe that *The Times* had not been abused by other papers recently, whereupon Northcliffe replied that he need not worry, as 'When I ... reveal my identity as controller ... you will get all the abuse you want.'[41]

Once *The Times* deal was done, Lord Northcliffe went on holiday to Seville, during which, Evelyn Wrench recalled, 'He seemed more carefree then than I ever remember him.'[42] On their long walks in the countryside, Northcliffe repeatedly told Wrench that he believed he would become one of the two or three top people in the newspaper industry. In one walk among the Moorish ruins of Alcala, ten miles from Seville, Northcliffe discussed with Wrench the difficulty in finding 'generals' for his undertakings. This was certainly to become a problem for him at *The Times*, where the culture of the paper meant that any reforms he wanted to undertake for the sake of efficiency, higher circulation and profitability moved at a glacial pace, to his extreme frustration, and eventually to his irritation and fury.

There was a collegiate atmosphere at *The Times*; all of the people at the top of the newspaper had clerical, Oxford or classical backgrounds, and some had all three.[43] They saw themselves as a collective body serving the public interest, and not primarily as a profit-making enterprise.[44] Buckle himself was conscientious: he read every letter the paper was sent, could quickly digest any amount of complex information, and often stayed at the paper until the early hours of the morning. For all the high moral tone of the paper, however, it was a loss-maker, and Northcliffe set about trying to change that without altering the fundamental character of the paper, which he genuinely revered.

Northcliffe's detractors accuse him of being a vandal who deliberately set out to destroy the traditions of *The Times*, strip it of its human assets, force it to follow his right-wing political line, and turn it into a cash-cow and a threepenny version of the *Daily Mail*. They are wrong. He did want it to break even or make a profit, but through increased circulation and ending the inefficiencies of a business that had not been examined systematically in decades. He always recognised the differences between his two major papers, referring to Carmelite House as 'the dog-fight' – which he loved – but wanting Printing House Square to retain its serene, cogitative ambience.[45] He once likened the idea of popularising *The Times* to putting 'a Punch and Judy show in Westminster Abbey'.[46] He therefore banned neologisms – it had to be 'motor house' rather than 'garage', for example – writing that 'American is very amusing to talk, but it should not be allowed to be printed in *The Times*.'[47]

'His ambition was to maintain its traditions,' Louise Owen recalled of Northcliffe's stance.

Only those in close association with him during those early days know of the struggle he had, and the obstacle-makers he encountered; it was like knocking his head repeatedly against a brick wall. He devoted much of his precious time to improving the appearance of the paper; the ink, printing, publishing and advertising. He had great difficulty ... in introducing electric light into some parts of Printing House Square, and how he urged and urged the late Mr Moberly Bell to save his energy and time by dictating his letters.[48]

As Northcliffe faced inertia rather than outright opposition from Printing House Square, he resorted to humour. He would recall how Printing House Square had been built on the site of an ancient monastery in Blackfriars and described the editorial team as 'Ye olde Black Friars'.[49] He also called them 'Old Gang' and 'giant tortoises',[50] and occasionally told them that their 'screeds' were not 'of great interest to ye publique'.[51] On one occasion, he likened Printing House Square to a 'barnacle-covered whale', 'giant sloth', and 'a cross between a Government office and a cathedral'.[52] He criticised the 'mephitic [noxious] atmosphere of Printing House Square', joking that the sub-editors had a 'morbid taste for ancient news', and believing that *The Times* motto was 'News, like wine, improves by keeping.'[53] When some ancient weaponry, including muskets and spears, were found in the cellars of 'that vast and gloomy labyrinth hidden away near St Paul's', he joked that 'they're to arm the staff with, if anyone brings you a piece of news'.[54]

'Did you know there was a sub-editor of *The Times* who once spiked an elephant?' Northcliffe was fond of relating. 'Yes, an elephant escaped from a circus in South London and went careering around the streets. When this sub-editor received an account of the incident, he stuck it on the waste-file with other rejected copy. It was too interesting!'[55] In fact, it was the *Daily Mail* that had failed to report Jimmy Dunn's story that lions, tigers and snakes were roaming around Birmingham's Corporation Street railway station after the train carrying Bostock's Menagerie crashed there. It was spiked because the news editor assumed that Dunn, who had been sent to Birmingham to report the annual meeting of the British Temperance Society, was drunk.[56]

Northcliffe took his time revamping *The Times*, investing £60,000 in replacing the old Kastenbein and Hoe presses with state-of-the-art Monotype typesetters and Goss presses.[57] Although there were thirty sackings in July, the rest of the staff kept their places; meanwhile, S. J. Pryor was brought in to advise on home news, Kennedy Jones 'shadowed' Buckle, and Reggie Nicholson became Moberley Bell's assistant, prompting a bitter Harcourt Kitchin to resign in dudgeon, denouncing what he called 'the formation of a Northcliffe Party in

Printing House Square'.[58] As well as introducing pictorial adverts, shaking up the typography and offering discounted advertising and subscription rates, Northcliffe 'appointed a penny-pinching day editor, Hugh Chisholm, on the assumption that a Scotsman would save him money'.[59]

For all the accusations made by Kitchin and others about Northcliffe as proprietor, when comparing a copy of *The Times* of the day before he bought it in March 1908 with one of the day before he died, the most noticeable phenomenon is how alike they are in terms of the huge amounts of content. There are a few more signed articles in the later paper; early on in his proprietorship Northcliffe asked why so many *Times* articles were unsigned, and was told that 'the real reason is that these fellows would ask for more money. The reason publicly given is that it gives *The Times* a great air of mystery and it all belongs to the great custom.'[60] Northcliffe never minded paying more money and believed that 'signing a man's work makes him work better'.[61]

~

Northcliffe's relationship with Buckle started off well. On 20 June, he told the editor that 'the paper has, in my view, been so uniformly good for so many days past that I should like to take this opportunity of thanking you and your staff for its alertness accuracy variety and maintenance of tone ... if the present level can be maintained ... the journal will prosper and gain its old place in the respect of the country.'[62] Buckle replied that 'the new arrangements and your vigorous personality have infused hopefulness and buoyancy into us all. It has been, if I may say so, a matter of very special satisfaction to me to find that the things I care about most in the paper are highly valued by you.'[63] On 9 July, Northcliffe wrote to Lord Esher, the chairman of the government's Committee of Imperial Defence, describing *The Times* as 'a newspaper not run as a profit-making machine at all. *The Times* is, in my life, what a yacht or racing stable is in others – it is merely my hobby.'[64] Yet unlike a yacht or most racing stables, it was not a hobby that he would allow to lose money in the long term. 'Northcliffe regarded *The Times* as a national monument much like

Westminster Abbey,' wrote the historian A. J. P. Taylor. 'He wished to preserve it and believed that running it at a profit was the only way of doing so.'[65]

'I am not, nor ever shall be, the "Chief" of *The Times*,' Northcliffe told Wickham Steed, 'I do not interfere in the conduct of the paper ... *The Times* is conducted entirely by Messrs Walter, Buckle, Bell, Chirol and Monypenny who understand the task better than I ever could.'[66] Northcliffe told Steed in September 1908 that he wanted to remain in the background and study *The Times* thoroughly before making any changes, although Steed thought that 'the process of adapting himself to something he had not created was plainly irksome to his energetic temperament'.[67] Bell had put the two men together, telling Steed that Northcliffe was 'one of the most interesting and inspiriting men I have ever met'.[68] Steed agreed, adding, 'and clear-eyed in regard to German policy'.

Relations were to worsen with Bell, especially after it took a whole year for Northcliffe to persuade him to use the same internal accounting system at *The Times* as for all the other Northcliffe papers. When tempers ran high on one occasion, Northcliffe telegraphed Bell's wife to say, 'If I am worrying Mr Bell, please let me know. I fear he does not understand my rough ways.'[69] Yet Bell ought to have taken little solace from this as, shortly afterwards, Northcliffe wrote to another member of *The Times* staff. 'You are too easy with Bell. He only understands the coke hammer.'[70]

CHAPTER 9

'Der Tag Will Come': The German Threat

April 1908–December 1909

'Our tons of ink make millions think.'[1]

LORD NORTHCLIFFE

On 3 April 1908, Sir Henry Campbell-Bannerman, the Liberal prime minister, retired through ill health, and was dead within the month. Herbert Asquith took his place, with David Lloyd George as chancellor of the exchequer, Sir Edward Grey as foreign secretary and Winston Churchill as president of the Board of Trade. Soon afterwards, Northcliffe wrote to Lloyd George to complain that there was a feeling in France that the British government was pro-German. It was the first connection Northcliffe had had with the Welsh dynamo. Their careers were to become closely intertwined, for occasional good but also much ill.

Lloyd George replied that he was 'genuinely surprised' at Northcliffe's news as the only pro-German on the Liberal side was Lord Rosebery – 'and I sometime wonder if he is even a Liberal at all! Haldane, of course, from education and intellectual bent, is in sympathy with German ideas, but there is really nothing else on which to base a suspicion that we are inclined to a pro-German policy at the expense of the entente with France.'[2] Richard Haldane, the secretary for war, was a Scot who had been educated in Germany and admired German philosophy, but was not markedly pro-German in politics or foreign affairs.

The Liberal politician with whom Northcliffe came into contact most at this period was Churchill, whom he liked personally but sparred with politically. Churchill sat for Manchester North-West and, under the custom of the day, he had to re-fight his seat on being appointed to the cabinet. When Northcliffe's *Manchester Courier* lambasted him during the by-election on 20 April, Churchill responded with an attack on its proprietor in a speech delivered at Strangeways Labour Hall in Manchester, in which he called Northcliffe 'a millionaire situated at a great distance from the constituency and an individual who cares nothing about the interests of the people who live in the constituency'.[3] Two days later, he added that 'Lord Northcliffe may placard the walls with the lies out of which he made his millions.'[4]

'My dear Churchill', Northcliffe wrote on 11 May,

> I was amazed to hear ... that you considered our criticisms a personal matter. There was a well understood agreement between us that we should use our stage thunder in the furtherance of our mutual interests. You have criticised me very hotly in and out of Parliament and I have never felt the least put out about it ... As we have got to live together more or less in public life and in more ways than you know, for, I hope, a great many years, I propose we take a walk in St James's Park some morning this week and thrash this matter out.[5]

Three days later, Churchill complained bitterly when the *Courier* accused him of breaking parole when he had escaped from his Boer prisoner-of-war camp in Pretoria in 1899, and threatened to sue for libel. 'Personally, I have nothing to do with the matter,' Northcliffe replied on 13 May. 'I am advised, and indeed consider that any endeavour to connect me with something over which I have no control: which took place when I was absent from England, and in a matter in which I am only one and not by any means the largest shareholder, would be an act of grave injustice, and I shall personally consider it an act of hostility.' After saying that no-one in London had heard of the matter, he added, 'When you get into your work and get the annoyances of electioneering out of your brain, this irritation will cease ... I do trust that in future you will neither deduce or attach importance to rumour or listen to the words of busybodies.'[6]

Churchill backed down from suing Northcliffe personally, but he did successfully take legal action against the *Courier*. 'I am very glad that this is now out of the way,' Churchill wrote to Northcliffe on 24 June, 'for although it would not have impaired our personal relations, it was an embarrassment and a nuisance.'[7] Northcliffe replied the same day commending Churchill's 'tact and conciliatory spirit'.[8] 'My feeling towards you have always been of admiration and esteem, and I shall look forward to a long, if somewhat critical friendship.'[9] They certainly had that. In August, Northcliffe gave Churchill a walking stick as a wedding present, whereupon Churchill thanked him for 'a token of peace and amity from you ... I shall often use and always value it.'[10] In fact, Northcliffe was trumped when the king gave Churchill a gold-topped malacca cane as a wedding present, which he understandably used instead.

~

On 13 July 1908, Frederick W. Wile, the American-born Berlin correspondent of the *Daily Mail*, published an interview with a German privy councillor, Herr Rudolph Martin, who had told him that, as a result of some recent twelve-hour Zeppelin flights, 'England is losing her insular character by the development of airships and aeroplanes.' He also declared that Germany would soon be able to 'transport 350,000 men in half an hour during the night from Calais to Dover ... We would conclude no peace until a German army had occupied London.'[11] This was no more than the *Daily Mail* had been saying for some time but, as well as Herr Martin, they had also heard from no less a figure than Sir Hiram Maxim, the inventor of the machine-gun, that 100,000 German soldiers could be landed in England in a single night by aeroplane. Also, Major B. F. S. Baden-Powell, president of the Aeronautical Society of Great Britain and brother of the hero of Mafeking, warned that 'a dozen great

Dreadnoughts would be helpless when faced with the task of repelling a swift fleet of foreign airships sailing high above the earth'.[12]

Only six days after Herr Martin's interview was printed in the *Mail*, Kaiser Wilhelm gave an interview to Dr William Bayard Hale, an ordained minister and respected literary editor of the *New York Times*, on the imperial yacht *Hohenzollern*, anchored off the Norwegian coast. Under the mistaken impression that Hale was a confidant of President Theodore Roosevelt, the Kaiser spoke with impetuous frankness. 'Germany is expecting to fight England,' Hale noted afterwards, 'and, in my judgement, the Emperor does not care how quickly.'[13] Wilhelm said the Boer War had been 'a war against God' which had started Britain's degeneration, and her alliance with Japan was a betrayal of the white race. Only German–American amity could defeat the 'Yellow Race' and ensure the future 'belongs to the Anglo-Teuton'.[14] 'The Japanese are devils,' stated the Kaiser. 'That is a simple fact.'

As well as predicting an inevitable war and deriding Edward VII and the British government, the Kaiser looked forward to the inevitable dismemberment of the British Empire.[15] He was essentially offering Roosevelt an anti-British alliance, telling Hale that 'it's been on my mind for four or five years ... Some fine day the world will wake up and read a quiet little agreement between Germany and the United States. Oh – ho ho! I wonder what my friends across the Channel will say to that!' At this point, the Kaiser 'laughed loudly, and made a dance step on the deck'.[16]

The German authorities understandably refused to allow the interview to be published in anything other than a profoundly bowdlerised form, but Dr Hale sent a detailed report with the original wording to William C. Reick, one of the owners of the *New York Times*. The *New York Times* refused to publish either version, but showed the original to Roosevelt, who also opposed publication on the grounds that it jeopardised world peace. By then, however, Northcliffe had obtained a summary account of the interview from a senior member of the *New York Times* editorial staff with whom he had a (presumably financially beneficial if underhand) 'working arrangement'.[17]

Instead of publishing this undoubted scoop – which moreover
fitted in perfectly with his own long-held views about the danger
posed by Imperial Germany – Northcliffe passed the interview summary on to Sir Edward Grey via Grey's private secretary William
Tyrrell, a habitué of Sutton Place. Grey thanked Northcliffe for
sending him it and showed copies of it to the king. Why had the
newspaperman in Northcliffe not leapt at the chance of embarrassing
the Kaiser whom he so feared and despised? Perhaps he was protecting his unnamed source at the *New York Times*. Perhaps he feared
that coming third hand it might be untrue and that publication in
The Times – especially once the Kaiser had inevitably denied and
denounced it – would result in another debacle for the paper, along
similar lines to the Charles Parnell libel case. Perhaps Northcliffe
recognised how catastrophic such a revelation might be for the
cause of peace.

Northcliffe certainly acknowledged the geopolitical dangers
involved, writing to *The Times* Vienna correspondent on 6 September
of the need for reticence in Anglo-German affairs. 'Silence and
preparation will do more good for peace, in my judgement, than
brilliant "beats" [scoops].'[18] A week earlier, he had already told the
journalist Arthur Mee, 'Nearly all wars begin by suspicions, and
suspicions can best be allayed, in my judgment by saying nothing.'[19]
Northcliffe occasionally did suppress information on national interest grounds; during the Great War, he refused to publish evidence of
corruption in the Royal Navy Aid Service because it would damage
British prestige, telling the first lord of the Admiralty, 'The perpetual
washing of dirty linen in public is not a grateful task.'[20]

'The prevailing sentiment among large sections of the middle
and lower classes of my people is not friendly to England,' Kaiser
Wilhelm told the *Daily Telegraph* in an interview in October 1908.
'Germany is a young and growing empire. She has a worldwide
commerce which is rapidly expanding, and to which the legitimate
ambition of patriotic Germans refuses to assign any bounds ... She
expects those interests to go on growing, and she must be able to
champion them manfully in any quarter of the globe. Her horizons
stretch far away.'[21] He considered himself a military expert, was

certain that Germany needed war with Russia sooner rather than later, and believed his civilian statesmen did not understand the international situation simply because they were civilians.[22]

Northcliffe believed that the notorious *Telegraph* interview – along with the Kruger Telegram, Tangier provocation, Hale interview, Rudolph Martin's threats, the speeches of von Bülow and others, but pre-eminently the massive naval construction – constituted clear evidence of Germany's threat to the balance of power in Europe. On the Kaiser's last visit to Britain in November 1907, Northcliffe attended the Court Ball held in Wilhelm's honour at Windsor Castle. 'I have escaped from the wily Kaiser, my dear,' he telephoned Louise Owen – with whom he was probably by then having an affair – shortly before midnight. 'It was made known to me that he wished me to be presented to him. I thought otherwise, so here I am at home. Just going to bed.'[23]

In January and February 1908, there were full-blown war scares, which were not eased by the news that Count Zeppelin had now perfected the design of his eponymous dirigible airship. 'I know them,' Northcliffe told Evelyn Wrench of the Germans in April 1909. 'They will bide their time, but *Der Tag* will come. Remember what I say.'[24] Nor did he confine his warnings to employees. 'For many years prior to 1914,' recalled Owen, 'he had correspondents in Germany gathering details about naval and military progress, activity at Krupps, and industrial conditions. This information was tabulated and sent by him to our leading politicians, some of whom were grateful, others not.'[25]

In 1909, the Admiralty publicly admitted that by 1913 Germany's strength in Dreadnoughts, the gold standard of battleships, would match that of the Royal Navy. The *Daily Mail* had long championed the cause of naval strength, coining the phrase 'Battleships are cheaper than battles.'[26] For all the truth of that, they were still extremely expensive and the Asquith government showed little interest in incurring the vast new extra expenditure that would be necessary. The *Daily Mail* has been criticised for making such statements as 'There is nothing between sea supremacy and ruin' (17 March 1909) and 'A weak navy or command of the sea' (7 January

1910), but in the face of Germany's naval construction programme, both were justified.

Occasionally, Jackie Fisher, the First Sea Lord, would supply J. L. Garvin at *The Observer* with secret details of the German programme, rather in the manner that various well-placed patriots in the War Office, Admiralty and Intelligence services kept Winston Churchill informed of the Luftwaffe's building programme in the latter half of the 1930s. 'The one topic of conversation was the naval situation,' Wrench told his parents about a lunch with the Northcliffes and J. L. Garvin in 1909, 'and we all listened to Garvin holding forth. He is full of Jackie Fisher, and says we must lay down eight Dreadnoughts this year and not one less. The Chief says the country must insist, so I am sure we will get them. The strength of the Navy is the only subject talked of in London.'[27] Staying at Sutton Place that April, he noted, 'It was a case of Dreadnoughts from morning till night.'[28] It was largely Garvin who started the cry of 'We Want Eight and We Won't Wait', a popular movement for building more Dreadnoughts that was picked up by other newspapers and in the music halls.

In the second week of December 1909, Robert Blatchford, the socialist editor and proprietor of the *Clarion*, wrote a series of ten articles for the *Daily Mail* warning of German strategic ambitions after travelling extensively there. These were reprinted as a pamphlet that sold half a million copies.[29] 'I write these articles because I believe that Germany is deliberately preparing to destroy the British Empire,' Blatchford explained, 'and because I know that we are not ready or able to defend ourselves against a sudden and formidable attack.' He called for full-scale, two-year conscription and an immediate £50 million extra funding for the Royal Navy.

'As to the war question, it is one of the most difficult in the world at the moment,' Northcliffe wrote to the novelist John Galsworthy in April 1909. Galsworthy had written about Germany for the *Daily Mail*.

Nobody wants it in this country. I feel my own responsibility in this matter very greatly, and having German relations and knowing intimately the feeling in both countries, I wish to make the readers of my newspapers as well acquainted as it is possible to be with the exact state of affairs. Two of my greatest difficulties are, firstly, English ignorance of Germany, and, secondly, Germany's somewhat natural indignation at our suggestion that they should alter their navy to suit us.[30]

Those are not the words of a warmonger.

~

Ironically enough, hypochondria is a genuine illness, and Northcliffe convinced himself that he had been subjected to ptomaine poisoning (a form of bacterial food poisoning) on a return journey to England on the *Lusitania* in early 1909. His main symptom was extreme irritability, which he displayed towards Mary on occasion. 'Her life is not so happy as I should like to see,' noted Evelyn Wrench in his diary, 'but she is wonderful.'[31] Wrench put her unhappiness down to the fact that Northcliffe was 'not an easy husband', even though he had personally witnessed Mary's infidelity the previous year. Northcliffe meanwhile complained to Sutton that owing to a minor bout of malaria he had contracted in India in 1897, he was 'lacking interest in the sex, always a bad sign with your devoted chief'.[32] A brief bout of malaria over a decade earlier was unlikely to have led to a loss of libido in 1909. Much later, Geoffrey Harmsworth recorded Mary telling him that 'the reason why she didn't seek a divorce' from Alfred had been on the eminently sensible grounds 'that she realised that he was a great man and that she wouldn't have liked to break up his home and all that their life together had witnessed'.[33]

~

Northcliffe continued to be fascinated by the aeroplane and when in February 1909 Orville and Wilbur Wright undertook groundbreaking test flights at Pau in southwestern France, he went to stay at the Hôtel de Gassion there to watch them. (Nor was the sex interest entirely lacking; Kathleen Wrohan was staying in a nearby hotel, and Harry Pine the young chauffeur would drive her backwards and forwards throughout the holiday.) On 3 February, Wilbur Wright flew for five minutes and fifty-seven seconds, reaching an altitude of more than a hundred feet. 'What is happening here is that Wright is teaching men to fly,' Northcliffe told Bell on 5 February, 'and he estimates that by the end of the present year there will be over five thousand people in Europe capable of flying as well as he does. He says that a man can learn to fly in two days.'[34]

On 7 February, the Wright brothers lunched with Northcliffe and Wrench, the latter of whom found the brothers 'both charming, absolutely natural and without any "side"'.[35] Wilbur said that 'walking is a good deal more difficult' than flying, and gliding was 'the most delightful sensation he knows'.[36] He said that, over the next quarter-century, his planes would be used for military scouting at 35mph a mile above sea level.[37]

Northcliffe persuaded Arthur Balfour, then still the Conservative Party leader, to visit Pau, where on 10 February, while snow and bad weather were preventing flights, Wilbur explained the principles of flight to him. The next day, Northcliffe and Balfour joined in pulling the rope used to raise weights on the launching derrick for Wilbur's plane the Wright Flyer before witnessing his twenty-minute flight. Balfour said he could not resist 'taking part in the miracle' and ran alongside with his coattails flying, steadying one of the wings as it took off. 'It is the most wonderful sight,' he told a friend. 'I wish I could be flying with him.'[38] Five days later, Wilbur's wife Katherine became the first passenger in flight, for seven minutes and four seconds, and the day after that, the Wrights signed a contract for demonstration flights in Germany with August Scherl, the owner of the *Berliner Lokal-Anzeiger*, a leading newspaper in Berlin.

'I wonder if I may bore you on the subject of aeroplanes,' Northcliffe wrote to Robert Haldane, the secretary for war, on 19 February, 'which I have been studying for close on six years. I notice that the Germans and French have both military representatives here watching the Wrights' machine, which Mr Balfour came to see, and of which he will speak to you.' He told Haldane that he was 'constantly being chaffed' by the German and French observers 'with regard to the British Army aeroplane, which they have nicknamed

The Steamroller'. He suggested that Haldane should try to 'find out why it is that [the Wrights'] aeroplane gets off the ground and flies for ten minutes or ten hours if it chooses, and your Aldershot aeroplane, which is a very bad copy of the bad French aeroplanes, is unable to leave the ground'.[39] He pointed out that the American, French and Austrian armies were already training pilots and that 'these aeroplanes can fly to a height of up to about a mile ... it is almost impossible to hit them, but, as Mr Wright says, if out of ten aeroplane scouts you lost four, what matters? Compare the loss with that of ordinary scouting operations. Pray pardon this long effusion, but I think it is the duty of everyone who can to help, and I do happen to know something about aeroplanes.'[40]

Northcliffe then contacted Lord Esher. 'Our national muddle-headedness has rarely been seen to worse disadvantage than in this particular matter, aviation,' he wrote. 'The English aeroplane arrangements have been put in the hands of an American* who, on his own statements, knows nothing about aviation. He got the appointment because he knew something about kites. I see at length that his machine has proceeded seven hundred yards in a direct line, a feat that was accomplished on the Continent long ago by aer-oplanists ... I might as well attempt to produce my newspapers by the aid of a man who confessedly knew nothing of printing, having carefully chosen old-fashioned machines to begin with.'[41]

Haldane, who stated that 'aeroplanes would never fly' in 1907, had already turned down the idea of working with the Wright broth-ers, who approached the Germans, French, Spanish and Italians instead.[42] 'Numbers of inventors came to see me as the then respon-sible minister,' he wrote in his autobiography, 'including the brothers Wright, and I examined many plans and specifications. But I saw that those whom I interviewed were only clever empiricists, and that we were at a profound disadvantage compared to the Germans, who were building up the structure of the Air Service on a foundation of science.'[43] He therefore installed a Scientific Committee at the

* In fact, Lieutenant John William Dunne was Anglo-Irish, but he was indeed far behind the Wrights with workable aeroplane prototypes.

National Physical Laboratory at Teddington in 1909, rather than buying any prototypes of planes that had actually flown. He would only publicly commit himself to further scientific studies of the fundamentals of flight, rather than urgently investigating its military applications.[44] Such seeming disregard for the dangerous realities of the situation outraged Northcliffe, who repeatedly urged Haldane to buy aircraft and investigate their capacity to drop bombs on enemy ports, factories and cities.[45]

Haldane did not respond to Northcliffe's letter of 19 February until 4 May, and when he did it was merely to tell him what would be studied by which physicists and that the Scientific Committee at Teddington would come under the purview of neither the War Office nor the Admiralty, but the Treasury, 'and will serve as a connecting link between the two Departments each of which will have its own construction establishment'.[46] This struck Northcliffe as the worst of all worlds, and he regarded the Treasury's involvement as an indication of parsimony in an area which he was increasingly convinced might play a significant role in any future war with Germany. 'I hope you will not mind my saying,' Northcliffe replied on 10 May, 'that in certain directions the composition of the committee is one of the most lamentable things I have read in connection with our national organisation'.[47] This was because although there were distinguished scientists, there was practically no actual aviator on the committee at all, and Northcliffe felt the subjects it discussed were years behind the times. By total contrast with the work being done at Teddington on paper, 'The Wright aeroplane is a practical machine, the flight of which can be taught in three hours.'

Northcliffe suggested Charles Royce for the committee rather than a Mr Lanchester, who had refused to believe that the Wright aeroplane would ever fly. He advised sending 'any intelligent observer' to Germany for a few months, who could 'station himself close to one of the numerous balloon sheds. I am sorry to be so pessimistic, but this proposed waste of money and time investigating that which is already known to foreigners is indeed lamentable.'[48] Instead, Northcliffe proposed a 'practical sub-committee be formed and given authority to test, say, the Wright and Voisin planes, which can be bought for a thousand pounds each, and make as near a copy of a Zeppelin as possible'.[49]

Northcliffe did compliment Haldane on his innovation, the Territorial Army, but criticised 'the artillery, which is laughed at, the rifle, which is poor, and the short time of service' of its men.[50] He also suggested that press censors should be trained up immediately in order to have them in place for when war broke out, so that national morale would not suffer in the early stages of the conflict, as it had in the Boer War. 'The handling of the Press during war is, in my humble opinion, almost as important as the handling of the troops,' Northcliffe told Haldane. 'The training of press censors might be commenced this year.'[51] Nothing was done about that either.

Haldane replied on 18 May that 'The naval and military experts have demonstrated to the Defence Committee that dirigibles and still more aeroplanes are a very long way off indeed being the slightest practical use in war.'[52] He praised the way that the Prussian government had set up a chair of aviation at Göttingen ('my old university') and that 'no student was to be admitted who was not expert with differential calculus. The German General Staff knows how much has got to be learned before practical results can be obtained in this new region.' This was all utterly exasperating for Northcliffe, who had seen that the Wright brothers – whose only expertise had been in bicycles – had put Mankind into the skies before any expert in differential calculus.

While in 1909 there were no military aircraft anywhere in the world, by 1910 there were fifty, and by 1914 a thousand across all the major belligerents.[53] Britain could have been in the forefront of aerial warfare but, in 1909, the Sub-Committee of the Committee of Imperial Defence on Aerial Navigation reported that research on fixed-wing, heavier-than-air aircraft was not worthwhile and recommended that the government 'stop all the money at Farnborough which was being spent on aeroplanes'.[54] That same year, General Douglas Haig declared that 'Flying can never be of any use to the Army.'[55] By total contrast, Northcliffe ran a long and lonely campaign in his papers with dozens of editorials beseeching the government to prepare for a new form of warfare where air power could play a powerful part.[56] To him, Haldane's attitude seemed frustratingly complacent; the first parachute jump from an aeroplane took place in March 1912 and the first aerial bombing of London on 31 May 1915. Northcliffe was no warmonger in pointing out the dangers to British national security posed by powered flight.

~

It was almost a year after buying *The Times* that Northcliffe started to criticise it. 'I still find the paper dull and lacking initiative,' he told Bell on 9 February, beginning the micromanagement he directed towards his other papers.

> In the 'Wills and Bequests' you are not giving bequests, which are the interesting thing. . . . The more I begin to understand *The Times*, the more I realise that, inasmuch as you are obliged to carry every day an immense amount of tedious reporting only interesting to those concerned, it is essential for the general welfare of the paper in its competition with other newspapers it should have every day something of interest to ALL its readers.[57]

The next day he was suggesting how adverts should be grouped, pointing out that 'I have had much to do with the getting of small advertisements at various times in my career, and I never failed yet. As a matter of fact I have often suffered from too many of them. Until we made the rates of the *Daily Mail* impossible (two shillings a line) we sometimes had three weeks' supply in hand.'[58]

Four days later, Northcliffe asked William Kennedy Jones to find £5,000 a week that could be lopped off *The Times*' expenses. Before long, and for the first time in many years, *The Times* could pay a dividend on its preference shares. Northcliffe continued to be hands-on at the paper; he used his blue pencil to circle every instance – sometimes twenty times per edition – where there were misprints, smudges, 'letters or figures battered and indistinguishable or misplaced, spaced and leads not pushed down etc'. Anything that had already appeared in a rival paper such as the *Daily Telegraph* or the *Morning Post* he considered 'stale news' and marked out.

On 19 February, he went through a long list of news items that *The Times* had missed, and was perplexed that, while the army's aeroplane trials were indexed under 'Science, Art, Music and Drama', the Wright brothers' flights were under 'Sport, Agriculture and Country Life'.

'When I return I wish to devote as much time as I can afford to *The Times* in suggestion rather than criticism,' Northcliffe wrote to Bell on 20 February.[59] He then entered into a column-by-column critique of the most recent paper he could lay his hands on, having spent two hours over it 'in this delightful Pau sunshine'. He admitted that 'One can apply the same criticisms to every paper daily, but I want *The Times* to be above reproach.'[60] Bell replied that he needed 'no persistent urging that we devote more space to this and that', whereupon Northcliffe spotted the reproach and replied, 'I have not said that it is a failure ... When you know me better you will understand my method of criticising and cooperating.'[61] 'I am sorry that you take my criticisms so much to heart,' he wrote the next day. 'I will desist until I come back, but you have not convinced me on any point.'[62] Unable to stop himself, he ended with a reference to the *Telegraph*'s coverage of a speech by the astronomer Sir George Darwin 'which *The Times* missed'.[63]

Northcliffe was an obsessive perfectionist, but he did tell Bell that 'I do not want the staff to trouble to reply to the things I mention, nor to carry them out unless they think I am right.'[64] Nonetheless it was a foolhardy member of staff below the level of Buckle or Bell who told him he was wrong, as he sacked people easily in those days of short or even non-existent contracts and weak employment laws.* On one occasion he wrote to Bell about Printing House Square: '"Abandon hope all ye who enter here" should be written over the portals of that mid-Victorian barrack ... This particular brand of [the notoriously poisonous] Upas tree not only carries its victims back almost into the depths of ancestor worship, but inculcates into them a love of the

---

* One telephone conversation was reputed to have gone as follows: Northcliffe: 'Who is that?' Reply: 'Editor, *Weekly Dispatch*, Chief.' Northcliffe: 'You were the Editor.' [Brendon, *Eminent Edwardians*, p.27]

inaccurate and a perverted appetite for printers' errors.'[65] He then listed the 'howlers' he had spotted.

~

By mid-March 1909, Northcliffe had begun to criticise Herbert Asquith, telling Earl Grey, the governor-general of Canada, that he was 'not nearly strong enough for the job. Hence the constant revolts of Churchill and Lloyd George. I asked Winston the other morning what was wrong with the cabinet. He was perfectly frank and said that they had not got a master.'[66] The following month, Lloyd George unveiled his 'People's Budget' which found the £3 million of extra funding for the Dreadnoughts that the Northcliffe press had been demanding, out of a total of £16 million in additional taxes to come from taxes on liquor and land, the latter being a direct threat to the aristocracy. Northcliffe was in Germany when the controversial plans were announced, seeing the leading occulist Dr Solm over three weeks of treatment for pain in his eyes, who told him that he needed to take more holidays and wear dark glasses.

Although the *Daily Mail* criticised the People's Budget, stating that the 'Liberal Socialist theory of taxation is that one million citizens are to serve as the milch cows of the rest of the community', it also carried an interview with Lloyd George, with the leader column complimenting him personally.[67] Northcliffe was of course accused of opposing the Budget because he did not want to pay the higher taxes it advocated, but because he did not own land he was not personally as heavily affected as the aristocracy.[68]

In May 1909, Northcliffe and Mary undertook a 400-mile tour of Germany. He told H. W. Wilson that they 'were amazed at the vast industrial strides made in practically every town we came to. Every one of these new factory chimneys is a gun pointed at England, and in many cases a very powerful one. We have not seen one tramp on the roads or been asked for a single penny anywhere.'[69] They were impressed by the thousands of sixteen- and seventeen-hand horses, 'magnificent beasts', fearing that in wartime 'every horse here can be requisitioned by the government'.[70]

This was no paranoiac fantasy: state-sponsored breeding increased the ratio of horse to men in the German army from one in four in 1870 to one in three by 1914. In the first weeks of the Great War, Germany mobilised 715,000 private horses from the army's register and Austria-Hungary 600,000.

To Wilson's oleaginous request that he give more speeches in the Lords on defence matters, Northcliffe replied, 'As for my own speaking; I shall never make an orator.'[71] He was correct, but not every public figure knows that about themselves. When he returned to Britain in late May, Northcliffe acted to scotch the full-scale naval panic that had been gripping Britain all spring. The panic had been sparked by supposed night-time sightings of hostile airships overhead in Berkshire, Peterborough, Wisbech, Cardiff and places on the Norfolk and Essex coasts such as Clacton-on-Sea. The *Daily Mail* investigated them all, but failed to find any proof of any secret Zeppelin flights, although this did not prevent the Home Fleet being alerted by urgent telegrams about the possibility of a covert German attack.[72]

Historians such as Oron Hale and Zara Steiner have blamed Northcliffe personally for the 1909 Naval Panic, but in fact he was abroad at the time and on 21 May wrote a leader denouncing 'the phantom airship', the panic itself, and 'the harm it does'.[73] He described Britons who put about such stories as 'mere nervous degenerates' while pointing out that the real danger came from Germany's Navy Laws.[74] Meanwhile, the *Daily Mail* suggested that a Military Air Service be set up as soon as possible, which Haldane ignored but which shows that Northcliffe was one of the earliest advocates for what later became the Royal Flying Corps, and subsequently the Royal Air Force.

Another idea that Northcliffe championed, and which came to fruition in June 1909, was the Imperial Press Conference, intended to improve communication within the British Empire. He had supported Harry Brittain's idea from the start; he pledged £500 initially and offered more if necessary; he hosted the delegates at lunch at Sutton Place where he showed them his pet bear cub; and he acted as the conference's honorary senior treasurer. Sixty editors and proprietors from around the Empire, along with 600 from Britain, met to discuss how to coordinate support for the mother country in any future war. Lord Rosebery opened it, in Shepherd's Bush Exhibition Hall, speaking of an 'approaching Armageddon'.[75] The delegates met the king and the Prince of Wales, visited Oxford and Edinburgh, enjoyed a reception in Westminster Hall, heard speeches by Sir Edward Grey and Reginald McKenna, were treated to a Spithead Review of eighteen miles of warships, took tea on HMS *Dreadnought* itself, watched military manouevres at Aldershot, and were generally given the full red-carpet treatment of Edwardian Britain. For Evelyn Wrench, there was an element of bathos, because although he sat on the committee of the Imperial Press Conference, that week he also had to oversee the *Daily Mail*'s sandcastle-building competition at Margate.

One journalist who was present at the conference, Keith Murdoch from Australia, wrote to his father how Northcliffe was

> a prominent figure. He never speaks, but his management can be detected in all the arrangements ... He is tall, fair, with a large head and a very kindly face ... a clear-sighted, deep general capability. He seems to have great knowledge and to be simple and direct in his purposes. That, I think, is the secret of his success ... he knows what he wants and goes straight for it.[76]

As we shall see, Northcliffe was to become Murdoch's friend, mentor and role model.

~

On 19 June 1909, Northcliffe wrote to David Lloyd George to complain that foreign cars were being needlessly held up while being imported into Britain.[77] Lloyd George saw this as an opening for getting to know the most powerful newspaper proprietor in the country and replied immediately, inviting Northcliffe to the Treasury to discuss what orders should be given to customs officials. Although Northcliffe politely refused the invitation, saying, 'I am one of those people who believe that journalists should be read and not seen,' he did visit the peers' gallery of the Commons to watch Lloyd George in action, and was impressed by what he saw. He recognised a fellow energetic figure who got things done.

Northcliffe met Lloyd George for the first time in person on 3 August in the Chancellor of the Exchequer's office behind the Speaker's Chair in the House of Commons, along with Northcliffe's brother Cecil Harmsworth MP. 'Lloyd-G[eorge] exercising all his arts of persuasion to induce A[lfred] to support his schemes of Development, invalidity insurance, etc,' Cecil noted in his diary some time afterwards.

> For an hour and more Ll-G exercised all his arts to win N[orthcliffe]* to the Budget. It was a tour de force – the most remarkable I have witnessed of the little Welshman's wizardry. N[orthcliffe] was visibly impressed, not indeed by Ll-G's main Budget proposals but by Ll-G himself. Failing in one direction, Ll-G took up the question of Development and Road Improvement. Here he was on sure ground with N who expressed himself in full agreement with this part of the Budget. To explain it, Ll-G quoted from the Statement about it that he was to make in the House the following day. He went much further. He handed the document to N and said he might make any use of it he liked! N was astonished and incredulous. Did he mean in the *Daily Mail* going to press that evening. Ll-G said Certainly yes. Before the House heard it? And exclusively in the *Daily Mail*? What would the House say? What would other newspapers say? The Liberal newspapers? Ll-G was after big game and sticking at nothing to win it. He did win N as far as his Development and Road Improvement plans were concerned … So, the next morning the *Daily Mail* came out with its exclusive and premature disclosure and there were wigs on the green† for the Chancellor in the House and in the Press.[78]

---

* It was interesting that even his brother referred to him by his title.
† An eighteenth-century Irish expression for a fight, as wigs were liable to fall off on the grass.

Northcliffe was 'delighted' by what he called Lloyd George's 'splendid imprudence' and it briefly bought the Liberals some leeway with the *Daily Mail*.[79] Some might call a chancellor of the exchequer leaking Budget proposals more than imprudence, however splendid, and in 1947 Hugh Dalton was forced to resign over much less. But Lloyd George believed it was worth it. Although both *The Times* and the *Daily Mail* opposed the Budget, they were not so vociferous or personal as much of the rest of the Unionist press. In part, that might have been the effect that Lloyd George had had in charming Northcliffe, but it was also because of Northcliffe's uncanny ability to read public opinion, and rarely position his papers too far adrift of it.

In September, Lloyd George continued his charm offensive when he visited Bétheny, north of Rheims, to attend the first international flying competition, where only one of the entrants was British. Lloyd George told the *Daily Mail* journalist of 'how hopelessly behind we are in these great and historic developments. I really felt, as a Britisher, rather ashamed that we were so completely out of it.'[80] Northcliffe was at Bétheny too, and of course this sentiment precisely chimed with his. Yet when Northcliffe pressed Haldane to set up a British flying school, the war secretary once again refused to commit himself. When, in the Great War, Northcliffe took up extreme positions in support of Lloyd George and denigration of Haldane, these had been long in the making.

On 10 August 1909, having finally got *The Times*'s accounts out of George Buckle, and having discovered that it was still losing money despite the economies he had introduced, Northcliffe wrote to Bell about Buckle, saying: 'I am sure that you realise as well as I do that the old man is one of the most difficult characters with which to deal. He is perfectly straight, and yet most elusive; most amiable and gentle, and, on the other hand, inordinately vain and obstinate; most industrious, yet doing little real work; and, above all things, tactless.'[81] It became clear to Bell that Buckle would not remain in the post for too much longer.

Northcliffe left Southampton for Quebec on board the *Empress of Britain* with Mary, Bell and Evelyn Wrench. To take them on a

six-week, 9,000-mile land journey, the Pullman Car 'Independence'
was waiting as they landed, to be attached to their train. 'It was a
home on wheels,' recalled Wrench. 'There were four private cabins,
a dining room, an observation room where we spent most of the
day, and an observation platform at the rear, where we sat in hot
weather.'[82] Theirs was always the last carriage in the train, allowing an unimpeded view of the surrounding countryside. It was this
coast-to coast journey to Vancouver that left Wrench, already a
convinced imperialist, certain that 'empire building was really the
only thing worthwhile. I felt I must take a hand in it.'[83] He was
sent out to buy Northcliffe a copy of each newspaper that he could
find at each town they stopped at, staggering back to the train with
twenty or thirty American papers. Northcliffe then spent hours
poring over them, looking for ideas that would work in Britain.[84]

They saw the entirely new San Francisco three years after its
devastating earthquake and, when interviewed by the *San Francisco
Chronicle*, both Northcliffe and Bell stated that a German war was
as inevitable as the Franco–Prussian and Russo–Japanese Wars had
been. They visited Los Angeles, and then Arizona by the Santa Fe
railroad, saw the Grand Canyon, and then spent nine days going
back across the continent from San Francisco to Grand Falls,
Newfoundland. Northcliffe found the heat of Arizona unbearable,
thought Kansas was 'much like Norfolk', and was annoyed that the
only British news he could get in western Canada was about the
suffragettes rather than the Budget.[85]

The main reason for the trip was to attend the official opening
of Grand Falls in October. 'I am very sure that this investment of
ours out here is the best we could possibly make,' Northcliffe wrote
to Kennedy Jones. 'I have made the most minute enquiries into the
areas of our forests, and I believe that with proper fire protection
and careful cutting, they are limitless.'[86] When a sloppy *Times* journalist mistook the name of the town in a report, Northcliffe told
Jones, 'The thought that occurs to me every day about *The Times*
is, "Is it good enough?" It lacks initiative in policy and in news ...
It is very careless – Grand Rapids for Grand Falls – Good God! It
wants energising.'[87]

'For my part, 1909 has been a backbreaker,' Northcliffe wrote to
J. L. Garvin at the close of the year.

> *The Times* has been my chief difficulty. Reforming Printing House
> Square is like filling a pneumatic tyre with a leak in it; you get
> the tyre pumped up good and hard, as the Americans say, you are
> getting into your car to ride off, and bump, bump, bump, down
> you are on the rim again; and constant pumping weareth away
> the Chauffeur. Sometimes I long for a new set of tyres altogether,
> but that is impossible.[88]

Buckle defended his staff from Northcliffe's criticisms, especially
those of the Foreign News Department, making it clear that the
sacking of people 'will be a serious matter for me, if I am pressed ...
to make myself the instrument of getting rid of colleagues'.[89]

Buckle generally supported Northcliffe's innovations in news
gathering, production, distribution, advertising and other aspects
of the business, but he fought hard for his editorial independence,
recognising that the paper's strength lay in not being, as he put it to
a future editor, 'a mere mouthpiece of Northcliffe, or a more respectable echo of the D[aily] M[ail]'.[90] To give him his due, Northcliffe
recognised that too.

To Northcliffe's recurrent cycle of overwork and exhaustion was
added his fear that *The Times* was turning into what he called 'a
financial Niagara'.[91] 'So long as we squabble and misunderstand each
other,' he had told Buckle on 23 December, 'the exercise of initiative
is impossible.'[92] Earlier that month, he had been the defendant in the
High Court in a case of wrongful dismissal brought by Annesley
Kenealy, the sister of the *Daily Mirror* editor Alexander Kenealy.
Northcliffe had sacked her for introducing her own views opposing
vivisection into a profile of Sydney Holland, the chairman of the
London Hospital. Rufus Isaacs demolished her case and the jury
found for Northcliffe, but his experience in the witness box had
been stressful.

In the general election campaign of January to February 1910,
Northcliffe energetically supported the tariff reform Unionists and

ensured that in the key battleground seats in Lancashire, East Anglia and north-east England there were special election editions of the *Daily Mail* that attacked the free trade Liberals. But the additional stress of the election took its toll and, as the election neared its close, Northcliffe, who was suffering from a combination of exhaustion, neurasthenia, irritability, inflammation of the pancreas, bronchial trouble and indigestion, seems to have undergone something akin to a nervous breakdown. The society doctor Bertrand Dawson* sent him to a clinic in Manchester Street in London, which Northcliffe nicknamed 'the Asylum' and which he told Sutton was 'like a prison'. A complete six-month rest-cure was prescribed, although Northcliffe continued constantly to comment on the content or appearance of almost every page of each of his newspapers. On top of all his other worries, Kathleen Wrohan, who was in her late thirties, wanted children.

She acquired a son on 25 August 1910 (at least according to a register of 1939, as the birth was not registered at the time). The parentage of Alfred John Francis Alexander Wrohan remains uncertain, as does that of the other two children Kathleen later acquired, as no birth certificates have ever been found for them. On the day that baby Alfred was probably born, Northcliffe was on board the *Mauretania* docking at New York with Mary and his sister Violet Grace, and he did not return until October.

Northcliffe instructed Henry Arnholz to set aside £1,000 per annum for the first three years of baby Alfred's life and then £6,000 per annum thereafter. Trusts were set up for the benefit of Mrs Wrohan and the children, including the Q Trust which held shares in the Pictorial Newspaper Company and lasted more than half a century. In 1911, Northcliffe had an income of £118,000, some 2,360 times the average labourer's wage of £50 a year, and the modern equivalent of more than £14 million.[23] For a lady in her late

---

* Northcliffe might have approved of Dr Dawson's decision to kill King George V in January 1936 by injecting his jugular vein with morphia and then cocaine, because it was done so that his death was announced in the morning edition of *The Times*, rather than the 'less appropriate ... evening journals'. [Francis Watson, 'The Death of George V', *History Today*, No. 36 1986]

thirties who had arrived penniless from Ireland eight years earlier, Mrs Wrohan had done well for herself. The names she chose for the child perhaps surprisingly included that of her husband Francis, the policeman from Dublin to whom she was, technically, still married.

By 18 September, Mrs Wrohan was staying at the Hôtel Meurice in Paris – where she said she was 'on business' – telling Arnholz to let Northcliffe know that 'the new relation is stronger ... and now gains weight rapidly' and informing him of her plans to move to a yet grander house, No. 5 Carlton House Terrace.[24] The next year, when on 3 March Mary went to South Africa on a health trip, Mrs Wrohan sent 'the small boy to Cimiez on the 5th to be with his Daddy'.[25] Here was a clear indication that she expected Northcliffe to believe that he was the father.

CHAPTER 10

CONSOLIDATING CONTROL
AT *THE TIMES*

December 1909–November 1911

'He did not fight with the "Old Gang" over power. He
fought with them, and got them out, because they were
incapable of producing an efficient newspaper.'[1]

A. J. P. TAYLOR, *Politics in Wartime* 1964

Northcliffe was by now enough of a public figure for two West
End plays satirising him to be produced in quick succession.
Arnold Bennett's 1909 comedy, *What the Public Wants,* was the
portrait of a media baron, Sir Charles Worgan, who was obsessed
with profits and the bottom line. 'I've revolutionised journalism,'
Worgan boasts in the play, 'and I'm only forty'. Written in 1909 but
staged the following year was *The Earth*, by the Jewish-Irish actor-
playwright J. B. Bernard Fagan, which featured a press proprietor,
Sir Felix Janion, who resorts to sexual blackmail in order to prevent
the introduction of a minimum wage for his employees. 'My dear,'
Northcliffe told Louise Owen, 'I could have done it so much better;
I should have torn him to shreds had I been the author.' When
years later Fagan was cited in a divorce case, Northcliffe ensured
maximum publicity for it, including on the news-stand poster-bills.
'He put me on the boards,' Northcliffe quipped, 'now I'll put him
on the bills.'

While he couldn't do much to prevent such satire when it came to his public profile, Northcliffe was careful to keep his own private life out of the public eye. Having successfully hidden the existence of his first illegitimate child, Alfred Benjamin Smith, Northcliffe was keen to hide the existence of a mistress from the public. For the owner of *Home Sweet Home*, *Home Chats*, the religious paper *Sunday Companion* and other publications which ultimately depended on Christian morals and Victorian values, to be publicly revealed to be unfaithful to his wife would have risked damaging charges of hypocrisy which would undoubtedly have had commercial implications. Northcliffe certainly had enough rivals, detractors and political opponents who would have revelled in such a fall from grace. He therefore put into action a cover-up operation involving George Sutton, his friend and lawyer Henry Arnholz, Evelyn Wrench, various brothers of his, doubtless his wife Mary, his other mistress Louise Owen, and other employees and enablers, which ensured that his name was not publicly connected with that of Kathleen Wrohan until 1971, almost half a century after his death.

Since September 1908, Northcliffe had been giving Kathleen Wrohan £8,000 per annum, something approaching £1 million in today's money.[2] Described as a 'hard-core spendaholic' by a modern historian, she somehow overspent even that enormous sum.[3] Her dress bills, large numbers of servants in big houses in the grandest areas of London, and lavish hospitality in Biarritz and the south of France probably accounted for a good deal of it, and, as will become clear, she was not saving anything.

It appears that Mrs Wrohan had other concerns on her mind. While staying at the Hotel Bellevue in Cannes, she wrote to Arnholz saying that 'a friend' was anxious to know

what are the regulations about the registrations of births in England ... How soon after a birth must the declaration be made? *Must it be done by either the father or mother – or both? Must the name of both father and mother be given and the address* ...? Are witnesses necessary at the time of making this declaration ... Is it absolutely necessary to register a birth at all?[4]

Alongside this fairly pointed question, she also enclosed her bills from Debenham & Freebody for a 'real Peruvian chinchilla' and a stole and muff. 'I hope you don't mind being bothered with my bills,' she wrote. 'It's such a trifling little business I hesitated before troubling you.' In fact they came to £2,110 and, despite her income from Northcliffe, she expected him to pay for these too.

Having spent at least two months at the Manchester Street clinic, Northcliffe grew tired of 'the Asylum' and took the Villa Sainte Baume at Valescure near Cannes for the next part of his rest-cure. He later claimed that he had had double pneumonia in 1910, which might well have been one of his ailments, but it was probably not the only one. 'I recover or recuperate very slowly,' he told Sutton on 1 April. 'If I get back to *Sturm und Drang* by June I shall be lucky. I am still in bed twenty or twenty-two hours of the twenty-four.'[5] Two days later, Mary told Sutton, 'He makes a little progress every day, but is still very easily fatigued – nervous – and a long way off work yet.'[6]

On 3 April, while Mary was therefore still staying at the villa, Northcliffe wrote to Arnholz saying he would pay off 'K''s debts, but 'over a long period, finance slowly', enclosing an initial cheque for £500. 'It is a difficult personal kind of business,' he wrote, which he thought 'good practice and experience for you. Do not spare her letters on the subject. She is very unbusinesslike and needs kindly keeping up to the mark.'[7]

At some point in early April, Northcliffe seems to have told Mary that although he wanted the villa to be essentially a private hospital, he thought it would be more peaceful if she were absent. She moved out, leaving the coast clear for Mrs Wrohan. 'Presumably she knew nothing of the mistress who was being whisked along the coast-roads, in and out of hotels and villas,' claimed one biographer,[8] but since Sutton, Pine, Arnholz, Wrench and especially Mary's lover Reggie Nicholson all knew about Kathleen, Mary almost certainly did too, and possibly did not mind handing over the job of nursemaid to the mistress.

After Arnholz replied to Mrs Wrohan that it was illegal not to register a birth in England, she wrote from the Hôtel Les Roches

Rouges in Agay, asking 'Are the rules less strict in France or Ireland, do you think?'[9] On 18 April, she euphemistically reassured Arnholz that 'the "elder brothers" [code for Arnholz and his colleagues] need not worry about my running up bills'.[10] Three days later, she wrote:

> I am very greatly distressed that you should have thought it necessary to write to the Chief about the Debenhams bill. Your [sic] worrying him about details ... If you knew the state of his health and nerves and how we are all working to keep *little* worries away from him you would understand what I mean. Sutton and I are very angry with you!! ... The Chief's health is very critical – the sudden opening of a door drives him frantic – and your letter yesterday set him back a week. Now this is quite private. We don't want people to know he is so ill. When more money is required for the bills it will be sent you, but don't go and write long legal letters that would upset anybody – oh dear! I wish I were near you. The ears of the elder brothers would get boxed and not on my own account at all, but only because you've gone and upset the Chief about nothing.[11]

Two days later, Kathleen said she was taking a furnished house at No. 40 Grosvenor Street for 500 guineas a year, which she wanted Arnholz to sign for her as she claimed to 'know nothing about leases'. (Arnholz knew enough about them not to agree to this.) She signed nonetheless, and the census return shows that by April 1911 she had a butler, cook, two housemaids, a kitchen maid and footman living there.[12] On 25 April 1910, still occupying the villa in France, she reported that 'our friend is making some progress the last day or two. The doctor came out and insisted on everybody leaving the villa except Sutton and the necessary servants, and the absolute quiet has had a good effect on the nerves.' When Arnholz apologised for his behaviour but pointed out that he worked for Northcliffe and 'no man can serve two masters', she replied that she agreed 'though he often tries to serve two mistresses!!!'[13] She had no idea when she would be back from the Riviera to take up residence at Grosvenor Street. 'It entirely depends on the invalid who does not like being left quite alone.'[14]

On 25 May 1912, Kathleen Wrohan acquired a baby girl, which she named Katherine Dorothea Geraldine Mary Northcliffe Wrohan, names which weirdly included tributes to Northcliffe's wife and mother, and possibly to Dorothea Glasgow. Including Northcliffe's name might have been a tribute, or possibly an insurance policy. Since Rebecca Bjorklund of Vancouver, Katherine Wrohan's adopted son's daughter, does not share DNA with either the descendants of Lord Northcliffe's brother nor with those of Beatrice Maud Cromie's sister, we can assume that if Kathleen Wrohan was indeed Beatrice Cromie, Louise Owen was correct when she said that Kathleen Wrohan's children were adopted rather than her and Northcliffe's biological offspring, in contradiction to Paul Ferris's assertions in his 1971 book *The House of Northcliffe* that they were the couple's illegitimate children.

On or near 14 April 1914, Kathleen Wrohan acquired a third child, John Harold Northcliffe Wrohan, probably in Paris. The baptismal register on 22 April at St Martin-in-the-Fields on Trafalgar Square gave her home address as No. 23, Avenue du Bois, Paris, and the date of birth was (possibly incorrectly) stated to be 'about mid-March'.[15] According to the register, John was 'the adopted son of Francis and Kathleen Wrohan', even though no-one called Francis Wrohan existed. Mrs Wrohan clearly did not consider herself to be under oath when it came to official paperwork.

Like the previous two children that she acquired, John was generously provided for through family trusts, again implying that Northcliffe probably – but not certainly – believed they were his. Yet we now know for certain that they were not. The adoption theory has been supported through DNA evidence from a descendant of John Harold. Their DNA has been compared to two descendants of Lord Northcliffe's parents and, although their relationship is close enough that shared DNA would be detected, no DNA is shared. Therefore, despite the strong hint given by Kathleen in his baptismal name, John Harold Northcliffe Wrohan was not the biological son of Lord Northcliffe.

~

Important events were taking place in London while Northcliffe was recuperating in France. Lloyd George's extremely radical People's Budget finally passed on 28 April 1910, and Edward VII died on 6 May, by which time Northcliffe was in the Ritz in Paris, still 'so weak' as he told 'Darling Mums'.[16] 'That great picture of the King lying with the Queen's roses by his side is one of the most beautiful ever produced,' he told Kennedy Jones of a photograph in *The Times*, 'not only in my opinion but in that of all the people here who have seen it'.[17] When Andrew Caird informed him that the *Daily Mail* could not get the access it needed to the king's funeral, Northcliffe wrote to Kennedy Jones.

> I do not like the Paper to use that word 'can't'. The occasion is one demanding immediate reform of the *Daily Mail* picture department, which should now be put into keen competition with the *Mirror* picture department. One secret of the success of the Amalgamated Press has been that we established competition *within* which destroys competition from without. We must now work up such competition between the *Mail* and the *Mirror* to the highest point. Both will benefit and the outsider will suffer.[18]

This was debatable, and led to some extraordinary scenes as each paper tried to outdo the other over illustrations. Because the *Daily Mirror* press time was 6.30pm and the *Daily Mail*'s was midnight, the *Mail* was able to scoop the *Mirror* using the *Mirror*'s own pictures, something that Northcliffe allowed but understandably the *Mirror* staff resented, and went to great lengths to prevent. On one occasion, an assistant art editor called Bartholomew even smashed a photographic plate across his hand, cutting himself deliberately, so that the *Mail* couldn't have it. On another, he used greasepaint to make himself look ill, and when the *Daily Mail* messenger arrived for the plates, it turned out that Bartholomew had taken them to the hospital with him.[19]

Back in England in early June, but still not feeling strong enough to return to the office, Northcliffe entertained Teddy Roosevelt at Sutton Place. The former president had previously been staying at

Chequers in Buckinghamshire with the Conservative MP Arthur Lee and his wife Ruth, who also came to Sutton Place. 'What people try to get into the papers is seldom news,' Northcliffe once told Arthur Lee, 'but what they try to keep out nearly always *is*.'[20] Lee noted how Mary Northcliffe was

> lovely to look at. She knew how to make the best of her every point, was always perfectly dressed, and everything in her garden was as finished and exquisite as her own person. Although extremely feminine, and the most sympathetic and loyal of friends, she had few illusions about Northcliffe, who, whilst lavishly generous about money and gifts and almost courtly in his outward devotion, took little pains to dispel the impression that he esteemed Mother above all other women.[21]

He was right about Northcliffe's generosity; in a will drawn up on 18 August, Mary would receive £10,000 per annum for life and St James's Place.* But it cannot have been an easy time for Mary.

Years later, Northcliffe's niece Enid Stokes recalled how a new coolness descended over Mary's relations with her husband's family. Before 1910, she wrote:

> Mary had been wonderful with presents, each one of so many carrying so much thought. She hung about for hours at the docks to welcome mother [Northcliffe's sister Geraldine] home from India and filled her room with flowers; one particular basket survived for years with green ribbon twined round the handle printed with letters of gold: 'Welcome Home'. All this seems to have come to an end in about 1910, presents and all. I don't know why, but expect that her expanding horizons and diminished affection for Uncle Alfred, caused her to lose interest in his family. She continued to be an excellent hostess for him, and I saw her at very rare intervals when she had become very artificial.[22]

---

* Whereas Louise Owen only got a £1,000 bequest, the same as his other secretary Miss Skipper.

~

By the autumn of 1910, Northcliffe had not wholly recovered from whatever had afflicted him in the first half of the year, and it worried Harold Harmsworth enough to write to him on 2 November to say that 'if anything did go wrong, what does it matter if the dividends of Amalgamated Press are 25% instead of 40% if, when the dividends are 25%, you are in good health, and when they are 40% you are in bad health?'[26] Northcliffe was well enough to arrange to go walking with H. G. Wells in order to talk about matters of state.

The failure of a Constitutional Conference to agree on reform of the House of Lords on 28 November made another general election inevitable, and it took place between 2 and 19 December 1910. Northcliffe ordered the news editor Walter Fish to keep Lord Roberts's demand for National Service at the forefront, but instead the election was again fought on food taxes, and Northcliffe could not persuade Austen Chamberlain and the rising Unionist MP Andrew Bonar Law to give any public assurances on the matter. 'You know I am a very keen tariff reformer,' he told Lord Robert Cecil, who wanted the Tories to promise a referendum on the issue, 'but that is not the discussion at the moment.'[27] He promised the party leader Arthur Balfour to use his newspapers to support the Unionists, but over food taxes he told Cecil, 'I hate this present situation.'[28] On 29 November, Balfour came out in favour of a referendum on tariff reform, admitting to Austen Chamberlain that it was partly under pressure from the *Daily Mail*.

Northcliffe again supported tariff reform candidates across the country, such as Leo Amery, who had been a member of the Milner Kindergarten, to whom he wrote, 'My Press is at your disposal; and I hope Mrs Amery does not mind the photographers, who are absolutely essential. To be unknown by the democracy is to be damned by them.'[29] The results of the December election were largely unchanged from the January one, and gave the Asquith Government a majority of 126 for their House of Lords and Irish Home Rule proposals, four more than after the previous election. 'Not before in my lifetime has our country been so greatly in need of leadership,' Northcliffe wrote to Balfour on 13 December, 'for, I notice, from a careful study of the German Press – of what it is printing and what it is not printing – that our friends across the North Sea are in no wise slackening their preparations, while we are amusing ourselves with an unnecessary General Election.'[30]

During the election, Northcliffe had been surprised at how unprofessionally politicians had gone about trying to get the best publicity for their speeches. 'I sometimes feel that I should like to compile a little book for public speakers and their relation to the modern press and telegraph wire,' he told Lord Curzon on 18 December.

> I will send you a few of my thoughts. 1. In making an important speech, decline to speak at any place unprovided with ample telegraph service. 2. Decline to speak later than half past seven. 3. Send *The Times* a little précis beforehand for the leader writers. 4. Let *The Times* know if the speech is going to be important or not. I refer to *The Times* not because of my connection with it, but because all the other newspapers base their report on those of *The Times*.[31] Public men do not seem to realise that the whole newspaper situation has changed in the last ten years. Newspaper trains used to leave London at 5.15am. They now begin to leave at 1.45am ... Churchill is very well aware of all these arrangements and while much of the reporting of his speeches is due to merit, a good deal is due also to his practical common sense in seeing the situation as it is. Speakers, however distinguished, who go to small places to speak, where perhaps there is only one wire and one operator, cannot possibly expect good reports. The modern newspaper, in my opinion, has entirely superseded the meeting, at any rate in a general election.[32]

~

Early in 1911, Northcliffe found the person he would like to replace George Buckle as editor of *The Times*. He had first been introduced to Geoffrey 'Robin' Robinson in June 1908 by Leo Amery, who had brought him to dinner at St James's Place. After Eton and Oxford, where he took a double first in Mods and Greats, in 1898 Robinson became a fellow of All Souls, and afterwards a member of Milner's Kindergarten and the editor of the *Johannesburg Star*. In January 1909, he wrote a five-page letter to Northcliffe with ideas 'for improving the supply of news from England to the Colonies' that might also be seen as an extended application for the job that Buckle had occupied for almost thirty years.[33] Northcliffe had replied that the matter was 'one to which I gave a great deal of attention while in Canada', while Lord Grey wrote to Robinson from Ottawa that 'Lord Northcliffe is your champion. Harness his energy to your team, and he will help you accomplish your desire.'[34]

Robinson went to Sutton Place to stay for four days in January 1911. 'He was entirely frank,' he later recalled of his host, 'talked of the great traditions of the Walter proprietorship, of his present difficulties, of the staff and of urgent problems.'[35] On the Friday, Northcliffe offered Robinson the position of informal assistant to Buckle, and told a friend of Robinson, a Yorkshireman, 'Behind his quiet manner ... he had one of the ablest brains in England.'[36] 'Rather nervous about it but much too attractive to refuse,' noted Robinson, who took up the post on 14 February.[37] That spring, Northcliffe and Robinson went on several walks on Hampstead Heath together, and soon they were addressing letters 'My dear Robin' and 'My dear Chief'.

On 26 January 1911 the shattering news arrived that the Canadian and United States governments had agreed a draft reciprocal trade agreement removing and reducing tariffs on a wide range of goods. Northcliffe had long feared and warned against the weakening of imperial ties that such an agreement might portend, and his leader in the *Daily Mail* made his feelings clear. 'The scheme of Imperial Preference, of which Canada was the cornerstone, is dead, and the sooner we realise this the better ... But the breach in the Imperial Fabric is not past mending. Imperial Federation is not dependent on Imperial Preference or on any fiscal firm. It is dependent on forces of race and blood.'[38] He was correct that, in Canada, neither the farmers of the west nor the manufacturers of the east had seemed much interested in Imperial Preference, but with the threatened removal of tariffs with their giant neighbour to the south, Canadian manufacturing interests started to court the constructive British imperialists who had since 1903 tried to rally Dominion support for tariff reform, hitherto without much success.[39]

Although the reciprocity agreement was eventually abandoned after the Canadian Conservatives won the September 1911 elections, by then the ructions had already riven the tariff reform movement in Britain. For Northcliffe, this meant parting ways with J. L. Garvin, whose *Observer* continued to argue that Imperial Preference (including food taxes) had a future, and who attacked the stance of the rest of the Northcliffe press three times in February 1911 alone. In reply, the *Daily Mail* ran editorials such as 'The End of the Food Tax', contradicting *The Observer*.[40] 'The Tory split on food taxes has developed into a furious newspaper war,' the radical journalist H. W. Massingham noted, with Mr Garvin and Lord Northcliffe as 'rival generalissimos'.[41] In the end, Northcliffe telegraphed Garvin: 'Either you get out or I do!'[42] From most proprietors, this would mean the departure of the editor rather than the proprietor, but not this one.

Northcliffe admired Garvin personally, had holidayed with him and still thought him 'the greatest journalist in England', despite profoundly disagreeing with him over food taxes.[43] Rather than simply sacking him, therefore, Northcliffe sold *The Observer* to the American William Waldorf Astor for £45,000 with Garvin still in place. 'The break in 1911 reflects credit on both men,' records the historian of these events, Dr A. M. Gollin. 'So far as I am concerned, *The Observer* is nothing,' Northcliffe told the MP Max Aitken on 21 February. 'It is everything to Garvin. Under no circumstances will I continue in *The Observer* with Garvin. I am extremely fond of him, but I think he acted with great unwisdom in declining to take a mere two-hour railway journey to discuss this matter.'[44]

With *The Observer* no longer waging a civil war within his newspaper stable, Northcliffe was able to fight a campaign against food taxes that was ultimately successful, getting them dropped from the Unionist platform by Arthur Balfour's successor Andrew Bonar Law in 1912. Fourteen years later, Max Aitken (by then Lord Beaverbrook) explained how Northcliffe had forced his friend Bonar Law, an Ulsterman who had been born in Canada and brought up in

Glasgow, to abandon food taxes as part of the Unionist programme. It had been a brilliant campaign, he explained, because instead of simply attacking the policy, Northcliffe had first deliberately created an air of mystery about Bonar Law's intentions. 'We were informed that the whole political world was talking about no other question,' Beaverbrook, who had been advising Bonar Law at the time, recalled.

> And by these mysterious hints and allurements the prophecy fulfilled itself and the boast became true ... At last, when the public was really excited – then, and not till then – Lord Northcliffe unmasked his batteries and aimed a shower of journalistic shot and shell on the hostile position. He demanded the abandonment of food taxes by the Conservative Party on the ground of its unpopularity in the constituencies ... and this decision Bonar Law accepted.[45]

'You are my worst enemy,' Law told Northcliffe. 'Oh no! I am your best friend,' replied Northcliffe. 'I have taken the millstone of food taxes off your shoulders. You could never have won an election on the food tax.'[46] As the Unionists had lost three in a row with them in the manifesto, Northcliffe was probably right.

At the same time as dealing with the *Observer* Reciprocity crisis, Northcliffe took on *The Times* senior management over the ratification of the Declaration of London. This saw him attempting to interfere with the editorial policy of the latter paper for the first time. The Declaration was an international agreement on the maritime rights of neutral countries in any future war, and specified which articles carried in ships could be considered contraband. It therefore sought to limit the Royal Navy's capacity to seize property on the high seas in wartime, which Northcliffe feared would blunt the naval blockade of Germany that some strategists believed would be needed to starve it into surrender. Buckle, Valentine Chirol, James Thursfield, the *Times* naval expert, and the Foreign and Imperial Desk of the paper, however, as usual supported the government. There is no indication that Northcliffe manufactured this crisis, since he sincerely believed that the Declaration would be disastrous, but it did bring to a head long-simmering resentments between the 'Old Gang' and the 'Northcliffe Party' at Printing House Square.

Northcliffe declared that its ratification would constitute 'an injury to the Empire' as it would hinder Britain's power to deny war materiel to an enemy. *The Times* directors pointed out that when buying the paper he had signed Article 10 of the Articles of Association agreeing 'that on all existing political questions the independent attitude of the paper shall be maintained as heretofore'.[47] Northcliffe replied that he would not allow a paper he owned to support the Declaration, telling Buckle that he did not 'propose to devote one farthing of my fortune to be used in connection with that which would injure this country'.[48] He was threatening to pull his huge investment programme.

'I entirely agree with you that Northcliffe's action in this matter is in direct contravention of our agreement with him,' Bell wrote to Chirol on 7 March. 'The matter is one of principle ... But it seems to me that opposition is quite certain to result in the complete annihilation of *The Times* as it has existed for the last eighty years ... What would you think of a general who gave up the citadel because the enemy had twice broken through his lines, or wasted the whole of his defensive force upon the defence of one not vitally important outwork?'[49]

Faced with a stand-off, *The Times* stopped opining on the subject of the Declaration either positively or negatively, and after the *Daily Mail* organised a rally in London against it, at which Balfour spoke, the House of Lords refused ratification. Nonetheless, both Buckle and Chirol saw it as the beginning of the end of their editorial independence. Northcliffe's views on a newspaper's relations with the government were put forthrightly to the *Daily Mail*'s managing director Thomas Marlowe on 10 February, when he complained that a *Mail* writer was considered pliable by ministers: 'The *Daily Mail* was not made by licking ministers' boots ... A newspaper is meant to publish news, and not to please highly-placed people.'[50]

Although it was not now hitting the million mark it had enjoyed during the Boer War, the *Daily Mail* was still easily Britain's bestselling newspaper, and Northcliffe took a close interest in every page or every edition. 'I notice that interesting pieces of news are being cut,' Northcliffe complained to Marlowe. 'Take for example "Girl Killed by a Whirlwind". Surely that is a very strange piece of news; it is buried on page five.'[51] 'We have a habit of dropping our topics,' he later complained, 'as is witnessed by the matter of paper bag cooking, which we left just as it was getting interesting.'[52] There was a strong element of bathos in his notes to Marlowe when, after discussion of the newspaper and its headlines, he would then turn to specifics, with advice such as, 'Two things I would hammer at, London Street Noises and the Ugly and Bad Stamps. Complaints are coming from all over the country about these stamps. They are ugly, badly gummed, and a very bad piece of economy.'[53]

~

On 5 April 1911, Charles Moberly Bell collapsed and died at his desk at *The Times* while writing a letter to a Liberal MP.* He was sixty-four. There were inevitably accusations, both at the time and later, that he died 'from overwork because of Northcliffe's incessant demands upon him', but that was untrue, as Northcliffe was constantly urging him to take holidays.[54] On 24 January, he had written to Bell's wife to say, 'I only wish that he could be induced to do what I did – cut himself off from work and worry until the doctor approves.'[55] Northcliffe used the opportunity to appoint Reggie Nicholson as managing director with a seat on the board, further tightening his grip on Printing House Square three years after buying it.

The death of Bell meant that the last bastions of the Old Gang could be politely removed from Printing House Square. George Buckle was retired on 31 July 1912, to be replaced by Geoffrey Robinson on a salary of £2,000 a year.[56] 'I hope and believe that we shall work well together,' Northcliffe wrote to Robinson on 8 August. 'I do not think that either of us are unreasonable people, and

---

* The unfinished letter accused the Asquith Government of legalising burglary and larceny in the new Copyright Bill.

I know that we have many Imperial ideas in common.'[57] It was clear that although Robinson inherited Buckle's editorial independence over the writing of leaders, he was expected to listen to Northcliffe's polite requests, which often sounded more like orders. 'Will you please see that the Festival of Empire and the Pageant of London get a special notice on Bank Holiday Monday in *The Times*,' Northcliffe asked on 3 August. 'I mean a really good notice.'[58]

Robinson always reacted immediately to his 'dear Chief' and, initially at least, tended to agree with him. 'Yes, it was rather a sloppy paper,' he wrote in a typical reply to a criticism.[59] It was a sign of how highly Northcliffe rated Robinson that he kept every letter from him, however mundane. Valentine Chirol* left *The Times* in December, privately complaining that he had been 'eased out'. His place was taken by Henry Wickham Steed, the paper's Vienna correspondent. Steed was already someone to whom Northcliffe turned, along with Robinson, for foreign policy insights, especially since Garvin's eclipse.

Northcliffe kept up his pressure for a military flying corps and, on 12 May 1911, a sobering demonstration took place at Hendon Aerodrome where his friend Claude Grahame-White, flying at 2,000 feet, managed to drop a 100lb sandbag directly onto the outline of a battleship. The implications ought to have been obvious to an audience that included Richard Haldane, Arthur Balfour and Reginald McKenna, the first lord of the Admiralty. It should have been the day that the British Establishment's view of warfare changed entirely, as the broad outlines of everything from Pearl Harbor to the sinking of HMS *Prince of Wales* and *Repulse* in 1941 were suddenly revealed to an incredulous audience. Yet it did not, and there was no change of policy.

After Northcliffe flew aboard Louis Paulhan's Farman military biplane in a cross-country flight from Versailles through the valley of the Chevreuse on 28 May, he was forced to send a telegram three days later that stated: 'I hereby promise not to go in any aeroplane or flying machine whatever without the written consent of my

---

* Who is credited with having invented the term 'Middle East'.

mother. Alf.'[60] Geraldine was not about to lose her eldest boy in one of the still-common accidents of the day. That October, he visited his childhood home, Sunnybank Cottage in Chapelizod in Dublin, which he had bought in July 1904 in an unmistakable sign of happy early childhood memories. 'I think of you every second,' he wrote to Geraldine from Ireland, 'and thank God I have had such a good and brave a mother.'[61]

Northcliffe might have had more influence on government defence and air policy if he had socialised with ministers, but he felt that it compromised his integrity as a newspaperman – and he never much liked politicians as a class. When Churchill invited him to join his new political dining club called the Other Club before its inaugural dinner on 18 May, he replied, 'I would be delighted to join your Club were it not that long ago I came to the conclusion, from my own experience and that of others, that a man who owns newspapers should not belong to clubs of any kind. It was for that reason that I resigned from membership of the Carlton and some other clubs some years ago.'[62] He did attend the Other Club's second dinner, which nonplussed its historian since no guests were allowed. Northcliffe's name, he records, 'appears under that of the chairman. No reason is given for his appearance, and he never came again.'[63]

In July 1911, the German government sent the gunboat *Panther* to French-protected Morocco, forcing Russia to warn Germany of her support for France. Lloyd George took a similarly tough line in a speech at Mansion House on 21 July. As the Second Moroccan Crisis rumbled on, Northcliffe wrote to Churchill on 18 September to say that Germany was 'bluffing her way into a position that will bring about a considerable reduction in the size of her head'.[64] He told Churchill that 'my newspapers have never been provocative about Germany. Germany resents my printing the facts about her forces and intentions.'[65] Around this time, Northcliffe told Churchill that a German cousin of his 'says that his people are like land-crabs: if we advance, they retreat: if we retreat, they advance'.[66] On 23 October, Churchill became first lord of the Admiralty and, in a speech at Guildhall on 9 November, he stated that 'the maintenance of naval superiority is our whole foundation. Upon it stands not the Empire only, not merely the great commercial prosperity of our people, not merely a fine place in the world's affairs. Upon our naval superiority stands our lives and the freedom we have guarded for nearly a thousand years.'[67]

Complimenting him on this tough stance, Northcliffe told Churchill,

> You will find that a firm attitude towards Germany will meet with the usual result in dealing with this greatly misunderstood, hysterical people ... I judge public men on their public form, and I believe that your inquiring, industrious mind is alive to our national danger.[68]

The letter was written on 11 November, a day that was to have a terrible significance to both men before the decade was out, but neither can be blamed for anything worse than wanting to ensure that Britain and her empire were ready for what was about to be unleashed.

CHAPTER 11

The Road to War

November 1911–July 1914

'His love for our Empire was the one passion of his life; it became almost an obsession. He did all that man could to further its interests, and link up our scattered possessions with an unbreakable chain of love and understanding.'[1]

LOUISE OWEN, *The Real Lord Northcliffe* 1922

After attending the Motor Show in November 1911, John Prioleau, a former music correspondent of the *Daily Telegraph*, was asked to report to Northcliffe at St James's Place at 8am. 'In those days he conducted a large proportion of his work in bed, between the hideous hours of 6am and 10am,' Prioleau recalled years later in an unpublished posthumous memoir. 'I found him in bed, surrounded by the day's newspapers. There was no time wasted. "I liked your purple description of *Salome* at Covent Garden. What strikes you as the most outstanding feature of the Motor Show?"' Prioleau replied that motoring was going to get cheaper as cars were being built better and lasting longer. Northcliffe, who by that time owned ten motor cars, hired him on the spot as motoring correspondent of both the *Daily Mail* and *The Times*. 'You know, it's great fun owning a newspaper,' he said as he got out of bed. 'You can make thousands of people do almost anything, though you can never make them think alike ... It's fun. Now it's up to you to make people buy cars. Do it. Goodbye.'[2]

In fact it was more of an au revoir, as Prioleau became a friend and confidant of Northcliffe's. As he put it, he was taken 'suddenly and without warning under the notice and deep into the sphere of Lord Northcliffe, a position not without its imminent and permanent dangers'.[3] Charlie Hands told Prioleau that 'from now on until you are sacked or dead, expect trouble of every kind. You will be in the centre of a storm-cycle that never dies down. But it will be worth it, if you can stand it.'[4] Prioleau recalled of Northcliffe that

> His nature ... was such an odd complexity of qualities, good, bad and trivial ... His character had a hundred different facets and, though certainly no Puck, he derived an inexhaustible and often mischievous delight in showing the right ones to the wrong people ... He was, according to some people who knew him, a ruthless and unjust employer, a benevolent tyrant, a simple soul who became rich by accident and managed his papers by luck, a bully, the first and cleverest journalist in the world, a man of great natural affection. ... nearly all these critics were correct.[5]

~

On 13 November 1911, Andrew Bonar Law took over from Arthur Balfour as leader of the Conservative Party in the House of Commons. (The title 'Leader of the Conservative Party' did not exist during Northcliffe's lifetime.) 'I am very pleased that our pro-spective leader is a Canadian,' Northcliffe told Max Aitken. 'On the two occasions I saw Bonar Law I liked him immensely: and I do not suppose that I shall have any difficulty in giving him my full support, though I am not, as you know, a strict Party man.'[6]

Northcliffe's usually astute political instincts – except in any issue concerning Judaism – deserted him in his stance towards Votes for Women, which he could not take seriously. In February 1912, he told Lord Curzon that his papers were 'going to do anything they can for the anti-suffrage party, but I am one of those people who believe that the whole suffrage movement is a bluff ... If it were not for the support of one or two wealthy women of my acquaintance we should hear very little of the matter.'[7] He refused an invitation to appear on a public platform at the Albert Hall to oppose female franchise, not because he did not believe in the cause but, as he told Lord Cromer, because newspaper owners 'should be read and not seen. The less they appear in person the better for the influence of their newspapers. That is why I never appear on public platforms.'[8] He recognised the power of the mystique surrounding the powerful press proprietor and did not want to dilute it by sitting on a podium, even alongside Curzon and Lord Chancellor Loreburn. Nonetheless, as he told Lord Roberts at this time, 'I am rapidly getting back to the firing line. I have been there since I was fifteen, and needed a year for reflection and rest, more especially after the reorganisation of *The Times*.'[9]

The year 1912 was to be dominated by domestic news, especially the Ulster Unionists' resolve to repudiate the authority of any Irish Parliament set up under Home Rule, and labour unrest in Britain after the miners balloted in favour of striking on 18 January. Northcliffe feared mob rule, especially once the transport workers and dockers joined in, and ordered that it be called 'the black strike'. As *Daily Mail* journalist Tom Clarke recalled, 'It was obvious his sympathy, so often with the workers, was against them in this case.'[10] *Daily Mail* reporters tracked down striking miners who were enjoying themselves at the seaside and dog races while workers from other industries suffered from the 'creeping paralysis' they had imposed on the economy. Yet even as the economy faced severe strains, Northcliffe set up a competition with a £50 prize for 'the finest new rose not yet in commerce', to be called *The Daily Mail* Rose.[11]

~

The sinking of the *Titanic* in the early hours of 15 April 1912 was covered by *The Times* with 'astonishing speed, accuracy and completeness'.[12] The report of 16 April started on page nine ('*Titanic* Sunk. Terrible Loss of Life Feared. Collision with an Iceberg') with two inches of headlines. It listed the first-class passengers (which included Northcliffe's friend Bruce Ismay, the White Star Line chairman, who survived, and the pioneering journalist W. T. Stead, whom

Northcliffe admired, who perished) and the expected underwriters' loss at Lloyds. For weeks, the paper gave the tragedy great prominence with breaking news. When the managing editor of the *New York Times* visited London years later, he was shown the famous *Titanic* edition of *The Times* and was told: 'We keep this as an example of the greatest accomplishment in news reporting.'[13] Northcliffe came up with the idea of a Women's Fund in memory of the men who had put women and children first, and on 23 April he wrote to Thomas Marlowe about the captains of Atlantic liners. 'The poor payment of these men is a world scandal. I wired you this morning to take it up.'[14] Rather strangely, when writing from the mid-Atlantic on his way to Quebec only four months later, Northcliffe told his mother: 'This morning we passed many beautiful icebergs, very lovely things.'[15]

~

On 18 September, Sir Edward Carson held a mass demonstration against Irish Home Rule in Enniskillen, and ten days later he signed the Ulster Covenant, the first of 470,000 people to do so, which promised to defeat Home Rule by force if necessary. Although Northcliffe and Geoffrey Robinson opposed Home Rule out of a belief in imperial unity, the former told the latter that he had 'not cared for the violent Ulster language of Bonar Law, Carson and others'.[16] His maternal aunt, Margaret Bell of Armagh, similarly disapproved of Carson's extremism. As with the Parliament Bill, Northcliffe was no last-ditcher, unlike the new leader of the Unionist party Bonar Law, who had already publicly stated that he could 'imagine no length of resistance to which Ulster will go, in which I shall not be ready to support them', which plainly included an armed uprising in the northern part of Ireland. This was denounced as treason by Liberals, and Northcliffe plainly was not willing to go along with a civil war which would have direct implications for his cousins on his mother's side of the family.

Meanwhile, Northcliffe and Churchill stuck to their agreement to be antagonistic in public but friendly in private. At a constituency meeting in Dundee on 11 September 1912, Churchill spoke of how

> the whole great [Unionist] party machine, led by Lord Northcliffe
> in his aeroplane, is energetically appealing to the working man to
> resist the unjust taxes and destroy the Insurance Act. ... I would
> gladly make a bargain with Lord Northcliffe, who is a very impor-
> tant figure in the politics of this country, and he on this subject is
> the leader of the Conservative party.[17]

A month later, in a postscript to a letter thanking Northcliffe for
a stick with which he could protect himself from the suffragettes,
Churchill, the First Lord of the Admiralty, asked, 'When do you
want me to take you down in a submarine?'[18] He repeated the offer
in April 1913, promising 'return to the surface guaranteed for both
or neither'.[19] There was a good deal of this kind of teasing banter
between the two men around this time. Northcliffe replied he would
be 'very glad' to go in a submarine, but 'please do not trouble to come
yourself', writing that 'If anything goes wrong with the submarine
with *both* of us in it, I am sure it would be a cause of satisfaction to
many.'[20] It was a frank acknowledgement of his own unpopularity
in government and Establishment circles, as well as Churchill's in
Unionist ones. In June 1913, Northcliffe gave Churchill a small ivory
statuette of their mutual hero, Napoleon.

Churchill's friendship with Northcliffe proved to be of inestimable
value in late 1912 when British politics was shaken by the Marconi
Scandal. Four senior Liberal politicians – Lloyd George, Rufus
Isaacs (the Attorney-General), Herbert Samuel (the Postmaster-
General), and Lord Murray (the government Chief Whip) – had
bought shares in the American subsidiary of the Marconi wireless
company when at least some of them knew that the parent company
was about to receive a large contract from the British government.
Moreover, Isaacs' brother Godfrey was managing director of the
parent company, and accusations of insider dealing left the politicians' careers – and perhaps the survival of the Liberal government
itself – in dire jeopardy. Churchill, who was entirely uninvolved in
the speculations, intervened with Northcliffe, who promised him
that his papers would treat the scandal on non-partisan lines.

Northcliffe liked and respected Rufus Isaacs, his barrister in the

Lever soap trial, and Harold Harmsworth asked his brother to 'soft-pedal' the scandal because Isaacs, Murray and Lloyd George were all friends of his who had stayed in his villa at Cap Martin, from where Murray had sent a crucial telegram in which he inquired after his shares in American Marconi.[21] Northcliffe duly soft-pedalled and on 21 March 1913 Lloyd George wrote 'to thank you for the chivalrous manner in which you have treated the Attorney-General and myself over the Marconi case. Had we done anything of which men of honour ought to feel ashamed we could not have approached you on the subject.'[22] Northcliffe replied, 'I adopted my line about this Marconi business because five minutes' lucid explanation showed me that it was the fairest one. Moreover I am neither a rabid party man nor an anti-Semite.'[23] (The fact that the Isaacs brothers and Samuel were Jewish had been seized on by anti-Semites such as G. K. Chesterton, Horatio Bottomley, Leo Maxse and Hilaire Belloc.)

Yet when it emerged that Lloyd George had in fact bought more shares in the American company after the initial tranche of April 1912, an angry Northcliffe wrote to Churchill on 11 April 1913 to complain that,

> Your Marconi friends stage-manage their affairs most damnably. For a couple of clever people [that is, Lloyd George and Rufus Isaacs], I cannot understand such muddling. ... though, as a matter of fact, the whole Marconi business looms much larger in Downing Street than among the mass of the people. The total number of letters received by my newspapers has been exactly three – one of which was printed – the other two were foolish ... My own belief is that both of them throughout the whole matter have greatly lacked sense of proportion and foresight.[24]

Northcliffe's protestations about not being anti-Semitic were contradicted on 7 May when he wrote to Robinson, who wanted to hound the four ministers out of office, to say that

> I should be very sorry to have any difference of opinion with you, especially at the present juncture when the paper looks like

emerging from its present forty-year slough of despond ... Even
if public opinion were as you say, which I entirely doubt, I am not
the least afraid of public opinion. I stood up against it here in the
Dreyfus Case. I took my life in my hands prior to the Boer War
and in connection with Mr Rhodes, when a pamphlet was placed
in every seat in the House of Commons accusing me of being paid
by Mr Rhodes. History has justified me in both cases. Rhodes was
grievously indiscreet, but he was not corrupt. I am not comparing
a Welsh solicitor [Lloyd George] and Jew barrister [Rufus Isaacs]
with C. J. R.[hodes], but I see around me exactly the same kinds
of minds as that with which I was faced before.[25]

He also thought it contrary to natural justice to blame Isaacs for the
faults of his brother, as 'I have been so attacked myself'[26] (although
in fact it was much more the case that his brothers were attacked
because of him). On 6 June 1913, the day after Churchill admitted
to Northcliffe that Lord Murray had also bought Marconi shares,
Northcliffe replied: 'I have made some bad bungles myself, but the
stage-managing of this business beats any record of mine.'[27]

As far as scandals went, Northcliffe was tiptoeing close to one
himself, as shown in *The Observer* on 13 April: 'We give below a list
of the box-holders for the ensuing opera season at Covent Garden,
which opens to-morrow week, April 21, with *Tannhäuser*.[28] The
King was in box 66, but in box 52 were Sir Edward Stern, Mrs Paris
Singer, Mrs Wrohan, Miss Faith-Moore and in box 53 were Arthur
Wagg, Esq., Lady Northcliffe, W. M. G. Simper, Esq.' A coincidence,
or had Northcliffe mischievously (or cruelly) paid for adjoining boxes
at the Royal Opera House for his wife and mistress?

~

On 26 November 1913, *The Times* went so far as to predict that 'war
is possible' within a year over something as seemingly unimportant
as what was taking place between Austria-Hungary and Serbia,
because of 'the larger issues which are said to lie behind it'.[29] Britain
was the only European country without conscription, and in the next
leader it urged that 'Our military forces ... are below the standard

which our interest requires ... and the British people as a whole ...
have not yet accepted the universal duty of manhood in its country's
defence.' Northcliffe was meanwhile contributing £250 quarterly to
Lord Roberts's National Service League.

Northcliffe's attempt to set up a Berlin edition of the *Daily Mail* –
with its stated ambition of bringing the British and German peoples
together – was suppressed by the authorities after a single issue.[30] Back
in 1902, after his first visit there, he had written that Germany was
'new, masterful, alive, brutal and horribly *nouveau riche*'.[31] Detractors
applied precisely that description to Northcliffe himself, but the
fact remains that – like Winston Churchill before the Second World
War – he was the first, loudest and most consistent in warning about
the threat that Germany posed to the balance of power in Europe,
and thus the world. Like Churchill, he was to be denounced as a warmonger – indeed he still is today – for pointing out the true nature of
Germany before that country deliberately started a terrible world war.

In late December 1913 and early January 1914, Northcliffe
'goaded' one Jewish member of *The Times* staff, the assistant foreign
editor D. D. Braham, into resigning and demoted another, David
Cowan, the chief foreign subeditor. In so doing, he told Robinson that
'he didn't like Jews in high places!'[32] Steed told Evelyn Wrench forty
years later that, with war coming, 'Northcliffe thought all Jews were
pro-German and one could not have two of them in key positions.'[33]
Northcliffe's official biography admitted that he 'was perversely given
to goading the susceptibilities of both Jews and Scotsmen', and disgracefully asserted that he 'was susceptible, like many Englishmen, to
the ancient fear of Jewish willpower with its enormous unconcern for
other people's ideals'.[34] That book also sought to excuse Northcliffe
on the grounds that one of his best friends – Henry Arnholz – was
Jewish, to whom 'he gave tokens of his regard in the form of jewelled
tiepins which have acquired heirloom value in the solicitor's family'.
Yet Northcliffe even managed to perpetuate anti-Semitic tropes while
doing this: one tiepin was in the form of a snipe fowl and his attached
message read 'Note the long bill!'[35]

With the *Morning Post* and the *Daily Telegraph* only costing a penny but *The Times* threepence, on 5 May 1913 Northcliffe embarked on a price war, cutting *The Times* to twopence and advertising it as 'the easiest paper to read'. This failed in the short term, with circulation only climbing from 41,000 to 47,000, not enough to offset the loss of revenue. He tried to encourage Geoffrey Robinson to make the paper more light-hearted, joking about how boring Bell and Buckle's paper had been: 'Under the old regime I should have expected the first leader this morning to have been Cambridge Mathematical Tripos, or, if they were in very gay mood, Land Taxation in the City.'[36]

'Fearful worry and chaos in the office,' noted Robinson in his diary in January 1914. 'N[orthcliffe] raging about and giving contradictory orders.' The next day, he recorded the staff being 'worried with all this lunatic raging and nagging'.[37] It was clear that the price cut to twopence had not worked in boosting circulation significantly so, on 16 February, Northcliffe invited Robinson to France for two days to discuss – during a walk and drive in Fontainebleau Forest – 'the 'tremendous undertaking' of reducing it further to only one penny, a risk which Northcliffe described as 'quite the greatest business responsibility I have ever undertaken in my life'.[38]

The announcement of the price reduction caused a sensation, and on Sunday 15 March the presses ran through the night at Printing House Square, not stopping until 11am the next morning, by which time 281,000 copies had been produced. From a circulation of 47,000 in February 1914, *The Times* was averaging 145,000 by April, and stayed there.[39] This was half as much again as the highest figure it had ever reached, on the Prince of Wales's marriage to Princess Alexandra in March 1863. A delighted Northcliffe told Robinson: 'I hear that the old lady of Printing House Square gathered up her skirts and shrieked at the sight of a man under her bed in the face of a real increase in demand for *The Times* for the first time since her middle age.'[40]

The new paper contained all the standard material, but also book reviews and lighter and more varied articles with a better layout. By the end of 1914, the *Times Literary Supplement* could be sold separately at one penny every Thursday, which was also a great success and soon averaged sales of nearly 42,000 a week. There were other popular supplements, such as a regular publication on the British Empire, and the price cut meant that, by the eve of the Great War, *The Times* was finally a viable commercial enterprise after six years of Northcliffe's ownership. His timing could hardly have been better, as the outbreak of war meant that people felt an overpowering need to be informed of the latest life-and-death developments.

Northcliffe's brilliance as a journalist was displayed to Tom Clarke when he became acting news editor of the *Daily Mail* over Easter 1914 and found that it was a very slow news day, except for a hit-and-run car accident in Lewisham, in which a man had been killed as he was cycling with his girlfriend. 'Work it up, work it up,' Northcliffe told the news conference. 'Start a hunt for the motorist who drove on; the *Daily Mail* must bring him to justice. What is the colour of the missing car? Call it "The Mystery of the Blue Car", or whatever the colour may be.' He then dictated the opening paragraph: 'A highway holiday starting in beautiful weather, with countless thousands of motors and bicycles on the road, bearing everywhere the huge population which is only beginning to enjoy the joys of open-air travel, has been marred by a highway tragedy.'[41] Northcliffe put the *Mail* crime expert on the hunt for the missing motorist, and roped in the Automobile Association and National Cyclists' Union to help in the search, and to denounce dangerous driving. Clarke was astounded by how Northcliffe had turned a slow news day into a nationwide campaign and man-hunt.

The Curragh Mutiny of 20 March 1914, during which British army officers based at the Curragh army camp in Ireland decided to refuse to take military action against the Ulster Protestants if called upon to do so, found Northcliffe, Robinson and *The Times* military correspondent Lieutenant-Colonel Charles à Court Repington all in agreement that Home Rule could not be imposed by force.[42] The genuine danger of civil war breaking out in Ireland led Northcliffe to make elaborate preparations to cover the emergency, which he and others believed might be the biggest news story since the Boer

War. Northcliffe himself went to Ulster, along with half a dozen of his reporters and cameramen, and he even chartered a steamer to carry the copy to Liverpool.

On 25 March, Robinson wrote a *Times* leader entitled 'The Plot that Failed' about 'a mischievous intrigue which has brought us within the last few days to the very brink of an unprecedented national disaster ... a rapid and secret coup d'état ... a deliberate conspiracy to provoke or intimidate Ulster at a moment when the peace of the Province was neither broken nor threatened.' He was referring not to the Curragh Mutiny but to the news that Winston Churchill and Jack Seeley, the secretary for war, had been considering sending a naval squadron to Belfast to intimidate the Ulster Protestants into accepting Home Rule. 'We acquit the PM, with his more responsible colleagues, of any effective share either in the conception or the mishandling of the plot,' Robinson wrote.[43] A few days later, Seeley was forced to resign and Asquith combined the post of war secretary with his premiership.

On 1 April, a British equivalent of Carson's Ulster Covenant was signed by Lords Milner and Roberts and tens of thousands of mainland Britons. As one might expect from an Anglo-Irish Protestant whose father revised for his exams with his sword on his lap, Northcliffe saw Irish politics in terms of the prestige of the British Empire, and he wanted Ulster excluded from Irish Home Rule. But he was not willing to countenance the use of violence, saying somewhat ambiguously that he 'had no sympathy for the Ulster resistance to Home Rule, except insofar as it must be resolved for the good of the Empire'.[44]

When Churchill suggested having lunch to discuss the situation, Northcliffe replied that

> I do not think these are lunching times. I have stood by you and [Lloyd] George on many occasions,* and have incurred plenteous abuse because of it, but as one who does happen to know the Irish people pretty well – I was born in Ireland, and have a home

---

* Principally a reference to the Marconi Scandal.

there, as you probably know – I can only regard recent outrageous threatenings as [an] aberration due to too much work. ... Any attempt to overcome the Ulster Protestants will mean Civil War.[45]

Northcliffe believed, wrongly, 'that the South of Ireland does not particularly want Home Rule ... Your position seems completely out of touch with the real views of the English as well as the Irish peoples.'[46] Churchill replied phlegmatically, 'My dear Northcliffe, our very pleasant personal relations have always proceeded on a basis independent of political differences on the one hand and of newspaper criticisms on the other ... Certainly, let us wait for better times.'[47]

On 25 May, the House of Commons passed the Home Rule Bill, and on 3 July, Northcliffe wrote to his staunchly Unionist mother from the Imperial Hotel in Enniskillen, 'I have seen enough of the drilling of these suspicious and determined Scotch and English Irish to know that they *cannot be put down* ... Red flags on all the churches everywhere and "We want no popery here" on all the walls. The girls wearing marigolds and other orange-coloured flowers.'[48] Three days later, he wrote that 'it is novel to be in a country that is obviously preparing for war ... The women are prepared, for ambulance, nursing, signalling and fighting too. I want to get back to arouse the English, but I must see more.'[49]

After he had seen more of the Ulstermen's preparations for civil war, Northcliffe let it be known to Lord Murray that he would be willing to brief Asquith on what he had seen and heard. On 10 July, Ulster's provisional government reaffirmed its determination to resist Home Rule by force, and that same day Asquith wrote of Northcliffe to his mistress Venetia Stanley:

I hate and distrust the fellow and all his works, and will never make any overture to him, so I said merely that if he chose to ask me directly to see him, and had anything really new to communicate, I would not refuse. I know of few men in this world who are responsible for more mischief, and who deserve a longer punishment in the next.[50]

It was an article of faith for Asquith and many Liberals that the
Ulster crisis was being whipped up by the Northcliffe press in order
to sell newspapers.

A secret meeting was nonetheless arranged between Asquith
and Northcliffe at Lord Murray's flat in Ennismore Gardens in
Knightsbridge, during which Northcliffe warned the Prime Minister
of what was about to happen in Ulster. Following a dinner party
given by Arthur Balfour soon afterwards, Lord Balcarres noted in
his diary that

> Northcliffe says the number of rifles is large, the amount of ammu-
> nition enormous. Stores of food are accumulated at all strategic
> points. Practically every motor in eastern Ulster is at the disposal
> of Carson. Meanwhile Captain [Charles Curtis] Craig* ... has
> effected the capture of all the petrol in Ulster. There is a strong
> desire to precipitate matters, not to await further shilly-shally on
> the part of the government ... Northcliffe stated categorically,
> though he could not quote his authority, that Asquith has at last
> begun to realise that words form an ineffective reply to rifles.[51]

Yet a conference held at Buckingham Palace between 21 and 24 July
failed to resolve the impasse and, on the 26th, more than a thousand
German-made rifles were delivered by nationalist sympathisers to
the Irish Volunteers from a private yacht at Howth Harbour, north
of Dublin. It is hard to escape the conclusion that if fighting had not
broken out in Europe in August 1914, it would certainly have started
shortly afterwards in Ulster, and Northcliffe did a public service in
warning Asquith about the extent of the Loyalists' preparations.

With civil war seemingly approaching in Ireland, Northcliffe
could be forgiven if, in common with most of the British press,
he initially failed to spot the implications of the assassination of
Archduke Franz Ferdinand in Sarajevo in Bosnia on Sunday 28
June 1914, for the event only received passing interest in the British

---

* MP for Country Antrim and brother of the first prime minister of Northern
Ireland, Sir James Craig.

national dailies across the whole political spectrum.[52] Coverage of Balkan politics before 21 July was minuscule compared to that of the Ulster situation and to the death of Joseph Chamberlain on 2 July. Thereafter, the reverberations of the assassination were hard to report, since the most important events were taking place in secret communications between Berlin and Vienna, in which the German government promised to support Austria's desire to punish Serbia, which was thought to have harboured the terrorist organisation responsible for the assassination, even if that were to lead to war with Serbia's protector, Russia. Only on 21 July did word start to leak of an impending Austrian ultimatum to Serbia, with all the implications that that might have for Europe.

CHAPTER 12

'THE ANGEL OF DEATH
IS ABROAD'

August–December 1914

'August 4, 1914: War declared. Lord Northcliffe has his
teeth sharpened.'[1]

E.V. LUCAS, *War Diary*

With Britain having become a near universally literate society by the
outbreak of the First World War, there were no fewer than seventeen
daily and evening papers published in London alone.[2] Although
daily sales figures are notoriously hard to estimate, it is probable
that the *Daily Mail* sold around 1.25 million, the *Daily Mirror* 1.2
million, the *Daily News* 375,000, the *Daily Express* 300,000, the
Daily Telegraph 240,000, and *The Times* 145,000.[3] More than
two-thirds of the morning metropolitan journals, an estimated
circulation of 3.625 million, were controlled by three companies, of
which Amalgamated Newspapers was much the largest, controlling
40 per cent of the morning, 45 per cent of the evening and 15 per
cent of the Sunday newspaper circulations in the United Kingdom.

In early 1914, Harold Harmsworth bought the *Daily Mirror*
outright from Amalgamated, and in 1915 he launched the very
successful *Sunday Pictorial*, establishing himself as an important
press proprietor in his own right, as he already owned the *Leeds
Mercury*, *Glasgow Daily Record* and *Glasgow Evening News*.[4] He

received a peerage in the 1914 New Year's Honours List, becoming Baron Rothermere of Hemsted in Kent. His relations with his brother remained close and co-operative.

In the coming war, the press would have unprecedented importance, since in the days before radio and television it was 'the principal, practically the sole, medium of communication between the nation's leaders and the public at large'.[5] Controlling 40 per cent of it naturally gave Northcliffe immense power, something of which he was of course constantly conscious, feeling the responsibility intensely.

The Times has been accused of warmongering in July and August 1914, and of deliberately advocating a war between the Great Powers.[6] Yet there is a world of difference between anticipating a conflict and encouraging one. Its leader of 22 July was entitled 'A Danger to Europe'; it covered what it called 'the growing tension between Austria-Hungary and Serbia', and stated that 'we have no wish to exaggerate the dangers which exist. A cool perception of their greatness may enable the Powers to conjure them before it is too late. There is no time to lose.'[7] This was not war-mongering, nor was it even the first editorial, which was about the Buckingham Palace Conference on Irish Home Rule. It also agreed with Vienna that 'The punishment of assassins ... is imperiously required by the first interests of society and by the conscience of mankind,' stating that 'The Government of Austria-Hungary have acted hitherto with comparative moderation.'

Wickham Steed wrote that leader after discussion with Northcliffe and Robinson, who 'agreed that *The Times* ought to speak, carefully and cautiously, but very firmly'.[8] It did recognise the possibility of the conflict widening, stating: 'It is not clear that Austria-Hungary, did she draw the sword, would localise the conflict if she could, and it is clear that the decision would not rest with her alone.'[9] It also predicted that a general European war would end in disaster for Austria, which it certainly did.

On 23 July, Austria-Hungary formally submitted an ultimatum to Serbia, and the next day Sir Edward Grey proposed a four-power mediation of the Balkan Crisis, while Serbia appealed to Russia for protection. Three days later, Austria-Hungary mobilised its forces on the Russian frontier. The following day, *The Times* responded to these momentous events with a leader entitled 'Europe and the Crisis' which stated that, with Serbia's moderate reply to the Austria-Hungarian ultimatum, 'the way to a peaceful settlement ought to stand open'.[10] Almost the whole of the article continued in the sense that 'there is still a breathing time ... the position is not desperate', pointing out that a war between Austria-Hungary and Serbia would be 'of the utmost danger to every Great Power in Europe', and stating that 'peace, indeed, is the first interest of the [Anglo-French] Entente and the first interest of England. Both will spare no efforts to preserve it.'

Of that leader's 153 lines, only twelve covered the question of what might happen were Germany to test the Anglo-French Entente, but they were uncompromising:

> Should there arise in any quarter a desire to test our adhesion to the principles that inform our friendships and that thereby guarantee the balance of power in Europe, we shall be found no less ready and determined to vindicate them with the whole strength of the Empire, than we have been found ready whenever they have been tried in the past. That, we conceive, interest, duty and honour demand from us. England will not hesitate to answer to their call.[11]

When the radical journalist C. P. Scott met Lloyd George that day, he said 'that Northcliffe wasn't fit to have a paper. I said ... that the article was not inspired by Northcliffe but by what *The Times* believed to be the views of the Foreign Office ... a *Times* man actually was allowed a room at the Foreign Office.'[12] Lloyd George corrected Scott's absurd untruth, although it was widely assumed abroad that *The Times* did represent the position of the British government. (Scott himself did not venture to write a leader on the war until December 1914.)

Austria-Hungary, supported to the hilt by Germany, considered Serbia's response insufficient and declared war on 28 July. The next day *The Times* leader, entitled 'The Efforts for Peace', stated that the news 'brings us nearer to the catastrophe that all the world apprehends'.[13] Yet even then the paper cannot be described as bellicose. 'There is reason to believe that in the most exalted quarter in Germany the maintenance of European peace is warmly and

honestly desired,' it stated, referring to 'the pacific leanings of the
Emperor'. The best way to keep the peace, the paper argued, was

> to make it clear to all that if [Britain's] friends are forced into
> such a war, England for her part will support them to the full.
> We have no selfish interests to serve. We have no direct interests
> at all, except those of seeing elementary fair play in the quarrel
> between Vienna and Belgrade ... It is our settled interest and
> traditional policy to uphold the balance of power in Europe ...
> To that Entente we shall remain faithful in the future, come what
> may, as we have been faithful to it in the past ... We shall spare
> no pains and refrain from no exertions to avert a calamity so dire
> to all the governments and all the peoples of Europe. But should
> our efforts in this prove vain, England will be as ready to stand by
> her friends today as ever she was to stand by them when she was
> aiding Europe to fling off the despotism of Napoleon.

The language might have been high-flown, but it was clear, sincere
and a good summation of British foreign policy for generations, and
could only be considered bellicose by powers that were intent on
upending the delicate balance of power in Europe.

On 30 July, Russia mobilised and Germany demanded in an
ultimatum that it cease doing so. The British press were split about
what to do next; the Northcliffe titles insisted that the government
announce its determination to support France and Russia in order
to deter Germany and Austria, but any such intervention was
strongly opposed by the radical and pacifist press, including the
Manchester Guardian, *Daily News* and *Liverpool Post*. Meanwhile,
the *Westminster Gazette*, *Daily Chronicle* and *Yorkshire Observer*
were 'clearly averse to taking a stand for or against neutrality'.[14]

The Times leader on 31 July argued that British mobilisation was
now necessary. 'Our duty is plain,' it argued.

> We must make instant preparations to back our friends, if they
> are made the subject of unjust attack ... The days of 'splendid
> isolation', if ever they existed, are no more. We cannot stand alone

in a Europe dominated by any single power, or any single group of powers. Were our friends to be attacked and conquered, not merely our position as a Great Power, but our safety within our own shores would be gone ... It is not merely our honour that bids us to be true to our friends. It is consideration for our own welfare and our own security ... We shall still work on for peace; work on for it to the very end; but the hour has come where we too may have to make instant preparations for war. The angel of death is abroad.[15]

Lord Fitzmaurice, a former Liberal minister, claimed that the Northcliffe press was waging 'a campaign to drive this country into joining the war', a stance taken by many commentators since, but in fact it merely wanted to be ready for a war that it believed, correctly, had already been determined upon by Germany.[16] On the very day that *The Times* ran its leader, the German army started to put its Schlieffen Plan into operation, which encompassed the invasion of neutral Belgium in a wide right-flank encircling movement that would swiftly capture Paris.

As France mobilised, Germany declared war on Russia and signed an alliance with Turkey on Saturday 1 August. The *Daily Mail*'s somewhat underwhelming headline that day was 'Bank Rate Doubled: King not to go to Cowes,' but *The Times* ran another rallying call, which stated that:

The policy to be adopted by Great Britain in the last resort remains clear and unmistakable. We desire peace and shall continue to do our utmost to preserve it. If we feel compelled to draw the sword, we shall do so with the utmost reluctance and without animosity. For us, whatever may befall, this cannot be a war of international hatred. We have nothing to avenge and nothing to acquire. In this vital issue we can only be guided by two considerations – the duty we owe to our friends and the instinct of self-preservation ... We dare not stand aside with folded arms and placidly watch our friends placed in peril of destruction ... We know full well that it will be our turn next. None would then raise a hand to save us.

Peace is not, at such a moment, our strongest interest, however dear it may be to us, and however earnestly we may strive to maintain it.[17]

In his autobiography published in 1924, Wickham Steed, who wrote that leader, referred to Saturday 1 August 1914 as 'the most terrible day of my life' because he feared that Britain would not 'stand firm' with France. He recalled a meeting in Northcliffe's office at Printing House Square along with Geoffrey Robinson and Thomas Marlowe in which

> Lord Northcliffe addressed me first and said very gravely, 'I have trustworthy information that the Government are going to "rat". We have hitherto taken a strong line in favour of intervention by the side of France and Russia. But, if the Government gives way, what do you think we should do?' 'We have no choice,' I answered. 'If the Government "rat" we must pull off our wigs and go bald-headed against the Government'. 'Would you attack the Government at a moment of national crisis?' asked Northcliffe. 'Certainly,' I replied.[18]

According to Steed's suspiciously perfect recall ten years later, he then painted a scenario in which Germany took Paris and 'the French make terms with the Germans and join them against us, as we should deserve to see them do'. It was certainly not an impossibility, and presaged the Vichy Government's actions against Britain after 1940.

According to Steed, Northcliffe then asked Marlowe ('the representative of his other newspaper') what he thought. 'Attack the Government in a moment of national crisis? Impossible! The country would never forgive us.'[19] Then Robinson was alleged to have suggested adjournment since, because there was no Sunday edition, they could watch developments for twenty-four hours before meeting again on Sunday afternoon. (Hamilton Fyfe, who was not present, ascribed this view to Northcliffe.[20]) According to Steed, before Northcliffe could reply, his telephone rang, and 'his face changed as he listened.' Northcliffe explained that he had been 'summoned urgently to see some important people'. It was Lord Rothschild and his younger brother who apparently 'summoned' Northcliffe; they told him that if Britain fought, 'the British Empire would be swept off the face of the earth in a few weeks.'[21] They therefore 'implored him to use his influence to keep England neutral'.[22]

Steed alleged in his memoirs that the Rothschilds were acting out of personal financial interests rather than wider national or imperial ones, and elsewhere in his memoirs he claimed that 'the power of international Jewry was the strongest' of the 'adverse influences' that sought to ensure that the people of central Europe 'should be permanently enslaved by a pan-Germanic Empire'.[23] Steed told the ad hoc editorial conference of 1 August that it was 'a dirty German-Jewish international financial attempt to bully us into advocating neutrality and the proper answer would be a stiffer leading article tomorrow'.[24] 'I agree with you,' said Lord Northcliffe. 'Let us go ahead.'[25]

Yet when Steed years later attempted to check his memories of the meeting against those of Marlowe, Marlowe contradicted him over several important aspects of it. Steed's allegations against the Rothschilds that Northcliffe came under 'short-sighted or unpatriotic pressure' can be safely dismissed as the sinister unsupported allegations of an anti-Semitic conspiracy theorist.[26] Even if the Rothschilds did believe that the peace route had not been exhausted by 1 August, they were not alone, as much of the liberal and radical press failed to stand up for the Entente. That day, the *Daily News* published a letter from A. G. Gardiner, who blamed 'the industrious propaganda of Lord Northcliffe' for Britain's 'anti-German frame of mind' and argued that there was nowhere in the world where British interests clashed with Germany's.[27] On the political left, it was assumed, in Michael Foot's words, that 'Northcliffe was the warmonger, helping to incite war against Germany to sell his newspapers.'[28] When figures on the left, such as H. G. Wells, wrote articles critical of Germany and in favour of prosecuting the war, Foot recorded that 'It was such an act of treachery that it seemed he would never be forgiven.'[29]

Yet it was Germany, not Lord Northcliffe, that started the First World War. It occupied Luxembourg on 2 August and the next day declared war on France and invaded Belgium, whose independence Britain, France and Prussia had guaranteed by treaty in 1839. 'We are feverishly organising in a bewildered sort of way for what may be the biggest war in history,' Clarke noted in his diary.[30] The *Daily Mail*'s special Sunday 'War Edition' featured a headline, 'Germany Begins War: Invasion of Luxemburg: Today's Cabinet,' unusually emblazoned in red ink. As one of its war correspondents, J. M. N. Jeffries,* was sent off to Belgium with two hundred gold sovereigns, Walter Fish reminded him that 'a deceased correspondent is of no use to this newspaper' before shaking him by the hand, saying, 'in case we don't meet again'.[31] The paper's leader emphasised sacrifice rather than vainglory: 'The shadow of an immense catastrophe broods over Europe today ... our duty is to go forward into the valley of the shadow of death with courage and faith – with courage to suffer, with faith in God and our country.'

The Times has been accused of understating the implications of war, and of fostering the idea that it would all be over by Christmas. This is untrue; its leader of 3 August, entitled 'The German Invasion', noted how

> The die is cast ... Europe is to be the scene of the most terrible war that she has witnessed since the fall of the Roman Empire. The losses of human life and in the accumulated wealth of generations which such a contest must involve are frightful to think on ... The blame must fall mainly upon Germany. She could have stayed the plague had she spoken to Vienna as she speaks when she is in earnest ... She has lived up to the worst principles of the Frederician† tradition – the tradition which disregards all obligations of right and wrong at the bidding of immediate self-interest.[32]

---

* Northcliffe tried to persuade Joseph Mary Nagle Jeffries to use his very unusual names in his byline instead of his unmemorable initials, but unusually for him he failed.
† A reference to Frederick the Great.

The Times sold 250,000 copies on the day war was declared, Tuesday, 4 August 1914. 'We go into this quarrel, if we must go into it, gravely and sadly,' stated its leader that day. 'But we go into it united ... It will cost us dear; we are under no illusion as to that ... We look not without uneasiness and not without sorrow, at the sacrifices which we know must come.'[33]

The day after the outbreak of war, Asquith appointed Lord Kitchener as War Secretary, the first time a serving officer had sat in a cabinet since General Monck during the Restoration of 1660. Northcliffe supported this appointment, not least because it meant that the post would not go to the obvious candidate – Lord Haldane, then Lord Chancellor. Haldane had modernised and reformed the British Army after its miserable performance in the Boer War and, between 1908 and 1912, had set up the Imperial General Staff, created the Territorial Army, and instituted the Officer Training Corps. Yet Northcliffe had built up an animus against him that was virulent and largely unfair.

Part of Northcliffe's anger against Haldane stemmed from his failure to heed his warnings about the threat from Germany in the air when Haldane was War Secretary. The Northcliffe press also argued that Haldane could not go to the War Office because his supposedly pro-German views would make him unacceptable to the French. Haldane had negotiated with the Kaiser in 1907 and 1909, and had him to lunch at his house at Queen Anne's Gate in May 1911, which was later held against him, even though other guests included Kitchener, Curzon and Robert Baden-Powell.[34] In 1912, he led the Haldane Mission to Germany to try to ward off hostilities. Disastrously, he was also once overheard telling a group of visiting German artists and writers that Germany was his 'spiritual home'.[35]

Yet none of this meant that the upstanding Scot was a would-be or actual traitor, which the press had already started to insinuate in an attack that has been described as 'as vicious and unjustified as any recorded in British history'.[36] Northcliffe did not initiate the assault on Haldane; that was done by the *Daily Express* and *Morning Post*, who criticised his supposed German sympathies, but he and Robinson did fail to print letters to *The Times* from Haldane's friends that attempted to portray him in a positive light.[37] Modern politicians sometimes complain of their rough handling by the press, but it is as nothing compared to what was meted out to Haldane during the first nine months of the Great War. It was alleged that he was a German spy; that the Kaiser was his illegitimate half-brother; that he had a secret wife in Germany; that the Haldane Mission had been intended to surrender the British Empire to Germany, and so on.

After one attack in the *Daily Express*, Haldane received 2,600 hate-letters at the House of Lords 'against my supposed disloyalty to the interests of the nation'.[38] He was nicknamed 'the Member for Germany' and had to be accompanied by a bodyguard throughout the war because of the number of death threats against him. Yet he never sued for libel, nor forced the press barons to try to defend their accusations and slanders in open court. As Lord Chancellor, he possibly felt legal action below him, or feared that a jury might acquit his persecutors, such was the level of popular anger against Germany.

The newspapers that took part in the lynching included *Blackwood's Magazine*, the *National Review*, *Daily Express*, *Morning Post* and the foamingly ultra-jingoistic *John Bull* edited by Horatio Bottomley, but *The Times* and the *Daily Mail* were also heavily responsible.[39] Deeply unattractive aspects of human nature were seen as this blameless patriot became the scapegoat on whom to focus the anger for the terrible losses that were beginning to be incurred on the Western Front.

~

On the day that the immensely popular Lord Kitchener was appointed secretary for war, an advert appeared in the *Daily Mail* stating, 'Your King and Country Need YOU'. This was then used by artist Alfred Leete as the basis for the recruitment poster, featuring Kitchener, stating 'Your Country Needs YOU,' which became an enduring wartime image.

Also on that day – 5 August – Northcliffe made an attempt to influence grand strategy in a very strange and potentially retrograde way. The Great War caught Britain underprepared on land, however powerful she was at sea. The Royal Navy had for years allowed Britain to maintain the largest empire the world had ever seen with military armaments and reserves that would be hardly enough for a third-class military power, and the British Expeditionary Force (BEF) consisted of only six infantry and one cavalry division numbering about 120,000, with fourteen infantry divisions and fourteen yeomanry cavalry brigades in a territorial reserve numbering about 275,000. Meanwhile, Germany had 870,000 regular soldiers and 4.3 million reservists.[40] Northcliffe did not understand that two other infantry divisions of the BEF were to be held back in case of a German invasion, while the rest was about to take its place on the left flank of the French army, and he became agitated at the idea of a Britain left naked to attack. Clarke wrote in his diary:

> To our amazement he declared quite vehemently that he was quite opposed to our sending our soldiers to France. 'What is this I hear,' he cried, 'about a British Expeditionary Force for France? It is nonsense. Not a single soldier shall leave this country ... What about invasion? What about our own country? Put that in a leader. Do you hear? Not a single soldier will go with my consent. Say so in the paper tomorrow.'[41]

Thomas Marlowe was astounded that the *Daily Mail* should suddenly (and vainly) oppose the whole strategic thrust of Britain's war effort, and a long and heated argument commenced. 'I gather there has been a great duel going on about it between the Chief and Marlowe,' Clarke noted later,

> and Marlowe seems to have won. The printers have had a lively night. They received two separate leaders, one prepared by the Chief and the other by Marlowe, and two separate articles and banner lines for the news page – one (by the Chief) against sending troops to France: the other (by Marlowe) ignoring the Chief's view. Both were prepared for publication in page form, and up to the last minute the printers did not know which of the pages would be passed for publication.[42]

In the end, Marlowe's leader was printed, albeit three-quarters of an hour late.

According to Beaverbrook, Northcliffe protested to Churchill against the deployment plans, but there is no evidence of this.[43] Northcliffe was concerned about the prospect of a German invasion of Britain well into the autumn of 1914, joking darkly to the American newspaper editor Arthur Brisbane on 26 October that 'We may not be preparing sufficiently for invasion. I am inclined myself to think that we are not – perhaps because I should be one of the first people to be hanged if the Germans got here.'[44]

There was in fact no prospect of the BEF not being deployed to the west of the French position, where it would be essential to help parry the Germans' thrust on Paris, although two divisions were held back until September in case of a German invasion. Fears that the deployment across the Channel might be costly due to German submarines proved unfounded; the first of the troops landed in France on 8 August and the whole operation saw no casualties.

Ten days later, George Curnock's despatch in the *Daily Mail* about the Connaught Rangers marching through Boulogne mentioned the fact that they were singing a little-known tune, 'It's a Long Way to Tipperary'. Northcliffe decided the song needed popularising and had the music printed in the paper, telling Clarke that 'We shall soon have everybody singing it.'[45] Today it is more emblematic of the war than any other song.

Northcliffe never believed that the Great War would be over by Christmas 1914, telling Steed on 6 August, 'This is going to be a long, long war.'[46] He gave interviews in the American press and elsewhere saying that it was going to last at least three years and he was highly supportive of Kitchener's plans to increase the army by half a million men. Northcliffe's fear of an imminent invasion was somewhat belied by his decision to send every correspondent who could be spared from London – and a dozen who were covering the expected civil war in Ireland – to France and Belgium to get as close to the fighting as possible. Star reporters like George Ward Price and Henry Hamilton Fyfe were sent to France where the *Continental Daily Mail* offices were kept open twenty-four hours a day, but it soon became clear that there would be a dearth of war correspondents because of a reluctance to discourage young men from joining the army.[47] Anything else would have been hypocritical given the newspapers' stance, but it did mean that men considered unfit and too old for service – and also women – were drafted in.

It soon became clear that Kitchener despised and distrusted journalists – he called them 'drunken swabs' – and the general headquarters of the BEF declared that no journalists would be allowed to go to the Front, allegedly in deference to French wishes and practice, so all battle reports had to come from serving soldiers rather than war correspondents.[48] This infuriated Northcliffe, who agitated against it endlessly, but initially to little effect. (There is no corroborating evidence for the allegation that he 'was so incensed by Kitchener's ban on correspondents going to the front that an interview at the War Office ended with Kitchener ringing for an aide to eject him'.[49]) In mid-August, Northcliffe ordered Ward Price to stay behind in Paris rather than going to the front because he had heard that 'The correspondents are going to be kept in cages like wild animals, and Paris provides a far better opportunity for you and the paper than the front.'[50]

That month, Parliament passed the Defence of the Realm Act (DORA), giving the government wide powers over what was allowed to be published in the press, which was restricted by censors who read the war correspondents' copy. F. E. Smith was put in charge of the government's Press Bureau that disseminated war news, which soon attracted the ire of journalists, editors and proprietors, who quickly dubbed it the Suppress Bureau. Northcliffe pointed out that because the German Army allowed journalists onto the battlefield, especially while it was moving forwards, it tended to get better coverage in the world's press. The situation even developed whereby the British press had to take its news in part from German newspapers. In late August, the *Daily Mail* was forced to offer to pay for letters sent by soldiers to their families to be printed.

Northcliffe was quite prepared to self-censor, and had no wish to print anything that might jeopardise military operations, but he was certain that the near-blackout of news was bad for national morale and international standing. His pre-war attempts to get Haldane's War Office to train censors for the coming conflict had failed, so there were numerous occasions when sheer ignorance meant that reports were censored unnecessarily and unprofessionally. On one occasion, a quotation of Robert Browning in *The Times* was changed by the censor from 'Twenty-nine distinct damnations' to 'different damnations', and on another an uplifting wartime quotation from William Pitt the Elder, Earl of Chatham, was forbidden because Chatham was a naval base.[51] Complaining to the prime minister was a waste of time: on 16 August, Asquith wrote to Churchill about how Northcliffe magnified 'the importance of the profession which he has done more than any living man to degrade'.[52]

The stories of German atrocities were reported in such a way that Northcliffe has been accused of 'fanning the flames of racial hatred during the war'.[53] On 10 August, the *Daily Mail* reported the destruction of a Belgian village by the German army as 'a monstrous crime against the law of nations'.[54] An editorial on 'German Brutality' two days later stated that

> In Belgium the Germans have treated the villages where any resistance has been offered to their attack with something approaching savagery. Peasants have been shot; houses have been wantonly burned; hostages have been seized and maltreated, or forced to march in front of German troops, where they would be most exposed to Belgian fire. Such are the methods of this people which claims the privileges of culture and civilisation.[55]

Although there was much criticism of the Northcliffe press's coverage of German atrocities in the Great War, in fact the Germans did behave brutally, and did everything mentioned in that report.[56]

On 1 September, the eyewitness article 'What I Saw in Louvain' – where the Germans murdered 209 civilians in four days in what is modern-day Leuven – was given thirteen paragraphs in the *Daily Mail*. Photographs of the deliberate burning of the medieval centre of the city – its Old Market, fourteenth-century Cloth Hall, 250,000-book University Library, and so on – were used extensively once it was recaptured. Around one-eighth of the city was destroyed, despite some reports in British papers that it was all 'no more than a heap of ashes'.[57] This overtly anti-German coverage has been condemned by Northcliffe's critics as 'violent appeals to hate and the animal lust for blood', yet in fact the *Daily Mail* tried to be as accurate as possible, and recent scholarship has confirmed that the German Army did indeed routinely behave with bestial cruelty to civilians in Belgium and France, and did indeed shell Rheims Cathedral.[58] The *Daily Mail* came up with a new hate-name for the enemy when, on 25 August 1914, five days after the Germans occupied Brussels, Lovat Fraser wrote an article entitled 'The March of the Hun'.[59] The term soon caught on.

On 8 January 1915, *The Times* reported that 'rape with every imaginable refinement of cruelty and bestiality marked the passage of the Huns with ghastly frequency. Irrefutable evidence has been collected ... a minute portion of the horrible German record.'[60] The report *The Times* used was an official one undertaken by Frenchmen of the highest integrity, including a president of the Cour des Comptes, an appeal court judge and a councillor of state, who, as the *Journal Officiel* noted, found that 'pillage, arson, rape and murder ... are the usual practice of the enemy'; that there were massacres of civilians at Lunéville, Gerbéviller, Nomény and elsewhere; and that officers took part in the massacre of civilians at Senlis.[61] 'The stories of rape are so horrible in detail that their publication would seem almost impossible,' stated *The Times*, 'were it not for the necessity of showing to the fullest extent the nature of the wild beasts fighting under the German flag for German ideals and civilisation.'[62] Racial hatred is always hard to avoid in a world war, but the stories that *The Times* reported were generally accurate, and the inaccurate ones – such as monks being used as bell-clappers – were sourced from impeccable newspapers such as *Le Matin*.

J. M. N. Jeffries, the *Daily Mail*'s Belgium correspondent, pointed out in his autobiography *Front Everywhere* that he and his colleagues in Brussels, Antwerp and Ostend were merely reporting what they saw and were citing only 'attested cases of named individuals'. They were under no pressure from Marlowe to print lurid stories unless there were multiple believable sources, which all too often there were.[63] German newspapers also printed atrocity stories, of course: on 1 December 1914, the *Norddeutsche Allgemeine Zeitung* informed its readers that Sikh and Gurkha troops crossed the lines to slit German sentries' throats so that they could drink their blood.[64]

On 25 August, Kitchener announced in the House of Lords that the first hundred thousand recruits were 'practically secured', hinting strongly that many more would be necessary. Northcliffe used his remarks to reinvigorate the campaign for compulsory military service should the voluntary system not provide enough recruits, which strongly contradicted the Liberal Party's view that the state did not have the right to compel citizens to bear arms and kill in its defence.[65] The Northcliffe press condemned what it called 'slackers' and 'shirkers' who they depicted as hiding behind those who had bravely stepped forward for Kitchener's New Army. 'It is a national scandal that the selfish should get off scot-free,' argued *The Times*, 'and if the voluntary system can do no better, it will have to be changed.'[66]

The recruitment system was absurdly haphazard, with men being accepted into the army from whatever trade, even from vital war industries like coalmining and munitions production. Nonetheless, in March 1915 Asquith told the Commons that the government was satisfied with its progress. It dawned far too slowly on the Liberal government that massive new armies would be needed, and that the war could not be fought by the Royal Navy blockade and a minimal British land army supporting a massive French one. Kitchener was reluctant to advocate compulsion, but Northcliffe recognised early on that it would be unavoidable.

Defeat at the battles of Namur and Mons on 22 and 23 August led to an Allied retreat from 24 August to 7 September, with the Germans crossing the Meuse on 26 August and entering Lille the next day. On 30 August, the same day that the Germans took Amiens, the Northcliffe press broke the news of the retreat from Mons to an astonished public in the *Weekly Dispatch* and a special Sunday edition of *The Times*. 'Our losses were very great,' wrote Arthur Moore in the latter. 'I have seen the broken bits of many regiments.'[67]

Although the Press Bureau had not tried to sugar the pill, calculating, correctly, that the defeat would be the spur to massive
recruitment, the widespread public dismay meant that next day it
was forced to issue a (false) correction of the stories. Asquith spoke
in the Commons of 'a very regrettable lapse' by the two papers,
enraging Northcliffe as the story was true and the Bureau censors
had passed the dispatches, with F. E. Smith saying 'We want reinforcements and we want them now.'[68] Fortunately, Northcliffe had
Smith's letter passing the report, and he ordered that it be printed in
facsimile on 1 September. On being told that the letter was private,
he insisted: 'Print it. Give it to me . . . I am not going to be attacked,
when I am right, without retaliation.'[69] Smith was forced to resign
from the Press Bureau and he blamed *The Times* and its untrustwor-
thy 'dirty dog' proprietor.

Churchill – who allowed no war correspondents on naval vessels –
was supportive of his best friend Smith, telling Northcliffe he could
not 'possibly shelter yourself behind the Press Bureau, although their
mistake was obvious. I never saw such panic-stricken stuff written
by any war correspondent before.'[70] Northcliffe replied that because
'*it was not only passed, but carefully edited, and accompanied by a
definite appeal to publish it*, there was no other possible conclusion
except that this was the Government's definite wish'.[71]

'People do not seem to know that a newspaper lives from one day
to another on public opinion,' Northcliffe told R. McNair Wilson
in reference to this incident. 'The Press can never be irresponsible.'[72]
Wilson recalled how a shadow darkened Northcliffe's face when he
added: 'I have been called an enemy of the British people because of
what *The Times* . . . published about the retreat from Mons. That
hurt me more than anything else in my life.'[73] It was true; H. A.
Gwynne of the *Morning Post* told his proprietor Lady Bathurst that
'the very existence of Northcliffe in a time like this is to my mind a
great national danger'.[74]

On 3 September, the Germans crossed the River Marne and got
to within twenty-nine miles of Paris. The French government moved
to Bordeaux, from where the *Continental Daily Mail* started to be
published on 7 September. By then, the battle of the Marne had

begun, which saved Paris and forced the Germans to retreat between 9 and 15 September, with the Allies retaking Rheims on the 14th. The next day, the *Daily Mail* staff returned from Bordeaux to Paris. Back in London, Northcliffe reappointed Hannen Swaffer to the *Daily Mail* in order to improve its pictures. 'I've got bad news for you all. Swaffer's back,' he told the editorial conference. 'Some of you don't like him. I know why. He's got more brains than anyone in this room except me.'[75] Swaffer was known for his waspish wit, once remarking that 'Freedom of the press in Britain means freedom to print such of the proprietor's prejudices as the advertisers don't object to.'[76]

The profound hostility that Northcliffe faced from the Asquith family is evident from a letter that the Prime Minister's son Raymond wrote to his wife Katherine on 10 September. It was about a dinner the night before where it was suggested 'that one of the British cable companies has been tampered with, and is somehow helping the Germans, and that Lord Northcliffe is or may be involved'.[77] The Asquith family were very free in making wild and completely unsupported accusations of treachery against Northcliffe on no evidence whatsoever, but with a good degree of condescension towards someone who had risen through journalism rather than the law, like Herbert Asquith. Three days later, Raymond wrote to his friend Conrad Russell repeating the gossip about Northcliffe being 'mixed up with a British cable company which has been bought by the Germans and gives away our secrets', but this time he admitted that it was unlikely to be true.[78]

～

After the battle of the Aisne in the second half of September, the Western Front stabilised and the line of trenches now stretched the 400 miles from Switzerland to the English Channel. In October, Northcliffe visited the Front where he met British, French and Belgian troops and charmed Major Ernest Swinton, the official War Office journalist. Because General Sir John French, the commander-in-chief of the BEF, could not meet him, he visited the front line in the purely nominal capacity of assistant to the chief scout of the

Belgian Army. Max Pemberton recalled Northcliffe sitting by the hospital bedside of an octogenarian Belgian woman who had been wounded by a shell-splinter in Furnes. 'What has she done that war should punish her?' Northcliffe asked him.[79]

When Winston Churchill went out to Antwerp in early October to try to bolster its defence, the Northcliffe press was highly critical, and when the city fell on 9 October, the *Daily Mail* ran an article entitled 'Who is Responsible?', which focused on Churchill. On 23 October, Robinson recorded in his diary: 'A talk with Northcliffe, broaching the subject of the Admiralty. I found him in the wildest state of mind denouncing ... [the First Sea Lord] Prince Louis [of Battenberg] for being a German.'[80] As with Haldane later on, the hounding from office of the honourable and patriotic Battenberg simply for having been born German was a discreditable episode in Northcliffe's war.

Similarly, Northcliffe's treatment of Major Sir Francis Trippel, a German-born professional fundraiser whom he had known since he had raised money for the 1908 London Olympics, was driven by anti-German bigotry. In April 1909, Northcliffe had given Trippel £500 'on account of your assistance in raising the Union Jack Club fund, the Cabmen's Fund, and your help with the Territorial Army'.[81] There had been a brief falling-out in 1912 when Northcliffe paid Trippel £100 for his help with the Antarctic Exploration Fund, rather than the £250 to which Trippel felt himself entitled but, nonetheless, in late October 1914 Northcliffe telephoned Trippel to warn him that he was being 'closely watched by detectives as a suspect individual, and that [his] whole record was being delved into'.[82]

Trippel was outraged that he was being treated almost as an enemy alien, considering that he had given 'the fullest information of my antecedents' when he had renounced his German nationality and become a naturalised British subject in 1892, since when he had been a commissioned officer in the British Army, raised money for endless patriotic causes, as well as having helped the *Morning Post* to raise a field force in the Boer War. He was the editor of *The Flag*, a journal published by the *Daily Mail*, and the only time he had been back to Germany in twenty-seven years had been to attend his father's funeral. 'I am quite ready to go to the front on active service should the call come,' Trippel told Northcliffe. 'No man could do more.'[83]

The Times Red Cross Fund, which Trippel helped to co-ordinate, had raised over £1 million, yet when in May 1915 he patriotically offered to set up a prize of £5,000 for the Admiralty 'to stimulate the invention of an effective defence to submarine and torpedo attacks', Northcliffe wrote to him,

> My dear Trippel, Can you not get into your thick Prussian* hide the fact that the best thing for ex-aliens is to be out of sight. I must write plainly for you go blundering about, and the more you flounder the more everyone becomes suspicious of you. Personally, I have always regarded you as a strictly honest but erratically impulsive individual, which rather agrees with the accounts published of you in the German newspapers which you probably never see. For goodness sake if you want to do anything, do it anonymously.[84]

Northcliffe had minimal contact with Trippel for the rest of the war, but by the summer of 1919 he was clearly on an unofficial blacklist. When Eugen Sandow, the father of bodybuilding, wrote to him, Northcliffe noted to his secretary H. G. Price: 'My dear Price, Is not Sandow a Hun? Find out, if so put him on the same list as Trippell [sic] for similar treatment, that is to say nothing doing. Chief.'[85] Sandow, who was a Prussian Jew and King George V's physical education instructor in 1911, was another naturalised Briton who had shown his loyalty to his adopted country by providing fitness training at his own expense for would-be recruits to the army since 1909. None of this was enough for Northcliffe, however, whose phobia about 'Huns' was lifelong. He only made an exception for his mother's two sisters, Grace and Caroline, who were married to Germans, to whom Northcliffe sent money during the war.[86]

During the First Battle of Ypres between 19 October and 22 November, the Germans failed to break through the Allied lines. Louise Owen, at the time still just his secretary, recalled Northcliffe

---

* Trippel was in fact a Rhinelander.

walking in his garden at Elmwood listening to the booming of guns across the Channel and remarking, 'I hope I shall live to see the end of this, and to keep an eye on the [peace] treaty. I know these crafty politicians and how they would sell their very souls for material gain.'[87]

In late November, Northcliffe produced a sixpenny pamphlet sarcastically entitled *Scaremongerings from the Daily Mail 1896–1914* which showed how prescient the paper had been about Germany's warmongering, while ridiculing the leading liberal newspapers and intellectuals who had taken pacific, or more often myopic, stances on Germany's armaments build-up. The response was predictably harsh, and on 1 December *The Star* wrote: 'Next to the Kaiser, Lord Northcliffe has done more than any other living man to bring about this war.' When he was shown this, he said that 'It is what you may expect. It only shows how angry they are about being shown up. It is not worth taking any notice of.'[88]

Northcliffe has been accused of hiding the realities of the war from the public, even of preventing the terrible facts of the war from penetrating to his Middle England readership. Yet that is quite untrue, as any reading of his papers proves. They did self-censor overt pacifism and defeatism, but not the dreadful realities of the conflict. 'All the spectacular side of the war has gone, never to reappear,' ran a typical report in *The Times* on 24 November 1914.

> Day after day the butchery of the unknown by the unseen. ... War has become stupid. Two lines of men entrench against each other ... The infantry trenches ... receive an uninterrupted rain of projectiles ... The strain on the infantry is tremendous, and it is endless ... At the cost of thousands of lives a few hundred yards may be gained, but rarely indeed does the most brilliant attack produce anything ..... Fresh troops brought up under cover of tremendous artillery fire which opens by surprise may effect a breach ... But only with heavy loss can such an attack be carried through.[89]

A week later, a correspondent described the Flanders battlefield as a modern 'charnel house'. There were articles on the sheer mathematical nature of the artillery war, and editorials on 'The Monotony of War' that described its 'sense of greyness and stagnation'. Soldiers' letters home were printed that emphasised how three days in the trenches had 'shattered every illusion about war. This siege warfare is a terribly dreary business, there is no romance in it.'[90] Far from hiding the truth, the Northcliffe press made clear the realities of Western Front combat from early on, and it never let up. To have attempted to hide the nature of a global conflict from the British public would have been impossible, and it would have gone against everything Northcliffe had been trying to do for years.

Another criticism of the Northcliffe press's coverage of the war was that it regularly employed archaic and euphemistic language that seemed increasingly out of touch with the terrible reality of the trenches. Headlines such as *The Times*'s 'Renewal of Youth' (16 February 1915), 'For Men Broken In Our Wars' (21 July 1915), 'Glorious Baptism of Fire' (4 September 1915), 'War and Sacrifice' (10 April 1916) and 'Heroes: Response to the Ideal' (18 August 1916) were later denounced as not reflecting the real experiences of the soldiers in the trenches, which was one of lice, rats, mud and the constant fear of death from sniper, bayonet, mortar and machine gun.[91] In Northcliffe's defence, however, there was plenty of truth about the nature of modern warfare in his papers. Readers of the day were used to euphemism, there was plenty of genuine sacrifice and heroism in the trenches, and there was a thin line between concentrating on the horrors of war and outright defeatism.

Such criticisms, both during the war and after it, had remarkably little effect on Northcliffe. 'I do not in the least mind personal attacks,' he told Lovat Fraser on 14 December, 'nor do I care what the public think of me. The fact that my newspapers are almost the only ones that are not shrinking rapidly at the present moment shows that my readers have faith in them. If the readers attacked me, I should begin to think that I am the wicked man the little tradesmen of Fleet Street believe me to be.'[92]

CHAPTER 13

THE SHELLS SCANDAL

January–May 1915

'His power was so considerable that it was of the utmost
importance in all matters of public interest to secure his
assistance or at any rate his neutrality.'[1]

LORD BEAVERBROOK on Lord Northcliffe,
Men and Power 1956

Lord Northcliffe visited the Front again in the New Year, increasingly worried that the enemy were winning the propaganda battle
in the United States, partly due to the Royal Navy's blockade of
Germany. A lifelong Francophile, who once told his chauffeur Harry
Pine that 'The French know how to live,' he also felt the government
was paying too little attention to Britain's most important ally.
Asquith might have been a perfectly adequate peacetime premier,
Northcliffe was starting to think, but he was no war leader. 'We are
not at law with Germany,' he said of Asquith's government. 'We are
at war with her.'[2]

Complaining about the government's 'meddling and dallying' to
the Northern newspaper proprietor Samuel Storey in mid-January,
Northcliffe said his papers were 'dealing very gently with the government now, because the public, who know nothing about the war, will
not tolerate criticism of our public men; but, believe me, we will not be
patient much longer.'[3] He was not appeased when Asquith appointed
Cecil Harmsworth as under-secretary at the Home Office in February.

On 2 February 1915, Northcliffe told Robinson that he was 'rather distressed' about *The Times*'s fall in circulation, and suggested there should be a leading article each day on something totally unconnected to the war. He did not want to reduce the price further, 'but it is obvious that the present rate of leakage will bring the ships on to the rocks again'.[4] With the rising cost of paper, even insulated as his empire was because of the operation in Newfoundland, his view was that 'we must issue small papers I fear'.[5] In fact, *The Times* stayed fourteen pages long and kept the same dimensions throughout the war, although the *Daily Mail* drastically reduced in size, from ten pages in August 1914 to only four by November 1918.

One result of trench warfare was that the original artillery shells, such as shrapnel ones that were intended for a more open kind of fighting, were no longer as useful as high-explosive shells, which it was hoped could damage dug-outs and even cut barbed wire. Almost throughout the war, the Germans built deeper and stronger dug-outs than the Allies, sometimes with extensive underground tunnelling. 'I hope that you will shortly receive the munitions for your great enterprise,' Northcliffe wrote to Sir John French on 3 March, prior to a major assault around the village of Neuve Chapelle intended to capture the Aubers Ridge and perhaps break through to Lille.[6] French replied three days later to say that he was sending his military secretary, Colonel Brinsley Fitzgerald, 'to talk with you on the subject ... He will express my views more clearly than could be done in writing ... *The Times* is doing a great work now for the Army out here.'[7]

The battle of Neuve Chapelle was launched on 10 March 1915 and failed within three days, largely down to the paucity of high-explosive shells available to French, who could not significantly damage the well-dug-in German positions with the necessarily short preliminary bombardment. On 15 March, Kitchener, the man ultimately responsible for what kind of shells were produced and delivered, had to make a statement to the House of Lords in which he admitted to having 'very serious anxiety' about the arrears in delivery of war materiel.[8] He blamed the trade unions and also stated that 'the temptations of drink account for this failure to work up to the high standard expected'.[9]

The afternoon closing of pubs had been introduced by the Defence of the Realm Act in August 1914, so that from the previous nineteen-and-a-half hours a day they were now only open five-and-a-half hours a day. Northcliffe was unpersuaded by Kitchener's attempts to blame trade unions and a drunken workforce for a lack of shells. Instead he believed it was the fault of a short-sighted government allowing munitions workers to join the army, Kitchener's mistaken concept of the nature of modern warfare, and the refusal of the War Office to extend munitions contracts to firms beyond the ones that the government had used for decades. Modern scholarship has generally supported Northcliffe's contentions over Kitchener's excuses. 'The suggestion that we shall have drinking to excess is untrue,' he told Robinson.[10]

Northcliffe had hailed Kitchener in both the Sudan Campaign in 1898 and the Boer War, and supported him in his spat in India against the Viceroy, Lord Curzon, in 1905. In 1914, he had pressed for Kitchener to become War Secretary. But now, armed with information from General French and Colonel Fitzgerald, he turned against him. Neither the Sudan Campaign nor the Boer War had featured long artillery preliminary bombardments of enemy positions, as were necessary at battles such as Neuve Chapelle. During what became known as the Shells Crisis, Northcliffe privately described Lord Kitchener of Khartoum as 'K of Chaos', 'the Cabinet's Old Man of the Sea' and 'a national great white elephant'.[11]

As one historian of the Shells Scandal has put it about the howitzers available to Sir John French:

The existing British model was deficient in range, and only in February did Kitchener approve a trial order for a new type. When the first batteries went out in March there were only 152 shells for each gun. Failure to perceive the scale of heavy artillery needs until this late stage put the British far behind the Germans and the French.[12]

This infuriated Northcliffe.

Less than a week after Neuve Chapelle, a further grave setback turned another senior government minister from a friend into an outright foe, when the Allied navies failed to force the Dardanelles Straits on 18 March 1915 in a campaign championed by Winston Churchill. Six Allied warships were sunk or disabled by mines or Turkish artillery fire, and the naval operation to sail through the Straits to Constantinople was called off until the Gallipoli peninsula on the western side could be secured by the Allies, despite its occupation by German-trained Turkish units.

In strategic terms, Northcliffe was a 'Westerner', someone who believed that the war would be won through a Clausewitzian decisive battle on the Western Front, rather than through geographically much wider assaults in places to the east like the Balkans, Mediterranean and the Middle East. Campaigns like the Dardanelles would only weaken the British Army in its hope to break through to Lille, and Northcliffe promised the prominent Westerner Sir John French that his newspapers would not 'cease to urge the sending of men to your army'.[13] The fact that Kitchener at least initially supported Churchill's plan to create an eastern diversion, aid Russia, and hopefully knock Turkey out of the war by seizing Gallipoli, only added to Northcliffe's doubts about the war secretary's competence.

On 25 March, once it was clear that Neuve Chapelle had been a costly failure, French wrote to Northcliffe essentially asking him to oppose the Gallipoli venture. 'I earnestly hope you will do your utmost in your powerful control of the Press to insist upon concentration of all available forces in this theatre,' he wrote.[14] Behind Kitchener's back, French was trying to recruit a press proprietor to oppose the government's grand strategy. That same day, *The Times* quoted French directly, complaining that his greatest problem was 'munitions, more munitions, always more munitions'.[15] It was meant as a spur to the workers in the munitions factories, but it could be read as an admonition to a government that was responsible for producing them. Four days later, French widened his needs to men as well, to Northcliffe's approbation. 'We have by no means enlisted all the men we shall want,' *The Times* wrote in favour of compulsory conscription. 'The country has courage; the Government apparently has not.'[16]

'My own most beloved and most dear,' Asquith wrote to his close friend and probable mistress Venetia Stanley at 3pm on 29 March. 'There is as you see in the Tory press a dead set being made against me personally. Witness the articles in *The Times* and the *Morning Post* ... McKenna came to see me just before lunch, with a tragic history of intrigue. The idea is that Lord Northcliffe (for some unknown reason) has been engineering a campaign to supplant me by Ll[oyd] G[eorge]!'[17] McKenna believed Lloyd George and Churchill were 'in it', but Asquith did not agree, correctly in Churchill's case. Asquith believed that the Cabinet would resign en masse sooner than see him displaced, and asked Venetia, 'Aren't you rather glad that ... all these men, mostly clever and able, all thoroughly competent, should ... be prepared to sacrifice everything personal or political for your true and devoted lover?'[18] As events were later to prove, Asquith had greatly misconceived the loyalty of his colleagues.

Later that day, David Lloyd George, according to Asquith,

vehemently disclaimed having anything to do with the affair. Kitchener, he claimed, is the real culprit because, in spite of every warning, he neglected up to the eleventh hour a proper provision of munitions ... As for himself (Ll G) he declared that he owed everything to me; that I had stuck to him and protected him and defended him when every man's hand was against him;* and that he would rather (1) break stones, (2) dig potatoes (3) be hanged and quartered (these were the metaphors used at different stages of his broken but impassioned harangue) than do any act, or say a word, or harbour a thought, that was disloyal to me ... His eyes were wet with tears, and I am sure that, with all his Celtic capacity for impulsive and momentary fervour, he was quite sincere.[19]

---

* Probably a reference to the Marconi imbroglio.

Perhaps Lloyd George had forgotten recently telling Sir George Riddell that Asquith lacked initiative and took no steps to co-ordinate and control the government.[20]

The exact nature of the relationship between the Prime Minister and Venetia Stanley, who was thirty-five years his junior, is the subject of a long-running, if still inconclusive, historical debate.[21] Roy Jenkins, Asquith's biographer, defended him from charges of infidelity, arguing that instead the relationship was merely epistolary, 'both a solace and a recreation, interfering with his duties no more than did Lloyd George's hymn-singing or Churchill's late-night conversations'. To this, the American historian Stephen Koss retorted: 'True enough, but the others, in their respective pastimes, did not make it a practice to divulge Cabinet proceedings or wartime troop movements.'[22] The most recent and comprehensive work on the subject, however, concludes that Asquith probably did have a three-year sexual affair with Venetia Stanley.[23]

Gladstone said he had known twelve prime ministers in his time and all but one* were adulterers. As well as Asquith and Lloyd George's affairs, Curzon conducted one with the novelist Elinor Glyn; Milner kept his mistress Cécile in south London and conducted a twenty-two-year affair with Violet Cecil before marrying her; Lord Carson's second wife was thirty years younger than him; Lord Horne was sung about in music-halls as 'Beaming Bert, that incorrigible flirt'; and Lewis 'Loulou' Harcourt committed suicide as accusations were emerging about pederasty.[24] Lord Northcliffe's affairs thus fitted into a sexual culture in which the uxoriousness of someone like Salisbury and Churchill was far from the norm.

~

In early April, Northcliffe made his third visit to the Front, and this time was invited to BEF GHQ to meet the commander-in-chief. 'Long talk with Sir John French,' he telegraphed to Mother on Easter Sunday, 5 April. 'Pleasant dinner, at which was the Prince of Wales. Off sightseeing today. Tomorrow [we] go [on] a long drive and stay

---

* He was probably referring to Lord Salisbury.

with [the French commander-in-chief] General [Joseph] Joffre. Your
devoted Alf.'[25] A letter to Alexander Kenealy, the former editor of the
Weekly Dispatch, gave an indication as to what had been discussed:
'All here most confident that by prolonged mass artillery fire on a
tremendous scale they can break the German line and the next few
weeks will be momentous in history I feel sure. General French is
calm, able and certain, and by necessity a terrific worker. I sat with
him till late last night. We need shells.'[26]

On his return, Northcliffe brought a seemingly live, ten-inch
shell into the lobby of Carmelite House, and placed it directly below
Andrew Caird's desk on the floor above, ordering that a sign saying
'Danger' was to be attached to it. 'See where it points,' he told Caird.
'What will happen to you if it goes off?'[27] Caird secretly ascertained
from the 3rd Field Artillery in City Road that it was in fact harmless,
but ordered his staff not to tell Northcliffe that he knew, as 'I don't
want to spoil his joke.'[28]

When Lovat Fraser wrote a *Times* leader on 'The Progress of
the War' on 12 April, it contained the sentence, 'There is a lull at
the Dardanelles at which we must not peer too closely.'[29] This was
because a great amphibious assault on the Gallipoli peninsula was
planned for 25 April. Fraser added that the abortive naval attack
of 18 March had 'revealed much valuable information regarding
the character of the work yet to be done'. Northcliffe exploded at
this over-optimistic 'Easterner' approach. In a long letter to Lovat,
he complained bitterly that the government was making error after
error. 'I very rarely interfere with the editorial writing in the *Times*,
but I must say that this morning's leading article distresses me
greatly and I know that the Editor is in accordance with my views.
Anyone who has studied the war knows that our army in France is
unable to move.'

Clearly having been briefed by French, Northcliffe claimed there
were three reasons for the British Army's inactivity: 'many of the
shells' were going to the Dardanelles instead of France; Kitchener
had earmarked the 29th Division to do the same; and the government
had not taken advantage of offers from small contractors to supply
shells. 'Why should we not peer too closely into the scandal of the

Dardanelles?' he demanded.[30] He told Fraser that Joffre had 'told me personally' that the result of the Dardanelles campaign would be 'greatly to hearten the Germans', and that 'It was heralded by a blare of trumpets that made a ridiculous fanfaronade throughout the world'.[31] Northcliffe continued:

> The whole effect of your column is to whitewash the Government and mislead the public. When recently I saw those splendid boys of ours toiling along the roads to the front, weary, but keen and bright-eyed (many of whom have given up rosy prospects and happy homes), I could not help feeling very, very bitter at the thought that many of them were on the way to certain mutilation and death by reason of the abominable neglect of the people here.[32]

Referring to Kitchener's excuses for the shell shortages, Northcliffe said that on his visits to the Front he had 'talked with hundreds of people ... and know that, while we are talking about the alleged drunken habits of the working man (in which I do not believe), the guns at the Front are starved for want of the only means of putting an end to this frightful slaughter of the best which any nation has to give'.[33] Fraser replied from his home in Slough that 'we can only say "Drop it" if we believe the [Gallipoli] operation to be impossible; and we do not know that it is. We cannot expose these blunders and mistakes in an operation that is about to be renewed. To do so would be to encourage the enemy and inspirit the Turks.'[34] He added that Kitchener had told him that the reason he was holding troops back in Britain was that 'He will not send over his new armies for Sir John to waste.'[35]

Fraser presciently told Northcliffe that 'The time will come when we shall have to say that we cannot win this war with a Cabinet of tired lawyers, but we must first be very sure of our ground, and not move unless the country will be with us. Remember that if that time comes we shall probably have to arraign Lord Kitchener also, and that will be a very big and difficult thing.'[36] Northcliffe had been warned.

One side-effect of Kitchener's accusations against the working man was that, on 15 April, Lloyd George wrote to Northcliffe to recruit his newspapers to the national drive for sobriety, saying, typically flatteringly, 'we cannot act unless we have practically the unanimous support of the leaders of the nation. Your influence is essential.'[37] The king took the pledge not to drink any alcohol for the duration of the war; Lloyd George did too, but failed to keep to it. Churchill was much more rational.

On 20 April, Asquith tried to defend his government's position in a speech at Newcastle that argued that the army did indeed have enough ammunition, which he had been assured by Kitchener was the case. 'I saw a statement the other day,' he said in a clear attack on the Northcliffe press, 'that the operations ... of our army ... were being crippled, or at any rate hampered, by our failure to provide the necessary ammunition. I say there is not a word of truth in that statement, which is the more mischievous, because, if it were believed, it is calculated to dishearten our troops, to discourage our allies, and to stimulate the hopes and activities of our enemies.'[38] By attacking Northcliffe's patriotism in his Newcastle speech, the Prime Minister had made a very powerful, dangerous, bitter, unforgiving and unrelenting enemy for life.

In response to the Newcastle speech, *The Times* expressed 'deep disappointment' over Asquith's 'somewhat petty attempts to prove that he and his colleagues have made no miscalculations and no mistakes'.[39] The *Daily Mail* pointed out that the speech could not be reconciled with Kitchener and Lloyd George's public admissions of a shell shortage. Nor was it only the Northcliffe press that attacked the speech; so did the *Pall Mall Gazette* and *Daily Express*, the latter calling it 'mischievous to a degree'.[40] 'Spent an hour with Northcliffe,' Lloyd George's friend George Riddell wrote in his diary at that time, 'who spoke in contemptuous terms of Asquith and Kitchener. He said that the former was indolent, weak, and apathetic. He exercises no control over various departments. He will never finish the war. L[loyd] G[eorge] may be the man. He is the best of the lot.' A week after the Newcastle speech, Colonel Repington slipped into an article the view in the BEF that it was held back by a 'want of artillery ammunition ... and there is not a man in the Army who is not aware of the fact'.[41]

Asquith himself was proud of his speech, but on 21 April the Unionist Opposition adopted a position that the Northcliffe press had been advocating for some time, for a new ministry of munitions that would institute national industrial mobilisation and go beyond the traditional armaments contractors and government arsenals in the production of shells.[42] Whoever was to provide them, the heavier shells could not arrive too soon: on 22 April, a German offensive led to the Second Battle of Ypres, which continued until 25 May and saw them launch the first great poison gas attack of the war on the Western Front. Northcliffe's response was to write a leader advocating the Allies' use of gas 'to help us advance into Germany'.[43]

When the Allied forces – including large Australian and New Zealand contingents known as the Anzacs – landed at Gallipoli on 25 April 1915, they failed to make the headway that Churchill, Curzon and other Easterners in the War Council had hoped. Asquith failed to call any War Councils between 19 March and 14 May, even though this was the period when the whole nature of the expedition fundamentally changed. Meanwhile, Admiral Jackie Fisher, the First Sea Lord, showed growing opposition to the whole operation. Northcliffe was an old and close friend of Fisher and an admirer of his, and as the news from Gallipoli got worse, Northcliffe became ever more convinced that Churchill should resign. On 29 April, *The Times* editorial described the reverses at Gallipoli as 'a very considerable disaster'.[44]

'I am keenly alive to my responsibilities,' Northcliffe told Riddell on 4 May. 'I am not carrying on *The Times* and the *Daily Mail* from a business point of view. I have a huge income, and might spend my time fishing and amusing myself, but I feel my responsibility to the nation. I feel that I must remain to guide and criticise.'[45] His consciousness of these responsibilities occasionally made him tetchy and difficult to those around him, and it led to a deterioration of relations between Northcliffe and Geoffrey Robinson at this time. Sadly, we only have Robinson's side of the story as related in his diary, and he might have been exaggerating while he let off steam about his boss, who naturally emerges very badly from it. Quotations from the period from 26 to 30 April include: 'Involved in a typhoon with Northcliffe at Perth – raging about nothing at all and generally upsetting things and depressing me!!'; 'The typhoon continued – violent telegrams about blameless leaders, etc, etc. I got into a hopeless state about ever doing anything with the paper'; 'What is one to do against these brainstorms?'; and 'A not quite intelligible state of agitation'.[46]

Northcliffe feared that the Asquith government might invoke the DORA powers to strengthen censorship, especially of soldiers in the trenches who were complaining about the lack of high-explosive shells. On 1 May, he wrote to Sir John French about what he called 'the palpable endeavour of the Government to silence the army' and argued that 'As a further result of secrecy, Mr Asquith is able to assure the nation that your operations have never been hampered by want of ammunition.'[47] He further believed that 'The inevitable result of secrecy will be eventually to cast blame upon you. If the public believe you have 750,000 men, which they do believe, and that you have ample ammunition, which is also believed, it is natural they should ask, "Why is our position in Flanders obviously not improving?"'[48] He suggested that French make 'a short and vigorous statement' that would 'render the Government's position impossible, and enable you to secure the publication of that which would tell the people here the truth and thus bring public pressure upon the Government to stop men and munitions pouring away to the Dardanelles, as they are at present.'[49]

Yet instead of taking a dictatorial attitude, in fact Asquith was experiencing self-doubt, as he wrote to Venetia Stanley at midnight on 3 May. 'I sometimes think that Northcliffe and his obscene crew may perhaps be right – that, whatever the rest of the world may say, I am, if not an imposter, at any rate a failure, and *au fond*, a fool. What is the real test?'[50] Northcliffe would have had a pithy answer to that rhetorical question.

~

The German submarine U-20's torpedoing of the ocean liner *Lusitania* off the southern coast of Ireland on 7 May 1915, with the loss of 1,198 lives, 128 of them American, was described as 'Premeditated Murder' by the *Daily Mail*'s headline the next day. It was all the more personal for Northcliffe as he and Mary had sailed in her five years earlier. Also, in March 1915, Reggie Nicholson had married Natalie Pearson, whose parents perished in the attack.

The war was brought even closer to Northcliffe the next day when his nephew – his sister Geraldine's son Lieutenant Lucas King (known as Luke) – was killed at Ypres. The 4th Battalion of the King's Royal Rifle Corps was in the line east of Bellewaarde Lake and had endured a day of fierce fighting, with shrapnel and high explosives taking a heavy toll. By mid-morning, the shelling was so severe that very little of their trenches remained and it was estimated that around 300 men and three officers of the battalion had been killed. King's body was never retrieved and Northcliffe was said to have exclaimed in his grief for his nephew, 'Kitchener murdered him!'[51]

The following day, Sir John French embarked upon the Battle of Festubert, an attack on Aubers Ridge that failed on the first day after he ran out of shells. The 88,615 eighteen-pounder high-explosive shells that were delivered to the British Army in the whole of May 1915 amounted to half the 176,000 rounds of 77mm shells that the French Army fired on 9 May alone.[52] French later recalled in his autobiography how that day his mind 'was filled with keen anxiety. After all our demands, less than 8% of our shells were H.E., and we only had sufficient supply for about 40 minutes of artillery preparation for the attack.'

French watched the Aubers Ridge from the tower of a ruined church, and nothing

> had ever impressed me so deeply with the terrible shortage of artillery and ammunition as did the events of that day ... I clearly saw the great inequality of the artillery duels, and ... I could see that the absence of sufficient artillery support was doubling and trebling our losses in men. I therefore determined on taking the most drastic measures to destroy the apathy of a Government which had brought the Empire to the brink of disaster.[53]

This determination was compounded when he returned to GHQ and found a telegram from Kitchener 'directing that 20% of our scanty reserve supply of ammunition was to be shipped to the Dardanelles'.[54] This comprised 20,000 rounds of ammunition. In his anger, French showed the letter to his old friend Colonel Repington, the military correspondent of *The Times*.

This was not just a shells scandal, but a heavy gun scandal too. In May 1915, the French had heavy artillery in a healthy ratio of 1 to 2.3 to their field guns. By contrast, the British equivalent was 1 to 20.[55] The French and Germans had recognised the necessity of producing far more munitions at the time of the battle of the Marne in 1914, but the British War Office failed to diffuse contracts across the country's entire engineering capacity, instead concentrating it in the traditional main armament firms.[56] It was not until March 1915 that precision engineering firms started getting contracts for munitions, too late for French's offensives at Neuve-Chapelle and Festubert.

There was also a political rule 'that businessmen offering assistance should not belong to firms with contracts', with Asquith telling George Macaulay Booth, deputy director of Munitions, that he did not want another Marconi Scandal. (Booth retorted that 'businessmen, unlike politicians, could not survive even one scandal'.)[57] On 4 April, Booth was put in charge of the War Office Armaments Output Committee, which recognised that the approved list of munitions providers needed to be drastically widened. It was sensible, but astonishing that the war should have been going on for over eight months before anyone spotted it.

'The magnitude of the manufacturing problem posed by the war was only beginning to be understood in May 1915,' writes an historian. 'By the end of June 1915 some 2,306,800 shells, mostly of light calibre, had been delivered by the manufacturers. Only 1.75% of these were 6-inch or over. At the end of the war some 217,041,200 had been made, 17.5% of which were 6-inch or over.'[58] Similarly, only 1,081 new guns or howitzers had been delivered by the end of June 1915, including only thirty-seven six-inch calibre or above. By the end of the war, the figures were 26,916, including 5,756 of the higher calibres. Northcliffe was accused of exaggerating the Shells Scandal, but these figures belie that.

On 10 May, *The Times* ran an anonymous article by Repington stating that the failure at Festubert on 9 May had been because 'we had not sufficient high explosive to level his parapets ... after the French practice' and the infantry had found 'many entanglements still intact'.[59] The headlines included 'Need for Shells', 'British Attack Checked' and 'Limited Supplies the Cause'.[60]

Though not naming Kitchener, *The Times* ran a strong leading article placing the blame on the War Office. The key sentence that somehow evaded the censor's blue pencil was 'The want of an unlimited supply of high explosive was a fatal bar to our success.'[61] Four years later, the American journalist Isaac Marcosson was to write, 'Never before perhaps in the history of ... war have sixteen words in a newspaper produced such epoch-making results.'[62] Kitchener immediately realised that Sir John French had either encouraged or inspired Repington's article.[63]

Even further against military protocol, French sent two of his staff officers, Colonel FitzGerald and Captain Freddy Guest, to show the entire correspondence between himself and Kitchener over munitions to Lloyd George and the two most senior Opposition politicians, Andrew Bonar Law and Arthur Balfour. These revealed the huge discrepancies between what French had said was needed and what had been delivered. These leaders all saw the opportunity not merely for establishing a munitions ministry separate from the War Office, but also – if the war continued to go badly and press coverage stayed highly critical – even perhaps to force Asquith to widen his ministry from a purely Liberal into a genuinely national government. As one historian has put it, 'The Shells Scandal assumes a larger importance as a question that dramatised for the public the fundamental question of the domestic war effort.'[64]

On Saturday 15 May 1915, the immensely popular and prestigious Admiral Jackie Fisher sensationally resigned as first sea lord over the Dardanelles campaign, blaming Churchill for its failure. Asquith ordered him 'in the King's name' to return to his post, but he did not.[65] This was the spark that was to bring to an end the last Liberal government in British history, especially once expertly fanned by Northcliffe. After the resignation had been confirmed, Bonar Law and Lansdowne wrote to Asquith to say that major changes in the government were needed. That afternoon, the War Council met for the first time in five weeks to debate strengthening the force in the Dardanelles, as Churchill strenuously advocated. Kitchener did not want to do this but, along with Curzon, feared the effect an evacuation would have on Muslim opinion throughout the empire.

Northcliffe met Lloyd George for an hour on Monday 17 May to discuss the crisis, which he later told Riddell had been 'very useful'.[66] The extent to which Northcliffe conspired with Lloyd George during these fraught days is still subject to debate, but their interests certainly aligned in wanting Lloyd George either to become Secretary for War instead of Kitchener or to head a new ministry of munitions separate from the War Office, preferably in a national rather than exclusively Liberal government. Along with a good deal of Fleet Street, the Northcliffe press wanted Churchill to leave the Admiralty instead of Fisher, and Lloyd George was not about to stick by his friend and political ally of ten years if it might be detrimental to his own career. When Bonar Law met Lloyd George on the morning of the 17th, he warned that the Unionists would abandon the party truce agreed at the outbreak of war – by which they did not stand candidates against one another in by-elections – if Churchill remained at the Admiralty.

Northcliffe saw the opportunity for using Unionist discontent to secure several things for which he had been advocating for months – in some cases years – such as military conscription, a new ministry of munitions and a national register of manpower, as well as the conscription of industry into the war effort. He aimed at Total War in a way Lloyd George but not Asquith might effect. Robinson possibly mistook his truculence and 'rages' for excited determination at being instrumental in effecting a revolution in the way the war was being fought. On 18 May, a stinging leader in *The Times* demanded Churchill's resignation from the Admiralty.

On the morning of 19 May, Kitchener asked Lord Esher to discover whether the rumours were true that Lloyd George wanted to

displace him at the War Office. That evening, having taken soundings, Esher reported that 'it seems that the Harmsworth plot is to
get him to the W[ar] O[ffice] if they cannot get him to 10 Downing
Street. It seems to me incredible but there may be something underlying the press reports.'[67] Yet for all the politicians' and journalists'
doubts about him, ordinary Britons still held Kitchener – or at least
the poster version of him – in great veneration.

Northcliffe was thus consciously taking his career into his hands
when, on Thursday 20 May, he personally wrote the leading article
and chose the headline 'The Tragedy of Shells: Lord Kitchener's
Grave Error' for the next morning's *Daily Mail*. Robinson, always
essentially an Establishment man, privately thought Northcliffe's
campaign 'mischievous and unnecessary' and only gave it lukewarm
support in *The Times*.[68] In the words of Tom Driberg, a journalist
and later Labour MP, 'Northcliffe's principal instrument in this
campaign had to be the *Mail*.'[69]

It was to be by far the most consequential article – for good and
ill – ever published by any of Northcliffe's papers in his lifetime,
and thus deserves extensive quotation. 'After vast losses we are just
where we were six months ago on our little line in the Franco-Belgian
frontier,' Northcliffe wrote,

> The real difference in our position is that we have embarked on the
> colossal Dardanelles expedition, of which the German newspapers
> give accurate particulars that are not permitted to be published
> here. We are fighting two great wars at once, and with the wrong
> kind of shell … We *know* that constant appeals for big explosive
> shells have been made to Lord Kitchener from the Front. We
> *know* that until the revelation from *The Times* correspondent, the
> Government itself did not know of these appeals. Sir Alfred Mond
> often tries to tell us that it is only *now* that the need for these
> essentials to success and the preservation of our men has become
> known to our soldiers. That is, in plain English, a lie. Thousands
> of homes are mourning today for men who have been needlessly
> sacrificed. No-one, not Caesar, Alexander nor Napoleon could
> supply men and ammunition to a country unprepared for war. But

there were scores of men, in Parliament and out of it, who could
have read the appeals for High Explosive shells and who could
have organised the factories for making them ... As is not uncommon with men of sixty-five years of age, Lord Kitchener tried to
do everything himself. The war grew more and more serious, more
and more men were required, and the appalling circumstance
arose that whole regiments of the flower of the Empire have been
blotted out of existence. That is why we criticise Lord Kitchener.[70]

The editorial went on to make other serious accusations – 'What we
do know is that Lord Kitchener has starved the Army in France of
High Explosive shells' – and it called explicitly for the removal of
both Kitchener and Churchill, stating that the army and navy should
instead be 'placed in the best available hands'.[71] The specific mention
of Sir Alfred Mond, a rich industrialist and Liberal MP for Swansea,
seems strange, unless it was because of his German and Jewish background. Mond had indeed stated that the war would be brief and
would cost 300,000 British jobs, but that had been back in August
1914 and he had made no such statements since then.

What caused utter outrage throughout Britain was Northcliffe's
ad hominem attack on Kitchener in his editorial. 'It has never been
pretended that Lord Kitchener is a soldier in the sense that Sir John
French is a soldier,' he wrote of the victor of the battle of Omdurman.
'Lord Kitchener is a gatherer of men – and a very fine gatherer
too.' This struck readers as faint praise for the man who had won
the River War in the Sudan. 'His record in South Africa as a fighting general,' Northcliffe went on, 'was not brilliant.'[72] Here, too,
Northcliffe was opening himself to severe criticism as Kitchener had
been Roberts's chief of staff and successor as commander-in-chief in
the ultimately victorious Boer War.

'The admitted fact is that Lord Kitchener ordered the wrong
kind of shells ... the same kind of shell he had ordered against the
Boers in 1900. He persisted in sending shrapnel – a useless weapon
in trench warfare.' Northcliffe was thus accusing Kitchener of
that most common of errors – fighting the last war – but it was
far from an 'admitted fact' that Kitchener had ordered shrapnel

shells, rather than high-explosive ones, out of nostalgia or atavism. Nobody else had predicted 400 miles of trenches in a matter of months after the outbreak of war. Moreover, Northcliffe alleged that Kitchener had been

> warned repeatedly that the kind of shell required was a violently explosive bomb that would dynamite its way through the German trenches and entanglements and enable our brave men to advance safely. The kind of shell our poor soldiers have had caused the death of thousands of them. Incidentally it has brought about a Cabinet Crisis and the formation of what we hope is going to be a national Government.[73]

The leader was journalistic high-explosive dynamite to fire against the government, and Northcliffe knew it. Showing it to a sceptical H. W. Wilson, he told him 'the thing has to be done! Better to lose circulation than lose the war.'[74] (Another, later, version has Northcliffe saying, 'Better lose circulation than lose the British Empire.'[75]) When he took it to Thomas Marlowe, the editor sought to warn him too. 'You realise, I suppose, that you are smashing the people's idol?' 'I don't care,' Northcliffe replied. 'Isn't it all true?'[76] 'Quite true,' replied Marlowe, who had recently met some of French's staff officers himself, 'but it will make the public very angry. Are you prepared for the consequences?' 'I don't care tuppence for the consequences,' said Northcliffe. 'That man is losing the war!'[77] In fact, this editorial was going to cost him many thousands of pounds. Only one person was allowed to alter the editorial before publication, and that was Mother, to whose house in Totteridge he drove that night, and her changes were more of emphasis than material.

Northcliffe knew from Asquith's Newcastle speech that he would most likely be accused of aiding and abetting the enemy with his editorial, and with his sixth sense for public opinion he prepared himself for the rage that it was about to engender, assuming that it would only be short term before he was proved right. 'On the night when the *Daily Mail* printed it,' recalled Henry Wickham Steed years later,

I found Lord Northcliffe sitting in the editor's room at *The Times* office with an expression more grim than I had ever seen on his face or ever saw again. In after years he often referred to his article and maintained that it had been necessary. 'I did not care whether the circulation dropped to one copy and that of the *Daily Mail* to two,' he would say. 'I consulted no one about it* except my mother, and she agreed with it. I felt the war was becoming too big for Kitchener, and that public belief in him, which was indispensable at the outset, was becoming an obstacle to military progress. Therefore I did my best to shake things up.'[78]

On his way into the office on Friday 21 May, Northcliffe told Pine, his chauffeur, 'I wonder what Lord Kitchener thinks of the *Daily Mail* today – I'll bet it made him jump! I mean to tell the people the truth and I don't care what it costs.'[79] It was to cost a good deal, as the universal fury that met the editorial meant that the circulation dropped by 238,000 copies overnight, and then continued to fall. Both the *Mail* and *The Times* – despite Robinson's refusal to join the criticism of Kitchener – were ceremonially burnt on the floor of the Stock Exchange, Baltic Exchange and Liverpool Provision Exchange, amid cheers for Kitchener from 1,500 brokers.† People sent pieces of charred *Daily Mail* to Northcliffe in the post. Trade unions passed motions condemning the buying of the *Daily Mail* by their members. A placard reading 'The Allies of the Huns' was hung outside the *Daily Mail*'s City office, while Northcliffe had to be given special police protection.[80]

The gentlemen's clubs of St James's cancelled their subscriptions to the *Daily Mail*, though they could not bring themselves to go quite that far over *The Times*. The *Mail* was banned at many public libraries and at the Oxford Union.[81] A. G. Gardiner, never one to let an anti-Northcliffe opportunity go by, called for his arrest under

---

* He had forgotten Wilson and Marlowe by the time he retold the story.
† Who might have held a private grudge against Northcliffe for establishing the Daily Mail Exchange to help readers in their share transactions without paying stockbrokers' commission.

the Defence of the Realm Act, adding that 'the Government have hesitated to deal with him, chiefly no doubt out of respect for our tradition of a free press and free criticism, but there comes a time when even the freedom of the press must give place to the safety of the State. That time has come.'[82] Not to be outdone, the novelist Arnold Bennett described Northcliffe as 'this frenzied office boy who skulks behind his newspapers – this unscrupulous adventurer whose whole career has been a record of vulgar sensationalism'.[83]

Northcliffe was attacked by the *Daily News*, *Star*, *Spectator* ('outrageous'), *Nation* (for spreading the 'poison of uncertainty'), and many other weekly magazines. When Hannen Swaffer chaffed him about his rivals wanting him to be sent to the Tower of London, Northcliffe replied: 'All they've got to say about me, when I tell the truth about shells, is that I own *Comic Cuts*! And it's a fine paper. It makes a lot of money and it's always clean. I wish I could say the same about some of their divorce reports.'[84] To Tom Clarke he noted that 'We are getting a lot of free advertising from competing newspapers.'[85] The sole paper from outside the Northcliffe stable to support him was Garvin's *Observer*.

Northcliffe was hanged in effigy, and 5,000 (overwhelmingly abusive) letters were received in one day. When a professor wrote to say that his views were 'written for the gutter from the gutter' and accused him of political ambition, Northcliffe replied, 'I am not a politician, nor am I interested in such people.'[86] When, as early as 11am on 21 May, Valentine Smith, Associated Newspapers' circulation manager, told Northcliffe that the editorial had already led to at least 100,000 cancelled subscriptions and that he was being 'bombarded with orders reducing supplies', Northcliffe replied 'I don't care,' albeit now in a quieter tone. 'What I wrote was true. Our men out there are being killed because there are no shells to smash down the German defences. I'm determined that they shall have them.'[87]

Just as seriously for his papers' financial future, there was a boycott organised by advertisers who were fearful of being tainted by association with Northcliffe. He remembered who they were for years afterwards, and eventually made them pay financially for what he saw as their disloyalty and cowardice. Even four years later, he could remember the names of the Pall Mall clubs that had cancelled their subscriptions.[88]

'On the very day that the *Daily Mail* was burnt in the City of London and advertisers were cancelling their contracts by the thousands,' Evelyn Wrench later wrote, 'I recall walking with him through the peaceful passages and purlieus of the Temple. Never did Northcliffe appear to me of more heroic mould. Northcliffe knew his facts were right, he was intensely patriotic and nothing would deflect him from the course of telling the people the truth.'[89] Wrench saw him on several occasions during the Shells crisis; 'He never showed to greater advantage. He was entirely single-minded. He was not playing for his own hand. He was sincerely convinced that Kitchener was a muddler.' Northcliffe told Wrench, 'I will continue to tell the truth in my papers.'[90]

'All day the telephones have been buzzing with protests from readers,' Tom Clarke noted in his diary on 21 May,

> and intimations that they will never buy our 'damned rag' again … Hundreds of abusive letters and telegrams are coming in. A bank manager telephoned me tonight to say that all his staff had agreed to buy the *Daily Mail* no more … The evening papers castigate us furiously … There's a special police guard at Carmelite House, and all the gates are locked … At five o'clock we sat awaiting the Chief. Wearing a blue suit, a green slouch hat, and chewing the end of a big cigar, he came quietly in and, dropping into an easy chair, said 'I have thrown off another string of pearls for you today.* … What's the news?' When the *Star* and other papers attacking him were produced, also the report of the Stock Exchange burnings, he threw them aside and said, 'That shows they don't know the truth. Why, even today General French has told Asquith that, if things don't improve, he will leave his job to come to England and stump the country to acquaint the people with the true state of affairs at the front.'[91]

---

* That is, written another leader.

It was not true about French; Northcliffe said it to keep up morale, despite saying that he alone was reporting the truth.

Hannen Swaffer was also in the *Daily Mail* conference that day. He recalled that on Northcliffe's entry, the staff stood up as usual. Northcliffe put on his big horn-rimmed spectacles and sat in an armchair beside Marlowe's desk. 'Have you seen *The Star*, Chief?' asked Marlowe. 'No,' joked Northcliffe, 'I never read those racing papers.' 'You'd better look at it.'[92] On the top of the fourth column of the front page of the 6.30pm edition was the headline '*Daily Mail* burned on the Stock Exchange'. Having glanced at it, Northcliffe said, 'I don't know what you men think and I don't care. *The Star* is wrong and I am right. And the day will come when you will all know that I am right. Fish, what's on the schedule?'[93] They then discussed the next day's paper.

That evening, Northcliffe went back to see his mother. 'I motored alone with him to dine at Totteridge the day the *Mail* was burnt on the Stock Exchange,' recalled Max Pemberton's son Arthur about the journey. 'I shall never forget his intense patriotism and his unaffected calm on that occasion.'[94] In many ways, Friday, 21 May 1915 was Lord Northcliffe's finest hour. Tom Driberg described his struggle over shells as 'unquestionably the most patriotic of all Northcliffe's campaigns'.[95] Years later, Northcliffe was to tell Isaac Marcosson that he 'was animated in this matter by two fundamental principles. One was truth and the other was necessity.'[96]

One of Northcliffe's favourite phrases was 'Every knock's a boost', and the shells article served to remind ordinary soldiers on the Western Front that there was someone willing to take on the Establishment so that they might have the correct type and number of munitions needed to support them before they went 'over the top'.[97] While *The Daily Mail* and *The Times* were being burned at the Stock Exchange, the future journalist Linton Andrews was in the trenches and 'felt that Northcliffe was the soldier's friend. Cruel experience of battle frustration, slaughter, and wounds convinced us that he was right.'[98] When officers serving at the Front wrote letters home to support Northcliffe's allegations about the lack of high-explosive shells, they were refused publication by the Press Bureau censors, so they posted them to Northcliffe who sent them on to Lloyd George and Curzon. 'They know the truth,' Clarke noted in his diary of the politicians, 'and it will let them see how the Press Bureau is keeping it back.'[99]

It helped Northcliffe's position enormously that, after the stabilisation of the Front in 1914, the *Continental Daily Mail*, which was published in Paris, reached the troops with great regularity on the date of issue and thus gained a large readership amongst the men in the trenches.[100] Other weekly publications such as *John Bull*, *La Vie Parisienne* (for the illustrations of young ladies that adorned many a dugout), *Bystander* and *Punch* were read, and kept up the troops' spirits, but the *Continental Daily Mail* was the paper of choice for the other ranks of the BEF, not least because it was perceived to stick up for their interests.[101]

Many senior army officers were nonetheless highly supportive of Kitchener over the shells controversy, perhaps unsurprisingly as he controlled all promotions. General Douglas Haig wrote to Kitchener's secretary Oswald Fitzgerald about how 'thoroughly disgusted we all are here at the attacks which the reptile Harmsworth press have made on Lord Kitchener'.[102] General Ian Hamilton, who commanded the Gallipoli campaign, wrote to Kitchener that 'They say a nation gets the Press it deserves, but surely the British Empire has never done anything bad enough to earn itself a Harmsworth!'[103]

In one important sense, Northcliffe had blundered badly. The outpouring of support for Kitchener made him virtually impregnable at the War Office.[104] By 25 May, Asquith had concluded that he was now permanently unsackable.[105] After he received the Order of the Garter in the next Birthday Honours list, Kitchener joked: 'I suppose for the future if I want anything, I have only got to get French to write me up!'[106]

Dangerously, the article also provided a political atmosphere in which the government could seriously consider limiting press freedom; several ministers supported what Margot Asquith, the Prime Minister's wife, approvingly described as 'an attempt to muzzle Northcliffe'.[107] Lord Esher 'begged' Asquith to close down Northcliffe's papers.[108] He later complained to Buckingham Palace officials that the Northcliffe press was acting like the Spanish Inquisition, and ought to be brought under control by law.

On 21 May, *The Times* had published a letter under the heading 'The Need for Compulsion' from a Major E. H. Richardson of Grove End, Harrow, who had been a military attaché to the French Army, stating that 'The last of the French reserves are out, and at the present moment young raw recruits are being called out.'[109] In England, by contrast, 'I came across scores of lusty, able-bodied young men walking about in smug complacency, utterly callous and indifferent to the anguish of their brothers, so long as they got their war bonus.' The French Army complained about this to the French Embassy in London, which in turn complained to the War Office, which decided to prosecute *The Times* under the DORA regulations for 'publishing information which might be directly useful to the enemy'.[110] Late on the evening of Saturday 29 May, *The Times* was therefore served with a summary injunction to appear at the Mansion House magistrates court early on the morning of Monday 31st, with the hope that Northcliffe would have no time to prepare a defence.

J. E. Mackenzie, the former Berlin correspondent of *The Times* who produced the daily digest of the enemy papers entitled 'Through German Eyes', happened to be in the office when the summons was served. He promptly amassed articles in many German papers such as the *Frankfurter Zeitung* and *Kölnische Zeitung*, as well as public debates in the French Assembly that proved that the state of French reserves was common knowledge. This gained a long enough adjournment at Mansion House for Northcliffe to secure Gordon Hewart QC (who would later become a Lord Chief Justice) to represent him. 'The Government thought it had found a sturdy cudgel wherewith to beat *The Times* and Lord Northcliffe,' recalled Wickham Steed, 'and would not let it go.'[111] Steed persuaded Paul Cambon, the French ambassador, to deny that the prosecution was being brought on the insistence of the French government, which was used by Hewart in his cross-examination of the War Office colonel who had given the opposite impression at the initial hearing. The magistrate then dismissed the government's case as baseless.

On the morning of Sunday 23 May, Northcliffe drove over to

Lloyd George's house at Walton Heath in Surrey. According to the diary of Lloyd George's extremely well-informed secretary and mistress, Frances Stevenson, Northcliffe

> was all for C[hancellor, her shorthand for Lloyd George] taking over Munitions, and not allowing the Tories to get it. He told C that they had begun intriguing already against the Liberals, and he was afraid the [coming] national government would not last long. He also told C that they had been trying to bribe the Harmsworth Press, offering to make Lord Northcliffe's brother B[onar] Law's assistant at the War Office if Northcliffe backed Bonar Law for the War Office and he succeeded in getting in. Dirty work when the country is in peril![112]

On 26 May 1915, Asquith formed a coalition government with the Unionists. Churchill was demoted from First Lord of the Admiralty to a ministry without portfolio, and replaced by Balfour; Lloyd George was appointed to the new Ministry of Munitions; Kitchener stayed on as War Secretary; Reginald McKenna took Lloyd George's job as Chancellor of the Exchequer, and Bonar Law became Colonial Secretary. Despite being Asquith's closest friend in politics, Haldane lost his post as Lord Chancellor. Northcliffe was unhappy about the promotion of McKenna, whom he did not rate, and of course about the retention of Kitchener and the refusal to have Fisher back at the Admiralty. He was delighted by the demotion of Churchill, the appointment of Carson – whose iron toughness he admired – as Attorney-General, and especially the departure of Haldane. His papers therefore welcomed the National Government, which the *Daily Mail* thought 'will satisfy the country'.[113] Northcliffe meanwhile wrote to Lloyd George to say that he had the 'heaviest responsibility that has fallen on any Briton for a hundred years', thereby equating it with Wellington's responsibility in June 1815 to defeat Napoleon at the battle of Waterloo.[114]

CHAPTER 14

GALLIPOLI AND CONSCRIPTION

May 1915–May 1916

'Lord Northcliffe was undoubtedly the most powerful
newspaper owner that has yet existed in this, or perhaps
in any country, and during the war he was at the height
of his power. Such a phenomenon no government could
wisely disregard.'[1]

ALFRED DUFF COOPER, *Haig* 1935

'Hundreds of letters continue to pour in daily protesting against the
Kitchener attack,' noted Tom Clarke on 27 May 1915, but nonetheless Northcliffe wrote the 'splash' headline 'Truth WILL OUT:
The Shell Scandal' for an article about the effect of the shortage of
high-explosive shells, which quoted Lord Lansdowne, the Duke of
Rutland, Bishop Furse, and recently returned Western Front officers
in support. He kept up private pressure too, writing to Lord Curzon,
the new Foreign Secretary, to say that:

Quite apart from the horrors that have taken place owing to the
lack of explosives, there are many revelations concerning the
shocking lack of preparation of what are called Kitchener's Armies
at home. After ten months there is a vast shortage of rifles, and
practically no machine guns or ammunition for practice ... I do
not publish this matter, as it might be valuable information for
the Germans, but I certainly think it should be known to those

like yourself who have taken upon themselves the responsibility of membership in this Cabinet.[2]

Sensing that a change of policy might be possible with the new government, Northcliffe also redoubled his efforts over compulsory military conscription. On 27 May, *The Times* carried a letter from Lord Milner suggesting that 'The State ought not to be obliged to tout for fighting men. It ought to be in a position to call out the number it wants, as and when it wants them, and to call them out in the right order.'[3]

Although *The Manchester Guardian* attacked Northcliffe's campaign as 'the victory of German methods' and the same kind of militarism against which Britain was fighting, Lloyd George's first speech as minister of munitions on 3 June acknowledged that compulsion might be necessary so as not to lose the war.[4] He recognised that organised labour was presently opposed, but 'If Germany wins, God help labour in this country.'[5] The next day, Margot Asquith hectored Kitchener for his supposed weakness over the press, saying 'You look like a strong man but you aren't! Why didn't you have that cur Northcliffe arrested!'[6] She also told her husband that 'I must get someone to explain why we allow Northcliffe to write any and every lie that he thinks "copy".'[7]

Margot, easily the most outspoken consort ever to occupy Downing Street, was right to hate and fear Northcliffe. At the printers' charity dinner the following day, Northcliffe was in the chair and told Riddell that 'he intended to attack Kitchener again, and also to attack Asquith, of whom he spoke in slighting terms'.[8] He also predicted that 'someone will turn up. The war will disclose a genius.' He then suggested that it might be Lloyd George.[9]

Earlier that day, Churchill made a speech in Dundee that Lovat Fraser depicted to Northcliffe as a 'mad and wicked proposal' to do no less than 'muzzle the Press'.[10] To loud cheers, Churchill had told his constituents:

I do not think that the newspapers ought to be allowed to attack the responsible leaders of the nation, whether in the field or at home, or to write in a manner which is calculated to spread doubts and want of confidence in them or in particular operations, or to write anything which is calculated to make bad blood between them. I apply this not only to the admirals and generals, but to the principal ministers at home, and especially the heads of the great fighting departments.'[11]

The reference was clearly to his falling out with Jackie Fisher over Gallipoli, and he went on to say that 'No other nation now at war would allow the newspapers such a licence in the present time, and if there is to be criticism, if there must be criticism, first, it should be only the loyal criticism of earnest intention.'

Churchill condemned 'irresponsible or malicious carping' and claimed that 'owing to war conditions, Parliament observes a voluntary but severe restraint, and when many of the subjects cannot be freely discussed without giving information to the enemy, then the balance of society is no longer true and grave injury results from the unrestricted action of the newspapers.'[12] As well as this clear assault on press freedom, Churchill also defended Haldane, saying that 'I deeply regret that he has ceased to fill the great office which he adorned. No more sincere patriot has served the Crown.'[13]

Fortunately for Northcliffe, Churchill's clear intimations in favour of increased censorship – or perhaps even nationalisation of the press for the duration of the war – were not taken up by Asquith. Churchill, Margot, her stepson Raymond Asquith, Lord Esher, A. G. Gardiner and so many others routinely ascribed malicious (and often pecuniary) motives to Northcliffe, as did even political allies like Bonar Law who, in July, described him in a private letter as 'one of the most jumpy of men and rushes at everything without regard to anything except his own vanity'.[14] Few wished to contemplate the possibility that Northcliffe genuinely thought the war was being prosecuted badly and was patriotically speaking truth to power.

One day around this time, Northcliffe and J. A. Hammerton left Fleetway House in Farringdon Street, where Amalgamated Press was based, and were walking to lunch in the private room at Printing House Square. As they reached the corner of Ludgate

Circus, Hammerton said that he thought Northcliffe was 'going to come out on top' over the Shells Crisis. 'I can see him now,' Hammerton wrote seventeen years later, 'instantly reacting to this piece of casual slang, stopping for a moment or two on the thronging pavement and saying in his gravest manner, "Never say that again. I don't want to come out on top. I want Britain to come out on top. Where I come out doesn't matter. Never suggest such an idea to anybody. I don't like to hear it."'[15] For Hammerton, 'He was so swift in his rebuke . . . and so earnest in his manner that he impressed me with the conviction of truth. I did not doubt then, nor do I now, that what he said he felt.'[16]

On 6 June, prior to a ninety-minute conversation with Northcliffe at Walton Heath, Lloyd George told Riddell that Kitchener had indeed 'covered up and distorted the figures' over ammunition.[17] After the meeting, he said of Northcliffe, 'He is a most extraordinary person.'[18] The next day, Margot predicted to her step-daughter Violet Asquith that 'Northcliffe will try to run Ll[oyd] George against father now! I see tiny signs of it.'[19] Maurice Bonham Carter, Asquith's private secretary and Violet's fiancé, could not spot it, though, and, at the time of Lloyd George's passing of the Munitions Bill, wrote to Violet saying that Lloyd George 'was of course accused of deep intrigue with N[orthcliffe], but that I never believed – but he certainly was playing with fire'.[20] Raymond Asquith hated Northcliffe quite as much as Margot did, telling his wife Katherine that he had 'got to the stage now when I would rather beat Harmsworth than beat the Germans. He seems to me just as aggressively stupid and stupidly aggressive as they are, and much less brave and efficient.'[21]

If there was an active conspiracy between Northcliffe and Lloyd George to make the latter prime minister, it was not a very effective one; there were nineteen months of stalemate and slaughter between the formation of the National Government and the fall of Asquith. There is certainly nothing to suggest a conspiracy in either Lloyd George's or Northcliffe's extensive private correspondence, although of course the avoidance of putting anything on paper is not disproof of a plot. Much more likely is that both men were simply responding to political events as they unfolded, while both having the strong belief that Lloyd George would be a far superior premier to Asquith.

On 9 June, Margot upbraided Lloyd George for telling Churchill that he 'thought Northcliffe a hero', which Lloyd George denied doing, but when he said that Northcliffe 'had done the right thing over the shells', Margot told him he had 'said a very wrong and very foolish thing ... mark my words, I've said this before and I'll say it again as a warning, Lord Northcliffe will run you against Henry [that is, her husband Henry Herbert Asquith]. He has already tried and he will go on and I shall back *Henry* to score if this happens.' Lloyd George smiled and said, 'My dear friend, wicked I may be, but I'm not a damned fool. As I said to Winston, "Do you really think I don't know what Northcliffe is? Why, he'll turn on me and stab me in the back at any moment."'[22] 'Then why do you praise him?' Margot asked.

> He is responsible for many, many deaths in this Ypres line by deliberately fostering and encouraging the generals to quarrel ... It's a low thing just to sell your papers to write sensational reports – 'Great Shell Scandal, Shortage' etc, etc, for all the German papers to copy ... Northcliffe has run his paper for himself, he doesn't know there is a war going on. He has got no heart. He's a regular Yankee, and has missed a *great* opportunity.[23]

A good deal of this strange rant was frankly unhinged, especially the part about the Second Battle of Ypres, but Margot had spotted early on Northcliffe's desire to put Lloyd George in her husband's place. On 15 June, she wrote to her stepson Arthur 'Oc' Asquith: 'That vile paper *The Times* (& *Daily Mail*) is running conscription for all it is worth ... Northcliffe ought to be shot but it's too good a death.'[24] As for her insight about Northcliffe running Lloyd George against her husband – 'I saw it like fish in a glass bowl (I'm really a sort of political clairvoyante)' – it hardly took much psychic power to spot that Lloyd George would be the obvious vigorous, energetic alternative to the lethargic, distracted, unmartial Asquith.[25]

'Mr Asquith, do you take an interest in the war?' Lady Tree asked him politely one day.[26] He passed the remark on, commenting that she had 'a good though often disguised sense of humour'. Even Asquith's admiring biographer Roy Jenkins admitted that Asquith 'was too eclectic to fill his mind with any single subject and too fastidious to pretend to an enthusiasm which he did not feel'.[27] By total contrast, Northcliffe believed, as he told Wickham Steed, that 'In these great days, the breath of war is the breath of life, and the spirit of sacrifice is the spirit of regeneration.'[28]

~

The war was never far away: London suffered its first Zeppelin raid on 1 June 1915 and, when telephoning Riddell from Elmwood on 13 June, Northcliffe said that he could hear the guns of the Battle of Artois booming across the Channel. Two days later, he wrote to tell Lloyd George that he believed 'the hushing up of the Dardanelles difficulty to be a fatal blunder'.[29] The next day, *The Times*, which had tended to be more circumspect under the Establishment man Robinson, summed up its complaints about the government succinctly, mentioning 'the waste of public money in camps and ships, the gross injustice of the present methods of promiscuous recruiting, the refusal to face the truth about our various campaigns, above all the deplorable lack of foresight about munitions of war'.[30] It was a formidable list.

On 29 June, Walter Long, the Unionist minister for local government, introduced the National Registration Bill in the Commons, which became law on 15 July and compelled every individual to state whether their occupation was 'serving war purposes'. This was not enough for Northcliffe, whose papers called for the immediate conscription of able-bodied males. By July, the *Daily Mail*'s circulation was back above a million; in the light of this, the paper was proudly describing itself as 'The Paper That Revealed the Shell Tragedy'.[31]

While Asquith, Long and several other ministers did not think compulsion was necessary since men were still volunteering in large numbers, Lloyd George, Curzon and Churchill did support it, because they believed the war was likely to go on for a long time. For Britons to accept mass compulsion for the first time in their history,

however, they needed to be persuaded, and Northcliffe was crucial
to that process. Kitchener refused to say that compulsion was necessary as he thought it bad for morale, but he was publicly asking for
an army of between seventy and a hundred divisions, which would
require one and a half million more men, at a time when the present
recruitment rates would only produce one million.[32] Northcliffe was
in advance of his times during this great debate: in the Second World
War, there was no discussion about the right of the state to compel
its citizens to defend it.

On 1 July, Northcliffe lunched with Sir George Riddell at *The
Times* offices. 'Northcliffe, laughing, said he would not trust his
money to Lloyd George,' Riddell recorded in his diary afterwards.
'He is too venturesome. N described LG as a *simple* man, who may
easily be ruined by his enemies and rivals!'[33] Riddell correctly disagreed as to Lloyd George's simplicity, but did not trouble to argue
further. Three days later, Northcliffe arrived at Walton Heath at 3pm
and stayed for another ninety minutes to discuss the ammunition
shortage. He was, as Lloyd George told Riddell, 'very gloomy. He
prophesied ... that a great national disaster is impending, probably
within a fortnight or three weeks, and that the present ministry
will be swept away. He expressed his anxiety that L[loyd] G[eorge]
should survive the flood.'[34]

At the meeting, and in clear contravention of the Official Secrets
Act, Lloyd George showed Northcliffe a War Office paper contain-
ing the amounts of ammunition ordered and supplied which seemed
to show that during March, April, and May 1915 only about 50,000
high-explosive shells per month had been supplied to the army in
France and in the Dardanelles.[35] That further convinced him of the
deleterious effect the Gallipoli campaign was having on the Western
Front, and puts into context Robinson's diary entry of 6 July that
Northcliffe was 'on the warpath about a long dispatch from Ian
Hamilton about the Dardanelles ... N[orthcliffe] kept me on the
go from early morning.'[36] By 13 July, Margot Asquith's estimation
of *The Times* and *Daily Mail*'s coverage of the war was that 'one
can only imagine that Lord Northcliffe is pro-German and expects
Germany to win. I think the Coalition idiotic to let him squeal and

scream. As for Geoffrey Robinson, editor of *The Times*, I will never shake hands with him again.'[37]

At a luncheon at the Ritz on 15 July given by his employees in honour of his fiftieth birthday, Northcliffe said that he had no regrets about criticising the government. 'If only all this munition problem had been tackled six months ago, things would have been in a very different state.'[38] He added that if any employee

> did not feel like going through with it under his leadership, now was the time for them to quit. He said his papers had been burned on the Stock Exchange; maybe they would burn Carmelite House next. He did not care. He had other plant and resources. They would have to destroy him or supply the troops with shells. Every farthing of his personal fortune was going into this struggle. He was liable to be ruined. He warned them of that; and again said those who could not go all the way with him should quit now.[39]

There was a slightly histrionic edge to all this of course and, when Northcliffe went to Boulogne at dawn the next morning for his fourth visit to the Front, Robinson privately called it 'a blessed riddance'.[40]

The combination of hatred and paranoiac fantasy that sometimes affected people regarding Northcliffe was on full display in August 1915 when J. C. C. Davidson, Bonar Law's private secretary and a lifelong Establishment insider, wrote to the colonial administrator Douglas Jardine about the question of National Service. 'The Harmsworth Press has taken it up and that, of course, is the first reason for suspicion,' Davidson wrote. 'I think that the days of *The Times* are numbered. Northcliffe is, I understand from those who know him and have dealt with him, convinced that Germany is going to win and he is therefore determined to be on the winning side.'[41] Quite how a demand for conscription could be construed as pro-German Davidson failed to explain, but he added that 'Except for a very very few cranks there is no single respectable person in the country, certainly no member of the Cabinet, whether Tory or Liberal, who thinks conscription either necessary or even possible.

We are not a military nation: we do not require an army on a conti-nental basis.'[42] It showed the challenge Northcliffe faced in order to get conscription adopted and the depth of hostility he faced, even to the extent of accusations of incipient treachery.

Lieutenant-General Sir Frederick Stopford's botched amphibious landings at Suvla Bay on the Gallipoli peninsula on 6 August drew a predictably caustic response from Northcliffe, who wrote to Carson, another sceptic, that 'The Germans are intimately informed of our impending catastrophe. Can nothing be done to minimise it?' He added of Kitchener that 'Your speeches suggest that my newspapers have some motive in criticising him. I do not know Lord Kitchener personally, but for ten months he had the power of Oliver Cromwell as to shells. Today he has the same power as to compulsion. I don't trust Lord Kitchener.'[43] As for the growing Anglophobia in France, Northcliffe boasted that 'The Times and Daily Mail secret service abroad is I think at least as good as your Government's.'[44] The dividing lines between egotism, vanity and megalomania are thin and porous, and Northcliffe's last sentence at least crossed from the first into the second, although he was still a long way from the last.

When the government finally brought in a national register for con-scription in mid-August, the Daily Mail noted that it still lacked the power of compulsion. Northcliffe had been advocating conscription since the outbreak of war, besides having been for years an active supporter of Alfred Milner's National Service League. In mid-August, he stepped up the campaign in the Mail, believing it vital to maintain Britain's credibility with her less reliable allies such as Russia and Italy, as well as being a military necessity in itself. On 16 August, the Daily Mail printed a pro-conscription form to be cut out, filled in and sent to the government. The paper criticised the 'unfairness' of the recent national register as it had no power over 'slackers'.[45]

Although Lloyd George supported the campaign for National Service, for many Liberals it was a profoundly difficult moral ques-tion as to whether the state had the right to force its citizens to fight, and thus perhaps die, for it. Northcliffe was convinced that the state certainly did have that right, and indeed under the present German onslaught might not survive without it. Over the following weeks and months, the Northcliffe press urged the government to pass compulsory military service for every able-bodied male. After the King told Milner at Windsor that he disapproved of the idea, Milner, in his biographer's words, 'attributed the King's disapproval to dislike of Northcliffe'.[46] Milner nonetheless wrote to the king afterwards saying that Northcliffe's agitation had rendered it 'impossible for those who honestly believe that the adoption of National Service . . . essential to avert defeat, to sit still and do nothing'.[47]

Asquith was trying to fight a world war in a way that did not require Total War, yet a world war against Imperial Germany could not be fought on the same basis as the Sudan War or Boer War, with limited involvement from the population at home. Instead it required the harnessing of all national resources, foremost amongst which was manpower, with the state stepping in to direct it. Conscription was necessary in a war of attrition, and was employed by all the other Great Powers. The sooner it was instituted, the more training the citizen's army could have before it was flung into the trenches.

Most modern historians recognise that the Great War could not have been won without conscription, and the Unionists at the time understood that it could not continue to be fought on a purely volunteer basis. It was estimated that there were about 650,000 men who were eligible but not volunteering, whom the Northcliffe press unhesitatingly described as 'slackers' and worse. In the autumn, Lord Derby, the national director of recruiting, instituted a scheme whereby all able-bodied eighteen-to-forty-one-year-olds were asked voluntarily to 'attest' to their willingness to serve in due course. Northcliffe supported this last call for volunteers, despite it falling short of compulsory conscription, because of the unspoken proviso, which Kitchener supported, that if it failed to plug the gaps in recruitment then compulsion would be used. (The Derby Scheme was greatly helped by the sense of horror when the Germans executed the British nurse Edith Cavell by firing squad at dawn on 12 October 1915 in Brussels.)

On 18 August, Margot wrote a 'Very Secret' letter to Arthur Balfour asking 'Are we – the Government – really powerless to deal with Northcliffe? You don't perhaps see the *Daily Mail* (*I* don't – but it is sent to me in batches of letters from strangers cursing Henry and the Cabinet for what I agree appears weakness in not dealing with Northcliffe).'48 In this, Margot joined a long list of people – then as now – who claim never to have read the *Daily Mail* yet who seemed to have a very good idea of what was in it. She advocated using Defence of the Realm Act provisions, and if that did not work, suggested that 'we should take powers', saying, 'I warn you that Northcliffe has backed himself to break this Cabinet and he will do it.'49

~

For all that Northcliffe could at times be tough and ruthless, there was a soft side to his character that came through in his touching love for children. When, in September 1915, J. M. N. Jeffries visited Elmwood to discuss the progress of the war, he arrived at the same time that a group of thirty or forty young orphan girls from a nearby convent were playing games and having tea on the lawns along with several of their nuns. 'Whatever emotions Lord Northcliffe gained from his achievements in the great world,' Jeffries noted, 'amongst these children it was plain to see that he enjoyed pure felicity. He shook hands with them, patted their heads, rumpled their hair, called them one and all "my dear", took part in their games of ring-o'-roses. He beamed at the nuns and chaffed them.'50 There were unlimited chocolates. When they left, Jeffries noticed Northcliffe 'leaning stretched far out of a low casement window, waving his hand loosely from the wrist in "bye-bye!" fashion to the departing children'. Even when they had turned the corner and gone, he 'stayed in the window and gazed up the empty drive, pensively, with his hand slowed but still waving up and down, for a minute or more'.51

Louise Owen recalled how much Northcliffe loved his illegitimate child Alfred Benjamin Smith, writing of how 'It was most pathetic to see Northcliffe hungering for the affection of this boy. That great paternal love of which he was capable centred in his son, and Northcliffe was anxious for him to live in a suitable, homely atmosphere.'52 He was also kind to Mrs Wrohan's adopted children, and we cannot know whether he knew they were not his own. In June 1946, his former private secretary Humphrey Davy recalled Northcliffe playing with the two boys and a girl at Elmwood, which was

> the place where he most liked to entertain friends who frequently came on visits. There none of his guests were more welcome than three children. At one moment he would be engaged in discussing important press or political matters on the telephone with one of his directors or editors, and then, when that was over, he would go back to the room where the children were. There he would sit down on the floor – which children much prefer to being perched up on chairs – and continue playing with them; joining in their fun as if he were an elder brother, as happy as a sand-boy and free from all their cares. The little visitors called him 'Harmy'.[53]

Meanwhile, Mary found love. It is likely to have been in the autumn of 1915 that her relations with Sir Robert Hudson, the chairman of the finance committee of the Red Cross and a former chief agent of the Liberal Party, moved beyond the purely friendly. They had first met in October 1914 when Mary joined the committee. Once Hudson helped set up *The Times* Red Cross Fund, which raised millions of pounds for wounded soldiers, Northcliffe and Hudson became friends. Mary was setting up a hospital for wounded officers at No. 16 Grosvenor Crescent in Belgravia and it is likely that both that and her weekly lunches for Red Cross workers at St James's Palace provided opportunities for Mary and Robert's attraction to blossom into love.[54] She certainly worked hard for the organisation; Mary's Red Cross's Pearl Necklace Scheme strung together enough donated pearls for forty-one necklaces, which in total fetched £100,000 at auction.

Hudson began to be invited to Sutton Place and to the house that Northcliffe had bought for Mary at Crowborough after Kathleen Wrohan had installed herself and the three children in a cottage on the Elmwood estate. Mary did not seem to mind being displaced by Wrohan, as she did not like Elmwood as much as Crowborough. When in 1916 Northcliffe published his book *At the War*, he praised Hudson highly, despite almost certainly by then knowing that he was sleeping with his wife. As with Reggie Nicholson, it was a privilege only granted to close and trusted friends, and effectively prevented any scandal emerging during the lives of any of them.

~

On 7 September, the *Daily Mail* ran an article entitled 'Recruiting by Blackmail', which argued that 'The country ... does not understand sneaking and haphazard compulsion under the guise of "moral pressure" excited by irresponsible canvassers on behalf of the Government that has not the moral courage to apply [compulsion] itself.'[55] *The Times* made similar points three days later in 'The Government and the Pink Forms', which complained of 'a fresh campaign of private pressure' rather than compulsion.[56] These articles were referred to the Attorney-General, who decided that the case for prosecution under DORA was too weak. The government nevertheless did have extensive powers, as Asquith told the king, 'to suppress by executive action offending newspapers without previous prosecution'.[57] It was a tribute to the democracy and freedom of speech for which Britain was fighting that the Northcliffe press was allowed to publish throughout the First World War, but there had already been some dangerous moments, and more were to come.

In late September 1915, Keith Murdoch, the thirty-year-old Australian journalist whose United Cable Service was housed in Printing House Square, wrote a devastating twenty-five page report about the Gallipoli campaign which he sent to Northcliffe – who made sure copies reached Lloyd George, Lovat Fraser, Charles Repington and other Westerners sceptical of the Gallipoli expedition – as well as to the Australian prime minister Andrew Fisher. Murdoch personified precisely the kind of driven ambitious young men from the empire whose careers Northcliffe liked to promote, and Lloyd George saw the value of the report – which recommended the recall of Sir Ian Hamilton – in bringing the Gallipoli expedition to a close. Northcliffe wrote to Murdoch on 30 September to say that were he an Australian and

in the possession of the information that you have, involving as it does the lives of thousands of your and my compatriots, I would not be able to rest until the true story of this lamentable adventure was so well known as to force immediate steps to be taken to remedy the state of affairs. The matter has haunted me ever since I learned about it, and I am glad to hear from Mr Lloyd George that your letter had produced a good result in regard to one thing.[58]

Northcliffe was probably referring to Asquith's decision to print the report as a cabinet paper for the Dardanelles Committee. Murdoch, meanwhile, met both Arthur Balfour and the Labour leader Arthur Henderson, and was soon to meet Sir Edward Grey, Reginald McKenna, F. E. Smith and General Callwell, the director of military operations, to discuss the paper. Sir Ian Hamilton was offended that a critical letter by a journalist was elevated by Asquith into a state paper without him even seeing a copy, and Murdoch's statement damning the conduct of the campaign thus went unanswered, but once trumpeted by Northcliffe, it went a long way towards the government losing faith in the failing expedition over the following three months. When, on 18 October, Sir Edward Carson resigned from the government over the Gallipoli campaign, *The Times* hailed him as 'a man who has foreseen a long series of blunders into which the want of a policy has led us, and has striven to warn his colleagues and has failed'.[59] The final report of the Dardanelles Commission was not published until well into 1919, because it was highly critical of the government's lack of control at every level.

The next threat to the Westerners' strategy was the sending of an expedition to Salonika to support Serbia and oppose Bulgaria in early October, which some suggested might be augmented by a large army taken from France. 'Northcliffe sent a man today to Joffre to warn him what was in the wind,' noted Repington in his diary, 'and another to [Georges] Clemenceau, who is of our way of thinking.'[60] On 15 October, the *Daily Mail* stated that no politician should interfere with the plans of the general staff, and especially not Churchill, 'a megalomaniac politician' who in Gallipoli had 'risked the fate of our Army in France and sacrificed thousands of lives to no purpose'. It was an indictment that effectively ended friendly relations between Churchill and Northcliffe, at least for the time being.

When George Riddell called on Northcliffe on 21 October, he

found him still full of prophecies and criticism ... The management of the Gallipoli campaign has been scandalous; the Balkan
negotiations have been muddled, and there is no proper military
plan; the defence of London [from Zeppelins] has been neglected
and mismanaged; the condition of affairs in Russia is most serious,
and in France the recent offensive has been the most costly victory
ever secured by British arms.[61]

In fact, the battle of Loos, fought between 25 September and 8
October, was a German victory that cost more than 59,000 British
Empire casualties. Northcliffe predicted that the government would
fall in three months to be succeeded by a five-man Committee of
Safety, after which there would be a revolution.

'When the true story of the Gallipoli campaign is published,'
Northcliffe told Riddell, 'the public will be aghast.'[62] He had been
talking to Lloyd George on the telephone the previous evening,
'but you can tell him he will be one of the five and that he will find
Carson a stout-hearted companion'.[63] When Riddell reported the
conversation to Lloyd George, he replied that 'The reorganisation
of the Cabinet is what is wanted; we are sure to be beaten under
our present regime.'[64] He also told Lloyd George's secretary Frances
Stevenson that, with regard to conscription, 'the unfortunate part is
that although the Northcliffe Press are absolutely right in their estimate of the situation, yet the very mention of Northcliffe makes all
the Liberals see red, so their judgement is absolutely warped by party
hatred and jealousy.'[65] Stevenson worried that meeting Northcliffe
so often might damage her lover's prospects, writing the following
January that 'Of course Northcliffe's few harmless visits to D[avid]
have been magnified in the City into endless secret conclaves, and I
must say I think this has done D[avid] a little harm with his Liberal
friends, for Northcliffe is not trusted, nor does he deserve to be.'[66]

Sir John Simon, the Home Secretary, agreed. On 1 November,
a secret Press Bureau report entitled 'The Northcliffe Press and
Foreign Opinion' was circularised to the Cabinet; it emphasised

the constant use that German newspapers such as the *Frankfurter Zeitung*, *Kölnische Zeitung* and *Berliner Tageblatt* were making of *The Times* and *Daily Mail*'s criticisms of the war effort in their propaganda.[67] The report effectively accused Northcliffe of printing material helpful to anti-British elements around the world, especially in the United States, by citing conscription, the Shells Crisis and the Dardanelles as issues over which he was supposedly giving comfort to the enemy. Simon was ready to prosecute Northcliffe, and even to suppress his papers, but the Cabinet had more respect for freedom of the press than the Liberal minister did.

A warning shot was fired across Northcliffe's bows five days later, however, when a generally Tory-supporting newspaper, *The Globe*, which had been founded in 1803, was indeed suppressed under DORA for 'publishing false statements tending to depress His Majesty's subjects and give comfort to the enemy', after it wrongly reported that Kitchener had resigned from the government, when in fact he had merely left on a fact-finding mission to Gallipoli.[68] The paper was allowed to publish again after its editor apologised, but the precedent had been established that the Cabinet could close a newspaper almost at will.

'It is said this is the first time in history that an English newspaper has been suppressed by the Government,' wrote Michael MacDonagh, an Irishman who was working for the Northcliffe press, in his diary.[69] In fact, there had been others, such as John Wilkes's *North Briton* in the 1760s. In January 1916, Northcliffe told Repington that he was worried that the government might impound the huge amounts of paper that he had 'so carefully collected for his various journals, and distribute them among the Radical papers that are short'.[70] That never happened, but to have raided Northcliffe's stockpiles in the name of fairness would have been a clever way for the government to damage him.

Northcliffe welcomed Churchill's resignation from the Cabinet on 26 November over the proposed evacuation of Gallipoli, and two weeks later he wrote to Marlowe, 'I wish you would not start "booming" Churchill again. Why do you do it? We got rid of the man with difficulty, and he is trying to come back. "Puffing" will bring him back.'[71] In fact, Churchill had bravely volunteered to serve in the trenches, something that, as a married man of forty-one, he was not required to do.

By mid-December, it was clear that the Derby Scheme had failed, despite doughty support from newspapers such as the *Daily Mail*. Instead of raising the necessary half a million men, only 340,000 had stepped forward. Compulsion thus returned to the top of the political agenda. The need for a radical overhaul was underlined on 19 December when Sir Douglas Haig, a strong Westerner, replaced Sir John French as commander-in-chief of the BEF, ostensibly because of French's mishandling of reserve divisions during the battle of Loos, but almost certainly also because of his disloyalty in the spring.

That same day, the British Army started to evacuate Gallipoli. Nothing so became the Allied Army on the peninsula there as the leaving of it, with no casualties incurred. On 21 December the *Daily Mail* described the whole expedition as having been a 'stupendous blunder', which has been echoed by most modern military historians, although today they ascribe the blame more widely than merely to Winston Churchill, the main scapegoat.

On 23 December, another revolution in the higher direction of the war took place when General Sir William 'Wully' Robertson, another committed Westerner, became Chief of the Imperial General Staff, with control over strategy being wrested from Kitchener, who protested but did not resign as War Secretary. Northcliffe can take some credit for this change because he initiated the first cracks in the edifice that was Kitchener's reputation.

'I am not anxious about the ultimate end of the war,' Northcliffe told H. W. Massingham, editor of *The Nation*, on Christmas Eve. 'What does trouble me is the holocaust of those splendid men.'[72] It was clear whom he blamed, complaining to Geoffrey Robinson on 30 December that

> nearly every day in some part of *The Times* or another appears a puff of Kitchener. Twice this week he has been unnecessarily referred to in a leading article ... Lloyd George assures me that this man is the curse of the country. He gave me example after

example on Sunday night of the loss of life due to this man's inept-
itude. Is it not possible to keep his name out of the paper? He is
the creature of publicity and lives by publicity.[73]

On 6 January 1916, the Cabinet finally agreed to conscript unmarried
men, with only Sir John Simon resigning over the issue. 'The End of
the Voluntary System', announced the *Daily Mail*, cheekily adding,
'And Sir John Simon'.[74] Passions ran high on the issue. 'Warning
to Lord Northcliffe,' read one anonymous letter sent to Carmelite
House. 'If the Compulsion Bill is passed, you are a DEAD man. I
and another half-dozen young men have made a pledge – that is, to
shoot you like a dog. We know where to find you ... BEWARE.'[75]
    The Military Service Act was passed on 9 February, rendering
conscription compulsory for all unmarried men and childless wid-
owers between the ages of eighteen and forty-one. Milner in the
Lords, Carson in the Commons, and Northcliffe in the press soon
started to bring pressure to bear on the government to extend it to
married men also. In January 1916, Lloyd George told Riddell that,
over conscription, the press had performed what 'should have been
performed by Parliament' – the job of reflecting public opinion.[76] As
one modern historian has put it, 'It seemed more likely that the press
was reflecting Northcliffe.'[77]
    In early February, the question arose of who should be the
first minister of air defence, charged with protecting Britain from
Zeppelins. Rather naively, Clementine Churchill wrote to her
husband Winston in the trenches on 8 February to say, 'I cannot
make out why Northcliffe does not wish you to be air minister.'[78]
In fact, Northcliffe's own name was starting to be bandied about,
both as a long-standing expert on air power and dirigibles, and
also as someone with a reputation for getting things done in large
organisations. 'Northcliffe would not be a success,' Lloyd George
nonetheless told Riddell. 'He has no experience of acting with
equals. He would be specially handicapped in a cabinet of twenty-
two. He would be overcome by the inertia and combined opposition
of his colleagues – trade unionism is strong among politicians – that
is the trouble during a war like this ... He is best where he is. Alone

he might organise the air defence very well; but many others could do that.'[79]

The observation about the trade unionism amongst politicians was a shrewd one, and Northcliffe would have agreed with that, if not necessarily with everything else that Lloyd George had written. Less defensible was Frances Stevenson's diary entry on 12 February which noted that Riddell believed that

> If Lord N[orthcliffe] once gets a footing inside the Government, he will not rest until he is made Dictator. I think there is something in it. Lord N[orthcliffe] is unscrupulous and a dangerous man, in spite of, or perhaps because of, his very smooth exterior. I do feel that D[avid Lloyd George] should not have too much to do with him. N[orthcliffe] will use him for his own ends and throw him over when he has no further use for him.[80]

There was some irony in her accusing Northcliffe of unscrupulousness, as he was a complete novice compared to her lover.

On 24 February, Lord Derby, who chaired the Cabinet committee charged with finding an air minister, contacted Northcliffe, who suggested the names of four businessmen, including Sir William Lever, implying that he no longer resented the soap debacle. It was obvious to outsiders that the army and navy ought not to run two parallel air services, but such was their rivalry that neither service was willing to give up the prize of overall control of both. The issue of which service the air minister should come from lay unresolved and when in May Asquith appointed Curzon to chair a new Air Board, the *Daily Mail*'s headline was 'What Does Lord Curzon Know About Aircraft?'[81]

Northcliffe visited the Front in late February 1916 alongside Wickham Steed, where he observed what was then the largest battle in the history of the world. When the Germans announced on 26 February that they had captured Fort Douaumont, the fall of Verdun seemed imminent, so the pair went to Verdun to, in Steed's words, 'report as eyewitnesses upon the truth or falsity of the German claim'.[82] German submarines in the Channel prevented a crossing until the 28th, when they found 'a cockleshell of a steamer' whose shallow draught was thought to render it immune from torpedo attack. 'I had never travelled with Northcliffe before,' Steed recalled, 'and his cheerfulness and patience under discomfort won my admiration and that of our [French military] companions ... There were but three berths left ... He insisted on tossing for them, and, having lost the toss, curled himself up in a mackintosh on a seat.'[83]

There were problems about getting to General Philippe Pétain's headquarters at Verdun, including a snapped gearstick in one car and a drunken driver for the car that replaced it, an overheated radiator (which they filled with snow), closed roadblocks, fears of air-raids, another car that broke down, and 300 refugees packed into the dining room of the Hôtel du Commerce at Souilly. The latter had reduced them to eating stale bread 'garnished with some Worcester sauce Northcliffe had found in a cupboard' and drinking water 'tempered with brandy from Northcliffe's flask'. When they finally hitched a lift on a military lorry, 'Northcliffe was given the seat of honour beside the driver' whom he recognised as an old acquaintance, the proprietor of a garage at Biarritz.[84] On the journey, Steed wore a waterproof cap, snow boots, and waterproofs buttoned over a fur coat. 'Anything less military than your appearance I cannot imagine,' commented Northcliffe. 'You look like a cross between a chauffeur and a bumboat* woman.'[85]

'Can you stop them, General?' Steed asked at lunch with Pétain on 4 March, and was told that 'positions are being prepared on every ridge as far back as Bar-le-Duc. If they get through I shall want to know why.'[86] Northcliffe and Steed then motored back to Paris over eight hours through the snow, bursting two tyres on the Châlons plain and reaching Paris exhausted at 11pm. 'Now,' Northcliffe told Steed, 'no supper or we shall both fall asleep. We must turn out that dispatch.'[87] Steed, who had interrogated surprisingly helpful Brandenburger prisoners, dictated the military part of the 6,000-word article while Northcliffe wrote everything else. At 2.30am, Northcliffe appeared in Steed's room asking him to revise and incorporate his part into Steed's, as the chill he had caught in

---

* A small skiff that sold provisions to moored or anchored ships.

the lorry 'had developed so violently that he could scarcely speak or see'.[88]

'Though not an exceptionally strong man,' Steed wrote of Northcliffe on that trip,

> he had borne exceptional strain and fatigue, with little sleep and less food, from the Thursday afternoon until 2.30am on Sunday, his mind being constantly on the alert and his pencil continually jotting down impressions in his notebook. No better companion in an adventure could be imagined. But I noticed also that his mind worked curiously. We both saw the same things; but I saw them in a matter-of-fact way while he saw and recorded them, unconsciously I believe, in a form which the public would most readily understand. His impressions were received through a medium of what might be called the public eye in miniature. His mind was wholly governed by an intense determination to help in winning the war, and all his observations were, in a sense, automatically censored by this resolve.[89]

'What he saw in and around Verdun left its mark on Northcliffe,' wrote his nephew Geoffrey Harmsworth years later. 'He had seen the horrors of war in the eyes of men who had suffered in ways that were new in human experience.'[90] The article appeared in the British and American press on Monday 6 March. Because the French censor had insisted on a more optimistic ending, Steed had written 'Verdun is unlikely to be taken' as the penultimate sentence. When he saw it, Northcliffe 'was filled with dismay. "I never prophesy," he declared, "and this conclusion implies a prophecy".'[91] Fortunately it was a correct one, for Verdun never did fall to the Germans, despite it becoming the charnel-house of French youth.

The five-column article was entitled 'Verdun: An Eye-Witness Account: German Motives and Losses: The Efficient French', and it grabbed the readers' attention from the first line: 'What are the secret motives underlying the German attempt to break the French line at Verdun, in which the Crown Prince's army is incurring such enormous losses?'[92] It had lines such as, 'The Germans made a good many of the faults we made at Gallipoli,' and plenty of exciting passages – 'the blazing dirigible crashing to the ground' – but also sheer propaganda, such as, 'The French losses are, and have been, insignificant.' In asking whether the Germans believed that taking Verdun might win them the war, Northcliffe wrote that 'The Germans are so wont to misread the minds of other nations that they are quite foolish enough to make themselves believe this or any other foolish thing.'[93]

~

On 22 April, H. G. Wells wrote to Northcliffe to say that Britain ought to be a republic. 'We want a Revolution,' he stated. 'And there is nobody in the country with the imagination, the instruments and the prestige for revolution except yourself. The war has brought you into open and active conflict with the system as it is ... What you don't seem yet to publicly admit is that to quarrel with one system is to incur the obligation of starting another. You could make that formulation possible.' He wanted a new 'republican British Empire' which would be 'such as the world has never seen'.[94] Northcliffe replied politely to this nonsense, offering to arrange for Wells to visit the Front.

'I find the only way to get anything done is to attack the coalition incident by incident, muddle by muddle,' Northcliffe wrote to Wells. 'It makes one's blood boil to know that while France has called up boys and men of fifty, our Army Pay Department is packed with young men doing the clerical work of girls.'[95] Of Wells' request that he go into the government himself, Northcliffe wrote truthfully: 'I have no ambition in this matter, and am not likely to give up the strength of my presses for the powerlessness of a portfolio.'[96] He especially did not want to be part of such a large Cabinet. 'Unfortunately owing to the manipulation of the Press by self-advertising quacks the wrong men often rise to the surface,' he told Wells. 'You must have noticed that in the scientific world as well as in that of politics. I am eternally thinking of the problem of winning the war. It is curious that the composite psychology of these twenty-three men always produces the same results – firstly, secrecy; secondly "too late".'[97]

The Easter Rising in Dublin from 24 April to 1 May 1916 had

Northcliffe fuming that the Press Bureau refused permission for his newspapers to cover it, despite their being the first with the news. 'There's Ireland in revolt,' he told the *Daily Mail* conference on 28 April, 'Kut on the eve of falling,* no "big push" ready on the Western Front, the Army calling for more men, and amid all this Asquith holds on to office and says "Wait and See".'[98] While it is hardly in newspaper proprietors' interests for nothing ever to go wrong, this was a formidable list of problems twenty months into the war. When conscription for married men was introduced in early May, the socialist intellectual Beatrice Webb wrote in her diary that 'The Northcliffe Press has won hands down,' but it did not seem that way to Northcliffe at the time, who saw it as yet another example of the Asquith government acting too late.[99] 'There are mothers here who have given four or five sons and are willing to give others,' he wrote to the Wright brothers' sister Katherine, 'anything rather than that our Empire and our little island should be under the heel of Germany.'[100]

The conscription struggle had left Northcliffe impressed with the new head of the army, telling Evelyn Wrench at lunch on 7 May that 'Sir William Robertson is the man who has come out strongest out of all the recruitment shilly-shallying as he absolutely stood out for the number of men he wants. Apparently, Kitchener has been very weak all through and could never make up his mind.'[101] Relations with Geoffrey Robinson were also relatively good, and the editor was able to take Northcliffe to task for his attacks on Curzon knowing nothing about aerial warfare. 'He lost his temper at first, but otherwise took it well,' recorded Robinson. 'I hope it may do good.'[102] Little could be done about Northcliffe's growing contempt for Asquith, however, and by late May Riddell was certain that 'There is no doubt that Lloyd George and Northcliffe are acting in concert ... Lloyd George is growing to believe more and more that he (LG) is the only man to win the War. His attitude to the PM is changing rapidly. He is becoming more and more critical and antagonistic. It looks as if Lloyd George and Northcliffe are working to dethrone Mr A[squith].'[103]

---

* The 8,000 British soldiers in Kut-al-Amara surrendered to the besieging Ottoman army on 29 April, in one of the worst defeats of the Great War.

CHAPTER 15

DETHRONING MR ASQUITH

May–December 1916

'He was "The Chief" to every one of us, and his proudest
boast was that he was a working journalist.'[1]

HANNEN SWAFFER, *Northcliffe's Return* 1926

On 23 May 1916 Northcliffe made one of his rare speeches in the
House of Lords. It called for the creation of an air ministry rather
than merely an air board, as well as increased provision for the
training of pilots, faster approval of grants to foster new inventions
in aeronautics, and larger government subsidies to aircraft manufacturers. 'This machine has entirely changed the position of our
kingdom from being an island to being part of the continent,' he told
their lordships about the aeroplane. 'We cannot, therefore, model
our air ministry on that of any other country.'[2] He nonetheless suggested adopting the German system 'of central assemblage of aircraft
parts ... at great central factories'. Radicals often complained about
how little Northcliffe spoke in the Lords, thinking that, as Tom
Clarke summarised, 'he ought to say what he has to say there, and
not only in his newspapers, where his critics cannot hit back'.[3] On
this occasion, he was listened to with respect, as his expertise in the
subject of air power was widely acknowledged.

The House would not have been so generous had they known
about the way in which Northcliffe was to greet the shocking news
that Lord Kitchener had drowned aboard HMS *Hampshire* when

it was sunk by a German mine off the Orkney Islands on the night of 5 June. 'Providence is on the side of the British Empire after all,' he is said to have exclaimed.[4] Another version has him telling his mother that 'The British Empire has had the greatest stroke of luck in its history.'[5]

Lloyd George took over as Secretary for War on 7 July, but the arrangement made with Kitchener the previous year still stood, with military strategy remaining firmly in the hands of the High Command, specifically William Robertson and Douglas Haig. Although Northcliffe welcomed Lloyd George's promotion, and was the first person to visit him at the War Office on the 8th, he firmly supported the status quo by which the generals stayed in control of the way the war was fought. That way had already been severely put to the test on the opening day of the Somme Offensive on 1 July when British casualties reached nearly 60,000 men, ten times that of the Germans. By the time the battle ended on 8 November, seven miles had been taken at the staggering cost of 620,000 Allied troops killed, wounded or captured.

At his first Cabinet meeting as president of the Board of Agriculture on 12 July, Lord Balcarres observed 'Asquith somnolent – hands shaky and cheeks pendulous. He exercised little control over debate, seemed rather bored, but good-natured throughout. After a complicated discussion on franchise he exclaimed, "Well, this is the worst mess I've ever been in" – "And you have been in a good many, haven't you," said Bonar Law and we all laughed (outwardly).'[6] With more than 19,000 men killed on the first day of the Somme Offensive, franchise reform was not in fact the worst mess Asquith had ever been in. Balcarres noted how the Cabinet 'is a huge gathering, so big that it is hopeless for more than one or two to express opinions on each detail – great danger of side conversation and localised discussions'.

In the third week of July, Northcliffe headed a delegation of newspaper proprietors on another trip to the Front. Lloyd George had told Haig that he wished 'some special attention' to be paid to Lord Northcliffe there.[7] Haig was more than willing to do this for, as his biographer Alfred Duff Cooper later pointed out, 'In 1916 the owner of *The Times* spoke through its columns to an enormously increased circulation and was able to express the same opinions in a louder voice with larger headlines to the million readers of the *Daily Mail*.[8] Although the previous year Haig had privately equated Sir John French's friendship with journalists, including Northcliffe, to 'carrying on with a whore', he was now more than willing to step out on the tiles himself.[9]

Haig and Northcliffe met for the first time on 21 July 1916 at Haig's headquarters at Château Val Vion near Beauquesne on the Somme. Northcliffe recorded in his diary how

> Sir Douglas Haig is, and looks, about 54, a quiet, determined, level-headed, easy mannered, blue-eyed Scottish gentleman with a Scottish accent, neither optimist nor pessimist, the kind of man who sets puzzles for Prussians. I had twenty minutes with him alone before lunch, in which he showed me his successive maps of the German order of battle and the movements of their troops. He has a good chin and firm hands, which he uses in explanations.[10]

At lunch that day were Generals Launcelot Kiggell, Haig's chief of staff, and John Charteris, his intelligence chief.

After lunch, Northcliffe was driven to see the ruins of the town of Albert, six-inch guns being fired and 'more British troops than the Duke [of Wellington] ever commanded', including Gordon Highlanders, Lancashires and Anzacs. 'Brilliant day, desultory artillery fire, dust and sunshine,' he wrote. 'British orderliness everywhere.'[11] After dinner, he talked with Haig on the terrace of the chateau. 'He spoke of the wonderful bravery of the New Armies and the stubborn courage of the German machine-gunners ... The flashing 4th Army is keen and enthusiastic. He showed me his plan of proposed attack tonight, in which the French, as I found later, have disappointed him as to promised support.'[12]

The next day Northcliffe examined the ruins of Fricourt, witnessed a 'sharp bombardment' and visited captured German trenches, going on to General Sir Henry Rawlinson's divisional headquarters. 'Dusty but wonderfully interesting day on territory captured from Germans, my first experience thereof. General Trenchard, head of R[oyal] F[lying] C[orps], sat next to me at dinner and talked air matters. I suggested my old scheme of perpetual propaganda by [dropping] facsimiles of German prisoners' letters in Germany and German lines by aeroplane.' After dinner, he walked on the terrace with Trenchard. 'Guns and flashes again at night, sobbing and throating, I call it. Haig, unusual facial angle, delicate features, strong chin, of kingdom of Fife, east of Scotland, strong quill hands, no mysteries, no military swank, always at his maps and calculations.'[13] Northcliffe had formed a powerful admiration for the commander-in-chief of the BEF, even though he was a Scotsman.

On 23 July, Northcliffe met an eighteen-year-old who had shot down a German observation balloon, and was taken by Philip Sassoon, Haig's aide-de-camp, to Maricourt, the headquarters of the 5th French Army, where the British liaison to the French army, Captain Louis Spiers, took him to a place on the Somme 'where big shells came near'.[14] He had a fifteen-minute meeting with General Ferdinand Foch ('polite, well informed'); thereafter he visited a hospital ('smiling wounded and one dead man'), met German POWs at Rouen and, after touring a veterinary hospital at Le Havre, stayed at the Hotel Continental. 'The growling and roaring of the big guns made me feel that I was in a fog on the Atlantic,' he wrote.[15] After visiting a Belgian munitions factory and Canadian hospital the next day, 'We drove again through Albert, where I think the falling figure in the church of the Virgin and Child is falling more and more.' (A British artillery bombardment was to bring it down just before the end of the war.) 'This bloody and damnable war is a black pall on everything,' he noted on 29 July after seeing row upon row of corpses by the roadside.

On 1 August, Northcliffe wrote a long letter to Lloyd George, suggesting that the new war secretary

devote at least a fortnight to the front and behind the front. My first visit in September 1914 and later depressed me greatly. Today, as one who has spent his life in organising, I must congratulate ourselves on the wonderful machine that had evolved out of

chaos ... I find no waste of men or materiel. The confidence of
the army in Sir Douglas Haig is voiced by every man I have met
and I have specially asked wounded men if there be any sort of
complaint whatever and can't find one ... The spirit of the armies
here is superb. They, as the prisoners are evidence, have shaken
the very best that Prussia and Bavaria can produce. Our losses are
considerable but a great proportion are very slightly wounded ...
Our leader has the complete confidence of his army ... Any waver-
ing now will cost us eventual losses beyond calculation, alarm
France, and hearten a depressed Germany.[16]

That same day, Churchill wrote a memorandum for the War
Committee of the Cabinet that was highly critical of Haig's Somme
strategy, pointing out that the first two offensives of 1 and 14 July
had been expensive failures.

On 2 August, Northcliffe went to 'say goodbye to Sir D. Haig ...
He showed me his plans. Each time I see him I am convinced of his
qualities. We talked of the wobble of the politicians.'[17] For his part,
Haig recorded in his diary that 'Lord Northcliffe arrived today
and stayed the night. I was favourably impressed ... He was most
anxious not to make a mistake in anything he advocated in his
newspapers, and for this he was desirous of seeing what was taking
place. I am therefore letting him see *everything* and talk to anyone
he pleases.'[18] Northcliffe was given a special pass that enabled him
to go everywhere and also 'an unusually fast Rolls-Royce', which
particularly pleased him as the Red Cross car that Robert Hudson
had provided had broken down after twenty miles.[19] Lady Haig was
doubtful about Northcliffe receiving this special treatment, but her
husband replied: 'I myself was much exercised in my mind whether
to receive him or not. As a matter of fact, a man more unlike the
Daily Mail than Lord Northcliffe is, it is difficult to imagine.'[20] After
lunching with Northcliffe, he noted 'I quite like the man; he has the
courage of his opinions and thinks only of doing his utmost to help
win the war.'[21] Haig's charm offensive had succeeded, even if his
military one had not.

The next stage of Northcliffe's tour was to take him to Italy via neutral Switzerland, but on 4 August Northcliffe told Geoffrey Robinson that he did not want to embark on it while Haig was under pressure for his lack of success on the Somme, egotistically adding, 'People in high position here think I ought not to go to Switzerland, which is overrun by German agents who may nab me.'[22] Having assured Haig that Charles Repington, who was critical of Haig's attritional tactics, 'had no influence with *The Times*', he ordered Robinson not to allow Repington 'to vent his spleen' against Haig, saying 'The Colonel is highly unpopular in certain directions.'[23]

There had been a time when Northcliffe would unhesitatingly have supported his writers against any powers that be, but he now so admired Haig that he was willing to have his own defence correspondent censored. 'Sir Douglas Haig,' Northcliffe told Hudson, 'who I saw on many occasions, is the first British general in whom I have ever had any confidence, and his Staff form a combination that would be very difficult to beat.'[24] In fact, the Germans were beating it so badly that a new offensive had to be planned for 15 September.

When rumours reached Northcliffe that Churchill and F. E. Smith had circulated a War Committee paper criticising the Battle of the Somme for its inordinate losses, he immediately warned Sassoon, who replied that

> We have heard all about the Churchill Cabal from the King and his people who are out here this week. As you say it is not worth worrying about as I cannot believe that the carpings of a discredited and embittered gang will find credence among honest men. ... The War Committee are apparently *quite* satisfied now in the appreciation which the Chief [Haig] had already sent them proved a complete answer to Churchill's damnable assertions ... It would be disastrous if Churchill were to come back to power at this juncture with his wildcat schemes and *fatal* record.[25]

Sassoon, who was Jewish and homosexual, was not at all the kind of person with whom Northcliffe would have normally chosen to associate, but such was the latter's admiration for Haig that he suspended his prejudices, and indeed his journalistic impulses. He was also flattered by Sassoon, who asked him to revisit GHQ before he left the Continent, adding, 'Sir D. H. was enormously interested by your letter so do write again and let us keep in touch.'[26] They did indeed keep in touch throughout the war. Even when Northcliffe started to question the High Command's attrition strategy, he always blamed it on others rather than Haig himself.

～

After sixteen days with the army, travelling 700 miles and speaking to hundreds of British soldiers and German prisoners, Northcliffe stayed at the Ritz Hotel in Paris. 'Played nine holes at St Cloud with the Aga Khan,' he noted on 9 August.[27] He wrote Lloyd George a letter that proved that he had swallowed John Charteris's wildly over-optimistic analysis of the situation, repeating that Haig's staff organisation 'is as well-nigh perfect as it can be', adding,

> Ugly rumours are circulating in Paris ... that some of your col-
> leagues are dissatisfied with the losses ... The troops at the front
> do not consider the losses dear in view of the fact that a breach
> in the German fortifications has been made. The loss of young
> officers has been grievous, but compared to the disgraceful waste
> of life at Loos where nothing was gained, the one hundred thou-
> sand casualties of the battle of the Somme, which include many
> lightly wounded men, are trivial.[28]

Losses of that size would never have been trivial, but they might have been acceptable if a permanent breach in the German fortifications had indeed been made, but the German counter-attacks were such that breaches never lasted long before they were closed again.

Northcliffe wrote a long letter to Charteris from the Ritz about propaganda, which was highly prescient in view of his later wartime services in that field. He stated that, in his 'humble and uninformed opinion', several things needed to be done, namely:

> To overcome the belief that we ill-treat or kill prisoners. To
> scatter propaganda in the form of facsimile letters and also of

photographs of prisoners in their English camps eating, drinking, smoking, working, playing games, etc ... To realise that propaganda, like advertising, must be continuous and persistent. To place the whole thing in the hands of some alert man, who would do nothing else. To drop the leaflets from aeroplanes so that they scatter. If they are dumped they will no doubt be destroyed by order. The thing, in my judgement, should be done on a very large scale.[29]

'I know the German mind very well,' Northcliffe continued, 'and I know from a hundred sources that the average German soldier is sick of the war and deeply distressed at the letters he gets from home.'[30] Unfortunately, Charteris fully agreed with this incorrect analysis; the German army was in fact buoyed by its successes in rebuffing the Somme assaults. 'Like advertising, the results will take a long time to come,' Northcliffe told Charteris. 'I stake any reputation I possess, however, that you will get immense results eventually ... I believe this bombardment of the German mind is almost as important as the bombardment effected by guns.'[31] Charteris replied encouragingly, saying that some deserters had come over the lines in one batch that day, although he admitted that there were 'only ten in all'.[32] (The German Army on the Somme numbered fifty divisions.)

Northcliffe continued his Panglossian estimation of Haig's command with an article in *The Times* on 8 August in which he described conditions behind the lines in France as 'perfect'.[33] He wrote to Robertson to 'urge that what is taking place on the Somme must not be measured by metres. It is the first time we have had a proper scientific attack. There are no complaints of bad staff work, no complaints of lack of ammunition, no muddling.' He claimed the Germans had had 'their biggest shake-up of the year' and that the German losses 'are *known* to be immense'.[34] In fact, this was mere supposition by Charteris. Northcliffe also wrote to Thomas Marlowe informing him that 'We do not want pictures of the [captured] German aviators and soldiers, and especially we do not want pictures of English Tommies being kind to Boche prisoners, which pictures are engineered by the Government at home ... A great part of the Army are very angry about them and the whole French nation detest them.'[35] Such photos were fine for propaganda for the enemy but had no place in the *Daily Mail*.

Lloyd George was not taken in by Northcliffe's estimation of Haig's 'perfect' organisation. 'He is wrong this time,' he told Riddell. 'Things behind the lines require to be vastly improved. The transit arrangements are very bad. We rely too much on motor lorries; we should have more light railways ... We are using too much petrol and too many men.'[36] After receiving the second letter from Paris, the War Minister said 'Northcliffe is all wrong'.

By then Northcliffe and Wickham Steed were at the Italian front visiting the Second Battle of the Isonzo,* where they met King Victor Emmanuel III and his chief of staff Marshal Luigi Cadorna. 'The King, who is shorter than I expected, having to get a chair for me, speaks English extremely well, is well read, humorous,' Northcliffe noted in his diary,

> uses his hands a little, as all Italians do, evidently loves and sym-
> pathises with all his soldiers, knew all the various guns and shells,
> evidently knows the Germans, was amusing about the kaiser's
> extemporaneous oratory,† knows his war very well. Showed us a
> horrid weapon for killing gassed wounded, and part of a knout
> for beating soldiers with.[37]

Northcliffe was impressed by Cadorna too, and later told Evelyn Wrench he reminded him of John Pierpont Morgan.[38]

On hearing that the key town of Gorizia had fallen, Northcliffe and Steed decided to follow Italian troops into the city. Official permission was not given for this, but neither was it absolutely refused. 'We trudged', Steed recorded, 'across a battlefield strewn with the debris of war.'[39] Austrian shrapnel was still bursting at intervals over the

---

* There were to be no fewer than twelve battles of the Isonzo.
† 'He always knows what to say,' the King said of the Kaiser. 'If his car breaks down in a village, he is certain to pull out the name of a famous violinist who died or that of a medieval painter who was born there. I am a very poor hand at that trade.' [Steed, *Through Thirty Years* II, p.88]

main Isonzo bridge while the Italian pioneers were busy mending it. In his report in *The Times*, Northcliffe wrote: 'To have broken bread well inside enemy territory is a quite new experience in the war ... As recently as Tuesday [8 August] this despatch would have been dated Gorizia, Austria. Today, though pink and white Austrian shrapnel is still bursting fitfully over the town, Gorizia is firmly Italian.'[40]

After visiting Venice, Rome and Berne, admiring the Jungfrau mountain, and spending a week's motoring holiday in Spain and Portugal, Northcliffe returned to Haig's headquarters on 9 September, six days before the third offensive was launched on the Somme. 'I am entirely satisfied with the progress of the war,' he had told Robinson earlier, and he wrote to his mother that 'all goes extremely well in the War. You know how careful I have always been in my estimates of the progress.'[41]

On being shown a tank for the first time, Northcliffe's and Steed's first inclination was to laugh at its cumbersome size.[42] Yet the joke was on Northcliffe because as Steed recalled, when he tried to climb into one, 'his girth was some inches larger than the hole, he stuck midway and had to be pulled down to the inside by the feet while I sat on his shoulders above. Getting him out again was an even harder matter, though presently he emerged minus some buttons.'[43]

Later that day, Haig showed Northcliffe his top-secret plans for a fourth massive offensive on 15 September where it was hoped that a creeping barrage and tanks would effect the longed-for breakthrough. Haig wrote to his wife to say that Northcliffe had described Lloyd George as 'a shirt-sleeved politician* and he told me that L[loyd] G[eorge] does whatever he (Lord N) advises!'[44] Sassoon meanwhile privately recognised that Haig getting on with Northcliffe 'will prove as good as a victory ... one must do all one can to direct Press opinion in the right channel'. Sassoon regarded most journalism with contempt, joking to Lord Esher of Haig that 'apparently the British Public have much more confidence in him now that they know what time he has breakfast!'[45] Charteris's dismissive

---

* That is, an active one who took off his jacket, rolled up his shirt sleeves and got on with the job.

comment on Northcliffe was that 'We can count on his support until some new maggot enters into his brain.'[46]

After calling on his nephew Alfred Harmsworth, Leicester's eldest son, who had been seriously wounded, Northcliffe returned to England.[47] The first day of the fourth great Somme offensive, 15 September, was hailed with headlines such as 'Great Success on the Somme' in the *Daily Mail*, and a *Times* leader described 'the brilliant success of the new operations on the Somme'. For all the *Mail*'s lauding of the tank – 'a new type of heavy armoured car' – and the 'tactical use of aeroplanes and their remarkable feats of machine-gunning', the offensive failed due to German counter-attacks.[48] Raymond Asquith was killed on the first day, leaving his father devastated and depressed.

Before it was clear that the offensive had not led to a decisive breakthrough, *The Times* leader lauded Haig on 18 September and the next day Northcliffe wrote to Sassoon 'to dispel the idea that our victories are accompanied by great losses'.[49] Sassoon replied the same day saying '*how* much we all liked *The Times* leader of the 18th ... The C in C was *quite* delighted with it ... We are going on well, steady every day with comparatively few casualties – all according to plan and nothing haphazard. This is the only way to reduce these brutes ... Your articles have been acclaimed.'[50] Northcliffe was as susceptible to flattery as anyone else, and Sassoon laid it on. Northcliffe replied:

> My present move is to combat the statements that the offensives of July 1st and September 15th are practically a repetition of Neuve Chapelle – heavy losses and comparatively few results. It is difficult to explain to people, when these suggestions are poured into them, that Sir Douglas is destroying the enemy – men and *morale* ... One of the reasons why the task is a little difficult is that the public were so fooled about the Dardanelles, Loos, Neuve Chapelle and other Allied successes that they are sceptical.[51]

'The war is going splendidly,' Northcliffe told Keith Murdoch on 20 September. 'We have thrown up a military genius at last in

Haig and he is blasting his way into Germany by the only possible means. The Australians must be largely represented when we get to the other side of the Rhine if only for the sake of showing the girls there the kind of stuff that can be found in the five nations.'[52] Haig was not a military genius, but then few generals in that war were. He might have been employing the only possible means of assault, but the offensive was nowhere near blasting into Germany; rather it was only taking small amounts of territory at vast cost, as the large scales of the maps illustrating the articles in the papers showed all too clearly. Indeed, even when the war ended, no Allied troops were standing on German soil.

By that stage of the Battle of the Somme, Lloyd George, who was always sensitive to the political aspect of such heavy losses, had become intensely sceptical about Robertson and Haig's strategy of huge and bloody frontal assaults against well-dug-in German positions, although he was not yet as outrightly opposed to it as Churchill. For all that Northcliffe feared that Lloyd George might give Churchill some appointment at the War Office, he and Harold were ready to pay Churchill £250 for three thousand-word articles.[53] He saw no contradiction in paying Churchill the modern equivalent of £22,000 to hear his views on strategy while trying to stop him putting them into action. Northcliffe was always a newspaperman first, and knew that Churchill turned in excellent copy, on time and to the right length, and that his name sold newspapers.

On 24 September, Northcliffe warned Sassoon that Lloyd George had sought him out soon after his return from the Front to make five major criticisms of GHQ, and thus of Haig: that the staff was too large; 'too large casualties in proportion to the results gained'; lack of transport for the 'coming great output of shells and guns'; corruption in the Clothing Department; and 'our artillery [is] inferior to the French'.[54] Northcliffe told Sassoon that he was 'categorically denying the criticisms, which I told him frankly were based upon too slight acquaintance with our army'. He concluded that nonetheless Lloyd George 'is an excellent man – keen to win the war, but he has a habit of rushing in where angels fear to tread'.[55]

This was amply proved only days later when Northcliffe helped to set up Lloyd George's 'Knockout Blow' interview with the American United Press, in which he refused to consider a negotiated peace, which the *Daily Mail* printed in full on 29 September along with an appreciative leader. Months later, the pacifist Lytton Strachey wrote to J. C. Squire, editor of the *New Statesman*, to say that he refused to write for the magazine because 'what you are really promoting is the policy of the knockout blow – that is to say the wicked and irresponsible policy of the Northcliffe Press ... Whatever you might say, and whatever you might think, you are in fact a Northcliffian.'[56] It was the very worst thing for one intellectual to call another, and although Squire vigorously denied being any such thing, Strachey continued to boycott the *New Statesman* during his editorship.

Writing of Lloyd George and Churchill, Northcliffe told Sassoon on 2 October that

> You are dealing with people, some of whom are very thick-skinned, others very unscrupulous, but all afraid of newspapers. It was urgently necessary that they should be told ... "Hands off the Army" ... Personally I dread a peace made by these tricky people. If they are allowed to exalt themselves they will get a hold over the public very dangerous to the national interests. As far as lies in my power, I do not intend that they shall have that hold over the public and having let them know that whatever influence I possess is with the Army, I will now do my utmost for smooth working between them and GHQ.[57]

In his long-anticipated move against the generals, especially in supporting another Eastern strategy in Arabia and Roumania, Lloyd George clearly could not expect any support from Northcliffe, who was now wholly allied to the High Command. Those who argue that Lloyd George and Northcliffe worked closely together to bring down Asquith often fail to spot quite how far apart the two men were, both over strategy and over where ultimate power should lie in civil-military relations, with Lloyd George taking the constitutionally correct stance that it lay with the elected politicians.

On 4 October, Northcliffe told Repington to let Robertson know that he would support him in standing up to Lloyd George and that he also supported Robertson's call to raise the conscription age from forty-one to forty-five. Writing to Sassoon what he called 'a few little jottings from the Home Front' on 6 October, Northcliffe said of Geoffrey Robinson, who was going out to see Haig, 'He is the greatest friend Lady Northcliffe and I have in common. Eton and Oxford never produced a greater gentleman. In home political affairs, he is my mentor, just as Steed is in matters confidential.'[58] He was less polite about the Cabinet. 'They are a pack of gullible optimists,' he told Sassoon, 'the generality of them have the slipperiness of eels, but with the combined vanity of a professional beauty.'[59] Sassoon showed the letter to Haig and replied that Lloyd George and Churchill were 'an enemy that wants watching every instant of the day and night – but so long as you are watching we can feel quite unruffled out here'.[60]

The long-awaited clash over grand strategy between the politicians and soldiers – sometimes nicknamed 'the frock coats and the brass hats' – finally came to a head on 10 October 1916. Constitutionally it ought to have been the War Secretary who defeated the chief of the imperial general staff and dictated military strategy, but in this clash Lloyd George did not have the Prime Minister staunchly behind him, and he was opposed by other important elements such as the king and crucially the press, roughly 40 per cent of which was controlled by Northcliffe. When Lloyd George demanded military support for Roumania, a new ally which was under attack and about to go the same way as Serbia, Robertson threatened to resign. Robertson knew precisely how to appeal to Northcliffe. 'The Boche gives me no trouble compared with what I meet in London,' he wrote to Northcliffe. 'So any help you can give me will be of Imperial value.'[61]

On 11 October, Northcliffe went to the War Office and, finding that Lloyd George was out, told his private secretary J. T. Davies that 'If further interference took place with Sir William Robertson I was going to the House of Lords to lay matters before the world, and hammer them daily in my newspapers.'[62] Frances Stevenson's version, which presumably came from Davies, was that Northcliffe complained that Robertson 'could not sleep at night because of the interference of politicians'. She believed that Northcliffe was acting from pique; 'The fact of the matter is that Northcliffe is furious because D[avid] does not take his advice.'[63]

'This may seem a brusque and drastic thing to do,' Northcliffe reported to Sassoon of his remark to Davies, 'but I think I know the combination I am dealing with better than you folks who are so engrossed in your splendid and absorbing task.'[64] He explained his reference to 'the combination' as including the backbenchers Churchill and Carson, saying, 'I am a believer in the War Secretary to a very great extent, but he is always being egged on by Churchill, the Attorney-General [Carson] and other little but venomous people.' He was unconcerned about Churchill, whose career he had almost helped finish over the Dardanelles, writing that 'Winston has been going about libelling me in extra vigorous style, which is a good sign.'[65] In his daily 'Message From The Chief', he wrote to his executives that 'If we continue to grind into the public mind the horrible fact that political interference means an increase in the death roll of our army, Sir Douglas Haig and Sir William Robertson will not be as worried as they are at present. This was a scandalous attempt to weaken the Army in France at the moment of Victory – an attempt to send our soldiers on mad, wild expeditions to distant places.'[66]

That was unfair: Northcliffe could not have known it, but the fourth Somme offensive of 25 September was far from a 'moment of victory'. Indeed, the mad, wild expeditions were increasingly looking like those on the Western Front, rather than in 'distant places' like Arabia, where the Great Arab Revolt had been weakening and distracting the Ottoman Empire since June. In fact, it was more likely that 'political interference' would have led to a decrease in the death rolls rather than an increase, because there would have been fewer offensive operations. But in the absence of offensives, how was the war ever to be won? Repington recorded Northcliffe telling a go-between that he would 'support Lloyd George if the latter did not interfere with the soldiers'.[67] At a lunch of City bankers and businessmen in the Aldwych, Northcliffe even mischievously hinted that the government might make a secret peace with Germany, which was not its intention at all and probably a constitutional impossibility too.[68]

'As for Northcliffe,' Frances Stevenson noted on 12 October, 'everyone says he has gone mad – suffering from too-swelled head ... However, he will find that it doesn't pay to quarrel with D[avid].'[69] Repington told Robertson that Lloyd George was 'furious with Northcliffe now', but when Repington told Northcliffe that, Northcliffe 'said he did not care' and 'he had sent word through a mutual friend that he would support him [for premier] on the same conditions'.[70] The friend was probably Riddell, who noted Lloyd George's joke that 'Even the Almighty formed a Trinity. Northcliffe is a Unitarian. It is a poor sort of religion.'[71]

The headline in the *Daily Mail* on 13 October was 'Politicians and Casualties. Hands off the Army!' above an article which argued that the job of ministers and MPs was merely, in italics, *'the supply of More Men'*, not to decide how they were used, because *'Ministerial meddling means military muddling.'* Lloyd George's response was to tell Riddell that Northcliffe's vanity was 'colossal, that he wants to be a dictator' – but that he himself would not be dictated to.[72] Over lunch with Repington at the Carlton Club on 25 October, Lloyd George said that 'Northcliffe had abused him for not bowing to the soldiers in strategy ... He said that N[orthcliffe] was like a flea; he hopped about and you never knew where to catch him.'[73] It was an analogy which he had made before and to which he would often return in coming years.

'Discussion with politicians is hopeless,' Northcliffe told Sassoon at this time. 'They can beat you every time at your own game.'[74] He could be friendly enough with certain ones, but none were ever genuine friends with him, as both knew that he might need to turn on them, as indeed he frequently did. Judging by the people he invited to his annual all-male Friday-to-Monday at Elmwood that he held every autumn, for which the guest list rarely changed over the years, Northcliffe's closest friends were employees, acolytes, golfing and motoring enthusiasts, one of his father's friends, and, in Reggie Nicholson and Robert Hudson's cases, his wife's lovers. Certainly no politicians were ever invited.

~

When, on 30 October, it looked as if the *Telegraph* and *Observer* were becoming critical of the still-ongoing and extremely costly Somme offensives, Northcliffe told Sassoon that 'We ought to mobilise the Press against the Politicians. Unless we are careful the politicians will mobilise the Press against the Army.'[75] Northcliffe also pointed out that 'Now that almost everyone has lost someone in the war, it is very easy to arouse criticism.' Northcliffe already had lost one nephew who had been killed and another who had been severely wounded, and on 13 November, Lieutenant Vere Harmsworth, Harold's twenty-one-year-old son, was killed in action serving with the Royal Naval Division at Ancre.

The Battle of the Somme, which finally ended on 18 November, had cost the British Empire no fewer than 420,000 casualties. Margot Asquith knew whom to blame: not her husband or the generals, but the soldiers themselves. 'I know I know nothing,' she wrote to Bernard Freyberg VC, 'but it does strike me that the soldiers must be very wanting in cunning and cover and care. We always fling ourselves at death – we don't creep and crawl and always go too far ... Can it be right to lose nine to ten thousand in casualties every two or three days? Is there no way of *surprising* the enemy? I feel terribly unhappy over it all.'[76] For sheer ignorance of the realities of trench warfare, on so many levels, let alone the morality of blaming soldiers for their own deaths, those five sentences were hard to beat.

The fall of Herbert Asquith was sparked by a very minor issue, as major political events sometimes are. On 8 November 1916, a parliamentary bill to auction captured German assets in Nigeria to the highest bidder – rather than restrict the bidding to Britons – 'unhinged the House quite unexpectedly'.[77] Sir Edward Carson clashed with Bonar Law, the Colonial Secretary, and no fewer than sixty-five of the one hundred and thirty-eight Unionists present rejected their leader's call and voted with Carson. Law learnt from whips afterwards that the revolt had had nothing to do with Nigeria or German assets, still less himself, but rather a disappointment with the leadership of the National Government. Many MPs disliked

Alfred Harmsworth Sr, pictured here with his eldest child Alfred Harmsworth Jr, was a good-natured barrister with a drink problem. (Paul Ferris, *The House of Northcliffe*)

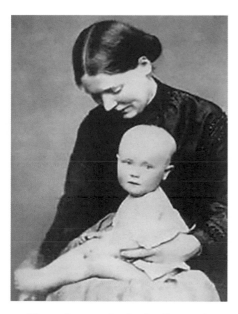

The real power in the family was its matriarch Geraldine Harmsworth (née Maffett), also pictured here *c*.1867 with baby Alfred Jr, who grew up worshipping his mother.
(J. Lee Thompson, *Northcliffe*)

Young Alfred was a daredevil bicyclist who thought nothing of riding scores of miles on his penny-farthing. He's pictured here wearing his bicycling club uniform aged about sixteen, *c*.1881.
(S. J. Taylor, *The Great Outsiders*)

Alfred's marriage to the beautiful and socially accomplished Mary Milner
began as a love match, before it became a marriage of convenience, due in part
to her inability to have children. (Trinity Mirror / Mirrorpix / Alamy Stock Photo)

Mary was an excellent hostess and
generous philanthropist, who entertained
Northcliffe's friends and guests with
aplomb. This portrait of her was painted
by Henry John Lintott.

(Nicholas Shakespeare)

Aged only thirty, Alfred Harmsworth
was about to became a power in the land
through his control of a huge proportion
of the British press. This portrait, by
Sir Leslie Ward, appeared in *Vanity Fair*,
16 May 1895.

(Heritage Images / The Print Collector / akg-images)

Lord Northcliffe was engaged in a number of affairs over the course of his marriage to Mary. Bettina Riddle von Hutten was a Philadelphia-born novelist. (*The Critic*)

Kathleen Wrohan, his mistress for nearly two decades, was an Irish adventuress with a mysterious past. (Teresa Stokes)

It was the success of the magazine *Answers* that allowed Alfred Harmsworth and his brother Harold to break into Fleet Street.
(The Harmsworth Connection)

Much of the Harmsworth newspaper empire was built on the vast sales of a large stable of magazines such as *Comic Cuts*.
(Spartacus)

Grand Falls in Newfoundland, the town that the Harmsworths carved out of virgin forest in a huge financial gamble, provided much of the paper for their magazines and newspapers. Here are the construction workers of the paper mill around 1906.
(Grand Falls-Windsor Heritage Society, A.N.D Collection; photograph by E.I. Bishop)

The Harmsworth brothers ensured that the printing presses here at Carmelite House in London and elsewhere were always the very latest cutting-edge technology, allowing them to out-produce and undercut their Fleet Street rivals. (ANL/Shutterstock)

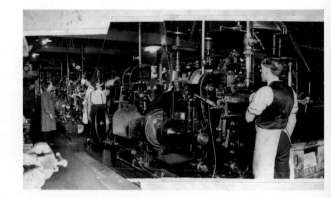

Harmsworth, by now Lord Northcliffe, was an early and proselytizing devotee of luxury, high-speed motor cars. Here he is around 1908 in an extravagant coat in front of Sutton Place, the Tudor mansion in Surrey that he leased between 1899 and 1917. (National Motor Museum/Heritage Images/Getty Images)

Wearing the same coat, Northcliffe, and Arthur Balfour behind him, pull the Wright brothers' plane into position in Pau, France, in 1909. Orville Wright is seen on the right, wearing a bowler hat, giving instructions.
(Trinity Mirror / Mirrorpix / Alamy Stock Photo)

Northcliffe and Henry Ford with a Deerborn tractor: as Chairman of the British War Mission to America in 1917, Northcliffe persuaded Ford to sell Britain thousands of tractors at cost price.
(SSPL/Getty Images)

Northcliffe is seen here with Winston Churchill in Paris. His friendship with Churchill was to founder irretrievably over the Gallipoli Expedition in 1915.

Northcliffe's press campaign was instrumental in replacing Herbert Asquith (left) with David Lloyd George (right) as prime minister in December 1916, but his relations with the latter soured soon after the Great War was won.

Often referred to as 'the Napoleon of Fleet Street', Northcliffe admired the audacity of the self-made emperor, as lampooned in this *Punch* cartoon of June 1917.
(Northcliffe Archive Papers)

XL. 13.

CARICATURE OF LORD NORTHCLIFFE. By K. Goetz.

Obverse:—Lord Northcliffe sharpening his pen; ink-pot containing "propaganda ink".
Reverse:—The Devil (the "Manufacturer of the Soul of the English people") feeding the blazing globe with the "Times", "Daily Mail", and other organs of the "Northcliffe Press".

BRITISH MUSEUM.   Printed at the Oxford University Press.

During the Great War, the Germans struck a medallion depicting Northcliffe, then Director of Propaganda in Enemy Countries in 1918, as being in league with Satan. (The British Museum)

Northcliffe on board the RMS *Aquitania*, embarking on his world tour in July 1921. Intended as a rest-cure for exhaustion, while travelling he would in fact catch the incurable disease that killed him. (Paul Thompson/FPG/Archive Photos/Getty Images; signature: Historic Collection / Alamy Stock Photo)

Asquith's dilatory nature; only two days beforehand, Lord Balcarres had noted in his diary of Asquith's opposition to the conscription of Russian Jews living in Britain. 'This is the only subject during a cabinet on which he has expressed any opinion with decision, since the beginning of July.'[78]

'Asquith's somnolence is heart-rending,' noted Balcarres on 18 November about the problem of food shortages due to U-boat action.[79] The next day, Lord Selborne, who had been president of the board of trade until June 1916, told Balcarres that he too 'used to groan at the poverty of direction shown by Asquith at Cabinet'.[80] This was at ministerial level; the dissatisfaction further down the Conservative party was even stronger. On 20 November, Lloyd George and Bonar Law met and agreed that a three-man war council needed to be imposed on Asquith, in which he would have no greater power than them.

By late November, Lloyd George wanted a reconciliation with Northcliffe; if he were to mount an internal coup against Asquith he would need press support. Similarly, Northcliffe had long wanted to be rid of Asquith and to be on the inside track and winning side. Arthur Lee MP, Lloyd George's private secretary, therefore told Robinson on the 28th that he 'thought it a pity that L[loyd] G[eorge] and Northcliffe had not for some time been on speaking terms'.[81] Robinson replied that Northcliffe 'was quite alive to L[loyd] G[eorge]'s great qualities and desire to win the war', and said that a meeting could easily be arranged. The two met on the morning of 1 December, just as Lloyd George and Bonar Law were about to demand that Asquith step back from the day-to-day higher direction of the war.

In a memorandum entitled 'The Political Upheaval of December 1916', Robinson later admitted that Northcliffe and Lloyd George

met frequently during the successive days, but nothing is more grotesque to suggest, as various newspapers soon began to suggest, that Lloyd George's revolt was the result of Northcliffe's inspiration, or the latter was in any sense the villain of the piece. It is true that the *Daily Mail* and the *Evening News* began a series of violent

attacks on the members of the ... Government, and assumed a
very intimate knowledge of Lloyd George's intentions, but this
had not in fact helped matters. If anything, it rather embarrassed
LG, as he himself told me afterwards, though it certainly gave
some colour to the popular impression that the thing had been
'engineered by the Northcliffe Press'.[82]

Northcliffe's daily diary ended in 1906 and was not to be resumed
until 1921, so we have no way of knowing how much contact there
was between the two men over the next week of intense political
intrigue. It is also important to remember that, in the December
Crisis, it was not just the Northcliffe press that thought Asquith
had to go. Back in April 1915, even C. P. Scott, the Liberal editor of
the *Manchester Guardian*, had concluded to a friend that the Prime
Minister was 'dead and buried – politically!'[83]

The hostility of the Northcliffe Press towards the Asquith government was unmistakable, however. Over the previous months, it had
denounced ministers for 'half-heartedness', 'flabbiness' and 'lack of
decision'. Asquith himself was 'feeble'; at sixty-eight, Arthur Balfour
was 'too old for the job' of first lord of the Admiralty; Edward Grey
was a 'semi-invalid'; ministers such as Reginald McKenna were 'limpets'. 'When will the war end?' asked one leader column. 'When we
have a government that is in earnest, knows the value of time, and
has a backbone.'[84] When people decried Northcliffe's ruthlessness in
attacking Balfour even though the latter had given him his peerage,
Evelyn Wrench pointed out that to Northcliffe 'the one essential
was to win the war and to achieve that end no consideration of past
favours or personal friendship was allowed to intervene'.[85] There
was something, in other words, almost noble and patriotic in his
monumental ingratitude.

Friday, 1 December saw a *Times* editorial entitled 'Weak Methods
and Weak Men' that urged a change of personnel at the top of
government. But at breakfast that morning with Riddell and Lord
Burnham, the owner of the *Daily Telegraph*, Lloyd George noted
that 'An alliance with Northcliffe is something like going for a walk
with a grasshopper.'[86] Lloyd George saw Northcliffe twice that day.

'Northcliffe has turned up again, grovelling, and trying to be friends with D[avid] again,' states Frances Stevenson's diary. 'He sees that the other game* will not work and if there is anything big happening Northcliffe would hate to be out of the know. But D[avid] has beaten him once again. He (N) acknowledges that D is the only man who can save the country, and N will back him.'[87] Apart from the fact that Northcliffe never grovelled, and especially not to politicians who needed him more than he needed them, it seems that this first meeting of the crisis went well.

The diary of Arthur Lee's wife Ruth tells a slightly different story: of Northcliffe telephoning Lee 'in one of his ugliest moods. He was very rude to A[rthur] about L[loyd] G[eorge] and said "I have wasted I don't know how many hours of my time on L[loyd] G[eorge] already and it isn't worth it. He will never really do anything and has not the courage to resign." He was so offensive that A[rthur] suggested that he would perhaps like to cancel the interview – but no, he did not want to do that and came after all.'[88] Later, Ruth wrote that the interview 'went off quite well after all. There were two of them in fact – one before L[loyd] G[eorge] saw Asquith, and one after.'[89]

When Lloyd George met Asquith on 1 December, he threatened to resign unless he chaired a new War Council consisting of himself, Bonar Law (at the Admiralty), Carson, and possibly Asquith's supporter Edwin Montagu, but not Asquith himself. Asquith recognised that this would leave him prime minister in name only, but his authority had already been damaged by a series of recent setbacks that included Loos, Gallipoli, Salonika, Romania and the Somme. Everyone, including Asquith, acknowledged that the present War Committee of ministers and officials was far too large for effective action. As Northcliffe later said, 'You cannot conduct war with a town meeting.'[90]

Writing of the December Crisis in his *War Memoirs*, published long after Northcliffe's death, Lloyd George sought to play down any involvement that the newspaper proprietor might have had on

---

* Stevenson believed Northcliffe wanted to remove Lloyd George from the War Office to give Robertson a free hand there.

events. 'I wish to confirm Lord Beaverbrook's statement that Lord
Northcliffe was never, at any stage, brought into our consultations,'
he categorically stated. 'He was not only left out of the negotiations,
but as far as I know he was not informed as to what was actually
taking place.'[91] Yet from Ruth Lee's diary it is clear that Lloyd
George saw Northcliffe both before and after his key meeting with
Asquith, which precipitated a full-scale political crisis over the weekend as Asquith tried to shore up support. Furthermore, although
Beaverbrook at some points downplayed Northcliffe's influence in
his book *Politicians and the War*, he did write of how he had been
'fully aware of the great influence Lord Northcliffe's attitude had on
the development of events'.[92]

On Saturday, 2 December, *The Times*'s leader was headlined 'The
Turning-Point of the War' and called for a small War Cabinet and

> a drastic reconstruction based wholly and solely on the qualities
> required in waging war; and the first of these is the capacity to
> organise the supreme authority itself. ... We have reached ...
> the turning point in this titanic struggle ... Victory may still
> be remote, but it was never more absolutely within our power.
> Nothing can postpone it, but a Government which fails through
> sheer unworldliness and irresolution to take advantage of its
> opportunities.[93]

It called for 'a very small, harmonious, resolute body of ministers,
an "inner Cabinet" ... to take every final decision, themselves as far
as possible exempt from departmental duties, and meeting daily for
action as a matter of course'.[94] Meanwhile, A. G. Gardiner's *Daily
News* predicted disaster for 'any government which lives by the
sanction of a press dictator'.[95]

Northcliffe visited Lloyd George at the War Office again on
Saturday afternoon, learning enough about his resignation threat 'to
put his *Evening News* to work placarding London with bills reading
"Lloyd George Packing Up"'.[96] He told Clarke that he wanted the
next day's *Daily Mail* placards to read 'Asquith a National Danger'.
Marlowe changed them to read 'The Limpets'.

On Sunday 3 December, Asquith provisionally agreed to Lloyd George's demand for a small War Council that would not include himself, while still trying to rally enough cabinet support to stymie that outcome. Lloyd George was thus unsure whether he would honour the agreement and, at 7pm that evening, he met Northcliffe at the War Office to discuss what to do if Asquith decided to call his bluff and accept his resignation. The historian A. J. P. Taylor believed that Lloyd George 'was insuring against failure. Being a poor man, he wanted a contract to write political articles for the *Daily Mail* and American papers. Northcliffe negotiated the contract.'[97] Taylor believed that after Lloyd George became prime minister, neither he nor Northcliffe admitted that that had been the subject under discussion that night. 'He naturally did not wish to confess that he had envisaged failure, still less that he had proposed to write for the *Daily Mail*, nor did Northcliffe wish to confess that he had missed a catch.'[98]

Years later, the meeting was something Lloyd George preferred to forget ever happened, and he flatly denied ever having seen Northcliffe at all on that Sunday evening.[99] Yet against his protestations there are the diary entries of Ruth Lee ('N[orthcliffe] saw L[loyd] G[eorge] at the War Office this evening'); the War Council secretary Maurice Hankey (who noted that Northcliffe was there that evening); and of Cecil Harmsworth ('Alfred has been actively at work with Ll-G with a view to bringing about a change').[100] C.P. Scott's diary records of that day that 'Ll[oyd] G[eorge] told me Northcliffe wanted to see me, so after leaving him I called at Northcliffe's house.'[101] Tom Clarke noted the next day that 'It is a remarkable thing that Northcliffe always seems to be near his mother in times of stress. He was with her yesterday afternoon. Then he came to town, saw LG, and then wrote a two-column article on the political crisis.'[102] The *Daily Mail* leader calling for 'A War Council That Will Act' appeared the next morning. Against Lloyd George's denial of Northcliffe's involvement at the key moment of decision, therefore, are the contemporary records of no fewer than five disinterested observers.

Yet it was *The Times* that caused Asquith to renege on his

agreement with Lloyd George on Monday 4 December, believing
that his war minister had acted in bad faith. 'Mr Lloyd George
has finally taken his stand against the present cumbrous direction of the war,' read the lead editorial in that paper, which was
entitled 'Reconstruction'. 'The gist of his proposal is understood
to be the establishment forthwith of a small War Council, fully
charged with the supreme direction of the war. Of this council Mr
Asquith himself is not to be a member ... On top of all this comes
the official announcement that the Prime Minister has decided for
reconstruction ... The conversion has been swift, but Mr Asquith
has never been slow to note political tendencies when they become
inevitable.'[103]

The article implied that Asquith had been extruded from the
higher direction of the war because of his inability 'to force the pace
of a War Council' and that 'We are within measurable distance of
having a small War Council as a super-Cabinet as advocated in these
columns for one and a half years.' The leader hailed this, stating that
'Mr Lloyd George has succeeded in impressing even the bitterest
of his opponents with his ... passion for victory.'[104] Asquith was
humiliated by what Maurice Hankey denounced as the 'intolerable,
one-sided, and obviously inspired leader'.[105]

The article has been described as 'the most celebrated single
piece of editorial writing for many a year before or after', yet in fact
although Northcliffe agreed with every word, he had not written it.[106]
In fact, Geoffrey Robinson had written the first half of it over the
weekend when he was staying at Cliveden in Buckinghamshire with
Waldorf and Nancy Astor, and the second half at Printing House
Square on Sunday evening after a long discussion with Carson.

In his memorandum, Robinson stated that his article 'was absolutely "uninspired" (in the sense that no-one suggested it to me) nor
did it ever occur to me when writing it, that I was "giving away"
information that was not known to a considerable circle. I had not
seen, or held any communication with, Lloyd George himself for
several weeks.'[107] Yet Robinson had seen Carson who was in close
touch with Lloyd George, and certainly knew Carson's views on the
proposed War Council, upon which he expected to serve.[108] Some

historians have doubted Robinson's claim that Northcliffe had no input into the article; as one biographer of the Asquith family puts it, 'The idea that the editor of a national newspaper would write a leading article during the gravest political crisis of the era without consulting his proprietor ... is preposterous.'[109]

Having heard from Edwin Montagu that Lloyd George had been closeted with Northcliffe the previous evening at the War Office (making him a sixth witness), Asquith not unnaturally assumed that Lloyd George himself had been the source of the editorial, which implied such bad faith that he decided to rescind his agreement to the War Council deal.[110] Montagu urged Asquith 'not to be put off by the Northcliffe article; he had never paid any attention to newspapers, why should he give up now because of Northcliffe?'[111] The answer was that the article 'showed quite clearly the spirit in which the arrangement was going to be worked by its authors', meaning Lloyd George.[112] The article also prompted some Liberals and three prominent Unionists – Lord Curzon, Lord Robert Cecil and Austen Chamberlain – to come out in favour of Asquith, which put some fight into the Prime Minister. Balcarres noted that in fighting for his premiership, Asquith was suddenly 'firm and vigorous, quite different from his own comatose and indolent self: he says he won't be a cypher'.[113]

'Such productions as the first leading article in today's *Times*,' Asquith wrote to Lloyd George, 'showing infinite possibilities for misunderstanding and misrepresentation of such an arrangement as we discussed yesterday, make me at least doubtful of its feasibility. Unless the impression is at once corrected that I am being relegated to the position of an irresponsible spectator of the war, I cannot go on.'[114] Lloyd George replied, probably untruthfully with regard to the first sentence as *The Times* was required breakfast reading for all politicians, let alone in a crisis such as this,

My dear Prime Minister, I have not seen *The Times* article. But I hope you will not attach much undue importance to these effusions. I had had these misrepresentations to put up with for months. Northcliffe frankly wants a smash. Derby and I do not.

Northcliffe would like to make this and any other arrangement under your premiership impossible. Derby and I attach the greatest importance to your retaining your present position – effectively. I cannot restrain, or, I fear, influence Northcliffe.[115]

With Northcliffe being the only person mentioned in a vital letter between the two leading protagonists of the greatest political crisis of the Great War, it is hard to accept the view of some historians that his influence during the December Crisis was marginal. (There are some historians who believe Asquith wanted to back out of the War Council idea anyway and used *The Times* leak for an excuse, but that does not lessen the importance of the article.)

After Asquith broke off negotiations, Lloyd George resigned from the government on Tuesday 5 December. Northcliffe might have had a hand in planning for this, which was always a likely contingency. 'Again and again Lloyd George threatened to resign but always flinched at the last moment,' Wickham Steed recalled in his memoirs. 'At last, Northcliffe's personal influence with him and the prospect of support from Northcliffe's newspapers helped him to make up his mind.'[116]

Eight months later, in August 1917, Lloyd George claimed to C. P. Scott about 'that strange creature Northcliffe ... for many weeks I never saw or spoke to him. In fact till forty-eight hours before the change of Government I had no communication with him. Then, seeing what was impending, he came to me. And yet people say that I conspired with him to upset the Government or that he used me to upset the Government.'[117] To this, Montagu said of Northcliffe: 'That is his way; he gets word of something that is going to happen, writes it up and then claims that he did it.'[118]

A key element was whether the Unionists under Bonar Law would go along with Lloyd George's attempted coup, especially if Curzon, Cecil, Chamberlain and perhaps others stood by Asquith. Ruth Lee's diary records of 5 December that 'Northcliffe telephoned as usual early this morning and wanted to know if A[rthur Lee] thought B[onar] L[aw] was hanging things up and playing false; if so he (N) would have the whole town placarded by 11 o'clock. But A[rthur] persuaded him to do nothing at present.'[119] In fact, Bonar Law and the Unionists also tendered their resignations that afternoon, forcing Asquith to resign to a sympathetic King George V at 7pm. Although he had resigned, Asquith was confident that Bonar Law and Lloyd George could not form a government out of the present House of Commons – especially considering the stance of the three senior Unionists – and that he would be recalled when that was clear. In peacetime, he might have been right.

'It had been a well-managed plot,' Cynthia Asquith wrote in her diary after a family dinner that night. 'According to Margot and others, Northcliffe had been to Lloyd George's house every day since the beginning of the war, the imputation being that George feeds him with Cabinet information, telling him the next item of the Government programme, so that he is able to start a Press agitation, and thus gain the reputation of pushing the Government into their independently determined course of action.'[120] This was completely untrue, but an accurate barometer of the family's paranoia about Northcliffe.

Lloyd George meanwhile summoned Robinson to the War Office to ask him to tell Northcliffe, according to Robinson's diary, 'that it did not help him when the *Daily Mail* and the *Evening News* assumed too intimate knowledge of his actions and intentions. Also that too much vituperation of individuals was not so useful as insistence that the whole system of Government was unsound and could not win the war.'[121]

On the morning of Wednesday, 6 December, *The Times* leader was entitled 'A Government in the Melting Pot'. The king sent for Bonar Law, who told him that he did not have the number of MPs necessary to form a government of Unionists, with the clear implication that he needed to call for Lloyd George. J. C. C. Davidson was concerned that Bonar Law would damage the Unionist party by agreeing to serve under Lloyd George, and wrote to Law's sister Mary, 'So far we have only heard Lloyd George thundering through the mouth of the Northcliffe press, the very exaggeration of which is tending every minute to discredit Lloyd George and that discredit will reflect upon anybody who supports him.'[122]

Certainly the *Daily Mail*'s support was vocal and, as Tom Clarke noted, 'our shout today across the splash page is "Bravo! Lloyd George" ... "Get a smiling picture of Lloyd George," said the Chief, "and underneath it put the caption Do It Now and get the worst possible picture of Asquith and label it Wait and See".'[123] When Clarke said that it was unkind, Northcliffe replied that it was 'nothing of the sort. Rough methods are needed if we are not going to lose this war ... it's the only way. This Haldane gang has dragged the country into a dangerous mess.' Another headline that Northcliffe inspired that day was 'Germans Fear Lloyd George: France Wants Him: The Empire Trusts Him.' The first two statements might have been true; the third not.

With Law having refused the premiership, in the afternoon the king asked Asquith to see whether he could reconcile his Cabinet. Yet Lloyd George had been busily ensuring that that would be impossible. He won over Balfour with the offer of the Foreign Office, and only hours after declaring that he would 'rather die than serve under L.G.', Curzon accepted the post of Lord President of the Council.[124] Lloyd George already had the support of Labour and 136 Liberals, and promised Unionists that if they supported him, no government places would be offered to Northcliffe or Churchill, no changes made in the army's high command, and no commitments would be given over either franchise reform or Irish Home Rule.[125] Before he had left office, he had reneged on all of those promises, but Unionists were not to know that at the time.

Over the coming days, Lloyd George also gave assurances that Northcliffe would not receive any preferential treatment above smaller newspapers over issues such as prosecutions under DORA, absurdly telling one deputation of Labour leaders that 'he personally would treat Lord Northcliffe in exactly the same way as he would treat a labourer'.[126] With all these guarantees being given, Lord Lansdowne was the only prominent Unionist to stand apart from the Lloyd George coalition.

Lloyd George was on safe ground in not offering Northcliffe office, since the latter was always perfectly open about the fact that he would refuse it. 'Ah,' he said of the *Daily News* prediction that he would be given a cabinet post, 'wouldn't they like to get me out of Fleet Street! It would ease the pressure on their papers. Would they not like it? I prefer to sit in Printing House Square and Carmelite House.'[127] Northcliffe enjoyed differentiating himself from politicians; for example, wearing suits at a time when the standard dress for Cabinet ministers was a frock coat with tails. 'Heaven forbid that I should ever be in Downing Street,' he replied the following month to a correspondent who suggested he ought to be prime minister. 'I believe the independent newspaper to be one of the future forms of government.'[128] It was an echo of what he had said in his *North American Review* article of 1901.

'We were all nearly sick with excitement and suspense,' noted Frances Stevenson in her diary on 6 December, the day before her lover became premier. 'Northcliffe apparently has the wires tapped, and knows the innermost secrets of what is going on.'[129] She was clearly as paranoiac as the Asquiths, but she also noted that Northcliffe told Lloyd George that Asquith was acting on McKenna's instructions. This was not true, but does prove that Northcliffe and Lloyd George were in communication on 6 December, as well as on several of the previous days.

'The London Liberal daily papers all this time are full of denunciations of Northcliffe whom they regard as the arch wrecker of the Asquith Government,' Cecil Harmsworth wrote in his diary. 'There is truth in this of course but not all the truth. Grave dissatisfaction with the PM's leadership has been growing apace among the Liberals in the House and has found expression in such staunchly Liberal papers as the *Manchester Guardian* and *The Nation*.'[130] Cecil was in a difficult situation and the next day he noted that, of his fellow Liberal MPs, 'half are burning with indignation at the way the PM has been treated by Ll-G and Northcliffe while the other half think that his habits of delay and indecision – the policy of "wait and see" – have been the main cause of merited misfortune.'[131]

Cecil and his brother Leicester did not attend the meeting of Liberal MPs at the Reform Club called by Asquith on 8 December as they had 'no wish to hear what might be said in criticism of Northcliffe who has had so large a share in the present upheaval'.[132]

In his speech there, Asquith admitted that *The Times* leading article of 4 December had begun the process that led to his fall. By the end of the month, Cecil was referring to his brother as 'the Kingmaker' and noting that Northcliffe was about to spend two hours with Lloyd George.

On the morning of 7 December, Northcliffe telephoned Arthur Lee 'and complained that he could not see LG "after all that my papers have done for him".'[133] Ruth recorded that he was 'feeling very ruffled, and especially disturbed about the Foreign Office, where he thinks things are worse than anywhere else'.[134] The *Daily Mail* and *Evening News* demanded that the Foreign Secretary Balfour and Lord Robert Cecil, whom Northcliffe thought too mild to be minister of blockade, should not be in the next government – one article about Balfour was entitled 'How to Lose the War' – but Lloyd George ignored them.

The same morning that Northcliffe called Lee, he also telephoned Cecil Harmsworth to read out the headline in the *Morning Post* – 'Who killed Cock Robin?' Cecil replied, 'You did.'[135] As Winston Churchill's son Randolph was perceptively to point out, Lloyd George's press campaign was 'a necessary part of the plan of action which started out with the limited intention of making Lloyd George chairman of the War Committee but which, owing to Asquith's mistaken judgement of the forces at work, ended in Lloyd George's arrival at 10 Downing Street'.[136]

That evening, George V summoned Lloyd George to Buckingham Palace and invited him to form a government. On leaving, the new prime minister went on to dinner not with his political advisors to discuss Cabinet-forming but with Lord Burnham and Sir George Riddell, illustrating the fact that 'Fleet Street in this era wielded more influence than ever before or since.'[137]

It is hard to disagree with J. C. C. Davidson's estimation of the December Crisis: 'That Asquith was outmanouevred there is no doubt whatever, but that the country under the prosecution of the war benefitted, there is also no question.'[138] Yet Lloyd George's promotion had in no way diminished the fundamental difference between him and Northcliffe, which was that Northcliffe thought that the generals should decide and control grand strategy whereas the new premier thought it should be the elected politicians. For all that Northcliffe helped Lloyd George into Downing Street, both men suspected that sooner or later there would be a clash.

~

On 8 December 1916, Lloyd George announced a five-man War Council comprising himself, Bonar Law, Curzon, Milner, and the Labour MP Arthur Henderson, of whom only Law had executive responsibilities, as Chancellor of the Exchequer and Leader of the House of Commons. Prominent absentees were Balfour the Foreign Secretary, Carson the First Lord of the Admiralty and Derby the Secretary for War. 'A National Government at Last' announced the *Daily Mail*, as 'Labour Joins Up'.

Describing itself as 'The Paper That is Combing <u>Them</u> Out', the *Mail* indulged in a particularly aggressive piece of journalism on a page entitled 'The Passing of the Failures'.[139] Across the photographs of various outgoing ministers, it wrote the reason that they had failed. Thus Churchill had the words 'Antwerp & Gallipoli' printed across his image; Haldane 'My Spiritual Home is Germany'; Simon 'No Compulsion. Down with *Daily Mail*'; Asquith 'Wait and See'; Grey 'Belgium, Serbia, Bulgaria, Greece, Romania'; and McKenna 'German Banks Still "Winding Up"', a reference to the length of time the previous chancellor had taken in liquidating German banks, which had long been a particular bugbear of Northcliffe's. Northcliffe had suggested the feature and proclaimed himself happy with the result.[140]

Some of those accusations were grossly unfair: Grey had stood by Belgium, for example. Churchill can be credited with saving Antwerp from the Germans for a vital week while the BEF raced to the sea to prevent an outflanking in October 1914, and the treatment of Haldane had been disgracefully xenophobic even for wartime. Asquith had told Opposition members to 'wait and see' four times in answer to questions on the Parliament Act Procedures Bill back in April 1914, not during the war, but the phrase stuck to him as it seemed to sum up his attitude. 'The Passing of the Failures' was the kind of journalism that in part explains why Northcliffe was hated and feared across much of the Establishment.

Was Northcliffe suffering from more than mere passing triumphalism after the fall of Asquith? Indeed, might he have fallen prey to megalomania, as several historians and biographers allege? Lord Beaverbrook claimed Northcliffe ostentatiously refused an invitation to Downing Street with the words, 'Lord Northcliffe sees no advantage in any interview between him and the Prime Minister at the present moment.'[141] A. J. P. Taylor points out that Beaverbrook was not with Lloyd George at this time, and as we have seen, Northcliffe complained to Arthur Lee that Lloyd George had not asked to see him.[142] Yet even if it were true, and even if Northcliffe had adopted the third person in the classic manner of royalty and megalomaniacs, he might have refused the offer out of concern for Lloyd George, who was facing a good deal of criticism for being seen as close to the press baron. 'Having destroyed one government,' the pro-Asquith A. G. Gardiner wrote in the *Daily News* on 9 December, for example, 'Lord Northcliffe is going to exercise the powers of a dictator over its successor.'[143]

Moreover, it was not necessary physically to go to Downing Street. On 10 February, Maurice Hankey, the new Cabinet Secretary, noted that at Walton Heath 'Lloyd George had a long talk on the telephone with Lord Northcliffe.'[144] Riddell wrote that at dinner Lloyd George claimed, 'I have told Northcliffe that if he endeavours to wreck this Government, I shall have to appeal to the House of Commons. The position is serious. I am very worried about the war.'[145] Northcliffe's supposed refusal of the possibly fictitious invitation to Downing Street has been put down to 'self-conceit' and worse, but there are other possible explanations.[146] (RSVPs often need the third person.)

There was no reason for Lloyd George to think Northcliffe might want to wreck his government at that point; indeed, quite the opposite. On 11 December, Northcliffe had written a United Press article entitled 'Fashioning the New England' which stated of Lloyd George, whom he praised as a 'human dynamo', that 'I believe that he will be at the head of the Government that wins the war.'[147] On the 12th, he sent a communiqué to his staff which read: 'We should now give all the publicity we can to the new men in the Government. We must do our best to get the new ministers known, and thus strengthen their position in the country. Their names must be given constant publicity.'[148]

He did not mind publicity for himself; that same day, *The Globe* newspaper ran an article about how 'Lord Northcliffe has just brought down the Asquith Cabinet [and] achieved probably the greatest journalistic feat in history.'[149] Robinson claimed that Northcliffe had approved the article beforehand, which he considered an 'outrageous and (as N knew) most dishonest puff'.[150] American newspapers were describing Northcliffe as 'Mentor of Ministers' and 'Breaker of Cabinets', and Margot Asquith certainly thought of him as the latter, writing in her diary of 'the Government smashed to atoms in the *greatest war* and at the most *dangerous* moment in the life of this country, and men put in its place of the lowest possible type (a *Press* Government – Lloyd George, Northcliffe, Rothermere, Aitken, Carson etc)'.[151] Four months later, she was still reproaching C. P. Scott for helping 'your friend Northcliffe ... in his conspiracy'.[152]

In the New Year of 1917, Northcliffe visited the Front yet again. Haig told him that the West must not be denuded of troops for Balkan and Italian offensives, such as those that Lloyd George and the French premier Aristide Briand envisioned. 'He is fully alive to his responsibility for putting Lloyd George into power,' Haig wrote in his diary on 6 January, 'and means to do his utmost to insist on him taking the advice of the General Staff.' He added that General Sir William Robertson had not impressed him, saying, 'You call him Wully. I think Woolly would suit him better because he is not firm enough.'[153] Haig then added to himself that 'There seems some truth in this opinion because the British Forces are not yet being concentrated at the decisive front, i.e. in France.'[154]

When Northcliffe got to Paris, he passed on his and Haig's thoughts to the former (and future) French prime minister Georges Clemenceau, another Westerner, and got into a row with Lord Milner. He warned Milner that he would turn his papers against the government unless they supported Robertson and Haig and did not 'scatter British forces in the Balkans'.[155] According to a letter to Beaverbrook from Sir Reginald Brade, the permanent under-secretary at the War Office, 'Lloyd George and Northcliffe quarrelled in Paris when they met during this week and the latter threatened to break the former. Salonika was the matter in dispute.'[156] Clearly Northcliffe needed to be moved away from the British political scene were Lloyd George to be able to take on the generals and what he saw as their horrendously expensive attritional Western Front strategy.

Since no press proprietor had ever wielded the kind of power that Northcliffe had, there were no historical precedents to indicate that he had gone too far. On 9 January, Colonel Repington visited him at 22 St James's Place and found Philip Sassoon there – 'We all agreed Britain's Salonika policy was disastrous.' He noted that 'N[orthcliffe] appears to have given L[loyd] G[eorge] a good piece of his mind in Paris,' saying that Lloyd George and the French prime minister Aristide Briand 'were not statesmen but only politicians' and that he was 'withdrawing all the reporters from Lloyd George and other ministers, and does not propose to see the War Cabinet men until he knows whether he may have to oppose them or not'.[157] The next day Northcliffe went to the War Office to tell Lord Derby that Sir John Cowans, the quartermaster-general of the British Army, was not to be dismissed.[158] All of this was far outside the normal purview of any previous press baron, however eminent, and Northcliffe was testing the limits of his new-found power. So far, he hadn't found many.

On 1 February 1917, Haig gave an interview to a group of French journalists and politicians at his headquarters which, in the view of his biographer Gary Sheffield, 'triggered a crisis that might have led to his being replaced as commander-in-chief'.[159] Haig said that the year 1917 would see 'the decision of the war on the field of battle' and made a statement about the Western Front being the decisive point, which Lloyd George interpreted as a direct criticism of his and Briand's plans for a Salonika campaign.[160] 'At best, Haig's comments were tactless,' concludes Sheffield. 'At worst, they could be seen as a calculated challenge to Lloyd George's authority by an over-mighty general backed by the Northcliffe press.'[161]

Once the remarks were translated from the French press and published in *The Times* on 15 February, alongside an article supportive of Haig, there developed a full-scale crisis in military-civil relations in which Northcliffe resolutely took Haig's side against Lloyd George. Although Derby, Balfour and Bonar Law all tried to defuse Lloyd George's anger and wish to remove Haig from his command, it was Northcliffe's advocacy and implied threats of withdrawal of political support that ultimately kept Haig in place. Lloyd George invited Northcliffe to a discussion in the cabinet room with him and Lord Curzon, after which Northcliffe reported to General Charteris that 'both of them seemed to take what I considered a ridiculously exaggerated view of a trifling incident, and I said so ... We had quite a hot argument for half an hour.'[162]

Neville Lytton, the head of Haig's press staff (and later the 3rd Earl of Lytton), believed that without Northcliffe's support, Haig's position would have become untenable. Soon after Lloyd George's death in 1945, Lytton quoted Northcliffe's words to him in February 1917: 'The little man (that was his way of describing the Prime Minister) came to me some weeks ago and told me that he would like to get rid of Haig, but that he could not do so as he was too popular. He made the proposition to me that I should attack him in my group of newspapers and so render him unpopular enough to be dealt with. "You kill him and I will bury him." Those were his very words.'[163] (Lytton considered that, for a prime minister to undermine a commander in that way, was 'not cricket'.) Despite being third hand, this is credible and was the way that Lloyd George sometimes behaved. Gary Mead, another of Haig's biographers, comments that 'Northcliffe, a monster in many ways but nonetheless intensely patriotic, declined to join the Prime Minister's intrigue, and the fuss over Haig's interview rapidly dissipated.'[164] It did, but Lloyd George was left with another strong reason to try to remove Northcliffe from day-to-day control of his newspapers.

～

At 11.30pm on 25 February, Elmwood was hit by a German destroyer shelling Broadstairs from three miles offshore. Three people were killed near the house, including a woman and her baby fifty yards away, and shrapnel rained down on its roof and a shell-hole in the gardener's cottage was later replaced by a window. Northcliffe was convinced the attack was a deliberate assassination attempt, telling his staff the next day that Elmwood had been 'lit up by twenty star-shells from the sea, so that the place was illuminated as if by lightning . . . The Authorities have no doubt that my house was aimed at and the shooting was by no means bad.'[165] He joked that the *Daily Mail* 'was nearly deprived of its chief proprietor last night – a source of mingled feelings amongst the staff'.[166] A modern historian believes the shelling was 'no coincidence . . . The Germans knew exactly how significant Northcliffe was in binding together British opinion.' Yet there is no actual evidence that the Germans were doing more than shelling a Kentish town, a not-unusual occurrence when they had the opportunity.[167]

On 19 March 1917, Northcliffe created a stir when *The Times* welcomed the Russian Revolution, led by Alexander Kerensky, which overthrew the Tsar. 'All lovers of liberty must sympathise with them,' it stated, 'and wish them success.'[168] Northcliffe supported Kerensky because he believed that he would keep Russia in the war, but two days later he also ran a letter from H. G. Wells entitled 'A Republican Society for Great Britain' which argued that the British spirit 'is warmly and entirely against the dynastic system that has so long divided, embittered and wasted the spirit of mankind'.[169] Wells later said that the article 'gave great offence in the highest quarters', meaning King George V. ' "There goes my earldom," said Northcliffe to me, with a gleam from the ineradicable schoolboy in his makeup.'[170]

Wells believed that Northcliffe was driven by the knowledge that he was an outsider. 'He knew the old social order accepted him, and his newly-titled brothers, by duress and with furtive protest and he felt the continual danger of treacheries and obstructions . . . The Court, the army people, the Foreign Office, treated him with elaborate civility but regarded him with hard, defensive eyes.'[171] Another outsider, Lloyd George, could occasionally enjoy Northcliffe's company, as on 29 March when, at a lunch at the Ritz given by Charles Repington, they discussed what their host called 'the Kaiser's pet ladies, of whom he seems to possess types in Norway, Venice, etc, as well as in Brussels. The PM much enjoyed this gossip, and his eyes twinkled as he listened to it.'[172]

The following night, Northcliffe had an even more convivial evening, one which ended with his being told news that would have a profound effect on his life. Since the mid-1890s, he had actively pursued a feud with Baron Herbert de Reuter, ever since the founder of the Reuters news agency had questioned whether a purveyor of 'lucrative unconsidered trifles designed to tickle the proletarian palate [that is, *Answers*] constitutes a qualification for . . . delivering to the general public serious intelligence of international importance'.[173] During the Jameson Raid and Boer War, and for years afterwards, the Northcliffe press regularly accused Reuters of falsifying news. After Reuter's death in 1915, the new head of the agency, Roderick Jones, saw an opportunity to patch up the quarrel as he 'felt it unfortunate to be in a state of almost continuous warfare with the most powerful newspaper proprietor of the age'.[174] He saw a chance for making peace when Northcliffe sent him an autographed copy of *At the War*, and Jones suggested a dinner with mutual friends, even though Northcliffe discouragingly told him that 'as he always went to bed early, he could not stay up later than nine o'clock!'[175]

They therefore dined at 7pm on 30 March 1917 and Jones invited the American ambassador Dr Walter Hines Page, the former Boer commando leader General Jan Christian Smuts, and his old opponent Dr Leader Starr Jameson to the private room of the Windham Club at 13 St James's Square. 'Northcliffe made no concealment of surprise and pleasure at his company,' and Jones recorded it as one of the most interesting evenings of his life.[176] 'All were in first rate talking form.' Northcliffe in fact stayed up until midnight, helped by 1827 Napoleon brandy, which was very rare for the abstemious Northcliffe. During the dinner, Page revealed off the record that the United States would enter the war one week later. 'My dear Roderick Jones,' Northcliffe said as they walked down the steps to his car, 'if dinners could always be like that one, I not only should dine out often, but I should stay late! I am grateful to you for an inspiring and indeed an historic evening.'[177] The feud was over. Indeed, the companies were to work amicably together on occasion. On 6 April

1917, the United States declared war against Germany. That meant that Lloyd George would require a high-level figure to lead a war mission to Washington to co-ordinate all the multifarious aspects of the new alliance.

~

On 16 April 1917, *The Times* ran an anti-German atrocity news story so bizarre that even a century later it almost beggars belief that it was printed in good faith. A report entitled 'Use of Dead Bodies: Callous Admission' on page seven – and then another story on page five of the next day's edition entitled 'The Germans and Their Dead: Revolting Treatment: Science and the Barbarian Spirit' – essentially claimed that a chemist, his assistant and seventy-eight men of the German Eighth Army Corps were boiling down their own soldiers' corpses to turn into pig food, fertiliser, glycerine, lubricants and soap.[178] The first article went into detail about how the corpses

> pass through a bath which disinfects them. Then they go through a drying chamber, and finally are carried into a digester or great cauldron [where] they remain from six to eight hours, and are treated by steam, which breaks them up while they are slowly stirred by machinery ... The fats are broken up into stearine, a form of tallow, and oils which require to be redistilled before they can be used. The process of distillation is carried out by boiling the oil with carbonate of soda, and some part of the by-products resulting from this is used by German soap-makers.[179]

It was an indication of quite how far the hatred and phobia about Germans had gone that *The Times* and *Mail* correspondents could have written, and *The Times* then print, such a fanciful and horrifying news item, which had black propaganda written all over it. Although General Charteris of course denied it at the time, British intelligence seems to have leaked the story a week earlier to a London-based Belgian émigré newspaper *L'Indépendance Belge*, which credited it to another paper, the Leiden-based *La Belgique*, which does not seem to have existed. Yet it was claimed in the article that eyewitnesses had testified that corpses were loaded off a train and boiled down in a corpse factory.[180]

In a German paper of 10 April 1917, the *Berliner Lokal-Anzeiger*, the war correspondent Karl Rosner had described a *Kadaververwertungsanstalt* (carcass utilisation establishment) where dead horses were boiled down for glue, which in the Northcliffe papers had been mistranslated as a 'Corpse Exploitation Establishment', that is, for humans.[181] 'Kadaver' means 'animal carcass' in German, not corpse, which led the philosopher Bertrand Russell and others to assume that it had been a deliberate mis-translation and the Corpse Factory story had been 'set going cynically' by Lord Northcliffe.[182] Yet in fact all the evidence suggests that Northcliffe had nothing to do with the story getting into his paper.

'In regard to the German Corpse Conversion Company,' he wrote in his communiqué to *Times* staff on 18 April, 'it is necessary that we reprint the evidence in facsimile from the German papers. *The Times* circulates largely in neutral countries in official circles, and I have little doubt that the Germans will attempt to deny their HORROR. The facsimile appeared in the *Daily Mail* this morning.'[183] On 2 April, *The Times* reproduced a facsimile of Rosner's original article, which mentioned 'a sickly smell in the air, as if glue were being boiled'.[184]

A month later, on 17 May, Northcliffe wrote in another communiqué that 'the Germans make no secret of the matter, and, owing to their ignorance of the psychology of the rest of the world, they were probably as much surprised at the way other countries received the news as we were at the fact that they utilised the bodies of the dead for commercial purposes.'[185] Although that was the last Northcliffe wrote on the matter, by then it had taken on a life of its own and, at the end of 1917, Amalgamated Press's *The Great War: the Standard History of the World-Wide Conflict*, which H. W. Wilson and J. A. Hammerton co-authored and which ultimately covered twenty volumes, still absurdly claimed that '*The Times* was right in this matter.'[186] It was not until 1925 that Charteris admitted that he had switched the captions on two photographs that had been leaked to the Belgian papers, one showing a train taking dead horses to the rear so that fat could be taken from them, and another showing a train taking dead Germans away for burial.[187]

~

In late April 1917, Frances Stevenson recorded that Lloyd George 'was rather depressed ... for Northcliffe has been to him the night before and told him that this Government is even more unpopular than the last! The truth is, that D[avid] is doing things without consulting or paying any heed to Northcliffe, and this rather riles the great man.'[188] It probably also added to Lloyd George's sense that the sooner that Northcliffe could be prised away from his newspapers, the better – although in reply to a letter from Sir Arthur Pearson congratulating him on chairing the Civil Aerial Transport Committee on postwar commercial aviation, Northcliffe said, 'I have no desire for any official positions, I can assure you.'[189]

In late May 1917, Arthur Balfour, who was on a visit to Washington DC, recommended to the Cabinet that a permanent British war mission needed to be established in Washington to liaise with the administration of President Woodrow Wilson and co-ordinate the activities of the burgeoning number of British agencies there, including the Admiralty, Treasury, War Office, Munitions ministry, Shipping Controller and Food Controller. At present there were too many conflicts of interest, overlapping responsibilities, and even instances of one British department bidding for supplies against others.[190]

'Although the person selected would no doubt have a lot to do with Americans,' Lloyd George noted in his war memoirs, 'his primary duty would be to control our own operations, including recruiting, purchase, manufactures, transport, and the priority of the various claims.'[191] Lloyd George later claimed that Northcliffe had been the Cabinet's choice not his, but on the day before the Cabinet met, Maurice Hankey had written of Lloyd George: 'This, of course, is really a dodge to get rid of Northcliffe, of whom he is afraid.'[192] A little later, Lloyd George told C. P. Scott that 'it was essential to get rid of him. He had become so "jumpy" as to be really a public danger and it was necessary to "harness" him in order to find occupation for his superfluous energies. "I had to do this," said Lloyd George, "if I was to avoid a public quarrel with him." '[193] Beaverbrook believed that Lloyd George was determined to bring Churchill back into the government, but recognised that he could not do so with Northcliffe in the country.[194]

It was with the greatest difficulty that Lloyd George got Balfour to agree that Northcliffe could take the role. Writing to his cousin Lord Robert Cecil, Balfour described Northcliffe as a 'vigorous hustler and loud-voiced propagandist'. On 28 May, Balfour told Cecil that he opposed sending 'a commercial man or Northcliffe' as it would have 'an unfortunate effect on the present and future relations of the two countries'.[195] Lloyd George persuaded Balfour to change his mind and, on 30 May, offered the job to Northcliffe over lunch in Downing Street. He accepted immediately.[196]

Northcliffe believed he could serve his country in a vital capacity at a crucial time in its history, but he also understood Americans better than most other Britons who were likely to be offered the post, having already visited the United States most years since 1894. Apart from the minor civil aviation job, it was the first public appointment he had ever held.

CHAPTER 16

THE BRITISH WAR MISSION

June–October 1917

'The Press? What you can't square you squash, what you
can't squash you square.'[1]

DAVID LLOYD GEORGE during the Great War.

Northcliffe left on the American steamer USMS *St Paul* on the
morning of Saturday 2 June, with no entourage except a valet. He
had been awarded very wide powers in his instructions, which were
bound to bring him into conflict with the British ambassador to
Washington, Sir Cecil Spring-Rice. All that the instructions said on
that score was that he would 'profit by the Ambassador's advice and
assistance, whenever these may be required'.[2]

Of course, Northcliffe knew perfectly well that Lloyd George's
primary motive in sending him across the Atlantic was to get rid
of him. He left no instructions whatever so far as *The Times* was
concerned, nor did he make comments on its conduct while he was
away. It was hardly the action of an interfering, megalomaniac proprietor. 'It is impossible to control a newspaper unless you sleep on
the premises,' Northcliffe told H. G. Wells on 21 May, putting his
papers' success down to 'the tact with which the Editor guides my
impetuosity'.[3] He did give general instructions to Steed to 'back the
soldiers'.

On 7 June, questions were asked in the House of Commons about
Northcliffe's mission, including the obvious one by Labour's Philip

Snowden about 'whether Lord Northcliffe has been appointed a member of the Government or the Diplomatic service; and, if not, why he has been selected to carry out an official mission?'[4] The minister did not know the answer, which was that Northcliffe was working in a special capacity that was neither governmental nor diplomatic. He also paid his own expenses, which amounted to £13,000. He had long criticised rich politicians who claimed expenses saying that 'They should not pile up debts for the British Empire.'[5]

Before leaving, Northcliffe told the American journalist Isaac Marcosson, who was also sailing on the *St Paul*, that he had a foreboding 'that the Germans would get him'. Indeed, some of the fifteen vessels in his convoy were sunk in the first twenty-four hours of the voyage.[6] 'He had a strong premonition he would not return,' recorded Sir Robert Hudson's tactful biographer J. A. Spender, 'and he solemnly charged Robert to guard and befriend his wife, while he was gone and if he should not come back.'[7] 'My task is a terrific one and most delicate,' Northcliffe wrote to Mary on board ship. 'I am sent forth literally to beg for assistance of all kinds and in colossal quantities and from a people whom certain of our public men and journals have attacked up till the past few weeks. Most fortunately, I have never allowed any criticism to appear in my Press.'[8] He ordered Arthur Willert, *The Times*'s Washington correspondent, that 'No criticism of the United States was to appear in my newspapers until the American Fleet bombarded Liverpool.'[9]

'If anything happens to me', he had written about Elmwood to George Sutton, 'I want you to have it, and after you the Boy, if he be a good boy and cares for it.'[10] The Boy probably referred to Alfred Benjamin Smith, but of course such a letter had no standing in law, as Northcliffe must have known.

While crossing the Atlantic, Northcliffe wrote an unusually self-reflective circular letter to his mother and siblings, stating that 'My domestic life, despite children that never came, is smooth and happy ... We have been married twenty-seven years, not many childless couples so happily.'[11] Yet he must have appreciated that almost every recipient of the round-robin knew perfectly well that Mary was living happily at Crowborough with Hudson. He went on to describe his newspapers and journals as his children, but then spoiled the touching metaphor by adding that his journals 'have been burned and banned at times for doing what they believed to be their duty, but they have huge followings'.

Northcliffe used the journey wisely, and Marcosson recalled how in his stateroom he blocked

> out a huge chart of organisation in the form of a pyramid with himself at the apex and the myriad subordinate British Missions in the United States radiating from it. When we got to New York he had the whole business definitely set down. It was typical of his energy that exactly one hour after we docked he was at a desk in an office on Fifth Avenue. He had rented it by cable and it was fitted up while we were at sea.[12]

When the ship docked on 10 June, Northcliffe was met by Willert, who found him in his trademark blue serge suit, soft grey hat and spotted tie, with malacca cane, 'compactly important, radiating expectant authority, standing out from his fellow passengers as a well-groomed horse from mules'.[13] Yet Sir Cecil Spring-Rice had not sent a representative from the British Embassy, whereupon, as Willert wrote in his autobiography years later, 'there ensued one of the most formidable expressions of temper that I have ever witnessed, if explosion is the right word for an outbreak of quiet concentrated anger'.[14] Spring-Rice's excuse was that he did not want to compromise Northcliffe's security by advertising his arrival, despite the fact that reporters and even cinematographers were covering his landing.

'Angry, very angry he certainly appeared,' Willert wrote, 'but he had a lively sense of the value of pretended anger,' and his threats to take the next ship home were obviously empty.[15] Northcliffe later showed Willert how he could throw his spectacles on the ground without breaking them as their metal frames were encased in rubber: 'You see, they don't break and there are times when doing that impresses people.'[16]

Although propaganda and publicity were not part of Northcliffe's official brief, he gave a press conference soon after he landed. Over the next few days in New York, staying at the Gotham Hotel, Northcliffe entertained an endless stream of callers: officials, newspapermen, friends and war workers. The important ones received a lunch 'washed down by a sweet white wine' at which, Willert recorded, 'Northcliffe was voluble and superficially frank, Napoleonic, domineering, downright in question and criticism, but genial.'[17]

As an old-school Establishment diplomat, Sir Cecil Spring-Rice believed that the dealings between the British and American governments should be conducted entirely through the diplomatic machine rather than through an ad hoc interloper and journalist. 'Northcliffe was the incarnation of all that he disliked in the twentieth century,' noted Willert, a 'vulgar parvenu in a private railway car basking in the adulation of the Press and giving bumptious interviews'.[18] Moreover, the Northcliffe press had been critical of him in the past, which he was convinced had been inspired by its proprietor personally.[19] Spring-Rice was the grandson of the Earl of Limerick, had gone to Eton and Balliol College, Oxford, and was Teddy Roosevelt's best man. Northcliffe saw him as the personification of the Establishment, what he called an 'all-covered-with-orders kind of person'.[20] It was clear there was going to be a clash, and it was not long in coming.

On 15 June, Northcliffe and Spring-Rice had a meeting in Washington with Josephus Daniels, the secretary of the navy, at which Northcliffe criticised the British government for 'stupid' censorship of maritime losses to submarines, arguing that public understanding the true situation would 'stimulate both patriotism and sacrifice'.[21] Counselor Polk of the US State Department noticed that although the two Britons 'were polite to one another ... it is easy to see they are not close friends'.[22] It was a huge understatement. That night at the embassy, Spring-Rice decided to have it out with Northcliffe.

Before the guests arrived at a formal dinner that Spring-Rice was giving in Northcliffe's honour, the ambassador showed him a pro-German American paper, the *Evening Post*, which had highlighted the Northcliffe press's criticisms of him in the past. 'He then suddenly rose,' Northcliffe told Lloyd George later, 'looked at me in a very queer way, and pointing his finger at me, said: "You are my enemy. Apart from these criticisms, you inserted four years ago an anonymous attack in *The Times* which nearly killed me; and Lady Spring-Rice declines to receive you on that account."'[23] Northcliffe commented to the Prime Minister that 'There are, fortunately, other charming ladies in Washington!'

Northcliffe had no idea what these criticisms were, but decided to go on the offensive. 'If you feel as you say you do towards me, I had better leave your house at once.'[24] Northcliffe walked towards the door, whereupon, recognising the embarrassment it would cause him to lose his own guest of honour just before the rest of the guests arrived, Spring-Rice 'rushed after me, put out his hand, and said: "We have to work together whatever we may feel about each other".'[25] Another account has Spring-Rice saying, 'This war makes strange bedfellows and we must work together whatever our personal feelings.'[26] Northcliffe then shook his hand, just as the French ambassador was announced – although in an account that President Wilson received it was the actual arrival of the French ambassador that prevented Northcliffe from leaving.[27] The phrase 'diplomatic incident' is usually reserved for spats between representatives of different countries, not of the same one.

Willert noted that Spring-Rice and Northcliffe entered the reception room to meet the French ambassador and other guests, 'the one looking grim, the other self-possessed and faintly amused'. Willert had warned that Spring-Rice had asked Northcliffe to arrive early for 'an exhibition of temper', and as Northcliffe passed Willert he whispered, 'You were right.'[28] Spring-Rice complained to Lloyd George about the Northcliffe press's 'anonymous and libellous' prewar criticisms of him, and told the Prime Minister that, at the end of their pre-dinner clash, 'I said that under present circumstances it would be childish and wicked to allow personal antagonisms to prevail over the public advantage. He entirely agreed and our personal relations have been very pleasant and friendly.'[29] The last sentence was untrue; in fact, they were unpleasant and fraught for the rest of Spring-Rice's embassy.

'My reception at Washington from the President downwards could not have been better,' Northcliffe reported to Lloyd George five days after the incident. 'My reception at the hands of the British Ambassador could not have been worse ... Sir Cecil Spring-Rice is an odd person. He is under the impression that anyone who comes here is a reflection on himself. He was rude to Sir Hardman Lever [the financial secretary to the Treasury] and ruder to me.'[30] Northcliffe later told Lloyd George's private secretary J. T. Davies that Spring-Rice was 'either overwrought by the strain of the war' or possibly 'not quite right in the head'.[31] (Against all that, Spring-Rice was also the poet who wrote the sublime words to the hymn 'I Vow To Thee My Country'.)

Spring-Rice believed (and probably hoped) that since President Wilson and Colonel Edward M. House, his closest advisor and confidant, were both liberal Democrats, they would not get on with a 'gutter-press Conservative', but they did. Indeed, they swiftly got on much better with the classless Northcliffe than they did with the upper-class Spring-Rice, who Wilson's biographer noted 'was often acutely paranoid – believing himself beset with German spies – and more generally inclined to adopt the manners of a viceroy than a diplomat'.[32] Ultimately, House, who had already been Northcliffe's guest at Sutton Place, informed the Foreign Office that the ambassador was 'unwilling to work cordially with his new colleague' and thus was 'temperamentally unfitted to cope with such complex and disturbed conditions'.[33]

Northcliffe first met Woodrow Wilson on 16 June, the day after the embassy imbroglio, and wrote to Mary that he was a

> determined looking gentleman with whom one would not care to be in an antagonism. He is about as tall as I am,* more slightly built, very quiet in his manner, compresses more meaning into a few words more than any other American I have met ... bears his worries remarkably well, is quite humorous and amusing and, incidentally, the most powerful individual in the world.[34]

---

* Northcliffe was 5' 10"; Wilson 5' 11".

As for Wilson's view of Northcliffe, Willert reported to Geoffrey Robinson, who had changed his name to Dawson for family reasons, that 'The President, who had expected a political ogre . . . has expressed himself to be agreeably surprised.'[35] 'The American Govt is very nice to me,' Northcliffe reported to his mother. 'They are a mighty people these Americans, and will end the war.'[36]

Oiling the wheels between Northcliffe and the two key Americans was Sir William Wiseman, head of British intelligence in the United States and a close friend of House. Northcliffe thought Wiseman 'well named' and came to trust him implicitly.[37] House was soon writing to Northcliffe, expressing his hope 'that you will call on me at any time that you think I can be of assistance'.[38] Another important figure that Northcliffe encountered was Major Campbell Stuart, whom he seconded to his mission as his own military attaché, the first Canadian to be appointed to the British diplomatic service. Stuart continued to work directly for Northcliffe for the rest of the latter's life, and rose to be chairman of *The Times*. (Stuart recorded how Spring-Rice's first comment to him on his arrival in Washington 'was an expression of regret that I had not been educated at Eton'.[39])

Northcliffe headquartered the War Mission at 671 Fifth Avenue in New York City, relatively far from the political decision-makers (and Spring-Rice), but the location made sense since it was the centre of news, food purchasing, steel, copper, oil, wheat, shipping, railway transport and, above all, finance.[40] A large number of *Daily Mail* employees were shipped over to work on overhauling British propaganda there, including Andrew Caird. Northcliffe made the six-hour journey to Washington once or often twice a week in his own Pullman with its drawing room compartment laid on by the United States government. (He thought it worthwhile noting to his mother that Henry, his Washington chauffeur, was not Russian but Jewish.)

Northcliffe took Bolton Priory for his country residence, overlooking Pelham Bay in Westchester County, New York. Set in fifty-five acres, with an English butler, gardener and cook-housekeeper (he appreciated her 'nice chops' and the fact that there was 'mustard on the table all the time'), he told his mother that his life there was 'about the most English thing in the United States'.[41] Yet for all the comfort, as Campbell Stuart pointed out, 'Life with Lord Northcliffe was a very different experience from the leisure of the Embassy.'[42] Northcliffe worked from 6am until he went to bed at 9.30pm, never took a weekend off, and avoided golf days in nearby Chevy Chase and society cocktail parties.

Northcliffe got a grip on the vast and growing British war mission immediately, helped by the War Cabinet's instructions that had given him the power of instant dismissal of officials. There were twenty-eight departments comprising 10,000 workers, with £80 million being spent monthly, including some money, as Northcliffe told H. G. Wells, being 'squandered ... and some swindling'.[43] He immediately placed all the British government departments, except the diplomatic, military and financial, under one head, with orders to put all information about experiences in organisation and manufacturing in Britain freely at the disposal of the US authorities. The historian of the war mission noted how 'The American officials were, from the very outset, able to give information of value – as, for example, certain suggestions which were made by their scientists in regard to gas warfare and were at once adopted by the British forces.'[44]

Britain had a vast range of contracts in the United States for everything from horseshoe nails to cargoes of wheat, and most needed to be increased significantly. One of Northcliffe's tasks was to induce the US government to supply the Allies with commodities at exactly the same rate at which the Americans themselves were supplied. He achieved this for steel and copper and several other important commodities.[45]

Northcliffe's first crisis arose almost immediately. On 28 June, Balfour warned Colonel House that Britain was in such dire financial straits because of the war – she had spent $3.7 billion and loaned $1 billion to her allies (including Russia) – that she might be forced off the Gold Standard, renege on her dollar debts and cease all purchases from the United States.[46] 'This is a staggering amount,' House told Wilson, 'and indicates the load Great Britain has been carrying for her allies.'[47] William Gibbs McAdoo, a tall good-looking man of fifty-four who was both the secretary of the Treasury and President

Wilson's son-in-law, became a vital figure in Northcliffe's work, whom he had to persuade that the British Treasury figures were real.

'I have met few men who had such a quick comprehension as Lord Northcliffe,' McAdoo recalled in his memoirs.

> It was never necessary to explain things to him twice. He reminded me more of the highest type of American business executive than any foreigner I have ever known. He was dynamic, his phrases were vivid, his ideas crisp and clear, and he had a way of getting down at once to the vital thought in any question under discussion.[48]

Northcliffe left the detailed financial negotiations to the experts Lord Cunliffe and Sir Richard Crawford, but, as McAdoo also noted, 'His strong point was in deciding how to do things – the shortest and surest road to accomplishment.'[49] Northcliffe needed to persuade McAdoo to extend a line of credit of $185 million a month for four months to prevent a complete breakdown of the dollar payments system.[50] He also insisted that Rufus Isaacs (by now Lord Reading) be appointed to negotiate the long-term Anglo-American financial relationship.

'Loan to us strongly opposed by powerful section of Congress,' Northcliffe telegraphed Steed. 'If loan stops, war stops.'[51] Northcliffe wrote to Lloyd George on 18 July:

> As you have landed me in the most difficult job I have ever had in my life, I want you to help me in every way in your power. Members of the Cabinet should understand that our attitude towards the United States Government is that of beggars ... It does not require any imagination to foresee great difficulty in obtaining money from the United States in the future.[52]

The Americans demanded proof that every penny they lent was directly used for winning the war, and regarded the appropriation of $185 million as a tremendous sum. 'When I repeat the Chancellor's statement that [the] war is costing us $50 million a day,' Northcliffe told Lloyd George, 'they are aghast.'[53] Lloyd George recalled in his memoirs how 'Northcliffe fretted and fumed and grizzled ... His work in America exposed some of his pettiness but it also revealed something of his greatness.'[54]

It was during the course of the ultimately successful financial negotiations that Northcliffe, with his natural sense for where power and influence lay, spotted quite how vital a figure Colonel House was in the Wilson administration. 'One of the reasons of his power is that he wants nothing for himself,' Northcliffe told his *Daily Mail* staff in a communiqué, in which he described House as 'gentle, quiet and unassuming ... He is now at the head of the United States politics and before the end of the war will be one of the heads of the world's politics.'[55] Northcliffe did not like to prophesy, but in this he was correct and the Northcliffe–House relationship became key to the Anglo–American one.

'I talk to Northcliffe as frankly as I can on all subjects,' House wrote. 'Northcliffe is a dominating man with boundless energy. I like him the more I see him.'[56] Northcliffe also established a good working relationship with Herbert Hoover, the director of the US Food Administration, who greatly impressed him. He also hugely admired Teddy Roosevelt, whom he nicknamed Emperor Theodore the First. 'I liked Roosevelt immensely,' he told his mother, 'but he is too much for my small luncheons.'[57] It was also good politics to keep Roosevelt at arm's length, as he was Woodrow Wilson's hated political enemy.

Northcliffe saw it as an important part of his duty to spread the message that the war which the United States had recently joined would be a long one, but that it had to be prosecuted to the utmost because it was a great struggle for civilisation. His lifelong reporter's practice of gauging opinion by speaking to everyone he met regardless of class was put to invaluable use as he toured the United States speaking to thousands of ordinary Americans. He also delivered set speeches to large audiences. On 21 July 1917, he spoke to a crowd of 14,000 people in Madison Square Gardens. Even electronically magnified, his weak speaking voice did not fill the arena in the way that booming American orators such as William Jennings Bryan and Bourke Cochrane did, but he was applauded for five minutes. It gave him the confidence to give public speeches everywhere he went, and his message of Anglo–American amity resonated well.

Northcliffe was constantly introduced as the man who gave Asquith the 'once over', the 'knock out', or as the man who 'put it over him', which was embarrassing when one of Asquith's sons was in the audience at a speech in Chicago.[58] Some of his radio speeches were syndicated nationally. 'I am supposed, in addition to my other duties, to be a sort of *Encyclopedia Britannica* about the war,' he told his mother. 'The American Government consults me about a hundred topics. Yesterday I had to address their Ministry of Munitions. One day this week I have to address their naval surgeons.'[59]

Northcliffe did indeed fret and fume and grizzle, as Lloyd George put it, especially over the way that the embassy did not put Britain's case aggressively enough in the United States. 'Ignorance about the war is absolutely colossal,' he told his mother and Mary, 'and lack of knowledge of our tremendous effort and mighty sacrifice deplorable. We have only ourselves to blame. If there is ever any hanging from lampposts, those who are responsible for our form of censorship should be the first to be strung up.'[60] He even met an American who thought that the Guards regiments were primarily engaged in 'guarding Buckingham Palace, and doing other work of that kind'.[61]

'Having made one's own way in life is a passport to American hearts,' Stuart wrote about the way that Northcliffe became popular in the United States. That said, Northcliffe had a US-appointed bodyguard called McCahill with him all the time he was there. When McCahill compared a threatening letter that had been left for Northcliffe at the Gotham Hotel to ones received by President Wilson's daughter Margaret, the sender was immediately consigned to a lunatic asylum. 'They do not waste much time in trying suspected people here,' Northcliffe told his mother, admiringly.[62]

When Northcliffe was travelling around the Continent, his vice-chairman Robert Brand took over in Washington. Brand was a Milner Kindergartener and fellow of All Souls, Oxford, and Northcliffe also surrounded himself with lieutenants of great intellects and capabilities, such as Sir Charles Gordon (later president of the Bank of Montreal), Sir Thomas Royden and Sir Hardman Lever. He told his mother that they were people who had 'come here to win the war in the only place it can be won – the United States'.[63]

It certainly was not being won by Sir Douglas Haig's offensive at Passchendaele in Flanders, also known as the Third Battle of Ypres, which was fought from 31 July to 10 November and which saw 275,000 casualties before all the ground that had been won had to be given up. 'GHQ could not capture the Passchendaele Ridge,' Lloyd George bitterly recorded in his memoirs, 'but it was determined to storm Fleet Street, and here [its] strategy and tactics were superb ... Lord Northcliffe had, ever since 1916, been the mere kettledrum of Sir Douglas Haig, and the mouth-organ of Sir William Robertson.'[64] He noted that, in September 1917, *The Times* had declared 'German Defence Broken' for a headline of a report of an attack in which only 1,000 yards had been taken on a narrow front with heavy losses. He complained that despite his desire to replace Haig and Robertson during Passchendaele, 'Northcliffe strongly supported both.'[65]

Meanwhile, in the drawing room of Violet Bonham Carter's house after lunch on 26 August, Cynthia Asquith heard J. A. Spender being 'very interesting about journalism and the personality, mentality, and tactics of Northcliffe. He says he employs vast armies of men with notebooks who go and listen in public houses and report on the tone and appetite of the moment for which the papers must cater.'[66] The Asquiths and their friends found the idea of finding out what ordinary people thought extraordinary and degrading, but in the rest of the world it was called journalism. (Similar haughtiness greeted George Sutton's ideas for trying to raise money for a Victory Loan in September, which included putting a tank in Trafalgar Square and illuminated green eyes in the lions on Nelson's column, both of which were stopped by J. C. C. Davidson.)

For all that Northcliffe needed to curry favour with President Wilson, he did not go along with Wilson's (at least publicly) altruistic view of why the United States was at war. Bravely, he stated what he saw as the truth in the journal *Current Opinion*, in an article entitled 'What America is Fighting For', in which he presented a far more realpolitik explanation as to why the United States needed to fight, arguing that the motive 'was not sympathy for any other nation, was not desire for gain, was not an abstract fondness for democratic as opposed to autocratic government: it was self-interest, self-preservation, self-respect. The American People are not fighting to make the world safe for democracy, but to make the world safe for themselves.'[67]

It was a hard-hitting article and came from Northcliffe's heart. His claims included: Austria was being 'used as a cat's-paw by the Hohenzollern gang'; 'The aim of the Hohenzollerns and of Prussian Junkerdom was to establish a world-domination'; 'The Archduke Franz Ferdinand was murdered (many believe with Prussia's connivance) after he had been made use of'; and 'King Ferdinand of Bulgaria, the Coburg fox, was taken out of his dissolute obscurity to be the tool of the real rulers of Bulgaria.'[68] He argued that the German theory of international relations 'is based upon the belief that the Germans are supermen, a chosen race, and that it is necessary for world-progress that they should forcibly impose their will on the world [and] no scruple about honour or pity must be allowed to stand in the way'.[69] It hardly needs stating that for all the absurdity of the conspiracy theory about Archduke Franz Ferdinand, other views from this article were well ahead of their time.

On 5 October, Northcliffe had a moment to reflect to his family about what he had achieved since the outbreak of war, and it is instructive what he chose to recall. 'I do not suppose many people have had such a kaleidoscopic life as I have had since the War began,' he wrote.

> First, those intense four days in 1914 of flogging those political jellyfish into action, then the row about Kitchener and the shells, and the bannings and burnings of my newspapers, then Ypres, Verdun, Gorizia and the Carso, among the Germans in Switzerland, then off to Spain, a few days salmon fishing on the Tay (six fish in one day), the battle of the Somme, more visits to France, more stirrings up of the Government, thirty-six hours in which to abandon the work of my life for this killing job of trying to push everything

available in the United States across the Atlantic to Haig and all the meat and wheat I can get for the people at home.[70]

Northcliffe believed that the work he was doing in the United States was hard, but the most important of his life.[71]

He met many of the most famous Americans of the day, including Orville Wright in Dayton, Ohio, to whom Northcliffe awarded the Albert Medal of the Royal Society of Arts, and Thomas Edison. Of the latter, he wrote to his mother: 'Old Edison, seventy years of age, alert as a young man and chewing tobacco all the time. He is very deaf, quite common, but has a magnificent head. I found that he had a wonderful memory and he recalled details of a conversation I had with him more than seventeen years ago. He is doing very good submarine work and hates the Germans like poison. They stole all his patents.'[72]

It was Edison who put Northcliffe in touch with Henry Ford, from whom Britain needed to buy 6,000 tractors at cost price. Because of bad treatment that the anti-war Ford had received from Spring-Rice, Northcliffe had to go to Detroit to, as he put it in a letter to Churchill, the new Minister of Munitions, 'eat humble pie'.[73] He ate it expertly, and also drove one of Ford's tractors. 'If he were introduced to you as a popular poet, preacher or actor, you would believe it,' he told his mother of Ford. 'He has the third largest income in the United States [and] was working at the bench seventeen years ago. Ford is no more interested in money than I am and knows about as much as I do about it.'[74] Three years later he said of Ford, with a chuckle, 'He is the only millionaire I have met with brains – except *me*.'[75]

Northcliffe did not shy away from visiting the pro-German areas of the United States.[76] In Chicago, the pro-German mayor asked him not to walk the streets despite his five giant bodyguards, but he turned out not to need them.[77] In a speech at the Cleveland Armory in isolationist Ohio, which he likened in size to the Albert Hall, there were overflow meetings outside.[78] His speeches never underplayed German power and the threat it posed, and forecast a long war with food rationing, but were optimistic about ultimate victory. He stressed the importance of self-sacrifice, the role of business, avia-tion and buying Liberty Loans. (He had a German U-boat brought

over to New York, which could only be inspected by buyers of a
Liberty Loan.)

Of the severe logistical problems involved in shipping the US's
million-man army to France, Northcliffe told his family: 'I am the
only Englishman over here who dares to suggest that anything at
all is wrong here. I wrap it up in a good deal of flattery and they
take it well.'[79] 'You may rely on me never to use minatory language,'
Northcliffe cabled to Balfour towards the end of his mission. 'I have
been dealing with these people for thirty years. Nothing can be
gained here by threats, much by flattery and self-abnegation.'[80]

Yet it was not all flattery and self-abnegation. When seated next to
the isolationist William Randolph Hearst at a banquet, Northcliffe
told him in a loud voice that he was fooling his readers and was
'backing the wrong horse ... and you ought to know it'. Hearst was
extremely sensitive to such accusations and, like Joseph Pulitzer back
on New Year's Day 1900, replied: 'Very well, Lord Northcliffe, I'll
give you the freedom of the New York American editorial page for
one day. You can write what you like in it.'[81] Bringing his fist down
on the table, Northcliffe accepted the offer and a speech he gave to
200 Midwestern editors from six states at Kansas City was printed.
Its headline was 'WAKE UP, AMERICA!' Back in London at The
Other Club, Lord Glenconner wagered Lord Beaverbrook £300 to
£100 that Northcliffe would not become prime minister 'before the
Armistice which in fact leads to peace'.[82] Glenconner won, but it
shows the prestige that Northcliffe enjoyed at the time, as well as
Beaverbrook's faith in him.

In his war memoirs, Lloyd George congratulated himself on
Northcliffe's appointment to the War Mission role, writing that 'it is
the wisdom of successful governments that it should harness power-
ful but unruly natural elements to some beneficent task. In the event,
Lord Northcliffe proved to be a striking success in his new role.'[83]
As a press proprietor, however, Lloyd George thought, Northcliffe

> was naturally impatient of even inevitable delays. Not accustomed
> to being thwarted or having his decision questioned or delayed,
> in his experience an order rung down the telephone had to be

executed forthwith ... He had thus acquired a telephone mentality. He was now in a world where the autocrat had to submit to being an all-round subordinate ... For a man of his dictatorial temperament and experience he did well.[84]

It was a fair estimation of Northcliffe's time running the British War Mission to the United States at a key stage of the Great War.

The admiration felt in Britain for Northcliffe's achievement in the US was not shared by everyone in the Establishment. In 1947, the Foreign Office veteran Lord Hardinge of Penshurst wrote in his memoirs, *Old Diplomacy*, that

> Lloyd George considered it desirable to send Lord Northcliffe, as a business hustler, to take Mr Balfour's place. Northcliffe went over, making no secret that he wanted to effect some big coup for his own glorification and admitting that he knew nothing of the blockade and other questions with which he had to deal. He was a complete failure and returned to England in a few weeks' time. The Americans felt they were as good businessmen as Northcliffe, and better hustlers than he, and they realised that he had none of the charm or distinction that had endeared Balfour to them.[85]

Every single sentence of that paragraph contains a factual inaccuracy, sometimes more than one, and the snobbery is palpable.

By October, with the difficult part of his job accomplished successfully and the War Mission on its feet, and, with a successor in Lord Reading well established, Northcliffe was, in the words of Campbell Stuart, 'growing weary of the War Mission post. More and more he had begun to feel that he had been sent to America to be got out of the way. He knew that his real importance and usefulness in life was as a newspaper proprietor. His mind was turning to war propaganda.'[86]

CHAPTER 17

'I WATCH THESE PEOPLE VIGILANTLY'

November 1917–January 1918

'He divided men into two classes – those who felt there
could be no way out except through victory, and those
who bewailed the loss of peace, or sought compromises,
or failed to bend all their energies to the hitting of the
enemy, constantly and hard by arms and by policy.'[1]

HENRY WICKHAM STEED on Lord Northcliffe
during the Great War

Northcliffe returned to Britain in November 1917 ahead of the
Conference of Allied Governments in Paris, which for the first
time would include the Americans, represented by Colonel House.
Northcliffe, Lord Reading and Campbell Stuart sailed across the
Atlantic in the blacked-out *St Paul*, 'with all lights out and submarines
lurking'.[2] Before they left, Lloyd George wrote to say that 'The War
Cabinet desire to express to you their complete satisfaction with the
manner in which you have fulfilled your mission.'[3] He also agreed to
the granting of a knighthood to the thirty-two-year-old Stuart, who
recalled how 'Northcliffe impressed upon me, looking back on his own
life, that honours are only really of value when you got them young.'[4]
On his return, Northcliffe set up the London headquarters of the British
War Mission opposite the Houses of Parliament at No. 29 Abingdon
Street and relinquished the American side of his activities to Reading.

The Balfour Declaration, which announced Britain's intention of giving a national homeland to the Jewish people in Palestine, was made on 2 November 1917 when Northcliffe was halfway across the Atlantic. With Geoffrey Dawson uninterested in Palestine and Northcliffe uncontactable, *The Times* was anodyne about it, not mentioning it in a leader until 3 December and then only in the context of Jews, Arabs and Armenians walking hand in hand for national redemption.[5] Steed supported the declaration because of his belief in 'the principle of nationality', that is, national self-determination as applied to small nations. He was a leading propagandist for the Czechs and Slovaks, Croats, Slovenes and Serbs destroying the Austro-Hungarian Empire, and extended the principle to the Jews in Palestine, despite his anti-Semitism.[6] Northcliffe only opposed the declaration when it was too late, writing that Britain had 'without sufficient thought, guaranteed Palestine as a home for the Jews despite the fact that 700,000 Arab Muslims live there and own it'.[7] (Although they did indeed live there, in November 1917 it was owned by the Ottoman Empire that no longer controlled it.)

The outbreak of the Bolshevik Revolution in Petrograd (modern-day St Petersburg) on 6 November gave Northcliffe an enemy he was resolutely to oppose for the rest of his life. 'Bolshevism is the handmaiden of the servant races,' he said. 'Our race, thank God, is not a servant race.'[8] Typically, he was to make the common anti-Semitic error of supposing that because Jews were prominent in the Bolshevik high command, there was a conspiracy between Jews worldwide and Bolshevism per se.

Northcliffe arrived on 9 November to a country exhausted by the slaughter at Passchendaele. Although the lack of a breakthrough there tested his faith in the High Command and its attrition strategy – though not Haig personally – Northcliffe was also unimpressed by almost everyone in the government except Lloyd George himself. This became publicly clear after Lloyd George offered Northcliffe the about-to-be created Air Ministry at a lunch at Downing Street on 15 November. 'What happened thereafter,' writes an historian, 'became one of the most celebrated incidents of wartime politics.'[9]

The Air Board, which Lloyd George wanted to raise to the status of a ministry, was presided over by the sixty-one-year-old Lord Cowdray. In his war memoirs, Lloyd George claimed that it was his intention 'to choose a younger and physically fitter man for the post of Air Minister. At a luncheon in Downing Street, in the course of a conversation with Lord Northcliffe, I sounded him on the subject without making any definite offer.'[10] Whether Lloyd George was being truthful or not, Northcliffe certainly left Downing Street thinking the offer had been made, and Colonel House's diary at the time recorded that Lloyd George 'wished N[orthcliffe] to become Minister of the Air Services'.[11]

What Northcliffe did next was, as Lloyd George later complained, a 'lamentable breach of my confidence, and ... one of those lapses into blundering brutality to which his passion for the startling gesture sometimes led him'.[12] For Northcliffe refused the offer not in a private note to the Prime Minister, but in a letter published on the leader page of *The Times*, a remarkable breach of etiquette that has rightly been described as 'gratuitously insulting' to Lloyd George and which the War Cabinet denounced as 'mischievous'.[13]

'Dear Prime Minister,' the letter from Abingdon Street read, 'I have given anxious consideration to your repeated invitation that I should take charge of the new Air Ministry. The reasons which have impelled me to decline that great honour and responsibility are in no way connected with the office which is rightly to be set up.' Instead, Northcliffe wrote, the reasons were that,

> Returning after five months spent in the virile atmosphere of the United States and Canada, I find that ... while the United States has instantly put into operation Conscription, over which we wobbled for two years, and is making short work with sedition-mongers; while Canada had already given such proofs of thoroughness as the disenfranchisement of conscientious objectors and the denaturalisation of all enemy aliens who have been naturalised in the last fifteen years ... There are still in office here those who dally with such urgent questions as that of the unity of war control, the eradication of sedition, the mobilisation of the whole man and woman power of the country, and the introduction

of compulsory food rations ... I find that the Censorship is still being misused, and that men in various positions of authority, who should have been punished, have been retained and in some cases elevated.[14]

Northcliffe effectively used the offer of a place in the government as a peg on which to hang a manifesto denouncing that government. 'We have,' he continued, 'in my belief, the most efficient army in the world, led by one of the greatest generals ... but I feel that in present circumstances I can do better work if I retain my independence and am not gagged by a loyalty that I did not feel towards the whole of your Administration.'[15] His final sentence might still have been true, but by then was quite irrelevant, and read, 'I have none but the most friendly feelings towards yourself.' To make matters worse, Northcliffe had alerted the news agencies, so that Lloyd George found out about the letter from a telephone call from Lord Beaverbrook before the letter itself arrived at Downing Street. 'Never before had a prime minister been treated in such an insulting fashion,' wrote Frank Owen, one of Beaverbrook's editors.[16]

Lord Cowdray, who had naturally expected to be the new air minister, took 'bitter offence' and resigned from the Air Board immediately, even though the Air Force Bill was going through Parliament at the time, and he became a bitter enemy of Northcliffe's for life.[17] The *Westminster Gazette*, a Liberal paper that Cowdray controlled, now took a decidedly anti-Lloyd George turn.

'The old Northcliffe had returned,' wrote *The Times* historian, Stanley Morison, 'in full venom.'[18] Why did Northcliffe do it, and in that inexcusable manner? Morison put the rudeness and ruthlessness down to megalomania and the fact that 'his effort on behalf of Anglo–American relations and the policy of peace by victory had permanently exhausted him'.[19] Others have even, wrongly, seen in it a bid for dictatorial power for himself. A much more likely reason was that, returning from the United States, the journalist in Northcliffe wanted to make a splash by writing a public letter setting out his genuinely held views showing that he was retaining his freedom of manoeuvre and criticism, and could not resist the scoop that he knew his public refusal of office would constitute. Above all, he believed the government was not doing enough to prosecute the war in the key areas he mentioned in his letter. 'My direct and indirect connection with the government', he told the *Globe* three days later, 'convinces me that it needs wholesale revision; some of its members are tired and some unsuitable.'

Colonel House sat next to Queen Mary at lunch at Buckingham Palace on the 16th, and she cited the letter in *The Times* as evidence that Northcliffe would soon 'begin an attack on the ministry'. After lunch, House noted in his diary that 'Lloyd George and I stood apart telling jokes and laughing about his predicament with Lord Northcliffe.'[20] Yet that day House also told President Wilson that 'Northcliffe has been splendid.'[21] In the afternoon, House met Northcliffe and Geoffrey Dawson at Chesterfield House, the head-quarters of the American War Mission to London, where the former 'spoke of the Government's lack of efficiency. He thought there were only two men in it of any value, [Lloyd] George and Milner ... Northcliffe criticised Balfour's and Bonar Law's inefficiency and said they should be gotten rid of forthwith.'[22]

Other reasons advanced as to why Northcliffe so publicly dis-tanced himself from Lloyd George on his return from the United States have been that, over the issue of peace with Germany, he was beginning to suspect the government of going soft; he did not trust Lloyd George; and a suspicion that an individualist like himself could never fit into a Cabinet of equals.[23] There might also have been some self-realisation that he would not have prospered as air secretary, subject to criticism and cross-questioning from across the House of Lords dispatch box.

'You cannot rely on him,' Lloyd George told Sir George Riddell while playing golf the day after the letter was published. 'He has no sense of loyalty and there is something of the cad about him. You can see it in his face. He is angling for the premiership. His object is plain.'[24] Neville Chamberlain, the director of National Service, agreed, telling his sister Ida that Northcliffe 'has gone too far. He has been out of the country now for some nine months, and yet he has the impudence to come and lecture us on what we should do in all departments making things worse by holding up the Americans as shining examples for us to follow. And when he is asked to come and show us himself how to do it he replies, "No I think I can be more useful throwing mud from outside." Poor Cowdray!'[25]

In fact, Northcliffe had already shown in the United States how to run two far larger organisations than the Air Ministry, and Chamberlain, who had not supported compulsory conscription, had long been a butt of the Northcliffe press's attacks over the way he ran his department.[26] 'I know nothing of Mr Chamberlain,' Northcliffe had said of him in March 1917 (although, of course, he had known his father Joseph well). 'The only things of his that have come to my notice have been blunders.'[27]

Someone else whom Northcliffe considered a blunderer, but whom he liked personally and who had been brought back into the Cabinet while he was away in the States, was Winston Churchill. When he saw Churchill entering the Ministry of Munitions in Northumberland Avenue, Northcliffe called out from his car, 'Hullo, Winston! Are you after Lloyd George's job?'[28] Under normal circumstances, Churchill would have dealt him a crushing riposte, but even he could not trade quips with a passing car. Instead, a piqued Churchill returned an ivory statuette of Napoleon that Northcliffe had given him, with a note saying that he could 'no longer keep it as the gift of a courteous gentleman'.[29] 'Had I thought that the remark would have wounded you,' a suitably admonished Northcliffe replied, 'I would not for a moment have made it; and I ask you to accept an expression of my regret for having said it.' That did not mean, of course, that he had not meant it, although at this period at least it was not true; Churchill knew he owed his return from the political wilderness entirely to Lloyd George.

On 24 November, Northcliffe was awarded a viscountcy for his work as chairman of the War Mission. There have been plenty of press barons created in the history of Fleet Street, but very few press viscounts. It was particularly generous of Lloyd George considering the disrespect Northcliffe had shown him only eight days earlier, but then Lloyd George set little store by peerages except as a means of party funding. Unlike Northcliffe's barony, this was certainly not the work of the Crown: Colonel House noted how, at an audience at Buckingham Palace on the evening of 20 November, 'The King was full of Northcliffe and his dictatorial assumptions,' and then at dinner with Lloyd George and Reading that night, 'We talked of Northcliffe. He [Lloyd George] is evidently afraid of him and, unfortunately, Northcliffe knows it.'[30] Yet this was contradicted a few days later when, on 1 December, House noted that Lloyd George 'is constantly ridiculing Northcliffe ... I replied that I had learnt to like him and that he could send him to America [as ambassador] and we would welcome him.'[31]

On 26 November, two days after the bestowal of Northcliffe's viscountcy and three days before the Air Force Bill became law, came the news on 26 November that the new air minister would be his brother Harold, Lord Rothermere. Harold had been acting independently of his brother for some time, though relations between them were good, but to have one brother accepting the post so soon after it had been publicly and contemptuously turned down by another had Westminster and Whitehall in uproar, although that was not reflected in the large section of the British press that the two brothers controlled.[32]

On 27 November, Lloyd George left for Paris from Charing Cross for the key inter-Allied conference that Northcliffe had returned home in order to attend. Along with them came 107 other people for the meeting of the 'Big Four' – Lloyd George, Georges Clemenceau, House and Vittorio Orlando of Italy – in order to discuss the Italian and Balkan campaigns, more efficient use of railways and, most importantly, the creation of a Supreme War Council, a concept that Northcliffe had been pushing for months, believing that it would strengthen the French voice in British strategy-making.

On the day that the British government delegation left London for the conference, the Unionist former foreign secretary Lord Lansdowne visited Geoffrey Dawson at *The Times* and handed him a letter that he wanted published the next day. It was a call for a negotiated peace with Germany.[33] Dawson flatly refused to publish the letter in *The Times*, telling him that he ought to wait until after the Paris Conference was over, so Lansdowne went instead to

Lord Burnham at the *Daily Telegraph*, which published it the next morning. Northcliffe was furious that *The Times* had missed out on such a sensational scoop, telling Lloyd George that he would have published a 'stinging leader' directly next to it.[34] It could hardly have been more stinging than the leader the *Daily Mail* published on the 30th, which stated that 'If Lord Lansdowne raises the white flag he is alone in his surrender.'[35]

Dawson later said that his difference of opinion with Northcliffe over this matter was 'the sharpest they ever had'.[36] The row went to the heart of the difference between the two men. Dawson's argument was that it would have been irresponsible for *The Times* to start 'very public discussions that should be avoided' at such a sensitive time, whereas Northcliffe took the view that they were newspaper-men not politicians, that if public discussions were to be had they should be had in his papers, and that this was a major news story in which they allowed themselves to be scooped by their chief rival. Yet that did not prevent Northcliffe attempting to take the moral high ground publicly. On 30 November, *The Times* stated that it refused to publish the letter because 'we believe it reflects no responsible phase of British opinion. Yet it appeared in the *Daily Telegraph*. We are confident that in all the Allied countries it will be read with universal regret and reprobation.'[37]

It was the battle of Cambrai, fought between 20 November and 7 December 1917, that turned Northcliffe against 'Wully' Robertson and various other senior members of the High Command, though not Haig himself. In this he might have been following, or at least reflecting, public opinion, as historians recognise Cambrai, despite its witnessing the first notable tank advance, as having finally 'jolted the nation's confidence in the British High Command'.[38] It was remarkable that this had not happened sooner as overall Britain had lost 822,000 killed, wounded or missing on the Western Front during the calendar year 1916.

As with the Battle of the Somme, early in the battle of Cambrai the Northcliffe press had run exaggerated headlines about the like-lihood of victory. The *Daily Mail* hailed 'A Splendid Success' on 22 November, along with 'Haig Through the Hindenburg Line'. The papers advocated the ringing of church bells around the country on 3 December, which happened, including those of St Paul's Cathedral.[39] In *The Times*, phrases such as 'splendid victory', 'bewildering success' and the 'glorious battle of Cambrai' appeared under the headline 'The Victory'.[40] Yet that was before the inevitable German counter-attack,* the biggest since 1914, in which all the ground gained had to be conceded.

Once it became clear that Cambrai had not been a victory, the newspaper (and its proprietor) started to look foolish.[41] In General Charteris's biography of Haig, he wrote that 'When a few days later the news of the German counter-attack was published, there was a corresponding reaction. Unduly inflated hope yielded to a depression equally justified. The public felt they had been cheated. Lord Northcliffe himself led this new outbreak.'[42]

After the Allied Conference ended, Northcliffe visited the Front again, meeting Haig on 7 December, just as the battle of Cambrai ended. There was none of the warmth of the earlier encounters. In bitter hindsight, Charteris later wrote that Northcliffe had been 'very strong in his condemnation of the Government, much impressed with American methods as opposed to ours, and bubbling over with the importance of his own Mission and full of himself. Unfortunately D[ouglas] H[aig] was too preoccupied to respond and Northcliffe was rather wounded in his self-esteem.'[43]

Yet was it really affronted pride that led Northcliffe to leave the chateau remarking that he thought Haig's 'grasp of affairs was weakening, and that he doubted whether he could continue to support him'?[44] In fact, Passchendaele and Cambrai had changed Northcliffe's mind, as well as the embarrassment at having hailed the latter as a victory worthy of bell-ringing. Steed's view was that had Northcliffe not gone to the United States, 'his own view might gradually have been modified under pressure of circumstances instead of changing so suddenly' at the time of Cambrai, which 'convinced him

---

* 'Nothing is inevitable in history,' the author was told by Professor Norman Stone in his first supervision at Cambridge University, 'except German counter-attack'.

that there was something radically defective in the British military conception of the war'.[45]

Haig's official biographer, Alfred Duff Cooper, believed Northcliffe's abrupt change of heart might have been 'due to that lack of balance in his judgement which became increasingly noticeable towards the close of his life, we cannot tell'.[46] This is wrong; Northcliffe's mind did not become unbalanced until at least four years after he became disillusioned by the enormous loss of life on the Western Front during Haig's time as commander-in-chief. It has also been alleged that 'the underlying motive for Northcliffe's change of allegiance was undoubtedly the prospect of political office', yet he had publicly turned down political office only three weeks earlier, and in a manner that made it very unlikely that it would be re-offered anytime soon.[47] Haig himself believed that Northcliffe wanted to become secretary for war, and supported Derby all the more because of it, but there is no evidence for that either.

Writing privately to *The Times* staff, Northcliffe called Cambrai 'one of the most ghastly stories in English history'.[48] On 11 December, he warned Charteris that 'I have been informed indirectly that members of [the] Government consider that you have misled them by exaggerated statements as to [the] decline of German morale and the number of German reserves ... I am convinced that unless examples are made of those responsible and changes at once made in Headquarters Staff the position of the Commander-in-Chief will be imperilled.'[49] The next morning, under the sub-heading 'A Case for Inquiry', *The Times* opined that there should be a public inquiry over Cambrai where 'The charges of blundering should be sifted and the blame, if and where it is due, should take shape in the prompt removal of every blunderer.'[50] It expressed dissatisfaction with 'the fatuous estimates' of German losses and demanded an inquiry, one that was 'prompt, searching, complete, and free from all suspicion that those responsible, however remotely, are sitting in judgement on their own miscalculations'.[51] Everyone knew that meant Charteris.

Writing to Philip Sassoon on 13 December, but also intended for Haig, Northcliffe warned that Lieutenant-General Sir Launcelot

Kiggell, Haig's chief of staff, and Charteris 'seem to be persons considered incompetent by every officer with whom I spoke, without any exaggeration. My knowledge of the temper of the people (quite apart from the temper of the Government, which will fall if there are many more Cambrais) shows me that they are at the end of their patience ... Sir Douglas is regarded with affection in the army, but everywhere people remark that he is surrounded by incompetents.'[52] He wrote that 'in some quarters it is asked, what is the use of sending out men to be "Cambrai-ised"?'[53]

Two days later, Haig persuaded Charteris to resign. Derby told Haig that the War Cabinet had long distrusted Charteris's reports, yet in fact it was the Northcliffe press and its demands for a public inquiry that finally dislodged Haig's chief intelligence officer who had for so long produced over-optimistic assessments of the German forces, ignoring those with different opinions.[54] Early in 1918, Kiggell became governor of Guernsey.

'This Government is always on thin ice,' Northcliffe wrote to Andrew Caird on 3 January 1918. 'I watch these people vigilantly day and night.' It was not only Kiggell and Charteris who now found themselves out of a job at least partly due to Northcliffe. At the meeting at Chesterfield House on 16 November, Colonel House noted Northcliffe referring to Admiral Lord Jellicoe, the First Sea Lord, as 'the man who ran away from a fight', a reference to the battle of Jutland and an undeserved slur.[55] The Northcliffe press had hounded Jellicoe ever since the indecisive battle, and his sacking by Sir Eric Geddes, the first lord of the Admiralty, on Christmas Eve was widely seen as a sign of Lord Northcliffe's power. Jellicoe himself later noted that he knew 'from Carson that Northcliffe had frequently pressed both him and the Prime Minister ... to get rid of me'.[56] In fact, it was Jellicoe's failure to institute the convoy system before August 1917 that had lost him the government's confidence, and the stridency of press criticism over the summer of 1917 had if anything strengthened Jellicoe, because the government feared to let it appear that Fleet Street was dictating to it.[57]

By late 1917, the Northcliffe papers seemed so supportive of the government that wags dubbed them 'the Georgecliffe press'.[58]

Typically, A. G. Gardiner, the Liberal editor of the *Daily News*, was on hand to put the worst possible slant on it, writing that 'The democracy, whose bulwark is Parliament, has been unseated, and mobocracy, whose dictator is Lord Northcliffe, is in power.'[59] With Northcliffe now back in Britain permanently, Lloyd George looked around for another full-time job for him that might lessen the danger of his outright opposition.

~

One casualty of Northcliffe's change of stance over the High Command's conception of attritional strategy was Charles Repington, a convinced Westerner and the veteran military correspondent of *The Times* who, after a shaky start in 1914, had grown close to Haig, and who, along with journalists such as Leo Maxse, St Loe Strachey and J. A. Spender, had championed him against Lloyd George. On 16 January 1918, Repington resigned in dudgeon and joined the *Morning Post*, alleging privately that *The Times* had shown 'a subservient and apologetic attitude' towards the War Cabinet and 'neglect of the vital interests of the Army'.[60] He had been complaining to his diary since early December that 'My difficulties are that Northcliffe has tied himself to L.G.'s chariot wheels,' and that the Western strategy was under threat because of the almost one million men stationed in Mesopotamia, Egypt and Salonika.[61] A measure of Repington's egotism can be gained from his remark that it was because 'I am unable to get the support from the editor of *The Times* that I must have to rouse the country.'[62]

Northcliffe had been downplaying Repington's influence even while he was working for him, and Dawson was altering his copy, so Repington's departure was the honourable thing to do, even though his effectiveness was greatly diminished once he had left. He told Strachey that Lloyd George and Northcliffe 'are a curse to the country ... They are directing this odious campaign against the High Command and I can't think why the Army Council does not take up Northcliffe, Marlowe and [Lovat] Fraser and have them shot.'[63] Yet in fact Fraser was at the time himself criticising Northcliffe for censoring 'points which tell specially against Haig' and instead directing attacks on Robertson and Haig's underlings.[64]

'The stories of Passchendaele and Cambrai have made a very bad impression,' Northcliffe told Sassoon on 17 January, 'and the hushing-up of Cambrai has made it worse.'[65] Of the rumoured imminent removal of Robertson, he added that 'the War Cabinet will take the matter into their own hands. I believe it will have the support of ninety-five percent of the people. The fall of Jellicoe has not produced a murmur of disapproval, and Parliament and public are in a mood that will not brook the support of incompetence.'[66]

Lovat Fraser's articles in the *Daily Mail* – 'The Soldiers' Friend' as it described itself – attacked the squandering of manpower as 'the strategy of the Stone Age' and 'the ridiculous "theory of attrition"'.[67] This attracted a good deal of criticism from other papers, and the Unionist War Committee in Parliament even called on Lloyd George to denounce Northcliffe. The 22 January publication of Northcliffe's daily 'Message from the Chief' noted that the paper was 'getting plenty of free advertising' and that it recalled for him 'the good old days of the shells'.[68]

Yet just as that crisis had actually entrenched Kitchener in place, so Robertson and Derby were strengthened by the Northcliffe press's criticism, as Lloyd George knew he could not be seen to bow to it, any more than Asquith had with Kitchener. On the same day as Northcliffe's pugnacious message to his staff, Lloyd George told the king's private secretary Lord Stamfordham that he 'could have taken him out and shot him'.[69]

CHAPTER 18

PROPAGANDA IN ENEMY COUNTRIES

February–September 1918

'Words today are battles: the right words, battles won;
the wrong words, battles lost.'[1]

GENERAL ERICH LUDENDORFF, 1918

Far from upbraiding Northcliffe as the Unionists wanted, on 10 February Lloyd George appointed him as Director of Propaganda in Enemy Countries, reporting directly to him rather than to the new minister for information, Lord Beaverbrook (the former Max Aitken). Here was another example of Lloyd George's capacity to 'harness powerful but unruly natural elements to some beneficent task'. Choosing the title 'director' was deliberate; Northcliffe would not be a minister. When Lord Milner, C. P. Scott, Lord Balcarres and others protested about the appointment, the Prime Minister replied that *The Times* had been 'quite reasonable' when Northcliffe had been in the United States and 'It was necessary to find occupation for his abounding energies if he were not to run into mischief.'[2]

The task of undermining German and Austrian morale would fully occupy Northcliffe for the rest of the war. It was one he relished and at which he was, unsurprisingly, excellent. As his deputy director, he appointed Campbell Stuart, then the managing director of the *Daily Mail*, who was soon nicknamed 'Senior Wangler' for the conciliatory tact with which he disarmed the suspicion of various existing (and competing) organisations. The Marquess of Crewe put Crewe House – No. 15 Curzon Street in Mayfair – at the department's disposal, where Stuart lived 'in solitary grandeur'.[3] Northcliffe appointed Wickham Steed, then foreign editor of *The Times*, as his chief political advisor for his knowledge of eastern Europe. He also invited H. G. Wells to join the organisation as head of the German department. 'You want a social revolution,' he said as they met in the palatial splendour of Crewe House. 'Isn't our sitting here social revolution enough for you?'[4] Other members of the executive committee included Colonel Chalmers Mitchell and the historian R. W. Seton-Watson, with S. A. Guest as the technical advisor on how physically to get propaganda into the enemy countries.

Almost as soon as he started working there, the importance of the work of his new department was underlined for Northcliffe by the loss of another nephew and godson, the twenty-three-year-old Captain Vyvyan Harmsworth, Harold Rothermere's eldest son. He died in Mary's hospital, the Lady Northcliffe Hospital for Officers in London, on 12 February 1918, three months after he had been wounded at Cambrai while serving with the 2nd Battalion of the Irish Guards. A week after his death, he was awarded a posthumous Military Cross. 'We don't mind being killed but we object to being butchered,' Vyvyan had said to Northcliffe of Cambrai, and Steed wrote that his loss was 'a poignant grief' to Northcliffe that left him willing to listen to other arguments about how the war should be fought than ones based on attrition.[5] When, on 17 February, Sir William Robertson was replaced by Sir Henry Wilson as chief of the imperial general staff, the *Daily Mail* applauded. This was also a victory for Lloyd George, whose unofficial military advisor Wilson had been for some time, but also for Northcliffe, with whom Wilson, the ultimate Westerner, had been in close contact since before the fall of Asquith. They used to dine together occasionally as part of an influential, secretive group called the Monday Night Cabal.

The appointments of Northcliffe, Rothermere and Beaverbrook were attacked in the House of Commons by Austen Chamberlain, who had resigned from the government in July 1917. He argued that it was unconstitutional to have newspaper proprietors being 'members of, or ... intimately associated with, the Administration' and that Lloyd George and the government 'have surrounded themselves quite unnecessarily with an atmosphere of suspicion and distrust because they have allowed themselves to become so intimately associated with these great newspaper proprietors ... As long as you have the owner of a newspaper as a member of your Administration you will be held responsible for what he writes in the newspaper.'[6] He denounced the Northcliffe press's attacks on admirals and generals as 'deplorable and cowardly', but refused to put the matter to a vote. 'He is too genteel,' concluded Leo Amery, and the journalist F. S. Oliver commented that 'he must have included someone at Madame Tussaud's among his maternal ancestors'.[7] A later comment on Chamberlain was that 'he always played the game, and always lost it'.[8]

Lloyd George took three weeks to reply to Austen Chamberlain's attacks on the press barons, but on 11 March he described Northcliffe as

> one out of hundreds of great businessmen, who, in this great national emergency, have voluntarily and gratuitously given their services to assist the State in the work for which their experience has especially qualified them ... Lord Northcliffe, who, in addition to being a great news organiser, has made a special study during the war of conditions in enemy countries, was invited to take charge of that branch. He consented to do so without any ministerial position. No man better qualified for that difficult task could, in my opinion, be found in the Empire, and the Government are grateful to him for undertaking it.[9]

Before the department was created, British propaganda had largely consisted of leaflet distribution by agents and by limited airdrops, but this had not been very effective in attacking enemy morale.[10] Northcliffe wanted to expand the role of propaganda enormously, to destroy German morale by every means possible and, in particular, to tell the many non-Austrian peoples of the Austro-Hungarian Empire that they now had a chance for autonomy if the Hapsburgs were to lose the war. After Lloyd George declared that one of Britain's war aims was that 'genuine self-government on true democratic principles [would be] granted to those Austro-Hungarian nationalities who have long desired it', Northcliffe concentrated on getting that message across to the non-Austrians who made up the two-thirds of the Hapsburg Empire. The historian A. J. P. Taylor certainly believed that Northcliffe 'probably helped to destroy Austria-Hungary by his conduct of enemy propaganda'.[11]

At the prompting of H. G. Wells, but also in accordance with his own well-honed instincts for propaganda, Northcliffe concentrated on getting information to the Germans that accorded as closely as possible with the facts. By the spring of 1918, some of these – the number of American troops in France, the progress of the Allied campaigns against Germany's allies, the number of U-Boats sunk, and so on – did not need to be exaggerated to have a demoralising effect on German soldiers. Small balloons, which carried four pounds of leaflets each, were released when the wind was blowing from the south west. A string passing round separate bundles was fastened to the neck of the balloon, with a slow fuse attached to the string, which would burn through at the proper moment. Although the bulk of them fell in the German trenches or within ten to fifteen miles behind their front, others were designed to float into central Belgium and the occupied areas of France, and even on occasion across the German border.[12]

The key to the propaganda, as Steed pointed out in his memoirs, was that it was 'based upon the truth – truth as to policy, truth as to facts, truth as to intentions. Lying propaganda defeats itself sooner or later.'[13] By September 1918, the *Kölnische Zeitung* was complaining that 'In our dear Fatherland today we have great numbers of innocent and ingenuous minds who doubt the plain statements of the German Army reports but believe the false reports and omissions of the enemy.'[14]

A good deal of effort was put into getting stories into the papers of neutral countries, which would then reappear in German ones. Northcliffe was 'particularly pleased' with a dummy German trench newspaper put out by Crewe House, which presaged the kind of 'black propaganda' used by Sefton Delmer and the Political Warfare Executive in the Second World War.[15]

On 18 March 1918, Northcliffe wrote to Lord Reading, who by then was ambassador in Washington, that Lloyd George was 'whiter and older-looking than he was when you left. He has wonderful recuperative power; has the faculty of auto-stimulation by conversation, to a degree I have never seen in anybody else.'[16] He believed that 'when the election does come, the PM will sweep the country and eliminate a great many parliamentarians whose only desire is to unseat him.'[17] He was concerned that Lloyd George was overworking:

> Walton Heath is nominally golf on Saturday, but really dispatch boxes, telephones and visitors. Downing Street is a public breakfast, with thirty minutes' walk with someone who is trying to get something out of him. The War Cabinet right up till lunch; Americans and other foreigners at lunch; deputations and interviews in the afternoon, and perhaps another War Cabinet; boresome and intense people like me at about six; very often people at dinner.[18]

'Since dictating the above,' Northcliffe continued,

> I had a narrow escape of being bombed. Last night was not a favourable night for the Germans. There was no moon ... I was sleeping at my mother's house just across the border of Hertfordshire on the top of a hill near a village called Totteridge. Just after midnight the house, which is larger than your Embassy,* of the long, low order, shook exactly as in an earthquake, and I speak from the experience of the Riviera earthquake of twenty-five years ago ... above was the noise of one of the new super-Gothas [bombers].[19]

---

* The predecessor of the present, Lutyens-built British Embassy in Washington.

Visiting the crater the next morning, he found a hole as big 'as your large room in the Embassy' and the surrounding houses all destroyed, with windows smashed and doors blown in for a quarter of a mile all around. 'There was only one person killed – a conscientious objector – which seemed to give great satisfaction to the unfortunate homeless.'[20]

On 21 March, the German army, much reinforced after the signing of the Treaty of Brest-Litovsk with Russia three days earlier, opened the great Ludendorff Offensive (also known as the Second Battle of the Somme) in an attempt to break through before the Americans could arrive on the Western Front in force. On the 23rd, they shelled Paris. 'We are at the beginning of the great battle which may decide the future history of the world for some centuries,' Northcliffe wrote on the 24th to W. F. Bullock, the *Daily Mail*'s New York correspondent. 'I do wish that our American friends were quicker.'[21] It was a nerve-wracking time for the Allies as their armies were forced to retreat under powerful and successive hammer blows.

~

In early April 1918, as soon as the War Cabinet authorised the proclamation of Czech, Polish, Southern Slav and Roumanian independence from Austria after the war, the news was given via fifteen million leaflets distributed to the Austro-Hungarian army by an impressive array of methods, including being dropped by aeroplane, fired from 4,000 rockets, shot from 20,000 specially constructed rifles, and left behind by patrols and raids.[22] 'Slav Soldiers!' read a typical one, 'Czechoslovak and Serb, Croat and Slovene prisoners now in Italy are considered as comrades, in complete equality with the Italian soldiers. The same treatment will henceforth be given to all ... who may be made prisoners of war or who may come over to our lines.'[23] 'Czecho-Slovak soldiers!' read another, 'Italy has recognised the autonomy of the Czecho-Slovak army. It is fighting by our side under the glorious flag of the ancient kingdom of Bohemia.' Another read, 'Yugoslav soldiers! There will be a Southern Slav State!'[24] Meanwhile, the national songs of the Czechs, Slovaks and southern Slav peoples were blared across the trenches by gramo-phone and microphone.

Such was the power of the propaganda amongst the Southern Slav regiments of the Austro-Hungarian army that the Piave offensive of 10 April had to be postponed until the end of June, and on 22 April Lloyd George sent Northcliffe reports from military intelligence sug-gesting that the Austrians had replaced politically unreliable ethnic units in the front-line with Austrian ones.[25]

On 13 April, Northcliffe entered into an ill-considered correspond-ence with Leo Maxse in which he made a statement that has been used by his detractors to imply, wrongly, that he was a proto-fascist. Maxse had tried to persuade Northcliffe to leave his propaganda post and go into all-out opposition to the government. Maxse accused him of blindly following Beaverbrook and 'treating the War Cabinet as a sort of God Almighty' in his newspapers; 'I feared this would happen from the moment you took charge of the American mission, which was Lloyd George's only object in offering it to you.'[26] Clearly stung, Northcliffe replied, 'Whom would you suggest that I support? *Name them.*' All Maxse could think of was Robertson, who was hardly likely to appeal considering that Northcliffe had supported his dismissal only a few weeks beforehand.

Northcliffe – who sarcastically signed himself Beavercliffe – prom-ised that, 'When I find a dictator who is not afraid of the politicians, I shall support him.'[27] Yet this statement was meant no more lit-erally than that of Repington about the Army Council shooting Northcliffe. The meaning of the word 'dictator' was anyhow very different before the advent of Mussolini and Hitler, and much closer to the Ancient Roman idea of a leader who was given wide tempo-rary powers in a time of crisis. Dr Johnson's dictionary definition is of 'one whose credit or authority enables him to direct the conduct or opinion of others'.

At the time, Beaverbrook believed that Northcliffe was readying himself to become prime minister if the government collapsed after a successful Ludendorff Offensive that forced the BEF to evacuate the Continent, as British armies had been forced to do in the Seven Years War and the Napoleonic Wars (and later had to do from Dunkirk in 1940). He gave no evidence for that assertion, and indeed all the evidence contradicts it, including Northcliffe's letter on 25 March to R. B. Marston, the editor of *Fishing Gazette*, stating: 'I have no desire to be PM. I have twice refused Cabinet rank because I believe I can be more useful in my present position as an independent critic.'[28]

Although, of course, the premiership in a moment of existential national crisis is not the same as mere Cabinet rank, there had not been a prime minister from the House of Lords since 1902, and there would have been plenty of politicians in the Commons better qualified for the role and unconnected to the government, such as Carson (who had resigned in March) or even Austen Chamberlain. As it was, the Ludendorff Offensive sputtered out by the end of April. No-one could have known it at the time, but Germany's last chance of winning the war had passed.

On 7 May, a serious attempt was made to overthrow Lloyd George by Asquithian MPs when Major-General Sir Frederick Maurice, the director of military operations, wrote a letter to *The Times* accusing the Prime Minister and Bonar Law of giving false information to Parliament about the strength of the British Army in France. *The Globe, Morning Post, Westminster Gazette, Daily News* and *Daily Chronicle* were all critical of the government, but crucially not the Northcliffe Press, and the conspiracy collapsed two days later in the Commons when Lloyd George defeated Asquith by 293 votes to 106. 'You have no doubt read of the ridiculous attempt of the Old Gang to unseat him,' Northcliffe told Reading, saying that it had been co-ordinated by Colonel Repington, 'an ill-balanced disappointed man who we were very glad to get rid of at Printing House Square ... Robertson, Maurice and Jellicoe and all the rest of them have absolutely no following in the country, or in the Army and Navy.' Of Lloyd George, Northcliffe wrote: 'He is complete master of the country if he only knew it.'[29]

Yet that did not mean that Northcliffe was not critical of Lloyd George in private. 'The whole of these difficulties could be settled if the Prime Minister were a man of business, which he is not,' Northcliffe told Wells of the various issues their department had with the government over propaganda. 'That is not the way of our gifted orator.'[30] He was particularly irritated at the Army Council's refusal to allow aeroplanes to drop propaganda leaflets over enemy trenches on the Western Front. 'I would deluge the German people with all sorts of American and English views, whether I agree with them or not. I lately asked *The Times* to publish the great Socialist Manifesto. I do not agree with much of it, but I had hoped to send it to Germany.'[31] To Dawson he wrote: 'The difficulty of dealing with our PM is that you never know what he is up to. He is oblique, evasive and Welsh. In dealing with President Wilson, as I did for six months, one had a feeling of absolute confidence in the man. The one endeavours to cajole; the other commands. One is an intriguer; the other has no comprehension of such mental perverseness.'[32]

Northcliffe won his struggle over the use of aeroplanes. Like many businessmen who have been translated into government departments before and since, he was frustrated at the way that politicians and civil servants wanted to discuss issues, often in committee, rather than do what they were told by their CEO. 'I am delighted to hear that the War Cabinet have, at length, rendered it possible for us to carry out efficient propaganda in Germany,' he told Beaverbrook. 'I am sure that we shall now be able to get to work, but the incident makes one despair of the brains at GHQ.'[33] He also despised the Foreign Office, as he articulated to Lloyd George, probably referring to the recently deceased Cecil Spring-Rice: 'My experience of our ambassadors is that they have no comprehension of propaganda, which is, of course, a highly complicated system of advertising, and no part of their training.'[34]

In a letter in July Northcliffe referred to H. G. Wells as a 'genius', but as Campbell Stuart noted in his autobiography, 'In all organisations that deal with opinions, there inevitably arise great problems with the staff.' He likened it to running an opera house, and one of its undoubted divas was Wells. When Stuart discovered that one of Wells's secretaries was the son of a German enemy alien, he wanted the young man dismissed as Crewe House was a secret government facility. Northcliffe supported him and an angry Wells resigned. In his biography of Wells, Michael Foot claimed that his hero 'consented for a while to serve Northcliffe's wartime propaganda organisation, but he soon became disgusted by the evidence of how the good work done there was so much outweighed by the evil'. However, Stuart's account of Wells' departure from Crewe House is more credible than the idea that he had a crisis of conscience about the evil being done there.[35] Although at the time of his resignation, Wells wrote to Northcliffe to say that he hoped their friendship would not suffer ('You have the rare and precious gift of getting work out of discrete and various men'), in his memoirs *Experiments in Autobiography*, published after Northcliffe's death, Wells subjected him to numerous strictures.[36]

It was unsurprising that Northcliffe took Stuart's side, as he was always highly attuned to the supposed danger enemy aliens posed, complaining that not enough action was being taken against German banking interests in the City of London and, as he told a friend, 'about the Germans in our midst. Here in Broadstairs we discovered a niece of [former chief of the German General Staff Erich] von Falkenhayn married to a Spaniard – actually resident in a prohibited area!'[37] He particularly wanted Mr Justice Sankey's Aliens Advisory Committee to sit in public and, on 28 July, wrote a violently angry article for the *Daily Mail* that stated that

> The heart of every uninterned Hun must have leapt for joy when he read the fatal dictum that the work of these odious people was to be investigated in secret ... People suspect that our plans are sold to the enemy by Huns and semi-Huns who are allowed freedom of residence and occupation dangerous to the State. Who warns the Hun submarine commander of the departure of certain ships? Who keeps Berlin informed by means of easily camouflaged telegrams from Holland and Sweden, or across the Atlantic? ... Mr Lloyd George, who is entirely responsible for the present situation, will find himself heavily handicapped in the forthcoming General Election. Rightly or wrongly, our people believe that the lives of our soldiers and sailors are being sold. The Lord Chancellor, whose knowledge of modern Germany is slight, went out of his way to say that he did not believe in the Hidden Hand. Ninety per cent of people disagree with Lord Findlay in this remark. There

are so many mysterious happenings – all favourable to the enemy – which have taken place in the past four years; there are so many Germans in high places in this country, that the coincidence of the presence of the Germans and the mysterious happenings is one that is obvious to any person of average intelligence.[38]

The public, or at least the more gullible section of it, was much swayed at that stage of the war by conspiracy theories that can be grouped under the title 'The Hidden Hand', which essentially blamed treachery and espionage for the lack of victory. 'Those who invoked the Hidden Hand', writes an historian, 'all felt baffled and frustrated at Britain's inability to bring the war to a quick conclusion.'[39] The phrase had been in common currency since 1915 and, in November 1917, the Conservative backbencher Sir Henry Page Croft had called for political donations to be made public; 'We shall never arrive at a better state until the unseen hand in party politics is exposed.'[40] Arnold White's book *The Hidden Hand*, published in 1917, put forward wild conspiracy theories about German sympathisers, with Pemberton Billing MP and his friend Captain Spencer suggesting that the Germans had a 'Black Book' of 47,000 British sexual perverts who were vulnerable to blackmail for 'unnatural vices' (generally sodomy).

No theory was too far-fetched for wartime Britain: 'If Lord Kitchener is dead,' the *Financial News* claimed, 'the Unseen Hand killed him.'[41] Northcliffe believed, as he told Dawson on 5 July, that 'Accountants state that the Deutsche Bank in London holds cheques paid to prominent English people on account of profitable sales of German securities up to the time of the war.'[42] Yet in the winding-up of these German companies, 'somebody stops or delays the proceedings'. As we have seen in his paranoiac reaction to Lord Haldane and blacklisting of Sir Francis Trippell and others, Northcliffe's Teutonophobia was sometimes taken much too far.

By this time, Northcliffe was spending much of his time at Elmwood, suffering badly from acute bronchitis and letting his talented subordinates run Crewe House with the lightest of touches from him. 'I have been on the verge of complete recovery again and again,' he told Lord Burnham in mid-July, 'but have relapsed after every visit to London. Four and a half months of bronchitis has been a very disagreeable infliction. I wish I could pass it onto the Huns.'[43] J. A. Hammerton, who had known Northcliffe since 1905, recorded how he changed radically in appearance towards the end of the war. 'In truth he tended to grossness. Gone was the incisive outline of his once so pleasing face. The clean-cut cheeks and firm lips had become soft, enlarged, puffy. The eyes always brilliant and prominent were often bloodshot and had an uncanny stare in them.'[44] Northcliffe always feared that he was suffering from heart disease and told Robert McNair Wilson, *The Times'* medical correspondent, 'I do want to live long enough to see the end of the war because I think I can help, a little, until then.'[45]

By August 1918, more than 100,000 leaflets a day were being dropped over the German lines. 'Written in good, simple German,' recalled Steed years later, 'they told the truth which was being concealed from the German troops. They gave information of the progress of the war on all fronts, showed, by means of shaded maps, the ground the Allies had gained, gave a full record of German losses, and recorded the progressive increase of the American Army in Europe.'[46] As a result, Northcliffe became a hate-figure in Germany, denounced in German newspapers and magazines such as *Simplicissimus*, which printed a caricature of Satan telling him 'Welcome, Great Master! From you we shall at last learn the science of lying!'[47] General Von Hutier called him 'the Minister for the Destruction of German Confidence' and 'the most thoroughgoing rascal of all the Entente'.[48]

Northcliffe of course revelled in German hatred of him, and never more than when they minted a bronze medallion of him showing his head on the obverse side sharpening a quill pen and Satan on the reverse side stoking flames, with the caption 'The architect of the English people's soul.'[49] When he managed to get hold of a copy of it, he proudly displayed it on the mantelshelf of his office in Carmelite House.*

---

* Today it rests on the mantelshelf of the boardroom at Northcliffe House, the headquarters of the *Daily Mail*.

The Germans took Allied propaganda extremely seriously, and their commander-in-chief General Paul von Hindenburg put out a 'Manifesto to the German People', calling on them to reject the enemy's 'drum-fire of printed paper' which amounted to attacks on the German spirit. 'Besides bombs which kill the body, his airmen throw down leaflets which are intended to kill the soul.'[50] In his autobiography, Hindenburg admitted that 'this propaganda greatly intensified the demoralisation of the German forces',[51] Similarly, Erich Ludendorff described British propaganda as 'exceptionally clever, and conceived on a grand scale ... We were hypnotised ... as a rabbit by a snake.'[52] Neither recognised that Germany's invasion of Belgium, widespread shooting of civilians in Belgium and France, torching of medieval Louvain, sinking of the *Lusitania*, execution of nurse Edith Cavell, or first use of poison gas and unrestricted submarine warfare might have had anything to do with what Ludendorff described as 'a sort of moral blockade' in neutral countries.[53]

Hindenburg's manifesto reported that his men had handed in 84,000 leaflets in May, 120,000 in June, and 300,000 in July, therefore still leaving huge numbers that had got through. Crewe House issued 3.96 million leaflets in August, 3.72 million in September, 5.36 million in October and 1.4 million in November 1918. 'Hindenburg's manifesto was a great tribute to the success of your propaganda,' wrote an admiring Philip Sassoon to Northcliffe.[54] Sassoon would not have written positively if he had thought Northcliffe was antagonistic towards Haig, who had embarked on a major offensive on the Western Front which captured Peronne on 1 September and inaugurated the campaign that saw the Allies win victory after victory in the last hundred days of the war.

While these victories were taking place, Northcliffe pressed for the number of journalists allowed at GHQ to be at least trebled, writing to Sassoon from the Royal Marine Hotel in Nairn,

> I recently travelled by road from London to Scotland and passed through something like an avenue of wounded men – many blind, legless or one-legged; others armless or one-armed – yet others

crippled in other ways or facially malformed. It is deplorable to think that, while we have had these terrible losses, the families of these men should know so little of what they have done in the war. ... These doleful lists of casualties, unaccompanied by any personal accounts of the Army and of its Generals, have a depressing effect upon our people both at home and abroad.[55]

~

Northcliffe considered Lord Beaverbrook a friend and ally, as well as a business competitor, but that did not mean that he could not be harsh about his Ministry of Information. The day after a Commons debate in early August, he sent Beaverbrook what he called 'a friendly but frank letter' saying that he could not continue to support him in his newspapers 'unless you help me by cleansing your dud-ridden establishment'.[56] Of the Foreign Office he wrote that 'they are slow; they are Roman Catholic; they are inefficient', adding another prejudice to the list. 'I have made mistakes in choosing already,' Northcliffe admitted, 'but I have fired the mistakes. I shall make more and fire them. Those who are critics of inefficiency in government must be themselves efficient.'[57]

On 14 August 1918, Northcliffe convened a four-day Inter-Allied Propaganda Conference at Crewe House where forty delegates from Italy, France, the United States and Britain discussed how to coordinate their efforts. The declaration in favour of Yugoslavian and Serbian unity issued by the Italian government on 25 September was a verbatim copy of the resolution unanimously adopted by the policy committee of that conference. Simultaneously, Northcliffe set up, with Lloyd George's at least initial approval, an interdepartmental committee to prepare a draft peace programme, which by 19 October had produced a list of 'indisputable conditions' that must be met by any future peace treaty. A small secretariat comprising Steed, Colonel Chambers Mitchell, R. W. Seton-Watson, Hamilton Fyfe, S. A. Guest and C. J. Phillips drew up the final draft in Northcliffe's name.

On 20 September, Northcliffe made a speech demanding that Germany – which he called Prussia – must be made to pay 'town for town, village for village, ship for ship, jewel for jewel, picture for picture, dollar for dollar ... she must pay full compensation for all she has ... stolen, sacked and burnt.'[58] Northcliffe's demands did not seem so harsh at the time as they were made to sound once the Versailles Treaty was comprehensively denounced by John Maynard Keynes in his influential philippic *The Economic Consequences of the Peace*, which argued that heavy reparations against Germany would be counterproductive. When the book was published, Northcliffe gave Steed carte blanche to attack it.[59] In its review, it asked of Keynes: 'How could he place the Allies on the same moral level as Germany in regard to the war?'[60]

The standard view today is that because the Second World War broke out twenty years after the treaty was signed, it therefore must have been flawed. Yet as the historian Margaret Macmillan has pointed out, Adolf Hitler had plans of conquest and dreams of scourging the Bolsheviks and Jews that would have led him far beyond any frontiers that any peacemakers could possibly have agreed upon at Versailles, however generous they were to Germany. To blame Versailles for Hitler's war is to let him, Stalin, and the Western appeasers off the hook and, as Macmillan argues, 'to ignore the actions of everyone – political leaders, diplomats, soldiers, ordinary voters – for twenty years between 1919 and 1939'.

Another argument can be made, one that puts Northcliffe's understandable response after four years of slaughter in a much better light. 'Of course things might have been very different if Germany had been more thoroughly defeated,' Macmillan writes. Had the treaty actually been *harsher* on Germany – specifically if it had divided the country in half as happened in 1945 – then there might have been no via dolorosa for Europe to walk between 1936 and 1939. The problem with Versailles was not that it was 'Carthaginian', as Keynes described it, but that it was not Carthaginian *enough*. (When a member of the staff of the American general Mark Clark tried to persuade him of the dangers of imposing a Carthaginian peace on Germany in 1945, he lugubriously observed, 'Well, we don't get too much trouble from those Carthaginians nowadays.')

Theodore Roosevelt and others called for the Allies to capture

Berlin, which if it had happened would at least have blunted the Nazis' later claims that the German armies were never defeated in the field, but only stabbed in the back at home. A peace which partitioned Germany and Austria in 1919 – perhaps even returning her to the pre-Bismarckian days of a dozen leading states, or even the pre-Napoleonic days of scores of self-governing entities on the Holy Roman Empire model – might well have prevented the Second World War. The problem with the peacemakers of Versailles was that they were willing to wound but afraid to crush, although admittedly it did not look that way at the time. In retrospect, Northcliffe might well have been right in his call for 'the total dispersal of the German tribes'.[61]

CHAPTER 19

THE RIFT WITH LLOYD GEORGE

October 1918–April 1919

'Peace meant the beginning of another war for him.'[1]

ISAAC MARCOSSON on
Lord Northcliffe in November 1918

In early October 1918, Lord Northcliffe attempted an unwarranted power grab, which has been put down to incipient megalomania but was perhaps more explicable by the fact that there were no established boundaries between politicians and a press proprietor as unprecedentedly influential as him. After meeting Lloyd George at Sir George Riddell's house – Danny Park in Sussex – on 2 October, Northcliffe wrote to Riddell about the forthcoming general election. 'I do not propose to use my newspapers and personal influence to support a new Government elected at the most crucial period of the history of the British nations ... unless I know definitely, and in writing, and can consciously approve, the personal constitution of the Government.'[2]

It was a bold demand to make, but Northcliffe could hardly pledge his support for a government that he feared would be filled with people he had hitherto denounced, without looking hypocritical. There were active negotiations underway for a coalition with the Asquithian Liberals, with Asquith himself as lord chancellor, for example. Lloyd George wanted Northcliffe's blanket support regardless of the make-up of his government, a carte blanche which few press proprietors would ever have given to any politician, let alone Northcliffe, who felt that he had contributed greatly to putting Lloyd George into power and wanted some guarantees before he committed himself to keeping him there.

Riddell showed the letter to Lloyd George, who said he could give 'no undertaking as to the constitution of the Government and would not dream of doing such a thing'.[3] 'I communicated this to Northcliffe,' noted Riddell, 'who said very little.' There was very little *to* say; he had tried but failed. Lloyd George had rebuffed him with perfectly correct constitutional propriety, which was not the stance he had taken when leaking Budget secrets in 1909.

~

On 10 October, Alfred ('Bob') King, the fifteen-year-old son of Northcliffe's sister Geraldine, was one of 500 people who drowned when the RMS *Leinster* mail-boat was torpedoed by U-boat 123 in the Irish Sea, only ten days before German submarine warfare ended. He had been travelling back from Ireland to Holyhead to attend Winchester College. His parents had deliberately sent him and his brother Cecil on separate ships because of the risk, and Cecil suffered from survivor's guilt for the rest of his life. Northcliffe is criticised for his hatred of what he called 'the Huns', but the war did kill no fewer than four of his beloved nephews.

Northcliffe wanted Germany's unconditional surrender, fearing that otherwise they might somehow salvage their pre-war position under an armistice due to Allied weakness at the peace conference. His stance was clear from the *Daily Mail*'s description of the German request for an armistice as 'not peace but trickery'.[4] He therefore convened the Inter-Departmental Committee at Crewe House to agree the propaganda to be pursued over peace, comprising representatives from the War Cabinet, Admiralty, War Office, India Office, Ministry of Information, Colonial Office, Press Bureau and National War Aims Committee (a cross-party parliamentary organisation established to conduct propaganda within Britain).

The final draft of the committee's 'Memoranda on Propaganda Peace Policy' envisaged the restoration and indemnification of

Belgium; reconstruction of invaded provinces; compensation for civilian losses and injuries; restoration of Alsace-Lorraine to France; re-adjustment of Italian borders according to nationality; the break-up of the Austro-Hungarian empire; an independent Poland with access to the Baltic; Turkey's evacuation of Rumania, Serbia and Montenegro; a war crimes tribunal; and the loss of all Germany's colonies. It also provided for negotiations over war reparations, and for 'the establishment, constitution and conditions of membership of a League of Free Nations for the purpose of preventing future wars and improving international relations'.[5] A great deal of work had gone into this memorandum, and Northcliffe, Wickham Steed and Colonel Mitchell were scheduled to discuss it with Lloyd George at Downing Street on 19 October.

Two days beforehand, however, Lord Milner gave an interview to the *Evening Standard* which exacerbated all of Northcliffe's fears that the government might not press Germany into unconditional surrender, as Milner said he was looking forward to victory 'either by the unconditional surrender of Germany or by an armistice on conditions imposed by our military leaders'. He thought that the Germans could then be left to reform their domestic political system themselves under the principle of self-determination. 'What constitutes complete victory?' Milner asked rhetorically, before going on to say that 'when the Germans see the complete and ignominious defeat of militarism ... they will be as eager to do away with it as the Allies ... It is in the interests of the Allies to see a stable government in Germany.' Milner, fearing a Bolshevik revolution in postwar Germany, had adopted this conciliatory stance without prior consultation of his Cabinet colleagues, something Bonar Law highlighted in the Commons on 23 October.

The meeting at Downing Street was a disaster, as is clear from the accounts of it in Steed and Mitchell's autobiographies. Steed has Lloyd George saying 'I can't have this' about the memorandum, which the Prime Minister viewed as an attempt to circumscribe his freedom of movement over eventual peace terms, not unlike the way in which Northcliffe had earlier tried to circumscribe it over the personnel of his post-election government. 'It invades the sphere of government,' Lloyd George complained. 'Here you are laying down principles and conditions which only the Allied governments are competent to decide.'[6] When Steed pointed out that the Inter-Departmental Committee had been set up by the War Office with the approval of the War Cabinet, and both had been represented on it, and that it was intended as propaganda rather than policy, Lloyd George replied: 'Well, I cannot sanction it. I cannot allow you to bind the hands of the Government by announcing things of this sort.'[7] He spoke testily, and threw the document onto the table after reading it.

In Mitchell's account, Lloyd George also said, 'I can't have anything to do with this,' before going on to state that 'The Germans are going to surrender. I am a lawyer, and can tell you that possession is nine points of the law. We shall have them in the hollow of our hands.'[8] The Crewe House delegation were unimpressed, and Mitchell recalled their 'complete disillusionment as to the psychology of the PM'. Yet Lloyd George did allow the document to be considered point by point by Balfour, who suggested different wording over the German colonies but kept the fact that they 'shall in no case be returned to Germany'.[9] Eventually, the War Cabinet ratified it with Balfour's amendments, but only for use as propaganda rather than as policy points for any future conference.

In the meantime, Northcliffe concentrated his newspapers' fire on Milner. 'The whole tone of the interview,' argued the *Evening News*,

> with its readiness to make excuses for the Huns, was entirely antipathetic to the vast body of opinion in this country. We all know that as long as things appeared to be going well for the Huns ... the whole German nation endorsed and applauded the worst outrages. Lord Milner does not represent public opinion in this country. Whom and what does he represent in Paris?[10]

Articles such as these infuriated the many Milner Kindergarteners inside and outside government, especially after 4 November when the *Daily Mail* used the headline 'Lord Milner's Blunder', quite possibly a conscious reprise of the 'Lord Kitchener's Blunder' headline that ignited the Shells Crisis three years earlier.

On 22 October, in a formal speech to American officers outlining the approved peace programme of the Inter-Departmental Committee, Northcliffe attacked Milner's remarks, arguing that in Germany 'the way to create Bolshevism was to let the Hun off' and speaking of 'the real danger of social upheaval ... in this country ... if an unsatisfactory peace is made'.[11] Both *The Times* and *the Daily Mail* insisted on unconditional surrender, with the latter making the remarkable prediction of a 'Great War of 1938' should the victors not have 'seen the thing through' in 1918.[12]

On 3 November, the same day that an Allied armistice was signed with Austria-Hungary and the German Grand Fleet mutinied at Kiel, Northcliffe met Lloyd George and asked his permission to merge the Department of Propaganda in Enemy Countries and the British War Mission, which Lloyd George gave. He told Steed that Lloyd George 'had asked him to transfer the principal members of the Crewe House staff to Paris, and to make [Northcliffe] responsible for the British publicity arrangements at the peace conference. Lloyd George, Northcliffe told me, had urged him to take a house near LG's own headquarters.'[13]

In a formal letter after their meeting confirming their agreement, Northcliffe wrote to Lloyd George, 'In view of the urgency of the matter, I request that I be given, with the least possible delay, authority as Chairman of the British War Mission to undertake this Peace Terms propaganda in the closest collaboration with the various departments of state until the final peace settlement has been concluded.'[14] Lloyd George did not demur, although with a general election five weeks away on 14 December, he was unlikely to have frustrated the hopes of the controller of 40 per cent of the British press. Northcliffe knew it was an apposite time to ask the Prime Minister for what he needed.

It is hard to escape the conclusion that Lloyd George was stringing Northcliffe along in this matter, knowing that the conference would only take place once the election was safely won. Northcliffe has been accused of being deluded in thinking that he might play an official role in the peace conference, but if so the Prime Minister had not discouraged the delusion. All Northcliffe can really be accused of is naiveté that Lloyd George would really give him the key propaganda role before the Versailles Treaty was signed. The MP Sir Auckland Geddes saw both Lloyd George and Northcliffe separately before the election and 'each described the other as impossible and intolerable. They were both very tired men and had been getting on each other's nerves for some time.'[15]

On 4 November, Northcliffe published the peace policy document under his own name as an article entitled 'From War to Peace'. It was uncompromising. 'There can be no question as to the "Honour" of the German people,' Northcliffe wrote. 'If they feel humiliated, they must blame those who brought the humiliation upon them.'[16] He also stated that 'A League of Free Nations will replace the old system of a balance of rival powers.' The article consisted of thirteen desiderata to which the Germans must agree if they wanted peace. It was not long before wags nicknamed it 'Northcliffe's Thirteen Points', a play on President Wilson's Fourteen Points, which was official American peace policy.

Underlining the sheer geographical reach and influence that Northcliffe's name had in the world's press at that time, *The Times* announced that 'this article is appearing today in the leading papers in Canada, Australia, New Zealand, South Africa, Newfoundland, India, the British Dependencies, United States, South America, France, Italy, Spain, Switzerland, Holland, Norway, Sweden, Denmark, Japan and elsewhere. It will be circulated in Germany during the present week.'[17] Because it was distributed within Germany, Steed believed that 'it certainly helped to hasten the collapse of German resistance. In fact, it was the crowning achievement of Crewe House propaganda.'[18]

In the Commons that day, the Irish nationalist politician John Dillon asked Bonar Law 'whether the statement of peace terms published to-day over Lord Northcliffe's name in all the chief newspapers of the world is part of his official foreign propaganda; and, if so, whether the terms stated may be accepted as the official view of the British Government?'[19] Bonar Law replied that 'the article is in every sense the work of Lord Northcliffe. The British Government were unaware of it, and in no sense responsible for it.'

Yet while it might have been unaware of the article's publication, the War Cabinet had amended and approved the document on which it was based.

Much more serious was the attack that Sir Edward Carson, a friend and ally of Lord Milner, made on Northcliffe in a debate on the Ministry of Information on 7 November. 'I am quite alive to the fact that it is almost high treason to say a word against Lord Northcliffe,' Carson said,

> I know his power and that he does not hesitate to exercise it to try to drive anybody out of any office or a public position if they incur his royal displeasure ... I venture to incur even the possibility of the odium of this great trust owner, who monopolises in his own person so great a part of the press of this country, and has always for himself a ready-made claque to flatter him and to run any policies for him that he thinks best in his own interests.[20]

Carson then accused Northcliffe of trying to drive Milner out of office 'in the midst of a crisis like this, when every moment of Lord Milner's time and his brains must be concentrated upon events of the greatest magnitude in this world', before going on to say,

> For what? In order that Lord Northcliffe may ... get into the War Cabinet, so that he may be present at the Peace Conference, whenever it comes. The whole thing is a disgrace to public life in England and a disgrace of journalism ... I do hope that Members of this House, whether they agree with Lord Milner or whether they agree with any other minister, will see that, at all events, at a crisis like this, fair play, fair criticism, honest dealing, and decent life are necessary.

John Dillon then denounced Northcliffe as 'the Napoleon of Journalism ... collaring the press and turning it into a great machine of power'.[21] He went on to liken Northcliffe to Oliver Cromwell, warning that the government 'will have created a Frankenstein they cannot resist'.[22] Stanley Baldwin, the Financial Secretary to

the Treasury, calmed down the debate by pointing out that in fact
Northcliffe and his department were not part of the motion being
debated. Milner wrote to Carson to thank him for his defence, saying
that 'I have had a shower of letters from friends simply delighted with
the trouncing you gave Northcliffe. I certainly think it was high time
that somebody other than myself said something, if only to show that
there are other people in the world who are not afraid of Northcliffe.
I believe myself that he is only a scarecrow, but still the fact remains
that most public men are in terror of him.'[23]

Two days after the debate, there was a revolution in Berlin
which forced Kaiser Wilhelm II to abdicate, allowing an armistice
agreed for 11 November. 'We have to an extent hastened the end,'
Northcliffe told a lunch of fellow propaganda chiefs in Paris. 'Ours
has been a bloodless campaign and a costless one.' It was certainly
cheap: the entire work of Crewe House over nine months only cost
the taxpayer £70,000, in a war in which Britain was spending £7
million a day.[24]

'I can truly say that I have done my best,' Northcliffe told an
author in 1919, 'without any motive other than that of helping
to secure victory for the only race that can rule.'[25] Summarising
Northcliffe's activities, one of his biographers wrote that 'We should
be thankful for his confessedly rough ways, what he termed his
"flogging of jellyfish into action".'[26] Another added that 'It ought
never to be disputed that he was a great force in helping Britain and
her allies to grasp victory in the First World War.'[27] Yet Northcliffe
himself went too far when he claimed that 'Good propaganda had
probably saved a year of war, and this meant the saving of thousands of millions of money and probably at least a million lives.'[28]
In the words of Colonel House's biographer, Northcliffe set up 'the
most effective scheme of propaganda known to modern history.
Ceaselessly he poured into Germany the idea that unless the people
repudiated the old regime, their own ruin would be linked to that
of the Hohenzollerns. It acted as a subtle corrosive which ultimately
wore away the German "will to victory".'[29]

One person who emphatically agreed with that estimation was the
Kaiser himself. In February 1921, Lady Norah Bentinck published

a book about her meetings with Wilhelm II in Holland entitled
The Ex-Kaiser in Exile, in which he said of Northcliffe: '*Was für
ein Mensch!* [What a man!] If we had had Northcliffe, we would
have won the war.' He described Northcliffe as his 'deadly enemy',
saying '*Ach, diese propaganda von Northcliffe! Es war Ko-loss-
al!*'[30] ('Oh, Northcliffe's propaganda! It was tremendous!') Lady
Bentinck recorded how the Kaiser 'regards Lord Northcliffe with
intense bitterness', before observing that 'What Northcliffe thinks
today, England thinks tomorrow.'[31] The *Daily Mail* delightedly
serialised the book. That same year, the Kaiser published a book
entitled *Comparative History*, which sought to prove that Germany
was not to blame for the war. Among the key dates in the European
history between 1878 and 1914 that he instanced was 1896, when
'The *Daily Mail* is founded by Harmsworth – Northcliffe.'[32]

~

As soon as the Armistice was declared, Lloyd George changed his
mind about Northcliffe staying in charge of British propaganda,
and installed his close friend Sir George (soon afterwards Lord)
Riddell instead.[33] This led to a row at No. 10, during which Lloyd
George later stated that Northcliffe was 'visibly astonished and upset
at my declining to accede to his request' to an official role at the
conference.[34] At the end of the argument, the Prime Minister told a
protesting Northcliffe to 'Go to Hades.'[35] Instead, Northcliffe went
straight to Bonar Law at the Treasury to complain, but he supported
the Prime Minister. It was the last time that Northcliffe met either
man again.

For much of 1918 Northcliffe was ill, and towards the end of the
year it was discovered that he had a growth in his throat, an adenoma
that required serious surgery the following year. On 12 November,
the day after the armistice, Steed 'found him in bed almost gasping
for breath and unable to speak above a whisper ... he felt too ill
for serious work and had been ordered by his doctors to spend the
winter in the South of France'.[36] Ten days later, Northcliffe's doctors
confined him to Elmwood as the lump had become visible.

Lloyd George told Carson and Riddell, and later recorded in his

Memoirs of the Peace Conference, that Northcliffe had insisted on being one of the five British delegates to Versailles, which is not impossible considering how demanding he had been the previous month but ought not to be accepted as historical fact simply because Lloyd George alleged it.[37] The supposed demand has also been taken as prima facie evidence that Northcliffe was suffering from megalomania, and it has also been suggested that the discovery that there were limits to his power played a part in later destroying his reason.[38] Yet was the demand for a delegate's role even true?

Nowhere in Northcliffe's extensive correspondence with his closest advisors and lieutenants did Northcliffe evince a wish to be a delegate to the Conference. 'I have heard it said on many sides that Lord Northcliffe was embittered because he did not take part in the Peace Conference,' Louise Owen later wrote. 'That is not true. We often discussed the matter before the Armistice, and he repeatedly told me how urgent it was for him to watch, and use his newspapers to the best of his ability.'[39] 'I have always disbelieved it,' agreed Wickham Steed, who was Northcliffe's close advisor in London and Paris at that time, 'both because Northcliffe never gave me any hint that he cherished such an ambition, and because he was far too unwell to undertake work as exacting as that of a delegate to the Peace Conference would have been.'[40]

Sir Auckland Geddes later denied that Northcliffe had ever demanded to be a delegate to the conference, saying that if so, Lloyd George would undoubtedly 'have blurted it out all over the place and there would have been a cloud of witnesses'.[41] Similarly, Bonar Law's biographer Robert Blake wrote that 'It is possible that Lloyd George was wrong in believing that Northcliffe demanded a seat on the Peace Delegation, but Northcliffe did undoubtedly wish to control British propaganda.'[42] Whatever was the case, Northcliffe resigned as Director of Propaganda in Enemy Countries and head of the War Mission in the United Kingdom as soon as the war was over. 'I wish to assure you how grateful I am for the great services you have rendered to the Allied Cause while holding this important post,' Lloyd George wrote to him about the propaganda job. 'I have had many direct evidences of the success of your invaluable work and of the extent to which it contributed to the dramatic collapse of the enemy strength in Austria and Germany.'[43] The kind words belied the private animosity that had grown between the two men.

On 14 November, Arthur Henderson's Labour Party seceded from the Lloyd George coalition and became the official Opposition for the first time in history, a remarkable achievement less than twenty years after its foundation. Northcliffe resolved to give Labour some free space in his papers, while maintaining their ideological distance from the socialist message. Similarly, when Tom Clarke assumed it would be the right thing to support Lloyd George in the election, he was quickly disabused. 'I knew better next day. I thought I was going to be fired. It was obviously "go slow" on Lloyd George if one wanted to avoid trouble.'[44]

It was understandable, therefore, that Lloyd George became convinced that, as he later put it, Northcliffe had become 'the inveterate and implacable enemy of the Administration up to the very hour of his death'.[45] Geoffrey Dawson agreed, noting in his diary on 14 November that after Northcliffe arrived at Printing House Square, he 'said he'd served notice on LG that he could no longer support him'.[46] During this period, the pro-government Dawson's relations with Northcliffe collapsed. 'How can one work under these conditions?' he wrote three days later, after successfully refusing to have his pro-government leaders edited over the telephone from Broadstairs.[47]

Lloyd George was popularly seen as the man who won the war, and his coalition was clearly heading towards a landslide election victory, something that Northcliffe knew he could not prevent. Northcliffe therefore concentrated on specific issues rather than candidates. With his press deluged with letters about delays in demobilisation and fears of unemployment, he continued to champion soldiers' concerns, telling his brother Cecil that the veterans had been 'through horrors unspeakable, unwritable, unbelievable, and they must not be fobbed off with mere promises and speeches. I will see to it that they are not so treated.'[48] When the veterans returned from the war, Northcliffe was among the small group of industrialists who did not lower their pay, adding that 'In my opinion a worker who does not join a union is a fool.'[49] He promoted the idea of spending public money buying land for veterans to farm.

'More or less peaceful day after the storm and an effusive bulletin from N[orthcliffe] about my conduct of the paper!' wrote Dawson on 18 November. 'What a man!'[50] They were the same words the Kaiser had used. At noon on 24 November, Lloyd George had a conversation at No. 10 with Milner and Hankey about Northcliffe, 'who is becoming hostile. The PM discussed the alternatives of keeping him quiet by bringing him to the peace conference ... of taking no notice of him; or of attacking him.'[51] Rather than Northcliffe megalomaniacally trying to force himself into the conference, therefore, Hankey's diary entry makes clear that Lloyd George was actively considering inviting him, even if for entirely cynical reasons. Milner and Hankey instead thought that 'it would be good electioneering tactics to counter-attack him'. On 27 November, the Unionist MP Robert Sanders noted after a meeting with Lloyd George that 'He is evidently a little uneasy. He was anxious to know if anyone could get to Northcliffe. I was afraid not.'[52]

Northcliffe had given *The Times* relatively free rein since his return from the United States, but during the election he started to take a much closer interest in it – to Dawson's increasing ire. On 30 November, he complained that the paper had 'lagged woefully' in telling readers that Lloyd George was 'evading main issues' and accused it of being in league with German financiers who were decrying Germany's having to pay reparations.[53] Dawson saw this as the opening salvo in a more general attack on the relative editorial independence he had inherited from Buckle.

The *Daily Mail* was leading Northcliffe's various campaigns for early demobilisation, economic reconstruction (especially in housing), full reparations, pension reform, the expulsion of enemy aliens, the Kaiser to be put on trial, and so on. By contrast, *The Times* was even more moderate than the government. 'I ... do not propose to speak any more with two voices,' Northcliffe told Dawson. 'I have great responsibility in the ownership of *The Times*.'[54] He used it by urging a Carthaginian peace upon Germany during the election campaign, imploring the government not to go soft over reparations.

Northcliffe was particularly worried that Lloyd George would appoint a right-wing, Unionist-dominated government after the election that would not find the money for the radical postwar reconstruction he thought necessary, warning Dawson on 1 December that Sir George Younger, the chairman of the Conservative Party,

> who is an able political boss ... running the party of wealth, may impose upon the PM reactionary ministers who will not allow LG to carry out such reforms as will prevent revolution. I said to you quite frankly that, in my belief and from my study of history, revolutions have been produced by reactionaries* ... Unless *The Times* takes a very strong stand regarding the selection of the next Cabinet, the deadweight of the preponderance of reactionary Coalitionists will impose on the PM Old Gangers ... Such little things are enough to ignite the flame of revolution.[55]

Northcliffe ended by asking Dawson to use the columns of *The Times* to demand to know who would be in the new Cabinet.

The next day, Dawson made what he called 'a weary pilgrimage' to Elmwood, where he told Northcliffe that

> he was not playing a straight game in his own papers by nominally supporting LG, while doing everything to embarrass and undermine him; that I could not run *The Times* as an appendage of the *Daily Mail*; that he was using great and difficult international questions as election cries, etc., etc. ... He was extraordinarily elusive and difficult to keep up to the point; tried at one point to suggest a compromise or bargain; told innumerable obvious lies (e.g. that he had only stood by LG because all the world was against him, etc.).[56]

---

* A counter-intuitive point of view, but not as strange as it looks at first glance, and something that Alexis de Tocqueville might have argued. It would make an excellent university essay question.

In fact, that was not a lie; Northcliffe had indeed stuck by Lloyd George during the Marconi Scandal. Soon after his trip to Elmwood, Dawson told his friend, Bishop Michael Furse of Pretoria, that his relationship with his proprietor had broken down, possibly irretrievably. 'I foresee more rows,' he wrote, 'and I'm not sure that it isn't more honest to have no more association *at all* with a man whom at heart I regard as a fraud!'[57] He went on to describe Northcliffe as a megalomaniac.

Northcliffe's clash with Lloyd George came to a head again on 7 December when he telegraphed the Prime Minister, who was electioneering in Leeds, to say:

> The public are expecting you to say definitely [the] amount of cash we are to get from Germany. They are very dissatisfied with [the] phrase 'limit of her capacity' which [may] mean anything or nothing. They are aware France has an amount. I am apprehensive of serious trouble in the country on the matter.[58]

Lloyd George, who wanted Germany to pay around £24 billion, replied tersely: 'You are quite wrong about France. No ally has named [a] figure. Allies in complete agreement as to demand for indemnity. Inter-Allied Commission will investigate on behalf of all on identical principles. Don't be always making mischief. Lloyd George.'[59] Two days later, Eric Geddes told an audience in the Drill Hall in Cambridge that, regarding German reparations, 'I will squeeze until you can hear the pips squeak.'[60] Then, on 11 December, Lloyd George called for the 'fullest indemnities' and for the Kaiser to be put on trial, which he presumably knew was an impossibility since he was in neutral Holland which would not extradite him.

Lloyd George's landslide election victory was announced on 28 December and saw no fewer than 520 Coalition MPs elected to a House of 635, including 395 Unionists. Asquith lost his seat. 'The Prime Minister has an immense opportunity,' Northcliffe told Harold from La Dragonnière, his brother's beautiful villa in Cap Martin in the south of France, 'but I doubt whether he will take it. The country would support him in a clean sweep of Old Gang people. The nation would welcome it. The Foreign Office ... could be put right in three months. The Home Office in four weeks.'[61] Northcliffe was in pain with his throat. 'I must have coughed at least two hundred times daily,' he told his brother on New Year's Eve, explaining how 'The nocturnal noise spoils my sleep. Everything has something and I must not grumble.'[62]

Northcliffe's fatal flaw – anti-Semitism – was highly visible during this period when German bankers, economists and businessmen were warning that swingeing reparations would only create poverty and help German Bolshevism. 'I believe in neither bluff,' he told Harold. 'The pressure of the international Jew is, I hear, great. They had the nerve to send me a four thousand-word telegram from Berlin through Holland prepared by [Walther] Rathenau, the head of the Electricity Trust [Allgemeine-Elektricitäts-Gesellschaft] with its two hundred million pounds capital. I sent them a reply that I did not deal with Huns.'[63] Rathenau, a Jew, was assassinated in June 1922 by right-wing extremists for his advocacy of observing the Versailles Treaty.

Recognising that the postwar newspaper world would need new blood, Northcliffe promoted a series of people to key roles in the organisation, two of whom – O. J. Pulvermacher (the night editor) and Bernard Falk (the news editor) – were Jewish. Pulvermacher only recalled one act of overt anti-Semitism, when Northcliffe called him 'Oriental Pulvermacher'.[64] Falk had been an intrepid reporter, of whom the story was told that he had once dashed out into the middle of Piccadilly to flag down a speeding fire engine, shouting that he was a reporter and wanted to know where the fire was.[65] He was a regular butt of Northcliffe's anti-Semitic jokes, however, such as, 'You belong to the Jewish persuasion, don't you, Falk? Who persuaded you?'[66] At one point, Falk – who had his job to protect – said, 'Let's talk about the Scots for a change, Chief.'[67]

~

'I shall not come back until my throat is more normal,' Northcliffe wrote to Thomas Marlowe in January 1919 from France. 'I have now been afflicted ... since February 1918.'[68] He had a severe bronchial illness and had been unable to sleep on his left side for months, but the Riviera weather seemed to lead to an improvement. Although he appointed Marlowe chairman of Associated Newspapers on New Year's Day, it was clear that Geoffrey Dawson would not be editor of *The Times* for much longer. After seven years of referring to him as 'My dear Chief' and signing himself 'Robin', Dawson now addressed his letters to 'My dear Lord Northcliffe' and signing himself 'Geoffrey Dawson'. 'It was unfortunate for Dawson,' Campbell Stuart later recalled,

> that in the world in which he moved, there was much open criticism and dislike of Northcliffe, which so-called friends of Dawson did not hesitate to repeat to his Chief, probably with a little more gloss than was warranted. As these stories began to gather in momentum, I realised Dawson would soon be in difficulties, and I warned him, but he would not listen to me. Northcliffe was intensely sensitive, like most geniuses, and ultimately Dawson had to resign. This was the governing reason, not matters of policy.[69]

Dawson was also tired after editing the paper since 1911 and of his regular working hours of 10am to 3am.[70] On the afternoon of Sunday 5 January, on a flying visit from France, Northcliffe went to Printing House Square and remonstrated with Dawson that during the election, in the words of Dawson's diary,

> *The Times* had not spoken with his voice! He held me entirely responsible for LG's great majority!! ... In future he was going to take a more direct hand in the conduct of the paper – would appoint a managing director of his own, whom he would train – ... might even sell it – had had a huge offer, etc. I told him ... it wasn't my property and he could do as he liked. After this he became more reasonable, and produced some admirable sentiments about his feelings for the Army and for the poor, his abhorrence of large fortunes, his zeal for research, his dislike of the narrow attitude.[71]

When the new government was announced on 10 January, many of Northcliffe's fears about the Unionist right were justified, and a number of his old antagonists found prominent places in the Cabinet. Sir Eric Geddes became Minister without Portfolio, alongside Austen Chamberlain as Chancellor of the Exchequer, F. E. Smith (now Lord Birkenhead) was Lord Chancellor and Balfour stayed on as Foreign Secretary. Lord Milner was Colonial Secretary, and Churchill had two ministries: War and Air. Only Edward Carson failed to find a place in what otherwise can be seen as a Cabinet largely made up of Northcliffe's enemies. Of the seventy-seven members of the new government, all but ten had been ministers in the previous one, lessening the likelihood of Britain experiencing the sweeping changes to society and economics that Northcliffe thought necessary to prevent revolution.[72]

Cecil Harmsworth, with whom Northcliffe was friendly but not close, became Balfour's under-secretary but, as Northcliffe told Dawson, 'The giving of office, either to brothers or friends, will not move me to the extent of a single colon or comma.'[73] The way Sir George Younger had succeeded in 'stampeding' Lloyd George into appointing the Old Gang Northcliffe described as 'a scandal' to Andrew Caird.[74] He cantankerously criticised the *Daily Mail* night editor over an article that he considered too kind to the government with the jibe: 'No wonder people say they can tell the difference in the *Daily Mail* when I have left England.'[75]

'I'm not given to saying ... "I told you so,"' Northcliffe wrote to Dawson on 12 January – a surefire prelude to someone saying just that – 'but I saw the possibilities of the present deplorable Cabinet when I asked you to begin that campaign last summer. I blame myself greatly for my lack of vigour in regard to *The Times* when I was ill at Elmwood in November and December.'[76] The criticism was clear; he was in fact blaming Dawson greatly for a lack of vigour. He preposterously and egotistically claimed that Lloyd George, one of the least timid premiers in British history, 'knew perfectly well that I was the only force that could stop his really timid nature'. In a clear warning-cum-threat to Dawson, he added: 'Never again will I allow myself to be overruled in a matter like that. I am very willing to be

led in matters I do not understand, but I do understand character.'
As for Lloyd George's character, Northcliffe told Dawson, 'I now
earnestly commend to you a study of Welsh character and history.
The Welsh are illusive, cunning and always ingrate.'[77]

Yet Northcliffe was not wholly antagonistic towards the entire
government. When, in late January, Churchill sent him – 'for your
secret and personal information' – an advance view of the demobilisation plan for the British Army, based on the 'first in, first out'
principle that was popular with the troops, Northcliffe cabled back
immediately 'All my newspapers will do exactly what you wish on
the subject and you may show them this telegram of authority.'[78]
The scheme was a success, and was helped by Churchill distributing
200,000 copies of the *Continental Daily Mail* to the troops explaining it in detail.

The clash with Dawson finally came on 25 January, when
Northcliffe complained that the editor had not criticised the Foreign
Office for over-staffing because of his friendship with fellow Milner
Kindergartener Lionel Curtis. 'I have no intention of reverting to
the unpleasantness of December last, but I assure you that I cannot
acquiesce in any more of his kind of *non possumus*. If you do not like
my attitude, I beg you to do either one of two things – endeavour to
see eye to eye with me, or relinquish your position.'[79]

Dawson replied, categorically contradicting Northcliffe's allegation and adding that 'I shall be only too willing, as you know, to give
up the editorship of *The Times* whenever the proprietors desire it. If
I had consulted my own wishes, I should have done so before now,
but I thought it would save trouble to remain here till you were well
again and able to take a more active part in the conduct of the paper,
as you told me that you intended to do.'[80] Dawson had to consider
his lifelong friendship with Milner, his genuine admiration of the
handsomely re-elected coalition, and his frustrations with having
Northcliffe freed from his war mission and propaganda work,
as well as his frustration with a proprietor who was now clearly
attempting to curtail his editorial independence.

'I do not propose to terminate a long pleasant relationship by
acrimonious discussion,' Northcliffe replied on 6 February, before

doing just that by saying: 'It would have been fairer to the paper and me to have told me of your wish to resign before I left England for a probable absence of three to four months.'[81] In a memorandum he wrote at the time, Dawson commented on this 'new complaint that I had not told him before he left England of a situation which had arisen out of his own messages from abroad!'[82]

Northcliffe met Wickham Steed at Avignon on 6 February and, seated in the ferry boat that plied to and fro across the Rhone, the latter accepted the editorship – subject to certain conditions regarding his independence, such as that Northcliffe 'should not . . . promise to any statesman or political party the support of any of the newspapers which he controlled, without previous consultation and agreement with me'.[83] Northcliffe told Steed that he wanted him to direct the policy of the *Daily Mail* as well as *The Times* 'in order that his various newspapers might not advocate conflicting policies'. Buckle and Dawson had bridled at the jibe that '*The Times* was merely the threepenny edition of the *Daily Mail*.'[84] As Steed put it, 'I thought it better for the *Daily Mail* to be called a penny edition of *The Times*.'[85] That was not the way Marlowe was to see it.

'Parting with dear Robin is a personal grief to me,' Northcliffe told Steed of Dawson.[86] He wrote a gracious letter to the outgoing editor stating that 'the Paper has never stood in higher esteem both at home and abroad than under your leadership'.[87] When the resignation was announced, a notice in *The Times* stated that 'the position and influence of *The Times* today are due in no small measure to his energies, character and ability . . .'[88] Dawson was profoundly bitter over the way that, as he put it in his memorandum, he had to work 'under the strain of incessant demands from Lord Northcliffe . . . inspired at bottom by personal vanity and the intention to use the paper for his own political aggrandisement'.[89] These were both unfair; it was Northcliffe's paper, and his views had significantly diverged from Dawson's over the most important issue: support of the government. Northcliffe was not interested in aggrandisement but influence, which was not an illegitimate ambition for a press proprietor.

Dawson claimed that Northcliffe had twice told him that he

wanted to be a British plenipotentiary at the peace conference, otherwise 'he never confided any of his ambitions to me'.[90] Northcliffe was right not to, as Dawson openly derided Northcliffe to his friends. Dawson's hagiographical biographer Evelyn Wrench tried to defend this, saying that it was 'surely ridiculous to suggest that Geoffrey [Dawson] should not have discussed Northcliffe's opinion and policy with his intimates. Of course he did. Northcliffe's views were public property; he enjoyed the limelight in his latter years.'[91] Yet Northcliffe also had the right to expect a certain degree of personal loyalty from his most senior employee, the editor of his most prestigious paper.

~

On 5 April 1919, Lloyd George's irritation with Northcliffe's accusations of pusillanimity towards Germany over reparations, territory and its navy boiled over. 'What do you think of the disgraceful attacks on me in The Times and the Daily Mail?' he asked George Riddell. 'They call me a pro-German. That is a libel. I have a good mind to bring an action. I shall certainly say what I think about Northcliffe.'[92] The Prime Minister thought that the attacks were 'due to vanity and spleen ... His advice has not been asked about a single subject. I ran the election without him and I beat him. He is full of disappointment and bitterness.'[93]

Three days later, Lloyd George believed he had a further reason publicly to denounce Northcliffe, when no fewer than 370 MPs (including 233 Conservatives) signed a telegram to Lloyd George in Paris that had been organised by William Kennedy Jones MP, Northcliffe's former employee. The telegram stated that 'The greatest anxiety exists throughout the country at the persistent reports from Paris that the British delegates instead of formulating the complete claims of the Empire are merely considering what amount can be exacted from the enemy.'[94] Lloyd George decided to return to London, and told his fellow conferees at Versailles in a closed session that he would be back soon 'unless the House of Commons refuses me its confidence, in which case it will be Lord Northcliffe or [the newly-elected] Horatio Bottomley [with whom] you will be resuming these talks'.[95]

On 10 April, Northcliffe wrote to his brother Harold from Fontainebleau that 'The Germans are bluffing ... What can be inducing the PM to wobble on this matter? He is surrounded by "be-kind-to-Germany" people.'[96] (A *Daily Mail* headline of the period read: 'They Will Cheat You Yet Those Junkers.'[97]) Three days later, Northcliffe wrote to Kennedy Jones to say of Lloyd George 'That he is being bluffed is obvious. His entourage* say that the reason the peace terms cannot be published is that the British Government would fall at once, as the people would realise they had been had.'[98] He claimed that Edwin Montagu was drafting the terms and was influential on Lloyd George: 'The French are very much surprised to find a Jew engaged in this business. I am not anti-Semite [sic] as you know but it is a deplorable thing that after all our sufferings and the sacrifice of all the gallant boys that have gone that in the end we should be beaten by financiers.'[99] Of course, the assumption that financiers were necessarily Jewish was in itself an anti-Semitic trope.

On 14 April, Frances Stevenson noted that her lover, the Prime Minister, had made up his mind to attack Northcliffe 'and declare war to the knife'.[100] Sure enough, in the debate of 16 April 1919, Lloyd George launched a vigorous attack in response to Northcliffe's allegations of his taking a lenient stance in Paris.[101] In the course of the Commons debate, Northcliffe had been referred to by an MP as a 'reliable source', and this provided Lloyd George with a series of attack-points. He never mentioned Northcliffe by name, but made it perfectly clear whom he was attacking by references to Broadstairs. 'Reliable!' said Lloyd George,

That is the last adjective I would use. It is here today, jumping there to-morrow, and there the next day. I would as soon rely on a grasshopper. Still, I am prepared to make some allowance – even great newspapers will forgive me for saying so – and when a man is labouring under a keen sense of disappointment, however

---

* Possibly a reference to Harold's only surviving son Esmond, who was on Lloyd George's staff in Paris. On his election for Thanet aged twenty-one years and five months, he became the youngest MP in more than a century.

unjustified and however ridiculous the expectations may have
been, he is always apt to think the world is badly run.[102]

He accused Northcliffe of being 'deluded' by his acolytes into believing 'that he is the only man who can win the war, and he is waiting
for the clamour of the multitude that is going to demand his presence
there to direct the destinies of the world, and there is not a whisper,
not a sound, it is rather disappointing; it is unnerving; it is upsetting.
Then the war is won without him. There must be something wrong.
Of course it must be the Government!'
    'Under these conditions,' Lloyd George's vicious and wildly unfair
philippic continued,

> I am prepared to make allowances; but let me say this, that when
> that kind of diseased vanity is carried to the point of sowing dis-
> sension between great Allies, whose unity is essential to the peace
> and happiness of the world ... then I say that not even that kind
> of disease is a justification for so black a crime against humanity.

At the moment that he said the words 'diseased vanity', the Prime
Minister turned around to the government benches behind him and,
out of eyesight of the parliamentary reporters, tapped his temple,
indicating that Northcliffe had gone mad.[103] 'They still believe in
France that The Times is a serious organ,' he continued. 'They do not
know that it is merely a threepenny edition of the Daily Mail ... That
is my only apology for taking notice of that kind of trash, with which
some of these papers have been filled during the last few weeks.'
    Later in the debate he referred to 'wild men screaming through
the keyholes', which was doubtless another reference to Northcliffe.
In the light of what was to happen to Northcliffe, Lloyd George has
been credited with extraordinary prescience, but in fact Northcliffe's
mental illness did not descend for many months afterwards, and it
was no more than a cruel jibe and a hint at megalomania.
    'The House of Commons roared with delight at the PM's perfor-
mance,' noted a disappointed Steed. 'It showed no critical faculty
whatever.'[104] Certainly no one asked why, if Northcliffe's vanity was

so diseased, Lloyd George had given him control of all of Britain's war effort in the United States and all of her propaganda effort in enemy countries. Nor did anyone question whether Northcliffe was in France waiting for a call to power which never came, as Lloyd George alleged, or he was there on his doctor's orders prior to a throat operation, which Lloyd George knew to be the case.[105]

Neville Chamberlain was particularly delighted with the speech, describing it to his sister Ida as 'the most dramatic and thrilling episode of the last Parliament. His attack on Northcliffe was positively vitriolic.'[106] Cecil Harmsworth considered resigning from the government, but later concluded that 'both were controversial bruisers, given to very rough blows on the one side and the other exceedingly well able to look after themselves ... N was opposed to my resigning.'[107]

'I don't mind attacks,' Northcliffe told Louise Owen at Fontainebleau. 'As you know, I am used to them. But what does depress me is that the PM, at a time like this ... should occupy the attention of the House ... in abusing me. It shows the mentality of the premier, and how he lacks all sense of proportion. No ordinary man like myself should at this time figure so prominently before the world.'[108] Lord Robert Cecil told Lloyd George that he expected Northcliffe to 'burst', but in fact he sensibly did not react publicly at all.[109] He had seen during the Shells Crisis how a public spat with a popular figure could backfire – and Lloyd George had recently won the largest landslide in British electoral history, so he decided to play it sensibly, chipping away at Lloyd George rather than confronting him in his hour of triumph. 'Your handling of our petty PM was perfect,' Northcliffe told Steed when *The Times* did not rise to the bait.[110] They believed they had years to exact their revenge.

CHAPTER 20

PURSUING THE VENDETTA

April 1919–July 1921

'Better be blackguarded than ignored.'[1]

LORD NORTHCLIFFE, 1920

'We must be careful not to involve ourselves in *wrong* quarrels with the Prime Minister,' Northcliffe wrote to Tom Marlowe and five other senior *Daily Mail* executives on 22 April 1919, six days after Lloyd George's ad hominem attack in the Commons.

> I have no personal interest in him either way. When he is vigorous in fighting Germany I support him: when he sings his 'Be kind to poor little Germany' song, I oppose him. I notice a tendency in the staffs of my newspapers to hit back when the Prime Minister makes foolish remarks about me. I deprecate that attitude. Silence is a more effective and dignified weapon.[2]

Marlowe agreed with this stance, but when he said so in a long letter, Northcliffe admonished him for not dictating it. 'I am sorry to receive a letter in your handwriting,' he complained. 'It must have taken at least thirty-five minutes to write.'[3] He also encouraged his editor to work only five days a week, 'as I am going to'.

There is no indication that Northcliffe did work any less hard, despite his looming throat surgery. Every day there came suggestions about how his papers might be improved. He was delighted that the *Daily Mail* had instituted a film column 'at my suggestion', noting that the movie industry was already the sixth largest in the United States. He was attracted by the stardust of Hollywood celebrity – Douglas Fairbanks Snr and Mary Pickford spent part of their honeymoon at Elmwood Cottage after their wedding in March 1920 – but he also reserved the right to criticise movies in his pages.

In the month of May 1919, Northcliffe mentioned individual writers he wanted complimented; complained that during the hundred-mile journey from Sutton Place to Elmwood he did not see a single placard for *The Times* though many for the *Morning Post*; and insisted on a burglary at Clandon Park* being reported 'otherwise the paper is not a record'. He also wanted *The Times* weather map enlarged. The story was told of Northcliffe raging down the telephone to the editorial desk. 'What have you done with the moon? I said the moon – the *moon*. Someone has moved the moon! . . . Well, if it's moved again, whoever does it is fired!'⁴ Far from megalomaniacally believing that he could alter the heavens, in fact Northcliffe was angry that his readers were not able to find the weather report, which recorded the lunar phases, in its normal place in the paper.

'I was glad to see the prominence given to the Czechoslovak Musical Festival,' Northcliffe told Steed in May 1920, and said that he enjoyed 'the delightful article on rhododendrons', while also being pleased at the paper's medical coverage: 'I may say that the *Lancet* and the *British Medical Journal* do not like us, which is a good sign.' He demanded that the *Mail*'s Walter Fish send 'independent persons' to ascertain the attendance at cricket matches, complaining that space had been given to one at which only 600 spectators were present. 'Cricket reporters will not tell you,' he wrote. 'They would be afraid to lose their jobs.'⁵

Northcliffe continued to make asides in his almost daily communiqués. 'I hear that the car of the Editor was stolen from outside *The Times* the other evening,' read one. 'I wish they would steal the horses that are, I understand, still being used for the transport of *The Times* in the middle of the night.'⁶ He wanted more non-political

---

* The home of Northcliffe's friend the Earl of Onslow, close to Sutton Place.

third leaders, arguing that 'One light article always alters the whole tone of the paper, just as a single reed instrument changes the tone of an orchestra of sixty.'[7] Similarly, he pressed for shorter headlines on poster bills: '*The Fate of Turkey* is quite as well expressed by *Turkey's Fate*.'[8]

Northcliffe was hard to read: Linton Andrews was editing on a day when he condemned the *Daily Mail* news pages for being too full of politics and lacking in news that appealed to 'the human desire for something fresh'. They then received a cable from the United States stating that a gangster's pet canary had died and he had put it in a 'gold coffin and given it a funeral of sumptuous splendour, watched by a vast crowd'. Hoping to please Northcliffe, Andrews and the night editor gave it top billing on the news page the next day. Instead, Northcliffe 'blazed with wrath at the prominence given to what he seemed to regard as a silly triviality'.[9] Throughout his long career as an editor, however, Andrews constantly asked himself, 'What would the Chief have done?' and considered that 'It helped me to take a bold and resolute line.'[10]

Northcliffe's punishing work pace meant that the doctor who specialised in removing the adenoma of the left lobe of the thyroid gland refused to operate unless he gave up all work and rested completely. 'It is not a malignant growth as some people say,' Northcliffe told Beaverbrook, 'though it may become so if not excised'.[11] In an undated letter of this period, Beaverbrook wrote to Northcliffe to express how he felt 'overwhelmed by your praise, particularly when I reflect on the fact that you are the foremost figure in journalism in the whole world history of the profession'.[12]

~

At 4.28pm local time on 14 June 1919, the intrepid aviators John Alcock and Arthur Whitten Brown took off from Newfoundland in a Vickers Vimy Rolls-Royce* twin-engined biplane to fly across the

---

* 'The most important part of an aeroplane is its engine,' Northcliffe once told his staff. 'Always give the name of the engine.' [Andrews and Taylor, *Lords and Labourers of the Press*, p.58]

Atlantic Ocean. They landed at Clifton in Ireland at 8.40am the next morning, thereby winning the £10,000 *Daily Mail* prize money that Northcliffe had offered for the feat back in 1913.

Northcliffe sent Alcock 'a very hearty welcome to the pioneer of direct Atlantic flight. Your journey with your brave companion, Whitten-Brown, is a typical exhibition of British courage and organising efficiency.' He looked forward to the time when 'the American and British peoples will understand each other better as they are brought into closer daily touch ... I rejoice at the good augury that you departed from and arrived at those two portions of the British Commonwealth, the happy and prosperous Dominion of Newfoundland, and the future equally happy and prosperous Dominion of Ireland.'[13]

This was a highly political act: Ireland was then part of the United Kingdom and not a dominion. When Steed pointed out that to foreshadow dominion status for a future self-governing Ireland 'would be impolitic', Northcliffe replied that he was 'certain that Ireland would be a Dominion before many years are over', so the phrase was left in, to the fury of ultra-Unionists such as Sir Edward Carson.[14] Whitten-Brown later told Northcliffe that 'It would not have been possible for Captain Alcock and myself to have been in the fortunate position in which we are today, had it not been for your stimulus and efforts in the early days of flying.'[15]

Although he could not attend the vast *Daily Mail* luncheon at the Savoy to celebrate Alcock and Brown's achievement, Northcliffe did not entirely obey his doctors' demand for total rest. 'This morning's article on bee-keeping was, in my opinion, much too long,' he told Walter Fish the day before his throat operation on 18 June.[16] 'He faced it pluckily,' Steed recalled of the painful surgery. 'He knew that it might be fatal or that, should he recover from it, it might seriously impair his powers. But he took the risk almost gaily and said repeatedly that anything would be better than the suffering he had undergone during the past year.'[17] Northcliffe kept the three-inch adenoma that was cut out of his neck in a bottle to show to friends.

Two days after the operation, Northcliffe asked the woman who was head of his convalescent home to get him a Victrola vinyl record player, saying, 'I must have music the last thing at night, otherwise I cannot sleep.'[18] She persuaded him instead to hire a female violinist to play for him as she had a great belief in music as a healing power.[19] On the first evening, the violinist played Scarlatti, Rameau, Paradies and Bach. Northcliffe asked her which of Chopin's four *ballades* she could play and whether the four *scherzi* were in her repertory. His favourite was *Nuit de Mai* by Palmgren, but he also asked for Sibelius's *Valse Triste* and Rachmaninoff's *Prelude* because the nurses liked to hear it. 'To reach people's minds,' Northcliffe told her when they discussed newspapers, 'you have to exaggerate – *everything*.'[20]

As well as music, he was put on powerful painkillers – with mixed effects. 'Morphine had no effect on me,' he wrote to Marlowe, 'neither had opium, aspirin and other coal tars. What did act quickly was hyoscine – the excellent stuff that Dr Crippen gave to his nagging wife.'[21]

From 5 July, Northcliffe was back writing his daily letters to his editors, full of praise but with occasional barbs. His remarkable micromanagement can be seen in a note to his staff of mid-August about how 'There is much too much of the shortage of fried fish and movements in the eel market about the Home Pages just now.'[22]

The politicians also had a brief reprieve. 'While he is ill there is a truce as far as I am concerned,' Lloyd George told Riddell in mid-July, 'but when he recovers he will have to make up his mind what line he intends to take. If he goes on attacking me, I shall have something more to say about him. I don't propose to allow matters to rest. I shall let the public know and fully realise that he is my enemy.'[23] When the Lord Chancellor Lord Birkenhead tried to gain access to him, Northcliffe told Marlowe on 17 July

> I greatly dislike these politicians trying to see me over the heads of my editors. Moreover, I never allow them into my house and never go into theirs ... The Prime Minister, having taken occasion to attack a man whom he knew to be ill and not having the courage to apologise, will find that the difficulty will never be overcome so far as my Mother, my Wife and the Family are concerned.[24]

The diary of Lord Riddell – whom Lloyd George insisted on the King ennobling despite his having been cited in a divorce case – confirms that, despite his personal animosity, Lloyd George was constantly vacillating about how to deal with Northcliffe. He was even 'rather favourable' to the idea of offering him the role of lord-lieutenant of Ireland. When he heard that rumour, Northcliffe told his brother Cecil: 'Does any human being imagine that I would compromise my power and independence by a footman's job like that?'[25]

Northcliffe and Mary moved into No.1 Carlton Gardens in September, one of the grandest houses in London whose previous owners included Louis Napoleon, who kept a tiger cub there, and Lord Ripon, the viceroy of India (today it is the grace-and-favour residence of the Foreign Secretary). When he discovered that William Gladstone was another past resident, Northcliffe wrote to a friend,

> I have noticed a glowing glibness and verbosity on my part lately – a capacity for burying my friends under mountains of words. I know the reason. That dreadful old man lived here, and just as they tell us that the plague bacillus lingers in houses for centuries, so it is possibly with the bacilli of Word Disease.'[26]

Mary used Carlton Gardens when she was in London, but suffered from neuralgia (or at least claimed to) and was spending much of her time at Crowborough with Sir Robert Hudson.[27] 'I am very glad that you are staying on to look after the ladies,' Northcliffe wrote to Hudson in January 1920, thanking him for protecting his wife and her nursemaid in the countryside, presumably from the influenza still ravaging Britain.[28]

On the evening of 5 November 1919, Northcliffe invited Tom Clarke, who was being tried out as a future news editor, to his study on the fourth floor of the house. There he described what it was like to decide what a million people would read the next day and the responsibility of 'controlling the news for the world's best newspaper in the world's greatest city'.[29] He wanted more of 'our various crusades' in favour of free trade and against state control, subsidies and nationalisation.[30] He wanted campaigns opposing waste in government and in favour of buying British produce and manufactured goods wherever possible.

'LG in high spirits', Riddell noted on 8 January 1920, 'but much obsessed by Northcliffe and his alleged villainies'.[31] That same month, the government's introduction of auxiliaries for the Royal Irish Constabulary – known as the 'Black and Tans' – drew criticism from *The Times* once it became clear that it was an attempt to crush Irish nationalism by extreme force, amounting almost to government-supported terrorism. *The Times* instead put forward schemes for the island of Ireland that approximated to self-government as a Dominion, which infuriated Unionists who made up much of the paper's readership. '*The Times* can rarely have been more unpopular in England than during this period,' Steed later recalled of this crisis of his editorship.

> Its circulation fell. Members of the Government denounced it, in season and out of season, and through many official channels the story was spread that its policy was inspired by a personal vendetta of Northcliffe against Lloyd George. Northcliffe was, indeed, placed in a difficult position. He supported us steadily ... Strong pressure was also put on him by members of his family,* and he felt keenly the injustice of the insinuation that the policy of *The Times* was dictated by personal animosity on his part against the Prime Minister. He viewed with concern the falling circulation.[32]

Death threats were received at Printing House Square, which had to be guarded by special detectives night and day during this fraught period. On one occasion, a photograph with bullet holes marked in Northcliffe's forehead was hand-delivered to Elmwood.[33]

Hatred of Northcliffe in 1920 was not confined to Irish politics: in his memoirs *Combed Out*, published that year, the left-wing

---

* Almost certainly including Mother, whose obituary noted that 'In her, loyal Ulster had the most devoted and unswerving of friends.' [*Evening News* 31 August 1925]

Manchester Guardian's Berlin correspondent quoted an unnamed British soldier saying, 'I tell you straight, if I had the choice of killing a German soldier and killing Lord Northcliffe, I'd shake hands with the German and ask him to help me kill Lord Northcliffe and others like him. And I'm not the only one who's that way of thinking, I can tell you.'[34]

Northcliffe's Teutonophobia was undimmed even a year after the armistice. 'I am being pressed to push the Opera,' he wrote to Steed, 'which is supported by a number of people who were semi-Boche before the war and are now putting forward too much German music. New York and Boston have shown us a good example, but there they know the Hun.'[35] In the United States, German classical music and conductors had been banned during the war, while sauerkraut became 'liberty cabbage' and dachshunds 'liberty pups'.

~

On 30 January, Cecil Harmsworth advised his brother to 'get a little sunshine into your blood before the summer comes and Home Rule, Bolshevism, falling exchanges and a tottering Government absorb your energies'.[36] Since he was a member of that government, Cecil could also have added to his list serious and widespread strikes and the reparations issue, which gave Northcliffe's papers further opportunities to criticise Lloyd George. Yet it was not solely personal pique that led the Northcliffe press into opposition; there was a sound business reason too. It is perhaps a comment on human nature that newspapers which criticise governments tend to sell more copies than those which laud them. During one government crisis at the time, a joke did the rounds that reflected Northcliffe's power and suspected megalomania: 'The *bon mot* in the lobbies is that the PM has resigned and Lord Northcliffe has sent for the King.'[37]

Northcliffe supported the strike of the workers of the Pearl Insurance Company for the minimum wage in January 1920. During the course of it, he publicly returned a £500 cheque for Pearl's prospective advertising in the *Weekly Dispatch*, and donated

the same amount to the strikers' fund, adding £1,000 a week from
the *Daily Mail*. His timing turned out to be impeccable; the Pearl
management were on the brink of collapse and it only needed to be
paid for a fortnight. He did not allow his own workers to dictate
to him, however, and when in February a Mr Collett threatened to
resign if various conditions concerning an agricultural supplement
were not met, Northcliffe merely replied: 'Then you have resigned.'
He commented to Steed, 'That's that. ...This incident will give you
an idea of what I went through ten years ago in trying to restore
The Times to its original prestige.'[38] Writing to his secretary H. G.
Price from the *Daily Mail* offices in the Rue du Sentier in Paris the
following month, Northcliffe stated that he had 'a duty towards *The
Times* to perform and I'll perform it without regard to the feelings
of individuals'.[39]

Tom Clarke described Northcliffe's friend and protégé Keith
Murdoch as 'a big, hefty Australian, as jolly and mischievous as a
schoolboy' for whom 'Northcliffe has developed a warm personal
regard'.[40] Before returning home in early March, where he was to
build up a great newspaper empire, Murdoch wrote a heartfelt letter
to Northcliffe thanking him

> for all that you have been for me and done for me since I came
> here four years ago. I will not say more than that you have been
> the biggest influence and the biggest force over me here, largely
> on account of the many kindnesses you have shown me, but even
> more lately from the example I have steadily seen in you and the
> standard that you have set me. I am certainly coming back, but
> if I never met you again I would retain this influence to the end
> of my life.[41]

~

On 8 May 1920, *The Times* devoted an entire column of its news
page to a pamphlet translated from the Russian entitled *The Jewish
Peril: Protocols of the Elders of Zion*, which had been disgracefully
published by the Crosthwaite-Eyre family who owned the Eyre &
Spottiswoode publishers. The anonymous article was written by

Steed and subtitled 'The Jewish Peril: A Disturbing Pamphlet: Call for Inquiry'.[42] 'What are these Protocols?' the profoundly anti-Semitic Steed asked.

> Are they authentic? If so, what malevolent assembly concocted these plans and gloated over their exposition? Are they forgery? If so, whence comes the uncanny note of prophecy, prophecy in part fulfilled, in part so far gone in the way of fulfilment? Have we been struggling these tragic years to blow up and extirpate the secret organisation of German world dominion only to find beneath it another more dangerous because more secret? Have we, by straining every fibre of our national body escaped a Pax Germanica only to fall into a Pax Judaeica?[43]

Steed did not overtly endorse the *Protocols*, but he went into their accusations in detail, saying they were 'likely to perturb the thinking public'. It resulted in a storm of criticism, which to his credit Steed published, including letters such as that from a Mr A. J. Villers saying, 'Lloyd George and Clemenceau pulled by the Elders of Zion! What balderdash!'[44]

On 16 August, once Philip Graves, *The Times* correspondent in Constantinople, had exposed *The Protocols* as a Tsarist forgery, the paper printed a retraction entitled 'Truth At Last', admitting that 'What some took to be the imprimatur of *The Times* gave it unprecedented importance.'[45] The sheer extent of Steed's malign recklessness can be gauged even today, where on the internet it is alleged that *The Times* endorsed the *Protocols* and 'called Jews the world's greatest danger'.[46]

Although Northcliffe was not directly involved in the *Protocols* debacle, and did not bother to read the book when a copy was sent to him by the *Daily Mail*'s New York correspondent, Steed would probably not have published the original column if he had not known his proprietor fully shared his bigotry towards Jews.[47] Over copyright negotiations with William Heinemann in 1920, John Hammerton recorded in his book *With Northcliffe in Fleet Street* that Northcliffe told him, '"Never trust a Jew. He will be alright for a while, but

in the end he'll let you down." Many times this was repeated.'[48]
Elsewhere in the book, Hammerton noted that 'His expressed
distrust of Jews was probably some inherited peculiarity ... but it
persisted to the end of his days.'[49]

~

Fascinated by the potential power of the wireless, on 15 June 1920
Northcliffe persuaded Dame Nellie Melba to sing in the first radio
concert ever broadcast, at Marconi's wireless station in Chelmsford
in Essex. After a dinner of chicken and champagne at 7pm, she sang
the *addio* from *La Bohème* into a microphone that was attached to
a fifteen-kilowatt set, transmitting on a 2,800-metre wavelength.
'Never before has her wonderful voice gone into space and been
carried by all who had the means to hear within a range of a thousand miles,' reported *The Times* the next day. 'The apparent miracle
was achieved by the aid of the wireless telephone.'[50] She was heard
distinctly in Paris, Warsaw, Stockholm and Berlin, and on cruise
liners at sea. 'In London the concert was heard with extraordinary
clearness,' reported the *Mail*.

Northcliffe had a seven-valve 'radiophone' wireless set installed
in *The Times* offices, recognising its importance for the worlds
of entertainment, business and government, while fearing that it
would one day eclipse newspapers in the dissemination of news.
When an American friend told him that radio gave his children a
nightly bedtime story, Northcliffe saw it as a threat to his children's
magazine business too. It has been speculated that, had he lived, he
would have fought to prevent the BBC setting up its monopoly of
the airwaves in 1927.

A diva just as demanding as Dame Nellie Melba was Margot
Asquith, who wrote to Northcliffe in July requesting a *Daily Mail*
interview of herself to discuss her autobiography. It proved that
some people will do anything to promote their books, including even
appealing to the man who destroyed her husband's premiership. 'I
wonder what you *really* think of the government you created,' she
wrote, which, although meant as a criticism for bringing down her
husband, was also an acknowledgement of Northcliffe's power. 'I

hear you had a delightful party the other night but you never asked me!' she wrote to the man she so despised.

'I am sorry to hear about the book and the wretched price people say you obtained for it,' Northcliffe replied about her £12,500 *Sunday Times* serialisation deal. He believed that it was worth £20,000 and that she ought to have gone straight to him.[51] Margot responded by asking that it be reviewed in Northcliffe's papers, saying his letter 'made me smile. You were pulling my leg, I rather think', and making the 'purely commercial' suggestion of a *Times* article about the congratulations she has been receiving about her book.[52] She thought an interview of herself would also make a good change during the 'silly season' time when otherwise 'mixed bathing, bad grouse shooting with ugly snapshots of stupid swells on the moors will be your chief copy'.[53] Northcliffe asked Churchill to review the book, but was unhappy with his copy and asked him to 'ginger' it up. 'Winston at first seemed very annoyed,' he told Tom Clarke, 'and ready to let the whole thing go hang, but eventually he made a few alterations.'[54]

Turning down Churchill's offer to speak at an air conference in the autumn, Northcliffe explained on 8 July that 'On Monday next I am commencing a three months' course of severe treatment in the hope of getting rid of the laryngitis which makes me almost a prisoner.'[55] His doctors were emphatic that Northcliffe not speak in public until at least late October. In another sign that he was no jingoistic imperialist, Northcliffe congratulated Churchill for having dismissed Brigadier-General Reginald Dyer, the soldier responsible for the Amritsar massacre: 'Everyone that I meet is glad about the stand you took in connection with the unfortunate General Dyer. My knowledge of India is only that of a cold-weather tourist, but I did meet several General Dyers there, both military and civil.'[56] 'Unfortunate' was meant not in the sense of unlucky so much as calamitous.

~

The national coal strike that started on 16 October 1920 was the worst work stoppage in Britain since 1912, it involving more than a million miners and cost a total of sixteen million days lost. *The Times* was critical of the government, even though Lloyd George's tough action in invoking wartime-era powers might under other circumstances have won its support. There were half-hearted attempts by Riddell and Campbell Stuart to broker a peace, or at least an armistice, between Lloyd George and Northcliffe, but these foundered before the formidable egos and wounded pride of both men.

On the day that the strike was settled, 23 October, Riddell noted in his diary that Lloyd George was 'very critical about Northcliffe's actions, which he says make negotiations of this sort very difficult. He said, "What is Northcliffe at? Is he veering over to the Labour Party?"'[57] When Riddell told the Prime Minister that Northcliffe had been very ill and had had a swollen adenoma removed, Lloyd George replied, 'He has also got a swollen head. It is a pity they did not remove that too!'[58]

Trade union militancy reached Fleet Street in late November 1920 when the mechanical staff of the National Union of Journalists (NUJ) threatened strike action over the *Daily Mail's* editorialising against the demands of the National Union of Railwaymen. 'Allow me to express my surprise at the ingratitude displayed in your letter today,' Northcliffe replied to their strike threat. 'You must be aware that my press has always given great space to labour matters.' He went into the attacks his papers had received over the course of his career from the Asquith and Lloyd George Governments owing to their independent line on trade unionism, but ended by saying that 'Rather than be dictated to by anyone or any body of men, I will stop the publication of these papers and in view of your letter I have so informed the Newspaper Proprietors' Association.'[59] If the stoppage went ahead, he stated that 'the directors, immediately, and with the deepest regret, well aware of the suffering that it will entail upon you and your families, will issue legal notice to terminate all contracts throughout the building and will stop the publication of our four newspapers. This is not a threat. I never threaten. It is a fact.'[60] This was not an example of his deranged vehemence, as some detractors have alleged, but rather a principled stand for press freedom.

The NUJ called off the strike and continued negotiations on the basis of wage increases and the grading of wages for groups rather than individuals, which Northcliffe characterised as 'degrading' and complained that it would bring the profession of journalism down to the level of a mere industrial concern. The *Daily Mail* derided the union's plans as 'Jam Factory Journalism'.[61] It made Northcliffe nostalgic for the rugged individualism of the past. 'We were a flesh and blood lot in those days,' he lamented, 'and not a bun-and-glass-of milk-fed NUJers.'[62] Yet, when in December 1920 he found a female typist had been hired by the *Mail* for as little as £1 a week, he rang up the head of the department responsible and docked £1 a week off his salary, before ordering the company cashier to tell everyone he met that he had done so.[63]

'It is about time men had a new hat,' Northcliffe told a *Daily Mail* conference at Carmelite House in the autumn of 1920. Why not offer £100 for the best design of a new hat?'[64] He pointed out that there was a limited choice for male headgear – only the top hat, bowler, straw boater, trilby and flat cap – so 'a new-hat-for-men competition would be most amusing. Let reference be made to hat monotony.' This was clearly a *jeu d'esprit* and possibly a bid to increase circulation with a competition, yet it has been depicted by Northcliffe's detractors as a bid to bully Britons into wearing different headgear. 'The public refused to be ordered about on the subject of hats,' noted Tom Clarke on 1 November. 'Were it the best hat in the world, given away free, people would not risk ridicule by wearing it. Northcliffe, who hated failure, was angrily lashing out at all and sundry in the office who had the remotest connection with the stunt. He complained to me of the "bad taste of our propaganda", and told me to get some fresh minds on to it.'[65]

Northcliffe sent a free *Daily Mail* hat, which looked like a squared-off version of the bowler, to Churchill, who had long worn something vaguely similar, and to ex-King Manuel II of Portugal, who put it on for the photographers.[66] The lobby correspondents only managed to get two MPs to wear them. Ambitious reporters wore them when Northcliffe was in the office, but then swapped back to normal hats on their journey home.

On 18 December, an article entitled 'The New Press Gang' in a magazine entitled *Outlook* was highly critical of Northcliffe and he took strong exception to it. Believing that Lloyd George was ultimately behind it, he blamed it on Arthur Lee, whose wife Ruth he thought owned the publication. 'This ... parasite attacks me in his journal, kept by his wife's money,' Northcliffe wrote to one of his lieutenants about Lee. 'This is not an ordinary newspaper attack. I rather enjoy those.'[67] The Lees had been about to stay with the Northcliffes at the Villa Roquebrune in Cap Martin in January, but Northcliffe instructed Mary to cancel the invitation. When, on Boxing Day, Hudson wrote from 'this delectable villa' to say that in fact Lady Lee had sold *Outlook*, Northcliffe was unappeased and replied that nonetheless she was still a shareholder and Arthur a director. Although neither Lee had even known the article was going to appear, the invitation was indeed rescinded and the two couples' friendship of many years ended in acrimony.

Northcliffe's ruthlessness was reiterated a few days later on New Year's Eve 1921 when he wrote to Steed about *The Times*'s shaky financial position, which in large part was the result of the political positions Northcliffe himself had adopted on Ireland, industrial relations and Lloyd George. 'During 1920, the Paper has caused me more annoyance than any other big operation I have ever had,' he wrote. 'Unless the position improves, I shall most reluctantly transfer my obligation to other shoulders ... I am looking around.'[68] Steed replied that 'We shall make every effort to effect economy, to keep expenditure down, and to put things into good shape. You know that everything I can do will be done.'[69]

'He could be rough with us,' recalled Sir Linton Andrews in later life, 'but his cruel sarcasm and explosive wrath found in men of *The Times* ... his worst-suffering victims. Even those who hated the methods of an irritable perfectionist – methods that at times amounted almost to mental torture – had to admit that Northcliffe saved *The Times*. I cannot think that Charles Arthur Pearson or any other contemporary could have made so many and such drastic, wise and lasting improvements as Northcliffe did.'[70]

On 27 January 1921, after the oleaginous leader-writer H. W. Wilson urged – with lots of references to Napoleon – Northcliffe to enter politics, he replied, 'Do you realise the fact that, if I enter political life, I have to abandon all connection with the Press, which is my sole source of power? Mine is a new kind of position in the world. I have been more or less forced into it, but I prefer it to any other as a means of getting things done.'[71] Five days later, commenting on the first sixty pages of Wilson's draft biography of him, Northcliffe wrote,

> I have been trying to weed out the myths from your manuscript about me ... You refer to 'partners'. I have never had a partner in my life. Do you think that a barony was the first of my ambitions? I attach about as much importance to a dumb Parliament like this as I do to a breakfast. You have forgotten the five-day week – the biggest revolution I have ever effected.

It was true that Northcliffe had allowed his employees not to work on Saturday mornings, but it was typical of him to take credit for the way the practice had been adopted by the rest of society in the 1890s. The refusal to acknowledge Harold Rothermere as having been his partner was similarly egotistical.

In March, Northcliffe went on holiday to the south of France. He had been getting tired earlier in the evenings since his throat operation, and would often leave his own dinner parties at 9.30pm to go to bed, after making sure his guests had enough port, brandy, champagne and cigars. However, the level of his characteristic micro-management of his papers did not perceptibly lessen while on the Riviera. One telegram to George Sutton merely read: 'Photographs of unimportant weddings will hurt the paper. Chief.' A few days later, he complained that *The Times* index had given incorrect page numbers.[72] Nor was he above a certain degree of subterfuge: when it became clear that his newspapers were becoming highly successful at selling life and house insurance, he ordered to 'as far as possible, discourage talk' of this fact, fearing all the newspapers would copy the idea, 'as in the old days of *Tit-Bits* and *Answers*'.[73] Instead, 'I tell everyone that it is a very expensive boom, which we shall probably drop at the end of the year.'

Northcliffe's personal relations with Churchill continued to be friendly, who was attending the Cairo Conference at the time when Austen Chamberlain took over from the ill Bonar Law as leader of the Conservative Party, with the coveted post of chancellor of the exchequer going to Robert Horne rather than to him. An *Evening News* cartoon was drawn of Churchill, depicting him splashing paint on the Pyramids as he hears the news of the reshuffle from an Egyptian news-vendor. Northcliffe sent Churchill the original artwork. Ten years later, Churchill recalled how Northcliffe 'thought it splendid. He roared with merriment as he pointed its beauties out to me. I accepted the gift with a stock grin. Of course, it was only a joke, but there was quite enough truth in it for it to be more funny to others than to oneself!'[74]

In early April, from the Hotel Windsor at Menton, Northcliffe told Campbell Stuart that his throat vaccines had to be administered every eighth day. 'They can only be injected after a very quiet day, and for two days afterwards I am unable to do anything.'[75] Yet the very next day, he told his secretary Francis Humphrey-Davy – whom he somewhat unimaginatively nicknamed Humpty Dumpty – that because of the threatened general strike in Britain he did not like being so far away from the centre of events and would move to the Hôtel des Reservoirs in Versailles prior to coming home. He ordered his newspapers to adopt a moderate tone over industrial relations, explaining that 'we may be beginning an entirely new era in English history and must be scrupulously fair to all. Print both sides fully.'[76] Six days later, he warned his editors that 'By attacking Labour as a whole we should [i.e. would] antagonise them.'[77] One positive aspect of the crisis was that sales of the *Daily Mail* rose to 1.5 million daily, which he rightly thought an 'astonishing figure'.[78]

None of Northcliffe's editors made the mistake of thinking that his lengthy throat recuperation or his being on holiday might take the edge off his perfectionism. 'In my opinion, the whole of yesterday's paper was spoiled by the change made in one headline,' he told Marlowe on 21 April. 'I daresay you might find that difficult to understand, but just realise that, when a French *chef de cuisine* merely touches a dish with a morsel of garlic, he knows what he is doing. I begin to think nobody understands the psychology of the *Daily Mail* as I do. I invented those small articles and ran them in opposition to practically the whole office. They are now copied in London, the provinces, France, the United States, and even, I see, in Germany.'[79] Vanity and egotism, certainly, but this behaviour was not a prima facie case of megalomania.

On 24 April, Northcliffe told Steed that he had three potential buyers of *The Times* ready, and it was 'the urgent wishes of my medical and other advisers to get rid of a very trying responsibility'. To him, '*The Times* is just that last straw which makes the load unbearable.'[80] It must have been very trying for Steed to receive letters like that after only two bad issues, or at least ones that Northcliffe told him were bad. Steed replied that he felt that selling *The Times* would be 'a great turning point in your life' and that Northcliffe would regret 'having vacated the premier position in journalism'. He suggested he would be 'acquiring a burden of regret that would weigh you down'.[81] It was excellent advice, and Mother and Mary also seem to have been united in their opposition to his selling the paper – if he had ever really intended to – probably appreciating, like Steed, the overnight reduction in his power and influence if he did. He later denied he had ever considered selling, telling the *New York World* that 'The whole story was concocted by the German papers. I never explain or complain' – even though in the previous sentence he had done both.[82]

The quarter-centenary of the founding of the *Daily Mail* was celebrated in suitably grand style on Sunday 1 May 1921 at a gala luncheon for 7,000 people at Olympia, although Northcliffe was much annoyed on noticing a few empty seats.[83] The sheer size of the event has been described as 'strong proof of the megalomania that was gripping him', but it can just as easily be seen in those paternalistic days as a generous if grandiloquent gesture of gratitude to the enormous number of employees who had made his ascendance possible. Northcliffe progressed around the balcony to the cheers of his employees, with his Mother on his arm rather than Mary. 'I had my first glimpse of Northcliffe,' recalled an advertising manager of the occasion. 'He was of medium height, square shouldered, heavily built, clean shaven with a bulldog jaw, piercing eyes well set apart, a strong nose and a heavy hank of hair brushed over the left-hand side of his forehead ... He had an air of power and command.'[84]

The advertising manager at Olympia had thought Northcliffe heavily built, which is supported by the statistics. Northcliffe had kept detailed notes about his weight ever since 1900, complete with notes to himself about its fluctuations. On 7 October 1900, he was 11 stone 13lb 13oz ('down again thank goodness'), but by 12 June 1901 he was 12 stone 9lb 4 oz ('appalling'), and when he reached exactly 12 stone on 2 September 1903, it was a 'triumph of self-denial'.[85] He lost nearly twelve pounds in six weeks when he was ill in 1910, but counted himself a 'good boy' when he got down to 13 stone 2lb on 6 July 1911. His weight diary for 1917–21, which shows that he fluctuated between 13 stone 10lb and 14 stone 1lb ('horror'), was entitled 'A Fat Man's Gallant Fight Against Fate.'[86]

Because of Northcliffe's throat, a recorded address was played proposing the toast to the newspaper, in which he pointed out that the *Daily Mail* was the only newspaper in the world produced in more than one country. It was the only time his voice was recorded, and its somewhat staccato, relatively high-pitched Received Pronunciation accent is reminiscent of the abdication broadcast of Edward VIII and the announcement of the declaration of war by Neville Chamberlain in 1939. The grace before lunch was said by a clergyman who intoned that 'Thou hast endued thy servant Alfred with many singular and excellent gifts' and asked him to continue 'guiding aright the destinies of this great Empire'.[87] Less respectful was the *Morning Post's* jibe that, considering how many people he had sacked over the years, 'We understand that he has engaged the Salisbury Plain in order to give a summer picnic to those who *have been* in his employ.'[88] On the afternoon of the celebratory luncheon, Northcliffe went back to the office and nearly sacked Mr Purser the shorthand-taker for being too slow and losing his notes. 'It occurred to me that he had not put enough water with it,' he told Marlowe, implying that Purser had been drunk.[89]

Although he insisted on streamlined efficiency in his companies, Northcliffe was, as Clarke noted, 'unsystematic himself, especially with correspondence'.[90] He often received two hundred letters a day, of which his secretaries, who summed up the important ones for him in a paragraph each, got him to read a score when in Britain and a dozen when abroad, usually in trains or cars or at odd moments during the day. Even then, he 'looks at the most important letters and drops them on the floor ... His bedroom is littered with the most important documents and correspondence.'[91] By 1921, Northcliffe was sleeping with one of his correspondence secretaries, Louise Owen, which probably did not help matters.

In June 1921, the Jewish veteran *Daily Mail* legal advisor Charles Benham retired from the paper after many years' service, including on the board. Shortly beforehand, in an argument, Northcliffe had made what even his official biography described as an 'uncalled-for reference to Benham's ancestry'. Northcliffe gave him a smoked salmon to apologise, because he was 'the noblest Jew I know'.[92] Once again, there was a sting in the tail: when Hannen Swaffer remarked that Benham would probably have preferred a Gluckstein – a reference to the tobacconists Salmon & Gluckstein – 'Northcliffe was much amused.'[93] On another occasion, during an argument with Clement Shorter (a Gentile), he retorted: 'You are only a damned old Jew anyway.'[94] He had other perverse prejudices, and in June 1921 banned photographs of women wearing breeches as 'masculine tendencies in women are interfering with the birth-rate', a tendency he did not want to encourage by 'the power of suggestion'.[95]

～

After some tentative approaches via Birkenhead and Churchill, on 7 June Lloyd George attempted to re-establish working relations with the man who still owned four-tenths of the London newspaper market by circulation and whose support he suspected he might need were a truce to be signed with Sinn Fein and Ireland to be partitioned without bloodshed north of the forthcoming border. To protect against another bruising rebuff, as with the Air Ministry in 1917, a former *Daily Mail* writer Gerald Maxwell contacted Northcliffe to see whether 'a good undertaking could not be re-established' with the Prime Minister, who added that 'I have, of course, already ascertained that this is his desire.'[96]

Northcliffe's reply reflected a lifetime of experience, some of it painful:

> Politicians and newspapers and financiers and newspapers are better apart. Some politicians seem to think that newspapers act from personal motives. Mine certainly do not. I have often expressed my great admiration for the part the PM played in keeping up the public spirit during the war. When he does what my newspapers conscientiously believe to be right, they will say so. I do not think he has been right about Ireland [i.e. the Black and Tans], a country I know as well as some people, and I do not think he is right about national expenses, and I shall say so. But please disabuse your mind of the idea that I have any ill-feeling about the PM or any politician.[97]

Yet he was not being wholly open with Maxwell, and the next month he complained bitterly to Riddell, who passed it on immediately, about 'the PM's attack on him in early 1919, when ... he was about to undergo a serious operation which might have ended his life'.[98] Northcliffe understandably had plenty of ill-feeling towards the man who had accused him of having a 'diseased vanity'.

Apart from having been born in Ireland, buying his childhood home, visiting very occasionally, and having some cousins from his mothers' side whom he hardly knew, Northcliffe did not really know the country well, despite Kathleen Wrohan and Louise Owen both hailing from there. He took a commendably responsible stance during the partition of Ireland, however, that led to the independence of the southern twenty-six counties as Eire. With government policy about to change radically from coercion to negotiation, Northcliffe was ready to support it.

On 22 June, King George V opened the new Ulster Parliament at Stormont, using the opportunity to appeal for peace, and afterwards he wrote to thank Northcliffe for the support of his papers over the visit. Three weeks later, the British government signed a truce with Sinn Fein, prior to opening talks. Much of the Unionist party watched the partition of Ireland with trepidation, but Northcliffe did not add his voice to the doubters, which could have seriously disrupted and embittered the already difficult negotiations.

Northcliffe was deeply opposed to the proposed naval conference in Washington, however, as he feared it would make too many concessions to the Americans and Japanese at the expense of the Royal Navy. On 13 July, a *Times* leader accused the chief British negotiator Lord Curzon of having a 'pompous and pretentious manner' (which was true), 'business incapacity' (which was not), and 'obsequious docility', which was as untrue as it was rude.[99] Yet that was kind compared to Steed's estimation of Lloyd George in the leader, who wrote that 'Of all the statesmen in Europe, he is probably the most distrusted. It is notorious that no Government and no statesman in Europe who has had dealings with him puts the smallest confidence in him ... the great qualification needed from the representatives of the empire is a character for conspicuous straightforwardness and honour. We have many such men in our public life, but Mr Lloyd George is not one of them.'

This, along with a statement by H. W. Wilson in the *Daily Mail* that Lloyd George and Curzon did not represent British public opinion, resulted in Lloyd George stating on 18 July that because of the 'peculiarly offensive' attack on Curzon, the favours extended by the government towards the Northcliffe Press had been 'entirely withdrawn'.[100] Northcliffe saw this as a badge of honour, having spotted that because of strikes, a weak foreign policy, the partition of Ireland and scandals over the sale of honours, the tide of popular (and Unionist MPs') opinion had finally turned against 'The Man Who Won The War'.

CHAPTER 21

THE WORLD TOUR

July 1921–February 1922

'Wire mother's health and circulation figures.'[1]

LORD NORTHCLIFFE's orders on
leaving for his world tour, 1921

At lunch with Lord Riddell on 13 July 1921, Northcliffe 'said he
was a sick man and disheartened'.[2] His doctor Sir James Mackenzie
had recommended that he take at least six months off work, so
he decided to voyage around the world to recover his health and
spirits.[3] On 15 July, his fifty-sixth birthday and the day before his
departure, he held a conference of editorial staff in Room One of
Carmelite House to ensure that everyone knew the lines to take
when he was away. 'What was the best story in this morning's
Daily Mail?' he asked a sub-editor from behind his enormous
Napoleonic desk. 'Viscount Northcliffe is leaving tomorrow on a
world tour and will be away for several months,' said a brave if
cheeky sub-editor. A shocked silence descended on the room. The
sub held his breath. A stern-faced Northcliffe turned to Louise
Owen and, after a theatrical pause, said 'See that that man gets a
hundred pound bonus.'[4] The meeting dissolved into laughter, and
the sub breathed again.

On Saturday 16 July, Northcliffe left for New York on the first leg of his tour.* He took with him his friend John Prioleau, and secretary Harold Snoad, chauffeur Harry Pine and valet Frederick Foulger. Steed also crossed the Atlantic with them, en route to cover the Washington naval disarmament conference. Prioleau, a thirty-nine-year-old American Old Harrovian, had been the *Daily Mail*'s automobile correspondent before serving in naval intelligence during the war. They sailed on the 3,500-passenger Cunard liner *Aquitania*, which Northcliffe described as 'a country house at sea with just the right number of people', of which there were 600 in first class alone, whom Northcliffe listed as including 'ambassadors, theatrical managers, ladies described as film stars which is a new name for an ancient profession'.[5] Earl Inchcape, chairman of the Peninsular & Oriental (P&O) steamship line, ensured that Northcliffe cruised in the most luxurious cabins of the best liners available throughout the tour. Mary was, at least officially, too ill to go, although Northcliffe and Hudson stayed in contact.[6]

Before Northcliffe left, Louise Owen thought that 'He looked so tired and worn that I suggested he should go instead to a nursing home and take a thorough rest. "I have always wanted this trip," he said, "and the doctors tell me my mother is in splendid health, so I am taking this opportunity of leaving her for a few months."'[7] He arranged with his mother that they would read passages from Samuel Bagster's *Daily Light on the Daily Path: The Classic Devotional Book for Every Morning and Evening in the Very Words of Scripture* every day – she at 7am and he at 7pm – so that in the Antipodes they would be reading them at the same time. (He kept one watch always set to 'Totteridge time'.) Northcliffe's last words before he left were 'I shall pray every day for my mother.'[8] Prioleau recalled that during the world tour 'he would send her a cable every day, from wherever he might be, using the phrase "Lilac time" to mean that life was beautiful and gay. Sometimes he would receive a reply in kind, sometimes a reproof not to be disregarded.'[9]

---

* An eleven-second silent newsreel report on Northcliffe on board the ship and talking next to the beautiful tennis player Eleanora Sears can be seen in the Pathé online archives.

Northcliffe set himself the tasks of investigating the state of the British Empire in general and the Japanese threat to it and the United States in particular. His voyage took on some of the attributes of a royal tour: circumnavigating the globe, meeting distinguished people and attending grand receptions, and doing much sightseeing in that golden age of leisurely travel. Unlike most royal tours, however, Northcliffe's resulted in a book, *My Journey Around the World 1921–22*, which was published posthumously. *Punch* magazine joked that 'Lord Thanet's World Pilgrimage' aboard the liner *Megalomania* would include visiting the North and South Poles, climbing Mount Everest and descending to the centre of the earth.

Ministers were more concerned than satirical, with Neville Chamberlain worrying to his sister Hilda that Northcliffe 'is out to make every bit of mischief he can between this country, USA and the Dominions. It is really alarming to think what he can do when he goes on to Canada and Australia.'[10]

Two days into the crossing, Northcliffe was told of Lloyd George's statement in the Commons boycotting his newspapers. 'It is kind and characteristic of the PM to wait until I am in mid-Atlantic for one of his monthly attacks on *The Times* newspaper,' he sarcastically told the United Press correspondent in reply, claiming that it 'in no way affects our news services which are infinitely superior to those of the Foreign Office, whose communications to the Press as a rule show singular lack of accuracy'.[11]

Northcliffe landed in New York on 23 July, where he was surprised by the lack of chimney-pots, motorbikes and public clocks. He went to a suite at the Gotham Hotel to give a press conference where he applauded the United States' plans for the Washington Conference, with an implied rebuke to those of the British government. 'The papers here have been very kindly to me about the LG controversy,' Northcliffe told Sutton, 'which I thought best to drop in another country. If he comes here he will do so in an atmosphere of deep suspicion. His mental acrobatics are talked of by the best writers.'[12]

Since he had last been in the United States in 1917, the New York *Daily News* had been founded, an illustrated tabloid along the lines of the *Daily Mirror*. Northcliffe was invited to its offices and shown a copy by editors hoping for some words of encouragement. Wearing white gloves, he turned the pages of the paper as the black ink came off on them. 'You'll have to fix that,' was his sole comment to his somewhat crestfallen admirers.[13]

~

On 23 July, Northcliffe allowed Steed to give an interview to the *New York Times* in Northcliffe's name, which was published the next day. The interview caused great outrage, because Steed claimed that King George V had disagreed with Lloyd George over the Black and Tans and had told his prime minister: 'This thing cannot go on. I cannot have my people killed in this manner.'[14] Although Northcliffe and Steed described the published version of the story as 'this outrageous fabrication' – with Steed making the point that he could not have been present at a private audience between king and premier – Lloyd George took the opportunity of denying the King's remarks in the House of Commons as a 'complete fabrication'. He used the opportunity for another personal attack on Northcliffe, saying that he hoped Buckingham Palace's denial would 'sterilise the effects of the criminal malignity which, for personal ends, is endeavouring to stir up mischief between the Allies, and misunderstanding between the British Empire and the United States, and to frustrate the hopes of peace in Ireland'.[15] This was a slander of Northcliffe, for whom Anglo–American amity and peace in Ireland were lifelong goals, but he could hardly have expected anything less.

Although the story eventually died, decades later it turned out that Steed had indeed made off-the-record statements about the King's solicitude for his Irish subjects, with phrases that chimed with other statements the King had been making to ministers at the time. It turned out to have been Lord Stamfordham, George V's private secretary, who had told Steed what had been said at the private audience, so ultimately the source for the third-hand information to the *New York Times* journalist had been the monarch himself. Frances Stevenson noted in her diary that at the time, Lloyd George was 'simply furious' with Stamfordham for the leak. Yet, despite

knowing that the story was essentially true, in July 1921 Lloyd
George told C. P. Scott that he would like to sue Northcliffe over it. 'I
have been wanting to get at him for some time,' he said.[16] The Prime
Minister even consulted the solicitors Lewis & Lewis about the possibility of an action for criminal libel. 'This will do Northcliffe a lot
of damage both here and in America,' hoped Stevenson.[17]

Mary Northcliffe, who was friendly with Queen Mary, telegraphed her husband to say that she was 'greatly distressed and ill
with worry. Situation here intolerable. Quite understand you personally not responsible but you are regarded as responsible for your
staff. Fear personal position not much improved by denial. Do now
refrain from politics and take [a] complete holiday.'[18] 'I daresay you
saw a ridiculous fuss in the papers about something I was supposed
to say about the King,' Northcliffe told his mother. 'I am afraid I did
not fuss at all but went on with my golf and novel-reading as usual.'[19]
To brother Harold – who, along with John Walter (who was still *The
Times* chairman), Sutton, Hudson and others thought that Steed
should be reprimanded or even fired for his remarks – Northcliffe
added: 'Am not worrying and my golf excellent.'[20]

Sir Auckland Geddes, by now the British ambassador to
Washington, withdrew an invitation to the British embassy on 31
July on Curzon's orders, but Northcliffe had an eighty-minute interview at the White House with Warren G. Harding. The President
was a former newspaperman who had edited the *Marion Star* for
many years, whom Northcliffe told Stuart he 'liked immensely'. He
refused to tell journalists what was discussed; 'I have been in the
game too long myself.'[21] 'I do hope if you see that I have attacked the
Queen or the Prince of Wales, that you won't believe it,' he joked to
Hudson on 5 August about the Steed controversy. 'I have been in the
newspaper game since a child and do not ever remember being con-
victed of a foolish statement. I am, unfortunately, a far better known
individual than I knew, and it does not amuse me in the least.'[22]

From Washington, Northcliffe's party went by train to Toronto,
Winnipeg and Vancouver, the last of which he thought 'very fine'
and where he spoke to the Canadian Club about the need for the
unity of the English-speaking peoples, telling them that Germany

was 'unrepentant, vengeful and watchful'. Leaving Steed in British Columbia, Northcliffe boarded the SS *Makura* bound for Hawaii. Keith Murdoch came on board at Vancouver, and Northcliffe described him as a 'great travelling companion and a veritable dynamo of energy'.[23] They played golf together in Honolulu, saw flying fish being shot from boats, and watched a new sport called 'surf-riding' which was done on special boards. At the British Club there, the members of the Overseas Club all wore their badges as a mark of respect to Northcliffe. On the way to Fiji, the heat was so bad that he had to change his clothes four times a day. At night, he told his mother, 'I sleep in the costume you gave me on 15 July 1865.'[24] He declared himself 'quite frivolous', but could not approve of the daring backless gowns the young women were wearing in the evenings.

On 11 August, Northcliffe wrote a circular letter about his experiences to his secretary H. G. Price that was to be distributed to closest friends and family. 'Please send a copy to Mrs Wrohan,' he ordered, but 'on no account to a very talkative lady who would make some queer use of them, exactly what use I do not know'.[25] He was referring to Louise Owen. When Kathleen Wrohan replied to Price from the Corner House, a cottage in the grounds of Elmwood where she was living with a parrot, canaries, pigeons, dogs and her three adopted children, her signature had collapsed into illegibility, possibly as a result of heavy drinking.[26] She said that the enclosures were 'very interesting, but they were not intended for me, so in case someone who expects them should be disappointed, I am returning them'.[27] Price assured her that 'I sent it to you at the Chief's suggestion.'

'It is a triumph of Nemesis that I should be pursued round the world by a Monster partly of my own creating – the Press,' Northcliffe wrote in his circular letter.

It is quite out of bounds in North America ... If one goes quietly about one's affairs, one is called haughty, as I have been. So-called American geniality is mere curiosity. It is the curiosity of the village at the coming of the circus. The lack of privacy in

America was intolerable. The clicking of the camera was never out of our ears.[28]

He only recognised quite how much of a global celebrity he was when he embarked on this tour.

At 6am on 16 August, *Makura* crossed the Equator in eighty-five-degree Fahrenheit heat, reaching Suva in the Fiji Islands on the 22nd. They arrived in Auckland in New Zealand on 26 August, where they stayed a week and where Sir Francis Bell, the acting prime minister, spoke at a luncheon thrown by newspaper owners and the veterans of the Western Front. They cheered Northcliffe when it was recalled what he had done to draw public attention to the shells scandal. Northcliffe found New Zealand 'inconceivably interesting. I call it topsy-turveydom – parlour-maids in summertime earn seven pounds a week; tops of mountains are blown away sixty miles, your money in your pocket turns black with the sulphur in the air; there are wingless birds, forty-pound trout and caterpillars with trees growing out of their heads; and there are ferns as tall as Printing House Square.'[29]

On 2 September, Northcliffe's party left Auckland for Sydney across flat seas in hot weather aboard the steamer *Maheno*, arriving five days later. The part he had played in revealing the conditions in the Gallipoli campaign ensured him a hero's welcome in Australia, where he was impressed by everything he saw, noting 'butchers-shops are as plentiful as lamp-posts', 'two-foot carrots', 'one man in twenty is a giant' and 'watercress develops so rapidly that it blocks rivers'.[30] He travelled to Melbourne and Tasmania to repeat the two key messages of his tour: that Britons should emigrate to the empire, where prices were low and well-paid jobs were plentiful, and that Japan would one day threaten the English-speaking peoples in the Pacific, who should therefore not disarm their navies at the Washington Conference. 'You must increase your slender garrison by the multiplication of your people,' he warned Australians. 'Only numbers will save you.'[31] He did level some criticisms of Australia in his book, saying that 'They think they are invincible, they believe Australia alone won the war, and measure the rest of the world by its inferiority at cricket.'[32]

On 1 October, the 4,000-ton steam yacht SS *St Albans* left Sydney for Yokohama, having picked up Mary's brother Henry Milner, who Northcliffe told Sutton was 'my earliest boyhood friend' but who had fallen on hard times in Brisbane.[33] 'There is no doubt that my presence stirred his creditors, but they have been very patient. He is a most worthy man.'[34] Northcliffe bailed Henry out and brought him back to London. 'I have not been bored or homesick one day,' he added. 'I have not yet dreamt anything about the journeys, but almost every night I dream of Elmwood or my little bungalow. I have never dreamt about the business.'[35] Another dream was of being in 'a theatre in Birmingham trying to reach the front row of the stalls by walking along a narrow plank in the dress circle'.[36]

Despite that classic anxiety dream, on 16 October, having passed Thursday Island, Northcliffe wrote to Price: 'As you know, I am not doing any work in connection with the newspapers; I don't think of them or ever read them.'[37] This was clearly untrue, as in the same letter he wrote,

> Look at the map and realise that the Fiji Islands are covered [by *The Times* and *Daily Mail*] from Sydney! Sydney has as much connection with the Fiji Islands as London has with Bulgaria ... Bullock, of New York, covers Manila ... Let it be instantly understood, from now onwards, that *The Times* and *Daily Mail* correspondents, in the more remote parts of the world, should be one and the same man. Gott in Himmel! Think of Bullock being responsible for Manila![38]

Back in London, Stuart complained that he was left to run *The Times* 'subject to innumerable telegrams at all times of day and night as to what the absent proprietor wanted done. Some had to be acted upon, some had to be disregarded, some ought never to have been received.'[39] As with *The Times* takeover in 1908, everyone was given codenames for the telegraphic traffic to ensure privacy: Stuart was Crownstar, Steed was Hamwick, Sutton was Ontax, Price was Hengilpri, Mary was Carlton, Steed was Attaché and Northcliffe was Southdown.[40]

~

On 21 October, the *St Albans* arrived at Manila where Northcliffe emphasised to the local Rotary Club the need for Anglo-American co-operation in the face of what he called 'events which, possibly, we do not like to name', but which undoubtedly alluded to a Japanese attack on the more vulnerable British and American interests in the Far East.[41] He had one worry on crossing the International Dateline: 'I wire to mother every day. How shall I manage about Friday when there is no Friday?'[42]

Hong Kong, where he arrived on 27 October, Northcliffe saw as 'that young and lovely daughter of British enterprise'.[43] Arriving at Canton, hundreds of small boats came out to greet him. On 2 November, he saw the snow-capped and cloudless Mount Fujiyama, which he considered the world's most beautiful mountain.[44] He arrived in Tokyo by electric train three days later and stayed at the Imperial Court Hotel. Despite his public opposition to the renewal of the Anglo–Japanese Treaty of 1902, he was welcomed by the Japanese and was hospitable to their journalists, laying on geisha dancing at the Maple Club. He visited the Meiji Shrine, met the mayor of Tokyo, observed the Tea Ceremony, and compared the food at the Imperial Court Hotel to that of the Paris Ritz.

On the train to Kyoto, Northcliffe spotted a young Japanese man reading Harold Begbie's newly published book *The Mirrors of Downing Street*, which had snobbishly depicted him as 'the Spring-Heeled Jack of Journalism' and declared that he did not have 'a trained mind' that could 'support the burden of trying to think'. It also predicted that, at the Seat of Judgement, he would be forced to answer for the low 'moral and intellectual condition of the world'.[45] Northcliffe warned the reader that it was a 'very wicked book', thereby presumably increasing his interest in it.

It was the beauty of Kyoto and Osaka that led Northcliffe to realise why so many Britons loved Japan, but he still criticised the 'Japanese craze that affects so many English visitors who do not realise the other Japan – the Japan whose brutality is notorious, the Japan who is obviously trying to rule China in order that she may rule the world'.[46] This was ten years before Japan's invasion of China, and twenty years before she took control of one-eighth of the globe after attacking Pearl Harbor. Northcliffe only ever witnessed Japanese politeness and exquisite manners himself, but that did not affect his view of the atrocities committed both in the Sino–Japanese War of 1895 (which won it Taiwan) and in its Korean 'protectorate' after the Russo–Japanese War of 1904–05. Northcliffe deserves credit for his prescience over the threat Japan would pose to the American and British empires in the Pacific by 1941.

Northcliffe was sorry to leave Japan, having found its people to be 'poetic, fond of tradition, polite, brave', but nonetheless future enemies. He was in Beijing when the Washington Naval Conference opened, but he stayed in contact with Steed, urging him to push the anti-Japanese line. 'They are out to pull the leg of the Conference, and I rely upon you to stop them. They are as like Prussians as they can be – inquisitive, flattering, yea, verily, even goose-stepping. Go in and win.'[47]

Despite being on the other side of the world in Java, Northcliffe was capable, on 6 November, of ordering Thomas Marlowe to 'Give support [to] Birkenhead and Churchill' over the Irish situation, in which he hoped for an early peaceful settlement.[48] A problem arose when he received a telegram complaining that 'All your papers are supporting coercion of Ulster. Do you approve? Very anxious and concerned, Reply. Mother.' Coming from the eighty-three-year-old matriarch, the word 'reply' was an imperative not an interrogative, and John Prioleau later recalled that he had never seen Northcliffe more troubled than when he received this. It took him an hour to find a form of words to placate her. 'Very disturbed by your Ulster message, most darling one,' he replied. 'I hate to think that while I am whirling around the world you should be for a moment unhappy about a matter I am too far off to help.'[49] On 4 December, he telegraphed her to say, 'Dearest, believe papers [are] following only possible [policy for the] avoidance [of] civil war ... Devotion.'[50] It hardly appeased her, as shortly afterwards she telegraphed: 'Alfred – I cannot make up my mind which of your two principal papers is the more vulgar this morning.'[51] Sometimes, very powerful people have one person in their lives before whom they are rendered powerless, even craven. Northcliffe's mother Geraldine had the power to turn the Napoleon of Fleet Street into jelly.

'I don't think I have ever been so well in my life,' Northcliffe told Sutton from Peking (modern-day Beijing) on 12 November. 'I was flabby before I left home and sometimes a little worried about myself, though I did not tell anyone so. Here I feel full of the strength (and the stupidity) of a bull. Lord! what a lot I did not know! How big the great world is. How old fashioned our little island is becoming.'[52] He found the Grand Hotel de Pekin 'twice as big as the Ritz in London, and twice as good, but too much jazz', while Peking was 'the world's most wonderful city'.[53] He bought Ming-period porcelain and jade on Mary's instructions, and took back six bricks from the Great Wall for Sir Robert Hudson. On his way to Shanghai on 21 November, he saw Japanese troops in Shantung, and noted in his diary that 'They have as much right to be in Shantung as they have to be at Birmingham.'[54]

The next stage of the journey comprised visits to Singapore, Batavia (modern-day Jakarta) in the Dutch East Indies (where at a press dinner in his honour he sat beneath a portrait of the Kaiser), Indo-China (modern-day Vietnam and Cambodia) and Siam (modern-day Thailand). When his schedule clashed with those of the KPM Steamship Company, it changed its sailing dates for him. 'The accommodation for my party is better than on most yachts,' he noted.[55] He showed interest in everything: comparing Dutch imperialism to British (naturally unfavourably); the coffee, cocaine and vanilla of Batavia; flora and fauna; trade; how pro-German different places were; wireless telegraphy; propaganda ('Japan is easily the master-twister'), and diesel-engined ships. He visited malaria hospitals, tin mines and an opium factory in Thailand ('All the machinery came from Birmingham'); he watched the milking of a rubber tree at a plantation in Saigon, along with jujitsu and Thai boxing, and birds, especially storks and cranes. He visited an aerodrome at Don Muang with Prince Purachatra of Siam.[56] He crossed the Equator four times.

On 7 December, Keith Murdoch telegraphed from Australia,

where he was proprietor-editor of the *Melbourne Herald*, to say that he had an 'excellent chance' of taking a controlling stake in Sydney's *Evening News*. 'Feeling this is my big chance', said Murdoch, asking him to 'join financially with a few thousands'. Northcliffe replied immediately: 'Gladlyest invest five thousand* as encouragement to others and proof [of] my complete confidence in you. Fact you have one man control [is] essential [in the] newspaper business.'[57] By the end of the month, Murdoch was writing to 'My very dear Chief' saying that he had secured the *Evening News,* which 'opens up great chances'.[58] They were not passed up, and in later life Murdoch did not take exception to being nicknamed 'Lord Southcliffe'.[59]

'They appear to me to be the idlest people I have had to do with,' Northcliffe wrote of the Javanese on 9 December, 'the slowest, the stupidest, and untruthful to boot ... Only a patient people like the Dutch could stand it.'[60] He was much given to racial generalisations: after complaining about how fast his Javanese chauffeur drove, he complained that 'There are people who talk about giving these idiots self-government.'[61] The Berber people, however, were 'the best native [car] mechanics in Africa'.[62] 'Here we are again in hustling, noisy, rickshawing, cocktail and stinger-drinking Singapore,' he reported; at a meeting with the editor of the *Straits Times* at the Europe Hotel, 'We had to shout at each other to get above the noise of the motor-horns, the tramways, the Chinese clogs, the strange queer native shouting, the horrible expectoral noises, and always the hotel jazz band.'[63]

Northcliffe noted how the servants at Government House in Singapore still wore the livery of the East India Company, which had been established in the reign of Elizabeth I, and wrote about 'the little lizards which run about the ceiling all night calling "Chi Char" to each other whilst hunting flies and mosquitoes'.[64] 'Frederick, how can I smoke within the beastly mosquito curtain without setting fire to the hotel?' he asked his valet, along with 'Frederick, turn on the electric punkah' and 'Frederick, what about the ice water in the big thermos flask?'[65] Northcliffe also played practical jokes on Harry

---

* Equivalent to over a quarter of a million pounds today.

Pine, such as putting hairbrushes down his bed, which must have been tiresome.[66]

Sailing from Singapore to Indo-China, Northcliffe shared a steamer, the *Admiral Latouche Treville*, with 600 soldiers of the French Foreign Legion ('every kind of exile strayed from society'), six of whom absconded overboard and two others jumped naked into the shark-infested sea for a wager. 'I love our French friends,' he concluded, 'but the Almighty did not intend them to run ships.'[67] He was shocked by the Frenchwomen on board 'displaying a wealth of stocking not exceeded by the American ladies in their deck chairs – which I may say is "going some"'.[68] Although he was constantly conscious of the noises on board – chefs shouting, soldiers bugling, officers' dogs barking – he was able to sleep well. 'Human beings spend twenty-six years of their life asleep, without much trouble,' he noted. 'A maker of long voyages could do much more than that.'[69]

After visiting Saigon and Phnom Penh, where he was impressed by how tall King Sisowath Chamchakrapong of Cambodia's elephant-houses were, Northcliffe spent two days at Angkor Wat with Marshal Joffre.* 'Extraordinaryest reception because [of] my consistently Francophile attitude newspapers during war,' he telegraphed Price.[70] At Angkor Wat, he admired the 'extremely good-looking' nineteen-year-old new wife of the eighty-one-year-old king.[71] She was one of 200 wives and was covered in jewels from head to foot. He attended a ceremony there in the boiling heat with 'princes, princesses, mandarins, the King himself, all gorgeously arrayed in wonderful silks, and carried in tall palanquins dazzling in the sunshine ... the whole ending up with fifty magnificently caparisoned elephants.'[72]

On 21 December, Northcliffe ate a nine-course dinner with the King of Siam at the Ambara palace in Bangkok. 'I am quite aware that the Siamese want their case set forth in my newspapers,' he noted. 'But they do the thing courteously.'[73] He refused a Siamese decoration from the king – 'I haven't any Orders and I don't want

---

* A fifty-three-second silent Pathé newsreel of the visit can be seen at: https://www.britishpathe.com/video/a-great-journalist-1/query/Alfred

any' – but he did take a Christmas cracker from the table to give to Harry Pine.[74]

Soon after the dinner, while still in the royal palace, Northcliffe behaved disgracefully, displaying what was probably the first symptom of the horrific disease that was to kill him. As we have seen, he could be irritable on occasion, but there was almost always a specific reason for it and he was not physically violent. Yet after the dinner, when his secretary Harold Snoad failed to find a newspaper that Northcliffe needed, he shoved him violently out of his room and pushed him down some stairs, where he was fortunately picked up by four impassive purple-clad royal attendants.[75] 'My birthday', noted Snoad in his diary, 'the worst day of the tour so far. The Chief has been most offensive to me in the very worst degree.'[76]

Northcliffe tried to make it up to Snoad later, but without specifically mentioning the incident. From that moment onwards, his behaviour was to become ever more unpredictable, then genuinely megalomaniacal, then violent, and ultimately psychotic. It was all the result of the illness that he had contracted on the tour but of which everyone was at that point unaware. With mental illness now finally de-stigmatised, Northcliffe should no longer be held morally responsible for statements and actions made when he was in the grip of this terrible disease, as he has been by so many contemporaries and historians over the past century.

~

'My mother's birthday,' Northcliffe noted on Christmas Eve, 'which I carefully observed all that day.'[77] He took the private carriage of a train from Bangkok to Kuala Lumpur, capital of the Federated Malay States. 'Personally I have always liked the private car life,' he wrote, 'especially when the valet is in the next door room and you can get at him in the morning.'[78] There were drawbacks, however. 'Travelling in this fashion, one gets all the annoying experiences of Royalty. You have to be up at all hours to receive people, to grin and bow, make inane talk before cinematograph operators, and enjoy mighty little privacy.'[79]

At Penang, Northcliffe and Prioleau were carried 2,000 feet up to

Government House on sedan chairs by 'lusty fellows', which took over an hour. 'I don't like to see human beings carrying other human beings,' Northcliffe wrote to his family. 'But these cheery fellows shouted and laughed as we went up.'[80] They then took a four-day cruise to Ceylon (modern-day Sri Lanka), where at the Fort Station he noted that 'It seems ridiculous to imagine that any people who direct the simple operations of a railways station in such a chaotic fashion should ever be capable of directing the destinies of the land of their birth.' Of the Sinhalese he wrote, 'Like everybody else in the world they have a grievance, and, like all Orientals, they are quite ungrateful.'[81]

On 9 January 1922, Northcliffe saw India for the first time in a quarter-century. 'It is not a country I like,' he told his family.[82] 'That I have had nothing stolen from me is due to the fact that I never carry any money, preferring to live on my friends and companions.'[83] It was something else he had in common with royalty. At Madras he told his diary how

> Now and then a smooth-spoken native opens up conversation with me and I tell him that I don't know why we should keep the Mohammedans and Hindus from cutting each other's throats if they want to, and the various tribes from fighting each other ... I always tell them that they don't contribute a farthing to the British Navy, which keeps the Jap[ane]s[e] from biting them.[84]

He found India 'a wearisome country. Compare lovely Japan or charming little New Zealand. What do we want India for? Prestige? Perhaps. Cash? We certainly don't get any from it.'[85] He was certainly becoming disillusioned with Britain's mission in India.

'India is immense,' Northcliffe told his family, 'and among all these hundreds of millions of blacks there are only 180,000 whites, including our troops. How is the miracle done?'[86] There were roughly 250 million inhabitants of British India and a further 70 million in the princely states at the time. In part, he answered his own question five days later when writing about how the young Maharajah Ulwah was 'preposterously rich' and 'makes remarkable speeches in Etonian English, writes fair poetry, tames tigers for the shooting of his British guests, goes nowhere without white kid or silk gloves lest he be contaminated, and will enter no place where there is a dog. He is one of our props in India.'[87]

In mid-January 1922, Northcliffe stayed with Lord Reading at Viceregal Lodge in Delhi, where there were 800 servants. 'It is always on my mind that amidst the quiet British luxury of this house is the Spectre of Indian Agitation,' he wrote. As he went into dinner with red-coated servants salaaming, men wearing orders and no fewer than four monocles among the aides-de-camp, all Northcliffe could think of was Indian political unrest.[88] Back in Batavia, he had noted how 'the Dutch can't understand why we don't arrest [Mohandas] Gandhi. They say that the effect of our tolerance of his vagaries is to make the Orientals think we are afraid of him and them, which I suppose is true.'[89] Although Northcliffe visited several major tourist sites, such as the Pearl Mosque, Red Fort and Kashmir Gate, he noted that 'All are anxious here, very, very anxious – almost as anxious as in 1857,' the year the Indian Mutiny broke out.[90]

Northcliffe promised Reading that The Times would support him in his coming efforts to crack down on Indian nationalism, and sent out the reporter Arthur Moore to help with his publicity. With the future King Edward VIII about to come out to stay with the viceroy, Northcliffe made an extremely prescient comment: 'I am a bit worried about the Prince of Wales. I don't like the company he is keeping, especially the female company.'[91] For his part, the Prince of Wales joked that 'Lord Northcliffe has no daughter, but if he had he would make me marry her I am sure.'[92]

Sir Edwin Lutyens, the architect of the vast New Delhi site, took Northcliffe around it as it was being built and pointed out that the London Ritz could fit inside one of the arches.[93] Northcliffe thought it 'a wonderful prewar conception', but one which neither Britain nor India could now afford. 'The British pessimists say we shan't hold India long enough to see a Viceroy live in it,' he wrote, although 'I believe that it will be finished.'[94] Leaving Delhi for Agra and Muttra, he noted how tiny grey squirrels ran about in their thousands, which ought to have been a warning to him, having helped establish them at Sutton Place.[95] He also saw peacocks, parrots, flamingoes, the myna bird, Great Indian kites, ring-tailed doves and kingfishers. He thought the Taj Mahal 'the lovely white tomb of which the name of the architect is absolutely forgotten ... Photographs do no more than indicate what it is like.'[96]

On arriving in Bombay (modern-day Mumbai), he stayed at Government House but found that he had not been assigned a private railway car. 'I think it does people good to come down a peg,' he wrote in a sentence that rather belies accusations of megalomania.[97] He spent his time there 'interviewing natives, mostly distinguished ones, many extremists, and some moderates', as well as observing snake poison extracted for serum by the Pasteur Institute in Bombay, and watching the method by which plague-conveying rats' fleas were caught by the use of trained guinea-pigs.[98]

'I don't suppose that I shall ever see the Orient again,' Northcliffe wrote on board the luxurious P&O vessel SS *Naldera* as he left India, 'as I am anxious to visit South America, South and Central Africa, and the East of Africa too ... I shall have to do these strenuous parts of the world before I get too ancient.'[99] His lifelong, hitherto unquestioning faith in imperialism had been shaken by his journey, and he told his family that the prime minister of the Philippines had told him that 'It is better to have our own disorderly government rather than be interfered with by the Americans.'[100] Nor could he understand why Britons were fighting and dying for India on the North-West Frontier in the thankless task of preserving British India. 'The frontier is alive with tribes armed with modern weapons,' he wrote. 'Why shouldn't the talking Babus or Madrassees and others protect *themselves* against the wild people in the North?'[101]

For all that, Northcliffe told Sutton that 'John Bull is very much the top dog in the vast world of the Far East. How such a tiny island as ours does it, I do not know, but it does.'[102] But for how much longer? 'It has been my lot to stay lately in four houses in which my host has been labouring under intense anxiety,' he wrote later of the governors' mansions of Ceylon, Delhi, Bombay and Cairo. 'This British Empire business is no easy job.'[103]

'I am carefully keeping away from looking at my own papers,'

Northcliffe told Murdoch on 24 January as he sailed towards Aden. 'I have seen a few *Times* and six *Daily Mails* – extremely bad they look, especially the *Daily Mail*. It seems to have got muddled up, or I am perhaps seeing it with a fresh eye .... The heading on the front page is cramped up ... and the advertisements are too close to it. Perhaps the heading is too small.'[104] It was the letter of a controlling, obsessive professional speaking to another proprietor-editor, but not that of someone who was deranged.

Landing at Cairo on 30 January found Northcliffe in a contemplative mood as he read the devotional book by Bagster that his mother had given him, writing that 'Today it says inter alia, "It is good for a man that he bear the yoke of his youth". I do often ask that my early "success" may not have spoiled me, but I did bear some yoke, a good deal more, in fact, than I like to talk about.'[105] Staying with Lord Allenby, the high commissioner of Egypt, whom he admiringly described as 'large-headed', Northcliffe was amused to have been given the bedroom that Lord Kitchener had occupied as commander-in-chief of the Egyptian Army. 'I am writing this early in the morning on the last day of January in the bed of that Mammoth Myth,' he noted in his diary.[106] Around this time, he dictated notes of his trip to Snoad for six hours non-stop, but then did not read the typed result.

On 3 February, Northcliffe visited the Pyramids, 'which I have often seen before, and was very, very disappointed ... not so wonderful as they seemed to be when I saw them as a young man'.[107] Two days later, he joked to one of his secretaries that he had been warned that it was going to be very cold at his next stop in Palestine and that 'We must wear sheepskins – not the first time my affectionate critics will say this wolf has gone forth so clad.'[108]

Staying in Government House on the Mount of Olives in Jerusalem, Northcliffe visited the tourist sites of the Western Wall ('the Jews' wailing place' as he put it), the Church of the Holy Sepulchre, the Pool of Bethesda, the Mosque of Omar, and met the Emir Abdullah of Transjordan. 'I don't suppose anyone except a stone image can enter the country of Christ without deep emotion,' he wrote in his diary. 'I for one of millions cannot.'[109] He had been given an armed escort, which 'set a match to his explosive nature' because he said that 'the trouble must have arisen from the new [that is, Jewish] settlers'.[110]

He asked Norman Bentwich of the Palestine government to be taken to a Jewish settlement at Rishon-el-Zion, where 'the elders of the village came out to greet their guest and made a grateful speech', whereupon after being given lunch by them, as Bentwich later recalled, Northcliffe

> put his elbows on the table, and told them that the Jewish immi-
> grants were aggressive and bad-mannered ... England had sixty
> million Muslims and five hundred thousand Jews in her Empire.
> She would not endanger her Empire for them. They must go slow,
> work for good relations with their Arab neighbours, and teach
> the immigrants to be modest ... On the way back, as though
> conscious that he had been wilful, he spoke of his admiration for
> a number of Jews.[111]

'People daren't tell the Jews the truth here,' Northcliffe noted in his diary. 'They've had some from me.'[112]

The Times later reported that Northcliffe warned the Jewish settlers that the British were losing patience with Zionism and espe-cially 'the recent importation of undesirable Jews, Bolshevists and others' which 'was the partial cause of the regrettable troubles with the Arabs'.[113] In private, he described the mayor of one hamlet as 'a long established Russian Jew of the thin-nosed type', and wrote of 'Fords packed with queer-looking Jews, the males, old and young, with hanging side-locks.'[114] He told an Arab deputation at Gaza that he opposed the Balfour Declaration, adding in his book *My Journey Round the World* that 'Arabs and Christians have now joined up against the Jews. There is hatred and there has been bloodshed.'[115] He considered himself even-handed when he wrote that 'both sides are oriental liars ... All lie profusely, the Moslems outrageously, the Zionists artistically. The Orthodox Jews seem bit-terest of all.'[116] Of Jerusalem he wrote that 'In many ways the town must be a town of cosmopolitan parasites; doctors, nurses and the rest, including Jewish remittance men from many lands.'[117] 'The methods of Zionism arouse antagonism,' he told his family, asking 'Can Jews rule?'[118]

'I'm mighty keen to be back in that very small circle in which I live,' Northcliffe wrote from the train from Haifa to Port Said on 12 February, 'and mighty keen to help with my newspapers, but equally keen on setting out again and learning more of the world.'[119] He boarded the *Egypt* the next day, finding the sea 'like a Hampstead pond' as he passed Corsica.

'Every ship has its odd characters,' he wrote in his diary about himself. 'Former fat man, now in skeleton class, who beginning life as a reporter at sixteen, is now said to have more papers than he can count and more money than brains. Is finishing flash round world and ready for another tomorrow. Hasn't seen one rough or windy day.'[120] As he arrived at a foggy Marseilles on Saturday 18 February 1922, after seven months of travelling, he could not know that his roughest days lay ahead, and soon.

CHAPTER 22

DEGENERATION

February–May 1922

'"Harley Street Crisis" and "Deadly Cocaine" are good
topics but I should not put them side by side. Contrast is
the salt of journalism.'[1]

LORD NORTHCLIFFE's communiqué to his staff,
15 April 1922

'My world-whizz was finished,' Northcliffe wrote in his diary on 18
February 1922 after addressing, in French, the Marseilles Chamber
of Commerce.[2] 'I have further resolved that I was not built for any
kind of public life, that I hate crowds, demonstration, ceremonial,
and curiously enough, although I am one myself, reporters.'[3] He went
to stay at the Eden Hotel at Cap d'Ail, where Mary came out to join
him. Although he cabled his brother Harold to say 'energy doubled,'
others disagreed with this self-diagnosis.[4] Harry Pine's impression
was that during the world tour 'He got more irritable, and at times
looked very tired and rather ill.'[5] 'The robust figure, the upright
bearing, the buoyant manner were gone,' recalled his biographer
Max Pemberton. 'I saw a stooping, wizened, shrunken old man and
the first glance at him told me he was doomed.'[6]

Campbell Stuart later wrote that 'The tour, as I had prophesied,
was the worst possible remedy for a man of his disposition ... and
as soon as I saw him on his return I felt his days were numbered ...
Northcliffe became impossible, and I had to bear the brunt of endless

contradictory instructions complicated further by quarrels with his editor.'[7] In reality, instead of the world tour re-energising him as his doctors had hoped, he had contracted a rare and terminal illness somewhere on his trip called acute malignant infective endocarditis, which of course no-one knew at the time. It was a condition in which the tissues lining the inside of the heart and the heart valves become inflamed, sending sufferers mad. Furthermore, if Stuart, Pemberton and so many others really had thought Northcliffe's days were numbered, they did nothing to alert him, or Mary, or their colleagues, let alone his doctors, as the illness took irreversible hold.

As soon as he landed, Northcliffe began sending telegrams to the staff in London. 'Please ask members of conference what the word ectoplasm means in leading article,' he told Tom Clarke. 'Nobody in this hotel understands it. I have complained of this priggish nonsense before.'[8] To Marlowe: 'Did not like the article about the horrible and boresome French film *Atlantide*.'[9] To Frank Fitzhugh, editor of *Evening News*: 'Don't like vulgar tone of paper ... Try and get public school or university sub-editor. Follow dignity of *Evening Standard*.'[10]

'In view of the appalling gross figures just received am returning immediately,' Northcliffe told his senior management on 20 February. 'Figures are worse than I predicted two years ago. All those explanations and statistics with which it was attempted to dope me make very pathetic reading today.'[11] The paranoia evident in that sentence was a portent of much more to come as the illness from which he was suffering took a grip on him that it never loosened – but which those around him took months to recognise as a medical condition rather than the mere bullying ill-temper they had long known. Because he had always been vociferous in his comments, no-one noticed when, in due course, this tipped into mental instability, by which time it was too late to save him.

To mask the true situation further, the actual ideas that he wanted to discuss – to combine the foreign news services of the *Daily Mail* and *Times*, start a campaign to encourage imperial emigration, merge the Overseas Club's 26,000 members with the Colonial Institute's 16,000, and so on – tended often to be good and reasonable, and he added that he thought the papers had 'improved [over the] last few months barring monotony [of the] leading articles'.[12] Yet there were definite signs of his coming derangement, as when he physically threw a union official of the *Continental Daily Mail* from his hotel room during wage negotiations, calling him 'a damned ungrateful swine' and aiming a parting kick at him.[13]

There was also a good deal of paranoia in Northcliffe's telegram to Sutton from Monte Carlo:

> Returning with abundant proof that Hamwick [Steed] constantly censors messages from foreign correspondents and other matters. Let him know plainly that in future no such censorship will be permitted. His pro-Japanese censorship will require immense amount of explanation. It involved me in great personal difficulty in Far East. Am not cross with him but he must stop this sort of thing or [I] shall give Stuart instructions to overrule him failing which to call me up at night which will be the end of everything ... Read this telegram to him. Very wet here.'[14]

Back in May 1920, when the Allied Supreme Council Conference at Spa decided to give effect to the Balfour Declaration, the Zionist leader Chaim Weizmann stated publicly that 'I do not pay a mere compliment when I say that the Zionists the world over will never cease to be grateful for what the *Daily Mail* and *The Times* have done for them'.[15] It was a fine encomium. On 23 February 1922, however, the *Daily Mail* ran a leading article entitled 'What is Happening in Palestine?' that advocated an end to the immigration of 'unsuitable' Jews there. When Weizmann complained about that and other articles in the Northcliffe press, he was invited to Carlton Gardens to debate the issue against Leo Maxse, a lifelong anti-Semite who denounced radicals for disseminating 'Hebrew influences' through Parliament and the press, and who had denounced 'the International Jew, who is cosmopolitan and usually an enemy of England and a more or less avowed agent of Germany'.[16]

On Weizmann's arrival, Northcliffe was telling Maxse that

Zionism was 'a danger to the British Empire' because there were a hundred times more Muslims in it than Jews. 'He placed me on his right and Maxse on his left,' Weizmann later recalled,

> and said 'Now, Maxse represents England; you are a Jew; I am the umpire!' From this we inferred that we were to be asked to make our respective cases – but not at all. Lord Northcliffe proceeded forthwith to tell us all about it. This conception of the functions of an umpire was new to me, and suggested that I was probably wasting my time, so I shortly made my excuses and withdrew.[17]

Once Weizmann had left and Price asked Northcliffe whether he wanted the notes of what he had said typed up into a memorandum, Northcliffe replied, 'Good Lord, no! Forget it.'[18] Thereafter, Weizmann noted that 'Although *The Times* remained dignified – if mistrustful – on the subject of Palestine, the other Northcliffe papers ... launched into a virulent campaign against us.'[19]

The onset of megalomania was part of Northcliffe's medical condition, but it was not uniform and there were plenty of moments of lucidity, self-awareness and even modesty. When W. J. U. Evans, the managing editor of the *Evening News*, complained to him about a rude appraisal of the paper that had been put on the noticeboard at Carmelite House (and ripped down), Northcliffe replied that he liked 'frank criticism' and was not too 'swell-headed' not to know that he was surrounded by 'flatterers and sycophants'.[20] Northcliffe's practice of publicising his criticisms of each day's paper was unpopular among senior management, one of whom wrote of his resentment that 'the office boys could enjoy the criticisms of the various members of the staff'.[21]

On 2 March, a large meeting was held in *The Times* boardroom at which Price read out a communiqué to the staff from Northcliffe stating that 'readers have been deserting the paper for years and recent editorial gaffes are, I am sure, losing us more. The unpopular policies I do not mind. The blunders I do ... I am not going to be quite as gentle in the future as in the past.'[22] He added that the price of the paper would have to be drastically reduced. Steed was outraged at the implied criticism and spoke to Stuart about resigning. His lawyer, Sir Charles Russell, advised him not to, as he had noticed Northcliffe's 'abnormal' condition and strongly suspected he was dying.[23] Yet there were also periods of normality, even levity. 'The Times is getting on,' Northcliffe wrote in early March. 'It is advancing by leaps and bounds. "Twenty-Two Bishops Murdered" is equal to any attempt at a headline made by our American friends.'[24]

On 9 March, with his throat and eyes 'much inflamed', Northcliffe went to Pau in the foothills of the Pyrenees to recuperate. He put his illness down to the climate in Britain, in particular 'the sudden change after so many weeks in the tropics'.[25] Staying at the Hôtel de Gassion, he told Sir Roderick Jones that he was reading the best-selling novel If Winter Comes by A. S. M. Hutchinson, because, typically for him, 'I want to discover what it is that attracts hundreds of thousands of readers – what it is the crowd likes. I confess that to me it's like sawing through damp wood.'[26] They discussed the future of Reuters, and Northcliffe urged Jones to keep it independent. 'I am with you,' he told him. 'I'll go in with you. I don't want to make money out of the thing. I have made all the money I want. But I believe in Reuters and I believe in you.'[27]

On 14 March, Northcliffe met Lord Derby at Derby's flat in Paris. 'Fat Man hurrying from Cannes,' he told Hudson of the overweight former war secretary the day before the meeting. 'Imagine he is after [Lloyd] George's job.'[28] Derby had been ambassador to Paris from 1918 to 1920, but was in no position to unseat the prime minister, assuming that was even his intention. 'He was a different Northcliffe to what I had ever known,' Derby recorded after the meeting. 'Very moderate in his views; no abuse of the government and discussing Indian matters with great clearness having evidently a very intimate knowledge of all that was going on.'[29] Northcliffe told a different tale to Hudson, reporting: 'Did my best with him for ninety minutes alternatively threatening and blessing.'[30] Nothing came of the plot – if plot it even was.

Northcliffe had gone to Pau to reacclimatise, sleep and quieten his nerves, and Tom Clarke, who was invited down, noticed 'a tired-ness about his speech and actions', although he remained 'a very jolly host, full of jest and story'.[31] Clarke recorded how they stood together on 17 March looking across the roaring Gave du Pau river 'towards the majestic snow-capped Pyrenees beyond the nearer vine-clad hills' and Northcliffe saying, 'Do you know, I have never seen these wonderful mountains the same colour. I have seen them all colours. They will have changed again in another hour.'[32] He stuck to his diet, telling his mother his plan was to 'retain my figure and eat very little and only drink at one meal daily'. His physician Dr Philip Seymour Price later said that this probably hastened his demise, for 'Instead of half starving himself as he did, he should have taken as much food as possible.'[33] Sandy Thomson, Northcliffe's golf profes-sional and friend, found that his client was unable to concentrate on his game in the way that he had before, and was often exhausted by the twelfth hole.

The day after his walk with Clarke, Northcliffe cut the price of *The Times* to twopence, which, although it increased circulation by 50,000, was not enough to stem the losses that were amounting to £1,000 a week, leading Harold to warn his brother that there was 'such a thing as bankruptcy'.[34] 'There's my brother,' Northcliffe told Price, 'moaning about money again.'[35] Yet he promised the trade union leader George Isaacs and the fathers of the federated chapels (unions) at Carmelite House that no cuts in wages or changes in conditions would take place.[36]

Having resigned from the Newspaper Proprietors' Association over their policy of cutting wages in the post-war recession, Northcliffe refused to rejoin what he privately called one of the 'combinations of rich men for grinding down poor men'.[37] 'What a lot of rubbish people talk about trade unions not desiring to produce good work,' he said the following month. 'That is not my experience of trade unions when they receive proper treatment and modern machinery.'[38] The fathers of the chapels sent Northcliffe their 'heart-felt gratitude', but when they later asked for a pay rise, Northcliffe telegraphed Isaacs saying that 'Your people are asking for trouble and will certainly get it good and hard.'[39]

'I have spies everywhere watching my papers,' Northcliffe paranoically told Clarke at Pau.

> They tell me what they hear and what they think, not what they think I would like to hear. I have them in the most unexpected places – in the office itself, in railway trains, trams and tubes. Some of them are women. The chief spotter is Nemo.* They watch people everywhere and keep eyes and ears open. They know. They make daily reports. I compare all their reports.

Unsurprisingly, Clarke commented in his diary, 'This makes one feel a little bit uncomfortable.'[40]

Northcliffe's private life seems to have taken an unpleasant turn at around this time too. At some stage he telephoned Louise Owen and presumably subjected her to the same kind of paranoiac ranting as other staff members, but in her case they had been lovers, although it is impossible to say for how long. She wrote him a bitter stream-of-consciousness letter from Paris, complaining of her treatment at the hands of his other secretaries and warning him that she had written a series of articles about her life, possibly for blackmail purposes. 'I suppose you were too pompous to read them and your unwarranted telephonic abuse is still a mystery to me,' she wrote.

> Your tone was most Carson-like, so full of your own importance ... Now you are cold-shouldering me I am being received with open arms by others. Don't get annoyed if I extract a little limelight – you live in it, so you can't begrudge me a few rays. Seriously, I did think you would have apologised to me, never mind, perhaps my turn will come in Heaven where the tables might be reversed where I'll be hauling you over the coals (what a mixed metaphor) ... Everywhere you are surrounded by sycophants and liars who, while licking the carpet for you to walk over, do not hesitate to cheapen you in every way to their advantage ... How

---

* The codename or nickname of someone Clarke believed was an ex-officer who had convalesced in Lady Northcliffe's hospital.

else should I have heard from a dozen people of your journey to Vancouver with the friction (*sic*) editress* and from another dozen the history ... of the so-called Elmwood housekeeper [that is, Kathleen Wrohan] ... I fully realise how you dislike me for my plain speaking but you cannot deny my disinterestedness. It is only to your face I am so unpleasantly outspoken. To others ... I dwell on those qualities in you which I admire – your patriotism, your devotion to your mother, your courage in dealing with national affairs, your generosity and treatment of your staff (sometimes not) etc, etc. I doubt if I can ever help you as I would like to ... I know your influence is on the wane and you are not master of your own affairs. It is not possible for even a Caesar to thrive only on flattery. Wholesome if unpalatable truth is necessary for the greatest sometimes, and to quote your own words, 'Royalty so often hear the truth only too late.' Are you aware of the manner in which your instructions are received by *The Times* editorial staff including the two great S[utton] and S[teed] ... Yours L[ouise] O[wen]. PS What presents have you bought for Mary and me – you promised us both something very nice and if I am not a deserving case what has poor Mary done?[41]

With his mistress being so solicitous of his wife, it was probably a good time for Northcliffe to have moved to the Pyrenees.

By late March, Northcliffe was inviting staff members to Pau urgently and then only talking about the weather; sending telegrams that were even more peremptory than usual; sleeping the wrong way round in bed, with his head away from the wall.[42] One thing did not change, though. When Bernard Falk arrived at Pau, Clarke noted that 'the Chief has started his "Jew-baiting" fun. It does not embarrass Falk, who stands up to it with good-humoured assurance. Only once have I seen him get a little impatient, when Northcliffe introduced a Scots guest to Falk as "another of the faith".'[43]

---

* Northcliffe had presumably been engaged in another affair with a fiction editor when he was in British Columbia the previous year, as Bettina von Hutten had not been in his life for over a decade.

On discovering on 25 March that the *Daily Telegraph* was dropping its price, Northcliffe suddenly announced at 1.30pm on a Saturday lunchtime at Pau that *The Times* would be reduced even further and that it needed to be announced that same day. 'That will shake up the complacent elders of *The Times*,' he told his guests, exulting that 'the first they would know of it would be reading it in the *Evening News*'.[44] Lints Smith, a *Times* manager, had only just arrived at Pau and not yet unpacked his bag, but he had to catch the next train to Paris and then take a plane to London.

The readership of the *Times Literary Supplement* (*TLS*) had meanwhile fallen drastically, from an average of 31,864 in 1919 to 21,205 in 1922, although this was not the fault of its editor Brian Richmond so much as a doubling of its price to sixpence in July 1920. On 27 March, Northcliffe telegraphed Stuart to warn Richmond that 'Unless he can during present week greatly improve literary side ... to my entire satisfaction, [I] shall merge *Supplement* in[to The] *Times* beginning with Friday week's number.'[45] There was a myth that was believed for many years that the *TLS* was only twenty minutes away from being merged back into *The Times*, but in fact Northcliffe changed his mind unprompted the next day, satisfied that *The Times* book coverage could be improved without the loss of the *TLS* as a separate entity.[46]

On 29 March, *The Times* came out against Lloyd George attending the forthcoming European economic conference at Genoa, where it feared that the Bolsheviks would be seeking to legitimise their regime. 'Personally greatly dislike [the] idea [of the] British Empire shaking hands with murder,' Northcliffe telegraphed.[47] Talking to Clarke, he alleged that the Prime Minister 'had been duped by the Russians, and that the Americans had more sense and had wisely refused to have anything to do with Genoa'. In his diary Clarke recalls, '"Stand by France and Belgium" was the Chief's slogan in reference to the reported threat of Lloyd George to break with France if she did not fall in with the conference proposals.'[48] Northcliffe also complained 'that our politicians were under the thumb of the "propaganding Jews"'.[49] He flitted erratically from one subject to another, but ended, 'Don't be led by the Scots or the Jews.'[50]

The Lloyd George coalition faced major problems in the spring of 1922: income tax had risen 20 per cent to six shillings in the pound since 1918, there was an agricultural depression and trade slump, unemployment reached one million, unrest was seen in India, Egypt and Palestine, and there was a looming civil war in southern Ireland, with Protestants being burned out of their houses there. On 30 March, Lloyd George told Sir Edward Grigg that he would not give in 'to the howls of enemies like Northcliffe', but he did need the Genoa Conference to be a success.[51]

Northcliffe left Pau for Paris on 1 April, and Clarke 'noticed the heaviness of his eyes. He looked quite twenty years older. He seemed a little undecided in his movements ... and mumbled a word or two I didn't catch.'[52] This was his illness taking hold, for whatever else he was, Northcliffe was not a mumbler. The next day, he threatened to sack Sir Andrew Caird, his loyal deputy of many years, saying: 'You've got the paper in worst trap in its history and you apparently don't realise it ... Very few of our people understand about newspapers.'[53] Yet for all that, the same day he discussed with F. E. Bussy, his director of business ideas and development, the concept of announcing the news in 'sky signs' made from electric lights in Piccadilly Circus, years before it happened.

On 3 April, Northcliffe sent Clarke and Bussy off to see Fontainebleau Palace. 'You'll find Napoleon's hat there,' he told them. 'I once had it on. It fits me.'[54] Clarke later recalled that 'There was something that prevented one thinking him ridiculous. No ordinary man could have said that and not have known that he was making himself ridiculous.'[55] Northcliffe claimed to Clarke that he had signed a contract to spend £1m on new buildings and machinery, which was completely untrue. Clarke put it down as a joke in his diary, but in retrospect it was just another portent of something much darker that was happening.

That same day, Lloyd George again attacked the Northcliffe press and other journals in a Commons debate, saying that – judging by the criticism of the Genoa Conference – any new government 'would have its principles enunciated and expounded by the *Morning Post*, the *Daily Herald*, the *Westminster Gazette*, the *Daily Mail* and

Comic Cuts. I do not mention *The Times*, because that is only a tasteless rehash of the *Daily Mail*.'[56] He called his press opponents 'this grotesque conglomeration' and won by 379 votes to eighty-four.

The next day, 4 April, Northcliffe told his secretary that he needed to learn how to handle a revolver because his life had been in danger several times.[57] This too ought to have presented a large red flag to his staff, but in the Northcliffe Archives Papers is the receipt from Holland & Holland gunsmiths in Pall Mall for two thirty-two-bore Colt automatic pistols with holsters and ammunition, costing £15 five shillings and ninepence.[58] Perhaps one of the reasons that it took so long for those around him to recognise anything was wrong was that he continued to be lavish with his praise. On 5 April, he told the editorial team of the *Evening News* that the previous edition had been 'admirable in every respect, editorially, pictorially, makeup dignified and enterprising'.[59] No-one would have wanted to believe someone who had just praised them so generously was mentally ill.

In the car on the way to the Gare du Nord in Paris to catch the boat-train for Calais on 6 April, Northcliffe told Clarke,

> I can't go on working always. I have nothing more to work for. I have all the money and all the social position I want. Social position is nothing to me, and never has been anything. Titles don't appeal to me ... The important thing is poise. How a man handles a situation is much more important than the situation itself. Poise in all things and at all times. So few people have it.[60]

Nearing Calais, Northcliffe pointed out the camp Napoleon had built for the invasion of England, prompting Clarke to write that 'Napoleon is obviously always much in his mind.'[61] It was not a good sign with lunacy looming.

Further evidence of mental disturbance emerged on 11 April with Northcliffe's admonition to his staff that

> the copy of *The Times* delivered to me this morning, at Carlton Gardens, is dirty, and the paper is torn in several places. Prowling around Blackfriars Bridge and the office at 6.30 this morning, I

bought an excellent copy in the street ... I am again sending my
dirty copy down to the office ... The wags are setting to work now
to compare the comments of the *Literary Supplement* with those
of *The Times*, and I shall shortly be having Lord Northcliffe's two
voices in parallel columns. When that starts there will be trouble
of an explosive kind. I am a most unwilling controller and proprietor of *The Times* and would be most glad to be relieved of the
burden. I do not propose to be made ridiculous by the paper, as I
have been on so many occasions.[62]

Referring to oneself in the third person is always worrying, yet even
on that day he was able to praise cogently, saying that 'The paper
compares well with its competitors this morning ... The whole of the
Bill page is good and short ... All the leading articles were good this
morning.' The next day, he admitted that 'one of my Ferrets* went
down to Teddington looking for badly printed *Times* where he heard
they were being dumped. He could not get one, I am glad to say.'[63]

As Northcliffe's mind started to disintegrate, a hitherto largely
unacknowledged sexism started to emerge. 'Frighten her,' he told
Clarke about a woman whose work had displeased him. 'Women
have no sense of responsibility unless you frighten them. I understand women. They do not understand discipline unless they are
going to lose something.'[64] A few days earlier, Clarke had noted
how the Chief, who 'could never be accused of lack of a full-blooded
interest in pretty girls', had almost missed the train at Pau because
he was talking to Lady Jones, of whom he said 'So seldom one can
talk to an extremely good looking lady with brains.'[65] Such casual
sexism was common in the 1920s, of course, but Northcliffe had no
female friends or confidantes besides Mother, not even his former
mistresses.

By mid-April, paranoia was evident in his latest concern. 'There
are, as you all know, German shareholders in *The Times*,' he wrote
to an executive on 13 April. 'What we can prevent are the numerous attempts made to influence *The Times* by foreign governments,

---

* His nickname for his team of informants.

financiers, Jews, Christians, Jap[ane]s[e], politicians and ladies who are about to enter the Divorce Court.'[66]

Yet the next day he turned up at Carmelite House for the first time in many months, fizzing with ideas. Sitting in Room One with a mock-up of the sixteen-page Easter special edition in front of him and blue pencil in hand, he was in his element. Clarke noted 'the old eagerness in his manner', as well as the old ambition. 'I want to get this paper up to two millions,' he said (it was then averaging 1,668, 214). 'I want to turn the whole business on to the aggressive again.'[67] He wanted Miss Cohen, the editor of the Women's Page, to have twice the space, and an exclusive interview with the American world heavyweight boxing champion Jack Dempsey, who was about to arrive in Britain, and a 'streamer' leader across two pages in a new typeface. 'Surprise people,' he ordered, and he wrote an article entitled 'Watch Japan!' that warned that that country had a land hunger and military ambitions which would one day endanger China – 'for he who controls China controls the world'.[68]

~

The news of the Russo–German treaty signed at Rapallo on the Italian Riviera on 16 April utterly undermined the Genoa Conference before it opened. In addition to the American boycott, the French foreign minister and former president Raymond Poincaré also refused to attend the latter conference, fearing that France would be asked to compromise over German reparations. 'The London press – particularly the Northcliffe papers – pounded Lloyd George without mercy, or concern for accuracy,' writes an historian.[69] In the *Daily Mail* of 18 April, there was even an article about Lloyd George entitled 'The Man Who Didn't Win the War' which listed multiple reasons why he didn't deserve the popular soubriquet of The Man Who Won The War: his prewar opposition to building four extra Dreadnoughts; his 'instability of character'; the refusal to spend money on artillery during the Shells Crisis; the lukewarm support of conscription until Northcliffe had made it inevitable; support for 'sideshows' that 'endangered the whole position in France'; the attempt to dismiss Haig in February 1917, and various other supposed errors.[70] It was also alleged that he was presently losing the peace to the Russians and Germans. By contrast, the article stated, it was Northcliffe who had called all of those issues correctly, an indication that he had entered the megalomaniacal stage of his illness.

On Easter Sunday, Northcliffe's luncheon hostess overheard him swearing over the phone to the office, which was also out of character. Wholly in character, however, was his response when a shareholder demanded a special favour. 'Give him hell,' he told his secretary. 'I get lots of letters from shareholders. My reply is unprintable unless their request concerns the shareholders' profit, which they are, of course, entitled to know about.'[71]

Northcliffe's reorganisation of the *Daily Mail*'s advertising department on 28 April 1922 soon became part of Fleet Street lore. It was another sign that he was ill, although that was still not appreciated at the time. He had long complained that large advertisements were 'bludgeoning the rest of the paper ... Advertisements in ugly type spoiled the appearance of the news pages. He wanted things more balanced.'[72] Since he believed that the heads of departments had ignored his instructions over this, he went to Carmelite House and suddenly appointed Robert Glover, the commissionaire (or chief hall porter) of almost three decades, as 'censor of advertisements' with the task of making them smaller and less prominent.

Immediately afterwards, Dr Price saw Northcliffe 'sitting with his head in his hands, his shoulders heaving with laughter, like a schoolboy who has played a successful trick'.[73] Glover himself was embarrassed by his promotion, which Northcliffe celebrated at a lunch in his honour at Carlton Gardens. Northcliffe later put out a staff communiqué saying, 'The Old Man, the Mr Alfred of earlier days, may be off his head, but he has stopped the big bludgeoning advertisements getting into the paper.'[74] He then telephoned Clarke to claim that 'Someone has been saying I am off my head. Not you, is it, Tom?'[75] Clarke understandably forbore to say that the rumour had been started by Northcliffe himself.

Northcliffe's last appearance at Carmelite House took place at a retirement party for an employee on 4 May, coincidentally the twenty-sixth anniversary of the founding of the paper. That day also saw his last communiqué to *The Times*, which showed no trace of the mania that was gripping him: 'With the exception of a mistake in a picture caption in which Haig is said to be on the right of the picture when he is in the middle, and some bad printing in the advertisement of the vineyard opposite the picture page, I think this morning's *Times* is a very admirable newspaper.'[76]

The Genoa Conference opened on 10 May and, by the time it ended nine days later, it was clear that – as the Northcliffe press had predicted – it had been a fiasco, and deeply damaging to Lloyd George's already tottering prestige. He had conceived it bringing the pariah nations of Russia and Germany into the European fiscal and commercial system and revisiting the reparations levels for the latter. But the Treaty of Rapallo had only three weeks earlier created a new power bloc in Europe, and Britain had found no major allies to balance it. Steed had not wanted to attend the conference, but Northcliffe, who was thinking of demoting him to foreign news editor, demanded that he did, further damaging relations between them.[77]

At the Empire Press Union dinner on 11 May, Northcliffe was 'very fidgety and jumpy'.[78] Two days later, he asked Hudson to return or destroy every day the copies of his communiqués that he received from *The Times* and the *Daily Mail*, without giving a reason why. In reply to a long, rational telegram from Steed about the political situation, Northcliffe wrote: 'Amazed disgusted [by] your reply. Matter in other hands. See *Spectator*.'[79] Steed was nonplussed, yet he and the management of the papers continued to see Northcliffe's behaviour as irritable and erratic rather than as evidence of a mental illness.

It is questionable whether a wholly sane Northcliffe would have published his twenty-four-page pamphlet on 18 May entitled *Newspapers and Their Millionaires, With Some Further Meditations About Us*. He had long denounced the fact that newspapers tended to be owned by businessmen rather than by newspapermen, and as recently as 15 April had told his staff, after a visit to his Gravesend paper mills, that 'some of the multimillionaires who have plunged into Fleet Street in the last few years are trying to drive down these men's wages. One of them confessed to me frankly that he did not know the difference of a rotary machine from a rotarian or an autoplate from a linotype.'[80] Yet he had not publicly attacked his fellow proprietors before, and certainly not almost all of them at once.

In the pamphlet, he referred to 'our wise friend, Lord Beaverbrook' – who was not part of the wages-reduction movement – saying that he showed great initiative and his career was a credit to Canada.[81] But in his other remarks about his fellow press proprietors, he mentioned the Cadbury family that owned the *Daily News* and its 'most un-Quakerly references to myself'; Sir Edward Hulton, a 'millionaire by inheritance' who owned the *Evening Standard*, which, Northcliffe wrote, 'masks some curious publications in Manchester'.[82] Reading Lord Cowdray's *Westminster Gazette* 'reminds me of a man playing golf for the first time. If Cowdray would go down to the office and use a little of his foresight and great sense of humour he might one day be able to approach the inevitable, *the net sale certificate*.'[83] 'If you buy the *Daily Herald* and want the news,' Northcliffe wrote about the left-leaning journal, 'you must buy another newspaper.'[84] He explained his resignation from the Newspapers Proprietors' Association, calling it 'a combination in which capitalists ignorant of Fleet Street dictate terms to those who have spent their lives trying to understand the complex questions of a newspaper'.[85] The pamphlet elicited predictable outrage amongst the other proprietors. Northcliffe told Clarke not to print a photo of him in the *Daily Mail* advert for the pamphlet, as 'my mother says I look like a codfish'.[86]

Clarke noted around this time that Northcliffe 'has become rather difficult on the telephone lately, as if he were not speaking into the receiver, and making long statements, jumping quickly from one thing to another and then suddenly disappearing from the telephone'.[87] At Elmwood, the staff noted his 'permanent anger', and his demand for fire alarms to be installed throughout the property because 'people were coming down to London to set fire to the house'.[88] Because of his abuse, the head gardener and housekeeper left after eighteen years of working for him.

On the evening that his pamphlet was published, Northcliffe
made his last public appearance, at a dinner of the Australia and
New Zealand Club, where he announced that he would shortly be
visiting Germany. It did not take long for German newspapers to
say that he would not be welcome. The *Neueste Nachrichten* said
something that might have appealed to him, however, which was
that 'Nobody had been so hated in Germany since Napoleon.'[89]
The Times chairman John Walter later noted that there was
nothing wrong with Northcliffe in the business discussion they
held on 24 May, and the same day Northcliffe wrote Churchill a
perfectly lucid letter on the British embargo on Canadian cattle,
stating 'Were your Prime Minister not such a damnably bad tempered fellow, I should have written to him direct, but I have done
so through Lord Riddell.'[90] It was to be his last communication
with Churchill.

On 25 May, Northcliffe left for a continental tour along with
Sandy Thomson, Harry Pine and his valet William Brown. He
should have been receiving medical treatment instead. 'Alfred is
looking very ill and nobody seems to realise it,' Kathleen Wrohan
told Pine.[91] She refused to send the eleven-year-old Alfred to see
him at the Hôtel Christol in Boulogne, which Pine later recalled left
Northcliffe 'considerably upset', but was a correct judgment on Mrs
Wrohan's part.

Northcliffe travelled via Brussels to Germany under the pseudonym Leonard Brown. For someone already suffering from paranoiac
episodes, it was the very last place he should have visited, hated as he
was there for his wartime propaganda. 'I am not afraid for my life,'
he said, carrying his loaded Colt revolver. 'I shoot from the hip.'[92] On
the journey to Cologne, he stopped in some woods to practise firing
it, and sent a messenger ahead to tell his host, General Sir Alexander
Godley, commander of the British Army, that he could be recognised
by his grey Tyrolese hat.

On 31 May, Northcliffe arrived at Cologne. He was under the
impression that the Germans had given him poisoned ice cream and
went to bed. 'I have had a curious illness,' he telegraphed home.
'Some people think I have been poisoned. Personally I cannot believe

that but I know I have been very bad.'[93] The next day, Godley described Northcliffe as 'obviously a very sick man' who 'talked incessantly' about himself.[94] There was clearly a pressing need for urgent medical intervention.

CHAPTER 23

DEATH

June–August 1922

'*The Times* was dying when he took charge of it and living
when Northcliffe died.'[1]

LORD BEAVERBROOK, *Men and Power* 1956

On 2 June 1922, Northcliffe cabled Totteridge: 'Am very well and
always thinking of my darling Mother.'[2] At the same time, he told
Mary – who was holidaying at Évian on Lake Geneva with Sir Robert
Hudson, supposedly to help her neuralgia – that he had had a 'very
interesting and adventurous time among the Bosche'.[3] Back in Boulogne
on 3 June, he sacked Sandy Thomson for alcoholism and told Harry
Pine that he could smell gas in his bedroom.[4] He asked *The Times* to
send him a secretary, and they chose the twenty-seven-year-old Douglas
Reed, who wrote about the scene in his memoirs *Insanity Fair* in 1938:

> He lay in bed a very sick man ... a man disappointed, disillu-
> sioned, distrusting everyone, with rare moments of gentleness,
> knowing himself to be mortally ill and hating the knowledge
> that neither his brain nor his energy nor his wealth could over-
> come this enemy. The shadows were already closing relentlessly
> in on him ... A disproportionately massive head lay on the
> pillow, a greying forelock hung dankly down, greenish eyes*

---

* They were blue.

contemplated the world in general and myself in particular with malevolence.[5]

Northcliffe dictated long letters 'which mercifully never appeared' from his bed on subjects from 'the skinny shanks of a famous society lady* to the Jewish influence in English life'. He dictated a series of four articles entitled 'Incognito in Germany', the first two of which, emphasising Germany's prosperity and high birth rate, were published, but not the rest, which were unhinged. 'He felt himself surrounded by treachery,' Reed recalled. 'He put his hand under the pillow and brought out a little black silk bag. "Look at this", he said, 'it was left for me, for Mr Leonard Brown, by a man who wouldn't give the porter his name. How do they know I am here? Do you see the colour? It is the colour of death!'[6] Within days, Northcliffe had so abused Reed that he 'became a nervous wreck' and left.[7]

With John Walter now worried enough to try to sell his shares in *The Times*, on 4 June Northcliffe telegraphed Sutton to say, 'Please, please, please, please, please, please don't consult me about Old One.† Will do exactly what you choose. Wish to get as many shares as I can. Have absolute confidence in future, but shall make clean sweep of office ... Am very tired after anxious German visit.'[8] He asked Robert Hudson to get the best medical 'opinion as to my sanity ... I do not know but think that I am going mad. I dreamt the other night that I had run off with Princess Mary‡ and had started a boarding house at Blackpool, and she said to me, "Thank you, we are doing very well."'[9] He ended, 'Wire me at once to relieve my suspicions.' Meanwhile, Valentine Williams, the foreign editor of the *Daily Mail* and a bestselling novelist, resigned because Northcliffe had told him that he could not 'serve two masters'.[10] 'Had I put up with the Chief's bludgeoning', Williams told Clarke, 'that other self would have whispered for all of my lifetime in my ears that I was a moral coward.'[11] Such bludgeoning of employees had gone on for so

---

* Margot Asquith.
† *The Times*.
‡ The twenty-five-year-old Princess Royal.

long that, it was said, 'One journalist instinctively raised his hat and bowed when speaking to Northcliffe on the telephone.'[12]

'I always thought him a lonely man,' Tom Clarke wrote of Northcliffe later; 'rather splendidly and pontifically lonely. He so seldom sought advice, and treated it so roughly if he did not like it, that people hesitated to give it to him. When he spoke, everyone listened, usually without challenge. He suffered from too little opposition.'[13] It is perhaps therefore unsurprising that it was not until early June that Northcliffe's staff finally recognised that, in the words of a coded message from H. G. Price to Clarke on the 9th, their chief was suffering from 'a curious illness. He had been very bad, but he [Price] could not believe, as some people thought, that he had been poisoned in Germany.'[14] Sir George Sutton, Peter Goudie the manager-designate of *The Times* and Miss D. M. Rudge, a *Daily Mail* telephonist,* were sent to France right away. 'You gave my address away for the first time in your life,' Northcliffe telegraphed Price. 'I pray you never do it again. Nobody but Mother and you knows my new address on Monday, Leonard Brown, Hotel Royal, Évian-Les-Bans. Please post my letters with your own hand and don't use *Times* envelopes with name on back.'[15]

Later that day, Northcliffe sent a paranoiac telegram that covered four pages and demonstrated the full extent of his mental illness:

Dearest Price, you will leave *The Times* permanently instantly and go to much healthier place. You have nothing to do with *The Times*. You never had. As for P[rinting] H[ouse] S[quare], I hate it. Her Ladyship's lovely Chinese room which you'll have with its little anteroom and Mrs Price's room for your clerks is said to be the most beautiful business room in London. You know perfectly well people come to see it from America especially. The lavatories are equal to those in Carlton House ... You don't even know that

---

* And possibly also the head of his intelligence system, who was said to listen in on conversations and report them to Northcliffe. One such between Dawson and Nancy Astor was said to have helped lead to Dawson's departure from the editorship. [Thompson, *Northcliffe*, p.443 n52]

I have bought the entire Walter interest. I am a little distressed at what Lewis & Lewis said about your relations with my enemies in the office. I am going to smite them hip and thigh next month. You know there is a strong pro-Walter clan. You have been seen with them ... Lints Smith was one of their leaders. Detectives found that out. You have in fact been duped ... Sincerely hope you will not wear that grey suit in Ladyship's beautiful room. People don't wear grey suits in beautiful Chinese rooms. Blue serge is best ... There'll be over a hundred dismissals in the first week [of] July ... I risked my life all the time in Germany ... We want more men telephone operators. Fleetway House is the healthiest building I have ... Get rid of Snoad. He's talking ... Have you begun to be a pettifogging interferer. I don't think so. We have thirty years files to examine this summer ... Of course Mackenzie [the house manager at Elmwood] is going on July 1st. He's not quite right in the head. We are all getting much older except you and me ... I hate London and I loathe beastly dirty *Times* office ... I want my beautiful room for a smoking room at Elmwood. It cost twelve hundred pounds.[16]

There were plenty more telegrams in this vein, and one wonders what the telegram operators could have thought of it all as they took Northcliffe's dictation. The next day he told Price he was leaving for the Hotel Plaza Athénée in Paris, signing one long rambling paranoiac telegram, 'Your totally unhectic Chief.'[17]

At Boulogne station on Sunday 10 June, Northcliffe declared that Douglas Reed had tried to assassinate him and had accused him of 'unnatural vice' (that is, sodomy) with his valet William Brown. He then 'in a loud tone and in the presence of a number of people on the platform, blasphemously accused the Deity of the same vice'.[18] He then insulted all the railway officials present on the platform, as well as the train's conductor and ticket collector during the journey. When he arrived in Paris, he had to be helped along the station platform and, on arriving at the hotel, he saw Mrs House in the lobby and subjected her to what the colonel described as a 'crude embrace', leaving the couple deeply shocked. 'Northcliffe is gone!' House told Steed when Steed arrived that evening. 'He won't live long now.'[19]

'You must be prepared for a shock,' Peter Goudie told Steed. 'The Chief is not himself.' 'Does that surprise you?' asked Steed. 'Not altogether,' Goudie replied. 'I have seen it coming for some time.'[20] Steed was taken to see Northcliffe in his fifth-floor bedroom at 8pm. 'I found Lord Northcliffe in bed, scantily dressed, in a darkened room,' he later recalled. 'He seized my hand effusively, and said he had felt terribly the separation from me. He appeared excited and, calling for his valet, asked whether it were seventeen days or seventeen years since he had left England. Northcliffe, speaking in rapid, jerky sentences, said he had been nearly assassinated.'[21]

Northcliffe told Steed that Douglas Reed, 'a partisan of Lloyd George', had 'tried to murder him by hitting him on the head with a Perrier bottle' in Boulogne, but he 'had evaded the blow and had knocked out the man's eye with his stick'. Steed soon ascertained from William Brown that none of this was true. Northcliffe also told Steed that John Walter and Lints Smith 'had tried to jew [Steed] out of a £50,000 contract'.[22] In order to prove that he had been poisoned by the Germans, Northcliffe showed Steed his tongue, 'which was black. His lower lip bore a black scab, as though it had been burned. His eyes were wild, and I noticed ... that his left eye had a strange squint in an upward diagonal direction.'[23] His lower lip might well have been burned by trying to light cigars, which he was no longer able to do but nevertheless tried on numerous occasions.

On the 11th, Steed found Northcliffe sitting up in bed excitedly waving a Colt pistol around and claiming that a man had tried to enter his room and shoot him. It turned out that he had been alarmed by the shadow of his dressing-gown hanging on the bedroom door. He claimed that the Colt had been given to him by an American friend and had once been used to kill seven men in one day. (Steed later ascertained that it had been bought recently in Pall Mall, but that there were indeed seven cartridges in it.) Steed was understandably concerned that Northcliffe's 'finger was constantly on the trigger' as he explained to Steed that 'God talks to me. I don't believe in Christ except as a great man. You must pray.'

When Northcliffe was in the bathroom, Steed and Brown managed to remove the cartridges from the butt of the gun and replace them with an empty clip.

'Lord Northcliffe then spoke in the most obscene terms of his wife and Sir Robert Hudson,' Steed noted, and said that 'he would smash all his enemies. He would be a Cromwell. He had given orders for the dismissal of 150 Lloyd Georgians from *The Times*.' He also claimed that Lewis & Lewis had dressed private detectives as bricklayers and clerks to spy for him there. He then accused Steed of having murdered Sir Campbell Stuart and stated that Sir Basil Zaharoff, the (possibly Jewish) Greek industrialist and arms dealer, was 'the real King of England and "ran" Lloyd George'.[24]

At 5am on 12 June, Northcliffe told a group of *Times* and *Mail* staff members who were waiting for him in the lobby of the Hotel Plaza Athénée that he could shoot seven Germans through his jacket pocket. He then dictated a letter to *The Times* about Herbert Asquith's letter on aviation that described Mary Northcliffe as 'feline' and acting 'snappishly' and 'cattishly'.[25] Steed discussed the letter as though it were rational, and then quietly put it in his pocket.

At 8.30am, Northcliffe and his party took the private carriage of a train from the Gare de Lyon to Bellegarde, where they would meet Harry Pine in the Rolls-Royce and be driven to Évian-les-Bains, where it was hoped that Mary and Hudson would ensure his rest and he could receive medical treatment from his physicians Sir Frederick Treves and Dr Price, as well as a local specialist. He travelled with Steed, W. L. Warden (the editor of the Paris *Daily Mail*), Peter Goudie, Miss Rudge, Sisley Huddleston (*The Times* foreign correspondent), Stephen Dowling (a shorthand writer from the *Continental Daily Mail*), and a French doctor of whom Northcliffe 'shrieked that if he came into the room he would throw him out'.

As soon as the train left the station, Northcliffe summoned Sisley Huddleston to tell him that he was no gentleman because he had a red silk pocket handkerchief, 'his teeth were bad, his breath stank'.[26] (He presumably passed Northcliffe's test for having an unusual name, though.) Huddleston left the train at Dijon. The rest of the ten-and-a-half-hour journey was spent with Northcliffe dictating libellous telegrams (which Steed succeeded in suppressing) and 'a ceaseless stream of indistinct and mostly disjointed talk' with moments of 'uncanny lucidity'. 'Part of it was filthy beyond repetition,' Steed recalled.[27] After lunch, he told Miss Rudge improper stories, saying to Steed afterwards, 'Did I go a little too far with that girl? Don't you think I'm mad? Am I mad?' Steed assured him that he was merely very tired.

Pine and Hudson were waiting for Northcliffe at Bellegarde Station. Thirty-five years later, Pine recalled how he 'seemed to be in a state of collapse. I could scarcely believe my own eyes.'[28] During the fifty-mile journey to Évian, he 'talked incessantly, except that he fell for a moment into another fit of coughing, retching and shrieking'. 'Don't you know the road or do you?' he asked Pine, ordering him to drive faster. 'Go on, don't humbug about.'[29] Pine drove 'at breakneck speed', impressing Steed with his chauffeuring skills.

When they reached the Hôtel Royal in Évian, Northcliffe insulted the manager, pageboys and porter, and later also Mary, who was 'much upset'.[30] 'I am in a delightful place,' Northcliffe telegraphed his mother, 'where I intend to spend some time with my dear wife among wildflowers. Am therefore announcing my indisposition in newspapers though in reality [I] am perfectly well.'[31] The next day, he told her that the rumours of his illness, which were swirling around Whitehall, Westminster, Fleet Street and clubland, 'are untrue. I have been unwell but am now well again.' In fact, by then he was on morphine injected by Dr Price, as he refused to see Sir Frederick Treves, whom he called 'an old imbecile'. This put an end to his incessant talking, which had lasted from 5am on the 12th to 1am on the 13th.

On the 14th, Northcliffe was foully rude to everyone in his presence. 'The malice and concentrated venom of his abuse was such as to demand the utmost self-control on my part,' wrote Steed in his memorandum. When Mary came in to tell Steed it was time for dinner, Northcliffe 'launched into obscene talk of a kind that reduced her to a condition of trembling disgust'.[32] He was finally persuaded to see a French nerve specialist (because he was told that he was an expert in German poisons), whom he nonetheless violently abused and who may or may not have signed a document certifying him as insane.[33]

'Lord Northcliffe was never at any time certified insane,' Dr Price assured Northcliffe's brother Leicester in October 1926. 'I was with him every day of his last illness including the day of his death. There is a world of difference between insanity and the delirium caused by such an illness as his.'[34] Steed and others insisted that the unnamed French doctor had indeed certified Northcliffe as insane, which explained why he needed to be taken back to England immediately in order to prevent his being detained as a dangerous individual by the Prefecture of Haute Savoie.

Steed contacted a friend, Senator Victor Bérard, to arrange for President Poincaré to instruct the Prefect not to take any action pending Northcliffe's removal to London by special railway carriage.[35] By then, Sir Leicester Harmsworth had arrived at Évian to take charge, and along with others of the entourage he persuaded Northcliffe to return, explaining that their mother wanted to see him. Meanwhile, Steed intercepted all communications from Northcliffe, except the soothing ones to his mother. 'This business is the devil!' Hudson told Sutton on 16 June. 'He is driving everyone around him into a condition that will soon resemble his own state! Everyone is to be dismissed as soon as he gets back to London, so pack your kit!'[36] The *Daily Mail* announced that the third and fourth of Northcliffe's articles on Germany would be 'temporarily suspended' owing to his 'indisposition', and Steed had to rewrite the second one extensively as parts of it were unprintably insane.[37]

Northcliffe's journey from Évian to Victoria Station was, in Clarke's words, 'hedged around with mystery and hush-hush that we associate with the illness of kings'. He was back at Carlton Gardens by the evening of Sunday 18 June. A team of male psychiatric nurses were engaged, one of whom Northcliffe attacked with a poker on 30 June.[38] Although he was not allowed access to the telephone, he found one in Mary's room and gave orders for the sacking of dozens of members of staff, which were of course ignored. 'Listen to him,' Clarke was instructed by the doctors, 'don't argue, be happy in your conversation with him, say nothing to worry or annoy him. Agree with all he says. Take down any instructions he gives you.'[39] On one occasion, Northcliffe managed to get through to the night editor of the *Daily Mail* and said, in a ghostly whisper, 'I hear they are saying I am mad. Send the best reporter for the story.'[40] Meanwhile, Lints Smith had a police guard placed at Printing House Square in case Northcliffe should escape from Carlton Gardens.[41]

The distinguished doctor Sir Thomas Horder took charge of Northcliffe's treatment on the morning of 19 June, at the rate of £15 per consultation.* When Dr Price told Northcliffe that Horder, who had recently been knighted, was to attend him, Northcliffe shouted, 'One of George's† bloody knights', and took a revolver from under his pillow.[42] 'He was restrained by the nurse,' Horder recalled in 1954, 'and did not – as has been reported – fire at me. I learned afterwards that the revolver was not loaded.‡ After a time, the patient was persuaded to let me examine him. He was obviously a very sick man physically. Mentally, he was completely disorientated, very voluble and restless.' Horder ordered blood tests to be taken, which showed the streptococcus characteristic of septic endocarditis, a form of blood poisoning which brings on fever and delirium.

Although Steed, Cecil King (in his autobiography), and many others both at the time and since, and indeed several historians right up to the present day, confidently diagnosed Northcliffe with General Paresis of the Insane (GPI), which is seen in late-stage syphilis, that was not what afflicted him.[43] He passed the Wassermann test for syphilis. A letter to *The Times* in December 1971, from Horder's assistant Dr Lloyd-Jones, went into more detail about Northcliffe's illness, which was, he wrote,

> Bacterial endocarditis ... an inflammation of the inner lining of the
> heart and especially the valves. Incidentally Horder had established

---

* £870 in today's money.
† Lloyd George loathed being called George, which might have been why Northcliffe often called him that. [Roskill, *Hankey* I p.464 n1]
‡ In May 1952, Lord Beaverbrook claimed on television that Horder had seized the revolver from Northcliffe, but Horder told Rothermere the following month that there was 'not a word of truth' in it. [Northcliffe Archive Papers RPR.023]

his name by giving the first full account of this condition, and he was the recognised authority on it. Horder, who was a genius at diagnosis, could not possibly have missed the condition known as GPI ... He would have heard the rumours about the possible GPI ... and would have investigated that opportunity. ... Dr Liebman of New York ... was recognised as the leading authority on bacterial endocarditis in America. Horder took him to see Northcliffe, and Liebman entirely confirmed the diagnosis, and had no further suggestions as to treatment ... Dr Joekes [a Dutch bacteriologist working at St Bartholomew's Hospital] ... produced triumphantly a flask of broth into which he had injected some of Northcliffe's blood, and from which he had succeeded in growing the infecting organism ... This proved the diagnosis to the very hilt.[44]

On 20 June 1922, the *Daily Mail* announced on page 9 that Northcliffe was 'undergoing treatment for heart weakness accentuated by ptomaine poisoning'.[45] Meanwhile Mary, who had moved into the Ritz, had been told that her husband might be suffering from abdominal problems, whereas she knew full well that they were psychiatric. She therefore wrote anxious letters to Leicester and Harold complaining that she was not being kept fully informed of what was happening at Carlton Gardens, worrying that Northcliffe was not getting the best possible treatment. Her attempts to have Northcliffe declared insane were 'powerfully resisted' by Cecil and Leicester, however.[46] 'I was sent away because they [the brothers and doctors] thought it proper to do so,' she later wrote, but Leicester rejected her accusations, stating years later that 'It was one of her characteristics to pose as a martyr in some respect or another and always to have a grievance ... She was very trying during N's illness.'[47] On 4 July, Hudson wrote to Leicester of Mary: 'She is perilously near collapse, and how to keep her going under the strain of her anxiety is a problem.'[48] To this, Leicester noted in the margin, 'Bosh. She never looked so well.'[49]

The *Evening News* carried bulletins each day, such as that of 12 August: 'The patient's condition remains persistently grave.' The story naturally fascinated people, not least because of the seemingly huge political implications for the government of the removal of its most powerful critic. 'Northcliffe under restraint!' Frances Stevenson noted in her diary on 20 June. 'Rothermere told D[avid Lloyd George] that he had been queer for some time, but now he is really off his head ... D would like to get *The Times* and if it is to be sold will try and get it bought by a friendly syndicate.'[50]

On 11 July, Horder wrote to Leicester Harmsworth that his 'fears are confirmed' and that the streptococcus and 'other symptoms and signs' meant that he could not 'avoid the conclusion that the heart has become infected'.[51] 'Is Northcliffe dying?' Clementine Churchill asked her husband three days later. 'How queer if he and Lenin drop off the globe about the same time like sort of mental Siamese twins.'[52] In fact Lenin, who had survived an assassination attempt in August 1918, did not die until January 1924. 'He has streptococcus infection in his blood,' Churchill replied, 'and no one has ever got well from this particular disease. His brother is my informant. *Sic transit gloria mundi.** I cannot help feeling sorry – although God knows how cruel he was to me in those evil days of 1916.'[53] Of Lloyd George, Churchill continued, 'Our revered leader is no doubt greatly relieved.'

On 22 July, Geraldine Harmsworth was brought to her son's bedside. 'Is it his head?' she asked, perhaps recalling his headaches as a child. By early August, members of the public started to arrive at Carmelite House with suggestions for cures. One reader sent a hair from an elephant's tail, 'which is sure to bring good luck'.[54] On 4 August, Steed 'received a final, pathetic message' from Northcliffe about how his death should be covered: 'Give me a full page in *The Times* and a leading article by the best available writer on the night.'[55] 'We gave him more than that,' Steed recorded. '*The Times* owed and owes him lasting gratitude, for he rescued it from decline and did much to vitalise it.'[56]

'In spite of periods towards the end when he was very mentally disturbed, he had moments of complete lucidity too,' Mary Northcliffe recalled of this period thirty-four years later. She instanced his remark to her about Kathleen Wrohan: 'Don't worry about her; she'll

---

* Thus passes worldly glory.

die of drink.'[57] Even before Northcliffe's death, St John Harmsworth had written to say that the wages of Sophie Fenton, Mrs Wrohan's secretary, would no longer be subsidised by the estate.

'Poor wretch,' Churchill wrote to Clementine on 9 August, 'his worst enemies could not but grieve for him . . . It cannot be long now.'[58] That day, Horder decided that Northcliffe needed constant fresh air, which he could not get in his bedroom, so Humphrey-Davy asked the Duke of Devonshire whether a 'temporary small hut or shelter' could be constructed on the very extensive roof of his adjoining house, No. 2 Carlton Gardens. The Duke gave his permission, so a white pinewood hut was built for Northcliffe up there, to give the patient 'air and isolation' and keep him cool on the hot summer nights.[59] 'Work began at 9pm and by 11am the next morning the Chief was in it,' noted Clarke.[60] It was the kind of efficiency and organisation that he would have admired in happier circumstances. It took a pulley and tackle to get Northcliffe, who was on a stretcher 'full of morphia', up onto the roof, after holes had to be cut through the ceilings of two storeys.[61] The first night he slept there, the weather broke and it rained heavily, and he found the noise on the corrugated roof 'nerve-wracking', but that was soon fixed by covering the roof with tar felt.[62]

Alfred Harmsworth, first and last Viscount Northcliffe, died 'very quietly' at 10.12am on Monday 14 August 1922, having drifted into a coma a few days earlier.[63] He was fifty-seven. Vyvyan and Cecil Harmsworth were present, as was Dr Seymour Price. Northcliffe's last recorded words were: 'Give a kiss and my love to mother, and tell her she is the only one.'[64]

~

'The illness from which Lord Northcliffe suffered was infective or ulcerative endocarditis,' Dr Price told Tom Clarke on the day of his death.

It is probable that this fatal disease began insidiously months ago. In fact, it is not improbable that it started during his recent world tour. The trouble made slow progress until some two months ago, when there was a considerable amount of fever, progressive weakness, and the heart was obviously becoming embarrassed. The patient's whole being was poisoned by the germ which was circulating in his blood. His condition steadily became worse. Infective endocarditis is usually fatal. Very few patients recover from it, and in the case of Lord Northcliffe his extremely strenuous life, together with his war work, his world tour, his recent visit to Germany, and the noticeable loss of weight, had done much to undermine his constitution, and had lowered his resistance to such an extent that the germ (streptococcus) was able to find its way into the bloodstream. These germs exist ordinarily in the body, but it is easy to understand that, should they find their way into the bloodstream, the condition presents an extremely grave problem ... Every treatment known to medical science has been tried, without success ... He was aware of his grave condition, but refused to yield to the enemy.[65]

On 19 August 1922 the *British Medical Journal* noted that

The death of Lord Northcliffe from a typical attack of infective endocarditis, while in the prime of life and activity, is all the more deplorable because if he had realised the significance of the early symptoms from which he must have suffered it is practically certain that treatment could have been adopted which might perhaps have prevented the development of the complication from which he died. The acute disease to which he was a victim was due to an infection of the heart which on that account is frequently called malignant endocarditis. What seems probable is that he had, in fact, suffered from streptococcal infection for at least a year.[66]

That would have placed his initial infection when he was on the world tour he had undertaken as a rest-cure for his exhaustion.

The *Journal* speculated that the origin might have been in 'a septic infection around the roots of teeth' and that

the blood was invaded. Very often ... the infection, having reached the blood, attacks one of the valves of the heart which may have been damaged, perhaps by rheumatism, many years before. It is known that Lord Northcliffe had a cardiac murmur at least fifteen years ago; how long it had been present before that is not known ... Remittent fever, with its well-known accompaniments, exhausting the physical and mental powers of the patient, is one of the usual manifestations of the disease, which, in this instance, followed its almost invariable course.[67]

Today, Northcliffe would be treated by a cardiologist working in conjunction with a microbiology team. The initial treatment strategy would be intravenous antibiotics and potentially cardiac surgery to replace the infected heart valves if various conditions were met. An early identification of the condition, early antibiotic therapy and possibly cardiac surgery would have substantially improved his chances of survival.[68]

~

The popular response to Northcliffe's death was truly remarkable. 'His death caused a sense of public loss rarely felt on such a scale,' wrote Linton Andrews of the reaction.[69] J. L. Garvin, never an uncritical commentator about his former proprietor, 'felt as one might if Niagara itself were to cease and vanish'. In *Answers* thirty-four years earlier, Northcliffe had jokingly predicted that 'literary men and women would one day process to the tomb of the first editor in Westminster Abbey'.[70] In fact, he was buried at St Marylebone Cemetery in Finchley on 17 August, after a funeral at Westminster Abbey in which every seat was filled. It was as great a funeral as has ever been given a Briton who never held either political or military office.[71] The Prince of Wales was represented by a brigadier, the Diplomatic Corps attended in strength and even Lloyd George sent a representative. Hardened journalists such as Hannen Swaffer* wept during the ceremony, as had *The Times* writers when they were

---

* 'They said millions of words about Northcliffe when he was alive,' Swaffer wrote later, 'and when he died. For he was one of the most talked-about men in all the world.' [Swaffer, *Northcliffe's Return*, p.15]

composing Northcliffe's obituary.[72] As well as the great and the good
who sent wreaths, so did the cleaning staff at the *Daily Mail*.[73]

After the funeral, the cortège proceeded down a seven-mile route
to Finchley along 'a practically unbroken avenue of reverent spectators'.[74] Northcliffe had inaugurated the 'Soldier's Friend' column
of the *Daily Mail*, and one of the reasons that an estimated 7,000
people lined the route was that ex-servicemen saw him as having
been on their side in the Great War. As the coffin reached its resting place, an aeroplane tipped its wings in salute. He was buried
with a picture of his mother on his breast, and under his hands the
devotional book *Daily Light on the Daily Path* that he had taken
around the world to read simultaneously with her.[75] Her response to
her eldest son's death was to repeat constantly, 'It is the Lord's will.
It is the Lord's will.'[76]

Northcliffe had left instructions that he wished to be buried as
near to his mother as possible, as he assumed she would pre-decease
him, 'and I do not wish anything erect from the ground or any words
except my name and the years I was born and [died] upon the stone'.
When his mother died in August 1925 aged eighty-six, she was
buried next to him. The Harmsworth family bought a fifteen-acre
site in Kennington next to the Imperial War Museum which became
the Geraldine Mary Harmsworth Memorial Park.

Mary Northcliffe received messages of sympathy from George V,
Queen Mary, Queen Alexandra and five other members of the royal
family. These also came from the kings of Portugal, Siam and Egypt,
from President Warren Harding of the United States, Presidents
Millerand, Poincaré and Clemenceau of France, from the viceroy
of India, Marshal Foch, six serving premiers, Thomas Edison, the
Maharajah of Kapurthala, and the ambassadors of every major
country except Germany. Even the proprietors of *Punch* magazine,
which had satirised Northcliffe for so long, sent their condolences.
It was all a far cry from the days, only seven years earlier, when
Northcliffe had been abused as 'that frenzied office boy' and his
papers burned on the floor of the Stock Exchange.

~

Northcliffe's will was proved at £3,250,000 gross, more than £200 million in today's money. In it, he remembered his 6,000 employees; to each of whom he gave three months' salary. He had made several wills in his lifetime, with many codicils, including a death-bed one that was correctly disregarded, but there was a good deal of legal argument over them prompted by (separate) assertions by Mary Northcliffe and Louise Owen that they were being unfairly treated.[77] In the will that was finally proved – which had been made on 22 March 1919, just before his throat operation – a residuary trust fund was formed. The annual income from this was divided between large numbers of people for their lifetimes, including Lady Northcliffe (who got 25 per cent before her remarriage and 10 per cent afterwards), Northcliffe's mother (8 per cent), George Sutton (7 per cent), Northcliffe's sisters (2 per cent each), his mother-in-law (1 per cent), three of his brothers (varying from half a percent to 3 per cent), Henry Arnholz (3 per cent), Louise Owen (2 per cent), his secretary (1 per cent), Max Pemberton, Francis Humphrey-Davy and H. G. Price (half a per cent each), Thomas Marlowe and Charles Hands (quarter of a per cent each), as well as nephews and nieces.

There were also legacies of £1,000 – more than £60,000 in today's money – for each of the directors of *The Times*, and £500 for Sir Campbell Stuart, Evelyn Wrench and seven others. His and Mary's godchildren received £100, as did Andrew Caird, Bernard Falk, Walter Fish, Hamilton Fyfe, Peter Goudie, J. L. Garvin, Mrs Jealous of the *Ham & High*, Leo Maxse, W. Lints-Smith, Isaac Marcossen, O. J. Pulvermacher, Harold Snoad, Valentine Smith, Wareham Smith, Henry Wickham Steed, Sir Arthur Willert, H. W. Wilson and twenty-eight others. The fathers of each of the printing union chapels each received £50, and he also remembered his valet, Pine his chauffeur, his mother's attendant, his housekeeper and Sandy Thomson, his golf professional.

Harold Rothermere was given the final choice of purchaser for Associated Newspapers Ltd, as long as 'The concern it is sold to must have most of its members of British birth.' In the event, it remained in the family's hands, where it has stayed to this day. In order to pay the £2 million death duties on his estate and all his bequests, *The*

Times had to be sold. Sir Campbell Stuart handled the negotiations by which John Jacob Astor MP bought Northcliffe's interest, despite a formidable bid by a chagrined Lord Rothermere. Astor immediately replaced Steed with Geoffrey Dawson, who remained as editor until September 1941, and is today best known for his support for the policy of appeasement.

Had Northcliffe lived for another two months, he would have had the great satisfaction of seeing the fall of Lloyd George, Britain's last Liberal prime minister. 'It was a good thing that I did not get turned out while he was alive,' Lloyd George joked, 'or he would have claimed he had done it.'[78]

As Northcliffe had predicted, Kathleen Wrohan died shortly after, outliving him by a less than a year. He had not made provision for her or her children in his will, but had been very generous to them throughout their lives. She died of myocardial degeneration in the Cliff Coombe nursing home in Broadstairs on 4 July 1923 and was buried three days later. She was (probably) fifty-one. Rothermere sent 'some nice blue flowers' to her funeral, which was also attended by Leicester Harmsworth, Sir George Sutton, Mr Arnholz, Sophie Fenton and Dr Price. She left £100 to Harry Pine in her will, but the rest was divided between Alfred John Francis Alexander Wrohan, Katherine Dorothea Geraldine Mary Northcliffe Wrohan and John Harold Northcliffe Wrohan, her adopted children.

Mary married Sir Robert Hudson six months after Northcliffe's death, which was too soon for the family, and Cecil, who later became Lord Harmsworth, declined her request to give her away. She later said that her short marriage to Hudson, who died in November 1927, was the happiest period of her life.[79] Afterwards she lived in some style in Virginia Water in Surrey, continuing to raise money for wounded veterans. Northcliffe's niece Enid Stokes noted that when Mary was in her early nineties, she was 'spry ... as well as living a full social life at the Dorchester in the week'.[80] When Geoffrey Harmsworth visited her in 1948, she told him, 'Alfred was a *dear* – a genius – he could be everything – gentle and tender, then harsh and ruthless – but he should *never* have married. I am terribly proud of him, and he gave me everything.'[81] He noted that 'She found that

Hudson's personality contributed a calm and serenity which Mary had not known as the wife of Alfred.'[82] She died in July 1963, aged ninety-five.[83]

One strange epilogue to Northcliffe's life was the way, in that time of belief in spiritualism, the paranormal and mediums, that Arthur Conan Doyle, Hannen Swaffer and Louise Owen all separately tried to raise him in seances.[84] Swaffer even wrote a book about it in 1926 entitled *Northcliffe's Return*. While Northcliffe purportedly imparted some less than useful advice such as, 'Don't chew the end of your pencils when you write,' and, 'Juicy figs are much better,' he also supposedly informed Swaffer that 'I am not dead but alive. Can you imagine me inert? Was it my body that lived? It was my mind driven by my will. My mind still lives.'[85]

Thirteen years after Northcliffe's death, his friend and confidant, the journalist John Prioleau, wrote in his unpublished memoirs of his sense of loss: 'I missed him, flaring rages and all, for many years after he died something vital, inspiring, had gone out of my life ... Fleet Street was no longer the Street of Adventure.'[86]

CONCLUSION

THE NAPOLEON OF FLEET STREET

'There is a great art in feeling the pulse of the people.'[1]

LORD NORTHCLIFFE, *North American Review*
January 1901

'If Northcliffe could be ruthless, he could also be big-hearted and magnificently encouraging.'[3]

DAVID LLOYD GEORGE, *War Memoirs* 1933

'Northcliffe liked war-paint and blood-curdling howls. But he also made English newspapers the best in the world; and he established the freedom of the press on the only firm foundation ... newspapers have a right to exist only if they can pay their bills.'[2]

A. J. P. TAYLOR, *Politics in Wartime* 1964

Great men are seldom nice men. They can display assertiveness, ruthlessness and other unattractive features in their quest to change the world around them and to fashion it in their own image. There are plenty of occasions in these pages when Lord Northcliffe displayed traits of discourtesy and egotism which marred his personality. To set against all that, however, it cannot be denied that he was one of the great men of his era.

Wars are not won by milk and rosewater, and that was especially true of the First World War. It took someone of a harsh and inflexible resolve to propagate the fact that Herbert Asquith's Liberal government's havering over compulsory conscription before January 1916 might spell disaster on the Western Front. Northcliffe played an important part in replacing Asquith with David Lloyd George that December, which greatly energised the British war effort. Similarly, the merciless naval blockade that did so much to starve Germany into submission by November 1918 had long been advocated by Northcliffe. The fact that he controlled some 40 per cent of the British press meant that the government could not escape his ceaseless demands for a more vigorous prosecution of almost every aspect of the war.

Military historians will long debate the merits or otherwise of the attritional military tactics adopted by the British High Command on the Western Front, but Northcliffe's support of Sir Douglas Haig meant that they could be pursued until eventually, after the effusion of seas of blood, they helped deliver victory after victory in the final hundred days of the conflict.[4] In his seven visits to the Western Front, Northcliffe made his own estimations and stood by them. His opposition to the failing Gallipoli and Salonika campaigns helped doom both. Moreover, his direct personal contribution to the winning of the war – principally as the head of the British War Mission to the United States in 1917, and as the Director of Propaganda in Enemy Countries in 1918 – was considerable, as even his detractors accepted. Charles Seymour, Colonel House's biographer, wrote that 'Lord Northcliffe organised at Crewe House the most effective scheme of enemy propaganda known to modern history.' Its effectiveness was attested to by the Kaiser, Hindenburg and Lûdendorff.[5]

In 1984, the historian A. J. A. Morris blamed Northcliffe's 'jingo rags' and 'simple-minded, vulgar trash' for the enthusiasm with which Britons embraced the First World War.[6] Yet in fact Northcliffe got Britons psychologically ready for the struggle, explaining cogently why it needed to be fought. 'He was right to see the dangers of war with Germany,' writes the historian Paul Preston, 'and right again to flay the inert prosecution of that dreadful conflict once it came.'[7] The oft-made accusations that Northcliffe bore responsibility for the war breaking out can be safely discarded: that was the fault of Imperial Germany, with its sabre-rattling Kaiser, rearmament programme (especially at sea), militaristic society, Schlieffen Plan, blank cheque to Austria-Hungary over Serbia in July 1914, invasion of neutral Belgium, and so on.[8] By warning the British people of Wilhelmine Germany's intentions over many years, Northcliffe filled much the same role before the First World War as Winston Churchill did with Nazi Germany before the Second, including putting forward radical armament proposals to try to deter the enemy from going to war in the first place.

Many of the measures that were taken for granted by the time of the Second World War had been championed by Northcliffe during its predecessor. As an eloquent pioneer of military air power long before 1914, Northcliffe showed great prescience in recognising how important it could be in protecting Britain. Northcliffe's demand for air defence dwarfed all his other campaigns, including those for wholemeal bread, tramways, a new type of hat, tastier peas, daylight saving, telephones in police stations, and louder bells on fire engines. Similarly, he advocated the rationing of all primary foodstuffs, the employment of women for the factory jobs vacated by men going to the front, the convoy system, a small War Cabinet, a Munitions Ministry, and many other policies necessary to fight a Total War – and all in the era before such a concept existed.[9]

On occasion, Northcliffe's advocacy undoubtedly went too far, helping to create an unnecessarily hostile atmosphere towards conscientious objectors, German-born British citizens ('enemy aliens') and blameless public servants such as Lord Haldane and Prince Louis of Battenberg. His belief in the 'Hidden Hand' conspiracy theory was also reprehensible.

In calling for a national government in May 1915 and the Lloyd George coalition in December 1916, Northcliffe supported both wartime political developments that presaged Winston Churchill's own National Government coalition of May 1940. Another far-sighted attitude Northcliffe adopted long before the outbreak of the Great War was his strong advocacy of the closest possible Anglo–American ties; he was a supporter of the concepts of the Special Relationship and the united action of the English-speaking peoples even before Churchill provided those names for them. 'There is nothing I rejoice in so much as co-operation between the American and British peoples,' he wrote to Arthur Whitten Brown when he discovered that the aviator was an American who had been born in Scotland, 'the only thing that, in my opinion, can maintain the peace of the world'.[10]

'I have never seen any allusion to what is surely true,' wrote the diarist and novelist Marie Belloc Lowndes in August 1946,

> that among those few who helped to win the Battle of Britain, a place should be found for the man who was long dead when it took place ... From the day Northcliffe saw the brothers Wright try out their flying machine ... he realised what may be called the potentialities of flying. He spent large sums of money for air races round Britain and more important to him, his time and energy in encouraging the science of aeronautics.[11]

It was true; an historian has written of Northcliffe's £10,000 prize for a London-to-Manchester flight that 'This remarkable stimulus to mechanical flight cannot be overestimated.'[12] Yet Northcliffe's campaign has been damned as a failure by one detractor merely because 'Frenchmen won his aviation prizes.'[13] The point of the prizes was not that they should be won by the English-speaking peoples – as the largest of them was, by Alcock and Whitten-Brown – but that the world should be alerted to the military potential of manned flight. Louis Blériot's flight over the English Channel was just as capable as a non-Frenchman of demonstrating Northcliffe's point about the perils of Britain's new strategic position.

Overthrowing a prime minister in the middle of a world war was no small task, yet it had to be done. The talents and qualities needed for pre-war diplomacy and preparation are not the same as those required for the grand strategy-making and morale-boosting once blood has begun to be shed. Herbert Asquith had long outlived his value to wartime Britain by December 1916; Northcliffe recognised this and moreover was determined to do something about it. Even Asquith's supporter Sir Edward Grey was later to remark that

'Asquith's government has never acted except in response to public opinion and I am most grateful to *The Times* and *Daily Mail* for kicking it into action on many occasions.'[14]

'He confronted the Asquith and Lloyd George governments on almost every issue,' the historian Richard Davenport-Hines has correctly written of Northcliffe's contribution to victory in the Great War:

> Censorship, finance, recruitment, conscription, the shells shortage of 1915, munitions supply, war strategy, the blockade, food, foreign policy, air power, propaganda and peace terms were all the subjects of his campaigns ... No-one outside the General Staffs or the Cabinet had a greater impact on the British war performance. He helped raise money and recruits, improve munitions supply, demoralise the enemy and protect Anglo-American and Anglo-French relations.[15]

When Britain faced an existential struggle for survival in the Great War, Northcliffe's power was, in the words of his *Daily Mail* obituary, 'used to stimulate the determination of the country to greater efforts to achieve victory'. William Hughes, the prime minister of Australia, wrote in a eulogy that Northcliffe was 'one of the great forces for making for victory during the war'.[16] Northcliffe wanted no epitaph, but that would have made a fine one (especially if slightly better edited).

Northcliffe's dream of having journalists allowed at the front was not to be realised until after his death, but during the Second World War his contention that it would be good for national morale also proved correct. Northcliffe showed similar prescience in large things and small – be it the rise of China, decimal currency* or the neon lights of Piccadilly Circus. 'I am looking forward to the day,' he wrote to his secretary H. G. Price, 'when, inside your hat, there will be a small gadget enabling me to keep in touch with you wherever you are.'[17] (Price replied, 'God forbid.')

---

* He was a vice-president of the Decimal Association.

~

Half of Northcliffe's reputation must lie in the signal service he performed for Britain and civilisation in helping to save Europe – and thus, in the early twentieth century geopolitical context, the world – from the hegemony of Wilhelmine Germany. The other half lies in the fact that he was, in the words of *The Encyclopaedia of the British Press,* 'the greatest newspaperman'.[18] As the founder of the *Daily Mail, Daily Mirror* and countless magazines, the saviour of *The Times, The Observer* and the *Evening News,* and the owner of several other regional papers, as well as the *Continental Daily Mail* and the *Overseas Daily Mail,* not for nothing was he regularly described as 'The Napoleon of Fleet Street'.[19] Without him, several newspapers of today would not exist.

The praise for Northcliffe's journalistic genius was often tempered with personal criticism, but it was tremendous, from friend and foe alike: 'He understood popular journalism as it has never been understood before or since'[20] (Evelyn Wrench); 'Without doubt the most magnetic figure of his generation'[21] (Hamilton Fyfe); 'The superman of British journalism'[22] (J. A. Hammerton); 'As a material force, there has been nothing in journalism to compare with him'[23] (Northcliffe's *Guardian* obituary); 'Quite simply he was the greatest press lord of them all'[24] (John McEwen); 'The emperor of the British kingdom of ink'[25] (Anthony Howard). 'Whatever the political world may think of Northcliffe,' wrote Lord Beaverbrook, who was in a position to know, 'one factor can never be disputed. He was the greatest figure who ever strode down Fleet Street.'[26]

'Papers can be as transient as mushrooms and butterflies,' A. P. Wadsworth, the editor of *The Guardian,* said in 1955. 'A few papers rise and become great, decline and fade away leaving no trace except their mouldering files in library cellars.'[27] That tended not to be the case with the newspapers that Northcliffe brought into being or saved from bankruptcy.

'Northcliffe knew that content is all,' Sir David English, editor of the *Daily Mail* from 1971 to 1992, once said.[28] Northcliffe obtained that content by paying writers on acceptance, and at much higher rates than competitors, meaning that writers for Amalgamated Newspapers did not have to wait weeks for their pay.[29] He also paid high salaries to female writers before anyone else in Fleet Street, recognising the purchasing power women were increasingly wielding.[30] As well as wages, Northcliffe fought to raise the professional standing of reporters and sub-editors, and succeeded almost out of recognition.[31] He lifted circulations to heights never known before, and revolutionised the advertising industry. No less an American newspaperman than William Randolph Hearst stated of Northcliffe's edition of *The World* on New Year's Day 1901 that 'All of us newspapermen smiled patronisingly but continued to make our voluminous newspapers. It was not until years later that the success of the tabloid in England compelled its adoption in this country.'[32]

Northcliffe's personal defects – his vendettas, his petty cruelties, his rows and rages – have to be set against his great acts of kindness: the fund he set up for Boer War soldiers' dependents; his fondness and provision for Kathleen Wrohan's adopted children (assuming he knew they were not his); putting Elmwood's gardens at the disposal of local orphans; the 6,000 people he remembered in his will; the kerbside tramps he occasionally fed, watered and clothed; the millions he raised for the Red Cross during the Great War; his establishment of the braille edition of the *Daily Mail*; the money he provided for Westminster Abbey, the 1908 London Olympics, the Dover Patrol Memorial, and so on. These speak to a great generosity. 'Money does not bring happiness,' Northcliffe would say, 'but it can round off the corners of life, in that it enables one to travel, and to help crowds of lame dogs over stiles.'[33]

R. D. Blumenfeld, the editor of the competitor *Daily Express*, described Northcliffe as a 'cyclone of emotional contradictions'.[34] These contradictions were indeed profound. In these pages we have seen a tough, ruthless businessman for whom freshly cut flowers gave joy.[35] He entered Fleet Street as a freelance writer, but admitted that 'I do not think I ever, after I left school, took any pleasure in writing for its own sake.'[36] He wanted to make his name in Fleet Street, but used *noms de plume*. He was a prominent proponent of family values who kept a series of mistresses. He admired the British Empire, but only toured it comprehensively in the last year of his life, when he provocatively wondered aloud whether India was worth keeping. He cheerfully put up with immense discomfort when reporting from war zones, but would then complain about every bedroom he was shown in the Paris Ritz.[37] He was an ardent Unionist who supported the Irish peace treaty and partition. Northcliffe's mercurial, contradictory nature was summed up by J. A. Hammerton's description of his 'complex, elusive, headstrong, irritating, charming, unreasonable, gentle, rude, lovable, unforgettable personality'.[38]

~

'As regards abuse,' Northcliffe once said, 'I am a pachyderm.'[39] That was just as well, considering the amount of it he received. Indeed, the historian Richard Davenport-Hines considers that 'No Englishman in his lifetime was more abused.'[40] A. G. Gardiner, the editor of the *Daily News*, called Northcliffe 'a poisoner of the streams of human intercourse' and 'an unscrupulous enemy of human society' who had 'the common mind to an uncommon degree'.[41] Sir Ian Hamilton, whose career Northcliffe helped destroy over Gallipoli, wrote of 'that reptile Harmsworth'.[42] Sir John Simon wrote that 'He has sold his country for halfpence.'[43] Harold Begbie considered that 'He has no moral scruples in a fight, none at all.'[44] Lloyd George said Northcliffe 'had a bad effect on the public mind'.[45] A German-American writer called Hansen wrote colourfully in the early 1920s of how 'the Northcliffes send their Niagaras of slime through the soul of the English-speaking peoples'.[46] Ezra Pound, meanwhile, placed Northcliffe in Hell in his Canto XV. Evelyn Wrench, whose career Northcliffe had fostered, accused him in 1934 of a 'lack of character'. H. G. Wells, who as we have seen was hardly objective, accused the Northcliffe Press of 'an entire disregard of good taste, good value, educational influence, social consequences or political responsibility'.[47] Worst, and most unjustifiably of all, A. J. P. Taylor sought to persuade readers that 'It is difficult to resist the impression that [Northcliffe] was an early sketch for Adolf Hitler.'[48]

In 1922, the German political philosopher Oswald Spengler published the second volume of his *The Decline of the West*, in which he described how 'The dictator of the press – Northcliffe! – keeps the slave-gang of his readers under the whip of his leading articles, telegrams and pictures.'[49] Yet, in fact, no-one was being forced to part with their halfpennies, pennies and threepenny bits in order to buy Northcliffe's papers, let alone so many tens of billions of times across a third of a century. They did it because they thought that the leading articles, news and illustrations were better than any of his competitors' on the news-stands. Intellectuals might despise concepts such as market competition, but it explains Northcliffe's success far better than concepts of dictatorship and slave-gangs.

Other critics cited his 'overweening vanity'[50] (John McEwen), or described him variously as 'only a scarecrow'[51] (Lord Milner), 'a great journalistic Barnum'[52] (Lloyd George again), 'commonplace and flashy'[53] (C. P. Scott), 'a simpleton in Westminster'[54] (A. P. Ryan), 'the arch-scaremonger'[55] (Niall Ferguson) and 'Our Citizen Kane' who 'made his own sizeable contribution to filling the military cemeteries in Belgium and in France' (Anthony Howard).[56] Of course, Northcliffe would have welcomed all such criticism, so long as he had a chance to defend himself. 'When they cease to attack us,' he told Hannen Swaffer, 'they'll cease to read us. The day I do not find any attacks on me in the other papers I'll start a paper, all my own. To attack myself with. And there'll be some bite in it too.'[57]

Of one common accusation he was innocent. The charge of megalomania was regularly levelled at him, but only became true once he was suffering from the horrific disease that ultimately killed him. Before that – and for all his admiration of Napoleon – Northcliffe was perfectly sane, indeed profoundly calculating, rather than megalomaniacal. Megalomaniacs don't make self-deprecatory remarks and jokes, which he did constantly. 'My chief companion, Prioleau, and I, went around the world together without a cross word,' he wrote in a book. 'It says a great deal for Prioleau.'[58] When he did exceed his boundaries, as with Lloyd George in 1919, it was because there were no historical precedents for a press proprietor as powerful as him. Northcliffe was also innocent of what one biographer referred to as 'the violence that was part of his nature', which also only emerged when he was suffering from his undiagnosed endocarditis.[59]

Now that mental illness has finally been de-stigmatised, Northcliffe should no longer be morally blamed for it, as almost all his many biographers have hitherto done.

When *The Labour Leader* newspaper published its obituary of Northcliffe, claiming that 'Never by any chance did he offer to his readers anything that would make them think,' the future Labour chancellor of the exchequer Philip Snowden corrected it, saying that he had been a regular contributor to the Northcliffe press on socialist topics and had never had his copy altered by so much as a word or comma.[60] The historian Robert Blake's accusation that at times Northcliffe used language suggesting 'that he almost favoured a military dictatorship and the temporary suspension of parliamentary government' was similarly unsupported by anything other than unreliable second-hand evidence.[61]

There was a good deal of snobbery in the criticism of Northcliffe, and hatred of his unapologetically bourgeois, Conservative and Middle England *Daily Mail*, let alone of his magazines such as *Answers*, *Comic Cuts* and *Illustrated Chips*. The snobbery of the intellectual classes towards Northcliffe scarcely abated after his death. Reviewing the history of the *Times Literary Supplement* in 2001, the writer Joseph Epstein described him as 'blustery and profit-minded and [he] would have lowered the paper's standards but for fear of being identified for the philistine he indubitably was'.[62] In fact, it was Northcliffe's victory in the price war in early 1914 that saved the *Times Literary Supplement*, and a man less fearful of what the literary world thought of him is hard to imagine. Epstein admits that the *Supplement* 'in some years lost money', but apparently for a proprietor to care about that was to be reprehensibly 'profit-minded'. Northcliffe's idea that the *Supplement* should try to sell more copies has been described as 'bullying' by Bevis Hillier.[63] The assumption too often was that it is the duty of businessmen like Northcliffe to lose money so that *litterateurs* can enjoy high-minded magazines.

Although Northcliffe was constantly sneered at for not having 'a trained mind' – by which was meant that he had not attended Oxford or Cambridge – he was intelligent enough, having left school at sixteen, to read history and literature avidly, write three books and two pamphlets, have a considerable knowledge of press history, a fine taste in music, and be an observant commentator on his many travels abroad.[64] This was not 'intellectual obliquity', of which Piers Brendon accuses him, rather it was commendable self-education.[65] Tom Clarke's belief that Northcliffe was 'more interested in people than things' naturally made him suspect to intellectuals.[66]

The intellectuals' wider dismissal of Victorian villa life and its reading taste is reflected in criticisms such as, 'Suburbia's conservatism was espoused in the pages of its favourite newspaper, the Daily Mail [which] played a conscious role in constructing its audience's jingoism' and the accusation that 'An opportunity to coax the mind into greater rigour, discernment or discrimination was thrown away in pursuit of money.'[67] That readers largely stayed loyal can be put down to Northcliffe's sixth sense for what they wanted, while his commissioning of pieces by writers of the lasting quality of Joseph Conrad, Arthur Conan Doyle, H. G. Wells, Max Beerbohm and Rudyard Kipling reflected his belief that his readers appreciated literary style. He masterminded a revolution in the content and purpose of newspapers by giving the public what they wanted, rather than what others considered was good for them.

~

Much more acute criticisms might be made of Northcliffe than the sheer avalanche of hatred that greeted his attempt to put readable and entertaining and patriotic newspapers on the news-stands. For example, his opposition to sending the British Expeditionary Force to France in August 1914 showed absurd strategic caution, and his ad hominem attack on Lord Kitchener during the Shells Scandal which kept the War Secretary in situ for the rest of his life. Yet it was also in many ways Northcliffe's finest hour. As Hammerton later wrote, 'When Stock Exchange numbskulls publicly burnt the Daily Mail in their pitiful ignorance of the true state of affairs, the valiance of its proprietor stood at its highest.'[68]

Northcliffe can be accused of being an ingénu when it came to the ways of politics, often coming off worse against politicians, especially the most formidable of the era, David Lloyd George.

(The manner in which Northcliffe refused Lloyd George's offer of the Air Ministry in 1917 was reprehensibly rude.) Northcliffe did not much like politicians as a tribe, and the long list of those with whom he fell out – including Lord Rosebery, Winston Churchill, Arthur Balfour, Lord Milner, Edward Carson, Bonar Law, and most spectacularly Lloyd George – can be seen as testimony to his independent-mindedness rather than acts of personal treachery. It is not the job of press proprietors to get too close to politicians; they ought to behave in what they see as their readers' and countrymen's best interests. 'Unstable though he might have been', Sir Simon Jenkins has written, 'Northcliffe was never guilty of being under any politician's thumb for long.'[69]

Northcliffe was understandably accused of inconsistency, but he recognised that too much consistency in a newspaper was bad for circulation. Harder to justify than Northcliffe's behaviour towards politicians was the way that he also fell out with so many friends and colleagues. Captain Beaumont, Evelyn Wrench, H. G. Wells, Harold Begbie, Arthur and Ruth Lee, Generals Kiggell and Charteris, Charles Repington, Geoffrey Dawson and Sandy Thompson – all were eventually either thrown over by him or escaped, bruised, from his embrace. In that sense, Lloyd George's quip about Northcliffe being as constant as a grasshopper was justified. From the 1890s, his marriage to Mary was one of convenience and residual affection, and he also broke with his three leading mistresses Betsy von Hutten, Kathleen Wrohan and Louise Owen. His last words – instructions to tell his Mother that 'she is the only one' – were among the truest he ever spoke.

There was undoubtedly a Jekyll and Hyde aspect to Northcliffe, an analogy often used by those who knew him well. 'Some day Northcliffe will find his Boswell,' wrote Wrench. 'Hitherto none of his biographers has done justice to his many-sided personality and magnetism. Like most of us, Northcliffe had two sides to his character, but during those early years I rarely saw the Hyde – it was the Jekyll that I met.'[70] Steed felt the same, writing, 'It was possible to have a great affection for him, but, unfortunately there was another side of his nature capable of destroying one's sentiments towards him.'[71] Northcliffe himself might not have disagreed. Writing in his diary from Cairo on 1 February 1922, he observed: 'Yesterday, some of the papers here were very naughty about me. Today, all that I've seen are most flattering. I suppose there is something to be said for both points of view.'

The Jekyll and Hyde facet to Northcliffe's character was echoed by Norman Angell, who worked for him for ten years in senior positions yet nonetheless wrote in his memoirs that Northcliffe was 'a man whose politics I detested and whose influence on the public through his papers of enormous circulation I believed to be malign'.[72] Yet even the Nobel Peace Prize-winner Angell had to commend Northcliffe for the way he was able 'to reach the mind of the British public more successfully than any other man of his generation'.[73]

'He loved power and people,' Campbell Stuart wrote of Northcliffe. 'To him money was always a secondary consideration.'[74] J. A. Spender agreed, writing that money to Northcliffe was only ever 'the means to power, and he was entirely without purse-pride in any of the ordinary relations of life'.[75] Once Northcliffe had provided for himself and his family, escaping the grinding financial humiliations of his youth, he saw his life's work as what Steed called 'solicitude for the future welfare of Great Britain and of the Empire'.[76]

This is the key to understanding Alfred Harmsworth, Lord Northcliffe. He was a man driven first by money, then by power, but ultimately by an imperial patriotism that was neither commendable nor deplorable, but a mixture of both. The period of his greatest influence coincided almost exactly with the summit of British glory. The *Daily Mail* was founded the year before Queen Victoria's Diamond Jubilee, and he died just as the British Empire reached its largest-ever territorial extent, as a result of the post-war peace treaties. Imperialism was his lifelong creed, and his belief in the empire was messianic. When Germany threatened that empire, and thus everything in which he believed, Northcliffe threw his all into its defence – and especially his genius for connecting to the ordinary Briton.

Lord Northcliffe was a great man. Like many other great men, he had serious flaws, some forgivable, others not. But his achievements are inarguable: he was the greatest newspaperman in British history, and he made a major contribution to victory in the First World War. It is no exaggeration to say that he shaped the landscape of modern journalism and thus, in many ways, the mind of an empire.

ACKNOWLEDGEMENTS

I would like to thank Jonathan Harmsworth, 4th Viscount Rothermere, and his wife Claudia for making the extensive privately held Northcliffe Archive Papers and the Harmsworth Family Archive fully available to me for the writing of this book. Similarly, I would like to thank Vyvyan and Alexandra Harmsworth for their hospitality and generosity; they could not have been more helpful and it was a delight to get to know them. The Northcliffe Archive Papers, which make up the main body of the research for this book, are quoted by kind permission of the Daily Mail General Trust.

Geordie Greig helped me profusely with his advice, encouragement and insights, and by lending me books from his extensive library. I should very much like to thank him, and also Rupert Murdoch for his memories of his father's friendship with Lord Northcliffe.

One of the pleasures of writing this book has been being in communication with Prof. J. Lee Thompson, the author of a distinguished life of Northcliffe, whose knowledge and thoughts in innumerable emails has been invaluable.

In trying to establish the truth about Northcliffe's somewhat complicated family and love life, I have been immensely helped by the genealogist Angela Aldam of Family Folios and the DNA expert Amelia Bennett of Mia Genealogy for their excellent sleuthing in tracking down Northcliffe's two secret 'families'. I would also like to thank all those who so generously allowed themselves to be DNA-tested in order finally to bring to a conclusion various century-long family mysteries surrounding Northcliffe's relationship with Kathleen Wrohan. These included Rebecca Bjorklund, Wendy Croome, Lucas Stokes, Theresa Stokes, Ian Wrohan and others.

The cause of Lord Northcliffe's death has proved a source of controversy for nearly a century, so I decided to send all the known symptoms to some of the most senior doctors in the field. For their expert clinical diagnoses, I would very much like to thank Professor Ronak Rajani, consultant cardiologist in heart valve disease and cardiac imaging at the Cardiovascular Directorate of Guy's and St Thomas' NHS Foundation Trust; Dr John Klein, consultant micro-biologist at the Department of Infectious Diseases at Guy's and St Thomas' NHS Foundation Trust; and Professor Michael Henein, consultant cardiologist at The Harley Street Clinic.

Dambisa Moyo and Jared Smith were typically generous in their hospitality at Palo Alto while I was writing this book at the Hoover Institution at Stanford University, where I am honoured to be the Roger and Martha Mertz Visiting Fellow.

A large number of people have helped me over various aspects of Northcliffe's life (and death), and I would like to place on record my profound thanks to Kevin Beatty, the CEO of DMG Media; Professor Jeremy Black for showing me Desmond Rothermere's cor-respondence; Robin Brodhurst; Richard Cohen; Rod Christie-Miller and Alex Maunders of Schillings for interpreting Northcliffe's will for me; Lucien Forbes, Holly Rowsell and Robyn Warren of the Grand Falls–Windsor Heritage Society; the Rt Hon. Michael Gove for taking me onto the roof at Carlton Gardens where Northcliffe died; James Holland and Paul Beaver for Northcliffe's connections with the RAF; Ross Hunter, president of the Sylvan Debating Club; Roly Keating and Jacqueline Pitcher at the British Library; Alice Kelly at the Rothermere American Institute at Oxford University; Lord King for explaining the economics of Imperial Preference and tariff reform; Arthur King of the North Foreland Golf Club; Richard Langworth for his insights into Winston Churchill's rela-tionship with Northcliffe; John and Celia Lee for showing me Jean Hamilton's diary references to Northcliffe; Maria Lucas-Tooth at the Beefsteak Club; Robert Noel (Ulster King of Arms) and Adam Tuck (Rouge Dragon Puirsuivant) at the College of Arms;

Northcliffe's great-great-nephew Edward Parks for permission to reproduce Philip de Laszlo's portrait of Lady Northcliffe; Tim Pleydell-Bouverie; David Richards for his insights into Northcliffe's relations with Rudyard Kipling; Maiko Jeong Shun Rothermere; Jeremy Solel; Teresa Stokes for her research on Kathleen Wrohan, advice and insights and for letting me see family documents; and Lord Waldegrave and Stephanie Coane for allowing me to research in the Eton College Library at short notice.

For their immensely helpful comments on the manuscript, I would like to thank Richard Gohen, Adrian Fort, Zewditu Gebreyohanes, Augusta Harris, Jerry del Missier, and J. Lee Thompson.

My publishers Ian Marshall and Kat Ailes could not have been more good-natured and efficient, and of course my agent Georgina Capel has been both a rock and a saint.

This book is dedicated to Ian and Natalie Livingstone, whose creation and cultivation of the Cliveden Literary Festival, of which I am proud to be President, has been a great joy to me.

Andrew Roberts
London
January 2022

NOTES

Introduction

1 *Daily Mail*, 5 November 1903, p.5
2 Ibid.
3 BL Add MS 62391 f.55
4 Owen, *The Real Lord Northcliffe*, p.23

Chapter One: Youth

1 Spender, *Life, Journalism and Politics* II, p.165
2 Viollis, *Lord Northcliffe*, title-page
3 Ferris, *House of Northcliffe*, p.16
4 Ibid., p.11
5 Edwards, 'Geraldine Harmsworth', p.466
6 Wilson, *Lord Northcliffe*, p.22
7 Brendon, *Eminent Edwardians*, p.10
8 Clarke, *My Northcliffe Diary*, p.19
9 *Evening News*, 31 August 1925
10 Wrench, *Uphill*, p.141
11 Brendon, *Eminent Edwardians*, p.9
12 Edwards, 'Geraldine Harmsworth', p.466; Taylor, *The Great Outsiders*, p.3
13 Taylor, *The Great Outsiders*, p.6
14 Owen, *The Real Lord Northcliffe*, p.34
15 Fyfe, *Northcliffe*, p.23
16 Northcliffe Archive Papers RPR.022
17 Clarke, *My Northcliffe Diary*, p.106
18 Northcliffe Archive Papers RPR.027; Brendon, *Eminent Edwardians*, p.9; Edwards, 'Geraldine Harmsworth', p.467
19 Northcliffe Archive Papers RPR.022
20 Owen, *The Real Lord Northcliffe*, p.25
21 Northcliffe Archive Papers RPR.022
22 Thompson, *Northcliffe*, p.3
23 Northcliffe Archive Papers Harmsworth Chronology
24 Brendon, *Eminent Edwardians*, p.10
25 Sylvan History Committee, *The History of the Sylvan Debating Club*, p.11
26 Northcliffe Archive Papers Alfred Harmsworth Snr 1870 Diary
27 Ibid.
28 *Answers*, 28 May 1892
29 Thompson, *Northcliffe*, p.5
30 Pound and Harmsworth, *Northcliffe* p.29
31 Northcliffe Archive Papers Alfred Harmsworth Snr file
32 My thanks to Geordie Greig for showing me this letter.
33 Pound and Harmsworth, *Northcliffe*, p.35
34 Ryan, *Lord Northcliffe*, p.22
35 Wilson, *Lord Northcliffe*, p.36
36 Ibid.
37 Fyfe, *Northcliffe*, p.30
38 Ryan, *Lord Northcliffe* p.23
39 Taylor, *The Great Outsiders*, p.9

40 Brendon, *Eminent Edwardians*, p.12
41 Ibid., p.12
42 Oosterhuis, 'Cycling, Modernity and National Culture', p.236
43 Pemberton, *Lord Northcliffe*, p.23
44 Ibid., p.11
45 Pound and Harmsworth, *Northcliffe*, p.41
46 Ryan, *Lord Northcliffe*, p.31
47 Northcliffe Archive Papers *Fame and Fortune*, p.48
48 Owen, *The Real Lord Northcliffe*, p.14
49 Ryan, *Lord Northcliffe*, p.28
50 Ibid., p.29
51 King, *Strictly Personal*, p.60
52 *The Times*, 29 August 1922, p.13
53 Northcliffe Archive Papers Alfred Benjamin Smith file
54 Pemberton, *Northcliffe*, p.9
55 Andrews and Taylor, *Lords and Laborers of the Press*, p.50
56 Clarke, *My Northcliffe Diary*, p.133
57 Lawrence (ed.), *Journalism as a Profession*, p.59
58 Pemberton, *Northcliffe*, p.30
59 Northcliffe Archive Papers, *Photography for Amateurs*, p.1
60 *Youth*, 5 December 1883
61 *Sunday Times*, 10 October 1948
62 *Oldham Chronicle*, 23 May 1885; *The Graphic*, 23 May 1885; *The Architect*, 13 November 1885; *The Metropolitan*, 16 April 1887
63 Northcliffe Archive Papers RPR.020
64 Northcliffe Archive Papers RPR.017
65 Northcliffe Archive Papers Alfred Harmsworth Jnr 1886 Diary
66 Ibid.

Chapter Two:
'Schemo Magnifico'

1 Ferris, *The House of Northcliffe*, p.21
2 Donovan, *Conrad and the Harmsworth Empire*, p.157
3 Ibid.
4 Ryan, *Lord Northcliffe*, p.36
5 Thompson, *Northcliffe*, p.9
6 Finkelstein (ed.), *The Edinburgh History of the British and Irish Press*, p.56
7 Ibid.
8 Thompson, *Northcliffe*, p.9
9 *The Times*, 29 August 1922, p.13
10 Northcliffe Archive Papers Geraldine Mary Harmsworth File
11 Taylor, *The Great Outsiders*, p.14
12 Ferris, *The House of Northcliffe*, p.32
13 Northcliffe Archive Papers RPR.017
14 Northcliffe Archive Papers Harmsworth Chronology
15 Brendon, *Eminent Edwardians*, p.15
16 Camplin, *The Rise of the Plutocrats*, p.83
17 Finkelstein (ed.), *The Edinburgh History of the British and Irish Press*, p.132
18 *Answers to Correspondents*, 30 June 1888, p.1
19 Ibid., p.4
20 Ibid., p.7
21 Ibid., p.9
22 Northcliffe Archive Papers RPR.017
23 Ferris, *The House of Northcliffe*, p.8
24 Ibid.
25 *Answers to Correspondents*, 9 June 1888, p.1
26 *Answers to Correspondents*, 23 June 1888, p.9
27 *Answers to Correspondents*, 16 June 1888, p.3
28 Ibid.
29 *Answers to Correspondents*, 7 July 1888, p.13
30 *Answers to Correspondents*, 20 Oct 1888, p.2
31 Brendon, *Eminent Edwardians*, p.15
32 *Answers to Correspondents*, 1 Sept 1888, p.15
33 Ibid.
34 Griffiths (ed.), *Encyclopedia of the British Press*, p.292
35 Thompson, *Northcliffe*, p.11
36 Heffer, *The Age of Decadence*, p.544

37 Camplin, *The Rise of the Plutocrats*, p.83
38 Ryan, *Lord Northcliffe*, p.47
39 Thompson, *Northcliffe*, p.400 n21
40 Northcliffe Archive Papers, 21 July 1889
41 Ibid.
42 Ryan, *Lord Northcliffe*, p.51
43 Northcliffe Archive Papers Harmsworth Chronology
44 Marquis, 'Words as Weapons', p.468
45 Thompson, *Northcliffe*, p.14
46 Chapman, *British Comics*, p.25
47 *Comic Cuts*, 17 May 1890
48 Chapman, *British Comics*, p.11
49 Heffer, *The Age of Decadence*, p.544
50 Ryan, *Lord Northcliffe*, p.51
51 *Answers*, 23 July 1892
52 Northcliffe Archive Papers North.009
53 Greenwall, *Northcliffe*, p.43
54 Thompson, *Northcliffe*, p.33
55 Private Information
56 Brendon, *Eminent Edwardians*, pp.7–8; Taylor, *The Reluctant Press Lord*, p.113
57 Northcliffe Archive Papers RPR.006
58 Thompson, *Northcliffe*, p.400 n25
59 Northcliffe Archive Papers, Alfred Harmsworth Jnr 1891 Diary
60 Mackenzie, Harmsworth Publications, p.11
61 *Forget-Me-Not*, 12 November 1892, p.16
62 Brendon, *Eminent Edwardians*, p.18
63 *Forget-Me-Not*, 12 November 1892, p.3
64 Ibid., p.1
65 Pierce, *Lord Northcliffe: Transatlantic Influences*, pp.11–12

Chapter Three: 'The Gospel of Loyalty to the Empire'

1 Marcosson, *Adventures in Interviewing*, p.118
2 Northcliffe Archive Papers North.009
3 Ibid.
4 BL Add Mss 62380, Northcliffe Archive Papers, Alfred Harmsworth Jnr 1892 Diary
5 Pound and Hamsworth, *Northcliffe*, p.141
6 *Answers*, 23 July 1892
7 Pound and Harmsworth, *Northcliffe*, p.181
8 James (ed.), *Winston S. Churchill: His Complete Speeches* vol 1, p.28
9 Northcliffe Archive Papers North.009
10 Gardiner, 'Two Journalists', p.250
11 Northcliffe Archive Papers North.009
12 Thompson, *Northcliffe*, p.18
13 Northcliffe Archive Papers Alfred Harmsworth Jnr 1893 Diary
14 Ibid.
15 Brendon, *Eminent Edwardians*, p.20
16 BL Add MS 62382 f.3
17 BL Add MS 62382 f.5
18 Pound and Harmsworth, *Northcliffe*, p.161
19 Clarke, *My Northcliffe Diary*, p.24
20 BL Add MS 62382 f.32
21 *The Geographical Journal*, Vol. 60 No. 4, October 1922, p.320
22 Thompson, *Northcliffe*, p.46
23 BL Add MS 62382 f.18
24 Taylor, *The Great Outsiders*, p.27
25 BL Add MS 62382 f.38
26 Northcliffe Archive Papers North.009
27 Ibid.
28 Smith, *Spilt Ink*, p.25
29 Ferris, *The House of Northcliffe*, p.72
30 Pound and Harmsworth, *Northcliffe*, p.172
31 Northcliffe Archive Papers
32 Smith, *Spilt Ink*, p.89
33 Taylor, *Great Outsiders*, p.29
34 Finkelstein (ed.), *The Edinburgh History of the British and Irish Press*, p.642
35 Ryan, *Lord Northcliffe*, p.55
36 *Evening News*, 31 August 1894
37 Thompson, *Northcliffe*, p.25

38 BL Add MS 62179 f.174
39 Taylor, *The Great Outsiders*, p.28
40 Northcliffe Archive Papers
    North.009
41 BL Add MS 62382 f.42
42 BL Add MS 62382 f.49
43 BL Add MS 62382 f.46
44 BL ADD Mss 62292A f4
45 BL Add MS 62383 f.8
46 Thompson, *Northcliffe*, p.27
47 Northcliffe Archive Papers
    RPR.034
48 Marcosson, *Adventures in
    Interviewing*, p.119
49 Northcliffe Archive Papers
    RPR.017
50 BL Add MS 62382 f.54
51 BL Add MS 62383 f.6
52 BL Add MS 62383 f.26
53 Thompson, *Northcliffe*, p.28
54 Ibid., p.30
55 Ibid.
56 *Evening News*, 1 Jan 1896
57 BL Add MS 62384 f.3
58 *Evening News*, 2 Jan 1896
59 *Evening News*, 4 Jan 1896
60 Mallinson, *1914*, p.182; Hoyer,
    Blood and Iron, p.129
61 BL Add MS 62384 f.8
62 BL Add MS 62384 f.11
63 BL Add MS 62384 f.12

Chapter Four:
'We've Struck a Goldmine'

1   Clarke, *My Northcliffe Diary*,
    p.196
2   Ryan, *Lord Northcliffe*, p.58
3   Brooks, 'Lord Northcliffe and the
    War', p.186
4   Taylor, *The Great Outsiders*, p.31
5   Ibid.
6   Brendon, *Eminent Edwardians*,
    p.22
7   Ryan, *Lord Northcliffe*, p.74
8   BL Add MS 62384 f.21
9   Mackenzie, *The Rise and Progress
    of the Harmsworth Publications*,
    p.25
10 Chalaby, 'Smiling People Make
    People Smile', p.42
11 Donovan, *Conrad and the
    Harmsworth Empire*, p.157
12 Brendon, *Eminent

    Edwardians*, p.36; Koss,
    *The Rise and Fall of the Political
    Press in Britain*,
    p.368
13 Taylor, *The Great Outsiders*, p.32
14 Chalaby, 'Smiling People Make
    People Smile', p.35
15 Cranfield, *The Press and Society*,
    p.220
16 Jones, Kennedy, *Fleet Street and
    Downing Street*, p.149
17 Fyfe, *Northcliffe*, p.286
18 Clarke, *My Northcliffe Diary*,
    p.100
19 Brooks, 'Lord Northcliffe and the
    War', p.187
20 Fyfe, *Northcliffe*, pp.86–87
21 Clarke, *Northcliffe in History*,
    p.181
22 Brendon, *Eminent Edwardians*,
    p.25
23 Ibid.
24 Taylor, *Politics in Wartime*, p.154
25 Pound and Harmsworth,
    Northcliffe, p.200
26 Angell, *After All*, p.120
27 Thompson, *Northcliffe*, p.35
28 Clarke, *My Northcliffe Diary*,
    p.210
29 Angell, *After All*, p.120
30 Heffer, *The Age of Decadence*,
    p.547
31 Northcliffe Archive Papers
    RPR.022
32 Clarke, *My Northcliffe Diary*,
    p.22
33 Ibid., p.202
34 Ryan, *Lord Northcliffe*, p.42
35 Swaffer, *Northcliffe's Return*,
    p.21
36 Brendon, *Eminent Edwardians*,
    p.41
37 Clarke, *My Northcliffe Diary*,
    p.137
38 Angell, *After All*, p.121
39 Clarke, *My Northcliffe Diary*,
    p.186
40 Smith, *Spilt Ink*, p.35
41 *Advertisers Weekly*, 18 August
    1922
42 Smith, *Spilt Ink*, p.31
43 Nevett, *Advertising in Britain*,
    p.82

44 Brendon, *Eminent Edwardians*, p.36
45 Clarke, *My Northcliffe Diary*, p.218
46 Northcliffe Archive Papers RPR.022
47 Swaffer, *Northcliffe's Return*, p.29
48 Northcliffe Archive Papers RPR.022
49 Andrews and Taylor, *Lords and Laborers of the Press*, p.49
50 Clarke, *My Northcliffe Diary*, p.20
51 Northcliffe Archive Papers RPR.022
52 Owen, *The Real Lord Northcliffe*, p.8
53 Wrench, *Struggle*, p.310
54 English, 'Legend of "The Chief"', p.7
55 Brooks, 'Lord Northcliffe and the War', p.188
56 Clarke, *My Northcliffe Diary*, p.204
57 Ibid., p.279
58 Angell, *After All*, p.120
59 Griffiths (ed.), *Encyclopedia of the British Press*, p.184
60 BL Add MS 62384 f.21
61 Brendon, *The Life and Death of the Press Barons*, p.114
62 Taylor, *The Great Outsiders*, p.38
63 Ryan, *Lord Northcliffe*, p.75; Griffiths (ed.), *Encyclopedia of the British Press*, p.184
64 Northcliffe Archive Papers RPR.023
65 Mitchell, *My Fill of Days*, p.272
66 Thompson, *Northcliffe*, p.34
67 BL Add MS 62153 ff.1–2
68 Ryan, *Lord Northcliffe*, p.76
69 Pound and Harmsworth, *Northcliffe*, p.211
70 Griffiths (ed.), *Encyclopedia of the British Press*, p.434
71 Swaffer, *Northcliffe's Return*, p.31
72 BL Add MS 62397 f.148
73 Northcliffe Archive Papers Alfred Benjamin Smith file
74 Owen, *Northcliffe: The Facts*, p.43
75 Ibid.
76 Private Information
77 Pound and Harmsworth, *Lord Northcliffe*, p.208
78 Greenwall, *Northcliffe: Napoleon of Fleet Street*, 1957
79 Pemberton, *Lord Northcliffe*, p.222
80 Lucas, *Wisdom While You Wait*, p.60
81 BL Add MSS 62201 ff.20–21
82 Beefsteak Club Candidates' Book
83 *Daily Mail*, 9 October 1896
84 BL Add MS 62384 f.44
85 Northcliffe Archive Papers RPR.017
86 BL Add MS 62397 f.158
87 Brendon, *Eminent Edwardians*, p.39
88 Ibid., pp.39–40
89 BL Add MS62385 f.4
90 Northcliffe Archive Papers *Hard Truths from India*, Appendix
91 Ibid., preface
92 Ibid., p.1
93 Ibid., p.2
94 Ibid., p.2
95 Ibid., p.3
96 Ibid., p.8
97 Catterall et al (eds), 'Northcliffe's Legacy', p.54
98 *Daily Mail*, 6 January 1897
99 *Daily Mail*, 9 January 1897
100 Catterall et al (eds), 'Northcliffe's Legacy', p.58
101 *Daily Mail*, 14 July 1897
102 Jones, *Fleet Street and Downing Street*, p.146
103 BL ADD MS 62385 f.28
104 BL ADD MS 62385 f.28
105 Thompson, *Northcliffe*, p.44
106 Ibid., p.45
107 BL ADD 62386
108 Pound and Harmsworth, *Northcliffe*, p.235
109 Ibid., pp.235–236
110 Clarke, *My Northcliffe Diary*, p.144
111 Ibid., p.145
112 Ibid., p.146
113 Ibid., p.146
114 Wrench, *Uphill*, p.199
115 Mackenzie, *The Rise and Progress of the Harmsworth Publications*, p.40

116 Morison (ed.), *The History of the Times* IV Part 1, p.131
117 Angell, *After All*, p.96
118 Churchill Documents II, p.1012
119 BL Add MSS 62156 f.1

**Chapter Five:
'We Believe in England'**

1 Wrench, *Uphill*, p.149
2 Northcliffe Archive Papers RPR.023
3 BL Add MS 62155 f88
4 Randolph WSC Vol I, p.437
5 Taylor, *The Great Outsiders*, p.55
6 Heffer, *The Age of Decadence*, p.549
7 Morison (ed.), *The History of the Times* IV Part 1, p.131
8 Lawrence, *Journalism as a Profession*, p.59
9 Northcliffe Archive Papers RPR.022
10 Northcliffe Archive Papers RPR.022
11 Engel, *Tickle the Public*, p.67
12 Edwards, 'Alfred Harmsworth', p.463
13 Ryan, *Lord Northcliffe*, p.90
14 Ibid., p.90
15 Ibid., p.60
16 Lycett, *Rudyard Kipling*, p.319
17 Richards, *Rudyard Kipling: A Bibliography*, p.137
18 Rüger, 'Revisiting the Anglo-German Antagonism', p.591
19 Ibid., pp.604–605
20 Ryan, *Lord Northcliffe*, p.92
21 Gardiner, A.G., 'Two Journalists', p.251
22 Catterall et al (eds), *Northcliffe's Legacy*, pp.45–69; Silberstein-Loeb, 'The Structure of the News Market in Britain', p.75
23 Brendon, *Eminent Edwardians*, p.38
24 Clarke, *My Northcliffe Diary*, p.35
25 Ibid., p.36
26 Ibid., p.32
27 Ibid., p.33
28 Ibid., p.38
29 Greenwall, *Northcliffe*, p.134

30 Northcliffe Archive Papers RPR.023
31 Ibid.
32 Ibid.
33 Angel, *After All*, p.123
34 Ibid.
35 Pound and Harmsworth, *Northcliffe*, p.253
36 Hammerton, *With Northcliffe in Fleet Street*, pp.171–172
37 *Daily Mail*, 4 May 1900, p.4
38 Thompson, *Northcliffe*, p.74
39 Ibid., p.75
40 *Daily Mail*, 18 May 1900
41 Thompson, *Northcliffe*, p.75
42 Ryan, *Lord Northcliffe*, p.110
43 Blumenfeld, *RDB's Diary*, pp.95–96
44 BL Add MSS 62156 f.3
45 Thompson, *Northcliffe*, p.83
46 Peter Preston in *The Observer*, 21 May 2000; Taylor, *Reluctant Press Lord*, p.210
47 Pierce, *Lord Northcliffe: Transatlantic Influences*, p.19
48 Ibid.
49 Northcliffe Archive Papers, *Alfred Harmsworth's American Visit New York World*, 1 Jan 1901
50 Pierce, *Lord Northcliffe: Transatlantic Influences*, p.21
51 Brendon, *Eminent Edwardians*, p.24
52 Pierce, *Lord Northcliffe: Transatlantic Influences*, p.17
53 Harmsworth, 'The Simultaneous Newspapers of the Twentieth Century', p.74
54 Ibid., p.74
55 Ibid., p.79
56 Ibid., p.75
57 Ibid., pp.79–80
58 Ibid., p.80
59 Ibid., p.81
60 Ibid., p.81
61 Ibid., p.82
62 Ibid., p.83
63 Ibid., p.85
64 Ibid., p.87
65 Ibid., p.87
66 Ibid., pp.87–88
67 Ibid., p.88
68 Ibid., p.90

69 Ibid., p.90
70 Ibid., p.90
71 Northcliffe Archive Papers
    RPR.027
72 Clarke, *My Northcliffe Diary*,
    p.45
73 Brendon, *Eminent Edwardians*,
    p.37
74 Clarke, *My Northcliffe Diary*,
    p.49
75 Spender, *Life, Journalism and
    Politics* II, p.166
76 Northcliffe Archive Papers
    RPR.027
77 Ibid.
78 Engel, *Tickle the Public*, p.77

Chapter Six: *The Mirror and a Mystery Woman*

1   Woods and Bishop, *The Story of
    the Times*, p.205
2   *Daily Mail*, 16 August 1902
3   Thompson, *Northcliffe*, p.96
4   *Daily Mail*, 12 August 1902
5   Gollin, 'Lord Northcliffe's
    Change of Course', p.46
6   Potter, 'The Imperial Significance
    of the Canadian–American
    Reciprocity Proposals', p.84
7   http://gfwheritagesociety.ca
8   https://www.youtube.com/
    watch?v=gdloevfiU7M
9   Northcliffe Archive Papers
    Geraldine Mary Harmsworth File
10 Lawrence, *Journalism as a
    Profession*, p.53
11 Ibid., p.54
12 Ibid., p.55
13 Ibid., p.56
14 Ibid., p.55
15 Ibid., p.58
16 Ibid., p.58
17 Spender, *Life, Journalism and
    Politics* II, p.171
18 Gollin, *Balfour's Burden*, p.87
19 Ibid., p.197
20 Startt, *Northcliffe the Imperialist*,
    p.27; Gollin, *Balfour's Burden*,
    p.85
21 Gollin, *Balfour's Burden*,
    pp.84–85
22 Startt, *Northcliffe the Imperialist*,
    p.27

23 BL Add MSS 62154
24 Ibid.
25 Spender, *Life, Journalism and
    Politics* II, p.172
26 Ibid.
27 *Companion* Vol. II part 1,
    p.224
28 Gollin, *Balfour's Burden*, p.197
29 Ibid., p.198
30 Thompson, *Northcliffe*, p.108
31 Startt, *Northcliffe the Imperialist*,
    p.28
32 *Daily Mail*, 7 October 1903
33 Ibid.
34 Thompson, *Northcliffe*, p.108
35 Startt, *Northcliffe the Imperialist*,
    p.29
36 Pemberton, *Lord Northcliffe*, p.88
37 Sykes, *Tariff Reform in British
    Politics*, p.1
38 *Daily Mirror*, 1 November 1903
39 Jones, *Fleet Street and Downing
    Street*, p.228
40 Brendon, *Eminent Edwardians*,
    p.26
41 BL Add MS 62391 f.55
42 Thompson, *Northcliffe*, p.110;
    Andrews and Taylor, *Lords and
    Laborers of the Press*, p.186
43 Andrews and Taylor, *Lords and
    Laborers of the Press*, p.188
44 Williams, *Dangerous Estate*,
    p.225
45 Owen, *The Real Lord Northcliffe*,
    p.18
46 Andrews and Taylor, *Lords and
    Laborers of the Press*, p.189
47 Brendon, *Eminent Edwardians*,
    p.26
48 Wrench, *Uphill*, p.138
49 *Overseas Daily Mail*, 25
    November 1904
50 Wrench, *Uphill*, p.138
51 BL Add MS 62391 f.60
52 Northcliffe Archive Papers North
    .005
53 Gollin, *Balfour's Burden*, p.205
54 BL Add MS 62392 f.29
55 Gollin, *Balfour's Burden*, p.241
56 Northcliffe Archive Papers
    RPR.017
57 Ibid.
58 Ibid.

59 Bourne, *Lords of Fleet Street*,
    p.67
60 Ferris, *The House of Northcliffe*,
    pp.129–30
61 *Evening Standard*, 15 April 1908
62 *Evening Standard*, 26 Feb 1909
63 *Dublin Daily Express*, 15 Jul
    1909
64 Northcliffe Archive Papers
    NORTH.033
65 Ibid.
66 Croome, *Annie's Journeys*,
    pp.32–33
67 US National Archives,
    Washington, Record Group
    No 85 (i) index card for
    Lady Cathleen Wrohan, series
    M1480 roll 163 (ii) Manifest,
    Cathleen Wrohan, series M1464,
    roll 38
68 *Belfast Weekly Telegraph*,
    Saturday 15 June 1912, p.9

Chapter Seven: Liberal Dawn

1   Wells, *Experiment in
    Autobiography* II, p.696
2   BL Add MSS 62393 f.20
3   Gollin, *The Observer and J. L.
    Garvin*, p.306
4   Northcliffe Archive Papers
    RPR.023
5   Angell, *After All*, p.103
6   Ibid., p.104
7   Ibid., p.110
8   Ibid., p.110
9   Ibid., p.111
10 Ibid., p.112
11 Pound and Harmsworth,
    Northcliffe, p.291
12 *Daily Mail*, 9 October 1905
13 Gollin, *Balfour's Burden*, p.241
14 Searle, *Corruption in British
    Politics*, p.93
15 Taylor, *The Great Outsiders*,
    p.85; Brendon, *Eminent
    Edwardians*, p.27
16 Ramsden (ed.), *Real Old Tory
    Politics*, p.125
17 Chisholm and Davie,
    Beaverbrook, p.320
18 Searle, *Corruption in British
    Politics*, pp.93–94
19 King, *The Cecil King Diary*, p.345

20 BL Add MS 62393 f.47
21 Northcliffe Archive Papers
    Geraldine Mary Harmsworth File
22 *Saturday Review*, 16 December
    1905
23 Northcliffe Archive Papers
    RPR.020, Macmillan,
    Peacemakers, p.45, Brendon,
    Eminent Edwardians, p.27
24 BL Add MS 62384 f.27
25 BL Add MSS 62172 ff.6–7
26 MacDonagh, *The Last Kaiser*,
    p.291
27 BL Add MSS 62394 f.10
28 Startt, *Northcliffe the Imperialist*,
    p.29
29 BL Add MSS 62394 f.5
30 Pound and Harmsworth,
    Northcliffe, p.296
31 RRJ Churchill Collected Speeches
    I, p.561
32 Le Queux, *The Invasion of 1910*,
    p.550
33 Ferguson, *The Pity of War*,
    p.11; Hansard Vol. 160 cols
    656–662
34 Thompson, *Northcliffe*, p.134
35 Wrench, *Uphill*, p.154
36 Owen, *The Real Lord Northcliffe*,
    p.27
37 Bourne, *Lords of Fleet Street*,
    p.67
38 Wrench, *Uphill*, p.154
39 Northcliffe Archive Papers
    RPR.034
40 Ferris, *The House of Northcliffe*,
    pp.131–132
41 Northcliffe Archive Papers
    RPR.034
42 Northcliffe Archive Papers
    RPR.006
43 Wrench, *Uphill*, p.199
44 Ibid., p.200
45 Ibid., p.218
46 Ibid., p.174
47 Clarke, *My Northcliffe Diary*,
    p.85
48 Harmsworth, 'Simultaneous
    Newspapers of the Twentieth
    Century', p.82
49 Smith, *Spilt Ink*, p.79
50 Campbell, *F.E.*, p.173
51 Camplin, *The Rise of the
    Plutocrats*, p.73

52 Searle, *Corruption in British Politics*, p.128
53 Campbell, *F.E.*, p.174
54 Judd, *Lord Reading*, p.65; Campbell, *F.E.*, p.174
55 Judd, *Lord Reading*, p.65
56 Northcliffe Archive Papers RPR.034
57 Searle, *Corruption in British Politics*, p.129
58 Heffer, *The Age of Decadence*, p.556
59 Searle, *Corruption in British Politics*, p.129
60 *Daily Mail*, 15 November 1906, p.6
61 Gollin, *England is No Longer an Island*, p.193
62 Hales-Dutton, *Pioneering Places of British Aviation*, p.90; Northcliffe Archive Papers RPR.023
63 Steed, *Through Thirty Years* I, p.274
64 Ibid.
65 Pound and Harmsworth, *Northcliffe*, p.309

Chapter Eight: Taking *The Times*
1 May, *Critical Times*, p.95
2 Searle, *Corruption in British Politics*, p.97
3 Startt, 'G. E. Buckle, Lord Northcliffe and the Conservative Revolution at *The Times*', p.14
4 Jones, *Fleet Street and Downing Street*, p.261
5 Startt, 'G. E. Buckle, Lord Northcliffe and the Conservative Revolution at *The Times*', p.12
6 May, *Critical Times*, p.4
7 Kitchin, *Moberly Bell*, p.213
8 Steed, *Through Thirty Years* I, p.275
9 Jones, *Fleet Street and Downing Street*, p.262
10 Pound and Harmsworth, *Northcliffe*, p.310
11 *Daily Mail*, 8 January 1908, p.4
12 Morison (ed.), *The History of the Times* III, p.526
13 Wrench, *Geoffrey Dawson and Our Times*, p.63
14 Greenwall, *Northcliffe*, p.89

15 Wrench, *Geoffrey Dawson and Our Times*, p.63; *The Times, Times History* III, p.536
16 Greenwall, *Northcliffe*, p.89
17 Jones, *Fleet Street and Downing Street*, p.263
18 Thompson, *Northcliffe*, p.142
19 *The Times*, 18 January 1908, p.9
20 Thompson, *Northcliffe*, p.144; Spender, *Life, Journalism and Politics* II, p.165
21 Bell, *Life and Letters of C. F. Moberly Bell*, p.291
22 Northcliffe Archive Papers North.003
23 Ibid.
24 Ibid.
25 Ibid.
26 Thompson, *Northcliffe*, p.144
27 Ryan, *Lord Northcliffe*, p.120
28 Ibid.
29 Steed, *Through Thirty Years* I, p.275
30 Northcliffe Archive Papers North.003
31 Ibid.
32 Morison (ed.), *The History of the Times* III, p.557
33 Startt, 'G. E. Buckle, Lord Northcliffe and the Conservative Revolution', p.15
34 Northcliffe Archive Papers Geraldine Mary Harmsworth File
35 Morison (ed.), *The History of the Times* III, p.570; Northcliffe Archive Papers Geraldine Mary Harmsworth File
36 Edwards, 'Alfred Harmsworth', p.463
37 Bell, *Life and Letters of C. F. Moberly Bell*, p.296
38 Kitchin, *Moberly Bell*, pp.234–45
39 Woods and Bishop, *The Story of the Times*, p.204
40 *The Times*, 17 March p9
41 Northcliffe, *Newspapers and Their Millionaires*, p.20
42 Wrench, *Uphill*, p.195
43 May, *Critical Times*, p.6
44 Ryan, *Northcliffe*, p.139
45 Wrench, *Geoffrey Dawson and Our Times*, p.65
46 Brendon, *Eminent Edwardians*, p.33

47 Ibid.
48 Owen, *The Real Lord Northcliffe*, p.37
49 Andrews and Taylor, *Lords and Laborers of the Press*, p.168
50 Startt, 'G. E. Buckle, Lord Northcliffe and the Conservative Revolution', p.16
51 Brendon, *Eminent Edwardians*, p.31
52 Ryan, *Lord Northcliffe*, p.127
53 Brendon, *Eminent Edwardians*, p.31
54 Ibid., p.31
55 Ibid., p.30
56 Greenwall, *Northcliffe*, pp.127–28
57 Thompson, *Northcliffe*, p.146
58 Kitchin, *Moberly Bell*, p.276
59 *Oxford Dictionary of National Biography*
60 Northcliffe Archive Papers, *Times* Bulletins, 1919–1922
61 Ibid.
62 May, *Critical Times*, p.62
63 BL Add Mss 62243 ff.2–3
64 BL 62298
65 Taylor, *Beaverbrook*, p.135
66 Morison (ed.), *The History of the Times* III, p.652
67 Steed, *Through Thirty Years* I, p.277
68 Ibid.
69 Ryan, *Northcliffe*, p.123
70 Ibid.

Chapter Nine: 'Der Tag Will Come': The German Threat

1 Brendon, *Eminent Edwardians*, p.38
2 BL Add MS 62157 ff.1–2
3 WSC Coll Speeches I, pp.986–987
4 Ibid., p.998
5 WSC Docs Comp Vol. 3 Part 2, pp.791–92
6 Northcliffe Archive Papers; Churchill correspondence
7 Ibid.
8 Ibid.
9 Ibid.
10 Ibid.
11 *Daily Mail*, 11 July 1908
12 Gollin, *England is No Longer an Island*, p.49; *Daily Mail*, 11 July 1908

13 Menning and Menning, *Baseless Allegations*, p.37
14 Ibid., p.373
15 Ibid., p.379
16 Ibid., p.374
17 Ibid., p.377
18 Morison (ed.), *The History of the Times* III, p.653
19 BL Add MSS 62193
20 BL Add MSS 62153
21 Mallinson, 1914, pp.149–50
22 Ibid., pp.171, 176
23 Owen, *The Real Lord Northcliffe*, p.47
24 Ferris, *The House of Northcliffe*, p.153
25 Owen, *The Real Lord Northcliffe*, p.47
26 Startt, *Northcliffe the Imperialist*, p.37
27 Wrench, *Uphill*, p.223
28 Ibid.
29 Adams and Poirier, *Conscription Controversy*, p.20
30 BL Add MSS 62303
31 Thompson, *Northcliffe*, p.161
32 Ibid.
33 Northcliffe Archive Papers RPR.017
34 Northcliffe Archive Papers North.003
35 Wrench, *Uphill*, p.218
36 Ibid.
37 Morris, *Scaremongers*, p.210
38 Adams, *Balfour*, p.269
39 BL Add MS 62155 ff.79–80
40 BL Add MS 62155 f.80
41 Brett (ed.), *Journals and Letters of Reginald, Viscount Esher* II, pp.371–372
42 Koss, *Haldane*, p.144
43 Haldane, *Autobiography*, p.232
44 Campbell, *Haldane*, p.287
45 Ibid., p.285
46 BL Add MS 62155 ff.82–83
47 Ibid., f.84
48 Ibid., f.86
49 Ibid., f.86
50 Ibid., f.86
51 Ibid., f.87
52 Ibid., f.90
53 Jungdahl, *Public Influence on the Proliferation of Military Aviation*, p.36

54 Ibid.
55 Ibid.
56 Ibid., p.37
57 Northcliffe Archive Papers North.003
58 Ibid.
59 Ibid.
60 Ibid.
61 Ibid.
62 Ibid.
63 Ibid.
64 Ibid.
65 Ibid.
66 BL Add MS 62155
67 Ryan, *Lord Northcliffe*, p.98
68 Heffer, *Age of Decadence*, p.611
69 BL Add MSS 62201 ff.36–37
70 Ibid., ff.36–37
71 Ibid., f.37
72 Gollin, *England is No Longer an Island*, pp.52–54
73 *Daily Mail*, 21 May 1909
74 Ibid.
75 Pound and Harmsworth, *Northcliffe*, p.369
76 Zwar, *In Search of Keith Murdoch*, p.55
77 BL Add MS 62157 ff.9–10
78 Thorpe and Toye (eds), *Parliament and Politics*, pp.32–33
79 Brendon, *Eminent Edwardians*, p.45
80 Thompson, *Northcliffe*, p.177
81 Fritzinger, *Diplomat Without Portfolio*, p.386
82 Wrench, *Uphill*, p.228
83 Ibid.
84 Ibid., p.229
85 BL Add MSS 62196
86 Ibid., f.54
87 Ibid., f.56
88 Startt, 'G. E. Buckle, Lord Northcliffe and the Conservative Revolution', p.16
89 Ibid., p.18
90 Ibid., p.19
91 BL Add MSS 62243 f.156
92 Ibid., f168

Chapter Ten: Consolidation Control at *The Times*

1 Taylor, *Politics in Wartime*, p.152
2 Northcliffe Archive Papers NORTH.033
3 Taylor, *The Outsiders*, p.131
4 Northcliffe Archive Papers NORTH.033
5 Ferris, *The House of Northcliffe*, p.167
6 Pound and Harmsworth, *Northcliffe*, p.392
7 Northcliffe Archive Papers NORTH.033
8 Ferris, *The House of Northcliffe*, p.167
9 Northcliffe Archive Papers NORTH.033
10 Ibid.
11 Ibid.
12 1911 Census summary book RG78/14 registration district 5 sub-district 1 enumeration district 11 p.6, and RG14/424 schedule 126
13 Northcliffe Archive Papers NORTH.033
14 Ibid.
15 Ferris, *The House of Northcliffe*, p.193; baptism register of St Martin-in-the-Fields STM/PR/6/45 p.680 no.15
16 Northcliffe Archive Papers Geraldine Mary Harmsworth File
17 BL Add MS 62196 f.75
18 Ibid., f.74
19 Driberg, *Swaffer*, p.33
20 Clark (ed.), *A Good Innings*, p.102
21 Ibid., p.110
22 Private Information
23 Ferris, *The House of Northcliffe*, p.178
24 Northcliffe Archive Papers NORTH.033
25 Ibid.
26 Northcliffe Archive Papers Harold Sydney Harmsworth file
27 BL Add MSS 62311
28 Ibid.
29 BL Add MS 62157 f.160
30 BL Add MS 62153 f.41
31 Ibid., f.144
32 Ibid., f.145
33 BL Add MS 62244 f.1; Wrench,

Geoffrey Dawson and Our Times, p.62 n2

34 BL Add MS 62244 f.17–18
35 Wrench, *Geoffrey Dawson and Our Times*, p.78
36 Ibid., p.77 n1
37 Ibid., p.78
38 *Daily Mail*, 30 January 1911, p.6
39 Potter, 'The Imperial Significance of the Canadian–American Reciprocity Proposals', p.81
40 *Daily Mail*, 4 February 1911
41 Startt, *Northcliffe the Imperialist*, p.32
42 Gollin, *The Observer and J. L. Garvin*, p.284; Andrews and Taylor, *Lords and Laborers of the Press*, p.91
43 Wrench, *Uphill*, p.195; Sykes, Alan, *Tariff Reform in British Politics*, p.241
44 BL Add MSS 62161 ff.5–6
45 Chisholm and Davie, *Beaverbrook*, pp.275–276
46 Taylor, *Beaverbrook*, p.78
47 Bell, *Life and Letters of C. F. Moberly Bell*, p.292
48 Startt, 'Northcliffe the Imperialist', p.39
49 Bell, *Life and Letters of C. F. Moberly Belli*, pp.310–12
50 BL Add MS 62198 f.87
51 Ibid., f.99
52 Ibid., f.112
53 Ibid., ff.115–16
54 May, *Critical Times*, p.61; Gollin, *The Observer and J. L. Garvin*, p.307
55 Pound and Harmsworth, *Northcliffe*, p.409
56 BL Add MSS 62243
57 BL Add MSS 62244 f.50
58 Ibid., f.25
59 Ibid., f.28
60 Northcliffe Archive Papers North.002; Northcliffe Archive Papers Geraldine Mary Harmsworth File
61 Northcliffe Archive Papers Geraldine Mary Harmsworth File
62 BL Add MSS 62156 f.31
63 Coote, *The Other Club*, p.18
64 BL Add MSS 62156 f.32

65 Ibid.
66 Ibid.
67 Rhodes James (ed.), *Winston S. Churchill: His Complete Speeches* II, p.1892
68 Northcliffe Archive Papers; Churchill correspondence

Chapter Eleven: The Road to War

1 Owen, *The Real Lord Northcliffe*, p.43
2 Northcliffe Archive Papers RPR.020
3 Ibid.
4 Ibid.
5 Ibid.
6 BL Add MSS 62161 f.14
7 BL Add MSS 62153 f.156
8 BL Add MSS 62318
9 BL Add MSS 62155 f.144
10 Clarke, *My Northcliffe Diary*, p.51
11 BL Add MSS 62198 f.130
12 Pierce, *Lord Northcliffe: Transatlantic Influences*, p.30
13 Ibid.
14 BL Add MSS 62198 f.132
15 Northcliffe Archive Papers Geraldine Mary Harmsworth File
16 BL Add MSS 62244
17 James (ed.), *Winston S. Churchill: His Complete Speeches* I, pp.2010–2011
18 BL Add MSS 62156 f.44
19 Ibid., f.47
20 Ibid., f.48
21 Pound and Harmsworth, *Northcliffe*, p.441; Searle, *Corruption in British Politics*, p.194
22 BL Add Ms 62157 ff.22–23
23 Ibid., f.24
24 BL Add MSS 62156 f.49
25 BL Add MS 62244 f.117
26 Ibid., f.116
27 Northcliffe Archive Papers; Churchill correspondence
28 *The Observer*, 13 April 1913, p.8
29 *The Times*, 26 November 1913, p.13
30 Griffiths (ed.), *Encyclopedia of the British Press*, pp.184, 292

31 Brendon, *Eminent Edwardians*, p.34
32 Wrench, *Geoffrey Dawson and Our Times*, p.95
33 Liebich, 'The Antisemitism of Henry Wickham Steed', p.187 n29
34 Pound and Harmsworth, *Northcliffe*, p.447
35 Ibid., p.448
36 BL Add MS 62244 f.137
37 Wrench, *Geoffrey Dawson and Our Times*, p.95
38 May, *Critical Times*, p.92
39 McEwen, *The National Press During the First World War*, p.467; Thompson, *Northcliffe*, p.216
40 Brendon, *Eminent Edwardians*, p.34
41 Clarke, *My Northcliffe Diary*, p.56
42 Ryan, *Lieutenant-Colonel Charles à Court Repington*, p.136
43 *The Times*, 25 March 1914, p.9
44 *Oxford Dictionary of National Biography*
45 BL Add MSS 62156 f.57
46 Ibid., ff.57–58
47 Ibid., f.59
48 Northcliffe Archive Papers Geraldine Mary Harmsworth File
49 Ibid.
50 Jenkins, *Asquith*, p.319
51 Vincent (ed.), *Crawford Papers*, p.338
52 Bones, 'British National Dailies and the Outbreak of War in 1914', p.988

Chapter Twelve: 'The Angel of Death is Abroad'

1 Morris, *Scaremongers*, epilogue; Fyfe, *Northcliffe*, p.152
2 Bones, 'British National Dailies and the Outbreak of War in 1914', p.975
3 McEwen, 'The National Press During the First World War: Ownership and Circulation', p.466; Koss, *Haldane*, p.145
4 Pound and Harmsworth, *Northcliffe*, p.391
5 McEwen, '"Brass-Hats" and the

British Press During the First World War', p.43
6 Ferguson, *Pity of War*, p.217
7 *The Times*, 22 July 1914, p.9
8 Steed, *Through Thirty Years* I, p.410
9 *The Times*, 22 July 1914, p.9
10 *The Times*, 27 July 1914, p.9
11 Ibid.
12 Wilson (ed.), *The Political Diaries of C. P. Scott*, p.92
13 *The Times*, 29 July 1914, p.9
14 Hale, *Publicity and Diplomacy*, pp.461–463
15 *The Times*, 31 July 1914, p.9
16 Morris, *Scaremongers*, p.359
17 *The Times*, 1 August 1914
18 Steed, *Through Thirty Years* II, p.10
19 Ibid., p.11
20 Fyfe, *Northcliffe*, pp.173–174
21 Steed, *Through Thirty Years* II, p.11
22 Ibid.
23 Ibid., pp.389–390
24 Ferguson, *Pity of War*, p.195; Ferguson, *World's Banker*, p.963
25 Steed, *Through Thirty Years* II. p.8ff; *The Times, The Times History of the War* IV, p.208
26 Northcliffe Archive Papers; Steed, *Through Thirty Years* II, p.12
27 Marquis, 'Words as Weapons', p.469
28 Foot, *HG: The History of Mr Wells*, p.153
29 Ibid.
30 Clarke, *My Northcliffe Diary*, p.63
31 Jeffries, *Front Everywhere*, p.67
32 *The Times*, 3 August 1914, p.7
33 *The Times*, 4 August 1914, p.5
34 Koss, *Haldane*, p.71
35 *The Times*, 2 December 1914, p.6
36 Campbell, *Haldane*, p.184
37 McEwen, '"Brass-Hats" and the British Press During the First World War', p.45; Cudlipp, *The Prerogative of the Harlot*, p.96
38 Haldane, *An Autobiography*, p.283
39 Koss, *Haldane*, p.135
40 Terraine, *White Heat*, p.77

41 Clarke, *My Northcliffe Diary*, p.65
42 Ibid., p.67
43 Beaverbrook, *Politicians and the War*, pp.36–37
44 BL Add MSS 62180
45 Clarke, *My Northcliffe Diary*, p.67
46 Steed, *Through Thirty Years* II, p.33
47 May, *Critical Times*, p.101
48 McEwen, '"Brass-Hats" and the British Press During the First World War', p.46
49 Pollock, *Kitchener*, p.442
50 BL Add MSS 62210B
51 Wrench, *Geoffrey Dawson and Our Times*, p.116
52 Randolph Churchill, *Winston S Churchill*, Vol. II Part 3, p.1629
53 Brendon, *Eminent Edwardians*, p.50
54 Gregory, *The Last Great War*, p.48
55 *Daily Mail*, 12 August 1914
56 Gregory, *The Last Great War*, p.48
57 Marquis, 'Words as Weapons', p.487
58 Haste, *Keep the Home Fires Burning* pp83–84; Horne and Kramer, *German Atrocities 1914*, *passim*
59 Ferris, *The House of Northcliffe*, p.193
60 *The Times*, 8 January 1915, p.9
61 Ibid.
62 Ibid.
63 Jeffries, *Front Everywhere*, p.125
64 Knightley, *The First Casualty*, p.83
65 Little, 'H. H. Asquith and Britain's Manpower Problem, 1914–15', pp.398–400
66 *The Times*, *The Times History of the War* VI, pp.289–290
67 Taylor, *The Great Outsiders*, p.149
68 Brock and Brock (eds), *H.H. Asquith*, p.210 n5
69 Clarke, *My Northcliffe Diary*, p.68
70 BL Add MSS 62156 f.60
71 Ibid., f.61

72 Wilson, *Lord Northcliffe*, pp.205–206
73 Ibid.
74 Heffer, *Staring at God*, p.135
75 Driberg, *Swaffer*, pp.63–64
76 Brendon, *Eminent Edwardians*, p.35
77 Jolliffe, *Raymond Asquith*, p.194
78 Ibid., p.195
79 Pemberton, *Lord Northcliffe*, p.148
80 Wrench, *Geoffrey Dawson and Our Times*, p.111
81 BL Add MS 62167 f.13
82 Ibid., f.73
83 Ibid., f.80
84 Ibid., ff.105–07
85 BL Add MS 62197 f.30
86 Thompson, *Northcliffe*, p.4
87 Owen, *The Real Lord Northcliffe*, p.48
88 Clarke, *My Northcliffe Diary*, p.71
89 *The Times*, 24 November 1914; Ferguson, *Pity of War*, p.218
90 Bogacz, '"A Tyranny of Words": Language, Poetry and Antimodernism', p.651 n23
91 Ibid., p.643
92 Morris, *The Scaremongers*, p.1

Chapter Thirteen: The Shells Scandal

1 Beaverbrook, *Men and Power*, p.xxii
2 Brendon, *Eminent Edwardians*, p.43
3 BL Add MSS 62328
4 BL Add MSS 62245 f.1
5 Ibid., f.3
6 BL Add MS 62159 f.47
7 Ibid., f.50
8 Fraser, 'The British "Shells Scandal" of 1915', p.70
9 Hansard HL Deb 15 March 1915 Vol. 18 cc721–722
10 BL Add MSS 62245 f.5
11 Brendon, *Eminent Edwardians*, p.43
12 Fraser, 'The British "Shells Scandal" of 1915', p.74
13 Thompson, *Northcliffe*, p.235
14 BL Add MS 62159 f.56

15 McEwen, '"Brass-Hats and the British Press During the First World War', p.50
16 *The Times*, 29 March 1915, p.9
17 Brock and Brock (eds), *H.H. Asquith*, p.517
18 Ibid.
19 Ibid., p.519
20 Riddell, *Lord Riddell's War Diary 1914–1918*, p.65
21 Popplewell, *The Prime Minister and His Mistress*, p77–91
22 Koss, *Asquith*, p.141
23 Popplewell, *The Prime Minister and His Mistress*, p.91
24 Hague, *The Pain and the Privilege*, p.225
25 Northcliffe Archive Papers Geraldine Mary Harmsworth file
26 BL Add MSS 62234
27 Clarke, *My Northcliffe Diary*, p.72
28 Ibid.
29 *The Times*, 12 April 1915, p.9
30 BL Add MSS 62251 ff.115–16
31 Ibid., f.116
32 Ibid., f.116
33 Ibid., f.117
34 Ibid., f.119
35 Ibid., f.121
36 Ibid., f.121
37 Owen, *Tempestuous Journey*, p.286
38 Thompson, *Northcliffe*, p.239
39 *The Times*, 21 April 1915, p.9
40 Brock and Brock (eds), *H. H. Asquith*, p.564 n1
41 *The Times*, 27 April 1915
42 Brock and Brock (eds), *H. H. Asquith*, p.562; Fraser, 'The British "Shells Scandal" of 1915', p.71
43 Clarke, *My Northcliffe Diary*, p.73
44 *The Times*, 29 April, p.9
45 Riddell, *Lord Riddell's War Diary 1914–1918*, p.84
46 Wrench, *Geoffrey Dawson and Our Times*, p.125
47 BL Add MS 62159 ff.67–68
48 Ibid., f.68
49 Ibid., f.69
50 Brock and Brock (eds), *H. H. Asquith*, p.583
51 Pollock, *Kitchener*, p.442
52 Fraser, 'The British "Shells Scandal" of 1915', p.71 n25
53 French, *1914*, pp.356–357
54 Ibid., p.357
55 Fraser, 'The British "Shells Scandal" of 1915', p.74
56 Ibid.
57 Ibid., p.75
58 Ibid., p.84
59 *The Times*, 14 May 1915, p.8
60 McEwen, '"Brass-Hats and the British Press During the First World War', p.50
61 *The Times*, 14 May 1915, pp.9, 10
62 Marcosson, *Adventures in Interviewing*, p.124
63 Pollock, *Kitchener*, p.441
64 Fraser, 'The British "Shells Scandal" of 1915', p.85
65 Adams, *Balfour*, p.298
66 Riddell, *Lord Riddell's War Diary 1914–1918*, p.87
67 Pollock, *Kitchener*, p.442
68 Driberg, *Swaffer*, p.71
69 Ibid., pp.69–70
70 Northcliffe Family Archive, *Lord Northcliffe's Notes for Leader in the Daily Mail of Monday 24 May 1915*
71 *Daily Mail*, 21 May 1915
72 Ibid.
73 Ibid.
74 Pound and Harmsworth, *Northcliffe*, p.478
75 Northcliffe Archive Papers, *The Times AAA Journal*, p.8C
76 Pound and Harmsworth, *Northcliffe*, p.478
77 Ibid.
78 Steed, *Through Thirty Years* II, p.73
79 Pound and Harmsworth, *Northcliffe*, p.478
80 MacDonagh, *In London During the Great War*, p.67
81 Griffiths (ed.), *Encyclopedia of the British Press*, p.184
82 Northcliffe Archive Papers RPR.023
83 Ibid.
84 Swaffer, *Northcliffe's Return*, p.25

85 Clarke, *My Northcliffe Diary*, p.82
86 Andrews and Taylor, *Lords and Laborers of the Press*, p.46
87 Pound and Harmsworth, *Northcliffe*, p.478
88 Northcliffe Archive Papers *Times Bulletins 1919–1922*
89 Wrench, *Geoffrey Dawson and Our Times*, p.116
90 Wrench, *Struggle 1914–1920*, pp,134–135
91 Clarke, *My Northcliffe Diary*, p.79
92 Swaffer, *Northcliffe's Return*, p.23
93 Ibid., p.24
94 Northcliffe Archive Papers RPR.020
95 Driberg, *Swaffer*, p.69
96 Marcosson, *Adventures in Interviewing*, p.121
97 Stuart, *Opportunity Knocks Once*, p.75
98 Andrews and Taylor, *Lords and Laborers of the Press*, p.56
99 Clarke, *My Northcliffe Diary*, p.79
100 Edmonds (ed.), *The History of the Great War*, p.149
101 Edmonds et al, OH 1916 I, p.48
102 Thompson, *Northcliffe*, p.241
103 Hamilton, *Happy Warrior*, p.322
104 Repington, *The First World War I*, p.41
105 Adams, *Bonar Law*, p.188
106 Pollock, *Kitchener*, p.444
107 Asquith, *Diaries 1915–1918*, p.24
108 Lees-Milne, *Enigmatic Edwardian*, pp.269, 310
109 *The Times*, 21 May 1915, p.9
110 Steed, *Through Thirty Years* II, p.75
111 Ibid., p.76
112 Taylor (ed.), *Lloyd George*, p.54
113 *Daily Mail*, 26 May 1915
114 Thompson, *Northcliffe*, p.242

Chapter Fourteen:
Gallipoli and Conscription

1 Cooper, *Haig* I, p.341
2 BL Add MS 62153 f.165
3 *The Times*, 27 May 1915
4 Little, 'H. H. Asquith and Britain's Manpower Problem', p.405
5 Ibid.
6 Brock and Brock (eds), *Margot Asquith's Great War Diary 1914–1916*, p.149
7 Ibid., p.148
8 Riddell, *Lord Riddell's War Diary 1914–1918*, p.99
9 Ibid.
10 BL Add MSS 62251 ff.132–33
11 Rhodes James (ed.), *Winston S. Churchill: His Complete Speeches III*, p.2382
12 Ibid.
13 Ibid., p.2383
14 Blake, *The Unknown Prime Minister*, p.296
15 Hammerton, *With Northcliffe in Fleet Street*, p.23
16 Ibid.
17 Riddell, *Lord Riddell's War Diary 1914–1918*, p.100
18 Ibid., p.102
19 Pottle (ed.), *Champion Redoubtable*, p.62
20 Ibid., p.70
21 Jolliffe, *Raymond Asquith*, p.257
22 Brock and Brock (eds), *Margot Asquith's Great War Diary 1914–1916*, pp.153–154
23 Ibid., p.154
24 Pottle (ed.), *Champion Redoubtable*, p.77 n1
25 Ibid., p.62 n2
26 Jenkins, *Asquith*, p.348
27 Ibid.
28 Steed, *Through Thirty Years* II, p.121
29 BL Add MS 62157 f.30
30 Lloyd, *The Western Front*, p.119
31 Brock and Brock (eds), *Margot Asquith's Great War Diary 1914–1916*, p.ciii n2
32 Little, 'H. H. Asquith and Britain's Manpower Problem', p.409
33 Riddell, *Lord Riddell's War Diary 1914–1918*, p.108
34 Ibid., pp.109–110
35 Ibid., pp.109–110

36 Wrench, *Geoffrey Dawson and Our Times*, p.125
37 Brock and Brock (eds), *Margot Asquith's Great War Diary 1914–1916*, p.166
38 Wrench, *Struggle, 1914–1920*, p.142
39 Clarke, *My Northcliffe Diary*, p.83
40 Wrench, *Geoffrey Dawson and Our Times*, p.126
41 James, *Memoirs of a Conservative*, p.37
42 Ibid.
43 Colvin, *The Life of Lord Carson* Vol. III, p.73
44 Ibid., p.33
45 Thompson, *Forgotten Patriot*, p.319
46 Marlowe, *Milner*, p.243
47 Thompson, *Forgotten Patriot*, p.320
48 Clifford, *The Asquiths*, p.300
49 Ibid.
50 Jeffries, *Front Everywhere*, p.47
51 Ibid.
52 Owen, *Northcliffe – The Facts*, p.43
53 Northcliffe Archive Papers RPR.022
54 Spender, *Sir Robert Hudson*, p.130
55 Colvin, *The Life of Lord Carson* Vol. III, p.74
56 Ibid.
57 Koss, *The Rise and Fall of the Political Press in Britain* II, p.281
58 BL Add MS 62179 ff.58–59
59 *The Times*, 18 October 1915, p.9
60 Repington, *First World War* I, p.52
61 Riddell, *Lord Riddell's War Diary 1914–1918*, p.127
62 Ibid.
63 Ibid., pp.127–128
64 Ibid., p.128
65 Taylor (ed.), *Lloyd George*, p.71
66 Ibid., p.90
67 NA INF 4/1B
68 MacDonagh, *In London During the Great War*, p.86
69 Ibid.
70 Repington, *The First World War* I, p.115
71 BL Add MS 62199 f.44
72 Pound and Harmsworth, *Northcliffe*, p.493
73 BL Add MSS 62245 f.17
74 *Daily Mail*, 6 January 1916
75 Clarke, *My Northcliffe Diary*, p.88
76 Riddell, *Lord Riddell's War Diary 1914–1918*, p.151
77 Little, 'H.H. Asquith and Britain's Manpower Problem', p.405
78 Soames (ed.), *Speaking for Themselves*, p.171
79 Riddell, *Lord Riddell's War Diary 1914–1918*, p.154
80 Taylor (ed.), *Lloyd George*, p.98
81 *Daily Mail*, 13 May 1916
82 Steed, *Through Thirty Years* II, p.81
83 Ibid., p.82
84 Ibid., p.88
85 Ibid.
86 Ibid., p.89
87 Ibid.
88 Ibid., p.90; Pound and Harmsworth, *Northcliffe*, p.496
89 Steed, *Through Thirty Years* II, p.91
90 Pound and Harmsworth, *Northcliffe*, p.496
91 Steed, *Through Thirty Years* II, p.90
92 *The Times*, 6 March 1916, p.9
93 Ibid.
94 BL Add MSS 62161 ff.95–96
95 Ibid., f.97
96 Ibid.
97 Ibid., f.100
98 Clarke, *My Northcliffe Diary*, p.99
99 Cole (ed.), *Beatrice Webb's Diaries 1912–1924*, p.62
100 Northcliffe Archive Papers North.002
101 Wrench, *Struggle 1914–1920*, p.164
102 Wrench, *Geoffrey Dawson and Our Times*, p.133
103 McEwen (ed.), *The Riddell Diaries*, p.156

Chapter Fifteen:
Dethroning Mr Asquith

1 Swaffer, *Northcliffe's Return*, p.20
2 Hansard Lords 5th series, Vol. 22 col. 125
3 Clarke, *My Northcliffe Diary*, p.98
4 Taylor, English *History 1914–1945*, p.58
5 King, *Strictly Personal*, p.58
6 Vincent (ed.), *Crawford Papers*, p.356
7 Cooper, *Haig* I, p.340
8 Ibid., pp.340–341
9 Thompson, *Northcliffe*, p.254
10 Northcliffe Archive Papers, *Visit to the War Summer 1916*, p.9
11 Ibid.
12 Ibid.
13 Ibid., p.10
14 Ibid., p.10
15 Ibid., p.12
16 BL Add MS 62157 ff.35–36
17 Northcliffe Archive Papers, *Visit to the War Summer 1916*, p.22
18 Sheffield and Bourne (eds), *Douglas Haig: War Diaries*, p.208
19 BL Add MS 62169 f.8
20 Cooper, *Haig* I, p.342
21 Ibid.
22 BL Add MSS 62245 f.23
23 Cooper, *Haig* I, p.342; BL Add MSS 62245 f.24
24 BL Add MS 62169 f.8–9
25 BL Add MS 62160 ff.2–4
26 Ibid., f.5
27 Northcliffe Archive Papers, *Visit to the War Summer 1916*, p.22
28 BL Add MS 62157 f.38
29 BL Add MS 62159 ff.112–13
30 Ibid., f.113
31 Ibid., ff.114–15
32 Ibid., f.116
33 McEwen, '"Brass-Hats" and the British Press During the First World War', p.55
34 BL Add MSS 62245 f.30
35 BL Add MS 62199 f.48
36 Riddell, *Lord Riddell's War Diary 1914–1918*, p.208
37 Northcliffe Archive Papers, *Visit to the War Summer 1916*, p.26
38 Wrench, *Struggle 1914–1920*, p.170
39 Steed, *Through Thirty Years* II, p.103
40 Jeffrey, *1916*, p.84
41 BL Add MSS 62245 f.33; Northcliffe Archive Papers Geraldine Mary Harmsworth File
42 Steed, *Through Thirty Years* II, p.122
43 Steed, *Through Thirty Years* II, p.122
44 Sheffield and Bourne (eds), *Douglas Haig: War Diaries*, p.208 n1
45 Sheffield, *The Chief*, p.155
46 Charteris, *At GHQ*, p.157
47 Pound and Harmsworth, *Northcliffe*, p.505
48 *Daily Mail*, 16 Sept 1916
49 BL Add MSS 62160 f.17
50 Ibid., f.18
51 Ibid., f.19
52 BL Add MSS 62179 f.71
53 Repington, *The First World War* I, p.354
54 BL Add MSS 62160 ff.21–22
55 Ibid., f.22
56 Holroyd, *Lytton Strachey*, p.442
57 BL Add MSS 62160 f.35
58 Ibid., f.38
59 Ibid., f.38
60 Ibid., ff.36–37
61 Thompson, *Northcliffe*, pp.257–258
62 BL Add MSS 62160 f.45
63 Taylor (ed.), *Lloyd George*, p.115
64 BL Add MSS 62160 f.45
65 Ibid., f.46
66 Thompson, *Northcliffe*, pp.258–259
67 Repington, *The First World War* I, p.359
68 Ibid.
69 Taylor (ed.), *Lloyd George*, p.117
70 Repington, *The First World War* I, p.361
71 Riddell, *Lord Riddell's War Diary 1914–1918*, p.217
72 Ibid., p.171

73 Repington, *The First World War* I, p.374
74 BL Add MS 62160 f.53
75 Ibid., f.57
76 Clifford, *The Asquiths*, p.379
77 Adam, *Bonar Law*, p.222
78 Vincent (ed.), *Crawford Papers*, p.364
79 Ibid., p.365
80 Ibid., p.365
81 Wrench, *Geoffrey Dawson and Our Times*, p.140
82 Ibid.
83 Wilson (ed.), *The Political Diaries of C. P. Scott*, p.121
84 Morison, *Personality and Diplomacy*, p.8
85 Wrench, *Struggle 1914–1920*, p.162
86 Riddell, *Lord Riddell's War Diary 1914–1918*, p.225
87 Taylor (ed.), *Lloyd George*, p.130
88 Clark (ed.), *A Good Innings*, p.160
89 Ibid.
90 Marcosson, *Adventures in Interviewing*, p.126
91 Lloyd George, *War Memoirs*, pp.586–587
92 Beaverbrook, *Politicians and War* II, p.201
93 *The Times*, 2 December 1916, p.9
94 Ibid.
95 Thompson, *Northcliffe*, p.262
96 McEwen, 'Northcliffe and Lloyd George at War', p.663
97 Taylor, *Politics in Wartime*, p.153
98 Ibid.
99 McEwen, 'Northcliffe and Lloyd George at War', p.664
100 Thorpe and Toye (eds), *Parliament and Politics*, p.235; Clark (ed.), *A Good Innings*, p.161; Roskill, *Hankey* I, p.326
101 Hammond, *C. P. Scott*, p.205
102 Clarke, *My Northcliffe Diary*, p.106
103 *The Times*, 2 December 1916, p.9
104 *The Times*, 4 December 1916
105 Roskill, *Hankey* I, p.316
106 McEwen, 'The Press and the Fall of Asquith', p.881
107 Wrench, *Geoffrey Dawson and Our Times*, p.140; Marlowe, *Milner*, p.256 n22
108 Wrench, *Geoffrey Dawson*, p.140; Thompson, *Northcliffe*, p.426 n 77
109 Clifford, *The Asquiths*, p.384 n1
110 Churchill, *Lord Derby*, p.231
111 Jenkins, *Asquith*, p.448
112 Ibid.
113 Vincent (ed.), *Crawford Papers*, p.374
114 Thompson, *Northcliffe*, p.260
115 Lloyd George, *War Memoirs*, pp.586–587
116 Steed, *Through Thirty Years* II, p.131
117 Wilson (ed.), *The Political Diaries of C. P. Scott*, pp.297–298
118 Ibid., p.298
119 Clark (ed.), *A Good Innings*, p.162
120 Asquith, *Diaries 1915–1918*, p.242
121 Thompson, *Northcliffe*, pp.258–259 / Dawson diary, Dawson box 66 ff.181–4
122 James, *Memoirs of a Conservative*, p.46
123 Clarke, *My Northcliffe Diary*, pp.107, 20
124 Judd, *Reading*, p.133
125 Egremont, *Balfour*, p.280; Judd, *Reading*, p.133
126 Beaverbrook, *Politicians and the War*, p.512
127 Clarke, *My Northcliffe Diary* p108; Koss, Haldane, p.306; McEwen, 'Northcliffe and Lloyd George at War', p.665 n45
128 Ferris, *The House of Northcliffe*, p.202
129 Taylor (ed.), *Lloyd George*, p.133
130 Thorpe and Toye (eds), *Parliament and Politics*, p.236
131 Ibid., p.237
132 Ibid.
133 Clark (ed.), *A Good Innings*, p.162
134 Ibid.
135 McEwen, 'The Press and the Fall of Asquith', p.863
136 Churchill, *Lord Derby*, p.232
137 McEwen, 'The Press and the Fall of Asquith', p.864

138 James, *Memoirs of a Conservative*, p.45
139 *Daily Mail*, 9 December 1916, p.9
140 Clarke, *My Northcliffe Diary*, p.98
141 Beaverbrook, *Politicians and the War*, p.544
142 Brendon, *Eminent Edwardians*, p.42
143 *Daily News*, 9 December 1916
144 Roskill, *Hankey* I, p.329
145 Riddell, *Lord Riddell's War Diary 1914–1918*, p.231
146 Brendon, *Eminent Edwardians*, p.42
147 *Daily Mail*, 11 Dec 1916
148 *The Times, The History of the Times* IV Part 1, p.307
149 *The Globe*, 12 December 1916
150 Wrench, *Geoffrey Dawson and Our Times*, p.141
151 Clifford, *The Asquiths*, p.388
152 Wilson (ed.), *The Political Diaries of C. P. Scott*, p.267
153 Sheffield and Bourne (eds), *Douglas Haig: War Diaries*, p.267
154 Terraine, *Douglas Haig*, p.269
155 Charteris, *Field-Marshal Earl Haig*, p.258
156 Beaverbrook, *Men and Power*, p.47
157 Repington, *First World War* I, p.427
158 Ibid., p.428
159 Sheffield, *The Chief*, p.202
160 *The Times*, 15 February 1917, p.9
161 Sheffield, *The Chief*, p.203
162 BL Add MS 62159 f.142
163 Mead, *The Good Soldier*, p.277; Lytton, 'Some Incidents', p.70
164 Mead, *The Good Soldier*, p.277
165 Thompson, *Northcliffe*, p.269
166 Northcliffe Archive Papers, *Viscount Northcliffe 1922*, Vol. III
167 Heffer, *Staring at God*, p.519
168 *The Times*, 19 March 1917, p.9
169 *The Times*, 21 March 1917, p.9
170 Wells, *Experiment in Autobiography* II, p.696
171 Ibid.
172 Repington, *The First World War* I, p.500
173 Jones, *A Life in Reuters*, p.197

174 Ibid., p.198
175 Ibid., p.200
176 Ibid., p.201
177 Ibid., p.202
178 *The Times*, 16 April 1917, p.7; Neander and Marlin, 'Media and Propaganda', p.69
179 *The Times*, 17 April 1915, p.5
180 Neander and Marlin, 'Media and Propaganda', p.71
181 Ibid.
182 Ibid., p.73
183 Badsey, *German Corpse Factory*, p.242
184 Ibid., p.243
185 Ibid., p.259
186 Ibid., p.269
187 Ibid., p.326
188 Taylor (ed.), *Lloyd George*, p.157
189 BL Add MSS 62172 f.62
190 Lloyd George, *War Memoirs* I, p.1000
191 Ibid.
192 Roskill, *Hankey* I, p.391
193 Wilson (ed.), *The Political Diaries of C. P. Scott*, p.xx
194 Beaverbrook, *Men and Power*, p.64
195 BL Add Mss 49738; Lloyd George, *War Memoirs* I, p.1000
196 Lloyd George, *War Memoirs* I, p.1000

Chapter Sixteen:
The British War Mission

1 Ryan, *Lieutenant-Colonel Charles à Court Repington*, p.174
2 BL Add MSS 62157.ff.76–77
3 BL Add MSS 62161 f.125
4 HC Deb, 7 June 1917, Vol. 94 cc324
5 Northcliffe Archive Papers RPR.027
6 Marcosson, *Adventures in Interviewing*, pp.132–133
7 Spender, *Sir Robert Hudson*, p.151
8 Pound and Harmsworth, *Northcliffe*, p.536
9 Steed, *Through Thirty Years* II, pp.140–141; Thompson, *Northcliffe*, p.232

10 Ferris, *The House of Northcliffe*, p.203
11 Ibid.
12 Marcosson, *Adventures in Interviewing*, p.133
13 Willert, *The Road to Safety*, p.100
14 Ibid.
15 Ibid., p.102
16 Ibid.
17 Ibid., p.103
18 Ibid., pp.96–98
19 Ibid., p.97
20 Brendon, *Eminent Edwardians*, p.47
21 Thompson, *Northcliffe*, p.279
22 Ibid., p.280
23 Lloyd George, *War Memoirs* I, p.1004
24 Morison, *Personality and Diplomacy*, p.15
25 Lloyd George, *War Memoirs* I, p.1004
26 Willert, *The Road to Safety*, p.104
27 Morison, *Personality and Diplomacy*, p.15
28 Willert, *The Road to Safety*, p.103
29 Lloyd George, *War Memoirs* I, p.1005
30 Ibid., p.1003
31 LG Papers F41/7/8
32 Morton, *Woodrow Wilson*, p.29
33 Brendon, *Eminent Edwardians*, p.48; Willert, *The Road to Safety*, p.98; Morton, *Woodrow Wilson*, p.29
34 Thompson, *Northcliffe*, p.280
35 Ibid.; Willert, *The Road to Safety*, pp.104–105
36 Thompson, *Northcliffe*, p.279
37 Willert, *The Road to Safety*, p.102
38 Morison, *Personality and Diplomacy*, p.15
39 Stuart, *Opportunity Knocks Once*, p.54
40 Tracy, *Who's Who in the British Mission*, p.xi
41 Northcliffe Family Archive, *Lord Northcliffe's Letters to His Mother*, 26 July 1917
42 Stuart, *Opportunity Knocks Once*, p.57
43 BL Add MSS 62161 f.137, Thompson, *Northcliffe*, p.283
44 Lyddon, *British War Missions to the United States*, p.29
45 Northcliffe Family Archive, *Lord Northcliffe's Letters to His Mother*, 5 October 1917
46 Thompson, *Northcliffe*, p.282
47 Morison, *Personality and Diplomacy*, p.17
48 McAdoo, *Crowded Years*, p.400
49 Ibid., p.401
50 Thompson, *Northcliffe*, p.282; Morison, *Personality and Diplomacy*, p.17
51 Steed, *Through Thirty Years* II, p.143
52 Lloyd George, *War Memoirs* I, p.1006
53 Ibid., p.1007
54 Ibid., p.1008
55 Morison, *Personality and Diplomacy*, p.18
56 Ibid., p.19
57 Northcliffe Family Archive, *Lord Northcliffe's Letters to His Mother*, 18 September 1917
58 Ibid., 26 July 1917
59 Ibid., 26 July 1917
60 Ibid., 12 August 1917
61 Ibid., 18 September 1917
62 Ibid., 18 September 1917
63 Ibid., 26 July 1917
64 Lloyd George, *War Memoirs* I, p.1318
65 Ibid., p.1371
66 Asquith, *Diaries 1915–1918*, p.329
67 *Current Opinion*, October 1917, No. 63 p.236
68 Harmsworth, 'What America Is Fighting For', p.236
69 Ibid., pp.235–237
70 Northcliffe Family Archive, *Lord Northcliffe's Letters To His Mother*, 5 October 1917
71 Brendon, *Eminent Edwardians*, p.49
72 Northcliffe Family Archive, *Lord Northcliffe's Letters To His Mother*, 21 October 1917
73 Thompson, *Northcliffe*, p.286
74 Northcliffe Family Archive, *Lord Northcliffe's Letters To His Mother*, 21 October 1917

75 Clarke, *My Northcliffe Diary*, p.161
76 Northcliffe Family Archive, *Lord Northcliffe's Letters To His Mother*, 21 October 1917
77 Ibid.
78 Ibid.
79 Ibid., 5 October 1917
80 Seymour (ed.), *The Intimate Papers of Colonel House* III, p.90
81 Pound and Harmsworth, *Northcliffe*, pp.28–29
82 Coote, *The Other Club*, p.53
83 Lloyd George, *War Memoirs* I, p.1005
84 Ibid., p.1008
85 Hardinge, *Old Diplomacy*, pp.213–214
86 Stuart, *Opportunity Knocks Once*, p.64

Chapter Seventeen: 'I Watch These People Vigilantly'

1   Steed, *Through Thirty Years* II, p.34
2   Stuart, *Opportunity Knocks Once*, p.66
3   BL Add MS 62157 f.90
4   Stuart, *Opportunity Knocks Once*, p.67
5   *The Times*, 3 December 1917, p.9
6   Liebich, 'The Antisemitism of Henry Wickham Steed', pp.191–192
7   BL Add MS 62397 f.168
8   Brendon, *Eminent Edwardians*, p.39
9   McEwen, 'Northcliffe and Lloyd George at War', p.668
10 Lloyd George, *War Memoirs* II, p.1110
11 Thompson, *Northcliffe*, p.292
12 Lloyd George, *War Memoirs* II, p.1110
13 Miller, *Boom*, pp.378 n23, 186
14 BL Add MS 62157 f.94
15 *The Times*, 16 November 1917
16 Owen, *Tempestuous Journey*, p.421
17 Lloyd George, *War Memoirs* I, p.1112
18 Morison, *Personality and Diplomacy*, p.32
19 Ibid., p.34
20 Ibid., p.35
21 Intimate House to Wilson, 16 Nov 1917; Morison, *Personality and Diplomacy*, p.36
22 Morison, *Personality and Diplomacy*, pp.36–37
23 McEwen, 'Northcliffe and Lloyd George at War', pp.668–669
24 McEwen (ed.), *The Riddell Diaries*, p.205
25 Self (ed.), *The Neville Chamberlain Diary Letters* I, p.232
26 Grieves, *Politics of Manpower*, p.122; Self (ed.), *The Neville Chamberlain Diary Letters* I, pp.186, 192, 195; Dilks, *Chamberlain*, p.222
27 BL Add MSS 62157
28 Pound and Harmsworth, *Northcliffe*, p.496
29 Ibid.
30 Morison, *Personality and Diplomacy*, pp.39–40
31 Intimate diary, 1 December 1917; Morison, *Personality and Diplomacy*, p.40
32 James, *Memoirs of a Conservative*, p.68
33 Kerry, *Lansdowne*, pp.284–289
34 Riddell, *Lord Riddell's War Diary 1914–1918*, p.296
35 *Daily Mail*, 30 November 1917
36 *The Times, History of The Times* IV Part 1, p.337
37 *The Times*, 30 November 1917, p.9
38 Grieves, *The Politics of Manpower*, p.166
39 Cooper, *Haig* II, p.205
40 Charteris, *Field-Marshal Earl Haig*, p.287
41 Mead, *The Good Soldier*, p.461
42 Charteris, *Field-Marshal Earl Haig*, p.287
43 Charteris, *At GHQ*, p.273; Sheffield, *The Chief*, p.257
44 Charteris, *Field-Marshal Earl Haig*, p.287n
45 Steed, *Through Thirty Years* II, p.141
46 Cooper, *Haig* II, p.205

47 Bond and Cave (eds), *Douglas Haig*, p.189
48 McEwen, '"Brass-Hats and the British Press During the First World War', p.61
49 BL Add MS 62159 f.184
50 *The Times*, 12 December 1917, p.9
51 Ibid.
52 BL Add MSS 62160 f.101
53 Grieves, *The Politics of Manpower, 1914–18*, p.165
54 Mead, *The Good Soldier*, p.312
55 Morison, *Personality and Diplomacy*, pp.36–37
56 Bacon, *The Life of John Rushworth Earl Jellicoe*, p.378
57 McEwen, 'The British Press and the Fall of Asquith', p.66
58 Woodward, *Lloyd George and the Generals*, p.232
59 Willis, *England's Holy War*, p.245
60 BL Add MSS 62253
61 Repington, *The First World War* II, p.149
62 Ibid.
63 Thomson, *Northcliffe*, p.295
64 BL Add MSS 62251 f.143
65 BL Add MSS 62160 f.104
66 Ibid., f.105
67 Woodward, *Lloyd George and the Generals*, p.246
68 Thomson, *Northcliffe*, p.296
69 Woodward, *Lloyd George and the Generals*, p.246; Barnes and Nicholson (eds), *The Leo Amery Diaries* I, p.201

Chapter Eighteen: Propaganda in Enemy Countries

1   Marquis, 'Words as Weapons', p.468
2   Koss, *The Rise and Fall of the Political Press in Britain* II, p.327; Wilson (ed.), *The Political Diaries of C. P. Scott*, p.336
3   Stuart, *Opportunity Knocks Once*, p.68
4   Wells, *Experiment in Autobiography* II, p.697
5   Steed, *Through Thirty Years* II, p.144
6   HC Deb, 19 February 1918, Vol. 103 cc.656–57
7   Barnes and Nicholson (eds), *The Leo Amery Diaries* I, p.208
8   Macmillan, *Winds of Change*, p.174
9   HC Deb, 11 March 1918, Vol. 104 cc.41–42
10 Wells, *Experiment in Autobiography* II, pp.700–701
11 Steed, *Through Thirty Years* II, p.187; Taylor, *Politics in Wartime*, p.153
12 Steed, *Through Thirty Years* II, p.225; Lloyd George, *War Memoirs*, II pp.1873–1874
13 Steed, *Through Thirty Years* II, p.226
14 Ibid.
15 Pound and Harmsworth, *Northcliffe*, p.669
16 BL Add MSS 62156 f.85
17 Ibid.
18 Ibid., f.86
19 Ibid., f.87
20 Ibid., f.87
21 Thompson, *Northcliffe*, p.300 / 62209
22 Thompson, *Northcliffe*, p.301; Steed, *Through Thirty Years* II, p.205
23 BL Add MS 62163 f.29
24 Ibid.
25 Lasswell, *Propaganda Technique in the Great War*, pp.28–29
26 Fraser, *Lord Esher*, pp.391–392
27 Ibid., p.392
28 Pound and Harmsworth, *Northcliffe*, p.629
29 BL Add MSS 62156 ff.90–91
30 BL Add MSS 62161 f.142
31 Ibid., f.143
32 BL Add MSS 62245 f.128
33 BL Add MSS 62161 f.52
34 BL Add MS 62157 f.115
35 Foot, *HG: A History of Mr Wells*, p.177
36 BL Add MSS 62161 f.154
37 BL Add MSS 62245 f.127
38 BL Add MS 62199 ff.125–29; Messinger, *British Propaganda and the State in the First World War*, p.156

39 Searle, *Corruption in British Politics*, p.248

40 *Morning Post*, 23 November 1917

41 Searle, *Corruption in British Politics*, p.251

42 Ibid., p.270

43 BL Add MSS 62172 f.95

44 Hammerton, *With Northcliffe in Fleet Street*, p.104

45 Wilson, *Lord Northcliffe*, p.10

46 Steed, *Through Thirty Years* II, p.225

47 Messinger, *British Propaganda and the State in the First World War*, p.155; Ferguson, *Pity of War*, p.213

48 Andrews and Taylor, *Lords and Laborers of the Press*, p.57; Lasswell, *Propaganda Technique in the Great War*, p.3

49 Messinger, *British Propaganda and the State in the First World War*, p.154

50 Steed, *Through Thirty Years* II, p.226

51 Marquis, 'Words as Weapons', p.493

52 Ibid.

53 Ibid.

54 BL Add MSS 62160 f.117

55 Ibid., f.114

56 BL Add MSS 62161 f.55

57 Ibid., f.56

58 Thompson, *Northcliffe*, p.307

59 BL Add MSS 62247A f.84

60 *The Times*, 5 January 1920, p.17

61 Pound and Harmsworth, *Northcliffe*, p.760

Chapter Nineteen: The Rift With Lloyd George

1 Marcosson, *Adventures in Interviewing*, p.116

2 Koss, *The Rise and Fall of the Political Press in Britain* II, p.327

3 Riddell, *Lord Riddell's War Diary 1914–1918*, p.366

4 *Daily Mail*, 7 October 1918

5 Steed, *Through Thirty Years* II, pp.243–244

6 Mitchell, *My Fill of Days*, p.297; Steed, *Through Thirty Years* II, pp.244–245

7 Steed, *Through Thirty Years* II, p.245

8 Mitchell, *My Fill of Days*, p.297

9 Steed, *Through Thirty Years* II, p.246

10 *Evening News*, 28 October 1918

11 *Daily Mail*, 23 and 25 October 1919

12 Thompson, *Northcliffe*, p.310

13 Steed, *Through Thirty Years* II, p.249

14 Thompson, *Northcliffe*, p.310

15 Pound & Harmsworth, *Northcliffe*, p.682

16 *The Times*, 4 November 1918, p.9

17 Ibid.

18 Steed, *Through Thirty Years* II, p.246

19 HC Deb, 04 November 1918, Vol. 110 cc.1799–800

20 HC Deb, 07 November 1918, Vol. 110 c.2350

21 Messinger, *British Propaganda and the State in the First World War*, p.158

22 Ibid., p.159

23 Colvin, *The Life of Lord Carson* III, p.367

24 Steed, *Through Thirty Years* II, p.227

25 Northcliffe Archive Papers RPR.023

26 Andrews and Taylor, *Lords and Laborers of the Press*, p.62

27 Ibid., p.48

28 Marquis, 'Word as Weapons', p.493

29 Seymour (ed.), *The Intimate Papers of Colonel House* III, p.61

30 *The Times*, 6 February 1921

31 Bentinck, *The Kaiser in Exile*, p.63

32 Wilhelm II, *Comparative History*, p.49

33 Steed, *Through Thirty Years* II, p.249

34 Lloyd George, *Memoirs of the Peace Conference* I, p.176

35 Ibid.

36 Steed, *Through Thirty Years* II, p.249; Andrews and Taylor, *Lords and Laborers of the Press*, p.57

37 Lloyd George, *Memoirs of the Peace Conference* I, p.176;

Amery, *My Political Life* II, p.180; Riddell, *Intimate Diary*, p.3

38 Anthony Howard in *Sunday Times* 7 May 2000; Ryan, *Lord Northcliffe*, p.8; Macmillan, *Peacemakers*, p.45

39 Owen, *The Real Lord Northcliffe*, p.47

40 Steed, *Through Thirty Years* II, p.249; Andrews and Taylor, *Lords and Laborers of the Press*, p.57

41 Pound and Harmsworth, *Northcliffe*, pp.882–883

42 Blake, *Unknown Prime Minister*, p.391

43 BL Add MS 62157 f.129

44 Clarke, *My Northcliffe Diary*, p.117

45 Lloyd George, *Memoirs of the Peace Conference* I, p.176

46 Wrench, *Geoffrey Dawson and Our Times*, pp.169–170

47 Ibid., p.170

48 Thompson, *Northcliffe*, p.315

49 Taylor, *The Reluctant Press Lord*, p.196; BL Add MS 62197 f.27

50 Wrench, *Geoffrey Dawson and Our Times*, p.170

51 Roskill (ed.), *Hankey* II, p.25

52 Ramsden (ed.), *Real Old Tory Politics*, p.117

53 BL Add MSS 62245 f149

54 Ibid., f.149

55 Ibid., f.147

56 Wrench, *Geoffrey Dawson and Our Times*, p.179

57 Ibid., p.171

58 BL Add MS 62157 f.137

59 Ibid., f.139

60 Butler and Butler, *British Political Facts*, p.267

61 Northcliffe Archive Papers North.008

62 Ibid.

63 Ibid.

64 Greenwall, *Northcliffe*, p.140

65 Clarke, *My Northcliffe Diary*, p.123

66 Ibid.

67 Greenwall, *Northcliffe*, p.140

68 BL Add MS 62199 f.153

69 Stuart, *Opportunity Knocks Once*, p.92

70 BL Add MS 62160 f38

71 Wrench, *Geoffrey Dawson and Our Times*, p.180

72 Blake, *The Unknown Prime Minister*, p.399

73 BL Add MS 62245 f.161

74 Pound and Harmsworth, *Northcliffe*, p.693

75 Thompson, *Northcliffe*, p.320

76 BL Add MS 62245 f.161

77 Ibid.

78 Northcliffe Archive Papers; Churchill correspondence

79 BL Add MS 62245 f.163

80 Wrench, *Geoffrey Dawson and Our Times*, p.182

81 BL Add MS 62245 f.177

82 Wrench, *Geoffrey Dawson and Our Times*, p.183

83 Steed, *Through Thirty Years* II, p.286

84 Ibid., p287

85 Ibid.

86 *The Times, The History of The Times* IV Part 1, p.486

87 BL Add MS 62245 f.182

88 Wrench, *Geoffrey Dawson and Our Times*, p.187

89 Ibid., p.175

90 Ibid.

91 Ibid., p.190

92 Riddell, *Intimate Diary*, p.46

93 Ibid., p.265

94 Elcock, *Portrait of a Decision*, p.206; Steed, *Through Thirty Years* II, p.321

95 Elcock, *Portrait of a Decision*, p.206

96 Northcliffe Archive Papers North.008

97 Anthony Howard in *Sunday Times*, 7 May 2000

98 BL Add MS 62196 f.110

99 Ibid.

100 Taylor (ed.), *Lloyd George*, p.180

101 HC Deb, 16 April 1919, Vol. 114, cc.2952–3

102 Ibid., c.2953

103 Self (ed.), *The Neville Chamberlain Diary Letters* I, p.322

104 Steed, *Through Thirty Years* II, p.322

105 BL Add MSS 62201 f.96

106 Self (ed.), *The Neville Chamberlain Diary Letters* I, p.322
107 Thorpe and Toye (eds), *Parliament and Politics*, pp.293–94
108 Owen, *The Real Lord Northcliffe*, p.49
109 Alcock, *Portrait of a Decision*, p.208
110 Thompson, *Northcliffe*, p.327

Chapter Twenty:
Pursuing the Vendetta

1 Clarke, *My Northcliffe Diary*, p.182
2 BL Add MS 62157 f.141
3 BL Add MS 62199 f.187
4 Brendon, *Eminent Edwardians*, p.7
5 BL Add MSS 62201 f.196
6 Northcliffe Archive Papers *Times* Bulletins 1919–1922
7 Ibid.
8 Ibid.
9 Andrews and Taylor, *Lords and Laborers of the Press*, pp.60–61
10 Ibid., p.61
11 BL Add MSS 62161 f.62
12 Ibid.,ff.66–67
13 Steed, *Through Thirty Years* II, p.344
14 Ibid.; Colvin, *The Life of Lord Carson* Vol. III, pp.375–377
15 Northcliffe Archive Papers North.002
16 BL Add MSS 62201 f.218
17 Steed, *Through Thirty Years* II, p.339
18 Hirstfield, 'Lord Northcliffe as a Music-Lover', p.990
19 Ibid.
20 Ibid.
21 BL Add MS 62200 f.10
22 BL Add MSS 62247A f.30
23 Riddell, *Intimate Diary*, p.104
24 BL Add MS 62200 f.6
25 Riddell, *Intimate Diary*, p.160; Clarke, *Northcliffe in History*, p.176; Thompson, *Northcliffe*, p.336
26 BL Add MS 62169 f.114
27 Ibid., f.78
28 Ibid., f.89
29 Clarke, *My Northcliffe Diary*, p.132
30 Thompson, *Northcliffe*, p.332; BL Add MSS 62247A f.73
31 Riddell, *Intimate Diary*, p.159
32 Steed, *Through Thirty Years* II, p.352
33 Ibid.
34 Voigt, *Combed Out*, pp.118–119
35 BL Add MSS 62247A f.71
36 Pound and Harmsworth, *Northcliffe*, p.762
37 Vincent (ed.), *Crawford Papers*, p.338
38 BL Add MSS 62247B f.5
39 BL Add MS 62197 f.45
40 Clarke, *My Northcliffe Diary*, p.187
41 BL Add MS 62179 f116
42 *The Times*, 8 May 1920
43 Ibid.
44 Liebich, 'The Antisemitism of Henry Wickham Steed', p.181 n5
45 Ibid., pp.180–181
46 Ibid., p.183 n15
47 BL Add MS 62248A f.22
48 Hammerton, *With Northcliffe in Fleet Street*, p.11
49 Ibid., p.92
50 *The Times*, 16 June 1929, p.16
51 BL Add MSS 62356 f.131
52 Ibid., f.135
53 BL Add MSS 62367 ff.64–65
54 Clarke, *My Northcliffe Diary*, p.175
55 Northcliffe Archive Papers; Churchill correspondence
56 Ibid.
57 Thompson, *Northcliffe*, p.336
58 Ibid., pp.338–339
59 Ryan, *Northcliffe*, p.147
60 Pound and Harmsworth, *Northcliffe*, p.776
61 Thompson, *Northcliffe*, p.341
62 Ryan, *Northcliffe*, p.147
63 Clarke, *My Northcliffe Diary*, p.180
64 Brendon, *Eminent Edwardians*, pp.5–6
65 Clarke, *My Northcliffe Diary*, p.173
66 Pound and Harmsworth, *Northcliffe*, p.775

67 BL Add MS 62169 f.105
68 BL Add MS 62248A f.45
69 Ibid., f.49
70 Andrews and Taylor, *Lords and Laborers of the Press*, p.55
71 BL Add MSS 62201 f.143
72 BL Add MSS 62241 f.38
73 BL Add MSS 62187 f.11
74 Churchill, *Thoughts and Adventures*, pp.28–29
75 BL Add MSS 62241 f.52
76 BL Add MSS 62187 f.25
77 BL Add MS 62197 f.57
78 BL Add MS 62248A f.85
79 BL Add NS 62200 f.108
80 BL Add MS 62248A ff.97–99
81 Ibid., f.101
82 BL Add MSS 62366
83 Clarke, *My Northcliffe Diary*, p.206
84 Messinger, *British Propaganda and the State in the First World War*, p.148
85 Northcliffe Archives Papers North.021
86 Ibid.
87 Messinger, *British Propaganda and the State in the First World War*, p.148
88 Thompson, *Northcliffe*, p.351
89 BL Add MSS 62200 f.113
90 Clarke, *My Northcliffe Diary*, p.211
91 Ibid.
92 Pound and Harmsworth, *Northcliffe*, p.794
93 Ibid.
94 Hammerton, *With Northcliffe in Fleet Street*, p.93
95 Clarke, *My Northcliffe Diary*, p.217
96 Thompson, *Northcliffe*, p.353
97 BL Add MSS 62365
98 Riddell, *Intimate Diary*, p.307
99 *The Times*, 13 July 1921, p.13
100 Thompson, *Northcliffe*, p.356

Chapter Twenty-one: The World Tour

1 Owen, *The Real Lord Northcliffe*, p.26; Brendon, *Eminent Edwardians*, p.54
2 Riddell, *Intimate Diary*, p.307
3 Pound and Harmsworth, *Northcliffe*, p.815
4 Ibid., pp.799–800
5 BL Add MS 62169 f.122
6 Ibid., f.123
7 Owen, *The Real Lord Northcliffe*, pp.25–26
8 Ibid., p.26
9 Northcliffe Archive Papers RPR.020
10 Self (ed.), *The Neville Chamberlain Diary Letters* II, p.74
11 BL Add MSS 62367 f.62
12 BL Add MSS 62187 f.65
13 Pierce, *Lord Northcliffe: Transatlantic Influences*, p.23
14 Rose, *George V*, p.240
15 BL Add MS 62155 ff.70–72; Hansard 5th Series Vol. 145 cc.915–917
16 Wilson (ed.), *The Political Diaries of C. P. Scott*, p.396
17 Taylor, *Lloyd George*, pp.232–233
18 Northcliffe Archive Papers RPR.017
19 Pound and Harmsworth, *Northcliffe*, p.803
20 BL Add MSS 62367 ff.89–90, 83
21 Thompson, *Northcliffe*, p.360
22 BL Add MS 62169 f.125
23 Thompson, *Northcliffe*, p.362
24 Pound and Harmsworth, *Northcliffe*, p.807
25 Northcliffe Archive Papers RPR.034
26 Northcliffe Archive Papers NORTH.033
27 Northcliffe Archive Papers RPR.034
28 BL Add MS 62169 f.129
29 Brendon, *Eminent Edwardians*, p.54
30 Northcliffe, *My Journey*, p.37; Brendon, *Eminent Edwardians*, p.54
31 *The Times*, 3 October 1921
32 Northcliffe, *My Journey*, p.39
33 BL Add MSS 62187 f.95
34 Ibid., f.97
35 Ibid., f.94
36 BL Add MS 62169 f.143
37 BL Add MS 62197 f.78
38 Ibid.

39 Stuart, *Opportunity Knocks Once*, p.94
40 Northcliffe Archives Papers North.021
41 Thompson, *Northcliffe*, p.365
42 Ryan, *Lord Northcliffe*, p.19
43 Northcliffe, *My Journey*, p.153
44 Ibid., p.94
45 Begbie, *The Mirrors of Downing Street*, pp.62–63, 68
46 Northcliffe, *My Journey*, p.103
47 BL Add MS 62248B f.23
48 BL Add MS 62200 f.137
49 Pound and Harmsworth, *Northcliffe*, p.818
50 BL Add MS 62197 f.82
51 Northcliffe Archive Papers RPR.020
52 BL Add MSS 62187 f.105
53 BL Add MS 62179 f.144
54 Northcliffe, *My Journey*, p.150
55 BL Add MS 62397 f.3
56 Ibid., *passim*
57 BL Add MS 62179 ff.150–53
58 Ibid., f.156
59 Jenkins, *Market for Glory*, p.116
60 BL Add MS 62397 f.14
61 Ibid., f.15
62 Ibid.
63 Ibid., f.16
64 Ibid., f.20
65 Ibid., f.19
66 Northcliffe Archive Papers RPR.027
67 BL Add MS 62397 f.23
68 Ibid., f.25
69 Ibid., f.28
70 BL Add MS 62197 f.83
71 Northcliffe, *My Journey*, p.197
72 BL Add MS 62397 f.48
73 Ibid., f.73
74 Ibid., f.72
75 Thompson, *Northcliffe*, p.372
76 Pound and Harmsworth, *Northcliffe*, p.820
77 BL Add MS 62397 f.81
78 Ibid., f.76
79 Ibid., f.82
80 Ibid., f.98
81 Ibid., f.110
82 Ibid., f.114
83 Ibid.
84 Ibid.
85 Ibid.
86 Ibid., f.120
87 Ibid., f.130
88 Ibid., f.121
89 Ibid., f.8
90 Northcliffe, *My Journey*, p.240
91 Northcliffe Archive Papers RPR.027
92 Thompson, *Northcliffe*, p.366
93 BL Add MS 62397 f.123
94 Ibid.
95 Ibid., f.132
96 Ibid., f.136
97 Ibid., f.137
98 Ibid., f.138
99 Ibid., f.144
100 Ibid., f.145
101 Ibid., f.127
102 BL Add MSS 62241 f.147
103 BL Add MS 62397 f.161
104 BL Add MS 62179 f.162
105 BL Add MS 62397 f.157
106 Ibid., f.159
107 Ibid., f.165
108 BL Add MS 62197 f.233
109 BL Add MS 62397 f.168
110 Bentwich, *Wanderer Between Two Worlds*, p.123
111 Ibid., pp.123–124
112 BL Add MS 62397 f.177
113 *The Times*, 8 November 1922
114 BL Add MS 62397 ff.169–70
115 Ibid., f.168
116 Ibid., ff.169–71
117 Ibid., f.171
118 Ibid., f.173
119 Ibid., f.184
120 Ibid., f.187

Chapter Twenty-two: Degeneration

1 Northcliffe Archive Papers *Times* Bulletins 1919–1922
2 BL Add MS 62397 f.188
3 Ibid., f.189
4 Thompson, *Northcliffe*, p.380
5 Northcliffe Archive Papers RPR.027
6 Pemberton, *Lord Northcliffe*, p.247
7 Stuart, *Opportunity Knocks Once*, p.97
8 BL Add MS 62197 f.90
9 BL Add MS 62200 f.152

10 BL Add MS 62197 f.93
11 BL Add MSS 62187 f.158; BL Add MS 62241 f.163
12 BL Add MS 62197 f.97
13 Pound and Harmsworth, *Northcliffe*, p.831
14 BL Add MS 62197 f.98
15 *Daily Mail*, 7 May 1920
16 Koss, *Haldane*, p.150
17 Weizmann, *Trial and Error*, p.351
18 Pound and Harmsworth, *Northcliffe*, p.846
19 Weizmann, *Trial and Error*, p.351
20 Pound and Harmsworth, *Northcliffe*, pp.835–36
21 Wilson (ed.), *The Political Diaries of C. P. Scott*, p.419
22 Pound and Harmsworth, *Northcliffe*, p.830
23 *The Times, The History of the Times* IV Part 2, p.629
24 Pound and Harmsworth, *Northcliffe*, p.834
25 Thompson, *Northcliffe*, p.385
26 Jones, *A Life in Reuters*, p.245
27 Ibid., p.250
28 BL Add MS 62169 f.160
29 Churchill, *Lord Derby*, p.428
30 BL Add MS 62169 f.161
31 Clarke, *My Northcliffe Diary*, p.232
32 Ibid., pp.231–32
33 Pemberton, *Northcliffe*, p.246
34 Thompson, *Northcliffe*, p.385
35 Pound and Harmsworth, *Northcliffe*, p.835
36 BL Add MSS 62172 f.137
37 Thompson, *Northcliffe*, p.386
38 Northcliffe Archive Papers *Times* Bulletins 1919 –1922
39 BL Add MSS 62187 f.167, BL Add MS 62197 f.131 & 135
40 Clarke, *My Northcliffe Diary*, p.236
41 Northcliffe Archive Papers RPR.006
42 Clarke, *My Northcliffe Diary*, p.240
43 Ibid., p.238
44 Ibid., p.242
45 May, *Critical Times*, p.148
46 Ibid., p.151
47 BL Add MS 62197 f.157
48 Clarke, *My Northcliffe Diary*, p.273
49 Ibid.
50 Ibid., p.274
51 Thompson, *Northcliffe*, p.387
52 Clarke, *My Northcliffe Diary*, p.249
53 BL Add MS 62197 ff.191–92
54 Clarke, *My Northcliffe Diary*, p.252
55 Ibid., p.17
56 HC Deb, 03 April 1922, vol. 152 c.1891
57 Clarke, *My Northcliffe Diary*, p.254
58 Northcliffe Archives Papers North.021
59 BL Add MS 62197 f.203
60 Clarke, *My Northcliffe Diary*, pp.258–259
61 Ibid., p.261
62 Northcliffe Archive Papers *Times* Bulletins 1919–1922
63 Ibid.
64 Clarke, *My Northcliffe Diary*, p.263
65 Ibid., p.249
66 Northcliffe Archive Papers *Times* Bulletins 1919–1922
67 Clarke, *My Northcliffe Diary*, p.264
68 *Daily Mail*, 18 April 1922, p.9
69 Adams, *Bonar Law*, p.309
70 *Daily Mail*, 18 April 1922, p.6
71 Clarke, *My Northcliffe Diary*, p.268
72 Ibid.
73 Pound and Harmsworth, *Northcliffe*, pp.846–847
74 Ibid.
75 Clarke, *My Northcliffe Diary*, p.269
76 Northcliffe Archive Papers, North Messages to *The Times*, 20 April to 4 May 1922
77 Thompson, *Northcliffe*, p.388
78 Northcliffe Archive Papers RPR.023
79 BL Add MS 62248B f.107
80 Northcliffe Archive Papers *Times* Bulletins 1919–1922
81 Northcliffe Archive Papers, *Newspapers and Their Millionaires*, p.9

82　Ibid.
83　Ibid., pp.10–11
84　Ibid., p.11
85　Ibid., p.5
86　Clarke, *My Northcliffe Diary*, p.281
87　Ibid., p.283
88　Thompson, *Northcliffe*, p.391
89　Ibid., p.390
90　BL Add MSS 62156 f.67
91　Northcliffe Archive Papers RPR.027
92　Brendon, *Eminent Edwardians*, p.59
93　Thompson, *Northcliffe*, p.392
94　Pound and Harmsworth, *Northcliffe*, pp.860–861

Chapter Twenty-three: Death

1　Beaverbrook, *Men and Power*, p.61
2　Pound and Harmsworth, *Northcliffe*, p.863
3　Thompson, *Northcliffe*, p.392
4　Northcliffe Archive Papers RPR.027
5　Reed, *Insanity Fair*, p.58
6　Ibid., p.59
7　Northcliffe Archives Papers North.021
8　BL Add MSS 62187 f.177
9　Brendon, *Eminent Edwardians*, p.59
10　Clarke, *My Northcliffe Diary*, p.286
11　Ibid.
12　Brendon, *Eminent Edwardians*, p.3
13　Clarke, *My Northcliffe Diary*, p.19
14　Ibid., pp.286–287
15　Northcliffe Archive Papers RPR.023
16　Ibid.
17　Ibid.
18　Northcliffe Archives Papers North.021
19　Northcliffe Archive Papers RPR.023
20　Northcliffe Archives Papers North.021
21　Ibid.
22　Ibid.
23　Ibid.
24　Ibid.
25　Ibid.
26　Ibid.
27　Ibid.
28　Northcliffe Archive Papers RPR.027
29　Ibid.
30　Northcliffe Archives Papers North.021
31　Northcliffe Archive Papers Geraldine Mary Harmsworth File
32　Northcliffe Archives Papers North.021
33　Northcliffe Archive Papers RPR.027; *The Times, The History of the Times* IV, p.680; Northcliffe Archive Papers RPR.022
34　Northcliffe Archive Papers RPR.023
35　Ibid.
36　*Taylor, The Great Outsiders*, p.214
37　*Daily Mail*, 16 June 1922
38　Thompson, *Northcliffe*, p.395; Clarke, *My Northcliffe Diary*, p.291
39　Clarke, *My Northcliffe Diary*, p.292
40　Ibid., pp.25, 293–294
41　Northcliffe Archive Papers RPR.023
42　Beaverbrook, *Men and Power*, pp.90, 358
43　King, *Strictly Personal*, p.57; Brendon, *Eminent Edwardians*, p.5
44　*The Times*, 11 December 1971, p.13
45　*Daily Mail*, 20 June 1922, p.9
46　Northcliffe Archive Papers RPR.023
47　Northcliffe Archives Papers North.021
48　Ibid.
49　Ibid.
50　Taylor (ed.), *Lloyd George*, p.242
51　Northcliffe Archives Papers North.021
52　Soames (ed.), *Speaking for Themselves*, p.255
53　Ibid., p.257
54　Clarke, *My Northcliffe Diary*, p.297
55　Steed, *Through Thirty Years* II,

p.385; Northcliffe Archive Papers
RPR.023

56 Steed, *Through Thirty Years* II,
p.385

57 Northcliffe Archive Papers
RPR.017

58 Gilbert (ed.), *Winston S Churchill*
IV, Companion Volume Part 3,
pp.1951–1952

59 Northcliffe Archive Papers
North.021

60 Clarke, *My Northcliffe Diary*,
p.295

61 Ibid., p.294

62 Northcliffe Archive Papers
RPR.027

63 Ibid.

64 Owen, *The Real Lord Northcliffe*,
p.26

65 Northcliffe Archive Papers, *The
Times AAA Journal*, p.13; Clarke,
My Northcliffe Diary, pp.300–301

66 *British Medical Journal*, 19
August 1922, p.319

67 Ibid.

68 Email from Professor Ronak to
the author, 30 December 2021

69 Andrews and Taylor, *Lords and
Laborers of the Press*, p.61

70 *Answers to Correspondents*, 1
Sept 1888, p.15

71 Ryan, *Lord Northcliffe*, p.153

72 Ibid., p.13

73 Northcliffe Archive Papers
RPR.023

74 Northcliffe Archive Papers, *The
Times AAA Journal*, p.13

75 Owen, *The Real Lord Northcliffe*,
pp.26–27

76 Edwards, 'Geraldine
Harmsworth', p.467

77 Stuart, *Opportunity Knocks
Once*, p.97

78 Clarke, *My Northcliffe Diary*,
p.117

79 Northcliffe Archive Papers
RPR.017

80 Enid Stokes' unpublished memoir

81 Northcliffe Archive Papers
RPR.017

82 Ibid.

83 *Illustrated London News*, 8 Oct
1963

84 Swaffer, *Northcliffe's Return*,
passim

85 Brendon, *Eminent Edwardians*,
p.62

86 Northcliffe Archive Papers
RPR.020

Conclusion:
The Napoleon of Fleet Street

1   Harmsworth, 'The Simultaneous
Newspapers of the Twentieth
Century', p.79

2   Taylor, *Politics in Wartime*, p.150

3   Lloyd George, *War Memoirs* I,
p.1006

4   McEwen, '"Brass-Hats and the
British Press During the First
World War', p.53

5   Stuart, *Opportunity Knocks
Once*, p.67

6   Morris, *The Scaremongers*, pp.4–5

7   Peter Preston in the *Observer*, 21
May 2000

8   Smith, *Marshall Hall*, p.92;
Chalaby, 'Smiling People
Make People Smile', p.39;
Playne, *Pre-War Mind*, p.112;
MacDonogh, *The Last Kaiser*,
p.376

9   Ferguson, *The Pity of War*,
p.230; Morison, *Personality and
Diplomacy*, p.9

10 Northcliffe Archive Papers
North.002

11 Lowndes (ed.), *The Diaries and
Letters of Marie Belloc Lowndes*,
pp.272–273

12 Gollin, 'England is No Longer an
Island', p.45

13 Brendon, *Eminent Edwardians*,
p.5

14 Ibid., p.45

15 Richard Davenport-Hines in *The
Times Literary Supplement*, 21
June 2000

16 Ryan, *Lord Northcliffe*, p.11

17 Northcliffe Archive Papers
RPR.023

18 Griffiths (ed.), *Encyclopedia of the
British Press*, p.292

19 Ibid.

20 Wrench, *Struggle 1914–1920*,
pp.309–319

21 Crowson (ed.), *Fleet Street, Press Barons and Politics*, p.66
22 Hammerton, *With Northcliffe in Fleet Street*, p.22
23 Griffiths (ed.), *Encyclopedia of the British Press*, p.184
24 McEwen, 'Northcliffe and Lloyd George at War', p.651
25 *Sunday Times*, 7 May 2000
26 Ryan, *Lord Northcliffe*, p.10
27 McEwen, 'The National Press During the First World War', pp.465–466
28 English, 'Legend of "The Chief"', p.7
29 Pound and Harmsworth, *Northcliffe*, p.122; Andrews and Taylor, *Lords and Laborers of the Press*, p.45
30 Owen, *The Real Lord Northcliffe*, p.5; Andrews and Taylor, *Lords and Laborers of the Press*, p.45
31 Williams, *Dangerous Estate*, p.151
32 Pierce, *Lord Northcliffe: Transatlantic Influences*, p.30
33 Owen, *The Real Lord Northcliffe*, p.33
34 Brendon, *Eminent Edwardians*, p.38
35 Owen, *The Real Lord Northcliffe*, p.4
36 Ryan, *Lord Northcliffe*, p.31
37 BL Add MS 62392 f.16
38 Hammerton, *With Northcliffe in Fleet Street*, p.11
39 Northcliffe Archive Papers RPR.023
40 Richard Davenport-Hines in *The Times Literary Supplement*, 2 June 2000
41 Brendon, *Eminent Edwardians*, p.4; Angel, *After All*, p.129
42 Brendon, *Eminent Edwardians*, p.50
43 Ibid.
44 Begbie, *The Mirrors of Downing Street*, p.67
45 Thompson, *Northcliffe*, p.395; Riddell Diary title and page number
46 Gilman, Lawrence, 'Review of *Americans*', p.409
47 Heffer, *Age of Decadence*, p.544
48 Taylor, *Politics in Wartime*, p.150
49 Spengler, *The Decline of the West*, p.461
50 McEwen, '"Brass-Hats and the British Press During the First World War', p.59
51 Brendon, *Eminent Edwardians*, p.42
52 Thompson, *Northcliffe*, p.395
53 Hammond, *C.P. Scott of the Manchester Guardian*, p.97
54 Ryan, *Lord Northcliffe*, p.8
55 Ferguson, *The Pity of War*, p.22
56 Anthony Howard in *Sunday Times*, 7 May 2000
57 Swaffer, *Northcliffe's Return*, p.31
58 Northcliffe, *My Journey*, p.285
59 Ryan, *Northcliffe*, p.131
60 *Newspaper World*, 2 September 1922
61 Blake, *The Unknown Prime Minister*, p.294
62 *Times Literary Supplement*, 9 November 2001, p.9; May, *Critical Times*, p.95
63 *Literary Review*, December 2001, p.55
64 Begbie, *Mirrors of Downing Street*, pp.62–63, 68
65 Brendon, *Eminent Edwardians*, p.4
66 Clarke, *My Northcliffe Diary*, p.15
67 Kuchta, *Semi-Detached Empire*, p.29; Heffer, *The Age of Decadence*, p.544
68 Hammerton, *With Northcliffe in Fleet Street*, p.22
69 Jenkins, *Market for Glory*, p.33
70 Wrench, *Uphill*, p.141; Wrench, *Geoffrey Dawson and Our Times*, p.64
71 Northcliffe Archive Papers RPR.022
72 Angel, *After All*, pp.102–103
73 Ibid., p.111
74 Stuart, *Opportunity Knocks Once*, p.75
75 Spender, *Life, Journalism and Politics* II, p.166
76 Steed, *Through Thirty Years* II, p.340

BIBLIOGRAPHY

All books were published in London unless otherwise stated

BOOKS

Adams, R. J. Q., *Arms and the Wizard: David Lloyd George and the Ministry of Munitions 1915–16* (1978)
—, *Bonar Law* (1999)
—, *Balfour: The Last Grandee* (2007)
—, and Poirier, Philip P., *The Conscription Controversy in Great Britain 1900–18* (1987)
Addison, Adrian, *Mail Men: The Unauthorized Story of the Daily Mail* (2017)
Amery, L. S., *My Political Life*, vol. 2 (1953)
Andrews, L., and Taylor, H. A., *Lords and Labourers of the Press* (1970)
Angel, Norman, *After All* (1951)
Asquith, Lady Cynthia, *Diaries 1915–1918* (1968)

Bacon, Admiral Sir R. H., *The Life of John Rushworth Earl Jellicoe* (1936)
Badsey, Stephen, *The German Corpse Factory* (2014)
Barnes, John, and Nicholson, David (eds), *The Leo Amery Diaries, vol. 1, 1896–1929* (1980)
Baumgart, Winifred, *Imperialism: The Idea and Reality of British and French Colonial Expansion, 1880–1914* (1982)
Beaverbrook, Lord, *Politicians and the Press* (1925)
—, *Politicians and the War, 1914–1916* (1928)
—, *Men and Power* (1956)
—, *The Decline and Fall of Lloyd George* (1963)

Begbie, Harold, *The Mirrors of Downing Street* (1920)

Bell, E. H. C. Moberly, *The Life and Letters of C. F. Moberly Bell* (1927)

Bentinck, Lady Norah, *The Ex-Kaiser in Exile* (1921)

Bentwich, Norman, *Wanderer Between Two Worlds* (1941)

Birkenhead, Viscount, *Points of View*, 2 vols (1922)

Blumenfeld, R. D., *R. D. B.'s Diary* (1930)

Blake, Robert, *The Unknown Prime Minister: The Life and Times of Andrew Bonar Law 1858–1923* (1955)

Blunt, Wilfrid Scawen, *My Diaries* (1932)

Bond, Brian, and Cave, Nigel (eds), *Douglas Haig: A Reappraisal 70 Years On* (1999)

Bourne, Richard, *Lords of Fleet Street: The Harmsworth Dynasty* (1990)

Brendon, Piers, *Eminent Edwardians* (1979)

—, *The Life and Death of the Press Barons* (1982)

Brett, Maurice V. (ed.), *Journals and Letters of Reginald, Viscount Esher*, 2 vols (1934)

Brock, Michael and Eleanor (eds), *H. H. Asquith: Letters to Venetia Stanley* (1985)

—, *Margot Asquith's Great War Diary 1914–1916* (2014)

Brown, Sir Arthur Whitten, *Flying the Atlantic in Sixteen Hours* (1920)

Butler, David, and Buler, Gareth, *British Political Facts* (1994)

Campbell, John, F. E., *First Earl of Birkenhead* (1983)

Campbell, John, *Haldane: Forgotten Statesman who Shaped Modern Britain* (2020)

Camplin, Jamie, *Rise of the Plutocrats* (1978)

Camrose, Viscount, *British Newspapers and Their Controllers* (1947)

Cecil, Hugh, and Liddle, Peter (eds), *Facing Armageddon: The First World War Experienced* (1996)

Carson, William E., *Northcliffe: Britain's Man of Power* (1918)

Cassar, George H., *Kitchener: Architect of Victory* (1977)

—, *The Tragedy of Sir John French* (1985)

Catterall, Peter, Seymour-Ure, Colin, and Smith, Adrian (eds), *Northcliffe's Legacy* (2000)

Chapman, James, *British Comics: A Cultural History* (2011)

Charteris, Sir John, *Field-Marshal Earl Haig* (1929)

—, *At G.H.Q.* (1931)

Chirol, Sir Valentine, *Fifty Years in a Changing World* (1927)

Chisholm, Anne, and Davie, Michael, *Beaverbrook: A Life* (1992)

Churchill, Randolph, *Lord Derby* (1959)

Churchill, Winston S., *The World Crisis 1916–1918*, Part 1 (1927)
—, *Thoughts and Adventures* (1932)
Clark, Alan (ed.), *A Good Innings: The Private Papers of Lord Lee of Fareham* (1974)
Clarke, Tom, *My Northcliffe Diary* (1931)
—, *Northcliffe in History* (1950)
Cole, Margaret (ed.), *Beatrice Webb's Diaries 1912–14* (1952)
Clifford, Colin, *The Asquiths* (2002)
Colvin, Ian, *The Life of Lord Carson*, vol. III (1936)
Cooper, Alfred Duff, *Haig*, 2 vols (1935)
Courlander, Alphonse, *Mightier Than the Sword*, 1912
Cranfield, Geoffrey, *The Press and Society* (1978)
Crowson, N. J. (ed.), *Fleet Street, Press Barons and Politics: The Journals of Collin Brooks 1932–1940* (1998)
Cudlipp, Hugh, *The Prerogative of the Harlot* (1980)

Davenport-Hines, Richard (ed.), *Letters from Oxford: Hugh Trevor-Roper to Bernard Berenson* (2006)
Dilks, David, *Neville Chamberlain 1869–1929* (1984)
Driberg, Tom, *'Swaff': The Life and Times of Hannen Swaffer* (1974)
Driver, Hugh, *Lord Northcliffe and the Early Years of Rolls-Royce* (1998)
Dutton, David, *Austen Chamberlain: Gentleman in Politics* (1985)

Edmonds, Sir James (ed.), *History of the Great War: Military Operations France and Belgium 1916* (1932)
Egremont, Max, *Balfour: A Life of Arthur James Balfour* (1980)
Elcock, Howard, *Portrait of a Decision* (1972)
Engels, Matthew, *Tickle the Public: One Hundred Years of the Popular Press* (1996)

Ferguson, Niall, *The Pity of War* (1998)
—, *The World's Banker: The History of the House of Rothschild* (1998)
Ferris, Paul, *The House of Northcliffe: The Harmsworths of Fleet Street* (1971)
Finkelstein, David (ed.), *The Edinburgh History of the British and Irish Press*, vol. 2 (2020)
Foot, Michael, *The History of Mr Wells* (1995)
Fraser, Peter, *Lord Esher* (1973)
French, Field-Marshal Viscount, *1914* (1919)

Fritzinger, Linda, *Diplomat Without Portfolio: Valentine Chirol, His Life and The Times* (2006)

Fyfe, Hamilton, *Twells Brex: A Conqueror of Death* (1920)

—, *Northcliffe: An Intimate Biography* (1930)

George, W. L., *Caliban* (1920)

Gilbert, Bentley Brinkerhoff, *David Lloyd George: The Organizer of Victory 1912–1916* (1922)

Gilbert, Martin, *Winston Churchill and the Other Club* (privately printed) (2011)

Gilbert, Martin (ed.), *Churchill Companion Volumes*

Godwin, J. (ed.), *Eton: As She Is Not* (privately printed) (1883)

Gollin, A. M., *The Observer and J. L. Garvin 1908–1914* (1960)

—, *Balfour's Burden: Arthur Balfour and Imperial Preference* (1965)

—, *No Longer An Island: Britain and the Wright Brothers 1902–1909* (1984)

Greenwall, Harry J., *Northcliffe: Napoleon of Fleet Street* (1957)

Gregory, Adrian, *The Last Great War: British Society and the First World War* (2008)

Grieves, Keith, *The Politics of Manpower 1914–1918* (1988)

Griffiths, Denis (ed.), *The Encyclopedia of the British Press 1422–1992* (1992)

Grigg, John, *Lloyd George: The People's Champion 1902–1911* (2002)

—, *Lloyd George: From Peace to War 1912–1916* (2002)

—, *Lloyd George: War Leader 1916–1918* (2002)

Hague, Ffion, *The Pain and the Privilege: The Women in Lloyd George's Life* (2008)

Haldane, Richard, *An Autobiography* (1929)

Hale, Oron James, *Germany and the Diplomatic Revolution 1904–1906* (1931)

—, *Publicity and Diplomacy with Special Reference to England and Germany 1890–1914* (1940)

Hales-Dutton, Bruce, *Pioneering Places of British Aviation* (2020)

Hamilton, Ian, *The Happy Warrior: A Life of General Sir Ian Hamilton* (1966)

Hammerton, J. A., *With Northcliffe in Fleet Street* (1932)

Hammond, J. L., *C. P. Scott of the Manchester Guardian* (1934)

Hardinge, Lord, *Old Diplomacy* (1947)

Harmsworth, Alfred, Lord Northcliffe, *Ellen Terry Waltz* (1885)

—, *Motors and Motor-Driving* (1902)

—, *At the War* (1916)

—, *Newspapers and Their Proprietors* (1922)

—, *My Journey Round the World 1921–22* (1923)

Hart-Davis, Duff (ed.), *End of an Era: Letters and Journals of Sir Alan Lascelles from 1887 to 1920* (1988)

Hattersley, Roy, *David Lloyd George: The Great Outsider* (2010)

Heffer, Simon, *The Age of Decadence: Britain 1880 to 1914* (2017)

—, *Staring at God: Britain in the Great War* (2019)

Heffer, Simon (ed.), *The Diaries of 'Chips' Channon*, vol. 1 (2021)

Heuston, R. V. F., *Lives of the Lord Chancellors 1885–1940* (1964)

Hewins, W. A. S., *The Apologia of an Imperialisti*, 2 vols (1929)

Holroyd, Michael, *Lytton Strachey* (1994)

Horne, John, *German Atrocities, 1914: A History of Denial* (2001)

Hoyer, Katja, *Blood and Iron: The Rise and Fall of the German Empire 1871–1918* (2021)

Hui-Min, Lo (ed.), *The Correspondence of G. E. Morrison 1895–1912* (1976)

Hynes, Samuel, *A War Imagined* (1990)

James, Robert Rhodes, *Memoirs of a Conservative: J. C. C. Davidson's Memoirs and Papers 1910–1937* (1969)

— (ed.), *Winston S. Churchill: His Complete Speeches*, vol. 1 (1974)

Jeffery, Keith, *1916: A Global History* (2015)

Jeffries, J. M. N., *Front Everywhere* (1935)

Jenkins, Roy, *Asquith* (1964)

Jenkins, Simon, *The Market for Glory: Fleet Street Ownership in the 20th Century* (1986)

Jolliffe, John, *Raymond Asquith: Life and Letters* (1980)

Jones, Andrew, *The Buildings of Green Park* (2020)

Jones, Roderick, *A Life in Reuters* (1951)

Jones, Aled, *Powers of the Press: Newspapers, Power, and the Public in Nineteenth-Century England* (1996)

Jones, Thomas, *Lloyd George* (1951)

Jones, Kennedy, *Fleet Street and Downing Street* (1920)

Judd, Denis, *Lord Reading: Rufus Isaacs, First Marquess of Reading 1860–1935* (1982)

Kerry, Simon, *Lansdowne: The Last Great Whig* (2017)

Keynes, J. M., *The Economic Consequences of the Peace* (1919)

King, Arthur, and Lavender, Tony, *The History of the North Foreland Golf Club 1903–2006* (2007)

King, Cecil, *Strictly Personal: Some Memoirs of Cecil H. King* (1969)
—, *The Cecil King Diary 1970–1974* (1975)

Kipling, Rudyard, *Something of Myself* (1937)
Kitchin, F. Harcourt, *Moberley Bell and his Times: An Unofficial Narrative* (1925)
Knightley, Philip, *The First Casualty* (1975)
Koss, Stephen, *The Rise and Fall of the Political Press in Britain* (1990)
—, *Lord Haldane* (1969)
—, *Asquith* (1976)

Lasswell, Harold D., *Propaganda Technique in the Great War* (1938)
Lawrence, Arthur, *Journalism as a Profession* (2009)
Lee, Alan, *The Origins of the Popular Press in England 1855–1914* (1976)
Lee, Celia (ed.), *Jean, Lady Hamilton: Diaries of a Soldier's Wife* (2020)
Lee, John, *A Soldier's Life: General Sir Ian Hamilton* (2001)
Lees-Milne, James, *The Enigmatic Edwardian: The Life of Reginald, 2nd Viscount Esher* (1986)
Le Queux, William, *The Invasion of 1910* (1906)
Lennox, Lady Algernon Gordon (ed.), *The Diary of Lord Bertie of Thame*, vol. II (1924)
Lewis, William Roger, *In the Name of God. Go! Leo Amery and the British Empire in the Age of Churchill* (1992)
Liebich, Andre, *Wickham Steed: Greatest Journalist of His Times* (2018)
Lloyd, Nick, *The Western Front: A History of the First World War* (2021)
Lloyd George, David, *War Memoirs of David Lloyd George*, 2 vols (1938)
—, *Memoirs of the Peace Conference 1939*, vol. 1 (1939)
Lowndes, Susan (ed.), *Diaries and Letters of Marie Belloc Lowndes 1911–1947* (1971)
Lownie, Andrew, *John Buchan* (1995)
Lucas, Edward Verrall, *Wisdom While You Wait* (1903)
Lycett, Andrew, *Rudyard Kipling* (1999)
Lyddon, Colonel W. G., *British War Missions to the United States 1914–1918* (1938)

MacDonagh, Michael, *In London During the Great War* (1935)
MacDonogh, Giles, *The Last Kaiser: William the Impetuous* (2000)
Mackenzie, F. A., *The Rise and Progress of the Harmsworth Publications* (1897)
Macmillan, Harold, *Winds of Change* (1966)

Macmillan, Margaret, *Peacemakers: The Paris Conference of 1919 and Its Attempt to End War* (2001)

Magnus, Philip, *Kitchener: Portrait of an Imperialist* (1958)

Mallinson, Allan, *1914: Fight the Good Fight* (2013)

Marcosson, Isaac F., *Adventures in Interviewing* (1919)

Marlin, Randal, *Propaganda and the Ethics of Persuasion* (2000)

May, Derwent, *Critical Times: The History of The Times Literary Supplement* (2001)

McAdoo, W. G., *Crowded Years* (1931)

McEwen, John (ed.), *The Riddell Diaries 1908–1923* (1986)

McKinstry, Leo, *Rosebery: Statesman in Turmoil* (2005)

McLoughlin, Donald, *In the Chair: Barrington-Ward of The Times* (1971)

Marlin, Randal, *Propaganda and the Ethics of Persuasion* (2000)

Marlowe, John, *Milner: Apostle of Empire* (1976)

Mead, Gary, *The Good Soldier: The Biography of Sir Douglas Haig* (2007)

Menzies, Amy, *Modern Men of Mark* (1921)

Messinger, Gary S., *British Propaganda and the State in the First World War* (1992)

Miller, Russell, *Boom: The Life of Viscount Trenchard* (1988)

Mitchell, Sir Peter Chalmers, *My Fill of Days* (1937)

Moorehead, Alan, *Gallipoli* (1956)

Morris, A. J. A., *The Scaremongers* (1984)

—, *Reporting the First World War: Charles Repington* (2015)

Morison, Stanley, *Personality and Diplomacy in Anglo-American Relations, 1917* (1956)

Morton, Brian, *Woodrow Wilson* (2008)

Murray, Arthur, *At Close Quarters* (1946)

Nevett, Terry, *Advertising in Britain* (1982)

Newton, Lord, *Lord Lansdowne: A Biography* (1929)

Norwich, John Julius, *The Duff Cooper Diaries 1915–1951* (2005)

Otte, Thomas, *Statesman of Europe: A Life of Sir Edward Grey* (2020)

Owen, Frank, *Tempestuous Journey* (1954)

Owen, Louise, *The Real Lord Northcliffe* (1922)

—, *Lord Northcliffe: The Facts* (1931)

Oxford and Asquith, The Earl of, *Memories and Reflections* (1928)

Pearson, Hesketh, *The Whispering Gallery: Being Leaves from a Diplomat's Diary* (1926)

Pemberton, Max, *Lord Northcliffe* (1922)

—, *Sixty Years Ago and After* (1936)

Philpott, William, *Bloody Victory: The Sacrifice on The Somme* (2010)

Pinney, Thomas (ed.), *The Letters of Rudyard Kipling*, vol. 3 (1996)

Playne, Caroline E., *The Pre-War Mind in England* (1928)

Plumptre, George, *Edward VII* (1995)

Pollock, John, *Kitchener* (2001)

Popplewell, Sir Oliver, *The Prime Minister and His Mistress* (2014)

Pottle, Mark (ed.), *Champion Redoubtable: The Diaries and Letters of Violet Bonham Carter 1914–1945* (1998)

Pound, Reginald, and Harmsworth, Geoffrey, *Northcliffe* (1959)

Ramsden, John (ed.), *Real Old Tory Politics: The Political Diaries of Sir Robert Sanders 1910–35* (1984)

Reed, Douglas, *Insanity Fair* (1938)

Repington, Charles, *The First World War*, 2 vols (1920)

Richards, David, *Rudyard Kipling: A Bibliography* (2010)

Riddell, George, *Lord Riddell's War Diary 1914–1918* (1933)

—, *Intimate Diary of the Peace Conference and After 1918–1923* (1933)

—, *More Pages from My Diary 1908–1914* (1934)

Rose, Kenneth, *King George V* (1983)

Roskill, Stephen, *Hankey: Man of Secrets*, 2 vols (1970, 1972)

Ryan, A. P., *Lord Northcliffe* (1953)

Ryan, W. Michael, *Lieutenant-Colonel Charles à Court Repington* (1987)

Searle, G. R., *Corruption in British Politics 1895–1930* (1987)

Self, Robert (ed.), *The Neville Chamberlain Diary Letters*, vols 1 and 2 (2000)

Seymour, Charles (ed.), *The Intimate Papers of Colonel House*, vols 3 and 4 (1928)

Sheffield, Gary, *The Chief: Douglas Haig and the British Army* (2011)

Sheffield, Gary, and Bourne, John (eds), *Douglas Haig: War Diaries and Letters 1914–1918* (2005)

Smith, Sally, *Marshall Hall* (2016)

Smith, Wareham, *Spilt Ink* (1932)

Soames, Mary (ed.), *Speaking for Themselves: The Personal Letters of Winston and Clementine Churchill* (1988)

Spender, J. A., *Life, Journalism and Politics*, vol. 2 (1927)

—, *Sir Robert Hudson: A Memoir* (1930)

Spengler, Oswald, *The Decline of the West*, vol. 2 (1928)

Steed, Wickham, *Through Thirty Years*, 2 vols (1924)
Stuart, Sir Campbell, *Secrets of Crewe House* (1920)
—, *Opportunity Knocks Once* (1952)
Swaffer, Hannen, *Northcliffe's Return* (1926)
Sykes, Alan, *Tariff Reform in British Politics* (1979)
Sylvan History Committee, *The History of the Sylvan Debating
      Club* (1967)

Taylor, A. J. P., *Politics in Wartime* (1964)
—, *English History 1914–1945* (1965)
—, *Beaverbrook* (1972)
— (ed.), *Lloyd George: A Diary by Frances Stevenson* (1971)
— (ed.), *My Darling Pussy: The Letters of Lloyd George and Frances
      Stevenson 1913–41* (1975)
Taylor, Philip M., *British Propaganda and the First World
      War* (1982)
Taylor, S. J., *The Great Outsiders: Northcliffe, Rothermere and the
      Daily Mail* (1996)
—, *The Reluctant Press Lord: Esmond Rothermere and the Daily
      Mail* (1998)
Terraine, John, *Douglas Haig: The Educated Soldier* (1963)
—, *White Heat: The New Warfare 1914–1918* (1982)
—, *The Times, The Times History of the War*, 30 vols (1920)
—, *The Times, The History of the Times*, vol. 4, Parts 1 & 2 (1952)
Thomas, G. Holt, *Aerial Transport*, 1920
Thompson, J. Lee, *Politicians, The Press, and Propaganda: Lord
      Northcliffe & the Great War* (1999)
—, *Northcliffe: Press Baron in Politics 1865–1922* (2000)
—, *Forgotten Patriot: A Life of Alfred, Viscount Milner* (2007)
Thorpe, D. R. (ed.), *Who's In, Who's Out: The Journals of Kenneth
      Rose*, vol. 1 (2018)
Toye, Richard, *Winston Churchill: A Life in the News* (2020)
Tracy, Louis, *Who's Who in the British War Mission in the United
      States of America* (1917)

Vincent, John (ed.), *The Crawford Papers: The Journals of David
      Lindsay, twenty-seventh Earl of Crawford and tenth Earl of
      Balcarres 1871–1940* (1984)
Viollis, André, *Lord Northcliffe* (1919)
Voigt, Frederick Augustus, *Combed Out* (1929)

Washburn, Stanley, *Field Notes From the Russian Front*, 2 vols (1915)

Weizmann, Chaim, *Trial and Error* (1949)
Wells, H. G., *Experiments in Autobiography* (1934)
Wilhelm II of Germany, ex-Emperor, *Comparative History 1878–1914* (1922)
Wilkinson, Glenn R., *Depictions and Images of War in Edwardian Newspapers 1899–1914* (2003)
Willert, Arthur, *The Road to Safety* (1952)
Williams, Francis, *Dangerous Estate: The Anatomy of Newspapers* (1957)
Wilson, H. W., *The War Guilt* (1928)
Wilson, John, *CB: A Life of Sir Henry Campbell-Bannerman* (1973)
Wilson, Robert McNair, *Lord Northcliffe: A Study* (1927)
Wilson, Trevor (ed.), *The Political Diaries of C. P. Scott 1911–1928* (1970)
Woods, Oliver, and Bishop, James, *The Story of The Times* (1983)
Woodward, David, R., *Lloyd George and the Generals* (1983)
Wrench, John Evelyn, *Uphill: The First Stage in a Strenuous Life* (1934)
—, *Struggle 1914–20* (1935)
—, *Geoffrey Dawson and Our Times* (1955)

LEARNED ARTICLES

Bogacz, Ted, '"A Tyranny of Words": Language, Poetry, and Anti-modernism in England in the First World War', *Journal of Modern History*, Vol. 58 No. 3 (September 1986)
Bones, Adam James, 'British National Dailies and the Outbreak of War in 1914', *International History Review*, Vol. 35 No. 5 (October 2013)
Brooks, Sydney, 'Lord Northcliffe and the War', *North American Review*, Vol. 202 No. 717 (August 1915)
Chalaby, Jean, 'Smiling People Make People Smile: Northcliffe's Journalism', *Media History*, Vol. 6 No. 1 (2000)
Croome, Wendy, 'The Journeys of Annie Cromie', *Anglo-Celtic Roots Quarterly Chronicle*, Vol. 15 No. 2 (2009)
—, 'Henry James Cromie: A Life of New Beginnings', *Anglo-Celtic Roots Quarterly Chronicle*, Vol. 22 No. 3 (Fall 2016)
Donovan, Stephen, 'Conrad and the Harmsworth Empire', *Conradiana*, Vol. 41 No. 2 (Fall 2009)
Edwards, Ruth Dudley, 'Alfred Harmsworth', *Dictionary of Irish Biography* (2009)
—, 'Geraldine Harmsworth', *Dictionary of Irish Biography* (2009)

English, David, 'Legend of "The Chief"', *British Journalism Review*,
    Vol. 7 No. 2 (1996)
Fraser, Peter, 'The British Shells crisis of 1915', *Journal of Canadian
    History*, No. 18 (April 1983)
Gardiner, A. G., 'Two Journalists: C. P. Scott and Lord Northcliffe:
    A Contrast', *Nineteenth Century and After*, Vol. 11 (1932)
Gilman, Lawrence, 'Review of *Americans* by Stuart P. Sherman',
    North American Review, No. 808 (March 1923)
Gollin, Alfred M., 'No Longer an Island: The Phantom Airship Scare
    of 1909', *Albion*, Vol. 13 No. 1 (Spring 1981)
—, 'Lord Northcliffe's Change of Course', *Journalism and Mass
    Communication Quarterly*, Vol. 39 No. 1 (March 1962)
Gordon, Louis, 'The Unknown Essays of Vladimir Jabotinsky',
    Jewish Political Studies Review, Vol. 9 No. 1 (Spring 1997)
Harmsworth, Alfred, Lord Northcliffe, 'The Simultaneous
    Newspapers of the Twentieth Century', *North American
    Review*, Vol. 172 No. 530 (January 1901)
—, 'What America Is Fighting For', *Current Opinion*, No. 63 (July–
    December 1917)
Harvey, George, 'Northcliffe: The War of the War', *North American
    Review*, Vol. 206 No. 1 (July 1917)
Hirstfield, Isabel, 'Lord Northcliffe as a Music-Lover', *The Musical
    Times*, Vol. 72 No. 1 (November 1931)
Jungdahl, Adam, 'Public Influence on the Proliferation of Military
    Aviation 1907–1912', *Air Power History*, Vol. 60 No. 1
    (Spring 2013)
Kennedy, Thomas C., 'Troubled Tories: Dissent and Confusion
    Concerning the Party's Ulster Policy 1910–1914', *Journal of
    British Studies*, Vol. 46 No. 3 (July 1907)
Liebich, Andre, 'The Antisemitism of Henry Wickham Steed',
    Patterns of Prejudice, Vol. 26 No. 2 (2012)
Little, John Gordon, 'H. H. Asquith and Britain's Manpower
    Problem 1914–1915', *History*, Vol. 82 No. 267 (July 1997)
Lonsdale, Sally, 'The Emergence of the Press Baron as "Literary
    Villain" in English Letters 1900–1939', *Literature and History*,
    Vol. 22 No. 2 (2013)
Lytton, Neville, 'Some Incidents in the Life of David Lloyd George',
    Blackwood's Magazine (July 1945)
Marquis, Alice Goldfarb, 'Words as Weapons: Propaganda in
    Britain and Germany During the First World War', *Journal of
    Contemporary British History*, Vol. 13 No. 3 (July 1978)
Matin, A. Michael, 'The Creativity of War Planners: Armed Forces

Professionals and the Pre-1914 Invasion-Scare Genre', *English Literary History*, Vol. 78 No. 4 (Winter 2011)

McEwen, J. M., 'The Press and the Fall of Asquith', *Historical Journal*, Vol. 21 No. 4 (December 1978)

—, 'Northcliffe and Lloyd George at War 1914–1919', *Historical Journal*, Vol. 24 No. 3 (September 1981)

—, 'The National Press During the First World War: Ownership and Circulation', *Journal of Contemporary History*, Vol. 17 No. 3 (July 1982)

—, 'Brass Hats and the British Press During the First World War', *Journal of Contemporary History* (18 April 1983)

Menning, Ralph R. and Bresnahan, Carol, '"Baseless Allegations": Wilhelm II and the Hale Interview of 1908', *Central European History*, Vol. 16 No. 4 (December 1983)

Neander, Joachim, and Marlin, Randal, 'Media and Propaganda: The Northcliffe Press and the Corpse Factory Story of World War One', *Global Media Journal*, Vol. 3 No. 2 (2010)

Oosterhuis, Harry, 'Cycling, Modernity and National Culture', *Social History*, Vol. 41 No. 3 (2016)

Pierce, Robert N., 'Lord Northcliffe: Transatlantic Influences', *Journalism Monographs*, No. 40 (August 1975)

Potter, Simon J., 'The Imperial Significance of the Canadian-American Reciprocity Proposals of 1911', *The Historical Journal*, Vol. 47 No. 1 (March 2004)

Rüger, Jan, 'Revisiting the Anglo-German Antagonism', *Journal of Modern History*, Vol. 83 No. 3 (September 2011)

Silberstein-Loeb, Jonathan, 'The Structure of the News Market in Britain 1870–1914', *Business History Review*, Vol. 83 No. 4 (Winter 2009)

Startt, James D., 'Northcliffe the Imperialist: The Lesser-Known Years 1902–1914', *The Historian*, Vol. 51 No. 1 (November 1988)

—, 'G.E. Buckle, Lord Northcliffe and the Conservative Revolution at *The Times* 1908–1912', *Journal of Newspaper and Periodical History*, No. 7 (1991)

Taylor, Peter, 'The British Shells Crisis of 1915', *Journal of Canadian History*, No. 18 (April 1983)

Thompson, J. Lee, '"To Tell the People of America the Truth": Lord Northcliffe in the USA, Unofficial British Propaganda June–November 1917', *Journal of Contemporary History*, Vol. 34 No. 2 (April 1999)

INDEX